# Lecture Notes in Computer Sc

Edited by G. Goos, J. Hartmanis and J. van

**Springer**
*Berlin*
*Heidelberg*
*New York*
*Barcelona*
*Budapest*
*Hong Kong*
*London*
*Milan*
*Paris*
*Santa Clara*
*Singapore*
*Tokyo*

Mehmet Akşit   Satoshi Matsuoka (Eds.)

# ECOOP'97 – Object-Oriented Programming

11th European Conference
Jyväskylä, Finland, June 9-13, 1997
Proceedings

Springer

Series Editors

Gerhard Goos, Karlsruhe University, Germany

Juris Hartmanis, Cornell University, NY, USA

Jan van Leeuwen, Utrecht University, The Netherlands


Volume Editors

Mehmet Akşit
University of Twente, Department of Computer Science
Postbox 217, 7500 AE Enschede, The Netherlands
E-mail: aksit@cs.utwente.nl

Satoshi Matsuoka
Tokyo Institute of Technology
Department of Mathematical and Computing Sciences
2-12-1 Oo-okayama, Meguro-ku, Tokyo 152, Japan
E-mail: matsu@is.titech.ac.jp

Cataloging-in-Publication data applied for

Die Deutsche Bibliothek - CIP-Einheitsaufnahme

**Object oriented programming** : 11th European conference ;
proceedings / ECOOP '97, Jyväskylä, Finland, June 9 - 13, 1997.
Mehmet Akşit ; Satoshi Matsuoka (ed.). - Berlin ; Heidelberg ; New
York ; Barcelona ; Budapest ; Hong Kong ; London ; Milan ; Paris ;
Santa Clara ; Singapore ; Tokyo : Springer, 1997
    (Lecture notes in computer science ; Vol. 1241)
    ISBN 3-540-63089-9


CR Subject Classification (1991): D.1-3, H.2

ISSN 0302-9743
ISBN 3-540-63089-9 Springer-Verlag Berlin Heidelberg New York

Typesetting: Camera-ready by author
SPIN 10548830    06/3142 – 5 4 3 2 1 0    Printed on acid-free paper

# Preface

This volume constitutes the proceedings of the eleventh European Conference on Object-Oriented Programming, ECOOP '97, held in Jyväskylä, Finland, June 9 - 13, 1997. Since the first ECOOP conference in 1987, object-oriented technology has grown from a limited academic exercise to an industrial driving force. Currently, numerous commercial object-oriented software products are available for practical use.

Undoubtedly, object-oriented technology has stimulated the increasing awareness of software practitioners that the software development process is an engineering activity, and just like other engineering disciplines, there are some rules to obey if their goal is to create cost-effective products. For example, the concept of "real-world" modeling enhanced the consciousness that the main goal is problem solving, rather than programming. Similarly, object-oriented technology has helped many academic people in recognizing that the purpose is not only defining correct programs, but also adaptable, reusable, and cost-effective software products. More importantly, object-oriented technology has given to all of us, theoreticians and practitioners, the courage to state that software development can be based on theoretical principles and yet be applied in practical projects. The ECOOP '97 conference with its well-balanced technical program and other exciting activities is a "living proof" of this pleasant evolution.

The ECOOP '97 technical program consisted of 20 papers (selected from 103 submissions), three invited speakers, plus one panel. The program committee, consisting of 26 distinguished researchers in object-orientation, met at the University of Twente in The Netherlands during January 30 - 31 for the paper selection. All papers were reviewed by at least four members of the program committee. The topics of the accepted papers cover traditional ECOOP topics such as programming languages, types, implementation, and formal specifications, as well as some new topics such as design patterns, metaprogramming, and Java.

As for the invited speakers, we were very honored to be able to present the talks by Kristen Nygaard, the well-known pioneer of object-oriented programming languages with his work on Simula-67 which was born 30 years ago in Scandinavia; Gregor Kiczales, who is proposing a new direction in object-oriented research, called Aspect-Oriented Programming; and Erich Gamma, a European pioneer on patterns.

We would like to express our deepest appreciation to the authors of submitted papers, the program committee members, the external referees, Richard van de Stadt for organizing the review process, and many others who contributed towards the establishment of the ECOOP '97 technical program.

April 1997

Mehmet Akşit and Satoshi Matsuoka
ECOOP '97 Program Chairs

# Organization

ECOOP '97 was organized by the University of Jyväskylä, under the auspices of AITO (Association Internationale pour les Technologies Objets), and in cooperation with ACM SIGPLAN (Association for Computing Machinery, Special Interest Group for Programming Languages).

## Executive Committee

| | |
|---|---|
| Conference Chair: | Boris Magnusson, University of Aarhus, DK) |
| Program Chairs: | Mehmet Akşit (University of Twente, NL) |
| | Satoshi Matsuoka (Tokyo Institute of Technology, J) |
| Organizing Chair: | Markku Sakkinen (University of Jyväskylä, FIN) |
| Tutorials: | Erkki Lehtinen (University of Jyväskylä, FIN) |
| Workshops: | Antero Taivalsaari (Nokia Research Center, FIN) |
| Management, Exhibition: | Taru-Maija Heilala-Rasimov (Jyväskylä Congress, FIN) |
| Panels: | Jari Veijalainen (University of Jyväskylä, FIN) |
| Posters: | Pentti Marttiin (University of Jyväskylä, FIN) |
| Demonstrations: | Risto Pohjonen (University of Jyväskylä, FIN) |
| Other members: | Matti Rossi (University of Jyväskylä, FIN) |
| | Jonne Itkonen (University of Jyväskylä, FIN) |

## Sponsoring Institutions and Companies

Academy of Finland
University of Jyväskylä
City of Jyväskylä
Nokia Research Center
Finnair
Jyväskylä Science Park Ltd.

# Program Committee

Pierre America (Philips Research Laboratories, NL)
Elisa Bertino (University of Milan, I)
Toby Bloom (CMG Direct Interactive, USA, OOPSLA'97 Program Chair)
Frank Buschmann (Siemens, D)
Luca Cardelli (Digital SRC, USA)
Denis Caromel University of Nice - INRIA Sophia Antipolis, F)
Pierre Cointe (Ecole des Mines de Nantes, F)
Derek Coleman (King's College London, UK)
Theo D'Hondt (Brussels Free University, B)
Peter Dickman (University of Glasgow, UK)
Bjorn Freeman-Benson (Object Technology International Inc., CND)
Rachid Guerraoui (EPFL IN-Ecublens, CH)
Dieter Hammer (Eindhoven University of Technology, NL)
Urs Hölzle (University of California, Santa Barbara, USA)
Shinichi Honiden (Toshiba, J)
Mehdi Jazayeri (Vienna University of Technology, A)
Eric Jul (University of Copenhagen, DK)
Gerti Kappel (Johannes Kepler University, A)
Jørgen Lindskov Knudsen (Aarhus University, DK)
John Lamping (Xerox Palo Alto Research Center, USA)
Karl Lieberherr (Northeastern University, USA)
José Meseguer (SRI International, USA)
Oscar Nierstrasz (University of Bern, CH)
Atsushi Ohori (Kyoto University, J)
Jens Palsberg (Purdue University, USA)
Douglas Schmidt (Washington University, USA)

## Referees

# Contents

**Invited Talk 2**

**Implementation and Systems**

**Formal Methods and Specifications**

**Java**

# Patterns

# Invited Talk 3 (Abstract)

# GOODS to Appear on the Stage

## Invited Speech at ECOOP 97

Kristen Nygaard

Department of Informatics, University of Oslo
P.O.Box 1080 Blindern, N-0316 Oslo, Norway
e-mail: kristen@ifi.uio.no

**Abstract.** The lecture will trace the development of some important object-oriented concepts and point out the analogy between performances at the stage of a theatre and the operation of information systems (and program executions). This metaphor will be used in a description of the ideas pursued and developed in the GOODS Project (General Object-Oriented Distributed Systems), a three year project supported by The Norwegian Research Council, starting January 1997. GOODS aims at extending the framework of object-oriented programming to include a multi-layered approach to the organisation of the relationship between people, computer hardware, organisational rules and programs in general distributed systems. GOODS also aims at introducing general tools for specifying visibilities of objects (scopes) and the precise dealing with the identities of objects that exist in many versions in a distributed environment.

## 1  Introduction

### 1.1  Back to Research

When the ECOOP '97 organisers invited me to give this speech, they offered me the choice between giving my overview and evaluation of the first thirty years of object-oriented programming 1967-1997, or talking about my own current research and views about the future of object-oriented programming. Since I now have passed seventy years, the attraction of presenting nostalgic and grandiose reflections on the past has considerably diminished. Rather exasperated reactions: "What! Even more new crazy ideas!" than: "Impressive! The old man still has an audible voice and is capable of standing on his feet a full lecture."

My six-year political assignment as national leader of the campaign against Norwegian membership in the European Union was finished with our victory on the 28th November 1994. I was very much looking forward to returning to research. Research is more exciting than politics, but sometimes politics is more important. The first thing to do in 1995 was to get hands-on experience with the new generation of workstations and with multimedia hardware and software that had appeared since 1988. The second was to decide what kind of research I should engage in and then try to compose a new team.

I commented in a recent paper [Nygaard, K. 1996]: "Many people have observed that the research teams in which I have been active, usually have contained people much younger than me. I have been asked if that is so because I prefer to work with young people. The answer is no. I prefer to work with people who believe that my newest ideas are worth while working on, and themselves have ideas that fit in. Older, more established people usually did not believe that, and don't. There are exceptions, like the people in the BETA team. In the EU battle I was working in many teams, most teams composed by people from a wide age bracket. In research it has been different, as I have told." [IRIS 96]

During my six "political years" (1988-1994) I still was not inactive in research. I could see that ideas about the "theatre metaphor" that I had worked on (with Professor Dag Belsnes at the Norwegian Computing Center and the BETA team) in the late 1970s and early 1980s, became more and more relevant, and I made some efforts to generalise these ideas and integrate them with other ideas.

In 1991 I was asked by Professor Brian Randell to present my subjective views on the "Past, Present and Future of Programming Languages" at The 25th Anniversary Newcastle Conference in 1992. I had, of course, to put quite much effort into the lectures, and as a result a program for future research started to emerge. In 1995 it turned out that audiences were particularly interested in just the main points of that program. Not surprising, because of their relevance to distributed systems. It was time to start assembling a team and to apply for funding.

## 1.2 Overview

The format of an invited speech may be rather different from that of an ordinary reviewed paper. Many styles are allowed, and a personal note is expected. Strong opinions and postulated facts may be stated in absolute earnestness or with a tongue-in-cheek. The interpretation may be left to the audience. In these senses this is a typical invited speech.

The lecture starts (Section 1.3) with some quotations from the application that gave us some funds for my current project, the GOODS project. You will probably observe that we have embarked on a very ambitious endeavour: To extend the conceptual framework of object-oriented programming as in the SIMULA, DELTA and BETA-tradition to include also a joint description of the *performances* (program executions) according to their given *scripts* (by programs, constraints and other kinds of rules) by *ensembles* (of human actors and information processing equipment linked by *connectors* (communication channels)).

In Section 2 the most relevant elements for the GOODS conceptual platform are selected from earlier SIMULA, DELTA and BETA papers from 1963 on. In an article for a journal this would have had to be cut down to a series of references, tacitly making the assumption that the reader had these references available and, even more unrealistically, would have the interest and energy to look them up. The presentation is brief, but should at least give some clues to the world view of our understanding of object-oriented programming.

The theatre metaphor is introduced (in Section 3) through the system generator (process generator, phenomenon generator) concept from DELTA together with our definition of the model concept. The extension and initial exploration of this metaphor follows (Section 4), using "the play within the play"-example from Shakespeare's Hamlet, Act III, Scene II, introducing multi- layered actor/role and ensemble/performance situations.

We will (in Section 5) have a go at a general approach to scoping: The description/ prescription of visibility/accessibility of system properties, components and states from a given location in a performance (program execution).

The reference to the (Kabuki) theatre is made to point out that scoping problems also appear in the setting of the theatre and of other process generators. The analogy with the theatre is certainly exaggerated in the next section (Section 6), in the brief discussion of clones: many versions of "the same" object in a distributed environment:

In dealing with general object-oriented distributed systems we also need tools for identifying and distinguishing different versions of an object and of state descriptors providing partial descriptions of objects states at a given time.

The lecture ends with some points relating to scripts, (plays, programs, specifications) dealing with open and closed, persistent and transient scripts, and with analysis and design in system development (Section 7).

## 1.3 The GOODS Project

The Norwegian Research Council demands applications that are serious and worded in concise and preferably impressive terms. For these reasons we started our application for funds with these paragraphs [GOODS, 1996]:

"To master the complexities of interaction in information systems, the magnitude of these tasks and the needs for frequent restructuring, object-oriented techniques have become dominant.

The penetration of information technology into the co-operation patterns of modern organisations has made it an important and interesting task to extend the object-oriented paradigm to encompass and integrate not only the computer programs but also the hardware executing the programs, the human actors and the communication functions in information systems. This extension should be directly linked to implementable new basic language constructs, and it should address both the analysis and design, the implementation and use, and the maintenance of systems."

"The project will be linked to research efforts at the universities in Glasgow and Århus, and to a user organisation introducing very comprehensive information systems.The framework shall be closely related to object-oriented programming languages and lend itself to supporting staging, operation and maintenance in a variety of such languages."

"The problem area has been cultivated, particularly as a field in software engineering, and notions such as actors, roles and views have been explored, often in connection with standardisation efforts. *Our use of the theatre metaphor is oriented towards the introduction of basic language mechanisms for creating layered system organisations, and our approach is similar to that used in developing object-oriented programming.* (Italics added by KN.). It is a project within basic research, not a software engineering project, in a field that in our opinion is not yet sufficiently explored to be suitable for standardisation.

We will use the BETA programming language as our platform because of its conceptual simplicity and generality, based upon a modelling view of programming languages. We feel that BETA will be the best substrate for our conceptual approach, integrating "what is done"- and "how it is done"-descriptions.

To the project members' knowledge, there exists no unified high level description and programming language for this kind of systems. There are protocols and various standards (e.g. CORBA), but they do not describe systems at the (user) application level. There is also much work done on general referent models and associated sets of languages (RM-ODP, Referent Model - Open Distributed Processing). We intend to address very wide classes of systems in terms of concepts implementable in a unified, programming language that includes the structured introduction of open segments that will be closed by human actors."

I want you to observe that we point out that the results of the project should be applicable also in the contexts of other reasonably well-structured object-oriented programming languages.

The Norwegian Research Council decided to support the project with some resources during a three-year period, starting in January 1997.

The GOODS team (as of March 1997) consists of:

- Associate Professor Dag Sjøberg, working in the field of persistent object-oriented distributed databases.
- Ph.D.-student Ole Smørdal, working on combining activity theory and the theatre metaphor in object-oriented analysis and design.
- Ph.D.-student Haakon Bryhni, working on high speed communication protocols in distributed systems.
- Another Ph.D.-student, starting later this spring.
- The author.

The GOODS reference group consists of researchers participating in seminars and discussions of ideas:

- Professor Dag Belsnes
- Gisle Hannemyhr
- Øystein Myhre
- Associate Professor Birger Møller-Pedersen.

The GOODS team and reference group have contributed to this lecture with both ideas and useful comments.

# 2 The Conceptual Platform of Object-Oriented Programming

## 2.1 SIMULA I and SIMULA 67: System Description and Programming

The foundation of the GOODS project should be established by tracing and bringing together some of the important lines of thought from the SIMULA languages, the DELTA language and the BETA language, as well as from system development research in which I have participated. (The SIMULA languages were developed by Ole-Johan Dahl and me, and with Bjørn Myhrhaug as a particularly important member of the very competent teams that participated in our work.)

The SIMULA I language report from 1965 [SIMULA I, 1965, p.2] opens with these sentences:

"The two main objects of the SIMULA language are:

To provide a language for a precise and standardised description of a wide class of phenomena, belonging to what we may call "discrete event systems".

To provide a programming language for an easy generation of simulation programs for "discrete event systems"."

Since SIMULA 67 came later and has got a much wider use than SIMULA I, some seem incorrectly to believe that the former is "more object-oriented" than the latter. The central concept is in place in SIMULA I, but regarded as and named "process" and not "object" (which emphasises the substance aspect of the process). Classes are named "activities", and qualified references with inheritance did not appear until SIMULA 67:

" ... to achieve greater flexibility and unity, SIMULA has integrated the two kind of entities (*comment 1997*: passive "data carriers" and acting "event routines") into one. The basic concept in SIMULA is the *process*, being characterised by a *data structure* and an *operation rule*.

The individual members of the data structure of a process will be called attributes".

"Thus SIMULA may be used to describe systems which satisfy the following requirement:

The system is such that it is possible to regard its operation as consisting of a sequence of instantaneous events, each event being an active phase of a process.

The number of processes may be constant or variable and they all belong to one or more classes called activities.

Since the set of system times at which events occur forms a discrete point set on the system time axis, and since every action in the system is a part of an event, we will name these systems *discrete event systems*." [SIMULA I, 1965, p. 7-9].

SIMULA I was a simulation programming language that turned out to become a powerful general programming language. SIMULA 67 is a general programming language that also is a powerful platform for other, specialised programming languages, as e.g. simulation languages.

SIMULA 67 was triggered of by the invention of inheritance: "Usually a new idea was subjected to rather violent attacks in order to test its strength. The prefix idea was the only exception. We immediately realised that we now had the necessary foundation for a completely new language approach, and in the days which followed the discovery we decided that:

We would design a new general programming language, in terms of which an improved SIMULA I could be expressed.

The basic concept should be *classes of objects*.

The prefix feature, and thus the subclass concept, should be a part of the language.

Direct, qualified references should be introduced."

In SIMULA 67 the *object* is the fundamental concept, and categories of objects are called *classes*. Direct and *qualified references* are introduced, as opposed to the indirect, unqualified element references of SIMULA I. The need to combine the safety of qualified referencing (from Tony Hoare in 1965, see [Hoare, C.A.R., 1968]) with flexibility led to the *subclass* construct. That again to the powerful notion of *inheritance* which introduced the expressiveness of *generalisation-specialisation* into programming languages. As a corollary, the notion of *virtual quantities* and late binding followed.

Does inheritance belong to object-oriented programming as an essential aspect? Some people think so, I don't. The language mechanism of generalisation-specialisation is useful in a wider context. On the other hand, since the programming language constructs for inheritance were not available in 1967, we had to invent them because we needed them.

Apart from these important extensions, the basic perspective on computing from SIMULA I was carried over to SIMULA 67: The *program execution* was the fundamental phenomenon to be structured, generated, operated and observed, providing us with information. The program execution was a *model system* of the *referent system* whose *structure* was described by the program. The referent could be *manifest*, in the outside world, as e.g. a warehouse or a harbour, or *mental*, existing in peoples' minds, as e.g. an envisioned new VLSI chip or information system, or a combination of manifest and mental components. This approach is commonly called the modelling view, or the Scandinavian view on object-oriented programming.

If we compare with current object-oriented programming languages, we find that most of the basic language constructs were introduced first in the SIMULA languages of the 1960s. If Dahl and I had not invented SIMULA in the first half of the 1960s, what would now have been the state of object-oriented programming? Approximately the same as it is today.

Why? Because object-orientation is one of the basic ways of structuring an information process. If we had not invented it, someone else certainly would have done so, probably in good time before 1980. One may ask: Was object-oriented programming invented or discovered? Well, since it did not exist before SIMULA except as exemplified in a number of specialised programs, not bringing out the clean general and basic concepts, it was obviously not discovered. The correct answer is that SIMULA was derived. It was derived as the answer to the task to which Ole-Johan Dahl and I had dedicated ourselves: To create a language suited to the description of a very large class of systems - the class of discrete-event systems which Operational Research workers would want to understand, analyse, design and simulate on a computer. We succeeded, and it turned out that this class was so rich that it also encompassed most of the organisationally complex information systems we now want to create programs for. Also, object-oriented analysis and design are becoming key technologies in system development in general.

## 2.2  From DELTA to BETA

Already in 1963, extension of SIMULA into the world of real-time computing was considered [Nygaard, K., 1963], and in the SIMULA I report of 1965 it was stated [SIMULA I, 1965, p. 9] that: "By introducing suitable processes SIMULA also may be used to describe with the desired degree of accuracy continuously changing systems, as well as systems in which some processes have continuous changes, other processes discrete changes."The task of generalising SIMULA to cope with continuously changing states was put aside for the more imminently important development of SIMULA 67.

After the SIMULA efforts I moved into cooperation with the trade unions to evaluate the workplace impacts of information technology, build their competence in the field and start the study of participatory design. This was later followed up by research in system development in parallel with my programming language research.

In a paper from 1986 [Nygaard, K., 1986: "Program Development as a Social Activity"] I make the remark: "I have been criticized for not using more time in the 1970s to promote the SIMULA language. Many other people have done a much larger job than I. It was a conscious choice. Should a single idea or project use up your whole life as a researcher? SIMULA (and object oriented programming) is like a child: You have helped create it, you are responsible for its young years, you must see to that it gets a chance to succeed. Then your responsibility ends. You may be proud of it, wish it well, but realize that it will develop on its own and is no longer your property. Your duty is now to care for the new baby and then for any future children."

The task of generalising SIMULA was, however, addressed later, in the years 1973-75, by the DELTA team consisting of Erik Holbæk-Hanssen, Petter Håndlykken and myself.

DELTA's objectives are stated on p. 5 in the DELTA language report [DELTA, 1975]:"The purpose of this report is to develop a conceptual framework for conceiving systems, and an associated system description language. Our starting point has been a language which is designed as a tool for both system description and the writing of computer programs: the SIMULA language. We have, however, freed ourselves from the restrictions imposed by the computer, described above. We hope to have provided a tool which makes it possible to conceive systems in ways natural to human beings, using and extending the properties of programming languages, making it possible to combine algorithmic, mathematical and natural language modes of expression."

In the SIMULA development, the notions of process, object, class, system etc. were precisely introduced in programming language terms, but a careful examination of the concepts lacked. This analysis, redefinition and introduction of precise concepts was given in Chapter 3 of the DELTA Report (pp. 14-221), and that chapter became later the conceptual platform and reference for the corresponding platform for the

BETA language project. (In DELTA the basic concept is called a component. It is an object with a action substructure more complex than in SIMULA and BETA.)

The early work on BETA was started in 1975 as the Joint Language Project (JLP) and is described in [Kristensen, B. B., Madsen, O. L. and Nygaard, K., 1977]. On p.2 the initial purpose is stated as: "1. To develop and implement a high level programming language as a projection of the DELTA system description language into the environment of computing equipment. 2. To provide a common central activity to which a number of research efforts in various fields of informatics and at various institutions could be related."

In BETA a continuing discussion, development and critical evaluation of the concepts was an essential part of the project. (The BETA team consisted during the initial language development stage of Bent Bruun Kristensen, Ole Lehrmann Madsen, Birger Møller-Pedersen and me. Later many others have contributed, in Oslo and particularly in Mjølner Informatics, Århus, and the University of Århus.)

The confusion surrounding the system concept is discussed on pp. 14-15: "The underlying misunderstanding is that these questions and remarks imply that the quality of being a system is innate to certain collections of objects (living or inanimate).

In our opinion, any system definition must point out that a part of the world may be called a system when, and only when we *choose* to regard it in a certain way."

This points to the introduction in BETA of *perspective* as a fundamental aspect of system description and programming:

"A *perspective* is a part of a person's cognitive universe that may structure her or his cognitive process when relating to situations within some domain
- by *selecting* those properties of the situation that are being considered (and, by implication, those that are ignored), and
- by providing concepts and other cognitions that are being used in the *interpretation* of the selected properties."

(A discussion of the perspective concept is given in [Nygaard, K. and Sørgaard, P., 1987].) To regard a phenomenon as a system then becomes a choice of perspective:

A *system* is a part of the world that a person (or group of persons) during some time interval chooses to regard as
- a whole consisting of components,
- each component characterized by properties that are selected as being relevant and
- by state transitions relating to these properties and to other components and their properties.

In BETA once more the process is the basic concept:

A *process* is a phenomenon regarded as the development of a part of the world through transformations during a time interval. *Structure* of a process is limitations of its set of possible states and of transitions between these states.

Examples of structures are:

- Written and unwritten rules being obeyed
- The effect of programs
- Perspectives

The process perspective may be further specialised to that of *information process*:
A process is regarded as an information process when the qualities considered are:

- its *substance*, the physical matter that it transforms,
- its *state*, represented by *values* obtained by mapping of measurements of *attributes*, attributes being selected properties of its substance,
- its *transitions*, the transformations of its substance and thus its measurable properties.

A computer program execution is an information process. Its substance consists of what is materialised upon the substrate of its storage media, its state consists of the values of variables (which we observe or "read" as "2.35", "HEATHROW", "false" etc.), evaluated functions and references, its transitions of the sequences of imperatives being executed. Another common example is the operation of an information system with both computers and people carrying out actions, and with program executions and paper documents being operated upon by these actors.

Now we may give a definition of the science of informatics (computer science in US and UK):

*Informatics* is the science that has as its domain information processes and related phenomena in artifacts, society and nature.

And by applying the system perspective upon an information process we get:

An *information system* is a part of the world that a person (or group of persons) during some time interval chooses to regard as an information process with

- its *substance* consisting of components,
- its *state* being the union of states of each of the components
- its *transitions* being carried out by the components and affecting their properties and the properties of other components.

We are now able to give a precise general definition of object-oriented programming:

In *object-oriented programming* an information process is regarded as an information system developing through transformations of its state:

- The substance of the system is organised as objects, building the system's components.
- Any measurable property of the substance is a property of an object.
- Any transformation of state is the result of actions of objects.

In an information process organised by object-oriented programming there are no loose crumbs of substance lying around, every piece of substance is a part of an object. There are no aspects of state not related to an object, and no Acts of God, only acts of objects.

The three basic aspects of information process are, not surprisingly, represented by abstractions in programming languages: The *class declaration* abstracts and categorises *substance*, the *type declaration* abstracts and categorises value and thus *state*, the *procedure declaration* abstracts and categorises state *transitions*.

In my opinion *system-oriented programming* would have been a better term than object-oriented programming, but the term object from SIMULA stuck and there is no point in any attempt to argue for a renaming. Object-oriented programming may also be characterised as *substance-oriented programming*, and instead of talking about logic or constraint-oriented programming and functional programming, we could have referred to state and transition:

*State-oriented programming:* The computing process is viewed as a deduction process, developing from an initial state, the process being restricted by sets of constraints and by inputs from the environment, the information about the set of possible states being deduced by an inferencing algorithm.

*Transition-oriented programming:* The computing process is viewed as a sequence of transitions between representative (meaningful) states, in which transformations of inputs produces outputs that in their turn are inputs to new transformations.

The capabilities for *hierarchisation* are among the important characteristics of programming languages. A language should offer:

- *Substance hierarchies*, as exemplified by nesting in block-structured languages.
- *State hierarchies*, that is values associated with sets of states, and subvalues associated with subsets of these sets. This has been contemplated for BETA, and it is on the list of constructs that may be introduced in GOODS.
- *Transition hierarchies*, that is actions decomposed into subactions and subaction's subactions, as offered by the action stack mechanism.
- *Category hierarchies*, as offered by inheritance: as the class/subclass construct in SIMULA 67 (pattern/subpattern in BETA).

In the SIMULA languages, only unisequential and deterministic alternation (quasi-parallel) sequencing were available. In BETA the full range of sequencing categories, including concurrency, are available.


# 3 *The Theatre:* A Simple But Typical Process Generator

## 3.1 The DELTA System Generator

The DELTA Report [DELTA 1975, pp. 23-25] discusses the situation in which system descriptions are communicated between *communicators* (people, or e.g. from people to computing equipment):

"The considered system, being described, will be called the *referent system*. The communicator making the description will be called the *system reporter* (or just *reporter*).

The communicator using the description to make a model will be called the *system generator*. The communication process may now be illustrated by Fig. 1. This conceptual framework covers a wider set of communications situations, however.

The system reporter or the system generator, or both, may consist of a group of communicators. The model system may be either mental or manifest. If the language is a computer programming language, the system description is a computer program and the system generator may be a computer generating a manifest model system in the form of a program execution.

Another example is offered by the following chain:

The referent system is mental, consisting of an island, a group of shipwrecked people, a magician named Prospero with his lovely daughter Miranda etc.

The reporter is William Shakespeare.

The language is a version of English, in which the description is organised into acts, scenes and lines, the lines containing ordinary English.

The system description is a play: "The Tempest".

**Figure 1.** The DELTA System Generator

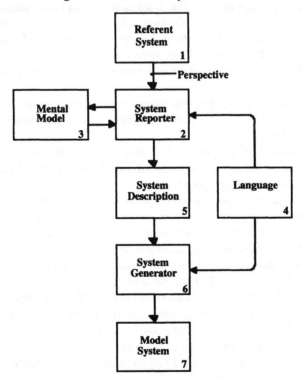

In many situations, the real purpose of the process is to generate a manifest model system which fulfils some purpose. Examples are: The performance of a play portraying the author's mental referent system. The operation of an information processing system, achieved by the execution of a set of programs (a system description) which describes the programmers' and system designers' mental referent system of what the (model) information processing system should do.

In relation to computer programming, we will understand the communication process in the following manner:

The programmer (reporter) will have a mental referent system of what the computer should do (the program execution), and his program is a description which make it possible for the computer to portray this mental referent system".

The notion of system generator was further discussed and decomposed in [Kristensen, B. B., Madsen, O. L. and Nygaard, K., 1977] on pp. 7-11: "In system programming it is, and to a much greater extent will become, necessary to control the components which are entering the program execution process: central processing units, storage media, data channels, peripheral equipment etc. This necessitates in our opinion a general conceptual approach to these apparently very different components. It will appear that a large proportion of the software complex now usually referred to as "basic software" and "operating system" will be regarded in our framework as being an integral part of the organisation of what we may call "logical components", as opposed to hardware components." "The "computer" concept is no longer useful for a precise discussion of the structure of the complex networks of interrelated computing equipment which we have to deal with in the computing systems of today and in the future. We shall regard such networks as system generators in the DELTA sense and introduce concepts in terms of which we may understand and describe such a network as a system generator."

"A system generator (computing equipment network) component upon which such systems may exist will be called a *substrate*. Disks, tapes, core storage, data screens are examples of substrates.

A system generator component which is able to change the state within a system (in the above sense of the term) will be called a *processor*. A central processing unit and a disk drive unit are examples of processors.

A system generator component which provides a connecting link between two components of theses categories (substrates, processors) will be called a *connector*. (It should be pointed out that the more complex "data channels" usually will have to be regarded as aggregates of substrates, processors and connectors at the basic "hardware level". They may be given a simpler structure at the "logical level".)

A collection of interacting substrates, processors and connectors will thus be called a system generator. We shall, in fact, understand any complex of computing equipment in these terms, any piece of equipment being regarded as belonging to one of the above component categories or as a subsystem consisting of such components. (A system generator may, of course, itself be regarded as a system.)"

The concepts of substrate, processor and connector were not further developed in the BETA language efforts. In the GOODS Project we will reexamine these concepts.


## 3.2   Models

When we relate to a situation, we cannot take into account at the same time all available information, we must always filter, select. This does of course also apply to modelling, and the perspective concept should to be introduced in any precise definition of the term *model*, as exemplified by Lindsjørn and Sjøberg in their ECOOP '88 paper [Lindsjørn, Y. and Sjøberg, D., 1988]:

"A phenomenon M is a model of a phenomenon R, according to some perspective P, if a person regards M and R as similar according to P.

We will call R the referent phenomenon (or simply referent) and M the model phenomenon (or simply model).

We will call P the perspective of the model M."

## 3.3  Performances and Ensembles

The theatre metaphor is a very useful one, since very many terms relevant to that world also have their counterparts in the world of information systems, and that analogy has been explored by many. In my own work we started using the metaphor in the DELTA project (as shown in the quotes above). Then Dag Belsnes and I explored the metaphor further around 1980. I have used it in my research, teaching and lecturing on programming languages in general and object-oriented programming in special, since then. Belsnes used our ideas in his 1982 paper "Distribution and Execution of Distributed Systems", [Belsnes, D., 1982], and they were used in Master Theses by Øystein Haugen [Haugen, Ø., 1980] and Hans Petter Dahle [Dahle, H. P., 1981]. In the BETA team, the metaphor was used in work on the safe dynamic exchange of BETA components during program execution (see [Kristensen, B. B., Madsen, O. L., Møller-Pedersen, B and Nygaard, K., 1986]) and in work by students of Ole Lehrmann Madsen and Bent Bruun Kristensen. Lindsjørn and Sjøberg gives a good example of the use of the metaphor in a multi-layered setting (see Section 4) in their ECOOP '88 paper.

(At this stage I want to remind you once more that I am not talking about what we have done, but about ideas for future work, to a varying degree based upon earlier work.)

By a performance we will understand a program execution in a computer, the operation of an information system containing people and computing artifacts, a performance of a play on a stage, as well as other processes created and stage-managed by a system generator in the sense we consider in this lecture.

A performance will be regarded as generated by an ensemble carrying out a script. In The American Heritage Dictionary of the English Language, [Third Edition 1992, Houghton Mifflin], we find:

"script (skrĭpt) noun ...

>   3.a. The text of a play, broadcast, or movie. b. A copy of a text used
>   by a director or performer. ... ".

I will use the term in a wider context, and include programs for computing artifacts and the sets of rules and conventions, written and unwritten, that provide the structure of performances.

In a performance on a theatre we identify subprocesses as the performance of roles in a setting given by backdrops, properties and costumes. Properties may also, however, "perform", representing something they are not. Consider, as an example, the daggers used for all the gruesome murders we witness on the stage and screen. All parts of the setting may impact upon the enacting of the roles (Noblemen are stabbed to death by daggers, Macbeth loses his head), they may themselves change state through actions in the performances of the roles: a door opened, a window pane splintered.

In SIMULA we united the "event routines" and the "passive data structures" into the powerful unifying concept of objects. I feel that the same conceptual unification must be made in our understanding of performances in general: Macbeth, the witches, the daggers, the tables, even Macbeth's decapitated head, all play roles in the performances.

Correspondingly, in a meeting the subprocesses of the meeting performance may be the roles of reviewers, secretaries, chairpersons, exam papers, ranking lists, database terminals, protocols with passed decisions. In informations systems all roles are present in the performance as objects, their substance and state being operated upon by the actions of the transitions, together constituting the object processes.

Roles are performed, enacted, embodied by actors -and in our terms - also by properties. Laurence Olivier performs Hamlet, a collapsible theatre foil performs in his hand in the fencing scenes. (Perhaps a stuntman had to take over the fencing for Olivier as he grew older.) An ensemble is a collection of the actors participating in a performance. The interaction between two role processes in a performance we will refer to as communication. The interaction between a role and the actor carrying out the script of the role we will refer to as interpretation, and we will say that the actor performs the role. The communication between two roles in a performance is implemented through communication between the two actors who interpret the roles.And the ensembles themselves are in an object-oriented perspective to be regarded as a a system of interacting object processes.

In the GOODS project we will have to consider the building up of simple ensembles from processors, substrates and connectors from very simple basic components. Then more complex ensembles may be constructed from these, incorporating also human actors.

In both SIMULA, DELTA and BETA all systems were block-structured and had a common outer, enclosing object, named the system object. All other objects were enclosed by, nested inside the system object, their life spans delimited within the life spans of their enclosers. This is illustrated on Figure 2. We will call this a nested structure, or simply a nest.

In order to refer to objects in a nest, we must use the DELTA terminology for describing object relations in object-oriented nested structures. They are illustrated in Fig. 2.

In Figure 2, the root of the nested structure is at the top. We will also use figures with the root at the bottom, as in Figure 3.

If a performance P1 shall act as an ensemble and perform another performance P3, P1 must know about P3 and be able to refer to it. This is outside the scope of the references in the SIMULA/DELTA/BETA languages. We have to introduce *external references*.

**Figure 2.** Nested Object Structures

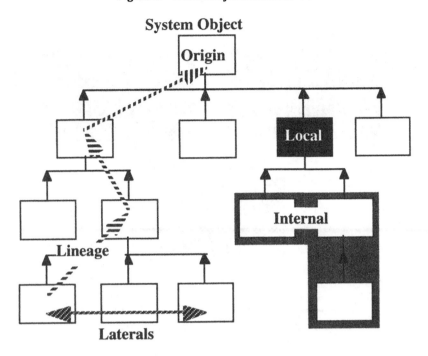

In distributed systems, the standard situation is that you are considering more than one nest, possibly widely separated, and any effort to make them have a common, enclosing system object will seem very artificial. This also necessitates external references if the nests shall communicate. External references then may be direct, or through a chain of nest-internal and nest-external references (Figure 3).

But the internal structure of P3 in Figure 3 may be unknown to P1. Should the external reference then be unqualified? I believe that instead the qualification of the external reference should be that of a pattern (class) containing the description of the characteristics of the *communication channel* and of the *communication protocol*. That is, the qualification of the *connector*.

In the case of a qualified external reference from P1 to P3, some kind of matching procedure will be necessary to secure that P3 will respond correctly to communication from P1. Also, the pattern used in this procedure could exploit the scoping capabilities proposed in Section 5 to specify the desired security from unwanted aspects of the communication.

In more complex situations, as in a networked environment, the organisation of the external references probably would be implemented through specialised performances in the net, functioning as name-servers.

**Figure 3.** Nests and External References

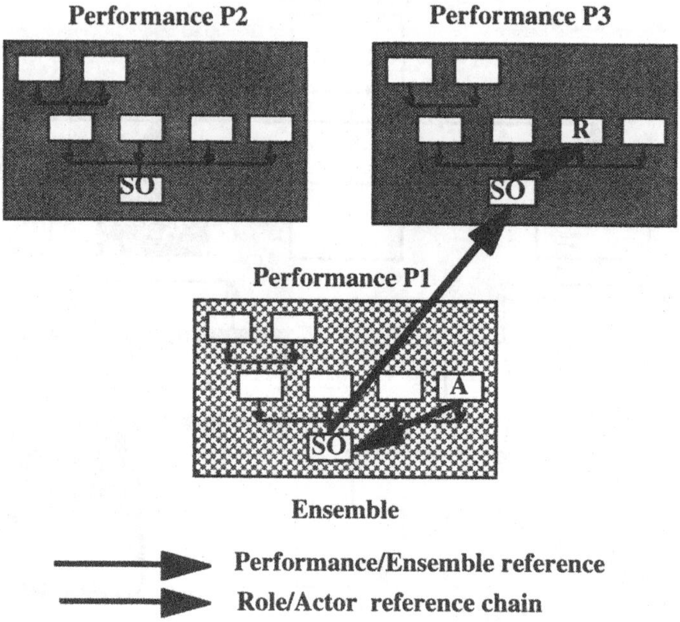

How is a new script entered? In the SIMULA/DELTA/BETA languages there are no direct language facilities for the production (through import or on-line programming) of new program segments that then are becoming scripts for new performances. *For the time being, I believe that a safe and understandable structuring of performances is best achieved by insisting that program segments produced within a performance may only be executed as a part of another, external performance.*

Programs may provide persistent or transient structure. In a database environment, the structure of the database is persistent. The structures of, e.g., the SQL queries operating upon the database are transient and should be generated by the database user processes (actors), and then performed by query processes.

The theatre metaphor may be generalised to systems where a set of performances are distributed to a set of locations called *stages* where they are performed by ensembles. The process of setting up and controlling the interplay between script and the ensemble in producing the performance is called *staging* or stage-management. (The sub-process of assigning actors to roles is traditionally called *casting*.)

*Hamlet, Act III, Scene II:* Staging, Layered Communication and Interpretation

The need for more complex models of information systems and system development became evident during the 1970s, as well as the need for involving the users. These activities started in a cooperation between the Norwegian Computing Center and the Norwegian Trade Unions in the early 1970s and spread (as "Participatory

Design" or "The Scandinavian School") to other countries. An overview is given in [Nygaard, K., 1986]. In [Nygaard, K. and Håndlykken, P., 1980, p. 169] it is stated:

" ... , the two main tasks for which the system specialist has a particular responsibility are:

the organisation of the proper cooperation of a large and varied group of information processing and communication equipment, many operating in parallel.

the design of the modes of expression available in the involved peoples' interaction with the information system - from their pushing of buttons, through their use of a limited set of rigidly defined transactions to their use of a programming language. If the sum total of a particular person's modes of expression in relation to the system is called his language, then it is seen that design and implementation of languages are essential tasks.

The "operating system" now becomes an integral part of organisational structure, and should (according to e.g. agreements, laws) be designed, or at least to a very great extent be modifiable locally."

The first extension of the theatre metaphor was inspired by "the play within the play" in Shakespeare's Hamlet. In Act III, Scene II Hamlet is staging a play with a troupe of touring actors. Later it is performed before the court, with Hamlet, the Queen (Hamlet's mother), the current King (Hamlet's uncle, brother of the now deceased King, Hamlet's father) in the audience. Hamlet has staged a play portraying his suspicions: The previous King is murdered by his brother, who pours poison in the King's ear while he is asleep in his garden (considered a fail-safe procedure at the time).

This results in a two-layered performance (see Figure 3): The top-layer performance is staged on a stage-within-the-stage. The roles of the King and the assassin are performed by 1st Actor and 2nd Actor as the main actors in the ensemble. They are communicating (interacting), and the King dies.

The lower-layer performance is the events in the court: Hamlet observing his mother and uncle, the King deeply disturbed by seeing his own crime re-enacted, etc. The two actors, 1st and 2nd Actor, are at this level roles performed by actors in the underlying ensemble, consisting of human actors.

In this layered situation, the Assassin cannot communicate with Hamlet in the audience. If that was attempted the structure of the situation would break down, and we would see what may be called "absurd theatre". Also, the actor playing the King may not address Hamlet, even if the communication between the King and Hamlet is implemented through communication between the actor playing the King and Hamlet, respectively.

This organisation of performances in layers is often used in building complex operating systems, but has not been supported by specific language constructs that may, I believe, result in easier, safer and more comprehensible implementations. The availability of tools for this layering may also facilitate the creation of general classes of distributed systems.

The analogy with computer-based performances should be obvious and is illustrated in Figure 4, in which we even have a stunt processor stepping in whenever the stunt of rapid multiplications is to be performed.

**Figure 4.** Hamlet, Act III, Scene II

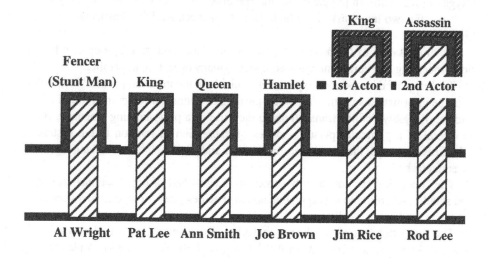

**Figure 5.** Computer Ensemble

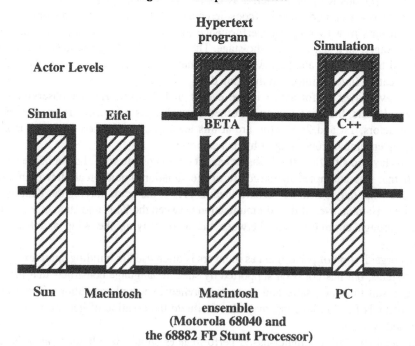

"When general object-oriented systems are considered, one needs also a generalisation of the theatre metaphor to multiple, communicating stages, as well as substages within a given stage. Our work till now shows that the generalisation to substages will not present large conceptual problems."

Some quotes from the GOODS project application:

"The actions are (will be) conceived as going on in layers, with hardware at the bottom, operating systems layers in between, and a final application task in the top layer. The structure of the application task, its program, is developed on the same equipment, and should get its proper place defined in a suitable layer." "A lower level object may at different stages at higher levels enact different views on this lower level object."

Figure 6 is from Lindsjørn and Sjøbergs ECOOP '88 paper and illustrates actors and performances at different layers in the construction and operation of a database.

**Figure 6.** Database Actors

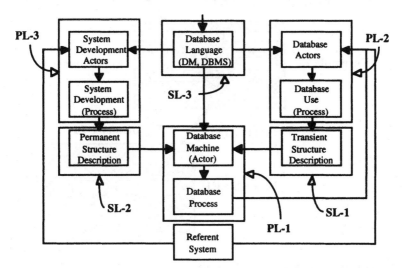

We find a similar multi-layered structure when we analyse process/structure layers in system development [Nygaard, K., 1986]:

*Process level 1:* The information process (e.g. program executions, data processing by people and machinery in offices, etc.).

*Structure level 1:* The limitations imposed upon this process by computer programs, machine hardware properties, written and unwritten rules of human behaviour etc.

*Process level 2:* The system development process, including programming as a partial process, that has the structure of the information process (or the modification of its structure) as its product.

*Structure level 2:* The limitations imposed upon system development by organization, existing knowledge, available resources etc.

*Process level 3:* The process of learning within organizations, the research process, the adaptation of organizations to a changed environment.

I feel that this scheme should be reexamined in the context of system development and staging of distributed systems.

Our current ideas for language constructs are illustrated by Figure 7.

**Figure 7.**  Performance Layers and Binding

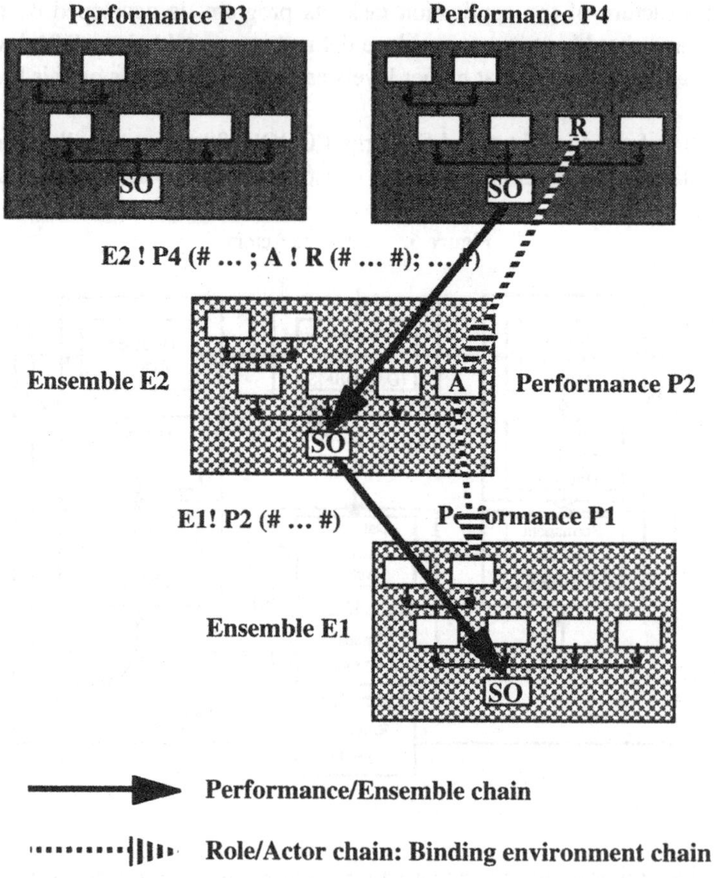

The basic imperative: "Let actor A perform role R!", or "Let A perform R!". In programming language notation:

A!R

(As an alternative we could write R!A, read as "Let R be performed by A!". The final choice will depend upon what seems most logical when the elaboration of the grammar and semantics of the imperative have been better worked out.)

Since there may be further specification to be given for the duration of this actor/role linking, the imperative should be augmented by a additional part:

A!R(#..... #)

For the time being, we feel that external references out of nests should be between performances. (We may change our minds.) Probably the actor/role linking should then take place through a linking of an ensemble E to a performance P. P then is a an existing (persistent program execution) performance or a reference to a program (script) that will generate a new performance accordingly:

E!P (# ... ; A1!R1 (# ... #); A2!R2 (# ... #); ... #)

Binding rules must then be established. The obvious one is that x in R is initially bound in P, normally, in its own environment. If no binding is found (not even in the system object of P, the last location examined), x is bound in the environment of A, that is, within E (with A as the first object and the system object of E as the last object to be examined for a binding). Binding of x to a specified identifier y in A's environment may be made by:

E!P(# ... ; A!R(# ... ; x:y; ... #); ... #)

This possibility makes it possible to provide a tailor made interface of an actor A (e.g. a document) to be used in a given setting (e.g. a meeting performance), and thus multiple interfaces to any object. When this is combined with the scoping possibilities discussed in Section 5, a very rich set of capabilities will be available.

The imperatives of the form E!P etc. do not belong within P. Do they belong within E, the ensemble, regarded as a lower level performance? Do they belong in a third performance, that of a Master Puppeteer, overseeing all performances, staging the stage managers? There are many possibilities, and it will be fun to explore them.

Will all the constructs proposed in this lecture and later in the GOODS project be implemented? If so, will the implementation be efficient, considering the basic nature of the mechanisms involved?

We intend to implement. We believe that implementations may be efficient, based upon experience with corresponding well-structured implementation of basic mechanisms earlier, dating back to SIMULA. But we cannot be sure.

Gisle Hannemyr in the GOODS reference group has pointed out that it will be very useful to be able to create, with little or moderate effort, a high-level implementation of a complex distributed system, even if it is not very efficient. Many of the crucial aspects may by this approach be evaluated before a more basic-level implementation is embarked upon.


## 4    *Black Objects, Kabuki and Scopes:* Precise Prescriptions of Visibility

Continuing our references to the theatre, I was very impressed by birds, dragons etc. in the Japanese Kabuki performances, carrying out very intelligent and most incredible feats. How? Simple: They were handled by stage workers dressed in black. Didn't this destroy the illusion? Not at all. The audience had worked the scoping rule into their conception of what they saw. They *knew* that people dressed completely in black were to be considered invisible.

By "scoping" we understand the mechanisms that in a program execution (performance) determine which other objects and object attributes are accessible at a given location and time. Those that are accessible, we call "visible". Certain aspects of scopes are determined by the language structure, by "structural visibility". Other aspects may, to have effect, be supplemented by "specified visibility", that is, by specific declarations.

DELTA is a block-structured language, describing nested object-oriented structures. In the DELTA report [DELTA, 75], Chapter 3, such structures are discussed in detail in order to describe precisely the interaction that may occur. Two levels of interaction (or, more correctly: *involvement*) are introduced (p. 112):

- "the "comprehensive" versions (*strong involvement*) assume that the acting component has *full information* about the other component's *qualification*, and that not only the *title* (class name) of the qualification is known.
- the "weak" versions (*weak involvement*) do not assume the full information about the other component's qualification, at most information about its (class, pattern) title."

Let C1 and C2 be objects within the same nested system (that is: with one system object enclosing all other objects), then [DELTA,75], p. 116:

"We will say that a component *C1 is perceived by another component C2* if and only if the state of the system is such that C1 is the value of some direct or remote, structural or specified reference of C2."

If C1 is perceived by C2, this implies that C1 may be weakly involved in C2's actions. If C1's attributes in addition are known to C2, then C1 may be strongly involved in C2's actions, and we will say that *C1 is recognised by C2*.

In [DELTA, 75] the conclusion of the discussion is (p. 125): "As we have demonstrated, a component may perceive any other component (object) with the preservation of security, if only the necessary precautions are taken. In fact, it also follows from the discussion that a component may also recognise any other component. It is thus possible to state the rule: Any component is structurally operable by any other component.

Should we state such a rule? If not, which rules should be imposed, and what should be their justification?"

In SIMULA the answer given is that lateral objects are structurally visible, but only accessible if they also are specified as visible by references. Enclosing objects are structurally visible and accessible without further specification. (See Figure 2 for explanation of the terms.) Scopes may in SIMULA be further detailed by specification of "hidden" and "protected" attributes.

Specification of scoping in BETA is discussed in [Kristensen, B. B., Madsen, O. L. and Nygaard, K., 1977] pp. 41-42 under the heading of "Interface specification":

"The set of possibilities available in the <interface description part> has not yet been discussed in any detail. Among the possibilities which may be useful we may mention, e.g.,

- the exclusion of any use of attributes of or references to (object) entities (only the entity itself and its internal entities being available).
- the exclusion of a specified list of identifiers (names and titles).

- the restriction to the use of only a subset of the imperatives of the language."

In BETA a very different answer was given than that of SIMULA: All objects and attributes that are structurally visible should be accessible, without restrictions imposed by the language designers. The rationale was that the scoping imposed is a part of the specification of the system at hand. Powerful tools for specifying visibility were discussed, but not worked out in detail and implemented.

In GOODS our attitude is that of the BETA language, and language constructs will be proposed. As of today, we are considering two general constructs for the declaration part of objects:

EXCLUDING <list of scoping clauses> and EXCLUDED IN <list of scoping clauses>.

A number of different categories of scoping clauses will be introduced:

- The non-terminal symbols of the BETA grammar are considered parts of the BETA language and a list of these non-terminals will be allowed as scoping clauses.
- Terms referring to internal, external, lateral and lineage objects, as well as their nesting level, in nested object-oriented structures.
- Names of attributes.
- Restriction from recognition to perception of objects that may be referenced.

The EXCLUDING declaration specifies terms that may not be used *within the local object* (where the declaration appears), and which object categories in the nested structure that may not be referred to or only perceived but not recognised.The EXCLUDED IN declaration specifies the contexts *outside the object* in which the object's descriptor and its attributes may not appear. Perhaps it will be convenient to introduce also as alternative versions ALLOWING and ALLOWED IN.

I believe that we may augment the set of options by creating clauses that prohibit binding of specified terms in the local performance, so that the binding is certain to take effect in the performing ensemble.

## 5 *Bring in the Clones:* Persistence in General object-oriented Systems

When objects are persistent, that is, when they have extended life spans and participate in a series of program executions, and also are moving between stages (locations), then more detailed and precise concepts are needed for distinguishing between objects stemming from the same source. (In addition to the problems of different versions of objects.) We may see objects that are cloned (copied) from one stage to another, the original still existing in the old location, or "transported", meaning that the original is deleted. We may have "dead" copies describing the state of the object at a specified time and location (state descriptor, snapshot, map), and active objects reconstructed from such a state descriptor. New structural attributes must be introduced in order to cope with these situations, and insight from recent work on persistent programming and object-oriented databases will be exploited in our work.

The notion of representative states were discussed in [Kristensen, B. B., Madsen, O. L. and Nygaard, K., 1977], pp. 41-42: "By a representative state we shall thus understand a state of aL- system component which has the property that it may be given a meaningful interpretation in terms of the task it performs in relation to other L-system components.

If a means is introduced of indicating stages of execution at which the state of a L-system component is representative in the above sense, then it is reasonable to require that

- execution of interrupts are initiated within an L-subsystem LSS, whose actions are executed by an L-processor LP, only when LSS as a whole is in a representative state.
- only values obtained in such representative states are read or assigned by other L-system components.

Similar notions have been treated by others, e.g. [Dijkstra, E., 1974].

When we create tools for dealing with multiple versions of an object and with (usually) partial maps of objects, it may be useful to insist that we from the outside of an object always may assume that it is in a representative state.

If we are to deal in general with persistent object, assuming that we only may interact with them in representative states, we must also provide for the preservation of information about their stage of execution, so that they may be reactivated and proceed with the execution of their associated actions. This, and other related problems, are of course addressed by researchers considering the notion of "live objects" existing on a variety of substrates. We will have to take into account the results already achieved by other researchers in this area.

## 6 *Authoring and Staging:* Programming from the Small to the Large and Systems Development

### 6.1 New modes of expression

In this section I will discuss matters relating to the writing of scripts:

- Different kinds of imperatives, introducing property descriptors, extending the imperatives of a programming language, dealing with the structuring of actions by human actors.
- The notion of open and closed imperatives, allowing for situations in which human actors may act (manouevering) according to motivations and rules that are not describable in programming language terms.
- Having a new go at the notion of contexts, trying to find a solution better than the half-baked ones offered by using inheritance.

- Linking the BETA fragment system alternative to multiple inheritance, program module reuse and program libraries to the new possibilities to defining contexts.

In DELTA the notion of actions had to be extended [DELTA 75, p. 172]: "The actions of a component (object) may be divided into the categories:

- time consuming actions, as, e.g. the heating of ore to the melting point within a furnace, or the traversing of a crane from one point to another, being executed during a time interval.
- instantaneous actions, as, e.g., the leaving of a queue, or the selection of which ship in a queue of waiting ships should be allowed to occupy an empty quay position in a busy harbour, being initiated, executed and completed at a discrete point in time."

(Remember that DELTA is a system description language in which both compilable and computer executable as well as non-compilable and non-computer executable description elements are available.) Since continuous changes of state had to be described, concurrency imperatives with property clauses were introduced, containing property descriptors. A property descriptor is set of relations, separated by commas and enclosed by braces. Examples of concurrency imperatives are:

- WHILE {temperature ≤ melting point} LET {temperature = start-temperature + F(Energy-supply(time))};
- WHILE {time < delivery time} LET {candidates work, each in isolation, on their written exam};
- LET {Evaluation of exam} DEFINE passed, mark;
- LET {x ** + y ** ≤ r **} DEFINE x, y;
- LET {Position of cardinals be inside conclave}; WHILE {no pope is elected} LET {Negotiations go on. Emit black smoke after each indecisive vote}; WHILE {Voting slips are burning} LET {Emit white smoke};

Concurrency imperatives and imposed property descriptors are discussed carefully in the DELTA report, including the duration of the imposition of a property descriptor upon its system environment. These language elements have to be reexamined in the GOODS project. By associating property clauses with objects in an action stack, a dynamically changing set of imposed condition may be described.

In programming languages, declarations are of course examples of property descriptors. More general constraints, described by property clauses have been treated in Alan Borning's work (see [Borning, A., 1981]), and extended availability of such tools in programming languages would be very welcome. However, this mode of expression often is the most natural one when describing the actions of people within the operation of an information system.

A performance of an information system will come to a halt if, at some step in the action sequence of a piece of computing equipment, no definite and precise next step is indicated. This will result in inactivity until a triggering interrupt arrives, from either some other artifact or from a human actor. For a human actor this is different. People may themselves decide which next action to choose in such situations, within the limits imposed. When no such choice exists, we will say that the next action (for a person or some artifact) is closed. When there is choice, the action is open. The actions within the performance then become depending upon the choices made by people in the situation, by what I call their manoeuvering. I think this term is quite suitable, as we may see from some of its meanings in a dictionary:

- A controlled change in movement or direction of a moving vehicle or vessel, as in the flight path of an aircraft.
- A movement or procedure involving skill and dexterity.
- A strategic action undertaken to gain an end.
- Artful handling of affairs that is often marked by scheming and deceit.

(The American Heritage® Dictionary of the English Language, Third Edition copyright © 1992 by Houghton Mifflin Company.)

The situation in the theatre corresponding to what is illustrated, is what is usually referred to as improvisation.

Often the situation is characterised by a manoeuvering in which there also exists a repertoire of available structured action sequences to choose between. This is a category of systems which semi-seriously may be referred to as PASTA systems (from PArtially STructured Activities). It is useful to point out that this mode of system description opens up for the inclusion very subjectively motivated actions, the details of which are unknown to those making the description.

## 6.2 From Simulation to Mediation

SIMULA, DELTA and BETA are languages that describe phenomena and concepts in the real world using objects and classes (patterns in BETA). Thus, object orientation is used to model the real-world domain that the information system is intended to maintain information about. Lately, there has been an attention to also capture aspects beyond this domain, and address the usage world, e.g., aspects relating to actors, communication, articulation of work, collective work arrangements, task flow, and work procedures. This is due to a shift of perspectives regarding the role of the computer in work settings; from a focus on the computer as means of control and administration of a real-world domain, to a focus that also include the computer as a mediator in the usage world, e.g., as in groupware or workflow applications.

Much work is invested in applying object-oriented technology to analysis and design in system development. We feel that more may be achieved than today.

In the GOODS project we will develop and use a conceptual framework for modelling computers incorporated into work arrangements based on activity theory ([Leontjev, A. N., 1983], [Engeström, Y., 1987]). Activity theory is used as a bridging link between the social concerns and the technical concerns as it address human work in a social context and has a strong emphasis on how artifacts (like computer systems) mediate human activity. Further, the theory distinguishes between four aspects of an activity:

*production*
(the production of the outcome of the activity, like a service or goods),
*consumption*
(the use of goods or services by clients/customers or citizens),
*communication*
and
*distribution*
(aspects of the collective work done in order to realise production). We explore using the notion of
*real-world modelling*
to address the production and consumption aspects and a
*notion of a theatre performance*
to address the distribution and communication aspects. ( This work has already started, see [Smørdal, O., 1996], [Smørdal, O., 1997])

## 6.3 In the large: Authoring and Staging

In the GOODS project we regard the concept of distribution in two ways:

- Multiple locations of stages. Still we may need to regard activity on multiple stages as belonging to one logical performance.
- Division of responsibilities. We want to address the responsibilities on objects to the performance as a whole. This include how actors interpret their role.

We argue that both of these interpretations of the concept of distribution are necessary to cope with complex systems, because notions of a whole (a performance), combined with layering (actor-role relationships) are powerful abstractions.

This naturally implies that "programming in the large" becomes an issue, because layering involves attaching various pieces of software to fulfil some function in the performance.

In the discussions of reuse, "programming in the large" has been a slogan. Now the notion of "design patterns" is attracting attention. Other approaches, like Ray Wellands "design zones", are also addressing the same set of problems. The GOODS project should provide a good basis for discussing these problems, and also contribute to solutions.

We will address the structuring of performances at two levels: Authoring and staging. This is due to a need within systems development to separate design of of-the-shelf software and software standards from the adaptation and integration of software in an organisation to fit the work.

When our general view is adopted, one also observes that this will lead to a way of specifying the proper place in the total picture of a number of programming tools, in particular program libraries. Since we will be using the same language approach for all aspects of the total process, we should achieve the "seamlessness" in concepts for the various stages of systems staging, operation and maintenance. Also, as far as we can see, a solution seems to be opening to the old problem of creating unions of contexts without resorting to multiple inheritance. (See, e.g., [Møller-Pedersen, B., 1977])

## 6.4 Research approach

In some of the main object-oriented language developments (SIMULA, Delta, BETA) a rich set of diverse examples were used to develop and test ideas. In the GOODS project the main examples, or scenarios, will be:

- The work in the Planning and Building Authority in the City of Oslo.
- The planning and production in a shipyard.
- The staging and performing of plays in a theatre.
- The development of concepts, the multitude of discussions and the writing of reports by research teams scattered geographically and in various kinds of locations (offices, meeting rooms, homes etc.).

The first scenario will be used extensively in close contact with the administration and specialists working in the Authority. The second and third will mainly serve to provide and test ideas. The fourth we want to establish as a factual networked cooperation system.

# 7 Conclusion

This manuscript has been prepared under extreme time pressure, since the invitation arrived very late. Other researchers whom I have consulted have stated forthrightly and gleefully that they were looking forward to nail me at ECOOP '97 because of the blunders to be expected in a paper not carefully prepared. Hopefully some of the less well-considered proposals will have been improved when the lecture is delivered. But certainly not all.

Also I may at that time be better oriented about the work of others in the same field.

I have, however, used the opportunity offered to give my account of the outline of the GOODS project at an early stage. The other team and reference group members might have preferred a different selection of points to be presented.

I hope that the lecture at least will be useful in bringing us in good and close cooperation with others sharing our interests.

# References

Belsnes, D., 1982: "Distribution and Execution of Distributed Systems", Report NR- 717, Norwegian Computing Center. Oslo 1982.

[BETA, 1993] Madsen, O. L., Møller-Pedersen, B. and Nygaard, K., 1993: "Object Oriented Programming in the BETA Programming Language", 357 pp. Addison-Wesley/ACM Press, ISBN 0-201-62430-3, 1993.

29

Birtwistle, G.M., Dahl, O.-J., Myhrhaug, B.and Nygaard, K., 1973: "SIMULA begin". Studentlitteratur, Lund and Auerbach Publ. Inc., Philadelphia, 1973.

Borning, A., 1981: "The Programming Language Aspects of ThingLab: A Constraint-Oriented Simulation Laboratory", ACM Transactions on Programming Languages and Systems 3(4), pp. 353-387, Oct. 1981.

Dahl, O.-J. and Nygaard, K., 1965: "SIMULA - a Language for Programming and Description of Discrete Event Systems". Norwegian Computing Center, Oslo 1965.

Dahl, O.-J., Myhrhaug. B and Nygaard, K., 1968, 1970, 1972, 1984: "SIMULA 67 Common Base Language", Norwegian Computing Center 1968 and later editions.

Dahle, H. P., 1981: "Observasjon av BETA-systemer" ("Observation of BETA Systems"), Report NR-707, Norwegian Computing Center, Oslo, 1981.

[DELTA, 1975] Holbæk-Hanssen, E., Håndlykken, P. and Nygaard, K., 1975: "System Description and the DELTA Language". Norwegian Computing Center, 1975.

Dijkstra, E. W., 1974: "Self-stabilizing Systems in Spite of Distributed Control", Comm. ACM 17, 11 (Nov. 1974), pp. 643-644.

Engeström, Y., 1987: "Learning by Expanding. An Activity-theoretical approach to developmental research". Orienta-Konsultit Oy, Helsinki, 1987.

Haugen, Ø., 1980: "Hierarkier i programmering og systembeskrivelse" (Hierarchies in Programming and System Description"), Master Thesis, Department of Informatics, University of Oslo, 1980.

Hoare, C. A. R., 1968: "Record Handling". In Genuys, F., ed., "Programming Languages", pp. 291-347. New York, Academic Press.

Holbæk-Hanssen, E., Håndlykken, P. and Nygaard, K., 1975: "System Description and the DELTA Language". Norwegian Computing Center, 1975.

Kristensen, B. B., Madsen, O. L. and Nygaard, K., 1977: "BETA Language Development Survey Report, 1. November 1976" (Revised Version, September 1977). DAIMI PB-65, September 1977, Dept. of Computer Science, University of Aarhus.

Kristensen, B. B., Madsen, O. L. and Nygaard, K., 1976-80, "BETA Project Working Note" 1-8. Norwegian Computing Center, Oslo and Computer Science Department, Aarhus University, Aarhus, 1976-80.

Kristensen, B. B., Madsen, O. L., Møller-Pedersen, B and Nygaard, K., 1983: "Syntax Directed Program Modularization". In "Interactive Computing Systems" (Ed. Degano, P. and Sandewall, E.), North-Holland 1983.

Kristensen, B. B., Madsen, O. L., Møller-Pedersen, B and Nygaard, K., 1983: "The BETA Programming Language". In "Research Directions in Object-Oriented Languages" (Ed. Shriver, B., and Wegner, P.), MIT Press, Cambridge, Massachusetts 1987.

Kristensen, B. B., Madsen, O. L., Møller-Pedersen, B and Nygaard, K., 1986: "Dynamic Exchange of BETA Systems", Unpublished manuscript, Oslo and Aarhus, 1986.

Leontjev, A. N., 1983: "Virksomhed, bevidsthed, personlighed" (English: "Activity, Consciousness, Personality"(?)). Forlaget Progress, Denmark, 1983.

Lindsjørn, Y. and Sjøberg, D., "Database Concepts Described in an Object-Oriented Perspective". In Proceedings of the European Conference on Object-Oriented

Programming (Oslo, 15th–17th August 1988), Gjessing, S. and Nygaard, K. (editors), pp. 300–318, Lecture Notes in Computer Science 322, Springer-Verlag, 1988.

Madsen, O. L., Møller-Pedersen, B. and Nygaard, K., 1993: "Object Oriented Programming in the BETA Programming Language", 357 pp. Addison-Wesley/ACM Press, ISBN 0-201-62430-3, 1993

Møller-Pedersen, B., 1977: "Proposal for a Context Concept in DELTA". DAIMI PB-83, DELTA Project Report No. 7. Department of Computer Science, University of Aarhus, Denmark, 1977

Nygaard, K., 1963: "Opparbeidelse av kompetanse innenfor Real-Time Systemer" ("Building Competence on Real-Time Systems"). Working Note September 19, 1963. Norwegian Computing Center.

Nygaard, K., 1970: "System Description by SIMULA - an Introduction". Norwegian Computing Center, Publication S-35, Oslo 1970.

Nygaard, K., 1986: "Program Development as a Social Activity", Information Processing 86, pp.189-198, Proceedings of the IFIP 10th World Computer Congress, North Holland, 1986.

Nygaard, K., 1992: "How Many Choices Do We Make? How Many Are Difficult?", pp. 52-59 in "Software Development and Reality Construction", Floyd, C., Züllighoven, H., Budde, R., and Keil-Slawik, R., editors. Springer-Verlag, Berlin 1992.

Nygaard, K., 1996: " "Those Were the Days"? or "Heroic Times Are Here Again"?" The Scandinavian Journal of Information Systems, Vol. 8.2, 1996.

Nygaard, K. and Håndlykken, P., 1980: "The System Development Process". In "Software Engineering Environments" - Proceedings of the Symposium held in Lahnstein, Germany, June 16-20, 1980. Hünke, H., editor, North Holland, Amsterdam 1981

Nygaard, K. and Sørgaard, P., 1987: "The Perspective Concept in Informatics", pp. 371-393 in "Computers and Democracy", Bjerknes, G., Ehn, P., and Kyng, M., editors, Abury, Aldershot, UK, 1987.

Smørdal, O., 1996: "Soft Objects Analysis, A modelling approach for analysis of interdependent work practices". In Patel D and Sun Y (eds.) Third international conference on object-oriented information systems (OOIS'96). (London, UK), Springer-Verlag, pp. 195-208, 1996.

Smørdal, O., 1997: "Performing Objects —A conceptual framework for object oriented modelling of computers incorporated into work arrangements". (Forthcomming).

Nygaard, K., 1992: "How Many Choices Do We Make? How Many Are Difficult?", pp. 52-59 in "Software Development and Reality Construction", Floyd, C., Züllighoven, H., Budde, R., and Keil-Slawik, R., editors. Springer-Verlag, Berlin 1992.

Nygaard, K., 1996: " "Those Were the Days"? or "Heroic Times Are Here Again"?" The Scandinavian Journal of Information Systems, Vol. 8.2, 1996.

Nygaard, K. and Håndlykken, P., 1980: "The System Development Process". In "Software Engineering Environments" - Proceedings of the Symposium held in Lahnstein, Germany, June 16-20, 1980. Hünke, H., editor, North Holland, Amsterdam 1981

Nygaard, K. and Sørgaard, P., 1987: "The Perspective Concept in Informatics", pp. 371-393 in "Computers and Democracy", Bjerknes, G., Ehn, P., and Kyng, M., editors, Abury, Aldershot, UK, 1987.

[SIMULA I, 1965] Dahl, O.-J. and Nygaard, K., 1965: "SIMULA - a Language for Programming and Description of Discrete Event Systems". Norwegian Computing Center, Oslo 1965.

[SIMULA 67, 1967] Dahl, O.-J., Myhrhaug. B and Nygaard, K., 1968, 1970, 1972, 1984: "SIMULA 67 Common Base Language", Norwegian Computing Center 1968 and later editions.

Smørdal, O., 1996: "Soft Objects Analysis, A modelling approach for analysis of interdependent work practices". In Patel D and Sun Y (eds.) Third international conference on object-oriented information systems (OOIS'96). (London, UK), Springer-Verlag, pp. 195-208, 1996.

Smørdal, O., 1997: "Performing Objects —A conceptual framework for object oriented modelling of computers incorporated into work arrangements". (Forthcomming).

# Balloon Types:
# Controlling Sharing of State in Data Types

Paulo Sérgio Almeida *

Department of Computing, Imperial College, London SW7 2BZ

**Abstract.** Current data abstraction mechanisms are not adequate to control sharing of state in the general case involving objects in linked structures. The pervading possibility of sharing is a source of errors and an obstacle to language implementation techniques.

We present a general extension to programming languages which makes the ability to share state a first class property of a data type, resolving a long-standing flaw in existing data abstraction mechanisms.

Balloon types enforce a strong form of encapsulation: no state reachable (directly or transitively) by a balloon object is referenced by any external object. Syntactic simplicity is achieved by relying on a non-trivial static analysis as the checking mechanism.

Balloon types are applicable in a wide range of areas such as program transformation, memory management and distributed systems. They are the key to obtaining self-contained composite objects, truly opaque data abstractions and value types—important concepts for the development of large scale, provably correct programs.

## 1  Introduction

Data abstraction mechanisms were introduced [8, 12] long ago and are used by most modern languages. While these mechanisms have proved successful when value semantics and named objects were the norm, this is not quite true in the case of dynamic linked data structures composed of unnamed objects and when assignment and parameter passing have reference semantics—something now common in object-oriented languages.

The use of dynamic linked structures is a source of errors due to the pervading possibility of sharing objects. The phenomenon of interference, for which solutions have been devised for the case of named objects [29], becomes considerably more complex, making it difficult to reason about programs or to perform program transformations such as parallelisation.

The contribution of this paper is a general language mechanism to control the complexity which arises from sharing unnamed mutable objects in dynamic linked structures, by making the ability to share state a first class property of a data type.

---

* On leave from Departamento de Informática, Universidade do Minho, Portugal. Partially supported by JNICT—PRAXIS XXI grant BD-3390-94.

In section 2 we explain the problem in detail. In particular we explain why the current data abstraction mechanisms do not provide appropriate support for managing the sharing of objects and discuss the fundamental flaw in the form of encapsulation provided.

In section 3 we describe balloon types: the basic idea, the invariant it enforces, and give an overview of the checking mechanism to enforce the invariant. This includes a 'simple rule' and a non-trivial static analysis which we developed formally as an abstract interpretation. We also introduce two important specialisations of balloon types—opaque balloon types and value types—and summarise the taxonomy of state sharing which results from balloon types. We end by discussing issues related to concurrency and distributed systems.

In section 4 we present the related work and finally the conclusions. The technical details of the abstract interpretation are somewhat involved and we do not describe them here, but we present in the appendix the most essential part.

## 2   State, Sharing and Encapsulation

### 2.1   Values, Objects and Aliasing

Language semantics for toy imperative languages associate a variable with a value. If we are to consider realistic procedural or object-oriented languages we must make the distinction between variables, objects and values. The concept of object is needed to reason about sharing, as it is meaningless to talk about the sharing of values [25].

This is true even in the case of primitive types like integer: integer variables denote objects that contain (representations of) values. We use this model to accurately describe the behaviour of a program when *aliasing* is present. In the case of integers, aliasing can be created when using call-by-reference. For example:

```
PROCEDURE f(VAR i:INTEGER, VAR j:INTEGER)
BEGIN
   WRITE i;
   j := j+1;
   WRITE i
END

VAR x:INTEGER;
BEGIN
   x := 1;
   f(x, x)
END
```

During the invocation of procedure $f$ variables $i$ and $j$ denote the same integer object: they are said to be aliases for the same object. The increment of $j$ changes the object which is also denoted by $i$. As such, the two write statements will result in '1' and '2'.

As in [15, 14] we will use the terms:

- *dynamic aliasing* when stack based *variables* (including parameters) are involved (as above),
- *static aliasing* when *state variables*[2] of objects are involved (discussed next section).

Dynamic aliasing has a lifetime which depends on the execution of functions, whereas static aliasing reflects the structure of the object graph.

Aliasing has been long ago recognised as a source of problems [13] and some attempts have been made to prevent it. The previous example would be invalid in Pascal [33], due to using $x$ twice as an argument, but in general dynamic aliasing cannot be prevented at compile time given parameter passing with reference semantics. An example is the call f(A[i], A[j]), when the indexes cannot be determined at compile time.

One nice property of integer objects is that they cannot be *statically aliased*: they cannot be shared by several state variables of objects.[3] This is a result of the assignment having value semantics: it copies the integer value. Consider the type Point, with state variables $x$ and $y$ of type Int:

```
Point = { x,y:Int }
p:Point;
...
p.x := 1;
p.y := p.x;
increment(p.y);
write p.x, p.y;
```

Programmers expect that the increment operation applied to $p.y$ does not affect $p.x$ and that the outcome of the program is '1 2'.

To summarise: in primitive types regardless of whether dynamic aliasing occurs (due to call-by-reference), static aliasing does not occur as the assignment has value semantics. The following cannot occur:

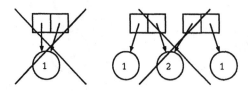

---

[2] We will use the term *state variables* for what in different places is referred to as instance variables or fields.

[3] This is assuming that languages impose some 'reasonable' constraints, like forbidding the explicit use of pointers and dereferencing. Such constraints tend to be incorporated in modern languages like Eiffel or Java. In languages like C++ [31] 'anything is possible', including storing in heap based objects pointers to stack based objects.

## 2.2 Sharing of State

In many object-oriented languages (eg. Smalltalk [10], Java [4]) variables of user-defined types are references to objects, and the assignment has reference semantics (copies just the reference). This makes sharing of objects by other objects (static aliasing) possible. As an example, consider the type Rectangle:

```
Rectangle = { p1,p2:Point;
              rotate(Int)
            }
r1,r2:Rectangle;
...
r2.p1 :- r1.p2;
r1.rotate(90);
r2.rotate(45);
```

As in Simula [8], we have used the ':-' notation for reference assignment. After the assignment both rectangles share a common point object. Consider the operation rotate which updates the point objects that constitute a rectangle; there would be interference between the two rotate instructions, as the first would modify a point that is accessed by the second.

Although sharing can be useful and may be desired in some cases, this is probably not what the users of rectangle objects would desire. They would expect that each rectangle is a self-contained object, and that operations on different rectangles do not interfere.

Programmers can obtain a copy of a point instead of copying a reference to it, but they can copy the reference accidentally. This can easily happen if the available assignment operator copies just the reference.

*Expanded types* were introduced in Eiffel [27], whereas originally user-defined types were always *reference types*. If a type is declared as expanded, variables will hold the object itself and not a reference to the object; also parameter passing and assignment copies the object.

Expanded types solve the problem in this particular case: the programmer just has to declare types Point and Rectangle to be expanded. This however makes it impossible to pass references to rectangles to a function so that the objects can be updated in-place. Moreover, it is not possible to have subtype polymorphism in expanded types.

## 2.3 Sharing and Unbounded Linked Structures

Expanded types provide insufficient support to prevent unwanted sharing. In the case of unbounded linked structures such as linked lists the recursive nature of these types prevents them from being declared as expanded. This means that even if one type is declared as expanded, objects of that type may need to reference a list, which cannot be an expanded type and may itself be shared.

Expanded types thus fail since they are not able to prevent sharing of linked substructures.

Consider a Shape type with several subtypes such as Rectangle and Polygon. Some of these types may require pointer structures such as a linked list of points in the case of polygon. Some of the structures may even contain cycles. Suppose we have an array of shapes and a loop which rotates each of the shapes in the array, as illustrated in Fig. 1.

```
Shape = { rotate(Int) }

Rectangle <: Shape
    = { p1,p2:Point }
Circle <: Shape
    = { c:Point; r:Real }
Polygon <: Shape
    = { List[Point] }
Graph <: Shape
    = { ... }

a:Array[Shape];
for i = 1 to N
  a[i].rotate(45);
```

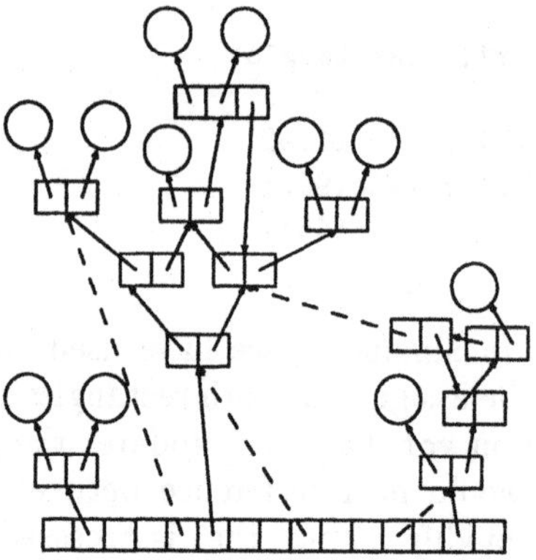

**Fig. 1.**

It could happen contrary to the programmer's intent that two shapes share the whole or part of the objects of their states, as illustrated by the dashed arrows. This would imply that performing a rotate on one shape would interfere with other rotate operations, contrary to the expectations of the programmer.

This pervading possibility of sharing state is what makes it difficult to reason about programs in procedural or object-oriented languages. Contrast the shapes example with plain integers:

```
a:Array[Int];
for i = 1 to N
  increment(a[i]);
```

Although trivial for integers, it can be extremely difficult for the compiler to determine in the case of shapes if the different iterations of the loop interfere. Providing an unchecked directive so that a programmer who 'knows' that they do not interfere gives that 'knowledge' to the compiler is dangerous. It can be the case that the programmer is wrong and they do indeed interfere, due to a bug in the implementation of some operation that causes the unwanted sharing.

## 2.4 Data Abstraction and Encapsulation of State

According to [32], a data abstraction is 'an object whose state is accessible only through its operations'. It may be thought that current data abstraction mechanisms are appropriate enough for controlling sharing of state. The problem is that currently they just control the access to the state variables and not to the whole reachable state; they consider it 'other objects'. However, to reason about program behaviour it matters precisely whether these 'other objects' are shared.

Only by thinking of the state associated with an object as the state directly or transitively reachable by the state variables is it possible to argue about whether the state is encapsulated (and not referenced by external objects), or is shared (and part of it is also referenced by external objects). This is how we see state and encapsulation of state.

The same view of state is expressed in [14], and a similar attitude towards encapsulation can be perceived in [5]. Also [15] has this interesting remark: 'the big lie of object-oriented programming is that objects provide encapsulation.'

A widespread misconception is that if encapsulation (as we see it) is wanted it is enough not to have functions of the type returning references to the state; this is definitely false:

- There can be interaction between the state and the parameters received by some function of the data type. This interaction can involve invocations of operations which may cause some object from the state to become referenced by an object reachable by a parameter or vice-versa, breaking the encapsulation of the state.
- The implementation itself, while manipulating several instances of the data type, may cause sharing of their states.

These situations may happen accidentally, contrary to the expectations of the implementor of the data type, with no warning or prevention by the compiler.

## 3 Balloon Types

Even if technically possible, a data type should not always enforce encapsulation of state. Although encapsulation may be wanted for some types, for others sharing may be needed. Designers of data types must be able to choose.

The point we make is that current languages do not provide a suitable mechanism for making this choice. One source of problems is precisely because this choice is not apparent (it may have not even been considered), and users of a data type may have wrong expectations about the behaviour in terms of sharing.

The basic idea of balloon types is precisely to make the ability of sharing state a first class property of data types, as important as the operations provided and their signatures. Among other things: it becomes part of a type definition, it is considered in type checking, it affects what code programmers are allowed to write, it is considered in the formal reasoning about programs, and it is used in compiler optimisations.

We propose a binary classification of data types with respect to sharing properties. Any type[4] is classified as either a *balloon* type or a *non-balloon* type.

- Balloon types are useful to prevent unwanted sharing of state, guaranteeing encapsulation of state. They result in cleaner semantics, being a means to prevent unexpected interference.
- Non-balloon types correspond to what current languages offer regarding user-defined types. They allow full freedom of sharing, being useful to represent linked structures with possible substructure sharing.

Balloon types have the properties that:

- Objects of a balloon type are unshareable by state variables of objects.
- All the state reachable by a balloon is encapsulated, in the sense that no part of it can be referenced by state variables of any 'external' object.

Some examples of balloon types are primitive types such as integer, real and boolean. People expect that they may be at most (and preferably not) dynamically aliased, but not statically aliased (not shared by different objects). There is no more than one object owner of an integer object, and there are no objects which can have a reference to part of the state of an integer object (a reference to some bit).

Programmers would probably choose 'shape' to be a balloon type to obtain 'nice' semantics in its use in programs. It would prevent accidental sharing even if each shape is a complex structure with internal sharing and even cycles, as illustrated in Fig. 2. In the loop example the balloon invariant would make clear to both programmer and compiler the absence of interference between iterations: performing a rotate on a shape a[i] would not affect a shape a[j] ($j \neq i$). This would make reasoning about the program easier and the compiler could perform loop transformations such as parallelisation. This is accomplished with an almost negligible syntactic cost; if we compare Fig. 1 with Fig. 2 there is only one extra keyword in the new program.

This figure also illustrates that in spite of the binary classification, both balloons and non-balloons can be used as part of the state of each other. This results in a hierarchical organisation of the graph of objects and in scalability of the control of sharing.

We consider static type checking as the useful thing to do regarding balloon types:

- Whether some type is a balloon type is declared by one keyword (such as balloon) in the definition of the type, and no syntactic cost is imposed on client code.
- A candidate implementation of the type undergoes a non-trivial compile-time checking which enforces the run-time invariant for objects of the type. The implementation may be accepted or rejected.

---

[4] We will use frequently 'type' as a short for data type (including primitive types), as we will not mention function types or higher-order types.

```
Shape = balloon { rotate(Int) }

Rectangle <: Shape
     = { p1,p2:Point }
Circle <: Shape
     = { c:Point; r:Real }
Polygon <: Shape
     = { List[Point] }
Graph <: Shape
     = { ... }

a:Array[Shape];
for i = 1 to N
  a[i].rotate(45);
```

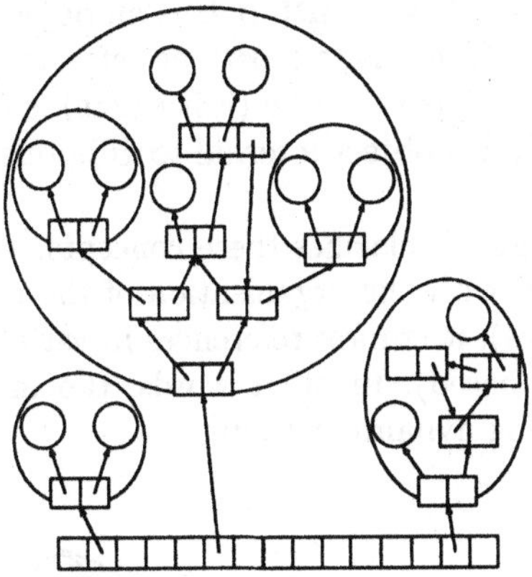

**Fig. 2.**

The emphasis is on extreme syntactic simplicity, placing the burden on the compiler. We consider this important for the success of the integration of balloon types in languages and the acceptance by programmers.

## 3.1  The Balloon Invariant

We now describe more precisely the run-time invariant which is enforced by balloon types. We remind that every object is an instance of either a balloon or a non-balloon type, and thus the terms balloon and non-balloon object. First we present some definitions.

Let $G$ be the undirected graph with all objects as nodes and all references between non-balloon objects and from balloon to non-balloon objects as edges.

**Cluster:** A cluster is a connected subgraph of $G$ which is not contained in a larger connected subgraph.

The graph $G$ serves only to define cluster. Consider from now on all objects and references in their state variables (at a given point in time).

**Internal:** An object $O$ is said to be *internal* to a balloon object $B$ iff :
   - $O$ is a non-balloon in the same cluster as $B$ or
   - $O$ is a balloon referenced by $B$ or by some non-balloon in the same cluster as $B$ or
   - there exists a balloon $B'$ internal to $B$ and $O$ is internal to $B'$.

**External:** An object is said to be *external* to a balloon object $B$ iff it is neither $B$ nor internal to $B$.

Now we can state the invariant.

**Balloon Invariant:** If $B$ is an object of a balloon type then:

$I_1$ There is at most one reference to $B$ in the set of all objects.

$I_2$ This reference (if it exists) is from an object external to $B$.

$I_3$ No object internal to $B$ is referenced by any object external to $B$.

Figure 3 clarifies these concepts. We should stress that the invariant is concerned with the organisation of the object graph (objects and inter-object references); it ignores references in variables from the chain of procedure calls (i.e. stack based). In other words, the invariant is concerned with static aliasing, ignoring dynamic aliasing.

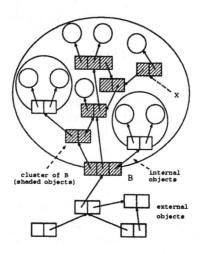

**Fig. 3.**

The invariant deserves some explanation, in particular why internal objects were not simply defined as the objects in the state of the balloon (that is, reachable by the transitive closure of the references relation). With such definition we would have the 'naive invariant'. However it would not be as useful or feasible of being enforced as the chosen invariant.

The reason is that during the execution of some operation of a balloon type several objects may be created. Some of them may be temporary, only referenced by local variables (or other similar objects), and not incorporated into the state of any 'external' object, being subject to garbage collection when the function terminates. The figure shows an object only referenced by a local variable ($x$).

While they exist these objects may store references to the state of a balloon. This violates the naive invariant as these objects are not part of the state of the balloon but have references to the state. Even if such did not actually happen, the mere possibility of it happening could lead to conservative rejection of code by a checking mechanism. For both these reasons, the naive invariant would make the set of valid programs unnecessarily restricted.

In the balloon invariant such temporary non-balloons are allowed and are classified as internal objects. The state reachable by a balloon object is a subset of the internal objects.

One consequence that can be derived from the invariant is:

$I_4$ From all objects that make up a cluster, at most one is a balloon object.

Furthermore, it can be shown that $(I_1 \wedge I_2 \wedge I_4 \Rightarrow I_3)$, which means that the invariant is equivalent to $(I_1 \wedge I_2 \wedge I_4)$. The balloon type checking mechanism enforces this last expression. $I_1$ is enforced by a simple rule concerning the reference assignment, while $I_2$ and $I_4$ are enforced by means of a static analysis of the candidate program.

## 3.2   Reference Assignment—the Simple Rule

**The Simple Rule:** A reference to a (pre-existing) balloon cannot be stored in any state variable of any object (by the reference assignment).

Which means that no statement like

```
x.v :- b;
```

is allowed when $b$ is of balloon type. It is important to note that the rule only mentions state variables of objects. This means that stack based variables and state variables of objects are treated differently by the type system.

The rule emphasises the difference between 'temporarily' *using* a reference to an object and *storing* the reference in some state variable of an object. This last case is what creates sharing of objects by other objects, and it is forbidden for balloon types.

By the simple rule, if only a reference assignment were provided by a language, no objects at all could have a reference to a balloon object. Such is made possible by providing the language with a *copy* assignment, as discussed below.

The simple rule is enough to enforce $I_1$, while allowing great freedom in the use of balloons: a reference to a balloon can be stored in variables, passed as argument to functions and returned from functions. The only case prevented is storing the reference in a state variable of some object. In particular, a function of a balloon type can safely return a reference to an internal balloon and client code can use the reference to invoke operations on it.

As an example consider a dictionary containing elements that can be searched using a key. Here the elements are shapes and the keys are strings. We define a function which invokes a search to locate a shape and then rotates and moves the shape:

```
DictShape = balloon Dictionary[Elem = Shape, Key = String];

rotate_and_move(ds:DictShape, name:String)
{
  s:Shape;
  s :- ds.search(name);
  s.rotate(45);
  s.move(10,15);
}
```

Here both shape and dictionary of shape are balloon types.[5] The simple rule allows the search to safely return a reference to an internal shape of the dictionary, as it will be forbidden to be stored in any object.

Balloon types can be important towards obtaining provably correct programs. The uncontrolled possibility of state sharing in current languages result in unexpected modifications to the state manipulated by the implementation of a data type. Quoting [23]: 'If modifications can occur elsewhere, then we cannot establish the correctness of the implementation just by examining its code; for example, we cannot guarantee locally that the representation invariant holds.' In balloon types—as opposed to current languages—the data type has complete control: the balloon invariant ensures that the only way a client can gain access to the state of a balloon is by a reference being returned by a function of the data type, as the search function above.

A function from a balloon type may decide to return a reference to an internal balloon specially if the (composite) value associated with this balloon does not matter for the representation invariant of the data type. Clearly, the contents of shapes are irrelevant to the implementation of the dictionary data type and returning a reference to an internal shape does not prevent reasoning about the correctness of its implementation.

### 3.3 Copy Assignment

The simple rule implies that state variables of balloon type can only be made to reference newly created balloons. Two cases should be provided for:

- The creation of an object using some constructor mechanism:
  ```
  x.shape := Rectangle(10,20,100,130);
  ```
- A general copy mechanism with the semantics of deep-copy (as in e.g. [19]), which creates a copy of a balloon and all its reachable state, while preserving internal sharing. It can be provided as a *copy assignment*:
  ```
  x.shape := s;
  ```

---

[5] Dictionary here is a generic type. The treatment of bounded polymorphism (as well as subtyping) is beyond the scope of this paper. Informally we can say that it will be more useful that 'balloonness' is not a property of a generic type itself but of its instantiations. An implementation of a generic type can be type-checked to access the correctness of its instantiation as balloon/non-balloon for each possibility regarding the type parameters being or not balloon types.

This copy assignment—which we denote by ':=' as opposed to ':-' for reference assignment—is the natural generalisation of the assignment for primitive types; it copies the (composite) value associated with the object. It emphasises 'obtain new object' as opposed to 'reference existing object'. To stress this we have used the ':=' notation in the constructor example above where no physical copy is involved.

We put the emphasis on observable behaviour and reasoning about the program rather than on an implementation directed definition. The copy does not have to happen physically, being subject to optimisation. This contrasts with current languages where it is close to impossible to optimise some built-in deep-copy mechanism. As a result, programmers rarely use it and suffer from unexpected interference or sometimes use it when it is not physically necessary.

Several possibilities for avoiding the deep-copy and performing only a pointer copy include:

- If the balloon which is the source of the assignment is not used subsequently until being 'released'.
- The balloon invariant does not have to hold physically: an implementation can share physically a balloon if that does not affect the outcome of the program. If the balloon remains immutable sharing becomes irrelevant.
- Using a 'copy on update': physically sharing a balloon and only copying it if some operation which causes updates is performed.

Although this kind of optimisations are the norm in functional languages, in current imperative languages the pervading possibility of mutable substructure sharing makes such optimisations unrealistic. The balloon invariant can make these optimisations more realistic; they will be the subject of further research.

## 3.4 Type-checking Balloon Types

We now give an informal overview of the balloon type checking mechanism. The full presentation involves some detail and is well beyond the scope of this paper. A detailed presentation will appear in [2].

The first point worth emphasising is that the non-trivial mechanism applies to checking the implementations (*classes* in object-oriented terminology) of balloon types. Each balloon class is subject to a static analysis which will decide its acceptance as the implementation of a balloon type.

In non-balloon classes there are no restrictions other than 'the simple rule' in the use of balloons and no restrictions in the use of non-balloons; non-balloon classes are not subject to static analysis. Interestingly, this is what happens in current languages: the simple rule is implicit for the only possible 'balloons' (the primitive types) as the assignment has value semantics, and no special restrictions exist for the 'non-balloons' (the user-defined types).

The essence of the checking mechanism is performing the inductive step of using the assumption that some types are balloons to check the implementation of some balloon type which uses them. Methods of a balloon class can manipulate the state of several instances of that class. Essentially the checking makes sure that, for any possible execution, the several balloons involved will remain balloons; or in other words, the invariant is preserved.

As an example, suppose a data type for arbitrarily large integers is required (BigInt). These can be represented by a linked list of plain integers whose size depends on how large the number is. BigInt being balloon guarantees that there will not be accidental sharing of parts of linked lists corresponding to different BigInts. A fragment of a possible implementation is given in Fig. 4.

```
balloon Int { operator + (Int): Int; ... }

balloon BigInt
{
private:
  Node  // nested declaration of a non-balloon type
  { public: val:Int; nxt:Node; }
  lst:Node;  // reference to the head of linked list
public:
  operator + (other:BigInt): BigInt
  {
    p,q,r:Node;
    carry:Int;
    num:BigInt;
    num :- new BigInt;
    num.lst :- new Node;
    r :- num.lst;  p :- self.lst;  q :- other.lst;
    r.val := p.val + q.val;
    if ( ... )
      then carry := 0;
      else carry := 1;
    while (p.nxt and q.nxt) do
      r.nxt :- new Node;
      r :- r.nxt;  p :- p.nxt;  q :- q.nxt;
      r.val := p.val + q.val + carry;
      ... // calc next carry
    ... // traverse the remainder of the largest BigInt
    return num;
  }
  ... // other operations on BigInt
}
```

**Fig. 4.**

The implementation manipulates the state of typically three[6] balloon BigInts, referenced by self, other and num. Three variables are used to traverse the

---

[6] It is possible that self and other refer to the same balloon. The analysis works under this possibility of dynamic aliasing.

linked list of Node (a non-balloon type). The analysis determines that during all possible executions these variables point to the above mentioned balloons, and that no statement creates sharing of states from any two different balloons. A statement like

```
r.nxt :- p;
```

would be rejected by the checking mechanism: the analysis would assess that $r$ and $p$ could point to non-balloons 'belonging' to different balloons, and that sharing would be created, breaking the balloon invariant. Note that here the simple rule does not apply because Node is a non-balloon type.

Although this is a simple example it serves to illustrate some points. Non-balloons play the main role in the checking mechanism. The task of the analysis is to make sure that for accepted programs both $I_2$ and $I_4$ hold. The analysis essentially takes care that:

- non-balloons in clusters containing no balloon—*free clusters*—are prevented from being *captured* by more than one balloon; or in other words, different clusters which may already have a balloon—*captured clusters*—are prevented from becoming linked (*merging* the clusters), and
- non-balloons in any free cluster $A$ are prevented from being captured by some balloon 'reachable' by $A$ (some balloon $B$ referenced by an object in $A$ or some balloon internal to $B$).

Although there may exist an arbitrarily large number of objects, in the body of a method there is just a small number of variables (parameters, self and local variables) from which to reach the graph of objects. The key to the analysis is to keep track, for these variables, of the possibility of:

- different variables pointing to objects in the same cluster,
- the cluster to which a variable points containing a balloon, and
- a free cluster 'reaching' captured clusters.

Variables of a balloon type other than the one being checked can be ignored. In this example Int variables are ignored because Int is a balloon type. This means that primitive types or other user-defined balloon types can be ignored. This is important because the size of the domains in the analysis grows exponentially with the number of variables in a method (see appendix).

Regarding the BigInt example, Fig. 5 shows one possible fragment of the object graph at some point in the execution of the '+' function. This scenario would be summarised by the static analysis as (using the notation described in the appendix, and $s$, $o$, $n$ as a short for self, other and num):

$$\boxed{\text{sp}}\ \boxed{\text{oq}}\ \boxed{\text{nr}}$$

which essentially states that:

- if the non-balloon to which $p$ points belongs to a cluster with one balloon, that balloon is the one pointed to by $s$ (and the analogous for $(o, q)$ and $(n, r)$), and

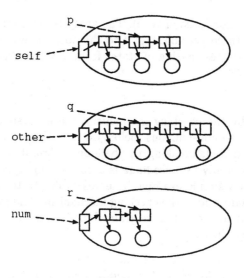

**Fig. 5.**

— $s$, $o$ and $n$ do not necessarily point to the same balloon.

Although that is not so in the `BigInt` example, the analysis considers the general case in which functions of a balloon type can have non-balloon parameters or result. Two restrictions are added to functions which are part of the interface of a balloon class $B$ (public functions); they are forbidden to:

— return a reference to a non-balloon which is internal to some balloon of class $B$.
— make a balloon of class $B$ capture non-balloons which come as parameters.

A special case of these restrictions is that in a balloon class there can be no public non-balloon state variables—as they are equivalent to a pair of get and set functions. The first restriction is necessary because a reference to a non-balloon can be freely stored in some object by non-balloon code. The second restriction applies because non-balloons that come as parameters may already 'belong' to some balloon (or they may be captured later). The static analysis that a balloon class undergoes enforces these restrictions.

In keeping track of the relevant information the analysis must consider all possible executions of the methods. To achieve this, each balloon class is subjected to a static analysis which includes fixed-point calculations due to loops and mutual recursion in functions of the class. However, it uses approximations of functions which are external to the class.

The less restrictive way to enforce the balloon invariant would be by considering information about the implementation of other types while checking some class. We note however that, although such mechanisms may be considered for optimisation purposes, they are unacceptable for type checking:

- Programmers expect to be able to construct modules, have them type checked and use them in other parts of the program. Furthermore, they expect to be able to change the implementation of a module without it affecting the type correctness of the rest of the program—as long as there is no change in the interface of the module.
- Libraries are an essential component and may be provided without source code or even be coded in different languages.

For these reasons, from the moment the idea was conceived (May 1994) the decision was for the checking mechanism to be modular, considering only the interface of other types. The simple rule was essential towards this, by allowing a reference to a balloon to be freely propagated without requiring any form of static analysis. Some construct for module of balloon type checking can be introduced (e.g. module as a set of classes). It can be useful if a group of classes cooperate tightly, typically some of them being auxiliary non-balloon classes used by some balloon class. These non-balloon classes are subject to the static analysis. The mechanism was developed considering this general case.

An advantage of not considering the implementation of other types is that the mechanism can be used in the presence of subtype polymorphism, which is essential in object-oriented languages. This because it is not relevant to know what code will be executed (which due to dynamic dispatch depends on the class of the object); only the type information regarding external functions is used.

The same applies to interfacing with code written in other languages. One example is the primitive types: the implementation of integers may be in assembly, without undergoing the static analysis we developed, but it is enough that integers are declared as balloon types to be considered in type checking user-defined code (as above), as long as the implementor of integers is trusted. This emphasises the importance of the knowledge obtained by making the ability to share state a property of a type, independently of whether the implementation is checked by the mechanism we have developed.

The static analysis was developed first as a global analysis of a program (which is not what intended) on which conservative approximations are made so that it becomes modular. It was developed using abstract interpretation [7], a semantics-based model for static analysis of programs.

In the appendix we describe the most essential element of the abstract interpretation: the way we abstract the relevant information about the concrete states. A reader who is not familiar with abstract interpretation can find a modern introduction and further references in [17].

## 3.5 Opaque Balloon Types

The main balloon mechanism focuses exclusively on the control of static aliasing—this is deliberate. The idea is that further constraints can be added on top of 'plain' balloons to focus on the control of dynamic aliasing, involving variables from the chain of procedure calls. An important specialisation is the concept of *opaque balloon types*.

Informally, an opaque balloon type has the added invariant that objects do not expose to clients any references to their internal state, even to be used temporarily by variables from some procedure: they represent *truly opaque data abstractions*, which guarantee that all the internal state remains unchanged between invocations of operations from the data type.

As an example, if the dictionary of shapes was an opaque balloon type, client code could not obtain a reference to a shape in the dictionary in order to update it in-place. It would only be possible to obtain a copy of a shape, which could be stored or operated upon with no effect on the shape in the dictionary.

Typical examples of opaque balloon types are the primitive types like integers. They are not simply balloon types, but opaque balloon types: there cannot be any reference to internal state of an integer (some bit) neither in external objects nor in variables from client code.

In terms of language use the situation is analogous to plain balloons: opaque balloons are declared using a keyword (such as `opaque`), and a candidate implementation undergoes a static check (on top of the plain balloon checking) in order to be accepted or rejected.[7]

## 3.6 Value Types

Typical primitive types like integer or boolean, are something more than just opaque balloon types; they can be said to be *value types*:[8] an integer variable is associated with an integer value. The important property for reasoning about programs using integer variables is that the value associated with a variable cannot change as a result of operations on other variables.

In object-oriented languages this property holds for primitive types because a variable contains an atomic representation of the value (as opposed to a reference to a possibly shared object) and parameter passing copies the value. However, if we are to be able to define value types in general (eg. for stacks or sets), the value will have to be represented by a group of objects and it is not possible for a variable to 'contain the value'. An example of this is the failure of expanded types in Eiffel to provide appropriate support for value types: by not being able to prevent sharing of linked substructures (as discussed above) they can lead to subtle interference, unlike in primitive types.

What is important is, not that the variable physically contains the object, which can be seen 'only' as an implementation issue, but that the group of objects that represent the value can only be accessed by the variable. This happens if:

- we have an opaque balloon type, and
- the variable holds the only reference to the opaque balloon object.

This means we can have the concept of value types as a (slight) specialisation of opaque balloon types. Value types will be declared by some keyword (such as

---

[7] The exact definition of opaque balloon types and respective checking mechanism are more involved than may be thought; they are beyond the scope of this paper.

[8] [18] also uses this term and discusses problems with expanded types in Eiffel.

value), and on top of the opaque balloon type checking, for value types the use of assignment or invocation with reference semantics will be forbidden in client code, being only allowed (deep) copy operations.

It is important to note that these copy operations are conceptual; they do not necessarily have to be performed physically. In fact, being only allowed assignment and parameter passing with copy semantics, the group of objects which represent a value will remain immutable after being computed and returned by some function in the implementation of the data type. This means that they can be physically shared and all conceptual deep copies in assignment or parameter passing in client code will be implemented as simple pointer copies.

In what concerns the implementation of a value type, if a function does not modify an object passed as parameter, the corresponding conceptual copy can also be optimised away. In the BigInt example no deep copies would exist at all. In other cases, even if some copy is needed, internal objects of value type can be physically shared, which means the copy does not need to be fully deep.

These situations are analogous to what happens in the implementation of functional languages. Indeed, user-defined value types can contribute towards bridging the gap between imperative and functional languages, concerning both programming styles and language implementation techniques.

Currently we have a gap between primitive types and user-defined types. With value types, the traditional behaviour concerning interference exhibited by traditional primitive types can be obtained in user-defined types if desired. This means primitive types can truly cease to be 'special'. We present in Fig. 6 the taxonomy of data types with respect to state sharing: the main binary classification in balloon/non-balloon and the two specialisations of balloon types.

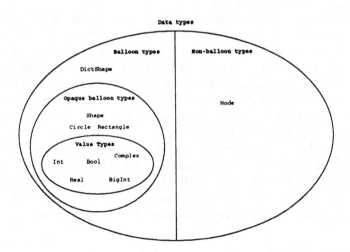

**Fig. 6.** Taxonomy regarding state sharing in data types

## 3.7 Concurrency and Distributed Systems

Balloons are a general concept. The balloon invariant can be regarded as a graph-theoretical notion: it describes a property of a graph with two 'kinds' of nodes. Balloons give structure to a global *state* (a pool of unnamed objects), regardless of the transient *computations* which are performed and their associated 'temporary views into the state' (i.e. local variables).

We have not mentioned issues such as object location: objects can reside in the memory of a machine, in a persistent object store, or be spread across a distributed system. Defining self-contained sets of objects, balloons are indeed relevant for distributed systems, as candidate units of object placement, migration, replication, and parameter/result passing to remote invocations. In the above cases, single objects would have a too fine granularity and would not be, in general, self-contained.

In what concerns computation, it does not matter whether we have sequential execution or several concurrent threads. The balloon invariant applies to both cases, as it ignores dynamic aliasing involving local variables of threads. An important point is that essentially the same checking mechanism can be applied to a concurrent model of execution. This is because the mechanism works under minimal assumptions about dynamic aliasing and does not consider the internal structure of objects. (Here we assume that local variables are private to each thread on only the pool of objects is shared.)

We make a clear distinction between (active) threads of execution and (passive) objects; and a corresponding distinction between local variables in threads and state variables of objects. In a model like *actors* [1], where objects are 'active', the distinction becomes blurred. However, in 'real' systems there are usually many more passive objects than active threads of execution; therefore, the distinction we make is important.

When several threads operate on shared data, concurrency control mechanisms are needed; balloons are also useful in this respect. In general, more than one thread can have references to a given balloon, being indeed unrealistic to try to prevent this from happening. What can be enforced is that only one thread 'enters' a balloon, by using balloons as the units of locking. A thread which enters a *plain* balloon $B$ can safely operate on any object in the cluster of $B$; however, it will have to perform locking of internal balloons, as dynamic references to these objects may exist in other threads.

Opaque balloons are particularly suitable as units of concurrency control: a thread which locks and enters an opaque balloon will be able to operate on *any* internal object with no need for further locking. This does not preclude intra-balloon concurrency: while 'inside' an opaque balloon, several sub-threads can be created to operate concurrently on different internal balloons.

## 4 Related Work

In [14] a taxonomy regarding the treatment of aliasing is described. There has been a lot of research on *alias detection*, and the interest has been progressively shifting towards dynamic data structures, two recent examples being [9, 30].

Much less has been done on *alias prevention*. A classic example which includes alias prevention for named objects is Reynolds' Syntactic Control of Interference [29].

A recent example regarding unnamed objects is [28]: it mentions unshareable objects (there can only be one pointer to them in the system) and unique pointers (from which assignment copies the pointer and nullifies the variable, i.e. moves the pointer). However, this proposal does not address substructure sharing: even if there is only one pointer to an u-object, it does not prevent sharing of objects reachable by the u-object. This means the usual subtle possibilities of interference can occur. A similar problem exists in expanded types in Eiffel which, as we have discussed, also fail to deal with substructure sharing.

Languages which offer *part objects* (like C++ and Beta [21, 26]) typically allow references (or pointers) to be obtained so that operations may be invoked on those part objects. These references to a part object may be stored by the invoked function in some object, creating sharing. Being such propagation of references allowed, physical containment can serve at most to bind the lifetimes of container and contained object. Moreover, with physical part objects it is not possible to have subtype polymorphism, as for expanded types.

The proposal for object-oriented databases in [20]—which uses the concept of *composite link* as a substitute to physical containment—is also concerned with relative lifetimes, and does not prevent part objects from being referenced by third parties, nor the existence of dangling references.

The principle of *design for analyzability* [11] is interesting, and our work can also be seen as an example of applying this principle. We present now the research on alias prevention for dynamic data structures we found more related to balloon types.

**Euclid's Collections.** The problem of aliasing was considered in the design of the language Euclid [22]. Pointer variables are declared as being pointers to a *collection*. A dynamically allocated object must be an element of a collection and it is enforced that pointers to different collections point to different objects.

The serious limitation is that collections are named entities like local variables of some procedure: it is not possible to have a collection as a member of a dynamically allocated object. This means that neither the number of collections can be related to the size of the object graph nor it is possible to obtain a hierarchical structure. As a result, collections are not appropriate as a means of organising the object graph.

**FX's Regions.** [24] describes an *effect system* with three base kinds: types, effects and *regions*. Effects describe the possible side-effects of an expression and regions describe the area of the store where those side-effects may occur. The effect system computes statically a conservative approximation of the actual side-effects that an expression may have. Regions are similar to collections and although more powerful they suffer from the same problem: they are named entities.

**Islands.** John Hogg's *islands* [15] proposal is more closely related to balloons. It represents an advance because, unlike collections or regions, islands impose a structure on the object graph without using named entities as units. This enables hierarchical structures to be described.

Similar to a balloon, an island defines a cluster of objects to which there are no references stored in external objects. There are however not only some differences in the invariants enforced, but major differences in the mechanisms:

– Islands have a considerable syntactic cost by requiring *access modes* to variables to be spread both in the signatures of all the methods in a class and in client code.

In balloons, one keyword in the definition of the type summarises the concept they represent, and no syntactic cost is imposed on client code.

– The detection by the compiler of whether a class is a *bridge* (entry to an island) is purely syntactic according to the access modes.

The use of a static analysis in balloons enabled minimising restrictions while maintaining syntactic simplicity.

– The knowledge that class $A$ is a bridge is not used to help in assessing whether a class $B$ (which uses $A$) is also a bridge. The knowledge that a class is a bridge is something that does not affect what code can be written (more than the individual signatures of the operations provided), and can be determined *a posteriori*, after the program is written.

Balloons are a full part of the type system: whether type $T$ is balloon or not affects what code can be written. Although we rely on static analysis, the mechanism is not an *a posteriori* alias analysis of a program. Using the knowledge that type $T$ is balloon is essential in checking the implementation of a balloon type which uses $T$. The use of induction is the essence of the balloon checking mechanism.

## 5 Conclusions

Although there has been much research on aliasing, most has been devoted to analysis techniques towards some optimisation: aliasing tends to be considered for implementation purposes and not as a first class entity in a type system. Moreover, not enough research has been devoted to obtaining concepts for grouping single objects into larger meaningful entities.

We have presented a mechanism which makes the ability to share state a first class property of a data type. Balloon types is an extension to programming languages which permits expressing and enforcing that all state reachable by an object is encapsulated: no external objects are allowed to have references to any object that is part of that state.

It allows designers of the data type to truly control what state is made available to be operated upon by the client, users of the data type to have confidence that the more pervasive form of interference does not occur and compilers to explore this knowledge to perform automatic program transformations.

The syntactic simplicity reflects the essence of the concept: a classification of data types according to the ability to share state. By the use of a static analysis as the checking mechanism it was possible to achieve this syntactic simplicity while avoiding imposing restrictions, otherwise unavoidable if the verification was purely syntactic.

The knowledge given by the balloon invariant can be seen to have wide usefulness. Some examples are program transformation for parallelisation or execution reordering and garbage collection. Being self-contained composite objects, balloons are suitable as units of locking and placement/copy/migration; this is specially important in concurrent and distributed systems.

Balloon types also constitute a valuable support for the development of large scale provably correct programs. Two specialisations of balloon types can be particularly important. Opaque balloon types represent truly opaque data abstractions. They are also the key to obtaining value types. These bridge the current gap between primitive and user-defined types: primitive types can truly cease to be 'special'.

Opaque balloons have so many 'nice' properties that it can even be argued that all balloons should be opaque: each type would be either a non-balloon type or an opaque balloon type (which includes value types). This is an important and non-trivial design issue which we have not attempted to resolve here.

### Acknowledgements

I thank Paul Kelly, Sophia Drossopoulou, and Sue Eisenbach for their comments to this paper. I also thank the anonymous referees for their comments.

# References

1. Gul Agha and Carl Hewitt. Actors: A conceptual foundation for concurrent object-oriented programming. In P. Wegner and B. Shriver, editors, *Research Directions in Object-Oriented Programming*, pages 49–74. MIT Press, 1987.
2. P. S. Almeida. *Control of Object Sharing (provisional title)*. PhD thesis, University of London, Imperial College, Department of Computing, 1997. To appear.
3. G. E. Andrews. The theory of partitions. In *Encyclopedia of Mathematics and its Applications*, volume 2. Addison-Wesley, 1976.
4. K. Arnold and J. Gosling. *The Java Programming Language*. Addison-Wesley, 1996.
5. Franco Civello. Roles for composite objects in object-oriented analysis and design. *Proceedings OOPSLA'93. SIGPLAN Notices*, 28(10):376–393, October 1993.
6. C. Clack and S. Peyton Jones. Strictness analysis—a practical approach. In *Proceedings FPCA'85*, volume 201 of *LNCS*, pages 35–49. Springer-Verlag, September 1985.

7. P. Cousot and R. Cousot. Abstract Interpretation: A Unified Lattice Model for Static Analysis of Programs by Construction or Approximation of Fixpoints. In *Proceedings 4th ACM Symposium on Principles of Programming Languages*, pages 238–252, January 1977.

8. O.-J. Dahl, B. Myhrhaug, and K. Nygaard. The SIMULA 67 common base language. Publication S-22, Norwegian Computing Center, Oslo, 1970.

9. R. Ghiya and L. J. Hendren. Is it a tree, a DAG, or a cyclic graph? A shape analysis for heap-directed pointers in C. In *Proceedings 23rd ACM Symposium on Principles of Programming Languages*, pages 1–15, January 1996.

10. A. Goldberg and D. Robson. *Smalltalk-80: The Language and its Implementation*. Addison-Wesley, 1983.

11. L. J. Hendren and G. R. Gao. Designing programming languages for analyzability: A fresh look at pointer data structures. In *Proceedings 4th IEEE International Conference on Computer Languages*, pages 242–251, April 1992.

12. C. A. R. Hoare. Proof of correctness of data representations. *Acta Informatica*, 1:271–281, 1972.

13. C. A. R. Hoare. Hints on programming language design. Technical Report STAN//CS-TR-73-403, Stanford University, Department of Computer Science, December 1973. Based on a keynote address presented at the ACM Symposium on Principles of Programming Languages.

14. J. Hogg, D. Lea, A. Wills, D. deChampeaux, and R. Holt. The Geneva convention on the treatment of object aliasing. Followup report on ECOOP'91 workshop W3: Object-oriented formal methods. *OOPS Messenger*, 3(2):11–16, April 1992.

15. John Hogg. Islands: Aliasing protection in object-oriented languages. *Proceedings OOPSLA'91. SIGPLAN Notices*, 26(11):271–285, November 1991.

16. Sebastian Hunt. Frontiers and open sets in abstract interpretation. In *Proceedings FPCA'89*, pages 1–11. ACM Press, September 1989.

17. N. D. Jones and F. Nielson. Abstract interpretation: a semantics-based tool for program analysis. In *Handbook of Logic in Computer Science*, volume 4: Semantic Modelling, pages 527–636. Oxford University Press, 1995.

18. S. Kent and J. Howse. Value types in Eiffel. In *Proceedings TOOLS Europe 96 (TOOLS 19)*. Prentice Hall, 1996.

19. S. Khoshafian and G. Copeland. Object identity. *Proceedings OOPSLA'86. SIGPLAN Notices*, 21(11):406–416, November 1986.

20. Won Kim, Jay Banerjee, Hong-Tai Chou, Jorge F. Garza, and Darrel Woelk. Composite object support in an object-oriented database system. *Proceedings OOPSLA'87. SIGPLAN Notices*, 22(12):118–125, December 1987.

21. Bent Bruun Kristensen, Ole Lehrmann Madsen, Birger Moller-Pedersen, and Kristen Nygaard. The BETA programming language. In P. Wegner and B. Shriver, editors, *Research Directions in Object-Oriented Programming*, pages 7–48. MIT Press, 1987.

22. B. W. Lampson, J. J. Horning, R. L. London, J. G. Mitchell, and G. J. Popek. Report on the programming language EUCLID. *SIGPLAN Notices*, 12(2), 1977.

23. B. H. Liskov and J. Guttag. *Abstraction and Specification in Program Development*. The MIT Press, 1986.

24. J. M. Lucassen and D. K. Gifford. Polymorphic effect systems. In *Proceedings 15th ACM Symposium on Principles of Programming Languages*, pages 47–57, January 1988.

25. B. J. MacLennan. Values and objects in programming languages. *SIGPLAN Notices*, 17(12):70–79, December 1982.

26. Ole Lehrmann Madsen, Birger Moller-Pedersen, and Kristen Nygaard. *Object-Oriented Programming in the BETA Programming Language.* Addison-Wesley, 1993.
27. Bertrand Meyer. *Eiffel: The Language.* Prentice Hall, 1992.
28. Naftaly Minsky. Towards alias-free pointers. In *Proceedings ECOOP'96*, LNCS 1098, pages 189–209. Springer-Verlag, 1996.
29. J. C. Reynolds. Syntactic control of interference. In *Proceedings 5th ACM Symposium on Principles of Programming Languages*, pages 39–46, January 1978.
30. M. Sagiv, T. Reps, and R. Wilhelm. Solving shape-analysis problems in languages with destructive updating. In *Proceedings 23rd ACM Symposium on Principles of Programming Languages*, pages 16–31, January 1996.
31. B. Stroustrup. *The C++ programming language.* Addison-Wesley, 1986.
32. Peter Wegner. Dimensions of object-based language design. *Proceedings OOPSLA'87. SIGPLAN Notices*, 22(12):168–182, December 1987.
33. N. Wirth. The programming language Pascal. *Acta Informatica*, 1:35–63, 1971.

# A   Base States in the Abstract Interpretation

Here we describe the way we abstract the relevant properties about concrete states. The presentation is divided in two parts. First we describe a domain, taking only $I_4$ into account. Then we present another domain, taking also $I_2$ into account. This last domain is obtained by refining each original state into several states.

## A.1   Enforcing $I_4$

Here we describe the abstract states used in the interpretation aimed at enforcing that 'from all objects that make up a cluster, at most one is a balloon object.'

From the set of concrete states $S$, we will use $S_4$ for the set of states in which invariant $I_4$ holds (valid states). Each element of $S_4$ is abstracted into an element of a finite set $C$. Elements of $C$ have the form $(p, b) \in \wp(I \times I) \times (I \to \{0, 1\})$ such that:

- $p$ is an equivalence relation on the set of identifiers $I$; defining a partition according to what variables reference objects in the same cluster.
- $b$ is a function from equivalence classes to $\{0, 1\}$; representing the number of balloons in the cluster corresponding to the given equivalence class. $b$ is presented as a function with domain $I$ and the invariant $(x, y) \in p \Rightarrow bx = by$.

All the characterisation of concrete states that is relevant to the presentation can be given by two functions (which only serve presentation purposes and are not used in the actual static analysis):

- $P: S_4 \to \wp(I \times I)$ maps a valid state to an equivalence relation on $I$. $(x, y) \in Ps$ iff in the state $s$, $x$ and $y$ reference objects in the same cluster.
- $B: S_4 \times \wp(I) \to N$ gives the number of balloons in all clusters referenced by the given set of identifiers in the given state.

The abstraction function $\alpha: S_4 \to C$ is defined in a straightforward manner in terms of $P$ and $B$:

$$\alpha = \lambda s.(Ps, \lambda x.B(s, \{x\})) \ .$$

While a concrete state in $S_4$ is abstracted to a single abstract state in $C$, an element of $C$ represents a set of concrete states. For a given abstract state $(p, b)$:

- If $x$ and $y$ are not both mapped to 1 by b, and are not in the same equivalence class (as defined by $p$), then in the corresponding concrete states $x$ and $y$ *definitely* do not reference objects in the same cluster.
  If they are both mapped to 1 by $b$ or belong to the same equivalence class, then nothing can be assumed: they *may or may not* reference objects in the same cluster.
- If $bx = 0$ it means that there is *definitely* no balloon in the cluster referenced by $x$. If $bx = 1$ it means that there *may* exist one balloon in the cluster referenced by $x$; this is included in:
- There is at most one balloon in the union of all clusters referenced by the set of identifiers in an equivalence class which is mapped to 1 by $b$.

This is given by the concretisation function $\gamma: C \to \wp(S_4)$:

$$\gamma = \lambda(p, b).\{s \in S_4 \mid \forall x, y \in I. \ ((bx = 0 \lor by = 0) \land (x, y) \notin p \Rightarrow (x, y) \notin Ps) \\ \land bx \geq B(s, px)\} \ ,$$

where we use the notation $px$ for $\{y \mid (x, y) \in p\}$.

States in S in which invariant $I_4$ does not hold (invalid states) are considered by adding a $\top$ to $C$, representing all states in S—both valid and invalid states. The abstraction and concretisation functions are extended to $\alpha: S \to C_\top$ and $\gamma: C_\top \to \wp(S)$ by making $\alpha(s) = \top$ if $s \notin S_4$, and $\gamma(\top) = S$.

The pair of functions $\alpha$ and $\gamma$ satisfy the expected property that the abstraction of a given concrete state $s$ represents a set of concrete states which include $s$. That is, for all $s \in S$:

$$s \in \gamma(\alpha s) \ .$$

The function $\gamma$ induces a partial order on $C$ such that $\gamma$ becomes an order-embedding of $C$ into $\wp(S_4)$. That is, for all $c_1, c_2 \in C$:

$$c_1 \leq c_2 \iff \gamma c_1 \subseteq \gamma c_2 \ .$$

This order is:

$$(p_1, b_1) \leq (p_2, b_2) \iff (b_1 \leq b_2) \land \forall x, y \in I. \\ ((x, y) \in p_1 \land (x, y) \notin p_2 \Rightarrow b_2 x = 1 \land b_2 y = 1) \\ \land (b_2 x = 1 \land (x, y) \in p_2 \Rightarrow (b_1 x = 1 \land b_1 y = 1 \Rightarrow (x, y) \in p_1)) \ .$$

Figure 7 shows the $C$ cpo in the case when $I = \{x, y, z\}$. We use a graphic notation to refer to elements of C. An element $(p, b)$ represented as $\boxed{xy} \ \overline{z}$ means that there are two equivalence classes defined by $p$—$\{x, y\}$ and $\{z\}$—and that

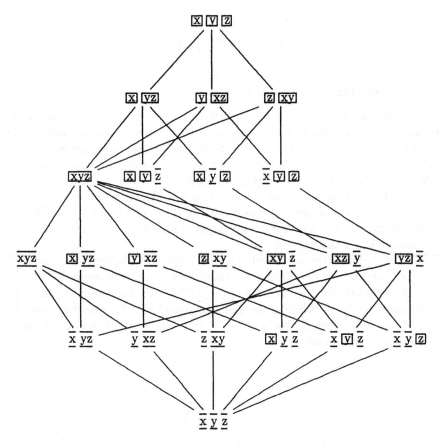

**Fig. 7.** The $C_{\{x,y,z\}}$ cpo

$b$ maps $\{x,y\}$ to 1, and $\{z\}$ to 0. With the given order we have for example: $\boxed{x}\,\underline{\bar{y}}\,\underline{\bar{z}} \leq \boxed{xy}\,\underline{\bar{z}}$ and $\boxed{xy}\,\underline{\bar{z}} \leq \boxed{x}\,\boxed{y}\,\underline{\bar{z}}$.

An important consequence results from ignoring other types while type checking a given class. During a 'pass' of analysing a function in a class $B$ the relevant set of identifiers $I$—which defines $C_I$—corresponds just to variables of class $B$ and of non-balloon types; variables of any other balloon type (like all primitive types) are ignored. This is important as the size of the corresponding $C_I$ has an exponential growth with the number of identifiers in $I$; more precisely:

$$|C_I| = \sum_{k=0}^{n} \binom{n}{k} B_k B_{n-k} \ ,$$

where $n = |I|$ and $B_i$ is the $i^{\text{th}}$ Bell number, the number of partitions of a set of $i$ elements, which can be calculated by (see eg. [3]):

$$B_0 \quad = 1 \; ,$$
$$B_{n+1} = \sum_{k=0}^{n} \binom{n}{k} B_k \; .$$

## A.2 Extending $C$ to Enforce $I_2$

By the simple rule, a reference to a balloon can be stored in some object only through the copy assignment, which gives a newly created balloon; therefore, the reference is stored in an external object. To enforce $I_2$—the only reference to a balloon $B$ is from an external object—we must prevent the external object which references a balloon from becoming internal. To do this, we must prevent any balloon $B$ from capturing non-balloons in a free cluster which references either $B$ or some balloon which contains $B$. (Only free clusters need surveillance, as non-balloons in captured clusters no longer can be captured; this is assured by the mechanism which enforces $I_4$.)

The abstract states as presented above partition variables according to clusters, but do not contain information about relationships between different clusters. As an example, the abstract state $\overline{\texttt{x}} \; \boxed{\texttt{y}} \; \boxed{\texttt{z}}$ can correspond to any of the three cases in Fig. 8. While in the first case (on the left) it would we acceptable to perform an instruction like 'y.a :- x', in the other two cases performing this instruction would break $I_2$.

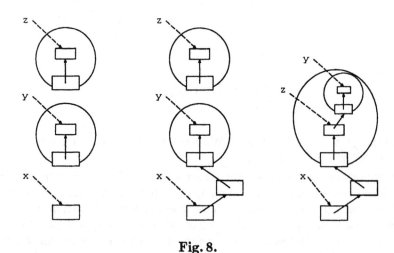

**Fig. 8.**

To enforce $I_2$, the previously described abstract states are refined in order to distinguish these situations: to a free cluster is now associated a set of which captured clusters *may be* 'reachable' by the free cluster. If a captured cluster is not in this set, then it is *definitely* not 'reachable' by the free cluster. (Every captured cluster is associated with at most one free cluster.)

The original state $\bar{x}\,\boxed{y}\,\boxed{z}$ is now refined into four states: $\bar{x}\,\boxed{y}\,\boxed{z}$, $\overline{x\boxed{y}}\,\boxed{z}$, $\overline{x\boxed{z}}\,\boxed{y}$, and $\overline{x\boxed{y}\boxed{z}}$. The three cases in Fig. 8 would now be abstracted as $\bar{x}\,\boxed{y}\,\boxed{z}$, $\overline{x\boxed{y}}\,\boxed{z}$, and $\overline{x\boxed{y}\boxed{z}}$ respectively. (Note how the nesting in the third case is not relevant; $y$ and $z$ could even refer to the same cluster, as before.)

We present in Fig. 9 a fragment of the extended $C_{\{x,y,z\}}$ cpo, corresponding to the three original states: $\bar{x}\,\bar{y}\,\boxed{z} \leq \bar{x}\,\boxed{yz} \leq \bar{x}\,\boxed{y}\,\boxed{z}$. (The full diagram for the extended $C_{\{x,y,z\}}$ cpo has 43 nodes and 91 edges and we do not present it here.)

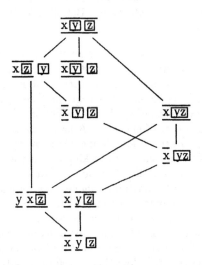

**Fig. 9.** Fragment of the extended $C_{\{x,y,z\}}$ cpo

## A.3 Control Flow

The domains described are not lattices (although that is the case when $I$ has just one or two elements); the concern was obtaining an abstract domain which represents the relevant information. We use these domains to describe the effects of the simple actions (the assignments).

For general control-flow commands we must have a lattice as there is the need for joins and fixed-points. For this we use a completion of the base domain, the lattice of order ideals (down-sets), having in mind that an actual implementation of the static analysis needs only manipulate their maximal elements, similarly to the frontier representation of a function [6, 16].

The analysis results in either $\top$ or a set of (incomparable) elements. If the result is $\top$ it is possible that the balloon invariant is broken at some point; otherwise the balloon invariant definitely holds at every point during the execution of the program. The (conservative) procedure for balloon type checking is thus to reject the program if the result is $\top$ and to accept it otherwise. A detailed presentation, including the abstract semantic functions, will appear in [2].

# Static Integrity Constraint Management in Object-Oriented Database Programming Languages via Predicate Transformers

Véronique Benzaken[1][2] and Xavier Schaefer[1][2]

[1] C.R.I., Université de Paris I - Panthéon - Sorbonne,
12 Pl. du Panthéon, 75005 Paris, France
[2] L.R.I., Université de Paris XI - Orsay, Bat. 490, 91405 Orsay Cedex, France

**Abstract.** In this paper, we propose an efficient technique to statically manage integrity constraints in object-oriented database programming languages. We place ourselves in the context of an extended version of the $O_2$ database programming language, and we assume that updates are undertaken by means of methods. An important issue when dealing with constraints is that of efficiency. A naive management of such constraints can cause a severe floundering of the overall system. Our basic assumption is that the run-time checking of constraints is too costly to be undertaken systematically. Therefore, methods that are always safe with respect to integrity constraints should be proven so *at compile time*. The run-time checks should only concern the remaining methods. To that purpose, we propose a new approach, based on *abstract interpretation*, to prove the *invariance* of *integrity constraints* under complex *methods*. We then describe the current implementation of our prototype, reporting many experiments that have been performed with it on non trivial examples.

Though our method is developed in the context of object-oriented database programming languages, it can easily be applied to the problem of static verification of object-oriented languages providing pre and post-conditions such as Eiffel.

## 1 Introduction

Efforts on object-oriented database programming languages have mainly been devoted to the integration of elaborated type systems and persistence mechanisms in a uniform way.

However, many specific database functionalities have not been taken into account by those works. In particular, functionalities such as view management, role definition and integrity constraints are either absent from, or only roughly supported by most (object-oriented) database programming languages. For the last five years, efforts in the database programming language community have been devoted to the definition of languages integrating such functionalities [AB91, SDA94, ABGO93, ABGO95].

Nevertheless, most object-oriented database programming languages are not able to take into account integrity constraints in a global and declarative way.

A great concern for database users is that the information stored should represent the real world faithfully. The data should respect at any moment a set of conditions, called *semantic integrity constraints*. For example, assume that our database stores persons who have a spouse, a reasonable integrity constraint imposed on these data could be:

*No person can be married to itself*

Integrity constraint management has always been presented as one of the great promises of database systems. To date, that *basic* facility should be provided by any object-oriented database system. However, no real database system has kept that promise in a satisfactory way.

One of the assumptions that has discouraged people from using integrity constraints is that constraints should be checked *systematically* at run-time, after each update. Despite the several optimisation techniques that have been proposed ([Nic79, LT85, HI85, BM86, KSS87, HCN84, WSK83, BDM88, BD95, Law95]) in order to improve dynamic checking, system performances are still greatly affected. Considering the efficiency problems that most database systems already have without having to deal with integrity constraints, one understands why integrity has more or less been left aside.

The situation can be significantly improved by detecting, at *compile time*, which updates preserve integrity. As in our framework such updates are undertaken by means of methods, a method that will never violate an integrity constraint should be proven safe at compile time. Indeed, the run-time checking of this constraint can be entirely avoided after the execution of this method.

To illustrate our motivation let us consider the simple example suggested previously. We consider a database that stores some information about people: their name and their spouse. The $O_2$ database schema of such a database could be as follows:

```
class Person inherit Object public type tuple (
                            name: string,
                            spouse: Person
                            )
method marry(q: Person)
end;
```

Consider the following constraint:

*"No person can be married to itself."*

Such a constraint will be written at the schema level in our extension of $O_2$:

```
forall x in Persons: x->spouse!=x;
```

where the notation x->spouse denotes the extraction of attribute spouse of object x and where Persons is defined in $O_2$ as the following persistent root:

```
name Persons: set (Person);
```

This command declares an entry point in the database as well as a container for objects which are instances of class Person. Let us now consider the following implementation of method marry

```
method marry(q:Person) in class Person{
  self->spouse=q;        <set the spouse attribute of the receiver to q>
  q->spouse=self; }      <set the spouse attribute of parameter to self>
```

That update can clearly violate the integrity constraint given previously, in particular when self is equal to q. The integrity constraint manager will therefore have to check the constraint after each execution of method marry. That can be done in several ways. It can either check the constraint as it is, i.e. check that (x->spouse!=x) for any Person x in the set Persons. It can also undertake an optimised run-time check. This test can be obtained with the techniques mentioned previously. In our case, such techniques can reduce the test to just testing that (self->spouse!=self) and (q->spouse!=q). An important point is that such an optimisation is possible only for very simple constraints. Most of the time, the run-time checking overhead remains. Moreover, such optimisations are unable to produce the "minimal" run-time test. In our case, the minimal test is just to check that (self!=q).

As far as the programmer is concerned, the best solution, in terms of efficiency, is not to let the system generate the run-time test. The programmer that wants to tune his database should introduce some "minimal" run-time test directly into the implementation of methods. Method marry becomes:

```
method marry(q:Person) in class Person {
  if (self!=q){
  self->spouse=q;
  q->spouse=self;}}
```

In that case, the overhead of run-time integrity checking can be avoided, as it is redundant with the precautions that have already been taken by the programmer inside the method. Also, the user does not have to suffer from mysterious program failures (due to constraint violations) anymore. However, we first have to make sure that those precautions are indeed sufficient, i.e. that this method will *never* violate the integrity constraint. That must be proven formally, automatically and at compile-time. The main contribution of this paper is to provide a technique for doing so as well as a prototype implementing it.

However, this technique should *not* be taken as an encouragement for the programmers to take specific precautions with respect to integrity constraints while writing programs. It just allows to *detect* such precautions, as far as they are taken.

Our approach undertakes a very detailed analysis of methods and provides some precise information on the impact they have upon constraints. Partial but reliable information concerning methods is obtained by means of a *predicate transformer*. A predicate transformer is a function that, given a method m and a constraint C satisfied by the input data of m, returns a formula $\bar{m}(C)$ that is satisfied by the output data of m. In other words, provided C is satisfied before an execution of m (which is the usual assumption as methods are run on a consistent state[3]), $\overline{m}(C)$ is satisfied after an execution of m. A method m is then safe with respect to constraint C if $\overline{m}(C) \Rightarrow C$ (C is a consequence of $\overline{m}(C)$). To prove the implication, we use a classical theorem proving technique based on the tableaux method (this method is shortly explained in Section 5.2).

Our approach reduces significantly the number of integrity constraints that have to be checked at run-time. It has been implemented and provides some positive results on some real, non-trivial examples. We believe it can greatly improve the overall efficiency of integrity management. We insist that it is *fully automatic*, in the sense that this technique is embedded in the compiler technology thus no human intervention is required at any stage.

Although our method is developed in the context of object-oriented database programming languages, it can also be applied to the problem of static analysis of object-oriented languages providing pre and post-conditions à-la Eiffel [Mey88, Mey91].

The paper is organised as follows. In Section 2 we informally present our framework: an object-oriented database programming language allowing the definition of integrity constraints in a global and declarative way. In Section 3 we describe an intermediate language in which complex instructions will be translated and give the reasons for such a translation. In Section 4, we define our abstract predicate transformer. We show how to handle simple methods, loops and recursion, and overriding. We describe in Section 5 the implementation of our current prototype and give results of experiments. In Section 6 we compare ourselves with different approaches that have been proposed in the database field. We finally conclude in Section 7.

# 2 An Object-Oriented Database Programming Language with Constraints

Our framework consists in a very simple extension of the $O_2$ programming language. The programmer can define, together with the usual classes and methods, some *semantic integrity constraints* which are well formed formulas on a specific language. However, we point out that using the $O_2$ language is not essential to our approach. We present, through examples, the ingredients of our language: classes and persistent roots, integrity constraints and methods. To focus on important issues, we will reduce the use of concepts that are not essential to our approach.

## 2.1 Classes and Persistent Roots

In order to illustrate the main concepts, let us start with the simple schema given in Figure 1.

---

[3] This corresponds to the classical notion of *consistency* in databases.

```
class Person inherit Object public type tuple(
        name: string,
        spouse: Person,
        bestfriend: Person,
        money: integer )
  method marry(q: Person);
        separate();
        spend(amount: integer);
        setbestfriend(p: Person);
        marry-and-separate(q: Person);
end;

class Parent inherit Person public type tuple(
        children: set (Person))
  method marry(q: Person);
        separate();
end;

class Employee inherit Person  public type tuple(
        boss: Person)
  method separate();
end;

name Persons: set (Person);
name Parents: set (Parent);
name Employees: set (Employee);
```

**Fig. 1.** A schema

We define three classes (Person, Parent and Employee). Both of them have tuple-structured types. A Person has a name, a spouse, a bestfriend and some money. The classes Parent and Employee inherit from Person, their respective types are subtypes of the one of class Person. Thus attributes name, spouse, bestfriend and money are inherited in classes Parent and Employee. Methods marry and separate have been redefined in class Parent and Employee. Such a redefinition obeys the covariant rule (see [BC96] for an enlightening discussion on the consequences in $O_2$ and [Cas96] for a more general framework). It differs from method overloading in languages such as C++ or Java in which methods are redefined on an invariant basis. The semantics of inheritance is the usual inclusion semantics. We also define three persistent names Persons, Parents and Employees, as a set of Persons (respectively Parents, Employees). Persistence is achieved by reachability from those persistent names. This means that every object reachable from those names is automatically stored on disk at the end of programs. Unreachable objects are garbage-collected.

## 2.2 Integrity Constraints

That schema is quite simple but many constraints can already be stated; some examples are:

- There must be at least one **Person** who is not married.
- A **Person** cannot be married to itself.
- No **Parent** can be married to one of its children.
- An **Employee** who is not married must have a boss.
- A **Person** must have some money.
- A **Parent** who is not married cannot have any children.
- There must be at least one **Person** who has no best friend.

All those constraints are given in Figure 2.

```
C1: exists x in Persons: x->spouse==nil;
C2: forall x in Persons: x->spouse!=x;
C3: forall x in Parents: !(x->spouse in x->children);
C4: forall x in Employees: x->spouse==nil ==> x->boss!=nil;
C5: forall x in Persons: x->money > 0;
C6: forall x in Parents: x->spouse==nil ==>!(exists y in x->children);
C7: exists x in Persons: x->bestfriend==nil;
```

**Fig. 2.** Integrity constraints

We have there a great variety of constraints. The constraints can be structural or on domains, they can involve very simple arithmetic (C5), tuples or sets. Most constraints that have several atoms are implication constraints (C4 and C6). We can briefly give a general syntax for constraints. It is simple and close to first order logic. We first define terms, that is, variables like p and q, constants like nil and more complex terms like p->spouse->spouse. Atomic formulas can be defined with standard predicates as ==, !=...and complex formulas can be built with the usual connectives "&&" (and), "||" (or), "!" (not), "==>" (implies). Quantification is also necessary. So, if "F" is a formula, then "forall p in S: F" and "exists p in S: F" are also formulas. We call that *range restricted quantification*, because the range on which the variable p varies is the set S. The semantics, i.e. the truth or falsity of those constraints with respect to a specific database should be clear. As usual, a database can be seen as a structure, that is a domain together with a set of relationships between elements of that domain. A database is coherent with respect to an integrity constraint C if it is a model of C.

```
method separate()          method spend(amount:integer)
in class Person {          in class Person {
   self->spouse=nil;}         if (self->money-amount>0)
                                 self->money=self->money-amount;}
```

```
method marry(q:Person)     method marry-and-separate(q:Person)
in class Person{           in class Person{
  if (self!=q){              if (self!=q){
   self->spouse=q;             self->spouse=q
   q->spouse=self;}}           q->spouse=self;}
                            for (u in Persons){
                              if ((u!=self) && (u !=q))
                                u->spouse=nil;}}
```

```
method setbestfriend(q: Person) in class Person{
    if (exists u in Persons: u!=self && u->bestfriend==nil)
       self->bestfriend=q;}
```

**Fig. 3.** Implementation of methods of class Person

## 2.3 Methods

Methods are building blocks which allow to update the persistent data stored in the database. If no precautions are taken by the application programmer, such updates could lead to inconsistent database states.

We give in Figure 3 the implementation of the methods defined on our schema. Those methods are safe with respect to at least one of the constraints previously declared.

Method **separate** in Figure 3 is obviously safe with respect to constraint C1: after the execution of **separate**, at least a Person x is such that x->spouse==nil, namely self.

As mentioned previously, method **marry** is safe with respect to C2. Method spend checks prior performing a withdrawal of money that the credit is still positive. Therefore it does not violate constraint C5. Method **marry-and-separate** first marries two persons self and q testing if self is different from q and then sets the spouse attribute of any person different from self and q to nil. Notice that this method performs complex statements such as an if embedded in a loop. This method is safe with respect to C2.

The previous methods are short (as methods often are), but non-trivial. However, the run-time tests that are undertaken are quite simple. Very often, the run-time tests that are necessary to write safe methods are more complicated and involve the use of *boolean queries*. Method **setbestfriend** for example makes use of those queries. Indeed, consider constraint C7 that says that at least one

Person has no best friend together with the following implementation for method
setbestfriend:

```
method setbestfriend(q: Person) in class Person{
    self->bestfriend=q;}
```

That method can clearly violate constraint C7, namely when the receiver is the
only person who has no best friend. To make that method safe, we have to test
that there is somebody else who has no best friend. This can be done in $O_2$ by
using a classical $O_2$ boolean query. The previous method made safe becomes:

```
method  setbestfriend(q: Person) in class Person{
    o2 boolean b;
    o2query(b,"exists u in Persons: u !=$1 && u->bestfriend==nil", self);
    if (b) self->bestfriend=q;}
```

That method is now safe with respect to constraint C7. To simplify the notations,
we generalize in the following the use of boolean queries and allow them to occur
directly inside if's, without using o2query and the working variable b, as shown
in Figure 3.

The following methods are defined or overriden for the subclasses Parent
and Employee. Method marry in class Parent has been overloaded, it is still
safe with respect to C2 but also with respect to constraint C3. Method separate
has been redefined in both classes Parent and Employee such as not violating
constraints C6 and C4 respectively.

```
method separate()              method separate
in class Employee{             in class Parent{
    if (self->boss!=nil)           if (!(exist u in self->children))
       self->spouse=nil;}             self->spouse=nil;}


method marry(q:Person) in class Parent{
    if (self != q && !(q in self->children) && !(self in q->children)){
       self->spouse=q;
       q->spouse=self;}}
```

Fig. 4. Implementation of methods for class Parent and Employee

When methods are overriden (as it is the case for methods marry and
separate) we shall adopt the following notation in the sequel. We note for any
overriden method m, $m = \{m_1, \ldots, m_n\}$ where $m_1, \ldots, m_n$ are all the different
implementations of method m in the system. For example, separate is formed
by three different implementations those in the classes Person, Employee and
Parent.

# 3   Translation of Methods into an Intermediate Form

The task of analysing computer languages can be difficult, particularly when dealing with object-oriented programming languages. Indeed, in such langages, objects that are involved in an update are reached in a *navigational* way. Defining an abstract interpretation directly on the source language can be a painstaking task, and proving that the abstract interpretation defined is *semantically founded* (which must always be done) can be very difficult. In order to compensate for that extra complexity, our technique is to:

– First, translate the source language into an intermediate form.
– Then, undertake the abstract interpretation on that intermediate form.

We give in this section a short illustration of the complexity problem that occurs in object-oriented langages. This illustration will help justify the intermediate language we consider in the next section. The complexity of instructions in object-oriented languages is due to the way the objects are referenced. Let us see a simple $O_2$ assignment instruction:

```
p->spouse->spouse=q->spouse
```

That update is not about p or q but about objects that can be *reached* from p and q. That instruction groups in fact two radically different operations:

– First, it determines the objects that are used for the update. To that purpose, it *navigates* along the paths defined by the attributes. In our case, the objects that are used in the update are denoted by p->spouse and q->spouse. Let us call them $o_1$ and $o_2$.
– Then, it undertakes the update. The update has become: $o_1$->spouse=$o_2$.

That decomposition has to be done formally and systematically. To that purpose we will use a simple new instruction:

```
forone object where condition do instruction.
```

That instruction executes *instruction*, where *object* denotes the only object that satisfies *condition*. With that new construct, the original instruction:

```
p->spouse->spouse=q->spouse
```

will be translated into:

```
forone o1 where p->spouse=o1
do forone o2 where q->spouse=o2
do o1->spouse=o2
```

That translation simplifies considerably the matter of defining an abstract interpretation for object-oriented programming languages. Indeed, with such a translation we can avoid defining a complex abstract interpretation for the assignment. We just have to define a simple abstract interpretation of the forone and we can consider without loss of generality assignments of the form: $v \to a = v$ instead of the more general form $v \to a = e$ (where $e$ denotes any expression).

The translation of database programming languages into that intermediate language is straightforward. We give in the following definition the syntax of the whole intermediate language we shall use.

**Definition 1.** *A method is a program* m = *instruction where* m *is the* name *of the method and instruction is the* body *of* m *that is syntactically defined as follows:*

instruction ::= *variable* -> *attribute* = *variable*
      |  instruction ; instruction
      |  { instruction }
      |  if condition then instruction
      |  forone variable where condition do instruction
      |  forall variable where condition do instruction

This definition deserves the following comments. We only consider instructions there and not methods returning expressions as we are only interested in updates (side effects) which can alter the integrity of data. Therefore, we do not have parameters in our syntax because we do not make any differences between methods parameters and global variables. Following [Cas96], self is just the first parameter of methods.

## 4 Safe Database Schemas via Predicate Transformers

We describe in this section our technique to prove automatically whether methods are consistent with respect to integrity constraints.

Our approach is an instance of abstract interpretation [CC77, CC79, JN95]. The aim of abstract interpretation is to provide, automatically and at compile time, some information on the possible run-time behaviour of a program. This amounts to doing, instead of a real execution of a program on a real environment, an *abstract execution* of that program on an *abstract environment*.

The program analysis framework we develop has been greatly inspired by the works of Dijkstra on predicate transformers [Dij76, DS90]. A (forward) predicate transformer is a function that given a program and a formula describing its input data, produces a formula describing its output data.

The application of predicate transformers to our problem is natural. The input data of a method m is described by an integrity constraint C. We apply the predicate transformer to m and C and get another formula (a post-condition) $\overline{m}(C)$ describing the output data of m. Formula $\overline{m}(C)$ is satisfied by any database resulting from an execution of m, provided C is satisfied before the execution. The main result of this section is that m cannot violate C if $\overline{m}(C) \Rightarrow C$ (C is a consequence of $\overline{m}(C)$).

Our technique undertakes a very detailed analysis of methods and provides some precise information on the impact they have upon constraints. Hoare and Dijkstra's main interest was to compute a so-called *weakest-precondition* in terms of a *post-condition* and a program. Hoare used some deductive rules to yield that pre-condition, whereas Dijkstra defined a backward predicate transformer[4]. An

---

[4] As opposed to forward predicate transformers, a backward predicate transformer is a function that, given a program and a formula describing its output data, produces a formula describing its input data

important result of their analyses is that they produce, for simple languages, the most precise information about program behaviour that can be obtained (i.e. strongest post-conditions or weakest pre-conditions). That implies that every property that is true of a program is *provable* (i.e. their method is complete). However, for some complex languages with some sophisticated features such as aliasing, Clarke [Cla79] has shown that completeness cannot be obtained. That has lead us to define an *abstract* forward predicate transformer, as it cannot claim to produce the most-precise information about program behaviour (i.e. strongest post-conditions). Still, it manages to produce some partial, but very useful information (as it is always the case in abstract interpretation). We will see later that this information yielded is sufficient to undertake program verification in even complex cases.

In the rest of this section, we shall first give the formal syntax of our formulas. We will assume without loss of generality that negation can only be applied to atoms[5].

We shall then define the abstract interpretation by induction, both on the structure of the method and the structure of the initial formula. For the sake of clarity, we shall first describe the abstract interpretation of simple instructions. To this end, we first define the predicate transformer for simple methods which do not contain loop instructions and are not overriden. We shall show how it is used to prove method safety. Then, we shall describe the predicate transformer for loops. This also suggests how recursion can be dealt with. Finally, we present the treatment of overriden methods.

## 4.1 Integrity Constraints

Integrity constraints are well-formed formulas on a first-order language. We use $a$ to range over *attributes* and $u, v$ to range over *variables*. Terms are defined by:

**Definition 2.** Let V be a set of variables, let C be a set of constants (0, 1, nil, etc), the set of terms is inductively defined by:

- For every $c$ in C, $c$ is a term,
- For every $v \in$ V, $v$ is a term
- Let t be a term and let $a$ be an attribute name then $t \rightarrow a$ is a term.

Formulas are constructed as usual by means of comparators ($<, >, =, \neq$) using the connectives $\wedge, \vee, \neg, \Rightarrow, \forall$ and $\exists$.

## 4.2 Simple Methods

**Definition 3.** Let m be a method (see Definition 1). We define the *predicate transformer* $\overline{m}$ of m, by induction, as follows ($\overline{m}$ denotes a formula). Let $\phi$ and $\varphi$ be two formulae:

---

[5] We can use the following rules to ensure that: $\neg(\phi \wedge \varphi) = \neg\phi \vee \neg\varphi$, $\neg(\phi \vee \varphi) = \neg\phi \wedge \neg\varphi$, $\neg\forall x \phi = \exists x \neg\phi$, $\neg\exists x \phi = \forall x \neg\phi$, $\neg\neg\phi = \phi$.

– Formula parse:

1. $\overline{m}((\phi)) \equiv (\overline{m}(\phi))$
2. $\overline{m}(\phi \wedge \varphi) \equiv \overline{m}(\phi) \wedge \overline{m}(\varphi)$
3. $\overline{m}(\phi \vee \varphi) \equiv \overline{m}(\phi) \vee \overline{m}(\varphi)$
4. $\overline{m}(\forall x \phi) \equiv \forall x \, \overline{m}(\phi)$
5. $\overline{m}(\exists x \phi) \equiv \exists x \, \overline{m}(\phi)$

– Method parse:

6. If: $m \equiv u\text{->}a=v$ then:
   - If: $\phi \equiv (x \rightarrow a = y)$
     then: $\overline{m}(\phi) \equiv (u = x \wedge u \rightarrow a = v) \vee (u \neq x \wedge u \rightarrow a = v \wedge x \rightarrow a = y)$
   - If: $\phi \equiv (x \rightarrow a \neq y)$
     then: $\overline{m}(\phi) \equiv (u = x \wedge u \rightarrow a = v) \vee (u \neq x \wedge u \rightarrow a = v \wedge x \rightarrow a \neq y)$
   - Else: $\overline{m}(\phi) \equiv \phi \wedge u \rightarrow a = v$

   where $\phi$ is a literal. If $\phi$ is not a literal[6], $\overline{m}(\phi)$ can be computed by parsing $\phi$ first using (1-5).
7. If: $m \equiv i_1; i_2$ then: $\overline{m}(\phi) \equiv \overline{i_2}(\overline{i_1}(\phi))$
8. If: $m \equiv \{i\}$ then: $\overline{m}(\phi) \equiv \bar{i}(\phi)$
9. If: $m \equiv \text{if } \psi \text{ then } i$ then: $\overline{m}(\phi) \equiv \bar{i}(\psi \wedge \phi) \vee (\neg \psi \wedge \phi)$
10. If: $m \equiv \text{for one } v \text{ where } \psi(v) \text{ do } i$ then: $\overline{m}(\phi) \equiv \exists v \, \bar{i}(\psi(v) \wedge \phi)$

We assume that there is no ambiguity between symbols. If necessary, we can always rename all the variables and parameters that are used in constraints and methods.

Clause 6 deserves an explanation. Let us assume that the update "$u\text{->}a=v$" is undertaken and that the formula "$(x \rightarrow a = y)$" is true before the update. Then, we either have $(u = x)$ or $(u \neq x)$, and a formula that is true after the update is respectively $(u = x \wedge u \rightarrow a = v)$ or $(u \neq x \wedge u \rightarrow a = v \wedge x \rightarrow a = y)$. The result follows: it is the disjunction of those two formulae. The other cases are similar.

We now have to prove formally that the abstract interpretation of a method gives some reliable information about the real behaviour of that method, i.e. that it is *correct*. In the following, we will have to interpret formulae with free variables. To that purpose, we will write $\mathcal{B}_\sigma$ the interpretation $\mathcal{B}$ provided with the assignment of free variables $\sigma$.

**Theorem 4.** Let $\mathcal{B}_{\text{old}}$ be a database, $m$ be a method, and $\mathcal{B}_{\text{new}}$ be the same database after an execution of $m$. Let $\phi$ be a formula, and $\sigma$ be an assignment for the free variables of $\phi$. We have:

$$\mathcal{B}_{\text{old}_\sigma} \models \phi \implies \mathcal{B}_{\text{new}_\sigma} \models \overline{m}(\phi)$$

that is, the abstract interpretation $\overline{m}$ of $m$ is correct

---

[6] A *literal* is either an atom or the negation of an atom. An *atom* is an expression $a(t_1, ..., t_n)$, where $a$ is a relation and $t_1,...,t_n$ are terms.

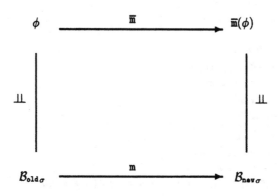

**Fig. 5.** Predicate transformer diagram

This relationship is illustrated by the diagram in Figure 5. That theorem is proven by induction on both formulas and instructions. The proof can be found in [BS95]. We have already said that we need some correct information about the run-time behaviour of programs. Moreover, that information must be precise enough to be useful. After all, we could define a predicate transformer that is correct, but does not provide any useful information. For instance: $\overline{m}(\phi) = \mathbf{true}$ for any method $m$ and any formula $\phi$. As it will be shown in Section 5, our predicate transformer is precise enough to allow us to prove method correctness for many non trivial examples.

We can now use that predicate transformer to tell whether a method might violate an integrity constraint. The following theorem is a consequence of Theorem 4.

**Theorem 5.** Let $C$ be a constraint and $m$ be a method. $m$ is safe with respect to $C$ if $\overline{m}(C) \Rightarrow C$.

The proof of this theorem can also be found in [BS95].

To establish that method $m$ is safe with respect to $C$, we have to prove that $\overline{m}(C) \Rightarrow C$. We point out that powerful methods have been developed in the field of automated theorem proving in first-order logic: resolution, paramodulation, tableaux method... We use the tableaux method exposed in [Fit90] because it does not impose any special normal form for the formula being processed. A property of all those proof techniques is that they are *complete*: if a formula is true, then those proof techniques find a proof for the formula in a finite time. The real problem occurs when the formula is *not* true. In that case, the theorem prover keeps on looking for a proof whereas none exists! Practically, theorem provers always look for a proof in a limited search space. So, our technique will:

- detect as being safe some safe methods (depending on the search space devoted to the computation).
- detect as being unsafe some safe methods and all unsafe methods.

## 4.3 Methods with Loops or Recursion and Overridden Methods

We show in this section how to deal with loops and recursion. For the sake of brevity, we shall focus on the loop. The generalisation to recursion should be clear. Database programming languages allow the use of a specific loop. In our kernel language, it is defined as:

forall *variable* where *condition* do *instruction*

The "forall" instruction executes "*instruction*" for every element, denoted by "*variable*", that satisfies "*condition*". A first approach is to look for the solution of the usual equation for loops[7]:

$$\overline{\text{forall}}(\phi) = \overline{instruction}(\overline{\text{forall}}(\phi))$$

The solution of that equation is the usual least fix-point of function $\overline{\text{forall}}$. However, in general, that fix-point cannot be computed (the computation may not terminate). We therefore have to undertake an analysis that is less precise, but which terminates, and yields some useful information. We use a technique, that allows to reach an approximation of the fix-point in a finite time. Intuitively, the idea is that if "*instruction*" is safe with respect to a constraint, then the overall "forall" instruction will also be safe provided that safety was guaranteed prior entering the loop (i.e., the constraint is a logical consequence of the current value of the predicate transformer). Suppose we are proving the safety of a method m with respect to a constraint $C$, and that m contains a loop. We define the predicate transformer of that loop as follows:

$$\overline{\text{forall}}(\phi) = \begin{cases} C & \text{if } \phi \Rightarrow C \text{ and } \overline{instruction}(C) \Rightarrow C \\ \text{true} & \text{otherwise.} \end{cases}$$

Each time we encounter a loop with a formula $\phi$ as input, we either replace it by $C$ if $\phi$ implies $C$ and the instructions contained in the loop are safe with respect to $C$, or by true otherwise. The abstract interpretation is still correct. Therefore the following holds:

**Theorem 6.** Let $\mathcal{B}_{\text{old}}$ be a database, m be a method with loop statements, and $\mathcal{B}_{\text{new}}$ be the database obtained after an execution of m. Let $\phi$ be a formula, and $\sigma$ be an assignment for the free variables of $\phi$. We have:

$$\mathcal{B}_{\text{old}_\sigma} \models \phi \implies \mathcal{B}_{\text{new}_\sigma} \models \overline{\text{m}}(\phi)$$

that is, the abstract interpretation $\overline{\text{m}}$ of m is correct.

The proof of this theorem relies on the fact that the composition of correct abstract interpretations is still correct. Again we have:

---

[7] We give a simplified version of $\overline{\text{forall}}(\phi)$. In the exact version, we have to take into account "*variable*" and "*condition*".

**Theorem 7.** Let $C$ be a constraint and m be a method with loops statements. m is safe with respect to $C$ if $\overline{m}(C) \Rightarrow C$.

In order to deal with loops, we have to include in the process of building our predicate transformer some theorem proving steps. Again for the same reasons that have been exposed in the previous section, for some safe methods with loops, safety cannot be proven. Safe methods can be detected as such if loops start from a coherent state (i.e. $\phi \Rightarrow C$ can be proven in the search space), and each iteration map a coherent state to a coherent state (i.e. $\overline{instruction}(C) \Rightarrow C$ can be proven in the search space). So, even when dealing with loops, we still have an efficient method for proving method safety. A similar method can be defined with respect to recursion.

We have described in this section a *program analysis framework* for the language defined in the previous section. We also have defined a very precise criterion to tell if a method can violate an integrity constraint. Our machinery can fail in proving the safety of some safe methods, but it will never manage to prove the safety of a method which is not safe. It errs on the side of caution (our technique is sound but not complete). On the basis of first experiments performed on our current prototype and reported in Section 5, we are confident that the proofs we are dealing with are simple and that many safe methods will be detected as such.

The application of our machinery to overridden methods is straightforward. Intuitively, an overridden method is safe if every branch defined for it is safe.

**Theorem 8.** Let $m = \{m_1, \ldots, m_n\}$ be an overloaded method. Let $C$ be an integrity constraint, m is safe with respect to $C$ if the following holds

$$\forall i \in \{1, \ldots, n\}, \overline{m_i}(C) \Rightarrow C.$$

## 5    Implementation

We present in this section the prototype that has been implemented. We are currently experimenting its behaviour on some real examples. We will give the results that we have obtained on the examples provided earlier. The prototype is in fact a pre-processor for $O_2$. It provides $O_2$ with an integrity constraint management facility. The integrity manager works with:

- an $O_2$ database schema together with a set of integrity constraints.
- a set of methods written in $O_2$.

For the sake of simplicity, the prototype only considers a significant subset of $O_2$ (namely, the instructions for which we have defined a predicate transformer). However, it can be extended to accept the whole $O_2$ language. We show in Figure 6 the general structure of the integrity constraint manager, and explain in the following the role of each part.

- First, a simple syntactical technique is used to show that some methods are safe with respect to some constraints. That component is a preliminary filter

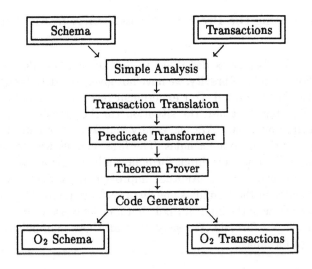

**Fig. 6.** structure of the integrity constraint manager

that only considers type information from the constraints and the methods. Roughly, it compares the types of the objects that are updated in each method with the types of the objects that are "constrained" by each constraint. This method has been presented with full details in [BD93, BD95]. It reduces the task of the next steps of the analysis in a significant way, and at a very low cost.

- After that, for methods that have not been proven safe, the more sophisticated method of *predicate transformers* is applied in different steps:

1. Methods and constraints are decomposed. In particular, methods are translated into the intermediate form to make the task of abstract interpretation easier.

2. For each method and each constraint, the predicate transformer is applied. Which method has to be checked with which constraint is determined by the first step mentioned previously.

3. An automatic first-order theorem prover based on the tableaux method is applied to the result provided by the predicate transformer.

4. The code generator finally takes into account the results of the analysis to generate the $O_2$ schema (if needed) and the $O_2$ methods. Checking algorithms are automatically generated if the safety proof for a method has failed. Those can be found in [BD93, BD95].

We will develop in the following several important points about the whole process. The first show how the predicate transformer is put into practice in the prototype. This will provide an explanation as to why the tableaux method has been chosen. We will then present briefly that method and give the results of our experiment.

## 5.1 Implementing the Predicate Transformer: from Theory to Practice

The predicate transformer as described in Section 4 is not directly suited to automation. For the sake of brevity, we have not given any details concerning the size of the formulas generated. Our experiment has shown that those formulas can be quite big, but that also the situation can be greatly improved by the use of appropriate heuristics. We use a very simple and pragmatic method to reduce the size of the output formulas. The first obvious way to do that is to simplify the input formula. The input formula can be simplified when it includes redundancies or contradictions. Another improvement, which is less trivial, is to include explicitly in the formula some facts that are implicit in that formula. This increases the size of the input formula but has the consequence of decreasing the size of the output formula. We insist that all those manipulations preserve the semantics of formulas.

**Normalisation** First, we systematically put the input formula into disjunctive normal form. It is first put into prenex form (i.e. quantifiers come first), and the matrix (i.e. the part of the formula that is not quantified) is put into disjunctive normal form. Therefore, each formula is of the form:

$$Q_1 x_1, \ldots Q_n x_n, E_1 \vee \ldots \vee E_m$$

where the $Q_i$'s are quantifiers and the $E_i$'s, which we shall call *environments*, are a conjunction of literals $(L_1 \wedge \ldots \wedge L_k)$. The cost of normalisation is not too expensive, as the initial formula (the constraint) is usually small, and each step of the analysis keeps the formula normalised.

**Dealing with Contradictions and Redundancies** Once the formula has been normalised, we make a simple analysis of each environment to get rid of contradictions and redundancies. The search for those is very limited (we would otherwise need a theorem prover). The redundancies we deal with are very simple: when a literal occurs twice in an environment, one occurrence can obviously be removed. Moreover, when a contradiction is detected in an environment $E$, $E$ can be removed from the disjunction of environments. We point out that such a removal should be done *before* applying the predicate transformer. The reason for that is illustrated below. Consider the following environment:

$$E \equiv (\text{p}{\rightarrow}\text{spouse}{=}\text{q} \wedge \text{p}{\rightarrow}\text{spouse}{\neq}\text{q})$$

That environment is contradictory ($E \Leftrightarrow \textbf{false}$). It should therefore be discarded in the list of environments (because $A \vee \textbf{false} \Leftrightarrow A$). Let us see what would happen if it was not discarded. Consider the following instruction $i$:

$$i \equiv \text{r->spouse=s}$$

The result of the predicate transformer on $i$ and $E$, $\bar{i}(E)$, is given below:

$((r=p \land p\rightarrow spouse=s)\lor(r\neq p \land p\rightarrow spouse=q \land r\rightarrow spouse=s))$
$\land$
$((r=p \land p\rightarrow spouse=s)\lor(r\neq p \land p\rightarrow spouse\neq q \land r\rightarrow spouse=s))$

It is not a contradiction, and cannot be removed from the list of resulting environments. However, it results from an initial situation which was impossible, and should therefore not have been considered. Much efficiency can therefore be gained when reducing the initial formula. The rules that are used to detect contradictions are the axioms of equality (reflexivity, symmetry, transitivity) and functions $(x = y \Rightarrow f(x) = f(y))$. For the sake of efficiency, the search space for contradictions is voluntarily limited.

**Making the Input Formula more Explicit** Another improvement can be obtained by including in the input formula some information that is implicit in that formula. For instance, consider the following environment:

$$E \equiv (q\rightarrow spouse=p \land q\rightarrow spouse=q),$$

and the instruction $i$:

$$i \equiv \text{p->spouse=q}$$

The result of the predicate transformer is given below:

$((p=q \land p\rightarrow spouse=q)\lor(p\neq q \land p\rightarrow spouse=q \land q\rightarrow spouse=p))$
$\land$
$((p=q \land p\rightarrow spouse=q)\lor(p\neq q \land p\rightarrow spouse=q \land q\rightarrow spouse=q))$

After simplification (applying normalisation and discarding contradictions and redundancies), this leads to:

$((p=q \land p\rightarrow spouse=q)$
$\lor$
$(p\neq q \land p\rightarrow spouse=q \land q\rightarrow spouse=p \land q\rightarrow spouse=q))$

However, a smaller formula can be obtained if we include in the input formula some of its consequences. For instance we can deduce (by transitivity of equality) from the previous environment $E$ the following one, which is equivalent:

$$E' \equiv (q\rightarrow spouse=p \land q\rightarrow spouse=q \land p=q ),$$

The result of the predicate transformer for $E'$ and $i$ is:

$((p=q \land p\rightarrow spouse=q)\lor(p\neq q \land p\rightarrow spouse=q \land q\rightarrow spouse=p))$
$\land$
$((p=q \land p\rightarrow spouse=q)\lor(p\neq q \land p\rightarrow spouse=q \land q\rightarrow spouse=q))$
$\land$
$(p=q \land p\rightarrow spouse=q)$

Again after simplification this reduces to:

(p=q ∧ p→spouse=q)

This shows how one can greatly improve the process of generating our post-condition, yielding a formula which is much more compact and can be dealt with more efficiently. Our experiment has shown that in some cases, it has allowed to reduce and simplify the output formula in a drastic way (from a formula with hundreds of literals to a formula with just one literal). Notice that all the optimisation techniques presented here are obviously valid and are automatically undertaken by the prototype.

## 5.2 The Tableaux Method

This section provides the main reason why the automatic theorem proving technique chosen is the tableaux method. The predicate transformer produces a formula which is (nearly) in disjunctive normal form. The resolution method requires that the formulas be in conjunctive normal form (after skolemisation). The cost of going from one normal form to another is so high that it cannot be done in a reasonable time. That is why we need to use a method that does not require the formulas to be in clausal form. The tableaux method is a refutation method. In order to prove that $F \Rightarrow G$, that method proves in fact that $F \wedge \neg G$ is unsatisfiable (contradictory). In order to do that, it develops a tree, called a tableau, which has several branches. A tableau is of the form:

$$[\text{branch}_1, \text{branch}_2, ..., \text{branch}_n]$$

Each branch is of the form:

$$[\text{formula}_1, \text{formula}_2, ..., \text{formula}_m]$$

In fact, each branch is a conjunction of formulas, and a tableau is a disjunction of branches. Note that any formula can appear on branches (they don't have to be normalised). A tableau is developed with *tableau expansion rules*. The tree is expanded only up to a certain "depth". Then, a "test for closure" is done on that tree, which amounts to an instantiation of free variables that reduces the tableau to a contradiction. The reader can find more details about automatic theorem proving techniques in [Fit90].

## 5.3 Practical Experiments

The prototype that is implemented consists of approximately 4000 lines of C code. We have chosen C for the sake of efficiency, although Prolog or Lisp might have been better languages for formula manipulation. The syntactic analysis of the input files is done with Lex and Yacc. The actual code is not very complicated as the abstract predicate transformer approach is well suited to implementation. It is very modular, and much of it consists of well-known procedures such a basic formula manipulation (normalisation, substitutions...). We give below the post-condition that is generated by the predicate transformer for method **marry** in class **Person**:

```
method marry(q:Person) in class Person{
   if (self!=q){
      self->spouse=q;
      q->spouse=self;}}
```

The pre-condition is constraint C2:

$$\text{C2: forall x in Persons: x->spouse!=x;}$$

The prototype uses a Lisp-like structure for formulas. For instance, constraint C2 is written:

$$\text{(forall x (|| (notin x Persons) (!= (spouse x) x)))}$$

Terms like x->spouse are written (spouse x), formulas like (x==y) are written (== x y), etc. The post-condition is:

```
(forall v0 (forall v1 (||
(&& (== (spouse q) self) (== (spouse self) q) (notin v0 Persons)
(!= self q) (!= self q))
(&& (== (spouse q) self) (== (spouse self) q) (!= (spouse v0) v0)
(!= self q) (== v0 self) (!= v0 q) (!= self q) (!= v0 q))
(&& (== (spouse q) self) (== (spouse self) q) (!= (spouse v0) v0)
(!= self q) (!= v0 self) (!= self q) (== v0 q) (!= v0 self))
(&& (== (spouse q) self) (== (spouse self) q) (!= (spouse v0) v0)
(!= self q) (!= v0 self) (!= self q) (!= v0 q))
(&& (notin v1 Persons) (== self q))
(&& (!= (spouse v1) v1) (== self q)))))
```

The tableaux method is then applied to prove that the post-condition implies the constraint. Our experiment has been done on a Sun sparc (sun4m) server running Solaris 2.3 OS. The complete safety proof takes less than 1 second. The integrity constraint manager has been run on all the examples given above. The results of that experiment are given Figure 7.

The times given are only a rough guide of the efficiency of the method. They show that, in many cases, a proof can be obtained quite fast (see method **separate** with constraint C1). In some other cases, although quite simple, the proof might need some extra time (for instance, method **spend** with constraint C5).The reasons for such differences between proofs are not clear. A further study should focus on the assessment of the cost of the analysis. However, we insist that our method is run at *compile-time* and once and for all. Therefore, such costs can be afforded by the system.

# 6  Related Work

The study of integrity constraints in database systems has been a topic of large interest [Sto75, Nic79, GM79, CB80, LT85, HI85, BM86, KSS87, HCN84, WSK83, BDM88, SS89, Law95].

| method | class | constraint | time |
|---|---|---|---|
| separate | Person | C1 | 0.18s. |
| separate | Employee | C1 | 0.27s. |
| separate | Parent | C1 | 0.29s. |
| separate | Parent | C6 | 1.23s. |
| separate | Employee | C4 | 1.10s. |
| marry | Person | C2 | 0.46s. |
| marry | Parent | C2 | 1.38s. |
| marry | Parent | C3 | 4s. |
| spend | Person | C5 | 1.32s. |
| marry-and-separate | Person | C2 | 0.65s. |
| setfriend | Person | C7 | 0.24s. |

**Fig. 7.** Results.

Several works concern the optimisation of checking: [Nic79, HI85] for relational databases, [BM86] for deductive databases, [BD95] for object-oriented databases, and [Law95] for deductive object-oriented databases.

In the context of active database systems, triggers are used to express integrity constraints [CW90, SKdM92, CFPT94, CCS94]. A trigger is composed by an event $e$, a condition $c$ and an action $a$. If $e$ occurs and if $c$ is satisfied then the action $a$ is executed. Depending from the context, the language used for expressing actions is more or less powerful (in [CCS94], message passing, for example, is possible).

However, triggers are far from the simple and declarative tool that integrity constraints should have been. Indeed, the definition and verification of constraints are merged in a single unit (the trigger). Integrity is spread out among several triggers and therefore the global vision of the application semantics is lost.

The subject of finding consistency proofs for transactions is not new: [GM79] gives some indications on how Hoare's logic could be used for that purpose. The invariance of integrity constraints is proven, by hand, for several examples. However, the ideas exposed are not formalised and no systematic procedure for obtaining such proofs is given.

Besides, [Cla79] has spotlighted the deficiencies of Hoare's logic for languages with complex features such as aliasing, side effects... that are shared by most database programming languages.

[CB80] attempt to give a logical method to assess database transaction semantics in general, with a particular interest for integrity constraints. Their work is closely related to [GM79], but uses dynamic logic. However, the problems about the formalisation and automation of the process remain. The work of [Qia90] is in the line of [GM79, CB80], and presents an axiom system for transaction analysis. However, the applicability of such an axiom system is unclear. [Qia93] asserts that conventional methods are not suited to automatic transaction safety verification and takes the opposite direction of *transaction synthesis*. [Qia93] justifies that new direction in the following way: "The generation of unnecessary constraint checking and enforcement code should be avoided. It should be noticed that such optimisation is out of reach for conventional program optimisation techniques, because conventional program optimisers do not have the ability to reason about integrity constraint." We show in this article that such is not the case. Conventional program optimisation techniques such as *abstract interpretation* can deal with that problem in an efficient way.

More recently, [Law95] has defined a way to obtain some *weakest-preconditions* for a very simple language, in the context of deductive and object oriented databases. The choice of that language is somewhat unrealistic as it does not allow basic constructs such as if's. His work focuses on checking the constraints at run-time, rather than proving at compile-time that constraints will be preserved by transactions. Instead of checking the constraint after the execution of the transaction, he checks the pre-condition before the execution, which avoids subsequent roll-backs.

[SS89] is, to our knowledge, the most in-depth application of the axiomatic method to our problem. It uses a complex theorem prover that uses Boyer-Moore's computational logic, based on higher-order recursive functions. Their theorem prover is in fact an expert system which uses a knowledge base where some properties of database constructs are kept. Some theorems are derived and the knowledge base grows. A complex strategy, with many heuristics, is used to improve the search process. Their knowledge base is first filled with axioms about basic language constructs. The main problem with this approach is that the consistency of those axioms is not guaranteed, particularly in the case of classical set theory (as mentioned by the authors). If those axioms are not consistent, then the expert system could prove just anything. Their approach is based on the confidence that no "surprising" properties can be derived from the axioms and is therefore not formally founded.

Our work differs from the other works on the subject of consistency proofs for transactions, in that we use the technique of *abstract interpretation*. The main advantage of this technique is that it focuses on operational issues rather than on mathematical relationships. Abstract interpretation is an elegant and unified framework to describe program semantics with algorithms that are very well suited to automation. Most other works (except that of [SS89]) attempt to clarify the semantics of updates in databases by linking it to logic. However, they do not suggest an effective way of undertaking program verification. Our method is, to our knowledge, the first approach based on first-order logic that has been implemented.

# 7   Conclusions

We have presented an efficient technique to deal with integrity constraints in object-oriented database programming languages that provide integrated facilities, as the extended version of $O_2$. This technique focuses on a compile-time checking of constraints. It first attempts to determine formally whether methods are consistent with integrity constraints. If such is the case, the cost of unnecessary run-time checking can be avoided. For the remaining methods (those who might violate integrity constraints), appropriate run-time tests are automatically inserted according to [BD95]. Our approach uses combined abstract interpretation and automated theorem proving techniques. Abstract interpretation provides, via an *abstract predicate transformer*, some partial information about the possible run-time behaviour of methods. This information is then dealt with by the theorem prover. No human intervention is needed, therefore the whole process is fully automatic.

A prototype which undertakes this method has already been implemented and provides some good results on some non-trivial examples. Ongoing experimentation focuses on the refinement and optimisation of the method. It should also give more information about the cost of this method.

Our approach is not restricted to the problem of statically handling integrity constraints in object-oriented database programming languages. It can also be adapted to static analysis of object-oriented languages providing pre and post-conditions such as Eiffel [Mey88, Mey91].

In our future research, we plan to develop some other abstract interpretation techniques. Particularly, we are currently developing a backward predicate transformer which, as opposed to the one presented in this article, will generate a pre-condition (rather than a post-condition). We hope that this latter analysis will allow us to detect some safe methods which are not handled by the forward predicate transformer described in this paper. Combining both analysis should yield some useful results. In particular, we believe that the backward analysis can be used for automatic repair of unsafe methods.

In the long term we plan to apply our method to dynamic constraints and to this end explore the domain of modal theorem proving techniques.

## Acknowledgements

We would like to thank Giorgio Ghelli and Atsushi Ohori who first recommended us to study abstract interpretation theory, Giuseppe Castagna for his suggestions and many valuable comments for improving this paper, and Serenella Cerrito, for reading an early version of this paper. We would also like to thank the reviewers for their precious remarks.

## References

[AB91]    S. Abiteboul and A. Bonner. Objects and views. In *ACM International Conference on Management of Data (SIGMOD)*, pages 238–248, Denver, Colorado, USA, May 1991.

[ABGO93]  A. Albano, R. Bergamini, G. Ghelli, and R. Orsini. An object data model with roles. In *International Conference on Very Large Databases*, pages 39–52, 1993.

[ABGO95] A. Albano, R. Bergamini, G. Ghelli, and R. Orsini. Fibonacci: a programming language for object databases. *VLDB Journal*, 4(3):403–444, July 95.

[BC96] John Boyland and Giuseppe Castagna. Type-safe compilation of covariant specialization: a practical case. In *ECOOP'96*, number 1008 in Lecture Notes in Computer Science, pages 3–25. Springer, 1996.

[BD93] V. Benzaken and A. Doucet. Thémis: a database programming language with integrity constraints. In Shasha Beeri, Ohori, editor, *Proceedings of the 4th International Workshop on Database Programming Languages*, Workshop in Computing, pages 243–262, New York City, USA, September 1993. Springer-Verlag.

[BD95] V. Benzaken and A. Doucet. Thémis: A Database Programming Language Handling Integrity Constraints. *VLDB Journal*, 4(3):493–518, 1995.

[BDM88] F. Bry, H. Decker, and R. Manthey. A Uniform Approach to Constraint Satisfaction and Constraint Satisfiability in Deductive Databases. In Missikoff Schmidt, Ceri, editor, *Proceedings of the EDBT International Conference*, LNCS 303, pages 488–505, 1988.

[BM86] F. Bry and R. Manthey. Checking Consistency of Database Constraints: A Logical Basis. In *Proceedings of the VLDB International Conference*, pages 13–20, August 1986.

[BS95] V. Benzaken and X. Schaefer. Abstract interpretation and predicate transformers: an application to integrity constraints management. Technical Report 1002, L.R.I, Université de Paris XI, 1995.

[BS96] V. Benzaken and X. Schaefer. Ensuring efficiently the integrity of persistent object systems via abstract interpretation. In S. Nettles and R. Connor, editors, *Seventh International Workshop on Persistent Object Systems*, Cape May, U.S.A, June 1996. Morgan-Kaufmann. To appear.

[Cas96] Giuseppe Castagna. *Object-Oriented Programming: A Unified Foundation*. Progress in Theoretical Computer Science. Birkäuser, Boston, 1996. ISBN 3-7643-3905-5.

[CB80] M. A. Casanova and P. A. Bernstein. A formal system for reasonning about programs accessing a relational database. *ACM Transactions on Database Systems*, 2(3):386–414, July 80.

[CC77] P. Cousot and R. Cousot. Abstract Interpretation: A Unified Lattice Model for Static Analysis of Programs by Construction or Approximation of Fixpoints. In *4th POPL, Los Angeles, CA*, pages 238–252, January 1977.

[CC79] P. Cousot and R. Cousot. Systematic design of program analysis frameworks. In *6th popl, San Antonio, Texas*, pages 269–282, January 1979.

[CCS94] C. Collet, T. Coupaye, and T. Svenson. Naos - efficient and modular reactive capabilities in an oodbms. In *Proceedings of the Twentieth International Conference on Very Large Databases (VLDB)*, pages 132–144, Santiago, Chile, September 1994.

[CFPT94] S. Ceri, P. Fraternali, S. Paraboschi, and L. Tanca. Active rule management in chimera. Morgan Kaufmann, 1994.

[Cla79] E. M. Clarke. Programming languages constructs for which it is impossible to obtain good hoare axiom systems. *Journal of the ACM*, 26(1):129–147, January 79.

[CW90] S. Ceri and J. Widom. Deriving production rules for constraint maintenance. In *Proceedings of the VLDB International Conference*, pages 566–577, Brisbane, Australia, August 90.

[Dij76]      E. W. Dijkstra. *A Discipline of Programming*. Prentice-Hall, 1976.

[DS90]       E. W. Dijkstra and C. S. Scholten. *Predicate Calculus and Program Semantics*. Texts and Monographs in Computer Science. Springer-Verlag, 1990.

[Fit90]      Melvin Fitting. *First-order logic and automated theorem proving*. Texts and monographs in computer science. Springer-Verlag, 1990.

[GM79]       G. Gardarin and M. Melkanoff. Proving the Consistency of Database Transactions. In *VLDB International Conference*, pages 291–298, Rio, Brasil, October 1979.

[HCN84]      L. Henschen, W. Mc Cune, and S. Naqvi. Compiling constraint checking programs from first order formulas. In H. Gallaire, J. Minker, and J.M. Nicolas, editors, *Advances in Database Theory*, volume 2. Plenum, 1984.

[HI85]       A. Hsu and T. Imielinski. Integrity Checking for Multiple Updates. In *Proceedings of the ACM SIGMOD International Conference*, pages 152–168, 1985.

[JN95]       N. D. Jones and F. Nielson. Abstract interpretation. In S. Abramsky, D. M. Gabbay, and T. S. E. Maibaum, editors, *Semantic Modelling*, volume 4 of *Handbook of Logic in Computer Science*, chapter 5, pages 527–636. Oxford Science Publication, 1995.

[KSS87]      R. Kowalski, F. Sadri, and P. Soper. Integrity Checking in Deductive Databases. In *Proceedings of the VLDB International Conference*, pages 61–70, 1987.

[Law95]      Michael Lawley. Transaction safety in deductive object-oriented databases. In *Proceedings of the Fourth International Conference on Deductive and Object-Oriented Databases, Singapore*, number 1013 in LNCS, pages 395–410. Springer-Verlag, Dec 1995.

[LT85]       J. W. Lloyd and R. W. Topor. A basis for deductive database systems. *Journal of Logic Programming*, 2(2), 1985.

[Mey88]      Bertrand Meyer. *Object-Oriented Software Construction*. Prentice-Hall International Series, 1988.

[Mey91]      Bertrand Meyer. *Eiffel: The Language*. Prentice Hall, 1991.

[Nic79]      J.M. Nicolas. Logic for Improving Integrity Checking in Relational Databases. Technical report, ONERA-CERT, 1979.

[Qia90]      Xiaolei Qian. An axiom system for database transactions. *Information Processing letters*, 36:183–189, November 1990.

[Qia93]      Xiaolei Qian. The deductive synthesis of database transactions. *ACM Transactions on Database Systems*, 18(4):626–677, December 1993.

[SDA94]      C. Sousa, C. Delobel, and S. Abiteboul. Virtual schemas and bases. In M. Jarke, J. Bubenko, and K Jeffery, editors, *International Conference on Extending Database Technology*, number 779 in LNCS, pages 81–95. Springer-Verlag, 1994.

[SKdM92]     E. Simon, J. Kiernan, and C. de Maindreville. Implementing high level active rules on top of a relational dbms. In *Proceedings of the Eighteenth International Conference on Very Large Database (VLDB)*, pages 315–326, Vancouver, British Columbia, August 1992.

[SS89]       T. Sheard and D. Stemple. Automatic Verification of Database Transaction Safety. *ACM Transaction on Database Systems*, 14(3):322–368, September 1989.

[Sto75]      M. Stonebraker. Implementation of Integrity Constraints and Views by Query Modification. In *ACM SIGMOD International Conference*, San Jose, California, May 1975.

[WSK83]      W. Weber, W. Stugky, and J. Karzt. Integrity Checking in database systems. *Information Systems*, 8(2):125–136, 1983.

# Issues with Exception Handling in Object-Oriented Systems

Robert Miller[1] and Anand Tripathi[2]
Computer Science Department
University of Minnesota
Minneapolis, Minnesota 55455 USA

## Abstract

The goals of exception handling mechanisms are to make programs more reliable and robust. The integration of exception handling mechanisms with object-oriented languages raises some unique issues. The requirements of exception handling often conflict with some of the goals of object-oriented designs, such as supporting design evolution, functional specialization, and abstraction for implementation transparency. This paper demonstrates these conflicts, illustrates that the use of exception handling in object-oriented systems poses potential pitfalls, and suggests that their resolution is one of the first steps necessary to make exception handling robust in object-oriented designs and languages.

## 1. Introduction

The general goals of object-oriented designs includes support for abstraction, design evolution, functional specialization, and conceptual modeling. These goals are supported by basic elements of object-oriented languages, which include constructs for supporting abstraction, encapsulation, modularity, and specialization and reuse through inheritance. Towards the building of robust and reliable systems, object encapsulation mechanisms create natural domains for confining the effects of errors within an object and propagating such effects in a well-controlled fashion across the object boundaries [11].

The importance of exception handling is for program reliability and robustness, since many object-oriented languages consider an exception to be some kind of error. Recovering from errors has traditionally been error prone, and is itself a significant cause of program failures. One study [5] has shown that perhaps two-thirds of a program may be for error handling. The rising importance of exception handling is evident in object-oriented languages such as C++ [20], Java [18], Ada [4], and Smalltalk [8].

By combining object-oriented design methods with exception handling techniques, it is hoped that more reliable error handling can occur within a program. However, exception handling often does not exactly fit into the object-oriented paradigm. We show in this paper that the needs of exception handling often conflict with the goals of object-orientation in the areas of object interface definition, composition relationships,

---

[1] E-mail rm@vnet.ibm.com. Currently with IBM, Rochester, MN.
[2] E-mail atripath@nsf.gov. Currently with National Science Foundation, Arlington, VA on a temporary assignment.

exception context, exception conformance, and program control flow. The conflict often manifests during the specialization of object functionality and design evolution.

The objective of this paper is to show, mainly through examples, why exception handling may need to conflict with traditional object-oriented goals. The purpose is to aid programmers that must write exception handlers and designers of exception handling mechanisms in avoiding the potential pitfalls that exception handling poses. With this insight, perhaps programmers and language designers can avoid these problems, and truly robust exception handling can be realized.

Section 2 of this paper provides background with terminology, exception models, and exception handling in some of the major object-oriented languages. We make a distinction between modeling and implementation domains because their exception handling requirements are different. Section 3 details four key areas of differences between the basic design goals of object-oriented systems and exception handling models: complete exception specification, partial states, exception conformance, and exception propagation. To keep the discussion focused, simple and somewhat contrived examples are used. Section 4 shows how these four differences can affect four of the major elements of object-oriented designs: abstraction, encapsulation, modularity, and inheritance. Lastly, Section 5 summarizes the conclusions of this paper.

## 2. Background and Related Work

Based on the work by other researchers in the field [9,12,23], we briefly describe the seminal concepts and terms related to exception handling models. Next, we discuss the different inheritance domains because there can be significant differences in the meaning that an exception can have in these domains. Finally, a brief overview of the exception handling models of some of the most common object-oriented languages is presented. The scope of this discussion is limited to the concepts that are relevant from the viewpoint of the central theme of this paper.

### 2.1 Terminology and Exception Models

Goodenough's work [9] forms the foundation of exception handling terminology and models. Over the past 20 years, there have been several further elaborations and extensions of these models. Goodenough considered exceptions as a means to communicate to the invoker of an operation various kinds of conditions, such as errors during an operation execution, classification of the result returned by an operation, or the occurrence of certain significant events (not necessarily failures) during the execution of an operation. Yemini and Berry [23] define an exception condition in an operation invocation as the occurrence of a state that does not satisfy the input assertion for the operation. Knudsen [12] defines an exception as a characterization of an unusual or abnormal condition that requires extraordinary computation. In many languages (e.g., C++, Java, Ada, Eiffel, and Smalltalk) an exception is normally viewed as an error.

An *exception* is an abnormal computation state. An *exception occurrence* is an instance of an exception. An exception can occur due to an *error* (an invalid system state that is not allowed), *deviation* (an invalid system state that is allowed), *notification* (informing an invoker that an assumed or previous system state has changed), or *idiom* (other uses in which the exception occurrence is rare rather than abnormal, such as detecting EOF). This paper deals mostly with errors, but touches upon deviations and notifications.

The terms *procedure*, *function*, and *block* are used in this paper in the usual sense, as implied in block-structured languages such as Algol-68, Pascal, or Ada. An *object* is an encapsulation of data and code that has a well-defined behavior. An *object's interface* (or *interface*) is the external view of an object that describes the object's behavior as a set of operations (i.e., functions, procedures, or methods) that can be invoked on the object, by its users. An *object context* (or *context*) is the information visible inside the object's encapsulation. This can include internal object variables and global variables.

An exception is *raised* when the corresponding abnormal state is detected. *Signaling* an exception by an operation (or a syntactic entity such as a statement or block) is the communication of an exception occurrence to its invoker. The recipient of the notification is a syntactic entity, called the *exception target* (or *target*); the originator of an exception is the *signaler*. The target is determined either by static scope rules or by dynamic invocation chain.

An *exception handler* (or *handler*) is the code invoked in response to an exception occurrence. It is assumed that the handler's code is separate from the non-exception (or *normal*) control path in the program. Searching for eligible handlers begins with the target (i.e., the search starts with the handlers associated with the target). An exception is considered *handled* when the handler's execution has completed and control flow resumes in the normal path. An exception handled by the target *masks* the exception from the target's invokers.

An *exception context* is the information available to the exception handler concerning the exception occurrence. The exception context may contain some data that is explicitly passed by the signaler, as in CLU and C++. Additionally, it may contain information implicitly passed by the language runtime; for example, the name of the method or the class that signaled the exception. Guide [13] allows a handler to distinguish between exceptions by additionally using the class and method names of the signaler.

*Exception propagation* is the signaling of an exception to the target's invoker. There are two ways to propagate an exception: *implicit* (i.e., automatic), and *explicit*. In some languages, e.g. Ada, an unhandled exception is implicitly propagated. The second way is to require that any exception to be propagated must be explicitly signaled in a handler; CLU follows this approach. Such exceptions are also called *resignaled* or *reraised* exceptions. An implicitly propagated exception is automatically signaled and is the same as the original exception; on the other hand, a resignaled exception must be explicitly raised by the target's handler and can be different from the original exception. For explicit propagation, an unhandled exception (i.e., an exception not handled by any handler in the target) is either implicitly converted into some predefined exception by the exception handling mechanism, or the program is terminated.

An *exception model* defines the interactions between the signaler, target, and handler. The *termination model* automatically terminates the signaler, destroys any objects within the scope of the signaler, and considers the target to be the signaler's invoker. Once the exception is handled by the target, control resumes at the next statement following the target's syntactic unit. For example, if the target's syntactic unit is a statement or a block, then normal execution resumes at the next statement or at the next statement after the block, respectively. In the *resumption model*, computation continues from the point where the exception was originally raised. The *retry model* is a combination of termination and resumption; when the exception is handled, the signaler's block is terminated and then is re-invoked (or retried). The *replacement model* [23] is a variant of termination. The handler can return a value in place of the result expected from the signaler. The signaler's block is terminated and the result from the handler is returned to the signaler's invoker. Languages that allow a handler to replace a signaler's result include Guide [13]. Lastly, it is not required that a language only support one exception model, though that is usually the case. The main reasons for this restriction are ease of implementation and that one model can usually emulate the main characteristics of the other models (though it may be grossly inefficient).

## 2.2 Domains of Exception Handling

There are two views (or *domains*) of inheritance [22]: *modeling* and *implementation*. The modeling domain is for conceptual inheritance, while the implementation domain is for code reuse. *Subtyping* is conceptual specialization, while *subclassing* is implementation reuse of code classes. With respect to exception handling, the two domains can be quite different: exceptions in the implementation domain are generally considered to be errors, while exceptions in the modeling domain are generally considered to be deviations.

In the implementation domain, one major concern is reliable programming. Program failures are often caused by unexpected conditions that cause an error and the error is not properly handled. Unexpected conditions are often treated as exceptions, so an exception handler effectively becomes an error handler. The typical exception model in object-oriented languages is termination because the termination model is considered easier to implement than other models, and it is usually safer to destroy an object that has signaled an exception and restart the computation than trying to restore the object to a consistent state. Over the years, experience has indicated that (a variant of) the termination model is easier to use than the resumption model in the implementation domain [21]. One reason is that it is hard for a handler to know the system state for all situations in which the handler may be invoked, so it is easier to terminate (or cleanup) to a well-known system state rather than proceed and possibly cause more problems by making an incorrect assumption. In [13], arguments are made against resuming a signaler inside an encapsulation after the execution of some actions by a handler outside the encapsulation. This makes it difficult to prove the correctness of an interface by only examining the encapsulated implementation.

In the modeling domain, a major concern is flexibility [2]. An example from [2] illustrates the use of exceptions in the modeling domain. A real estate database has fields for the address and price of each listed house. An exception occurs for two kinds of contradictions within the database: the database constraints may need to be violated occasionally, and some subtypes may need to violate parts of the supertype definition. An example of violating a constraint is if the house is in a foreign country. If the price of the house is in the foreign currency, then, depending on the exchange rate, the price field may be exceeded. Another example is if a new subtype for address is defined for a foreign country, it may not be a proper subtype of its parent type because the parent may have fields that have no meaning to the child. An example is US and Canadian addresses: US states are not a subset of Canadian provinces, or vice versa. Such abnormal cases are considered as acceptable deviations in the modeling domain.

Most languages are designed for the implementation domain since everything (including modeling domain abstractions) must eventually be implemented. However, in the modeling domain an exception is not an error that may compromise program reliability, but is instead a way of increasing program flexibility. An exception cannot be considered an error and the use of the termination model in a similar fashion as in the implementation domain may not allow exceptions as deviations. It would seem that the resumption model would be more suitable for modeling domain exceptions.

There is another way that the mixing of the two domains affects exception handling: an exception context may need to be modified as an exception is signaled from one domain to the other. To illustrate this, assume an accounting spreadsheet program is executing within an environment, such as an accounting framework that provides features unique for accounting. The accounting program and framework could be in the modeling domain, while runtime libraries used by the framework are in the implementation domain. Within the program, an arithmetic operation in a library routine signals an overflow exception. The operation knows the exception occurred during an integer addition, so resignals to the framework an 'integer addition failed' exception. The framework, in turn, resignals the exception to the program as a 'tally operation failed' exception. The same exception has had its abstraction (and so its context) changed from integer overflow in some hardware register to a tally operation failing. Another program, say a database, could also encounter the same integer overflow exception, but the exception's changing abstraction may follow a completely different path than that of the accounting program.

This example raises two significant issues regarding how to adequately represent the difference in abstraction that an exception represents. The issues are how does an exception context get modified during exception propagation, and what is the form of the exception propagation (along the invocation chain or along the class hierarchy) that can correctly represent the change of domain.

## 2.3 Exception Handling in Object-Oriented Languages

Exceptions are represented in a variety of ways in the various object-oriented programming languages. At one end, Beta [15] does not provide any special constructs or primitives to represent and handle exceptions. Instead, Beta uses its basic language constructs (such as *virtual patterns*). At the other end, some systems [7] use a special class of objects to represent exceptions that have certain predefined operations, such as *signal* or *raise*. In between are languages such as Guide [13] that represent exceptions as symbols, which can be organized according to some inheritance hierarchy. Such an organization permits incremental specialization of exceptions and their handlers, and can provide default and generic support for exceptions defined at the higher levels of the inheritance hierarchy.

There are many variations on representing exceptions as symbols. In CLU, an object-based language, exceptions are represented as symbols with an associated set of typed parameter objects that can be used to pass information from the signaler to the handler. In C++, an exception is represented by an object which is not necessarily differentiated from other objects of the computation. An object representing the exception is created when an exception is raised.

Representing exceptions as objects allows inclusion of context information that can be explicit (passed by the signaler) as well as implicit (passed by the runtime) to communicate to the handler the nature and cause of the exception. Guide [13] implicitly provides the handler with the names of the class and the method that signaled the exception. In C++, context-related information is explicitly passed to the handler with the object that is created when the exception is raised.

Many languages have been concerned with the ability to determine, at compile time, the set of exceptions that an operation can raise. For this reason, the interface of an object should also list the set of exceptions that an operation can raise [9,14,23]. In general, an attempt to propagate to the invoker an exception not in this list can cause the program to terminate. In C++, it leads to the execution of a function named *unexpected*, which can be redefined by the programmer.

The propagation of exceptions along the dynamic invocation chain is considered to increase reusability so that the invoker of an operation can possibly handle it in a context-dependent manner. This can help in increasing the usability of an object in a wider context. However, the goal of compile time determination of a possible set of exceptions requires disallowing automatic propagation of exceptions along the dynamic invocation chain. All exceptions propagated from an operation to its invoker should be either explicitly propagated or resignaled. If an unhandled exception is not explicitly propagated, it is either considered a fatal error or is implicitly propagated after being changed to some predefined general exception, such as *FAILURE* in CLU or *UNCAUGHT_EXCEPTION* in Guide.

In Smalltalk-80, exceptions are handled by the object encountering the abnormal condition. There is no propagation along the dynamic invocation chain. There are three selectors defined for each class to deal with exceptions. Two of these have predefined meanings, and the third selector, called *Error*, is used to communicate all programmer defined errors. Thus, the meaning of *Error* may become overloaded, as there is no way to define new exceptions.

In Eiffel, exceptions are defined as the violation of certain assertions on the object state or the pre- or post-conditions of an invoked operation. A handler is attached to a method as a *rescue clause*, which can possibly direct the re-execution of the method using the *retry* statement after it has restored the object to a consistent state. Any termination of a method through the rescue clause results in the failure of the operation. Within a rescue clause, the exception can be determined by comparing a predefined variable called *exception* with an exception name. The exception names form a global name space.

In Beta [15], there is no explicit construct to represent exception conditions. When an abnormal condition is detected, an appropriate pattern, which is a Beta object, is invoked. This pattern defines the exception handler for the detected condition. Beta's approach is like building "fault tolerant encapsulations" [6] that try to handle abnormal conditions within the object at the points where they arise. The program or object's enclosing scope is terminated if the exception cannot be handled within the object. An exception condition is detected and handled as part of the normal flow of execution. For that reason, the concept of searching for a handler does not exist in Beta. The *inner* construct and virtual patterns of Beta together provide a way for an invoker of an operation to affect the handling of an exception inside the object. The code extension (called *binding*) given by the invoker at the time of an invocation is executed by substituting it in the operation's code at the place where *inner* is declared. The *inner* mechanism also allows a subclass to extend or augment the exception handling of the parent class. This use of *inner* can often require a careful understanding of the pattern's code.

## 3. Exception Handling vs. Object-Orientation

Many other researchers [e.g., 2,7,13,19] have recognized that exception handling may have different requirements than object-orientation. It is this paper's position that the differences are more like conflicts because exception handling can contradict the conventional object-oriented paradigm. As noted in Section 1, exception handling is often error handling, which is notoriously difficult to do. The conflicts can lead to a 'false sense of security' [3] that exception handling in object-oriented languages will automatically yield more robust programs. To the contrary, the conflicts may lead to a less robust program. To begin the discussion, it is necessary to see how exception handling may differ from object-orientation. The differences to be discussed in this paper are:

- Complete exception specification.
- Partial states.
- Exception conformance.
- Exception propagation.

### 3.1 Complete Exception Specification

The object interface is the outside view or specification of the object. In many languages, the interface only contains a list of the exceptions that an interface method may signal (an *exception specification*). However, this does not unambiguously define the exception behavior of the interface. We use a new term, *complete exception specification*, that extends upon an exception specification in the following ways:

- Exception masking: how is the abstract state of an object affected if the implementation masks an exception.
- Exception consistency: each exception that can be signaled has an associated meaning that is consistent regardless of the signaling location.
- Exception context: what is the exception context provided for each signaled exception.
- Object state: the state of the object immediately prior to the exception signaling is indicated within the exception context.

A complete exception specification is similar to a normal (non-exception) interface in two ways. The exceptions that can be signaled are similar to the *return codes* that the interface defines. Exception consistency is similar to a return code having the same meaning, regardless of the location in the implementation from where the code is returned.

None of the remaining extensions have equivalents in a normal interface. The exception masking equivalent would be similar to the normal interface detailing how an internal call is handled within the interface implementation. Exception context's equivalent is similar to the interface being able to return different types of results. Lastly, object state for the normal interface is usually assumed to be valid upon return. An explicit declaration of state is unnecessary for the normal interface but may be necessary for exception handling.

The key difference between exception handling and normal object-orientation is that more information is revealed in the exception specification. This is to provide enough information to the handler to allow recovery or termination. No known language implements a complete exception specification as outlined here.

### 3.2 Partial States

Normal object-orientation (i.e., without exception handling) generally considers an object state to be either *valid* or *invalid*. The difference with exception handling is that there is a third state, which we call a *partial* state. Such a state may arise in a collection of objects, called a *composition*, where some invariant relationships among the components (or members) are required to be maintained. A partial state occurs when all the component objects of a composition are valid, but the composition relationships are not satisfied, implying an invalid composition state.

For normal object-orientation, changing a component object of a composition from one state to another may transition through a partial state. Normal programming generally considers object state transitions to be atomic, so the partial state is not observable to the programmer. However, the assumption of atomic state changes may not hold for exception handling because an exception may occur before the state change has completed.

The major difference between exception handling and normal object-orientation is that exception handling cannot always assume that state transitions are atomic. No known language has a total solution for partial states. Languages that support finalization or destruction (e.g., Ada and C++) address, in a limited way, the problems due to partial states by keeping track of which objects have been created or destroyed. But they do not keep track of relationships between objects.

A partial state is, in general, an invalid state. The difficulty is in indicating to the users of the composition, and possibly composition members, what the partial state is. A possible indicator for an invalid state is for the object to signal a failure exception. However, several questions arise. If a failure exception is signaled, should the object be allowed to exist in an invalid state or be destroyed? Should an object in an invalid state be allowable due to unforeseen side-effects if the object is accessed again? How is a user of the composition informed that the object is in a different partial state than what is expected?

## 3.3 Exception Conformance

Conformance between types also includes exceptions in some languages. Assume that class $B$ is derived from class $A$ and is to be conformant with $A$. For all methods that $B$ inherits or redefines from $A$, $B$ cannot signal an exception that is not a subtype of an exception that can be signaled from the corresponding method in $A$. For example, if $A$ has method $M$ that can signal exceptions $E1$ or $E2$, then $B$ cannot extend or redefine $M$ with new exceptions that are not subtypes of $E1$ or $E2$. We call conformance between exception types *exception conformance*.

Exception handling may need to be non-conformant. For normal object-orientation, implementations can change without users needing to know. New functionality can be provided as a redefined virtual method, however, the redefined method must still be conformant with the original method interface. For exceptions, new functionality may need new exceptions that are not subtypes of exceptions from the parent method. The conformance rules would prevent the new functionality because the exceptions would be non-conformant. To make the exceptions conformant requires the parent methods to use sufficiently generalized exception types so that any possible new exception that may be signaled by a redefined virtual method would be a subtype. The generalized exception types may be so general that they have limited value in defining a clear and consistent exception interface.

The difference between exception handling and normal object-orientation is that methods can be overloaded to have similar meaning in a wide variety of situations, but exception information (particularly for errors) generally needs to be specific. The overloading of functionality is acceptable and often desirable, but the overloading of exception information is usually not. This difference clearly surfaces in conformance.

There is a conflict between exception conformance and complete exception specification. To have a complete specification implies exception conformance, but to allow evolutionary program development suggests exception non-conformance, which in turns suggests an incomplete exception specification.

### 3.4 Exception Propagation

In normal object-oriented programming, program control flow follows the call/return path. If method A calls B, which then calls C, then C will return to B which will return to A. It is not expected that code from A will execute before B and C return. Even if C is terminated, the normal flow would not expect code from A to execute before code from B. Suppose that C signals an exception, then, depending on how the exception is propagated, handler code from A may execute before code from B, or even before C returns or is terminated.

The key point is that exception handling differs from normal object-orientation because exception propagation can change the control flow. It becomes important for a programmer to understand the possible control flow change, so there are at least two paths (not one) that the programmer must consider: the normal path, and the propagation path.

## 4. Exception Handling and Object-Oriented Goals

The preceding section showed how exception handling is different in four ways from normal object-orientation. In this section we see how these four differences manifest themselves in four of the major elements of object-orientation: abstraction, encapsulation, modularity, and inheritance.

### 4.1 Abstraction

One goal of abstraction principles is to hide the implementation details of an object from its users and expose only the necessary functionality. There are two aspects of abstraction that are relevant here:
- Generalization of operations.
- Composition.

### 4.1.1 Generalized Operations

A goal of exception handling mechanisms is to generalize operations of an object and make them usable in a wider range of conditions [9]. Often this may require exposing more implementation details, as a part of the abstraction, to the object's users. We observe here that the motivation for introducing exception handling may sometimes impose conflicting demands in regard to hiding implementation details. The following example illustrates this point.

Consider the design of a fault-tolerant disk storage system that is required to be more reliable and available as compared to a single disk drive system. Suppose that this reliable disk system is implemented using two drives acting as a primary-backup pair. There are two opposite solutions to building such a fault-tolerant object [6]. One is to perform all recovery within the object in case of any exception and not propagate the exception to the object's users. The second approach is to mask exceptions within the object, and propagate only relevant exceptions to the object's users. With the first approach in implementing the desired reliable disk system, one can completely hide from the users the internal implementation detail that the disk system consists of a pair of disk drives. In case of a failure of one of the drives, it would be meaningless to inform the user that one of the drives has failed. Thus, the system would be working at a reduced reliability level without the user knowing of or correcting such a situation.

The second approach is to expose the primary-backup nature of the implementation as a part of the abstraction visible to the users. An exception can be signaled to the user in case of a failure of one of the drives. The reliable disk system's interface can also provide suitable functions to the users to perform appropriate reconfiguration (such as replacement of the failed drive with a new one) in the event of such an exception. This approach of communicating exceptions to the users gives a greater flexibility to recover from failures, but it involves making the abstraction closer to the implementation.

### 4.1.2 Composition

Composition is a form of abstraction by grouping together related objects and presenting them as a single entity. Recall from Section 3.2 that a partial state is one in which all component objects of a composition are in valid states, but the relationships between the objects are not. Each individual component object may have no indication that the composition is invalid. We show two examples in which partial states are important: exception masking by a component object, and a component object signaling an exception to the composition user.

A component object masking an exception may need to inform the composition that an exception has occurred that is of interest to the composition. Assume that a composition class C is defined that has an individual component object that is an array: *Array[100]*. Each element of *Array* has a field that is a pointer to another element of *Array*, so that the pointers form a doubly-linked list of *Array* elements. Suppose that *Array[50]* is to have its pointer field set to *Array[1]*, and vice versa. Assuming that *Array* is initialized in ascending index order, *Array[1]* will be pointing to *Array[50]* when an exception is signaled during the initialization of *Array[50]*. The *Array* code masks the exception, and as part of the masking the pointer for *Array[50]* is set to a predefined value, NULL. Class C methods cannot assume that the pointer fields represent a doubly-linked list anymore. Since the exception is masked, C cannot invoke its exception handler to even scan *Array* and perform consistency checks. The masking of the exception may require class C methods to assume the possible existence of partial states, which conflicts with the assumption of object-oriented programming that internal state transitions are atomic.

A component of a composition could signal an exception to a composition user. However, not only the user, but also composition members may need to be informed of the exception. Thus, an exception may not only need to be propagated upward to the composition user, but also across or downwards to composition members.

Suppose that, in the example above, the exception signaled from *Array[50]* during its initialization is not masked, and the exception is signaled to the composition *C*. Two problems can arise as described below: the possible inability of *C* to correct the invalid composition relationships, and the possible need to propagate the exception downward to a component object. First, *C* needs to know which element of *Array* signaled the exception so *C* can identify which composition relationships are invalid. Since an individual element may not know what its array index is, the exception context may not have any information as to which element signaled the exception. So, *C* may not be able to do any recovery since it cannot determine where the exception occurred. Second, it may be desired to undo the link that *Array[1]* has set pointing to *Array[50]*. Undoing of actions is normally considered an error recovery path and usually not a part of the normal execution path, hence *Array[1]* needs to have an exception signaled to it. It would be preferred if the exception is signaled to *Array[1]* before signaling the exception to *C* so that *C* need not concern itself with invalid composition relationships. To accomplish this, the exception from *Array[50]* would need to be signaled to *Array[1]*, then signaled to *C*.

As an aside, no known language propagates exceptions downward and upward in the fashion described here. When this situation arises in current languages, what may be done is to create a method that performs the undo. When *C*'s handler is invoked, the handler calls the undo method to simulate an exception being signaled. The difficulty arises in specifying in *C*'s handler all the composition members that may need to be undone if more than one member is affected. *C* may need to know details of composition member implementations in order to determine which members' undo methods need to be called; because the undo method is considered a part of the 'normal' code (because it is not in a handler), it could be used inappropriately within normal execution.

## 4.2 Encapsulation

The encapsulation defined by an object hides its internal implementation from the users. However, implementation details of a signaler can be exposed by an exception object if it contains information pertaining to the signaler's implementation that is more than what is permitted by the encapsulation. It is also possible that the parent classes of an exception object may have extra information, unknown to the interface, using which the exception handler may be able to deduce implementation details. A programmer may be tempted to use the extra information for error recovery, which may become invalid if the implementation is changed. There are two ways that extra information can be used detrimentally: trying to determine the location of the signaler, and accessing the signaler without using the established interface.

Using implementation details can be useful when determining why an exception is signaled. Often, one handler is enabled over a region of code. The handler may need to determine where in the region did the exception occur. If the handler has access to extra exception context information, then the handler may be able to use that to assume where the exception was signaled. However, if this information is easily available to the programmer, then there is a high probability that the programmer will use it.

For example, suppose that the exception context contains information about the location of the signaling operation in the code, and this information is available to a handler. Let's say that one particular signaling code location is within a library routine, and the programmer knows that this library routine is only called at one location within the implementation. The programmer can use this information directly in the handler. Of course, the potential difficulty is if the implementation code (or anything that it may invoke) is changed to use the library routine in a different way, the handler may perform the wrong action. However, if this is the only way for the programmer to determine why the exception was signaled, then there is a high probability that the programmer will use the extra information.

The second way to expose implementation is if the exception context contains a pointer to private data within the signaler. Suppose that the exception context contains a pointer to the static data area of the signaler, then the handler may view or modify the static data. Though the handler may not actually know how the signaler is implemented, it may be able to access private data within the signaler without using the signaler's interface.

## 4.3 Modularity

The goal for modularity is to ensure that the changes in one module have little effect on other modules. However, exception handling often increases the coupling between modules due to evolution of the modules. At the time the modules are designed, interfaces can be adhered to. After a module is designed and implemented, evolution in the form of incremental change can occur, which is one of the advantages of object-orientation. However, evolution of a design may require the redefined methods or new implementation of an object to signal some additional exception conditions to its users. The non-updated user modules of such an object may still continue to rely upon the validity of the original interface of the object. Evolution related problems can occur in three ways:

- *Exception evolution*: evolution of exception signaling by a method, leading to signaling of new exceptions while conforming to the current exception interface.
- *Function evolution*: evolution of the functionality of a method, leading to the definition and signaling of some new exceptions by the method not in the current exception interface.
- *Mechanism evolution*: evolution of the underlying implementation (or mechanism) used by a method, leading to the overloading of existing exceptions in the current exception interface.

Mechanism evolution is similar to function evolution and exception evolution. The difference with function evolution is that function evolution signals new exceptions not in the existing exception hierarchy, while mechanism evolution signals new exceptions that must be in the existing exception hierarchy. Mechanism evolution is different from exception evolution in the sense that it overloads the meaning of an existing exception.

### 4.3.1 Exception Evolution

Exception evolution is the incremental changing of exception signaling from a method. A typical example is exception specialization (creating a more specialized exception by subclassing from an existing one). To uphold modularity, the specialized exceptions should preserve *exception conformance* to remain compatible with existing exception handlers in any user methods and modules. The basis of exception specialization is that only those modules that want to use the specialization need to be changed, and other modules should not be affected. However, exception specialization can increase module coupling due to the side-effect the new exception creates because the new exception has to be handled by existing handlers in unchanged user modules.

The code of Figure 1 is used to illustrate, through an example, the issues that can arise due to exception evolution. This code is from a module that calls the *open* function of a file system module to open a file. Assume that *open* can signal the exceptions *FileErr* or *InputErr*. *FileErr* indicates a fatal error, while *InputErr* indicates a user error, e.g., non-existent path or filename, and is not fatal. The *FileErr* exception handler terminates the program, while the *InputErr* exception handler prompts the user for a new filename and retries the file open operation. When a file is already opened, *open* signals a *FileErr* exception. After the program in Figure 1 is designed, *open* is modified by the file system module so that an already opened file is not a fatal error. Therefore, a new specialized exception named *FileOpened* is defined indicating an already opened file. *FileOpened* cannot be derived from *FileErr* because *FileOpened* is not a fatal error. So, *FileOpened* is derived from *InputErr*. However, in Figure 1, if *FileOpened* is signaled, the *InputErr* handler gets invoked because *FileOpened* is derived from *InputErr*. The handler prompts the user for a filename, which is irrelevant for an already opened file. For *FileOpened* to be correctly handled by the modules that use this new version of the file system, all *InputErr* handlers in those modules need to be examined to determine the effect of signaling *FileOpened*. This illustrates an increase in module coupling.

```
try {
    open(file);
} catch(FileErr)  {...};
  catch(InputErr) {...};     // prompt filename and reopen
```

**Fig. 1.** Example of exception specialization problem

### 4.3.2 Function Evolution

Function evolution is the incremental changing of the functionality of a method. It affects exception handling because unchanged modules may have to cope with new exceptions that are introduced by the new functionality. An example of function evolution is the definition of polymorphic methods that incorporate new functionality. Virtual methods can be redefined as new subclasses are created, and can implement a completely new function. A redefined virtual method can signal a new exception that is not within any existing exception hierarchy of the method.

Figure 2 is a modified example from [22], and it is used here to illustrate the problems arising due to function evolution. The code shown there is from a module that uses an object of class *Window*. Class *Window* has a virtual method *drawFrame* that draws a window on the terminal. The code block shown in Figure 2 draws a window, and has an exception handler for *DrawErr* if the drawing operation fails. Suppose that the virtual method *drawFrame* is redefined by a new class, *TitleWindow*, that is subclassed from *Window*. *TitleWindow* places a text title in the window, and its version of *drawFrame* can signal *DrawErr* and a new exception, *TitleErr*, which corresponds to the increase in functionality provided by *TitleWindow*. If the code block in Figure 2 invokes *TitleWindow*'s version of *drawFrame*, a *TitleErr* exception would not be expected. All modules that could potentially use *TitleWindow* have to be examined to determine the effects of *TitleErr*. In general, exception handling in modules using *Window* objects may need to be changed appropriately, which may imply an increase in module coupling.

```
try {
      win.drawFrame()
} catch(DrawErr) {...}
```

**Fig. 2.** Example of function evolution

### 4.3.3 Mechanism Evolution

Mechanism evolution is the incremental changing of the implementation of a method, possibly using a different set of mechanisms to implement the same functionality. The problems in mechanism evolution arise when the new mechanism uses the existing exception hierarchy in the system. The new mechanism may have to overload the meaning of existing exceptions in the system, with the possible result of an unintended handler action by the user modules.

The code in Figure 3 is used here to illustrate the problems arising from mechanism evolution. The procedure *proc*, shown in this figure, reads from a file and transmits the data across a network to a target machine. It uses a file system module and a network module. There are two main classes of exceptions: *FileErr* (error signaled from the file system) and *CommErr* (error with the network communications). The code shown in Figure 3 has handlers for both types of exceptions. Suppose that the *FileErr* exception context contains the file name for which the *open* operation failed, and similarly *CommErr* contains information about the failed connection request. The handler for *FileErr* assumes the file to be read is non-existent or bad and creates it. The handler for *CommErr* assumes that the connection that is indicated by the exception object has a failure, and it then retries that connection. After the procedure *proc* is designed, suppose that the file system module is reimplemented as a network file system and the new implementation now also signals *CommErr*, which is a currently defined exception in the system, to also indicate a network error encountered by the file system. Now *FileErr* and *CommErr* may have overloaded meanings in the modules, such as *proc*, using the file system. This is illustrated in the situation when the network file system times out.

When the network file system times out, it can signal either *FileErr* or *CommErr*. Unfortunately, either exception can cause the wrong action to be performed by *proc*. If *FileErr* is used, then *proc*'s handler may attempt to recreate the file, and will fail again. When the network error that caused the timeout is corrected, the file system will signal another exception due to trying to create or overwrite an existing file. If *CommErr* is signaled to indicate the timeout, then the connection will be retried through the *CommErr* handler. If connection information is passed to the handler through the exception object, the connection that is to be retried would be the one to the network file system. In many network file systems, directly connecting to it is not allowed, so the connection may fail repeatedly inside the handler. The handler may go into a loop, trying the connection only to have it refused. This shows that changing an underlying mechanism may increase module coupling if existing exceptions are overloaded.

It is easy to see that exception conformance inhibits evolution. If exception non-conformance is allowed, would the effect be any different? Probably not, since the exception would not be recognized and eventually converted into an unhandled exception. What is needed is exception non-conformance and the ability to add exception handlers to existing code without the need to re-compile the code. Beta [15] supports this kind of augmentation of code, using its *inner* mechanism.

```
proc() {
        ...code...
        try {
                ...code...
                open(file);
                open(connection);
                ...code...
        } catch(FileErr)    {...}    // assumes file is bad or non-existent
            catch(CommErr) {...}   //assumes network connection terminated
```

**Fig. 3.** Example of mechanism evolution

## 4.4 Inheritance

The inheritance goal is to promote code reuse and conceptual specialization. The aspect to be considered here is the *inheritance anomaly*. An inheritance anomaly occurs when a subclass method has to re-implement a parent class method to get the derived class's functionality [16]. The anomaly can occur when a subclass's exception handling replaces rather than augments the parent's handling of exceptions. Beta [15] is one of the few languages that supports augmentation of the parent class code by a subclass, rather than completely rewriting the method's code. Therefore, some of the problems mentioned here do not apply to Beta. The inheritance anomaly due to exception handling can occur in two ways:

- A subclass wants to specialize or handle an exception that a parent class method is signaling.
- A virtual method is redefined to signal a new exception that is not expected by any of the ancestor class methods calling that virtual method.

To illustrate the first case, say a subclass wishes to signal a specialized parent class exception, but still inherit the parent's handling. In Figure 4, the *put* method from class *Buffer* is shown. All exceptions from *put* are resignaled as *PutErr*. Suppose that *BetterBuffer* is derived from *Buffer*. *BetterBuffer* wishes to add a new exception to its *put* method that further specializes memory exceptions. *BetterBuffer* does not want to re-implement the *put* method, only to signal a specialized exception. The inheritance anomaly may occur if there is no way for *BetterBuffer* to signal the new exception. The parent *put* method only signals *PutErr* exceptions, and *BetterBuffer* does not receive any other exceptions from *Buffer*. So, *BetterBuffer* cannot resignal any specialized exceptions. Prior to signaling *PutErr* from *Buffer*, it is needed to augment the exception handling of *Buffer* with the extensions desired by the *BetterBuffer* implementation. Here also we notice that Beta supports this kind of augmentation of parent methods using the *inner* mechanism.

Lastly, the inheritance anomaly may occur due to a virtual method call in a parent method. With virtual methods, the subclass may be designed after the parent class. If a redefined virtual method in a subclass signals certain exceptions not handled by a parent class method calling this virtual method, then the parent class method may need to be re-implemented. Using Figure 4 again, *put* uses a virtual method for *createElement*. If *BetterBuffer* has a virtual method for *createElement*, and that version signals a new exception unknown to the *put* method of *Buffer*, then *put* may need to be re-implemented. Suppose that the *createElement* method for *BetterBuffer* can signal a new exception indicating a buffer element creation error. If the parent *put* receives this exception (due to a virtual method call to *createElement*), *put* resignals the exception as *PutErr*. Users of *BetterBuffer* may be expecting the new exception, which will not be signaled by *put*. The anomaly is that the parent *put* may need to be re-implemented to accommodate the requirements of *BetterBuffer* users.

```
class Buffer
    put() throws PutErr {
        try {
            ...
            self.createElement();
            ...
        } catch(...) { throw PutErr; }
```

**Fig. 4.** Example of inheritance anomaly

# 5. Summary

In this paper, exception handling in object-oriented languages is examined to determine which object-oriented techniques do not quite fit with exception handling. The goal is to be able to better identify the aspects of exception handling that make it hard to use or understand. This identification may be of value to programmers and language designers who wish to use or design exception handling in a robust way.

Four aspects of exception handling that are different from normal object-orientation are identified:

- Complete exception specification: extra information may be needed in the exception specification (via the exception context) to provide information for the handler that is beyond what is in the object interface.
- Partial states: exception handling cannot always assume that state transitions are atomic.
- Exception conformance: functions can be overloaded to have similar meaning in a wide variety of situations, but exception information (particularly for errors) generally needs to be specific.
- Exception propagation: propagation can change the control flow, putting an extra burden on the programmer to understand at least two control paths: the normal execution path, and the exception handling path.

The above four differences can affect the major elements of object-orientation. The examination of the effects of exception handling on some of the object-oriented design elements leads to the following conclusions:

- Abstraction: generalization of operations and composition construction may involve changing of abstraction levels and dealing with partial states.
- Encapsulation: the exception context may leak information that allows implementation details or private data of the signaler to be revealed or accessed.
- Modularity: design evolution (function and implementation) maybe inhibited by exception conformance.
- Inheritance: the inheritance anomaly can occur when a language does not support exception handling augmentation in a modular way.

## Acknowledgments

The authors wish to express gratitude to the reviewers for their insightful comments and detailed suggestions in revising this paper to its current form. The first author is also grateful to IBM in supporting his efforts. The second author wants to thank NSF for providing him an opportunity to work on this paper.

## References

[1]    G. Booch, "Object-Oriented Analysis and Design with Applications, 2nd Ed", Benjamin/Cummings, 1994.

103

[2] A. Borgida, "Exceptions in Object-Oriented Languages", *SIGPLAN Notices*, vol. 21, no. 10, pp. 107-119, Oct. 1986.

[3] T. Cargill, "Exception Handling: A False Sense of Security", *C++ Report*, vol. 6, no. 9, pp. 21-24, Nov.-Dec. 1994.

[4] N.H. Cohen, "Ada as a Second Language, 2nd Ed", McGraw-Hill, 1996.

[5] F. Cristian, "Exception Handling", *IBM Research Report RJ5724*, 1987.

[6] C. Dony, "An Object-Oriented Exception Handling System for an Object-Oriented Language", in *Proceedings of ECOOP'88*, pp. 146-159, 1991.

[7] C. Dony, "Exception Handling and Object-Oriented Programming: Towards a Synthesis", in *Proceedings OOPSLA 90*, pp. 322-330, Oct. 1990.

[8] A. Goldberg and D. Robson, "Smalltalk-80: The Language", Addison-Wesley, 1989

[9] J.B. Goodenough, "Exception Handling: Issues and a Proposed Notation", *Communications of the ACM*, vol. 18, no. 12, pp. 683-696, Dec. 1975.

[10] J.D. Ichbiah, J.C. Heliard, O. Roubine, J.G.P. Barnes, B. Krieg-Brueckner, and B.A. Wichmann, "Rationale for the Design of the Ada Programming Language", *SIGPLAN Notices*, vol. 14, no. 6, Part B, Jun. 1979.

[11] A.K. Jones, "The Object Model: A Conceptual Tool for Structuring Software," in Operating Systems and Advanced Course - Lecture Notes in Computer Science, Vol. 60, pp. 7-16, Springer-Verlag, 1979.

[12] J.L. Knudsen, "Better Exception-Handling in Block-Structured Systems", *IEEE Software*, vol. 17, no. 2, pp. 40-49, May 1987.

[13] S. Lacourte, "Exceptions in Guide, an Object-Oriented Language for Distributed Applications", in *Proceedings ECOOP 91*, pp. 268-287, 1991.

[14] B. Liskov and A. Snyder, "Exception Handling in CLU", *IEEE Transactions on Software Engineering*, vol. SE-5, no. 6, pp. 546-558, Nov. 1979.

[15] O.L. Madsen, B. Moller-Pedersen, and K. Nygaard, "Object-Oriented Programming in the Beta Programming Language", Addison-Wesley, 1993.

[16] S. Matsuoka and A. Yonezawa, "Analysis of Inheritance Anomaly in Object-Oriented Concurrent Programming Languages", *Research Directions in Concurrent Object-Oriented Programming*, chapter 4, MIT Press, 1993.

[17] B. Meyer, "Eiffel: The Language", Prentice-Hall 1992.

[18] T. Ritchey, "Programming with Java!", New Riders, 1995.

[19] A.B. Romanovsky, L.V. Shturtz, and V.R. Vassilyev, "Designing Fault-Tolerant Objects in Object-Oriented Programming", in *Proceedings 7th International Conference of Technology of Object Oriented Languages and Systems (TOOLS Europe 92)*, pp. 199-205, 1992.

[20] B. Stroustrup, "The C++ Programming Language, 2nd Ed.", Addison-Wesley, 1991.

[21] B. Stroustrup, "The Design and Evolution of C++", Addison-Wesley, 1994.

[22] A. Taivalsaari, "On the Notion of Inheritance", *ACM Computing Surveys*, vol. 28, no. 3, pp.438-479, Sept. 1996.

[23] S. Yemini and D.M. Berry, "A Modular Verifiable Exception-Handling Mechanism", *ACM Transactions on Programming Languages and Systems*, vol. 7, no. 2, pp. 214-243, Apr. 1985.

# Subtyping Is Not a Good "Match" for Object-Oriented Languages*

Kim B. Bruce[1], Leaf Petersen[1]**, and Adrian Fiech[2]

[1] Williams College, Williamstown, MA, USA
[2] Memorial University of Newfoundland, St. John's, Newfoundland, Canada

**Abstract.** We present the design and rationale of a new statically-typed object-oriented language, $\mathcal{LOOM}$. $\mathcal{LOOM}$ retains most of the features of the earlier language **PolyTOIL**. However the subtyping relation is dropped from $\mathcal{LOOM}$ in favor of the matching relation. "Hash types", which are defined in terms of matching, are introduced to provide some of the benefits of subtyping. These types can be used to provide support for heterogeneous data stuctures in $\mathcal{LOOM}$. $\mathcal{LOOM}$ is considerably simpler than **PolyTOIL**, yet is just as expressive. The type system for the language is decidable and provably type safe. The addition of modules to the language provides better control over information hiding and allows the provision of access like that of C++'s friends.

## 1  Introduction

Most statically-typed object-oriented programming languages, including C++ [ES90], Java [AG96], Object Pascal [Tes85], and Modula 3 [CDG+88], suffer from very rigid type systems which can block the easy expression of programmers' ideas, particularly in the definition of subclasses. Other statically-typed object-oriented languages, such as Eiffel [Mey92] and Beta [MMMP90], are more flexible, but require run-time or link-time checks in order to eliminate holes in the type system. One important goal of our previous work in designing static type systems for object-oriented languages has been to design flexible, yet safe, static type systems (see for example [Bru93, Bru94, BSvG95]). In this paper we propose a fairly radical departure from previous statically-typed object-oriented languages by dropping subtyping in favor of a relation called matching and a new type constructor related to matching.

It has become clear in the last several years that the concepts of inheritance and subtyping in object-oriented languages are not at all the same. (See [Sny86] for early hints, and [CHC90, AvdL90, LP91] for more definitive treatments of the topic.) In earlier papers [Bru93, Bru94, BSvG95], we introduced the notion of *matching*, a relation between object types which is more general than subtyping.

---

* Bruce and Petersen's research was partially supported by NSF grant CCR-9424123. Fiech's research was partially supported by NSERC grant OGP0170497.

** Current address: School of Computer Science, Carnegie-Mellon University, Pittsburgh, PA, USA

A history of matching can be found in [BSvG95]. See also [AC95] for a discussion of explanations of matching in terms of F-bounded and higher-order subtyping.

An important feature of matching is that if two classes are subclasses, then the corresponding object types are in the matching relation. However, these types are not generally in the subtype relation if the language includes a type expression, *MyType*, standing for the type of *self*. Since *MyType* is extremely valuable, we end up with a mismatch between subtyping and inheritance.

The language PolyTOIL [BSvG95] supports both subtyping and matching. It also supports bounded polymorphism where the bounds on type parameters are given in terms of the matching relation. Unfortunately, the relations of matching and subtyping are similar enough that it might be difficult for a programmer to keep their differences straight. As a result we began considering the possibility of simplifying the language by dropping one or the other.

It was clear that matching was absolutely necessary in PolyTOIL in order to express the type-checking rules for subclasses, as well as to provide constraints for polymorphic operations and data structures. Subtyping was too restrictive to serve either of these purposes. Moreover, as we looked at the sample programs we had written in PolyTOIL, we noticed that we rarely used subtyping. In the presence of *MyType* and match-bounded polymorphism, we almost never needed to explicitly change the types of methods in subclasses.

With this in mind, we decided to be bold and investigate the results of eliminating subtyping in favor of matching. While this caused no problems with the inheritance mechanism, we did discover a few situations where we found it difficult to do without subtyping. To deal with this we introduced a new type constructor, $\#T$, which represents elements whose types match the type $T$. With this addition, we found that we had a language which was essentially as expressive as **PolyTOIL**, yet significantly less complex.

In the next section we review briefly the main features of **PolyTOIL**. In section 3 we introduce the language $\mathcal{LOOM}$. We pay special attention to the introduction of a new type constructor which can be applied to object types to form types which have properties similar to subtypes (but are less restrictive). In the following section we provide a brief overview of the technical results used to justify the use of the language: type-checking is decidable and the language is provably type-safe. We provide a brief overview of $\mathcal{LOOM}$'s module system in section 5. Finally in section 6 we summarize and evaluate the features of the language.

# 2   Introduction to PolyTOIL and Matching

In [BSvG95] we introduced **PolyTOIL**, a statically-typed object-oriented programming language which provides all of the usual constructs of class-based object-oriented languages. In particular, it supports objects which consist of instance variables and methods, and in which computation is based on message-sending. Reuse is supported via inheritance, subtyping, and a form of bounded polymorphism.

We refer the reader to [BSvG95] for the details of the language. We provide only a brief summary here. Relatively innovative features of the language include:

- The use of *MyType* in classes to refer to the type of *self*, the receiver of the message.
- The treatment of classes as first-class values of the language. They have types and can be both parameters to functions and returned as the results of functions.
- The separation of the inheritance and subtyping hierarchies, in order to avoid problems which can arise with so-called binary methods.
- The introduction of a new ordering called "matching", written $<\#$, which corresponds closely to type changes allowed in defining subclasses. Subtyping, written $<:$, is also supported.
- Support for a form of bounded polymorphism, called *match-bounded polymorphism* in which the bound is expressed in terms of the new matching ordering.

Within the scope of each object (or class), **PolyTOIL** defines a type identifier *MyType* that represents the type of the object itself. This type is "anchored" to the type of the object in which it appears, so that an appearance of *MyType* in the type of a method inherited from another class represents the type of an instance of the current class, rather than the parent class in which the method was defined.

Matching is a relation between types which is very similar to subtyping, but is designed to correspond better to the inheritance hierarchy of classes and objects. An object type $\tau$ *matches* an object type $\sigma$ in **PolyTOIL**, if for every method $m_i : \sigma_i$ included in object type $\sigma$ there is a corresponding method $m_i : \tau_i$ included in object type $\tau$ such that $\sigma_i <: \tau_i$ (where occurrences of the keyword *MyType* in the method types are treated as uninterpreted free variables).

The definition of subtyping for object types is similar to that for matching, but also requires that *MyType* only occur positively[3] in method types (see [BSvG95] for definitions and details). In particular, an object type with a method with parameter of type *MyType* cannot have any non-trivial subtypes. As a result, if a class has a method with a parameter of type *MyType*, then subclasses will not give rise to subtypes.

While $\sigma <: \tau$ implies that any element of type $\sigma$ can be treated as being of type $\tau$, the import of matching is weaker. If $\sigma <\# \tau$ then any message sent to an object of the type $\tau$ could also be sent to an object of type $\sigma$.

*MyType* and matching are crucial to the expressiveness of **PolyTOIL**. *MyType* is often used in expressing the types of methods whose types will need to change in subclasses. It appears frequently in association with *copy* or *clone*

---

[3] Roughly, an occurrence of an identifier is positive (or covariant) if it is on the left side of an even number of function types, and is negative (or contravariant) if it is on the left of an odd number of function types. In particular, if the return type of a function is *MyType*, then that occurrence of *MyType* is positive. On the other hand, if a parameter type of a function is *MyType*, then that occurrence is negative.

```
class Node(n: Integer)
   var
      val = n: Integer;
      next = nil: MyType;
   methods
      function getVal(): Integer  {return val.clone() }
      procedure setVal(newVal: Integer) {val := newVal.clone()}
      function getNext(): MyType {return next}
      procedure setNext(newNext:MyType) {next := newNext}
      procedure attachRight(newNext: MyType) {self.setNext(newNext)}
   end class;

class DbleNode(n: Integer)
        inherits Node(n) modifying attachRight
   var
      prev = nil: MyType
   methods
      function getPrev():MyType {return prev}
      procedure setPrev(newPrev: MyType){prev := newPrev}
      procedure attachRight(newNext: MyType) {self.setNext(newNext);
         newNext.setPrev(self) }
end class;
```

**Fig. 1.** Singly and doubly-linked node classes in **PolyTOIL**.

methods and so-called *binary* methods – methods whose parameter should always be the same type as the receiver. Bounded polymorphism based on matching proves to be a very useful tool in object-oriented programming – so much so that when programming in **PolyTOIL**, we found that it (in combination with the use of *MyType*) almost completely replaced the use of subtype polymorphism as a mechanism for producing generic code.

Figure 1 provides an example of *Node* and *DbleNode* class definitions. Notice that for *n: Integer*, class *DbleNode(n)* inherits from *Node(n)*. The occurrences of *MyType* in *Node* implicitly denote the type of objects generated by *Node*, while in *DbleNode* they denote the type of objects generated by *DbleNode*. It follows easily from the definition of matching in PolyTOIL that the types generated by these classes are in the matching relation. However they are not subtypes because *setNext* and *attachRight* have parameters of type *MyType*.

Nevertheless it is possible to define a polymorphic list class that, when instantiated with the type of objects generated by *Node*, will generate singly-linked lists, while if it is instantiated with the type of objects generated by *DbleNode* will generate doubly-linked lists. (See [BSvG95] for the code and details.) The fact that these types are not subtypes is not a handicap in using them in the ways intended.

These results suggested to us that subtyping might not be necessary at all.

At the same time, we began to feel that presenting programmers with both the subtyping and matching hierarchies on types in a single language might be confusing.

The paper [GM96] in ECOOP '96 presented a language TooL, which is more general than PolyTOIL in that the bound on polymorphic types and classes could be specified using either subtyping or matching, and type-checking of classes could be done assuming that *MyType* either matched or was a subtype of the intended type of objects generated by the class. After experimenting with the language, the authors decided the language was too complex for programmers, and suggested dropping matching. Based on our experience, we prefer instead to give up subtyping. In the rest of this paper, we describe the language $\mathcal{LOOM}$, which we designed as a simpler replacement for **PolyTOIL**.

## 3 $\mathcal{LOOM}$: Core Language

As a result of our concerns about the complexity of **PolyTOIL**, we developed the language $\mathcal{LOOM}$. $\mathcal{LOOM}$ retains the syntax and match-bounded polymorphism of **PolyTOIL**, but completely abandons the subtyping relation in favor of a simplified version of matching. As a whole, $\mathcal{LOOM}$ is a much simpler language than its predecessor.

In abandoning subtyping, we also decided not to allow the types of inherited methods to be changed when overridden. While this may seem like a step backwards in the design of more flexible type systems, our experience indicates that the presence of the *MyType* construct (standing for the type of *self*) combined with match-bounded polymorphism provides sufficient flexibility for redefining methods in subclasses.

Because we wish to have matching correspond to the changes in types allowed in defining subclasses, we provide a more restricted definition of matching in $\mathcal{LOOM}$ compared to that of **PolyTOIL**. We write object types in $\mathcal{LOOM}$ in the form

```
ObjectType
   m1:T1;
   ...
   mn:Tn
end;
```

or more compactly, $ObjectType\{m_1: T_1; \ldots; m_n: T_n\}$.

**Definition 1.** Given object types $ObjectType\{m_1: T_1; \ldots; m_n: T_n\}$ and $ObjectType\{m_1: T_1; \ldots; m_k: T_k\}$, define

$$ObjectType\{m_1: T_1; \ldots; m_n: T_n\} <\# ObjectType\{m_1: T_1; \ldots; m_k: T_k\}$$

iff $k \leq n$. The relation $<\#$ is referred to as "matching".

In both **PolyTOIL** and [AC95], the matching relation allowed the types of corresponding methods to be subtypes. Since the corresponding types must now be the same, a matching type simply is an extension of the original. It might seem that this would significantly impact the expressiveness of the language. While there are some occasions where this restriction forces us to introduce type parameters, it is our experience that most of the time when we wish to have a change in the type of a method, the use of *MyType* provides the necessary change implicitly.

## 3.1 Hash Types Replace the Use of Subtyping

In object-oriented languages, subtyping allows a value of one type to masquerade as a value of a supertype. This permits the definition of data structures and operations that treat heterogeneous objects with common functionality. This is primarily used in two contexts. The first is in applying functions to parameters which are subtypes of their declared type. The second is for assignments to variables. While the first problem can be handled fairly elegantly with match-bounded polymorphism, the second is essentially impossible in **PolyTOIL** without subtype polymorphism.

In those places where we might have passed in a parameter that was a subtype of the declared type of the parameter, we could instead provide the function or procedure with an extra type parameter that was bounded (using matching) by the originally declared type of the parameter. If we had *procedure p(w:Window)* in **PolyTOIL** taking a parameter of type *Window*, then it could also be applied to parameters which were subtypes of *Window*. In $\mathcal{LOOM}$ we could rewrite it as *procedure p'(T <# Window; w:T)* with appropriately modified body. This procedure is actually now more general than the original because it can be applied to objects whose type merely matches that of *Window* rather than being a subtype. In particular, if *Window* contains a method with a parameter of type *MyType*, there are many types which will match it, but none which are proper subtypes.

This rewriting of programs has one major disadvantage – it introduces extra type parameters into many of the method definitions. One of the advantages of subtyping is that it is possible to write one simple function definition with a parameter of a fixed type, yet apply it to arguments of many more types. We address this problem below.

The use of subtyping in assignment statements occurs frequently when defining heterogeneous data structures. In a language with subtyping, we can relatively easily create a data structure in which all data values are subtypes of some fixed type. For instance, in programming a graphic user interface one might want to maintain a heterogeneous list of windows. From the point of view of maintaining the list, one need only require that each list element supports certain window operations. This can be captured most naturally by assuming each has a type which matches some general window type, rather than using subtyping. (After all, some of the methods might include negative occurrences of *MyType*.) We wish to be able to handle this in our language.

In implementing these heterogeneous data structures, we often have an instance variable to which we wish to assign the values to be stored in the structure. Generally it is assumed that the type of the value to be stored is a subtype of the declared type of the variable. However, as above, we have found that assuming it matches the declared type is often a better description of what is actually needed. Unfortunately, we know no way of modeling the flexibility of subtyping for variable assignments using match-bounded polymorphism.

To solve these problems, we introduce a new type, $\#\tau$, for $\tau$ an object type. If a variable or formal parameter is declared to have type $\#\tau$ then it will be able to hold values of any type matching $\tau$.[4]

A simple example should illustrate the use of hash types. Suppose we have a class in **PolyTOIL** with an instance variable *aWindow* of type *Window*, and a method

```
procedure setWindow(newWindow:Window){aWindow := newWindow}
```

We can rewrite this in $\mathcal{LOOM}$ by changing the type of *aWindow* to be $\#Window$ and replacing the method by

```
procedure setWindow(newWindow:#Window){aWindow := newWindow}
```

Now we can pass a variable of any type matching *Window* to the method. Note that if *Window* had a binary method, then it has no subtypes, so only objects of type *Window* could be passed in to the original *setWindow*. However, there will be many types matching *Window*, so the revised method may be more flexible than the original.

The type-checking rules *Weakening* and *Subsump* in Appendix C state the essential properties of these new types: If $e$ has type $\tau$ and $\tau <\!\#\, \sigma$, then $e$ also has type $\#\sigma$. We refer to types of the form $\#\tau$ as "hash" types, in reference to the constructor.

We can now rewrite the procedure declaration above nearly as simply as with subtyping by writing *procedure $p'(w:\#Window)$* in place of the longer polymorphic definition above. Similarly we can declare a variable to have type $\#\tau$ if it is to hold values with types that match $\tau$.

## 3.2 A Heterogeneous Ordered List Program in $\mathcal{LOOM}$

Before presenting the syntax and type-checking rules of $\mathcal{LOOM}$ formally, we provide an extended example of a heterogeneous list program. We begin by defining parameterized singly-linked and doubly-linked nodes in $\mathcal{LOOM}$, and work up to defining a class which can be instantiated to provide either singly-linked or doubly-linked heterogeneous ordered lists.

In Figure 2 we provide examples of parameterized *HetNode* and *HetDoubleNode* classes in $\mathcal{LOOM}$. Unlike the earlier examples of Nodes from **PolyTOIL**, they are now parameterized by the type of value stored in the node as well as

---

[4] Some readers may find it useful to think of $\#\tau$ as an abbreviation for the type $\exists t <\!\# \, \tau.t$ of the second order lambda calculus. (See [CW85, MP88].)

```
class HetNode(T <# Object; v: #T)
   var
      value = v: #T;
      next = nil: MyType;
   methods
      function getValue(): #T  {return value.clone() }
      procedure setValue(newValue: #T) {value := newValue.clone()}
      function getNext(): MyType {return next}
      procedure setNext(newNext:MyType) {next := newNext}
      procedure attachRight(newNext: MyType) {self.setNext(newNext)}
   end class;

class HetDbleNode(T <# Object; v: #T)
         inherits HetNode(T,v) modifying attachRight
   var
      prev = nil: MyType
   methods
      function getPrev():MyType {return prev}
      procedure setPrev(newPrev: MyType){prev := newPrev}
      procedure attachRight(newNext: MyType) {self.setNext(newNext);
         newNext.setPrev(self) }
end class;
```

**Fig. 2.** Polymorphic singly and doubly-linked node classes.

the initial value for that node. The upper bound *Object* on the type parameter $T$ is a built-in type which every object type matches. (It is similar to class *Object* of Java.) Because the instance variable *value* is declared to have type $\#T$, it can hold a value of any type matching $T$. Similarly, the methods *getValue* and *setValue* use hash types. On the other hand, the instance variables *next* and *prev* can only hold values with type exactly *MyType*. Thus the *next* field of an object generated by class *HetNode* can only hold nodes, while the corresponding field from class *HetDbleNode* can only hold doubly-linked nodes. Note that for fixed $U <\# Object$ and $u: \#U$, *HetDbleNode(U,u)* inherits from *HetNode(U,u)*.

We can create new objects from the *HetNode* class by first supplying the parameterized class with actual parameters and then applying the *new* operation to it. Thus if $U$ is an object type and $u:\#U$, then *new HetNode(U,u)* results in the creation of a new node object whose *value* field is initialized to $u$.

The type of objects is written using the *ObjectType* constructor. The type functions *HetNodeType* and *HetDbleNodeType* defined in Figure 3 describe the types of objects generated by the classes *HetNode* and *HetDbleNode*.

The keyword *include* used in the definition of *HetDbleNodeType* indicates that all methods of *HetNodeType* are included in *HetDbleNodeType*, as well as the new methods declared there. This may be thought of as a form of inheritance for types. It is modelled on a similar construct in Rapide [KLM94a], and is

```
HetNodeType(T <# Object) = ObjectType
            getValue: Func():#T;
            setValue: Proc(#T);
            getNext: Func():MyType;
            setNext: Proc(MyType)
            attachRight: Proc(MyType)
        end ObjectType;

HetDbleNodeType (T <# Object) = ObjectType include HetNodeType
            getPrev: Func():MyType;
            setPrev: Proc(MyType);
        end ObjectType;
```

**Fig. 3.** Types for singly and doubly-linked node classes.

essentially the same as the use of *extends* on interfaces in Java [AG96].

It follows from the definition that if $U$ <# $Object$, then $HetDbleNodeType(U)$ <# $HetNodeType(U)$. Of course, there is an *implicit* change of type resulting from the occurrences of *MyType* in the types of *getNext*, *setNext*, and *attachRight*, but the definition of matching is sensitive only to *explicit* changes in types.

The use of *MyType* ensures that instance variable, parameter, and return types change appropriately when new classes are defined by inheritance, and new types are defined using *include*. The type checking rule *Msg* in Appendix C specifies that when a message is sent to an object whose corresponding method involves the type *MyType*, all occurrences of *MyType* in the method type are replaced by the type of the receiver. For example, if a *setNext* message is sent to an object, the actual parameter must have the same type as the receiver. In particular, if *sn: HetNodeType(U)* for some fixed type $U$, then the type of parameter *newActualNext* in *sn.setNext(newActualNext)* must also be *HetNodeType(U)* for the message send to be type correct. On the other hand, if *dn: HetDbleNodeType(U)*, then the type of *newActualNext* in *dn.setNext(newActualNext)* must be *HetDbleNodeType(U)*.

```
OrdEltType = ObjectType
            gt, eq: Func(#OrdEltType):Boolean;
            ...
        end ObjectType;

OrdNodeType = HetNodeType(OrdEltType);

OrdDbleNodeType = HetDbleNodeType(OrdEltType)
```

**Fig. 4.** Node types for ordered elements.

```
class OrdList(N <# OrdNodeType)
  var
     head = nil: N;
  methods
     function find(match:#OrdEltType): Boolean
       var
         current: N;
       { current := head;
         while (current != nil) & match.gt(current.getValue()) do
           current := current.get_next()
         end;
         return (current != nil) & (current.getValue()).eq(match))}

     procedure addNode(newNode:N)
       ...
  end;

OrdListType(N <# OrdNodeType) = ObjectType   -- parameterized type
     find: Func(#OrdEltType): Boolean;
     addNode: Proc(N);
  end ObjectType;
```

**Fig. 5.** Heterogeneous linked list.

We define *OrdEltType* in Figure 4 to be an object type which includes operators which allow comparisons with elements of any type matching *OrdEltType*. We wish to construct a heterogeneous list, each of whose elements has a type matching *OrdEltType*. The individual nodes holding those values will have type *OrdNodeType* if we wish to have a singly-linked list, or type *OrdDbleNodeType* if we wish to have a doubly-linked list (see Figure 4). However, because *OrdDbleNodeType* <# *OrdNodeType*, we can take advantage of the polymorphism by creating a list class which is parameterized so that the type of its nodes is a fixed type which matches *OrdNodeType*.

In Figure 5 we provide the definition of a parameterized class which generates heterogeneous lists of elements whose types all match *OrdEltType*. The figure also includes the type function *OrdListType* which describes the objects generated by the class.

Because *OrdList* can be applied to any type which matches *OrdNodeType*, we can easily instantiate the lists to be either singly or doubly-linked. Thus

$$slist := new\ OrdList(OrdNodeType)$$

creates a new singly-linked heterogeneous list, while

$$dlist := new\ OrdList(OrdDbleNodeType)$$

creates a new doubly-linked heterogeneous list. If *elt* has any type which matches *OrdEltType* then *slist.find(elt)*, *slist.addNode(new Node(OrdEltType,elt))*, *dlist.find(elt)*, and *dlist.addNode(new DbleNode(OrdEltType,elt))* are correctly typed message sends which look up or add new elements to singly or doubly-linked lists.

## 3.3   Type Checking and Hash Types

The rules for forming legal type expressions and defining matching in $\mathcal{LOOM}$ are given in Appendix B, while the most important type-checking rules can be found in Appendix C.

The type-checking rules for classes are in a slightly different style from those in [BSvG95]. This slight variation makes the proof of type-safety somewhat simpler. The keyword *self* is of type *MyType*, and represents the object from the outside. It is used as in the examples given earlier to send messages to the object executing the code, or it can be used to pass the object as a parameter to a method of another object. (The keyword *self* may be omitted in terms of the form *self.m()* in the implemented $\mathcal{LOOM}$ interpreter, as the interpreter can infer where it needs to occur.) The keyword *selfVar* represents the record of instance variables of the object, which are only visible within the object's methods. In the examples given earlier in this paper, if *v* is an instance variable, we have chosen to simply write *v* rather than *selfVar.v*. Again the interpreter will infer when this is needed and insert it if it is omitted.

The addition of hash types provides most of the original functionality of subtype polymorphism. It allows us to write heterogeneous data structures and to write functions that operate on all objects whose type matches their parameter. However there are some new wrinkles in type checking that should be noted.

As stated earlier, by the *Weakening* and *Subsumption* type-checking rules, it is possible for elements of a fixed type $\sigma$ to be assigned to a variable with type $\#\tau$ for $\sigma <\!\!\# \tau$, but not vice-versa. Similar rules hold for the correspondence between formal and actual parameters of functions and procedures.

We discussed above the type-checking rule for sending messages, *Msg*, which appears in Appendix C. For that rule, we needed to know the exact type of the receiver. But what happens if all we know about the receiver *o* is that it has a type of the form $\#\sigma$? If the method to be applied has a type $\tau$ in which all occurrences of *MyType* are positive (e.g., *MyType* does not occur as the type of a parameter), then one can apply the same typing rule. That is, the type of *o.m* is $\tau[\#\sigma/MyType]$. (See rule *Msg#* in the appendix.) It can be shown via an inductive proof that this rule is sound. However, if the method type $\tau$ includes a negative (contravariant) occurrence of *MyType*, then the rule does not hold.

A concrete example should help illustrate the reasons for the failure. Suppose *aNode* has type *#OrdNodeType*. Then *aNode.attachRight(bNode)* will not be well-typed. The value of *aNode* at run-time might be of any type matching *OrdNodeType*. If the value held in *aNode* actually has type *OrdNodeType* at run-time, then the type of the parameter *bNode* must be *OrdNodeType*. On the other hand, if the type of the value held in *aNode* is actually *OrdDbleNodeType* at runtime, then the type of the parameter *bNode* must instead be *OrdDbleNodeType*. Since we cannot determine the type of the value statically, we cannot determine which is the correct type for the parameter. (Note that having an actual parameter with type #*OrdNodeType* makes the situation even worse!)

Thus if the receiver of a message has a hash type, we cannot send it a binary message, or indeed any message whose type involves an occurrence of *MyType* in a contravariant position.

A practical consequence of this is that if we have a heterogeneous data structure, as is the case in Figure 5 above, we can only send non-binary messages to its elements (at least in the absence of a type-case statement – or equivalent – which allows the run-time checking of types). One might suspect that this is the reason why the type *OrdEltType* in the program has no binary methods. In fact, this simply results from thinking through the logical design of these methods. If *ge* and *eq* had types of the form *func(#MyType):Boolean*, then there would be no way of comparing successive elements of the list, since their values could be of incomparable types matching *OrdEltType*. In that case one could not send a comparison method to one using the other as a parameter. Thus it would be a logical mistake to try to use a binary method there.

It is also worth noting here that we would be stuck in this case in a language supporting subtyping as well. If the type $\tau$ of elements in the list had a binary method, then no proper subtypes of $\tau$ would exist, forcing the list to be homogeneous. In $\mathcal{LOOM}$, such binary methods might exist in $\tau$, as long as they aren't used in the methods of the heterogeneous data structure.

Finally in many cases where a binary method needs to be sent to a parameter $x$ with a hash type of the form #$\tau$, the function declaration can be rewritten to take an explicit type parameter $t <\!\#\, \tau$ and parameter $x\!:t$. In this way we have an explicit name for the type of $x$, and can provide an actual parameter for a binary method with a parameter which is also of type $t$.

Thus while this restriction on typing message sends corresponding to binary methods seems to be a limitation, the limitations are actually less severe than in languages with subtyping.

# 4 Decidability, Natural Semantics, and Type Safety

In this section we outline some important results for $\mathcal{LOOM}$ whose details will be provided elsewhere. These include the decidability of type checking for $\mathcal{LOOM}$, the provision of natural semantics, and the proof of type safety.

Pierce's [Pie92] results on the undecidability of subtyping in the second-order bounded polymorphic lambda calculus has caused designers of languages supporting bounded polymorphism to be concerned about whether their type systems are undecidable. While $\mathcal{LOOM}$ does not support subtyping, one might be concerned that match-bounded polymorphism could lead to the same difficulty. Luckily this turns out not to be the case. In fact the determination of whether two types match is relatively straightforward since one object type matches another only if the first type contains all of the methods (with corresponding types) of the second. As usual it is straightforward to replace the general transitivity rule for matching with a restricted rule which is computationally easy to deal with (and in fact we have included only this restricted rule in Appendix B).

The algorithm for type checking terms is fairly straightforward. As with **PolyTOIL**, the complexity of type-checking is non-polynomial in the worst case, since in contrived families of examples the type of a term can grow exponentially fast in the length of the term. In practice we find type checking in $\mathcal{LOOM}$ to be acceptably fast (at most quadratic in the size of the type).

In order to prove the type safety of $\mathcal{LOOM}$, we need to show that the type system is consistent with a semantics for the language. We can define a natural semantics for $\mathcal{LOOM}$ similar to that provided for **PolyTOIL** [BSvG95]. Once defined we can prove:

1. If a term of $\mathcal{LOOM}$ has type $\tau$ (possibly under some assumptions on free term and type variables) and if the evaluation of the term halts (when started with an environment and state that are consistent with the assumptions), then the value will also have type $\tau$.[5]

2. If a term is well-typed then the evaluation will not get "stuck". That is, it will not get to a point in the evaluation where the partial result is not a designated "reduced value", yet no computation rule applies.

The proofs of these results are similar to those in **PolyTOIL**, but are simpler because of the lack of subtyping. The only terms which require extra work are message sends to hash types, but a proof by induction on the structure of terms suffices to show that the type-checking rule is sound. Needless to say, the assumption that the method type includes only positive occurrences of *MyType* is crucial to the proof.

Details of the semantics, formal statement of the theorems, and the proofs will be given in an extended form of this paper.

## 5 Adding Modules to LOOM

As programmers and language designers have gotten more experience with object-oriented languages, it has become clearer that class boundaries are not always the correct abstraction layer for large programs. Interestingly it is the hybrid languages which have grown from ADT-style languages which have often provided the best support for this modularity. Thus Ada 95 [Int95] and Modula-3 [CDG+88] have introduced module structures which are distinct from classes. Pure object-oriented languages like Smalltalk and Eiffel have generally chosen to identify classes with modules, though newer languages like Theta [DGLM94] (which can be seen as a descendant of the ADT-style language, Clu) and Java [AG96] have also chosen to provide modules (called packages in Java).

---

[5] If $\tau$ involves free type variables then the type of the value will have a type obtained by replacing the free type variables of $\tau$ by corresponding values from the environment.

Modules provide three important functions in programming languages:

1. They provide a way of organizing code into manageable pieces and help with name-space management by only exporting names that are needed elsewhere.
2. They provide important abstraction barriers, lessening the dependence of a unit on the implementation details of another unit.
3. They provide support for separate compilation, aiding the programmer in debugging large programs as well as making it possible to provide reusable code in libraries in such a way that the original source code need not be revealed.

With strong language support for modules it should be possible to change the implementation of a type without changing its public interface and without requiring recompilation of other modules which import it. See [Jon96] for a more detailed discussion of modules.

We have chosen to follow the lead of languages like those in the Modula and Ada families and provide module interfaces which can be completely separate from the module implementation (e.g., the interface can be compiled before the implementation is written). A key issue is to provide a mechanism for revealing in the interface as much or as little as desired about the details of the implementation of a type.

In ADT-style languages it is typical for type definitions in interfaces to consist either of *manifest* types, in which all details of the type definition are revealed, or *opaque* types, in which only the name of the type is revealed. However in ADT-style languages, operations are defined externally from the type itself. Thus an opaque type will be accompanied by a collection of names of constants, functions, and procedures related to it that are to be exported (though their implementations are typically hidden).

In object-oriented languages, however, object types include the names and types of their methods. In ADT-style languages it is easy to reveal only certain operations, leaving others hidden in the implementation module. We can emulate this in object-oriented languages by providing partial revelations of object types as is done in Modula-3. That is, for each object type we only list those methods which we wish to publicly advertise. This can be expressed using the matching relation from $\mathcal{LOOM}$.

The following example is similar to one presented in [PT93]. If we declare

```
IntSetType <# ObjectType
              add: proc(Integer);
              remove: proc(Integer);
              contains: func(Integer):Boolean;
              intersect: proc(MyType)
           end;
```

in an interface, then we know that IntSetType has methods *add*, *remove*, *contains*, and *intersect* with the appropriate types. As before, we note that subtyping would not be an appropriate relation (even if it was supported in $\mathcal{LOOM}$)

because the fact that *intersect* has a parameter of type *MyType* implies that the given object type has no proper subtypes!

$\mathcal{LOOM}$, like **PolyTOIL**, allows the programmer to label methods as either Visible or Hidden, depending on whether or not we wish them to be available outside of the object's own methods.[6] Also an object's instance variables are not accessible outside the object's methods. Why then do we need the extra mechanism of partial revelations? The reason is that some objects might need to provide extra methods which are only accessible to a limited number of other types of objects. This is exactly the idea behind C++'s friends and is similar to the provision of different levels of access in Ada 95 and Java.

Let us continue with the example above of sets of integers. In order to implement the intersection operation efficiently we may need to have more access to the representation of the sets. Appendix A contains an example of a collection of $\mathcal{LOOM}$ modules which supports the efficient implementation of integer sets as ordered lists.

There are several points worthy of remark in this example. First notice that *OrdListType* is a manifest type. The user has full access to the type and to the class *OrdListClass* which generates objects of that type. However the type *IntSetType* is only partially revealed. Inside the implementation module it is defined as an extension of *OrdListType* (and hence matches *OrdListType*), but that information is not available outside of the implementation module. Hence one may not deduce in any other module that *IntSetType* <# *OrdListType*. This represents good programming practice since one should not in general be able to use list operations on sets. Notice also that because *OrdListType* is not exported by *Interface SetOfInt*, the name space is not cluttered up with details about lists.

A second important point about this example is that our (efficient) implementation of *intersect* depends on being able to use the fact that *IntSetType* is implemented as an ordered list. If, for example, all of the list operations (such as *first*, *next*, and *deleteCur*) were hidden methods, we would not be able to send the corresponding messages to the parameter *other*. If there were methods of other classes which also needed access to these non-exported methods, we would simply include their definitions in the same module. Thus we can achieve the effect of C++'s friends without letting the non-exported methods escape the module boundary.

This technique for providing information hiding while providing access by operations at the same level of abstraction is similar to that suggested in [PT93] and [KLM94b], where bounded existential quantifiers based on subtyping are used to perform the information hiding.

In summary, our implementation of modules in $\mathcal{LOOM}$ allows the programmer to specify how much information about an object type is revealed to other program units. While it is possible to have a totally opaque type, this should

---

[6] For simplicity, we have not labeled the methods in the earlier examples, though all would be labeled as *Visible*. Our use of *Visible* corresponds to C++ and Java's *public*, while *Hidden* corresponds to their *protected*.

be relatively rare with the object-oriented style of programming. The user can reveal all of the details of a type definition by providing a *manifest* type, or may reveal only a portion of the type by providing a matching bound on the type. Function, procedure, class, and other constant declarations can also be exported by placing them in a module interface. Our module design satisfies all of the goals listed at the beginning of this section.

## 6 Evaluation of LOOM

One of the most difficult decisions to make in designing a programming language is not so much what features should be included, but rather which features can (or should) be excluded. Based on our previous work, we concluded that subtyping was a feature that could be excluded from object-oriented languages. In this paper we presented the language $\mathcal{LOOM}$, which dropped subtyping in favor of matching, and added hash types.

Aside from subtyping, features of $\mathcal{LOOM}$ include all of those in our earlier language **PolyTOIL**. Because of the lack of subtyping, we decided not to allow types of methods to be changed when defining subclasses.[7] Similarly, matching now requires corresponding method types to be the same, rather than subtypes. To replace other uses of subtyping we introduced a new type constructor which can be applied to object types to obtain "hash types". With the addition of the hash types, the elimination of subtyping has very little impact on the expressiveness of the language.

Another advantage of $\mathcal{LOOM}$ is that the matching relation is relatively trivial, only allowing the addition of new methods to object types, as compared to subtyping, which is defined on all types and is often quite complex. The covariant and contravariant rules for subtyping functions are a good example of the complexity of subtyping that we can simply ignore in $\mathcal{LOOM}$.

Binary methods have been hard to express in most statically-typed object-oriented programming languages because they seem to require a *MyType* term representing the type of *self*, yet *MyType* and subtyping have not interacted well. See [BCC+96] for an exposition of the difficulties of handling binary methods in statically-typed object-oriented languages. In that paper, matching is suggested as one way of getting around these difficulties, but it is also criticized as not providing support for heterogeneous data structures. In this paper we have shown how to provide that support by the use of hash types.

One possible disadvantage of $\mathcal{LOOM}$ is that the programmer must explicitly mark the types of variables and formal parameters which are allowed to hold values of more than one type by declaring them with hash types. Variables and parameters with non-hash types are only allowed to hold values of the type with which they are declared. The programmer is required to "plan ahead" which slots are allowed to hold values which match because the typing rules for message sending are different for hash types than for regular types. It is worth noting in

---

[7] An early version of $\mathcal{LOOM}$ did allow types to be changed, but we decided that the gains were not worth the added complexity.

this regard that Ada 95 [Int95] also requires the programmer to mark the types of variables and parameters with the "*class*" suffix if values which are subclasses of the declared type may be used.

A complication of $\mathcal{LOOM}$ compared to **PolyTOIL** is that binary messages may not be sent to hash types. As discussed in the previous section, this has little practical impact since binary methods are generally not appropriate for heterogeneous data, and match-bounded polymorphism can usually be used in place of hash types where binary methods are needed.

We noted that the type-checking algorithm for $\mathcal{LOOM}$ is decidable, with low complexity in practice. Also, the static type system for $\mathcal{LOOM}$ guarantees that no type errors will occur during the execution of type-checked programs, so $\mathcal{LOOM}$ is type-safe.

$\mathcal{LOOM}$ also provides significant features for information hiding. All instance variables are hidden from clients, while methods are marked as being either visible or hidden in order to determine their visibility to clients. All instance variables and methods are visible to inheritors. We described briefly the module facility in the language which provides for separate compilation, restriction of the scope of names, and information hiding. Like Modula-3, it provides extra support for information hiding by the use of partial revelations of types. This fine control over information hiding can be used to provide objects defined in the module access to more features than those outside, providing a feature similar to C++'s friends. This also allows more efficient implementation of binary methods.

We are currently examining mechanisms to allow modules to support multiple interfaces. This would make it possible to provide different views of a module to different clients. For instance, a client wishing to define a subclass of a class in a module will need much more detailed information about the superclass than a client which simply wishes to be able to generate objects from the class and use them.

We have implemented an interpreter for $\mathcal{LOOM}$, which is based on the natural semantics of the language. In spite of the seemingly radical step of eliminating subtyping, our experience is that $\mathcal{LOOM}$ provides a conceptually simpler language than **PolyTOIL**, yet provides essentially the same expressiveness as the earlier language. It may be time to rethink the notion that subtyping is an essential part of object-oriented languages.

*Acknowledgements: The $\mathcal{LOOM}$ language design is due to Bruce and Petersen. A more complete description of the language design, type-checing rules, natural semantics, and the analysis of complexity of type-checking can be found in Petersen's honors thesis [Pet96]. The proof of type safety was done by Fiech with the assistance of Bruce, and was based on a similar proof for **PolyTOIL**. The $\mathcal{LOOM}$ implementation was primarily accomplished by Petersen with assistance from Hilary Browne, and was based on the **PolyTOIL** interpreter written by Robert van Gent and Angela Schuett, with assistance from Petersen and Jasper Rosenberg.*

# References

[AC95]   Martin Abadi and Luca Cardelli. On subtyping and matching. In *Proceedings ECOOP '95*, pages 145–167, 1995.

[AG96]   Ken Arnold and James Gosling. *Java*. Addison Wesley, 1996.

[AvdL90] Pierre America and Frank van der Linden. A parallel object-oriented language with inheritance and subtyping. In *OOPSLA-ECOOP '90 Proceedings*, pages 161–168. ACM SIGPLAN Notices,25(10), October 1990.

[BCC+96] Kim B. Bruce, Luca Cardelli, Giuseppe Castagna, The Hopkins Objects Group, Gary T. Leavens, and Benjamin Pierce. On binary methods. *Theory and Practice of Object-Oriented Systems*, 1996. to appear.

[Bru93]  K. Bruce. Safe type checking in a statically typed object-oriented programming language. In *Proc. ACM Symp. on Principles of Programming Languages*, pages 285–298, 1993.

[Bru94]  K. Bruce. A paradigmatic object-oriented programming language: design, static typing and semantics. *Journal of Functional Programming*, 4(2):127–206, 1994. An earlier version of this paper appeared in the 1993 POPL Proceedings.

[BSvG95] Kim B. Bruce, Angela Schuett, and Robert van Gent. PolyTOIL: A type-safe polymorphic object-oriented language, extended abstract. In *ECOOP '95*, pages 27–51. LNCS 952, Springer-Verlag, 1995.

[CDG+88] L. Cardelli, J. Donahue, L. Galssman, M. Jordan, B. Kalsow, and G. Nelson. Modula-3 report. Technical Report SRC-31, DEC systems Research Center, 1988.

[CHC90]  William R. Cook, Walter L. Hill, and Peter S. Canning. Inheritance is not subtyping. In *Proc. 17th ACM Symp. on Principles of Programming Languages*, pages 125–135, January 1990.

[CW85]   L. Cardelli and P. Wegner. On understanding types, data abstraction, and polymorphism. *Computing Surveys*, 17(4):471–522, 1985.

[DGLM94] Mark Day, Robert Gruber, Barbara Liskov, and Andrew C. Meyers. Abstraction mechanisms in Theta. Technical report, MIT Laboratory for Computer Science, 1994.

[ES90]   Margaret A. Ellis and Bjarne Stroustrop. *The annotated $C^{++}$ reference manual*. Addison-Wesley, 1990.

[GM96]   Andreas Gawecki and Florian Matthes. Integrating subtyping, matching and type quantification: A practical perspective. In *ECOOP '96*, pages 26–47. LNCS 1098, Springer-Verlag, 1996.

[Int95]  Intermetrics. *Ada 95 Reference Manual, version 6.0*. 1995.

[Jon96]  Mark P. Jones. Using parameterized signatures to express modular structure. In *23rd ACM Symp. Principles of Programming Languages*, pages 68–78, 1996.

[KLM94a] Dinesh Katiyar, David Luckham, and John Mitchell. A type system for prototyping languages. In *21st ACM Symp. Principles of Programming Languages*, pages 138–150, 1994.

[KLM94b] Dinesh Katiyar, David Luckham, and John Mitchell. A type system for prototyping languages. In *Conference Record of POPL '94: 21st ACM SIGPLAN-SIGACT Symposium of Principles of Programming Languages, Portland, Oregon*, pages 138–150. Association for Computing Machinery, January 1994.

[LP91]     Wilf LaLonde and John Pugh. Subclassing ≠ subtyping ≠ is-a. *Journal of Object-Oriented Programming*, pages 57–62, January 1991.

[Mey92]    B. Meyer. *Eiffel: the language*. Prentice-Hall, 1992.

[MMMP90]   O. Madsen, B. Magnusson, and B. Moller-Pedersen. Strong typing of object-oriented languages revisited. In *OOPSLA-ECOOP '90 Proceedings*, pages 140–150. ACM SIGPLAN Notices,25(10), October 1990.

[MP88]     J.C. Mitchell and G.D. Plotkin. Abstract types have existential types. *ACM Trans. on Programming Languages and Systems*, 10(3):470–502, 1988. Preliminary version appeared in *Proc. 12th ACM Symp. on Principles of Programming Languages*, 1985.

[Pet96]    Leaf Petersen. *A module system for LOOM*. Williams College Senior Honors Thesis, 1996.

[Pie92]    Benjamin C. Pierce. Bounded quantification is undecidable. In *Proc 19th ACM Symp. Principles of Programming Languages*, pages 305–315, 1992.

[PT93]     Benjamin C. Pierce and David N. Turner. Statically typed friendly functions via partially abstract types. Technical Report ECS-LFCS-93-256, University of Edinburgh, 1993.

[Sny86]    A. Snyder. Encapsulation and inheritance in object-oriented programming languages. In *Proc. 1st ACM Symp. on Object-Oriented Programming Systems, Languages, and Applications*, pages 38–46, October 1986.

[Tes85]    L. Tesler. Object Pascal report. Technical Report 1, Apple Computer, 1985.

# A  Sample LOOM Program for Integer Sets Using Modules

A row of "*"s indicates a module boundary. The intersection method of SetOfInt is destructive – the receiver of the message is updated to hold the value of the intersection.

```
Interface IntOrdList;

type

   OrdListType = ObjectType
      first: proc();
      next: proc();
      off: func():Boolean; -- is current elt off end of list?
      add: proc(Integer);
      deleteCur: proc();  -- current is next elt after deleteCur
      contains: func(Integer):Boolean;
      getCur: func():Integer
   end;


   OrdListClassType = ClassType ... end;
      -- class types include instance variable and method types
```

```
const

   OrdListClass: OrdListClassType;

end;
```

****************************************************

```
Interface SetOfInt;

type

   IntSetType <# ObjectType
      add: proc(Integer);
      remove: proc(Integer);
      contains: func(Integer):Boolean;
      intersect: proc(MyType)
   end;

const

   function newSet(): IntSetType;

end; -- Interface SetOfInt
```

****************************************************

```
Module Implements SetOfInt import IntOrdList;
-- SetOfInt is implemented as a specialized ordered list in order
-- to make the methods find and intersect more efficient.

type

   IntSetType = ObjectType include IntOrdList::OrdListType
      remove :proc(Integer);
      intersect: proc(MyType)
   end;

   ListSetClassType = ClassType
           include IntOrdList::OrdListClassType;
      methods visible
         remove :proc(Integer);
         intersect: proc(MyType)
      end;
```

```
const

    ListSetClass = class inherit IntOrdList::OrdListClass
        methods visible
            procedure remove(elt:Integer) is
                begin
                    if find(elt) then deleteCur()
                end;

            procedure intersect(other:MyType) is
                                        -- destructive intersection
                begin
                    first();
                    other.first();
                    while (not off()) and (not other.off) do
                        if getCur() < other.getCur() then
                            deleteCur()
                        else if getCur() > other.getCur then
                                other.next()
                            else
                                next();
                                other.next()
                            end -- else if
                        end -- if
                    end -- while
                    while not off() do
                        deleteCur()
                    end -- while
                end -- function
            end; -- class

    function newSet():IntSetType;
        begin
            return new(ListSetClass)
        end;

end -- Module
```

# B  Type Formation and Matching Rules

There are rules which determine which type expressions are well-formed. While there is not room to include these in this extended abstract, the well-formed type expressions are the following: a type variable or constant, a function type of the form *Func(σ):τ*, a polymorphic function type *Func(s <# σ):τ* where σ is an object type or type variable, a regular or polymorphic procedure type, a record type of the form $\{m_1:\tau_1;\ldots;m_n:\tau_n\}$, an object type of the form *ObjectType* $\tau$ (for $\tau$ a record type), an expression of the form *ClassType($\sigma,\tau$)* (for $\sigma$ and $\tau$ record types) which represents the type of a class whose instance variables have type $\sigma$ and methods have type $\tau$, or an expression of the form $\#\tau$ (where $\tau$ is an object type or variable).

Reference types are generated automatically by the system from variable declarations. The type of a variable holding values of type $\tau$ is written as *ref* $\tau$.

We say that $\{m_1:\tau_1;\ldots;m_n:\tau_n\}$ *extends* $\{m_1:\tau_1;\ldots;m_k:\tau_k\}$, if $n \geq k$. Matching is only defined on object types and variables.

$Var(\lessdot\#)$
$$C \cup \{t \lessdot\# \tau\} \vdash t \lessdot\# \tau,$$

$Refl(\lessdot\#)$
$$\frac{C \vdash \tau \lessdot\# Object}{C \vdash \tau \lessdot\# \tau,}$$

$Trans(\lessdot\#)$
$$\frac{C \vdash \tau \lessdot\# \gamma}{C \cup \{t \lessdot\# \tau\} \vdash t \lessdot\# \gamma},$$

$ObjectType(\lessdot\#)$
$$\frac{\tau \text{ extends } \tau'}{C \vdash ObjectType \; \tau \lessdot\# ObjectType \; \tau'},$$

# C  Selected Type-checking Rules for $\mathcal{LOOM}$

$C$ is a collection of type constraints of the form $t \lessdot\# \tau$, while $E$ is a collection of type assignments to identifiers. We have omitted many of the rules which are the same as for PolyTOIL. In particular we have omitted the rules for declarations and most commands aside from assignment.

$Assn$
$$\frac{C,E \vdash x: ref \; \tau, \quad C,E \vdash M:\tau}{C,E \vdash x:= M: COMMAND}$$

$Var$
$$C,E \vdash x:\tau, \quad \text{if } E(x) = \tau$$

$Function$
$$\frac{C,E \cup \{v:\sigma\} \vdash Block:\tau}{C,E \vdash \text{function } (v:\sigma) \; Block: \; (Func \; (\sigma):\tau)}$$

where $\sigma$ may be of the form $\#\gamma$.

$BdPolyFunc$
$$\frac{C \cup \{t \lessdot\# \gamma\}, E \vdash Block:\tau}{C,E \vdash \text{function } (t \lessdot\# \gamma) \; Block: \; (Func \; (t \lessdot\# \gamma):\tau)}$$

$$FuncAppl \quad \frac{C, E \vdash f \colon Func(\sigma) \colon \tau \\ C, E \vdash M \colon \sigma}{C, E \vdash f(M) \colon \tau}$$

$$BdPolyFuncAppl \quad \frac{C, E \vdash f \colon Func(t <\!\# \gamma) \colon \tau \\ C \vdash \sigma <\!\# \gamma}{C, E \vdash f[\sigma] \colon \tau[\sigma/t]}$$

$$Record \quad \frac{C, E \vdash a_i \colon \sigma_i, \text{ for } 1 \leq i \leq n}{C, E \vdash \{v_1 = a_1; \ldots; v_n = a_n\} \colon \{v_1 \colon \sigma_1; \ldots; v_n \colon \sigma_n\}}$$

$$Proj \quad \frac{C, E \vdash a \colon T, \ C \vdash T \ extends \ \{v_1 \colon \sigma_1; \ldots; v_n \colon \sigma_n\}}{C, E \vdash a.v_i \colon \sigma_i} \text{ if } 1 \leq i \leq n$$

$$Class \quad \frac{C^{IV}, E \vdash a \colon \sigma, \ C^{METH}, E^{METH} \vdash e \colon \tau}{C, E \vdash class(a, e) \colon ClassType(\sigma, \tau)}$$

where $C^{IV} = C \cup \{MyType <\!\# ObjectType \ \tau\}$,
$C^{METH} = C^{IV} \cup \{SelfVarType \ extends \ MkRef(\sigma)\}$,
$E^{METH} = E \cup \{self \colon MyType, selfVar \colon SelfVarType\}$
$MkRef\{v_1 \colon \sigma_1; \ldots; v_n \colon \sigma_n\} = \{v_1 \colon ref \ \sigma_1; \ldots; v_n \colon ref \ \sigma_n\}$
Neither $MyType$ nor $SelfVarType$ may occur free in $C$ or $E$.
$\sigma$ and $\tau$ must both be record types,
while the components of $\tau$ must be function types.

$$Object \quad \frac{C, E \vdash c \colon ClassType(\sigma, \tau)}{C, E \vdash new \ c \colon ObjectType \ \tau}$$

$$Msg \quad \frac{C, E \vdash o \colon \gamma, \ C \vdash \gamma <\!\# ObjectType\{m \colon \tau\}}{C, E \vdash o \Leftarrow m \colon \tau[\gamma/MyType]}$$

$$Msg\# \quad \frac{C, E \vdash o \colon \#ObjectType\{m_1 \colon \tau_1; \ldots; m_n \colon \tau_n\}}{C, E \vdash o \Leftarrow m_i \colon \tau_i[\#ObjectType\{m_1 \colon \tau_1; \ldots; m_n \colon \tau_n\}/MyType]}$$

Only if all occurrences of $MyType$ in $\tau_i$ are positive.

$$Inherits \quad \frac{\begin{array}{c} C, E \vdash c \colon ClassType(\{v_1 \colon \sigma_1; \ldots; v_m \colon \sigma_m\}, \{m_1 \colon \tau_1; \ldots; m_n \colon \tau_n\}), \\ C^{IV}, E \vdash a_{m+1} \colon \sigma_{m+1}, \ C^{IV}, E \vdash a'_1 \colon \sigma_1, \\ C^{METH}, E^{METH} \vdash e_{n+1} \colon \tau_{n+1}, \ C^{METH}, E^{METH} \vdash e'_1 \colon \tau_1 \end{array}}{\begin{array}{c} C, E \vdash class \ inherit \ c \ modifying \ v_1, m_1; \\ (\{v_1 = a'_1 \colon \sigma_1, v_{m+1} = a_{m+1} \colon \sigma_{m+1}\}, \\ \{m_1 = e'_1 \colon \tau_1, m_{n+1} = e_{n+1} \colon \tau_{n+1}\}) \colon \\ ClassType(\{v_1 \colon \sigma_1; \ldots; v_{m+1} \colon \sigma_{m+1}\}, \\ \{m_1 \colon \tau_1; m_2 \colon \tau_2; \ldots; m_{n+1} \colon \tau_{n+1}\}) \end{array}}$$

where $C^{IV} = C \cup \{MyType <\!\!\# ObjectType \{m_1\!:\tau_1; \ldots; m_{n+1}\!:\tau_{n+1}\}\}$,
$C^{METH} =$
$\qquad C^{IV} \cup \{SelfVarType \ extends \ MkRef(\{v_1\!:\sigma_1; \ldots; v_{m+1}\!:\sigma_{m+1}\})\}$
$E^{METH} = E \cup \{self\!: MyType, selfVar\!: SelfVarType,$
$\qquad\qquad super\!: MyType \rightarrow SelfVarType \rightarrow \{m_1\!:\tau_1; \ldots; m_n\!:\tau_n\}\}$
Neither $MyType$ nor $SelfVarType$ may occur free in $C$ or $E$.

*Weakening*
$$\frac{C, E \vdash e\!:\tau}{C, E \vdash e\!:\#\tau}$$

*Subsump*
$$\frac{C \vdash \sigma <\!\!\# \tau, \quad C, E \vdash e\!:\#\sigma}{C, E \vdash e\!:\#\tau}$$

# Near Optimal Hierarchical Encoding of Types

Andreas Krall[1], Jan Vitek[2] and R. Nigel Horspool[3]

[1] Institut für Computersprachen, Technische Universität Wien
Argentinierstraße 8, A-1040 Wien, Austria
andi@complang.tuwien.ac.at

[2] Object Systems Group, Centre Universitaire d'Informatique
Université de Genève,
24 rue Général-Dufour, CH-1211 Geneva, Switzerland
jvitek@cui.unige.ch

[3] Department of Computer Science, University of Victoria,
P.O. Box 3055, Victoria, BC, Canada V8W 3P6
nigelh@csr.uvic.ca

**Abstract.** A type inclusion test is a procedure to decide whether two types are related by a given subtyping relationship. An efficient implementation of the type inclusion test plays an important role in the performance of object oriented programming languages with multiple subtyping like C++, Eiffel or Java. There are well-known methods for performing fast constant time type inclusion tests that use a hierarchical bit vector encoding of the partial ordered set representing the type hierarchy. The number of instructions required by the type inclusion test is proportional to the length of those bit vectors. We present a new algorithm based on graph coloring which computes a near optimal hierarchical encoding of type hierarchies. The new algorithm improves significantly on previous results – it is faster, simpler and generates smaller bit vectors.

## 1  Introduction

Checking the type of a value is a common operation in typed programming languages. In many cases this requires little more than a comparison. But, modern languages – those which allow types to be extended – complicate matters slightly. Type tests must check for inclusion of types, that is, whether a given type is an extension (or a subtype) of another type. The subtyping relation, a partial order on types, written $<:$, is the transitive and reflexive closure of the direct subtype relation $<:_d$. The common practice for object-oriented programming languages is to derive $<:_d$ directly from the inheritance structure of a program. Thus, each class A defines a type A, and A is a subtype of B either if A = B, or if A inherits from B.

Type inclusion tests can occur so frequently in programs, particularly object-oriented programs, as to put a strain on the overall system performance. It is important to have type inclusion testing techniques which are both fast and constant-time. However, these techniques should also be economical in space.

The techniques developed in this paper are based on a scheme called *hierarchical encoding*. This scheme represents each type as a set of natural numbers. The sets must be chosen so that either

$$x <: y \Leftrightarrow \gamma(x) \supseteq \gamma(y) \quad \text{(top down encoding)}$$

or

$$x <: y \Leftrightarrow \gamma(x) \subseteq \gamma(y) \quad \text{(bottom up encoding)}$$

where $\gamma(x)$ maps type $x$ to its set representation. Thus, the set used for a subtype has to be a superset of the set representing its parent. The sets have a natural representation as bit vectors. An example for a small hierarchy is shown in figure 1 (top down encoding) and figure 2 (bottom up encoding). In the bit vector representation the test function for hierarchical top down encoding becomes

$$x <: y \Leftrightarrow \gamma(x) \lor \gamma(y) = \gamma(x)$$

or alternatively

$$x <: y \Leftrightarrow \gamma(x) \land \gamma(y) = \gamma(y)$$

which would be implemented in C code as

```
if ((type->code & parenttype->code) == parenttype->code)
    /* it is a subtype */
```

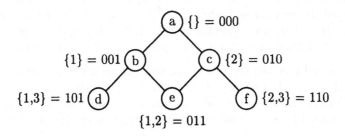

**Fig. 1.** Hierarchical encoding (top down)

The following sections briefly discuss previous work on type inclusion tests. Subsequently, we describe our new method which uses graph coloring techniques to find nearly optimal set representations for types in a multiple inheritance hierarchy. Finally, we present experimental results which show that our new method is significantly better than the main competing method on three counts. It generates significantly shorter bit vectors, it computes the vectors faster, and it requires less working storage.

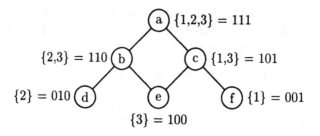

**Fig. 2.** Hierarchical encoding (bottom up)

## 2 Previous work

One 'obvious' algorithm for implementing the type inclusion test is that described by Wirth[Wir88]. To test if $x <: y$, the algorithm proceeds up the inheritance hierarchy starting from $x$ to see if $y$ is an ancestor. However, the algorithm does not run in constant time, which is a problem if the hierarchy becomes large, and the basic algorithm works only for single inheritance hierarchies. Generalizing the method to work with multiple inheritance, either by using backtracking or by constructing sets of parents, makes it slower still.

Another 'obvious' algorithm, and one which achieves a fast constant time test, is to use a precomputed matrix that records all possible relationships. An element $M[x,y]$ in the binary matrix holds a 1 if $x <: y$ and 0 otherwise. Although this implementation is used by some O-O languages, it has the drawback that the matrix can be very large. If there are 2000 types, the matrix will consume nearly 500 KB. (There are a number of schemes for compacting the matrix at the expense of making a look-up in the matrix much slower [DDH84].)

Cohen showed how the type inclusion test can be implemented in constant time using the concept of displays to precompute paths through the inheritance hierarchy[Coh91]. However, Cohen's method uses more memory than Wirth's and, in its original form, is applicable only to single inheritance hierarchies.

Caseau took a different path based on hierarchical top down encoding. He was inspired by a method originally developed for fast implementation of lattice operations [ABLN89] based on hierarchical bottom up encoding and adapted it to the type inclusion problem[Cas93]. Caseau's scheme computes a bit vector for each type. The bit vector represents a set of *genes*, where a gene is represented by a natural number. Each type that has only one parent in the hierarchy has an associated gene. A type with multiple parents has no associated gene. The bit vector for a type $T$ is computed as the set of all genes associated with itself and with all ancestors of $T$. Testing if $x <: y$ is implemented as a test to see if the set of genes for type $x$ is a superset of the set for $y$. Caseau's method requires that the type hierarchy be a lattice. This requirement may force extra nodes to be added to the hierarchy. Caseau gave an incremental algorithm for maintaining the lattice property and gave a backtracking technique for finding sets of genes and for updating previously computed sets of genes as the hierarchy is constructed in a top-down manner.

Problems with implementing Caseau's algorithm inspired us to develop our own method for finding sets of genes. We encountered situations where the Caseau algorithm produces incorrect results. Such an example is shown in figure 3. Even if we assume that the error can be corrected, Caseau's method for maintaining the lattice property may force the addition of an exponential number of additional nodes (and therefore also require exponential running time). The worst case is unlikely to occur in practice, but this is nevertheless undesirable behavior. We also discovered that the number of distinct genes used by Caseau's algorithm may be considerably more, sometimes by a factor of 4, than the optimal number. Since the number of genes determines the sizes of the bit vectors (and therefore determines the running time of the set inclusion test too), it is important to minimize the number.

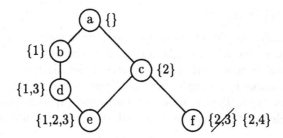

**Fig. 3.** An incorrect encoding produced by Caseau's algorithm

Habib and Nourine showed that constructing an optimal bit vector encoding for partially ordered sets is NP-hard [HN94]. They also showed in [HN94] and [HN96] that there exist some classes of lattices (distributive and simplicial lattices) where, for an optimal solution, all genes have to be different. For these classes of lattices, therefore, an optimal solution can be constructed in linear time. Partially ordered sets resulting from type hierarchies tend to be very different from distributive lattices, so their encodings are correspondingly an order of magnitude more compact.

## 3   Near optimal hierarchical encoding

Our near optimal hierarchical encoding algorithm is similar to Caseau's because it also relies on a top down encoding. But, unlike Caseau's algorithm, our algorithm does not require the hierarchy to have a lattice structure – it can encode any partially ordered set. We rely on balancing the height of the hierarchy and use graph coloring to find a near optimal solution. The algorithm was designed for fast execution (it has worst case quadratic run time complexity) for integration into compilers for object oriented programming languages with multiple inheritance or multiple subtyping. Instead of performing a full and slow search for optimal encodings, we have used simple heuristics to find a near optimal solution in a matter of seconds.

### 3.1 The basic algorithm

To make hierarchical encoding of partially ordered sets practical, we must avoid any restriction to lattice structures and thereby avoid the exponential behavior of lattice completion. We can easily eliminate such a restriction if we associate a gene (i.e. a distinguishing bit) with all nodes in the hierarchy. In contrast, Caseau's method associates a gene only with nodes that have a single parent. However, a better solution is to determine which nodes actually need a gene.

To find a correct hierarchical top down encoding, the following equation must be fulfilled in both directions:

$$x <: y \Leftrightarrow \gamma(x) \supseteq \gamma(y)$$

If a type with only one parent gets a gene and every type inherits all the genes of its super types, the left to right direction of the equation is fulfilled. The opposite direction is more difficult to achieve if the hierarchy is not a lattice. Consider the example hierarchy of figure 4. Types e and f both have more than one direct super type. Type e needs its own gene (4), otherwise its encoding would be included in the encoding of f – which wrongly would state that f is a subtype of e.

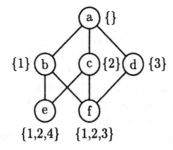

**Fig. 4.** Multiple inheritance type (e) needs a gene (4)

The solution to the problem is to give all types with multiple super types a gene if they would violate the above equation. So our algorithm just checks the above equation to determine which types require a gene. For the purpose of describing our algorithm, we first give some definitions:

| | |
|---|---|
| *parents(x)* | // all nodes which are a direct supertype of *x* |
| *children(x)* | // all nodes which are a direct subtype of *x* |
| *ancestors(x)* | // all nodes which are a supertype of *x* |
| *descendants(x)* | // all nodes which are a subtype of *x* |
| *singles* | // all nodes in the hierarchy with a single parent |
| *multis* | // all nodes with more than one parent |
| *needgenes* | // all nodes which need a gene |

All nodes $m \in singles$ need a gene and *needgenes* becomes *singles*. All nodes $m \in multis$ for which $\exists n \in multis$ and not $n <: m$ need a gene (and are added to *needgenes*) if

$$ancestors(m) \cap needgenes \subseteq ancestors(n).$$

For a correct hierarchical encoding it is not necessary for the genes to be distinct. Two genes can be the same if other genes ensure different encodings. For an example just take a hierarchy with two chains. The genes in one chain can be the same as in the other chain. Only the topmost node in each chain must be different to ensure correct encoding. In the hierarchy in figure 1, the genes of d and f can be the same. The different genes for b and c ensure a correct encoding.

Our algorithm determines which nodes cannot use the same genes. For each node, the set of conflicting nodes is determined and a conflict graph is constructed. An edge in the conflict graph means that two nodes are not allowed to use the same gene.

The conflict graph is constructed as follows:

- Every node conflicts with all descendants of its parents.
- In addition, a node $N$ conflicts with all ancestors of any descendants of $N$'s parents if these descendants are not descendants of $N$.

A correctness proof for the conflicting genes can be found in [Cas93]. It has to be modified slightly, since Caseau missed some cases for the second class of conflicts. The following pseudocode gives a more formal description of conflict graph computation.

```
for each x ∈ hierarchy do
    parx := parents(x)
    if parx = {} then parx := {x}
    for each y ∈ descendants(p), y ≠ x, ∀p ∈ parx do
        enter conflict between x and y in conflict graph
```

**if** $y \in multis, \neg(y <: x)$ **then**
$\quad \forall anc \in ancestors(y), anc \neq y$, enter conflict between
$\quad \quad x$ and $anc$ in conflict graph

After the conflict graph has been constructed, graph coloring is used to find a solution to the gene assignment problem. The hierarchical code for a node is then computed as the union of the genes for all its ancestors and for itself.

A better, near optimal, solution can be found if sets of children are subdivided and the hierarchy is *balanced* before the conflict sets are computed. The next two subsections describe both coloring and balancing in some detail. The main steps of the encoding algorithm are as follows (complete pseudocode can be found in the appendix).

mark all nodes in hierarchy which need a gene
split children lists and balance the hierarchy
compute conflict graph
color the conflict graph
compute code

## 3.2   Coloring the conflict graph

Computing the chromatic number of a graph (determining the minimal number of colors needed to color vertices of the graph) is a NP-complete problem. There exist backtracking algorithms which can compute the chromatic number for very small graphs (up to 100 vertices), there are probabilistic algorithms with almost polynomial run time [EL89] and there are genetic, tabu and hybrid algorithms for graph coloring [FF95]. But all these algorithms are unusable for the large conflict graphs which we must construct for type hierarchies. The graphs may have 2000 vertices and 200000 edges (see table 6).

There is, however, a class of very fast heuristic algorithms which give good results on most graphs and are used, for example, in graph coloring register allocators [BCKT93]. These sequential vertex coloring algorithms [MMI72] have a run time which is linear in the number of vertices plus the number of edges in the conflict graph [MB83]. All these algorithms order the vertices according to some predetermined criteria and color the vertices in this order. If no color, out of those used so far, can be reused for the current vertex, the number of colors is increased by one and the vertex is assigned the new color. Otherwise, one of the existing colors, one which does not cause a conflict for the current vertex, is selected.

[MMI72] presents two algorithms which give the best results: *largest degree first* ordering and *smallest degree last* ordering. *Largest degree first* ordering sorts the vertices by the vertex degree (number of edges from the vertex) and starts coloring with the vertex with the largest degree. *Smallest degree last* ordering recursively removes the vertex with the smallest degree together with all its edges from the graph and colors the vertices in reverse order of removal. Often the *smallest degree last* algorithm gives the best results.

Another possibility is to construct a vertex order from the structure of the hierarchy. The simplest order is generated by a top down, depth-first, traversal of the hierarchy. A different order is based on a topologically sorted order. Here, the top down traversal is modified so that it descends to a node $N$ in the hierarchy only if all parents of $N$ have already been visited. This traversal visits the nodes in an order similar to that assumed by Caseau in his algorithm. We will refer to this order as the *Caseau order*. An evaluation of all these algorithms shows that the *smallest degree last* algorithm gives the best results (see section 4 table 4). For many hierarchies, this algorithm finds an optimal result.

There are different strategies for choosing which color to reuse for the current vertex. If the colors are numbered in order of first use, two simple strategies are to use the color with (1) the smallest number or (2) the largest number. Another strategy is to choose the most heavily used color which does not cause a conflict. Table 5 in section 4 shows some results using these strategies. The strategy that selects the most used color weighted by the degree of the node often gave the best results in our experiments. Since there is no consistent winner, a mixed strategy which tries more than one method and then picks the best result might be appropriate.

In [MB83], an improvement to sequential vertex coloring is presented. If there is no unused color available, an color exchange is tried. First all conflicting colors are collected which conflict only once with the vertex to color. Then there is a search for a vertex which is not in conflict with one of these collected vertices and the new vertex. If such a vertex can be found, the colors can be exchanged and the new vertex can be colored. Unfortunately, we found that this color exchange strategy fails with the conflict graphs constructed for our type hierarchies. Our graphs tend to have so many edges that there are no nodes which can be exchanged. We assume the reason is that nodes near the top of the hierarchy conflict with nearly all nodes.

## 3.3 Splitting and balancing the hierarchy

Caseau noted in [Cas93] that the number of bits needed for hierarchical encoding is greatly influenced by the number of children at a node. If a node has $k$ children, then $k$ distinct genes are immediately needed to distinguish these children. To reduce this number when $k$ is large, we can either use more than one gene to distinguish the different children or we can split the children into smaller groups by adding additional nodes to the hierarchy. Using more bits to identify a type complicates the algorithm and makes it difficult to find a near optimal solution. Therefore, whenever a node had more than 8 children, Caseau split them into two groups and introduced two additional nodes as parents for those groups.

Repeatedly applying this technique reduces the total number of genes needed, but it far from being an optimal strategy.

We also use the idea of splitting children into groups but we attempt to balance the hierarchy when inserting new nodes. A lower bound on the number of genes needed for hierarchical encoding may be constructed as maximum over all weighted path lengths from the root node to a leaf node. The path length for a leaf node is

$$\sum |children(N)|$$

where $children(N)$ is the set of child nodes for node $N$, and the sum is made over all nodes $N$ on the longest path from the root node to the leaf node. Only child nodes which need a gene are counted for the path length. For hierarchies which are trees, the largest path length also provides the optimal solution. An optimal solution for the hierarchical encoding of trees can be constructed by splitting children lists and generating a balanced binary tree which minimizes the path length. A bottom-up algorithm can be used to balance the tree. The example in figure 5 shows the number of genes needed being reduced from 5 to 4 by balancing.

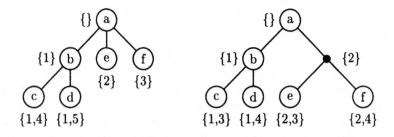

**Fig. 5.** Balancing a tree

An optimal balancing algorithm appears to be feasible only for tree-structured hierarchies. With multiple subtyping, the hierarchy has to be balanced to generate the minimal chromatic number for its conflict graph. Since computing the minimal chromatic number is NP-complete, the balancing problem is very likely to be NP-complete too. We therefore looked for a heuristic solution. In practice, most multiple subtyping hierarchies deviate only slightly from a tree structure. Heuristics based on the tree balancing method work satisfactorily when taking into account the characteristics of multiple inheritance hierarchies.

If we are balancing a tree, splitting the children into two groups can be performed arbitrarily. In the multiple subtyping case, children which share some common descendants should be assigned to the same group. If we did not do that, coloring is made harder because these common descendants would gain an additional parent node.

The splitting process is faster if it is performed in two stages. A 'presplitting' pass repeatedly performs a heuristic split into two groups and adds two parent nodes until the groups are smaller than a certain limit (currently 14 nodes) using precomputed path lengths. The second pass recomputes the path lengths after every split and does a more complicated split inserting one or two nodes.

The presplitting pass computes an optimistic path length for every leaf node. These optimistic path lengths are computed assuming fewer than three children per node. It is assumed that the hierarchy can be balanced without introducing nodes on the critical path. A leaf node's path length is propagated together with an unique number to all ancestors of the leaf node. During the propagation, larger path lengths overwrite smaller ones. Furthermore the set of all descendants of a node are computed as a bit vector. Using these sets, children which are detected to have overlapping descendant sets are placed in the same bucket. All children lists are sorted according to three criteria. The primary criterion is by bucket, the secondary criterion is by leaf nodes, and the third by the size of the path length. Then every list of children which is longer than the limit is split into two parts so that the lengths of both lists are smaller than the largest power of two which is smaller than the original length of the list.

The second splitting pass precomputes the correct path length after every split, and uses the sum of all children which need a gene on the path from the root to a leaf. The leaf's path length is again propagated to all ancestors. Then the ancestors of the leaf node with the largest path length are checked for a children list to split. This splitting takes care that ancestors of the leaf node are in the same list after splitting. The path lengths of the nodes are also taken into account and, depending on the circumstances, either one or two new nodes are inserted.

## 3.4  Space and time complexity

A careful implementation of the algorithm needs 19 milliseconds for the smallest hierarchy and 2 seconds for the largest hierarchy when encoding the hierarchy on an Alpha workstation with a 500MHz 21164a processor. The worst-case time complexity of the algorithm is quadratic. The average complexity is lower and depends on the number of edges in the conflict graph. The marking part is quadratic in the number of nodes that have more than one parent (i.e. the size of *multis*). Each splitting step during balancing is linear in the number of nodes, but since the number of nodes can be doubled this also implies quadratic complexity. Coloring is linear in the sum of nodes and edges in the conflict graph [MB83]. The number of edges is limited by the number of nodes squared, but usually is about twice as large as the average number of ancestors times the number of nodes. Table 1 shows the proportion of the total run time spent on each of the algorithm's subtasks (encoding the Geode hierarchy).

The space cost is dominated by the storage needed for the conflict graph. The graph is stored in two representations. One is a bit vector to provide a fast

| input management | marking | splitting | | conflict graph | graph coloring |
|:---:|:---:|:---:|:---:|:---:|:---:|
| | | pre | final | | |
| 6.6% | 6.2% | 3.1% | 58.4% | 21.3% | 4.4% |

**Table 1.** Execution profile of the encoding algorithm

check to see if a conflict has already been entered in the graph. The second is a list representation that allows fast sequential access to conflicting nodes. If space is a concern, computation time can be traded for space. It is not necessary to store the conflict graph – it can be computed twice. Initially, only the degree for each node is stored, and then the nodes are sorted according to decreasing degree. Subsequently, the conflicts are computed for each node and immediately colored. This increases the time, but reduces space requirements.

### 3.5   Incremental algorithm

The algorithm as presented above is not suited for incremental computation of the encoding bit vector. But if slightly worse encodings are accepted, it can be modified for incremental computation. An incremental algorithm can only be implemented in a top down manner where all super types of an added type have to belong to the hierarchy already. The main difficulties are that the size of the encoding could grow from one machine word to two (or from two words to three, and so on), as well as the space consumption and execution time consumption caused by a recomputation of the encoding, if the balancing or encoding changes.

The problem caused by increasing the number of machine words can be solved by linking at run time with different type checking subroutines which work for one, two, three or more machine words.

The current algorithm stores the complete bit matrix for fast computation of type inclusion tests. Additionally, ancestors sets and descendants sets are stored for faster determination of which nodes need a gene and for faster balancing. In an incremental algorithm, fast type inclusion can be performed using the bit vector encodings. Also the test whether a type with more than one super type needs its own gene can be performed using bit vector encodings instead of ancestor sets. Balancing could be replaced by a simpler splitting process which ignores the depth of the tree. Coloring could be carried out using an algorithm similar to the one proposed by Caseau.

## 4   Results

This last section evaluates different aspects of the algorithm and compares the performance of the algorithm with other approaches. As test data, we used a collection of class libraries compiled by Karel Driesen. We also obtained the Laure type hierarchy from Yves Caseau [Cas93] and the Java API library from Sun [GYT96]. Table 2 presents the relevant characteristics of those libraries. The number of classes varies from 225 to 1956, representing both big applications and libraries. The depth of the hierarchy ranges from 7 to 18. The first four libraries use single inheritance only; the others use multiple inheritance with up to 16 parents per class. Except for the three programs written in LOV (a language similar to Eiffel), the average number of parents is close to one. For the three LOV programs the average number of parents is close to two.

| library name | language | classes | depth | max parents | avg. parents |
|---|---|---|---|---|---|
| Visualworks2 | Smalltalk-80 | 1956 | 15 | 1 | 1 |
| digitalk3 | Smalltalk-80 | 1357 | 14 | 1 | 1 |
| NeXTStep | Objective-C | 311 | 8 | 1 | 1 |
| ET++ | C++ | 371 | 9 | 1 | 1 |
| Unidraw | C++ | 614 | 10 | 2 | 1.01 |
| Self | Self | 1802 | 18 | 9 | 1.05 |
| Geode | LOV(Eiffel) | 1319 | 14 | 16 | 1.89 |
| Ed | LOV(Eiffel) | 434 | 11 | 7 | 1.66 |
| LOV | LOV(Eiffel) | 436 | 10 | 10 | 1.71 |
| Laure | Laure | 295 | 12 | 3 | 1.07 |
| Java | Java | 225 | 7 | 3 | 1.04 |

**Table 2.** Hierarchy characteristics

Table 3 shows the main result, the number of bits needed for the encoding using three different splitting strategies combined with two different coloring strategies. The first two columns show the number of genes needed for encoding the original hierarchy. The next two columns show the genes needed for a hierarchy where all classes with more than 8 children have been replaced by a class that has two new classes as children, each having one half of the children of the original class. The last two columns show the results for a balanced hierarchy using the balancing algorithm described in the previous section. The two sequential coloring techniques use an ordering similar to that used by Caseau (top down after all parents of a class have been colored) and the smallest degree last ordering. Note that Caseau's algorithm cannot directly encode all our hierarchies because it requires every hierarchy to be a lattice; we only color the classes in a sequence which is similar to the ordering of his algorithm. To compare Caseau's results with ours, it is necessary to compare the column *Caseau* of *max 8 children* with the last column. Our algorithm can reduce the sizes of the encodings to one quarter of those produced by Caseau's algorithm.

Table 4 gives the performance using six different sequential coloring tech-

| benchmark | original hierarchy | | max 8 children | | balanced hierarchy | |
|---|---|---|---|---|---|---|
| | Caseau | smallest last | Caseau | smallest last | Caseau | smallest last |
| Visualworks2 | 420 | 420 | 124 | 124 | 50 | 50 |
| digitalk3 | 325 | 325 | 116 | 116 | 36 | 36 |
| NeXTStep | 177 | 177 | 92 | 92 | 23 | 23 |
| ET++ | 181 | 181 | 61 | 61 | 30 | 30 |
| Unidraw | 227 | 227 | 96 | 96 | 30 | 30 |
| Self | 297 | 297 | 180 | 180 | 55 | 53 |
| Geode | 404 | 403 | 231 | 228 | 110 | 95 |
| Ed | 128 | 126 | 90 | 80 | 62 | 54 |
| LOV | 130 | 127 | 92 | 86 | 68 | 57 |
| Laure | 34 | 33 | 34 | 33 | 23 | 23 |
| Java | 97 | 97 | 50 | 50 | 22 | 19 |

**Table 3.** Bit count of Caseau and near optimal coloring for different balanced hierarchies

niques. The first column (smallest first) is the worst ordering; it starts with the class which has the smallest degree (the smallest number of conflicting classes). Random ordering takes the classes in the order they are read in. Top down ordering traverses the hierarchy in a depth first manner from the root node down to the leaf nodes. The Caseau ordering also traverses the hierarchy top down, but it colors a class only after all parent classes have been colored. Largest degree first and smallest degree last are the orderings suggested by Matula [MMI72] and give the best results for our conflict graphs. The *lower bound* column gives an estimate for the lower bound using the largest path length as described in the previous section. This estimate is quite accurate for tree-like hierarchies but is only approximate for other hierarchies. In many cases, coloring needs the same number of colors as estimated by the lower bound and this shows that an optimal solution has been found. It is evident that conflict graphs resulting from single inheritance hierarchies can be colored optimally regardless of the algorithm used.

The quality of a sequential coloring algorithm not only depends on the ordering of the vertices but also on the color chosen if there is a choice of more than one non-conflicting color to reuse. The *last use coloring method* sorts the colors by their last uses and takes the first used color which does not conflict. The *largest coloring method* selects the color with the largest number while the *smallest coloring method* selects the color with the smallest number. The best color selection algorithms are based on an assumption that preferring a color which is heavily used should produce fewer conflicts later on. The *max use coloring method* counts the number of uses of each color and takes the most used one. The last two algorithms weight the use by the degree of the class. The *max sdl coloring method* weights the use count by the removal degree obtained by

| benchmark | smallest first | random | top down | Caseau | largest first | smallest last | lower bound |
|---|---|---|---|---|---|---|---|
| Visualworks2 | 50 | 50 | 50 | 50 | 50 | 50 | 50 |
| digitalk3 | 36 | 36 | 36 | 36 | 36 | 36 | 36 |
| NeXTStep | 23 | 23 | 23 | 23 | 23 | 23 | 23 |
| ET++ | 30 | 30 | 30 | 30 | 30 | 30 | 30 |
| Unidraw | 30 | 30 | 30 | 30 | 30 | 30 | 30 |
| Self | 60 | 57 | 56 | 55 | 53 | 53 | 47 |
| Geode | 140 | 122 | 120 | 110 | 99 | 95 | 42 |
| Ed | 84 | 72 | 68 | 62 | 57 | 54 | 30 |
| LOV | 86 | 73 | 79 | 68 | 59 | 57 | 31 |
| Laure | 24 | 25 | 23 | 23 | 23 | 23 | 23 |
| Java | 22 | 22 | 22 | 22 | 19 | 19 | 19 |

**Table 4.** Bit count of different coloring techniques

the *smallest degree last* ordering, and the *max ldf coloring method* weights the use count by the unmodified degree. The *smallest* coloring method and the three *max use* methods sometimes give different best results. Because the computation time for a coloring is small compared to the time needed to construct the conflict graph, it makes sense to try all four algorithms and take the best result.

| benchmark | last use color | largest color | smallest color | max use color | max sdl color | max ldf color |
|---|---|---|---|---|---|---|
| Visualworks2 | 50 | 50 | 50 | 50 | 50 | 50 |
| digitalk3 | 36 | 36 | 36 | 36 | 36 | 36 |
| NeXTStep | 23 | 23 | 23 | 23 | 23 | 23 |
| ET++ | 30 | 30 | 30 | 30 | 30 | 30 |
| Unidraw | 30 | 30 | 30 | 30 | 30 | 30 |
| Self | 54 | 53 | 54 | 54 | 53 | 54 |
| Geode | 97 | 97 | 95 | 95 | 97 | 95 |
| Ed | 56 | 56 | 55 | 56 | 56 | 54 |
| LOV | 60 | 62 | 59 | 61 | 62 | 57 |
| Laure | 23 | 23 | 23 | 23 | 23 | 23 |
| Java | 19 | 19 | 19 | 19 | 19 | 19 |

**Table 5.** Bit count of different color choosing techniques

Table 6 gives more data on the characteristics of the different type hierarchies with respect to the algorithm. It is evident that in most hierarchies the number

of types which need their own gene is small compared to the number of types
with multiple super types. The only exceptions are the three LOV hierarchies,
where half the types need their own gene. The column *balancing nodes* shows also
that the most added balancing nodes were needed for the Geode hierarchy. The
number of conflict edges increases if there is a higher use of multiple inheritance.
Computations of the encodings have been performed on an Alpha workstation
with a 500MHz 21164a processor. All computation times are in milliseconds.

| benchmark | type number | singles | multis | need gene | balancing nodes | conflict nodes | conflict edges | computaion time (ms) |
|---|---|---|---|---|---|---|---|---|
| Visualworks2 | 1965 | 1965 | 0 | 0 | 388 | 2353 | 62394 | 890 |
| digitalk3 | 1357 | 1357 | 0 | 0 | 298 | 1655 | 37871 | 426 |
| NeXTStep | 311 | 311 | 0 | 0 | 103 | 414 | 6141 | 30 |
| ET++ | 371 | 371 | 0 | 0 | 94 | 465 | 7997 | 39 |
| Unidraw | 614 | 604 | 10 | 4 | 164 | 772 | 13541 | 93 |
| Self | 1802 | 1741 | 61 | 22 | 465 | 2228 | 113489 | 1367 |
| Geode | 1319 | 614 | 705 | 384 | 796 | 1794 | 149052 | 1902 |
| Ed | 434 | 272 | 162 | 68 | 198 | 538 | 26885 | 136 |
| LOV | 436 | 271 | 165 | 70 | 217 | 558 | 30428 | 168 |
| Laure | 295 | 275 | 20 | 0 | 29 | 304 | 4823 | 21 |
| Java | 225 | 216 | 9 | 1 | 63 | 280 | 3509 | 19 |

**Table 6.** Complexity data of hierarchies

We compared the size of the tables resulting from a bit matrix representation
of the transitive closure of the subtype relation with our encoding (table 7). The
size of the table can be reduced by a factor of up to 31 for the test hierarchies.
The size of the bit matrix encoding increases by $n^2$ with the number of types. The
size of the bit vector encoding (for a hierarchy which is a balanced binary tree)
encreases by $2 * n \log n$. If the multiple inheritance portion is low, our algorithm
comes close to the logarithmic size increase.

## 5 Conclusion

We have presented a near optimal algorithm for finding hierarchical encodings
for type hierarchies. Our algorithm produces encodings which are up to four
times shorter than encodings generated by a previous algorithm (Caseau) and
therefore provide a faster type inclusion check for object oriented languages with
multiple subtyping. The algorithm is also an order of magnitude faster than the
previous algorithm which makes it practical for use in compilers. To evaluate

| benchmark | size of bit matrix | size of codes | reduction factor |
|---|---|---|---|
| Visualworks2 | 485.3 | 16.0 | 31 |
| digitalk3 | 233.4 | 11.0 | 21 |
| NeXTStep | 12.4 | 1.2 | 10 |
| ET++ | 17.8 | 1.4 | 12 |
| Unidraw | 49.1 | 2.4 | 20 |
| Self | 410.8 | 14.7 | 28 |
| Geode | 221.5 | 15.9 | 14 |
| Ed | 24.3 | 3.4 | 7 |
| LOV | 24.4 | 3.4 | 7 |
| Laure | 11.8 | 1.1 | 10 |
| Java | 7.2 | 0.9 | 8 |

**Table 7.** Table sizes and reduction factor

our algorithm, the complete source code can be obtained via world wide web at http://www.complang.tuwien.ac.at/andi/typecheck/.

# References

[ABLN89] Hassan Aït-Kaci, Robert Boyer, Patrick Lincoln, and Roger Nasr. Efficient implementation of lattice operations. *ACM Transactions on Programming Languages and Systems*, 11(1):115–146, 1989.

[BCKT93] Preston Briggs, Keith Cooper, Ken Kennedy, and Linda Torczon. Coloring heuristics for register allocation. In *ACM Conference on Programming Language Design and Implementation*, pages 275–284, Portland, June 1993. ACM.

[Cas93] Yves Caseau. Efficient handling of multiple inheritance hierarchies. In *Conference on Object Oriented Programming Systems, Languages & Applications*, pages 271–287, Washington, October 1993. ACM.

[Coh91] Norman H. Cohen. Type-extension type tests can be performed in constant time. *ACM Transactions on Programming Languages and Systems*, 13(4):626–629, 1991.

[DDH84] Peter Dencker, Karl Dürre, and Johannes Heuft. Optimization of parser tables for portable compilers. *ACM Transactions on Programming Languages and Systems*, 6(6):546–572, 1984.

[EL89] J. A. Ellis and P. M. Lepolesa. A Las Vegas graph coloring algorithm. *The Computer Journal*, 32(5):474–476, 1989.

[FF95] Charles Fleurent and Jacques A. Ferland. Genetic and hybrid algorithms for graph coloring. *Annals of Operations Research*, page to appear, 1995.

[GYT96] James Gosling, Frank Yellin, and The Java Team. *The Java Application Programming Interface*. Addison-Weley, 1996.

[HN94] Michel Habib and Lhouari Nourine. Bit-vector encoding for partially ordered sets. In *ORDAL'94*, LNCS 831, pages 1–12. Springer, 1994.

[HN96]    Michel Habib and Lhouari Nourine. Tree structure for distributive lattices and its applications. *Theoretical Computer Science*, 165:391–405, 1996.

[MB83]    David W. Matula and Leland L. Beck. Smallest-last ordering and clustering and graph coloring algorithms. *Journal of the ACM*, 30(3):417–427, July 1983.

[MMI72]    David W. Matula, George Marble, and Joel D. Isaacson. Graph coloring algorithms. In R. C. Read, editor, *Graph Theory and Computing*, pages 109–122. Academic Press, 1972.

[Wir88]    Niklaus Wirth. Type extensions. *ACM Transactions on Programming Languages and Systems*, 10(2):204–214, 1988.

# Appendix: the encoding algorithm

```
// definitions
parents(x)          // all nodes which are a direct supertype of x
children(x)         // all nodes which are a direct subtype of x
ancestors(x)        // all nodes which are a supertype of x
descendants(x)      // all nodes which are a subtype of x
mark(x)             // flag, is 1, if x need a distinguishing gene, 0 otherwise
length(x)           // longest path length between x and a leaf node
leaf(x)             // leaf node of the longest path which includes x
gene(x)             // gene number, bit position in bit vector
code(x)             // the bit vector of class x
singles             // all nodes in the hierarchy with a single parent
multis              // all nodes with more than one parent
needgenes           // all nodes which need a gene
```

```
// mark all nodes of hierarchy which need a bit
mark(s) := 1 ∀s ∈ singles
needgenes := singles
for each m ∈ multis do
    if ∃n ∈ multis, ¬(n <: m), ancestors(m) ∩ needgenes ⊆ ancestors(n)
    then mark(m) := 1, needgenes := needgenes ∪ {m}
    else mark(m) := 0
```

```
// balance the hierarchy
define compute_length(l ∈ Integer, leaf ∈ hierarchy, x ∈ hierarchy) as
    l := l + ∑ mark(childx), ∀childx ∈ children(x)
    for each parentx ∈ parents(x) do
        if length(parentx) < l then
            length(parentx) := l
            leaf(parentx) := leaf
            compute_length(l, leaf, parentx)
length(x) := −1 ∀x ∈ hierarchy
```

**for each** $leaf \in hierarchy, children(leaf) = \{\}$ **do**
    $length(leaf) := 0$
    $leaf(leaf) := leaf$
    $compute\_length(0, leaf, leaf)$
**for each** $x \in hierarchy, size(children(x)) > 2$ **do**
    split $children(x)$ and add one or two nodes to $hierarchy$
    if this is possible without increasing $length(y)$ for any $y \in hierarchy$

// compute conflict graph
**for each** $x \in hierarchy$ **do**
    $parx := parents(x)$
    **if** $parx = \{\}$ **then** $parx := \{x\}$
    **for each** $y \in descendants(p), y \neq x, \forall p \in parx$ **do**
        enter conflict between $x$ and $y$ in conflict graph
        **if** $y \in multis, \neg(y <: x)$ **then**
            $\forall anc \in ancestors(y), anc \neq y$, enter conflict between
            $x$ and $anc$ in conflict graph

// color the conflict graph
**for each** $x \in hierarchy$ in smallest degree last order **do**
    **if** $mark(x) = 1$ **then** $gene(x) :=$ the most used non conflicting gene

// compute code
**for each** $x \in hierarchy$ **do**
    $code(x) := \cup gene(ancx), \forall ancx \in ancestors(x)$

# An Extended Theory of Primitive Objects: First Order System

Luigi Liquori *

Dip. Informatica, Università di Torino, C.so Svizzera 185, I-10149 Torino, Italy
e-mail: liquori@di.unito.it

**Abstract.** We investigate a first-order extension of the Theory of Primitive Objects of [5] that supports *method extension* in presence of *object subsumption*. Extension is the ability of modifying the behavior of an object by adding new methods (and inheriting the existing ones). Object subsumption allows to use objects with a bigger interface in a context expecting another object with a smaller interface. This extended calculus has a sound type system which allows static detection of run-time errors such as *message-not-understood*, "width" subtyping and a typed equational theory on objects. Moreover, it can express classes and class-inheritance.

**Categories**: Type systems, design and semantics of object-oriented languages.

## 1  Introduction

The Abadi and Cardelli's Theory of Primitive Objects [3, 4, 5], supports method override, self-types, and (*self-type covariant*) "width" subtyping. No object extension is provided, since the objects have fixed size. In fact, the only operations allowed on objects are method invocation and method override. The objects are very simple, with just four syntactic forms, and without functions. The expressivity of the calculus is given via an encoding of the λ-calculus. The various fragments of this calculus have a sound type system that catches run-time errors such as *message-not-understood*, and a typed equational theory on objects.

The starting point of this paper is the first-order type system for the primitive object calculus, called $Obj1_{\prec:}$ [5]. We extend this calculus by allowing the dynamic addition and subsumption of methods, and we provide for a sound static type system and a typed equational theory on objects. We call this (conservative) extension $Obj1^+_{\prec:}$. The $Obj1^+_{\prec:}$ calculus allows a considerable number of programs to be typed that are not typable in $Obj1_{\prec:}$.

In this calculus, we distinguish between two "kinds" of objects-types, namely the *saturated* object-types, and the *diamond* object-types: if an object can be typed by a saturated object-type, then it can receive messages and override the methods that it contains. If an object can be typed by a diamond object-type, then it can receive messages, override some methods, and it can be extended

---

* Kindly supported by CSELT, Centro Studi e Laboratori Telecomunicazioni.

by new methods. On both types, a "width" subtyping relation is defined. This relation behaves differently depending on the shape of the object-type.

Summarizing, our calculus exhibits the following features:

- extendible objects with appropriate method specialization of inherited methods,
- static detection of run-time errors, such as *message-not-understood*,
- a "width" subtyping relation compatible with method extension,
- it can express classes and class-inheritance.

Moreover, the $Obj1^+_{\preceq:}$ type system can be extended with self-types by modeling the inheritance and the self-application semantics via *bounded universal polymorphism*. This (conservative w.r.t. $Obj1^+_{\preceq:}$) extension can be easily obtained with a very little cost with respect to the typing rules of $Obj1^+_{\preceq:}$ (see [16]).

This paper is organized as follows: in Section 2 we recall the untyped calculus of primitive objects, and we define the new calculus with method extension, its operational semantics and untyped equational theory. In Section 3 we present the first-order extension $Obj1^+_{\preceq:}$ with its typing and subtyping system. Section 4 is concerned with the type soundness and the typed equational theory on objects. A number of examples to give some intuition of the power of the extension are given in Section 5. Section 6 considers an interesting encoding of classes as objects that share a lot of similarities with the object-oriented language *Smalltalk-80* [15]. The last section is devoted to the comparison with the Lambda Calculus of Objects of [12] (and related papers [14, 10, 21, 9, 18, 8, 7]), Baby-Modula-3 of [1], and contains also open problems and the conclusions.

We assume that the reader is familiar with some object-oriented concepts such as delegation-based object calculi, type and subtype systems, self-types. Some knowledge of the seminal papers [12, 5] (and the above cited related papers) would be useful but not essential.

# 2　The Extended Primitive Calculus of Objects

## 2.1　The Abadi-Cardelli's Primitive Calculus

The untyped syntax of the Primitive Calculus of Objects is defined as follows:

$$o ::= s \mid [m_i = \varsigma(s_i)o_i]^{i \in I} \mid o.m \mid o.m \leftarrow \varsigma(s)o',$$

where in the term $[m_i = \varsigma(s_i)o_i]^{i \in I}$, $m_i$ $(i \in I)$ are method names, $o_i$ $(i \in I)$ are the bodies of methods, $s_i$ $(i \in I)$ are bound parameters referring to the object itself, and $\varsigma$ is a binder for the $s_i$. Hence, an object is an unordered collection of pairs of method-names and method-bodies. If $o$ reduces to $[m_i = \varsigma(s_i)o_i]^{i \in I}$, then the expression $o.m_i$ $(i \in I)$ stands for method invocation, and the expression $o.m_i \leftarrow \varsigma(s)o'$ $(i \in I)$ stands for method override. Let $o \triangleq [m_i = \varsigma(s_i)o_i]^{i \in I}$, and let $o\{s \leftarrow o'\}$ denote the substitution of the object $o'$ for the free occurrences of $s$ in $o$, and let, for $i, j \in I$, $m_i$ and $m_j$ be distinct methods. The operational semantics is defined as the reflexive, transitive and contextual closure of the reduction relation defined in Figure 1.

| | | | |
|---|---|---|---|
| (Select) | $o.m_j$ | $\overset{ev}{\to}\ o_j\{s_j\leftarrow o\}$ | $(j \in I)$ |
| (Override) | $o.m_j\!\leftarrow\!\varsigma(s_j)o'$ | $\overset{ev}{\to}\ [m_i = \varsigma(s_i)o_i, m_j = \varsigma(s_j)o']^{i\in I-\{j\}}$ | $(j \in I)$ |

Fig. 1. Operational Semantics for the Primitive Calculus

| | | | |
|---|---|---|---|
| (Select) | $o.m_j$ | $\overset{ev}{\to}\ o_j\{s_j\leftarrow o\}$ | $(j \in I)$ |
| (Override) | $o\!\leftarrow\!m_j = \varsigma(s_j)o'$ | $\overset{ev}{\to}\ [m_i = \varsigma(s_i)o_i, m_j = \varsigma(s_j)o']^{i\in I-\{j\}}$ | $(j \in I)$ |
| (Extend) | $o\!\leftarrow\!m_j = \varsigma(s_j)o'$ | $\overset{ev}{\to}\ [m_i = \varsigma(s_i)o_i, m_j = \varsigma(s_j)o']^{i\in I}$ | $(j \notin I)$ |

Fig. 2. Operational Semantics for the Extended Primitive Calculus

## 2.2 The Extended Abadi-Cardelli's Primitive Calculus

The Extended Calculus of Primitive Objects agrees with the following untyped syntax (which slightly differs from the one shown before):

$$o ::= s \mid [m_i = \varsigma(s_i)o_i]^{i\in I} \mid o.m \mid o\!\leftarrow\!m = \varsigma(s)o.$$

Here the $\leftarrow$ operator can be intended as an override or an extension operator according to whether the method $m$ belongs to the object $o$ or not. The semantics of the override and of the extension is functional: an override and an extension always produce another object where the overridden method has been replaced by the new body. Therefore, the operational semantics can be given as the reflexive, transitive and contextual closure of the reduction relation defined in Figure 2.

To send the message $m$ to the object $o$ means to substitute the object itself (i.e. $o$) in the body of $m$. As usual, we do not make error conditions explicit. We can derive an untyped equational theory from the reduction rules, by simply adding rules for symmetry, transitivity, and congruence, as shown in Figure 3.

Let $\overset{ev}{\twoheadrightarrow}$ be the general many-step reduction. The connection between equality $\overset{ev}{=}$ and reduction $\overset{ev}{\twoheadrightarrow}$ is given by the fact that the $\overset{ev}{\twoheadrightarrow}$ reduction rule satisfies the Church-Rosser property.

**Theorem 1 (Church-Rosser).**
   The relation $\overset{ev}{\twoheadrightarrow}$ is Church-Rosser, and if $\vdash o \overset{ev}{=} o'$, then there exists $o''$ such that $o \overset{ev}{\twoheadrightarrow} o''$ and $o' \overset{ev}{\twoheadrightarrow} o''$.

*Proof.* The proof is standard, following the method of Tait and Martin-Löf [6].

## 2.3 Evaluation Strategy

In this section, we define an evaluation strategy which is directly derived from that one defined in [5]. As usual the purpose of the reduction is to maps every

$$\frac{\vdash o_2 \stackrel{ev}{=} o_1}{\vdash o_1 \stackrel{ev}{=} o_2} \quad (Eq\text{--}Symm) \qquad \frac{\vdash o_1 \stackrel{ev}{=} o_2 \qquad \vdash o_2 \stackrel{ev}{=} o_3}{\vdash o_1 \stackrel{ev}{=} o_3} \quad (Eq\text{--}Trans)$$

$$\frac{}{\vdash s \stackrel{ev}{=} s} \quad (Eq\text{--}Var) \qquad \frac{\vdash o_i \stackrel{ev}{=} o_i' \qquad \forall i \in I}{\vdash [\mathtt{m}_i = \varsigma(s_i)o_i]^{i \in I} \stackrel{ev}{=} [\mathtt{m}_i = \varsigma(s_i)o_i']^{i \in I}} \quad (Eq\text{--}Obj)$$

$$\frac{\vdash o_1 \stackrel{ev}{=} o_2}{\vdash o_1.\mathtt{m} \stackrel{ev}{=} o_2.\mathtt{m}} \quad (Eq\text{--}Select) \qquad \frac{\vdash o_1 \stackrel{ev}{=} o_2 \qquad \vdash o' \stackrel{ev}{=} o''}{\vdash o_1 \leftarrow \mathtt{m} = \varsigma(s)o' \stackrel{ev}{=} o_2 \leftarrow \mathtt{m} = \varsigma(s)o''} \quad (Eq\text{--}Ext)$$

$$(\text{Let } o \stackrel{\triangle}{=} [\mathtt{m}_i = \varsigma(s_i)o_i]^{i \in I}) \qquad \frac{j \in I}{\vdash o.\mathtt{m}_j \stackrel{ev}{=} o_j\{s_j \leftarrow o\}} \quad (Eq\text{--}Select_{ev})$$

$$\frac{j \in I}{\vdash o \leftarrow \mathtt{m}_j = \varsigma(s_j)o' \stackrel{ev}{=} [\mathtt{m}_i = \varsigma(s_i)o_i, \mathtt{m}_j = \varsigma(s_j)o']^{i \in I - \{j\}}} \quad (Eq\text{--}Over_{ev})$$

$$\frac{j \notin I}{\vdash o \leftarrow \mathtt{m}_j = \varsigma(s_j)o' \stackrel{ev}{=} [\mathtt{m}_i = \varsigma(s_i)o_i, \mathtt{m}_j = \varsigma(s_j)o']^{i \in I}} \quad (Eq\text{--}Ext_{ev})$$

**Fig. 3.** Untyped Equational Theory for the Extended Primitive Calculus

closed expression into a normal form, i.e. an irreducible term (if we consider constants such as natural numbers we would naturally include them among the results). We define the set of results as follows:

$$v ::= [\mathtt{m}_i = \varsigma(s_i)o_i]^{i \in I} \mid wrong.$$

The result *wrong* denotes a run-time error which occurs when we send a message to an object which does not have any corresponding method, and therefore cannot respond to the message in question. The evaluation strategy *Outcome* is defined via a natural proof deduction system à la Plotkin [20] style and it is shown in Figure 4. The relation between $\stackrel{ev}{\twoheadrightarrow}$, $\stackrel{ev}{=}$ and *Outcome* is:

**Proposition 2 (Soundness of *Outcome*).**
   *If Outcome*$(o) = v$, and $v \not\equiv wrong$, then $o \stackrel{ev}{\twoheadrightarrow} v$, and $\vdash o \stackrel{ev}{=} v$.

*Proof.* By induction on the structure of the derivation of *Outcome*$(o)$.

   In Section 4 we will study the relations between the *Outcome* evaluation strategy and the objects typing, by showing the "Type Soundness", i.e. that every "well typed" program will not evaluate to the *wrong* result.

## 3   Types

The type system of the original Primitive Calculus of Objects is composed by several fragments, each necessary to give a correct type to different objects of

$$\frac{}{Outcome([\mathbf{m}_i = \varsigma(s_i)o_i]^{i \in I}) = [\mathbf{m}_i = \varsigma(s_i)o_i]^{i \in I}} \quad (Red\text{-}Obj)$$

$$\frac{Outcome(o) = [\mathbf{m}_i = \varsigma(s_i)o_i]^{i \in I} \quad Outcome(o_j\{s_j \leftarrow [\mathbf{m}_i = \varsigma(s_i)o_i]^{i \in I}\}) = v \quad j \in I}{Outcome(o.\mathbf{m}_j) = v} \quad (Red\text{-}Sel)$$

$$\frac{Outcome(o) = [\mathbf{m}_i = \varsigma(s_i)o_i]^{i \in I} \quad j \notin I}{Outcome(o \leftarrow \mathbf{m}_j = \varsigma(s_j)o') = [\mathbf{m}_i = \varsigma(s_i)o_i, \mathbf{m}_j = \varsigma(s_j)o']^{i \in I}} \quad (Red\text{-}Ext)$$

$$\frac{Outcome(o) = [\mathbf{m}_i = \varsigma(s_i)o_i]^{i \in I} \quad j \in I}{Outcome(o \leftarrow \mathbf{m}_j = \varsigma(s_j)o') = [\mathbf{m}_i = \varsigma(s_i)o_i, \mathbf{m}_j = \varsigma(s_j)o']^{i \in I - \{j\}}} \quad (Red\text{-}Over)$$

$$\frac{Outcome(o) = [\mathbf{m}_i = \varsigma(s_i)o_i]^{i \in I} \quad j \notin I}{Outcome(o.\mathbf{m}_j) = wrong} \quad (Red\text{-}Sel\text{-}Wrong)$$

$$\frac{Outcome(o') = wrong \quad o \equiv o'.\mathbf{m}_j \quad or \quad o \equiv o' \leftarrow \mathbf{m}_j = \varsigma(s_j)o''}{Outcome(o) = wrong} \quad (Red\text{-}Prop\text{-}Wrong)$$

**Fig. 4.** Evaluation Strategy for the Extended Primitive Calculus

this calculus. For example, to give a type to those objects which contain only methods whose results are not the object itself, a first-order fragment of the type system would suffice. On the other hand, to give a type to objects whose methods returns either *self* or an updated *self* (such as, for example, a **point** object with a **move** method), recursive-types are needed. Finally, in order to include a subsumption relation between objects, the authors extend this type system with existential-types [2]. Starting from the first-order calculus $\mathcal{O}bj1_{\prec:}$ [5], we extend its type system by allowing object-extension to be typed.

In the type system of $\mathcal{O}bj1_{\prec:}$, the object-types has the following form:

$$[\mathbf{m}_i : \sigma_i]^{i \in I},$$

where we assume that the $\mathbf{m}_i$ $(i \in I)$ be distinct and that permutations do not matter. When a method $\mathbf{m}_i$ is invoked, it produces a result having the corresponding type $\sigma_i$.

As clearly stated in [13, 4], subtyping is unsound when we allow objects to be extended. As a simple example of this problem, suppose to allow extension on objects and let

$$\mathbf{point} \triangleq [\mathbf{x} = \varsigma(s)1, \mathbf{y} = \varsigma(s)s.\mathbf{x}], \tag{1}$$

of type

$$\vdash \mathbf{point} : [\mathbf{x} : nat, \mathbf{y} : nat].$$

By subsumption (we allow for "width" subtyping, i.e. an object with some methods can be used in every context expecting an object with less methods) we get

$$\vdash \mathbf{point} : [\mathbf{y} : nat],$$

and by object extension we build another object

$$\mathbf{point'} \triangleq \mathbf{point} \mathbf{\leftarrow} \mathbf{x} = \varsigma(s) - 1,$$

of type

$$\vdash \mathbf{point'} : [\mathbf{x} : int, \mathbf{y} : nat],$$

which is obviously type-unsound, since

$$\mathbf{point'}.\mathbf{y} \overset{ev}{\rightarrow} [\mathbf{x} = \varsigma(s) - 1, \mathbf{y} = \varsigma(s)s.\mathbf{x}].\mathbf{y} \overset{ev}{\rightarrow} [\mathbf{x} = \varsigma(s) - 1, \mathbf{y} = \varsigma(s)s.\mathbf{x}].\mathbf{x} \overset{ev}{\rightarrow} -1,$$

with $\vdash \mathbf{point'}.\mathbf{y} : nat$, but $\nvdash -1 : nat$.

Therefore, we add in $\mathcal{O}bj1_{\preceq}^{+}$, another kind of object-type, that we call *diamond-type*, of the form:

$$[\mathbf{m}_i : \sigma_i \diamond \mathbf{m}_j : \sigma_j]_{j \in J}^{i \in I}.$$

The symbol $\diamond$ is used to distinguish the two parts of that object-type: the *interface-part* and the *subsumption-part*. The interface-part of a diamond-type describes all the methods (and their types) that may be invoked on the objects. The subsumption-part, instead, conveys information about (the types of) methods that are (or can be) subsumed in the type-checking phase. In fact, the subsumption-part lists (a superset of) the methods (and associated types) that can be "hidden" in the object.

Intuitively, a diamond-type $[\mathbf{m}_i : \sigma_i \diamond \mathbf{m}_j : \sigma_j]_{j \in J}^{i \in I}$ can be assigned to an object o with $\mathbf{m}_i$ and (some of the) $\mathbf{m}_j$ methods, and o responds only to the methods listed in the interface-part. Moreover, the object can be also extended with the $\mathbf{m}_j$ methods (of type $\sigma_j$) listed in the subsumption-part. At this regard, we observe that the addition of any "fresh" (i.e. unused) method $\mathbf{m}$ of type $\sigma$ is constrained to the prior introduction of $\mathbf{m} : \sigma$ in the subsumption-part of the diamond-type via an application of a subtyping rule (see Subsection 3.2).

Accordingly, the ordinary object-types $[\mathbf{m}_i : \sigma_i]^{i \in I}$ can be assigned to an object o which responds to $\mathbf{m}_i$ methods, and can be used in any context which does not extend the object o, but can override some methods, or send messages to them. In this way, ordinary object-types, here also called *saturated* object-types, can be assigned to objects which cannot be extended at all. Thus, we can distinguish two kinds of objects, with related object-types:

- objects which can be extended and overridden (typed by diamond-types of the shape $[\mathbf{m}_i : \sigma_i \diamond \mathbf{m}_j : \sigma_j]_{j \in J}^{i \in I}$);
- objects which can be only overridden (typed by saturated object-types of the shape $[\mathbf{m}_i : \sigma_i]^{i \in I}$).

Diamond-types allow to eliminate the unsoundness previously shown. In this calculus, the subsumption rule can "hides" a method by moving it from the interface-part to its subsumption-part, and a method $m$ of type $\sigma$ can be added to an object o only if $m : \sigma$ is contained in the subsumption-part of the diamond-type assigned to o. The usual type-inclusion between (extendible) points and colored points does not hold with diamond-types, i.e.

$$[\mathbf{x} : int, \mathbf{col} : colors \diamond] \not<: [\mathbf{x} : int \diamond]$$

(and this is sound because it is well known that subsumption is not allowed in presence of object-extension), but it holds instead (see the subtyping rules)

$$[\mathbf{x} : int, \mathbf{col} : colors] <: [\mathbf{x} : int]$$
$$[\mathbf{x} : int, \mathbf{col} : colors \diamond] <: [\mathbf{x} : int \diamond \mathbf{col} : colors]$$
$$[\mathbf{x} : int \diamond] <: [\mathbf{x} : int \diamond \mathbf{col} : colors]$$
$$[\mathbf{x} : int \diamond] <: [\mathbf{x} : int].$$

The first type-inclusion gives us the desired property of using a (non extendible) colored point in any context expecting a (non extendible) ordinary point, whereas the second one is necessary for method hiding in presence of object-extension. The third inclusion ensure that an object can be extended with a new (unused) method. The last inclusion says that a diamond-type with empty subsumption-part can be also considered as a saturated object-type (this property will be generalized in the subsumption rules also to diamond-types with non empty subsumption-part).

For instance, if we take the context $[\langle\,\rangle \leftarrow \mathbf{col} = \varsigma(s)red]$, then the "hole" $\langle\,\rangle$ can be filled both by a (color extensible) point object (in this case $\leftarrow$ denotes method extension) and by a colored point object (where $\leftarrow$ denotes method override).

As such, we can derive for the above (extendible) object $\mathbf{point}$ (1)

$$\vdash \mathbf{point} : [\mathbf{x} : nat, \mathbf{y} : nat \diamond],$$

and hence, by subsumption, $\vdash \mathbf{point} : [\mathbf{y} : nat \diamond \mathbf{x} : nat]$, but we cannot derive $\vdash \mathbf{point} \leftarrow \mathbf{x} = \varsigma(s) - 1 : [\mathbf{x} : int, \mathbf{y} : nat \diamond]$, since the typing of the method $\mathbf{x}$ does not satisfy the typing inside the subsumption-part of the diamond-type in question.

## 3.1 Types, Contexts, and Judgments

The set of types in $\mathcal{O}bj1^+_{<:}$ is defined by the following grammar:

$$\sigma, \tau ::= \omega \mid [m_i : \sigma_i \diamond m_j : \sigma_j]^{i \in I}_{j \in J} \mid [m_i : \sigma_i]^{i \in I}.$$

We omit how to encode basic data-types and function-types, which can be treated as in [5][1]. The type-constant $\omega$ is the supertype of every type.

---

[1] An arrow-types $\sigma \to \tau$ is codified in the object-type $[\mathbf{arg} : \sigma, \mathbf{val} : \tau]$.

We require that, in the diamond-type $[\mathbf{m}_i : \sigma_i \diamond \mathbf{m}_j : \sigma_j]_{j \in J}^{i \in I}$, the $\mathbf{m}_i$ with $i \in I$ (resp. $\mathbf{m}_j$ with $j \in J$) are distinct, and the interface- and the subsumption-parts be *disjoint* $(I \cap J = \emptyset)$, i.e. methods occurring in the former part are not occurring in the latter and vice-versa. The judgments have the following forms:

$$\Gamma \vdash ok, \qquad \Gamma \vdash \sigma, \qquad \Gamma \vdash \mathbf{o} : \sigma, \qquad \Gamma \vdash \sigma <: \tau,$$

where $\Gamma$ is a context which gives types to the free variables of $\mathbf{o}$, generated by the following grammar:

$$\Gamma \ ::= \ \varepsilon \mid \Gamma, s : \sigma.$$

By deriving the first two judgments we check the well-formation of the context $\Gamma$ and of the type $\sigma$, respectively, while with the third one we assign a type $\sigma$ to the expression $\mathbf{o}$. The last judgment is the usual subtyping judgment between types. We also decorate the language with types as follows:

$$\mathbf{o} \ ::= \ s \mid [\mathbf{m}_i = \varsigma(s_i{:}\sigma_i)\mathbf{o}_i]^{i \in I} \mid \mathbf{o}.\mathbf{m} \mid \mathbf{o} {\leftarrow} \mathbf{m} = \varsigma(s{:}\sigma)\mathbf{o}.$$

## 3.2 Subtyping

The subtyping relation allows to use an object of type $\sigma$ in any context expecting an object of type $\tau$, provided that $\sigma <: \tau$. The subsumption rule for objects

$$\frac{\Gamma \vdash \mathbf{o} : \sigma \qquad \Gamma \vdash \sigma <: \tau}{\Gamma \vdash \mathbf{o} : \tau} \quad (<:)$$

allows an object with more methods to be used in every place where an object with less methods is required. The most important subtyping rules are presented in Figure 5 (see Appendix for the full set of rules).

The $(Shift_\diamond)$ rule says that we can "hide" a method which belongs to the interface-part simply by moving it into the subsumption-part of the diamond-type. This rule is needed when we know that the hidden method will be added again. This subtyping rule allows to use subsumption over extendible objects.

The $(Extend_\diamond)$ rule says that an object with smaller subsumption-part can be used in any context which expects an object with a bigger subsumption-part. This rule is crucial to ensure that an object can be dynamically extended with fresh methods.

The $(Sat_\diamond)$ rule says that a diamond-type becomes a saturated object-type preserving only the methods in the interface-part. When this rule is applied, the "extendible" object to which is assigned a saturated object-type becomes a "non-extendible" one.

The $(Width)$ rule hides a method from the interface-part of the saturated object-type in question. Note that, when a method is hidden by using this rule, the hidden method cannot be recovered. We stress, again, that when a saturated object-type is assigned to an object, that object cannot be extended, but it can be used, subsumed and overridden. This subtyping rule correspond to the ordinary subtyping for objects of [5].

$$\frac{\Gamma \vdash [m_i : \sigma_i \diamond m_j : \sigma_j]_{j \in J}^{i \in I+K}}{\Gamma \vdash [m_i : \sigma_i \diamond m_j : \sigma_j]_{j \in J}^{i \in I+K} <: [m_i : \sigma_i \diamond m_j : \sigma_j]_{j \in J+K}^{i \in I}} \quad (Shift_\diamond)$$

$$\frac{\Gamma \vdash [m_i : \sigma_i \diamond m_j : \sigma_j]_{j \in J+K}^{i \in I}}{\Gamma \vdash [m_i : \sigma_i \diamond m_j : \sigma_j]_{j \in J}^{i \in I} <: [m_i : \sigma_i \diamond m_j : \sigma_j]_{j \in J+K}^{i \in I}} \quad (Extend_\diamond)$$

$$\frac{\Gamma \vdash [m_i : \sigma_i \diamond m_j : \sigma_j]_{j \in J}^{i \in I}}{\Gamma \vdash [m_i : \sigma_i \diamond m_j : \sigma_j]_{j \in J}^{i \in I} <: [m_i : \sigma_i]^{i \in I}} \quad (Sat_\diamond)$$

$$\frac{\Gamma \vdash [m_i : \sigma_i]^{i \in I+J}}{\Gamma \vdash [m_i : \sigma_i]^{i \in I+J} <: [m_i : \sigma_i]^{i \in I}} \quad (Width)$$

**Fig. 5.** Main Subtyping Rules for $\mathcal{O}bj1_{<:}^+$.

## 3.3 Typing

The main typing rules are shown in Figure 6 where we assume that when $i, j \in I$, $m_i \neq m_j$ (see Appendix for the full set of rules). In addition to these rules, we have also rules for well-formation of contexts. By inspecting the typing rules, one can see that the (*Object*) rule is the same as in $\mathcal{O}bj1_{<:}$ when we let $H_i \stackrel{set}{=} I$, and $[m_i : \sigma_i \diamond]^{i \in I} \triangleq [m_i : \sigma_i]^{i \in I}$ (in fact, in the original calculus, we can build only "fixed-size" objects). Also the (*Over*) rule is the same as in $\mathcal{O}bj1_{<:}$ if we assume $\tau \equiv [m_i : \sigma_i]^{i \in I}$. As such, $\mathcal{O}bj1_{<:}^+$ is a proper extension of $\mathcal{O}bj1_{<:}$. We only explain the (*Ext*) rule, the new one; firstly, one can see that we cannot extend an object whose object-type is saturated. Secondly, this rule allows one to extend an object with a new method if and only if that method is present in the subsumption-part of the diamond-type assigned to the object to be extended. But this condition can always be satisfied by a diamond-type thanks to the subtyping rule (*Extend*$_\diamond$). Finally, observe that this rule handles also the case where the method belongs to $\diamond$ but it has been already subsumed.

An important difference with [5] is that here the $\varsigma$-bound variables $s_i$ (referring to *self*) in the same object $\diamond$ can have different saturated object-types. This fits well with the semantics of the message send thanks to the presence of the subsumption rule (<:).

## 3.4 Typing à la Curry

We could also omit type-decorations inside $\varsigma$-binders and build a "type inference" version of $\mathcal{O}bj1_{<:}^+$, by adopting the untyped calculus instead of the explicitly typed one. The operational semantics, the typing and subtyping rules are the same as in Figure 2 and 5, and 6 (taking into account the modification in the

$$\frac{\begin{array}{l} \Gamma \vdash \sigma_i \quad \forall i \in I \\ \Gamma \vdash \sigma_j \quad \forall j \in J \quad I \cap J = \emptyset \end{array}}{\Gamma \vdash [\mathtt{m}_i : \sigma_i \diamond \mathtt{m}_j : \sigma_j]_{j \in J}^{i \in I}} \ (Diamond\text{--}Type) \qquad \frac{\Gamma \vdash \sigma_i \quad \forall i \in I}{\Gamma \vdash [\mathtt{m}_i : \sigma_i]^{i \in I}} \ (Sat\text{--}Type)$$

(Let $\tau_i \triangleq [\mathtt{m}_h : \sigma_h]^{h \in H_i}$).

$$\frac{\Gamma, s_i : \tau_i \vdash \mathtt{o}_i : \sigma_i \quad \forall i \in I \quad H_i \subseteq I}{\Gamma \vdash [\mathtt{m}_i = \varsigma(s_i : \tau_i)\mathtt{o}_i]^{i \in I} : [\mathtt{m}_i : \sigma_i \diamond]^{i \in I}} \ (Object) \qquad \frac{\Gamma \vdash \mathtt{o} : [\mathtt{m}_k : \sigma_k]}{\Gamma \vdash \mathtt{o}.\mathtt{m}_k : \sigma_k} \ (Select)$$

$$\frac{\Gamma \vdash \mathtt{o} : \tau \quad \Gamma \vdash \tau <: [\mathtt{m}_i : \sigma_i]^{i \in I} \quad \Gamma, s_k : [\mathtt{m}_i : \sigma_i]^{i \in I} \vdash \mathtt{o}' : \sigma_k \quad k \in I}{\Gamma \vdash \mathtt{o} \leftarrow\!\!\mathtt{m}_k = \varsigma(s_k : [\mathtt{m}_i : \sigma_i]^{i \in I})\mathtt{o}' : \tau} \ (Over)$$

(Let $\tau_k \triangleq [\mathtt{m}_h : \sigma_h]^{h \in H}$).

$$\frac{\Gamma \vdash \mathtt{o} : [\mathtt{m}_i : \sigma_i \diamond \mathtt{m}_j : \sigma_j]_{j \in J}^{i \in I} \quad \Gamma, s_k : \tau_k \vdash \mathtt{o}' : \sigma_k \quad H \subseteq I \quad k \in J}{\Gamma \vdash \mathtt{o} \leftarrow\!\!\mathtt{m}_k = \varsigma(s_k : \tau_k)\mathtt{o}' : [\mathtt{m}_i : \sigma_i \diamond \mathtt{m}_j : \sigma_j]_{j \in J-\{k\}}^{i \in I+\{k\}}} \ (Ext)$$

**Fig. 6.** Main Typing Rules for $\mathcal{O}bj1_{<:}^+$.

syntax). Type inference for primitive objects has been extensively studied in [19] (see also Subsection 7.1).

## 4 Soundness and Equational Theory of $\mathcal{O}bj1_{<:}^+$

In this section, we prove that the $\mathcal{O}bj1_{<:}^+$ type system is sound. Because of lack of space, all proof are omitted (the reader is referred to [16] for detailed proofs).

The following fact is crucial for subject reduction.

**Fact 3 (Sub Methods).**

1. If $\Gamma \vdash [\mathtt{m}_i : \sigma_i \diamond \mathtt{m}_j : \sigma_j]_{j \in J}^{i \in I} <: [\mathtt{m}_h : \sigma_h \diamond \mathtt{m}_k : \sigma_k]_{k \in K}^{h \in H}$, then $H \subseteq I$, and $J \subseteq K$, and $I \subseteq H \cup K$.

2. If $\Gamma \vdash [\mathtt{m}_i = \varsigma(s_i : \tau_i)\mathtt{o}_i]^{i \in I} : [\mathtt{m}_h : \sigma_h \diamond \mathtt{m}_k : \sigma_k]_{k \in K}^{h \in H}$, then $H \subseteq I$, and $I - H \subseteq K$.

The following two lemmas are useful for stating structural properties on objects and to guarantee that the calculus is closed under substitution.

**Lemma 4 (Generation).**

1. (Bodies) If $\Gamma \vdash [\mathtt{m}_i = \varsigma(s_i : \tau_i)\mathtt{o}_i]^{i \in I} : \tau$, then there exists $\{\sigma_i \mid i \in I\}$, such that $\Gamma, s_i : \tau_i \vdash \mathtt{o}_i : \sigma_i$, and $[\mathtt{m}_i : \sigma_i \diamond]^{i \in I} <: \tau$.

2. (Object) If $\Gamma \vdash [\mathtt{m}_i = \varsigma(s_i : \tau_i)\mathtt{o}_i]^{i \in I} : \tau$, then there exists $\{\sigma_i \mid i \in I\}$, such that $\Gamma \vdash [\mathtt{m}_i = \varsigma(s_i : \tau_i)\mathtt{o}_i]^{i \in I} : [\mathtt{m}_i : \sigma_i \diamond]^{i \in I}$, $\Gamma \vdash [\mathtt{m}_i : \sigma_i \diamond]^{i \in I} <: \tau$, and for all $j \in I$, $\Gamma \vdash [\mathtt{m}_i : \sigma_i \diamond]^{i \in I} <: \tau_j$.

*Proof.* Both parts can be proved by induction on the structure of derivations.

**Lemma 5 (Substitution).**
  *If $\Gamma, s : \tau \vdash o : \rho$ and $\Gamma \vdash o' : \sigma$ and $\Gamma \vdash \sigma <: \tau$, then $\Gamma \vdash o\{s \leftarrow o'\} : \rho$.*

*Proof.* By induction on the structure of derivations.

We can now prove the subject reduction theorem.

**Theorem 6 (Subject Reduction for $Obj1^+_{<:}$).**
  *If $\Gamma \vdash o : \sigma$ and $o \overset{ev}{\to} o'$, then $\Gamma \vdash o' : \sigma$.*

*Proof.* By cases on the definition of $\overset{ev}{\to}$, using Fact 3, Lemmas 4, and 5.

We can now prove the type soundness result that certifies that every well typed program cannot evaluate to the *wrong* result.

**Theorem 7 (Type Soundness for $Obj1^+_{<:}$).**
  *Let $o$ be a closed expression. If $\varepsilon \vdash o : \sigma$ and $Outcome(o)$ is defined, then $Outcome(o) \neq wrong$.*

*Proof.* By induction on the structure of the derivation of $Outcome(o)$.

Moreover it holds:

**Theorem 8 ($Obj1^+_{<:}$ has Minimum Types).**
  *If $\Gamma \vdash o : \sigma$, then there exists $\sigma'$ such that $\Gamma \vdash o : \sigma'$, and for any $\sigma''$, if $\Gamma \vdash o : \sigma''$, then $\Gamma \vdash \sigma' <: \sigma''$.*

*Proof.* The proof is standard and follows the guidelines of [5].

As in the original calculus, the lack of type-annotations inside $\varsigma$-binders destroy the minimum-type property for the type inference version of $Obj1^+_{<:}$ [5].

## 4.1   An Equational Type Theory for $Obj1^+_{<:}$

In this section we present the "typed" equational theory for $Obj1^+_{<:}$. We refine the untyped theory presented in Section 2 by introducing a typing judgment to ensure that equal (provable in the theory) terms have the same type. We introduce the judgment:

$$\Gamma \vdash o \overset{ev}{=} o' : \tau,$$

to describe the property that $o$ and $o'$ are provably equal in the theory with type $\tau$. Figure 7 presents the most important rules while the full set of rules can be found in the Appendix.

The relation between $\overset{ev}{=}$, $\overset{ev}{\to}$, *Outcome*, and the equational type theory is:

**Theorem 9 (Soundness of Outcome w.r.t. the Equational Theory).**
  *Let $o$ be a closed expression. If $\varepsilon \vdash o : \sigma$ and $Outcome(o) = v$, then $o \overset{ev}{\to} v$, and $\varepsilon \vdash o \overset{ev}{=} v : \sigma$.*

*Proof.* The proof follows from Proposition 2, and Theorems 6, and 7.

(Let $\tau_i \triangleq [\mathbf{m}_h : \sigma_h]^{h \in H_i}$, and $\tau_j \triangleq [\mathbf{m}_k : \sigma_k]^{k \in K_j}$, and $\tau \triangleq [\mathbf{m}_i : \sigma_i \diamond \mathbf{m}_j : \sigma_j]_{j \in J}^{i \in I}$).

$$\frac{\Gamma, s_i : \tau_i \vdash o_i : \sigma_i \quad \forall i \in I \quad H_i \subseteq I \\ \Gamma, s_j : \tau_j \vdash o_j : \sigma_j \quad \forall j \in J \quad K_j \subseteq I+J}{\Gamma \vdash [\mathbf{m}_i = \varsigma(s_i{:}\tau_i)o_i]^{i \in I} \overset{ev}{=} [\mathbf{m}_i = \varsigma(s_i{:}\tau_i)o_i, \mathbf{m}_j = \varsigma(s_j{:}\tau_j)o_j,]_{j \in J}^{i \in I} : \tau} \quad (Eq\text{-}Obj\text{-}{<}{:})$$

(In the next rules, let

$o \triangleq [\mathbf{m}_z = \varsigma(s_z{:}\tau_z)o_z]^{z \in Z}$, and $\tau_k \triangleq [\mathbf{m}_h : \sigma_h]^{h \in H}$, and $\tau \triangleq [\mathbf{m}_i : \sigma_i \diamond \mathbf{m}_j : \sigma_j]_{j \in J-\{k\}}^{i \in I+\{k\}}$).

$$\frac{\Gamma \vdash o : [\mathbf{m}_k : \sigma_k]}{\Gamma \vdash o.\mathbf{m}_k \overset{ev}{=} o_k\{s_k \leftarrow o\} : \sigma_k} \quad (Eq\text{-}Select_{ev})$$

$$\frac{\Gamma \vdash o : [\mathbf{m}_i : \sigma_i \diamond \mathbf{m}_j : \sigma_j]_{j \in J}^{i \in I} \quad \Gamma, s_k : \tau_k \vdash o' : \sigma_k \quad H \subseteq I \quad k \in Z-I}{\Gamma \vdash o \!\leftarrow\!\mathbf{m}_k = \varsigma(s_k{:}\tau_k)o' \overset{ev}{=} [\mathbf{m}_z = \varsigma(s_z{:}\tau_z)o_z, \mathbf{m}_k = \varsigma(s_k{:}\tau_k)o']^{z \in Z-\{k\}} : \tau} \quad (Eq\text{-}Ext^1_{ev})$$

$$\frac{\Gamma \vdash o : [\mathbf{m}_i : \sigma_i \diamond \mathbf{m}_j : \sigma_j]_{j \in J}^{i \in I} \quad \Gamma, s_k : \tau_k \vdash o' : \sigma_k \quad H \subseteq I \quad k \in J-Z}{\Gamma \vdash o \!\leftarrow\!\mathbf{m}_k = \varsigma(s_k{:}\tau_k)o' \overset{ev}{=} [\mathbf{m}_z = \varsigma(s_z{:}\tau_z)o_z, \mathbf{m}_k = \varsigma(s_k{:}\tau_k)o']^{z \in Z} : \tau} \quad (Eq\text{-}Ext^2_{ev})$$

**Fig. 7.** Typed Equational Theory for $Obj1_{<:}^+$.

As in the original calculus, we may find two objects which may give equal result for all their methods, and still be distinguishable in the equational theory. As a simple example of such two objects, let

$$o_1 \triangleq [\mathbf{x} = \varsigma(s{:}[\,])1, \mathbf{y} = \varsigma(s{:}[\,])1],$$
$$o_2 \triangleq [\mathbf{x} = \varsigma(s{:}[\,])1, \mathbf{y} = \varsigma(s{:}[\mathbf{x}{:}int])s.\mathbf{x}],$$

both of type $[\mathbf{x} : int, \mathbf{y} : int]$, but $\nvdash o_1 \overset{ev}{=} o_2 : [\mathbf{y} : int]$. More details can be found in [4].

## 5 Examples

In this section, we will present a few examples that help to illustrate the features of our first order type system.

*Example 1 (Method Specialization).* We show how our typing rules can capture the desired form of method specialization by extending the object $[\mathbf{x} = \varsigma(s{:}[\,])1]$ with a $\mathbf{y}$ field which depends on the $\mathbf{x}$ field, so building an (extendible) diagonal point. Consider the following object expression:

$$\mathbf{point} \triangleq [\mathbf{x} = \varsigma(s{:}[\,])1]\!\leftarrow\!\mathbf{y} = \varsigma(s{:}[\mathbf{x}{:}int])s.\mathbf{x}.$$

We can derive $\varepsilon \vdash \mathbf{point} : [\mathbf{x} : int, \mathbf{y} : int \diamond]$, with the following derivation:

$$\frac{\dfrac{s:[\,]\vdash 1:int}{\varepsilon\vdash [\mathbf{x}=\varsigma(s{:}[\,])1]:[\mathbf{x}:int\diamond]}\ (Object)}{\varepsilon\vdash [\mathbf{x}=\varsigma(s{:}[\,])1]:[\mathbf{x}:int\diamond\mathbf{y}:int]}\ (<:)\qquad \frac{s:[\mathbf{x}{:}int]\vdash s:[\mathbf{x}:int]}{s:[\mathbf{x}{:}int]\vdash s.\mathbf{x}:int}\ (Select)$$

$$\frac{}{\varepsilon\vdash \mathbf{point}:[\mathbf{x}:int,\mathbf{y}:int\diamond]}\ (Ext)$$

*Example 2 (Object-Internal Subtyping).* In this example we show that our type system allows also subtyping inside objects. We introduce $\lambda$-binders to denote functions (see [5]). Let the following object-types:

$$
\begin{array}{llll}
P_\diamond & \triangleq & [\mathbf{x}:int\diamond] & \text{(extendible point)}\\
P_{col,y} & \triangleq & [\mathbf{x}:int\diamond\mathbf{y}:int,\mathbf{col}:colors] & \text{(point extendible with }\mathbf{y}\text{ and }\mathbf{col})\\
2P_\diamond & \triangleq & [\mathbf{x}:int,\mathbf{y}:int\diamond] & \text{(extendible bidimensional point)}\\
CP & \triangleq & [\mathbf{x}:int,\mathbf{col}:colors] & \text{(non-extendible colored point).}
\end{array}
$$

For the object **foo**

$$
\begin{aligned}
\mathbf{foo}\ \triangleq\ &[\mathbf{addcol}=\varsigma(s{:}[\,])\lambda p{:}P_{col,y}.p{\leftarrow}\mathbf{col}=\varsigma(s'{:}[\,])red,\\
&\mathbf{select}=\varsigma(s{:}[\mathbf{addcol}{:}P_{col,y}{\to}CP,\mathbf{get\_p}{:}P_\diamond,\mathbf{get\_2p}{:}2P_\diamond])\lambda b{:}bool.\\
&\quad \text{if }b=true\text{ then }s.\mathbf{addcol}(s.\mathbf{get\_p})\text{ else }s.\mathbf{addcol}(s.\mathbf{get\_2p}),\\
&\mathbf{get\_p}\ =\varsigma(s{:}[\,])[\mathbf{x}=\varsigma(s{:}[\,])1],\\
&\mathbf{get\_2p}=\varsigma(s{:}[\,])[\mathbf{x}=\varsigma(s{:}[\,])1,\mathbf{y}=\varsigma(s{:}[\,])1]\\
&],
\end{aligned}
$$

we can derive

$$\vdash \mathbf{foo}:[\mathbf{addcol}:P_{col,y}{\to}CP,\mathbf{select}:bool{\to}CP,\mathbf{get\_p}:P_\diamond,\mathbf{get\_2p}:2P_\diamond]$$

and

$$\vdash \mathbf{foo.select}\ true:CP,\qquad \vdash \mathbf{foo.select}\ false:CP.$$

This is possible since $P_\diamond<:P_{col,y}$, and $2P_\diamond<:P_{col,y}$.

Note that other typing for **foo** are possible: among the others we mention the following interesting one:

$$\vdash \mathbf{foo}:[\mathbf{addcol}:P_{col,y}{\to}CP_y,\mathbf{select}:bool{\to}CP_y,\mathbf{get\_p}:P_\diamond,\mathbf{get\_2p}:2P_\diamond],$$

where

$$CP_y\triangleq [\mathbf{x}:int,\mathbf{col}:colors\diamond\mathbf{y}:int],$$

which allows one to type the interesting programs

$$\vdash \mathbf{foo.select}\ true{\leftarrow}\mathbf{y}=\varsigma(s)1:[\mathbf{x}:int,\mathbf{y}:int,\mathbf{col}:colors\diamond],$$

and

$$\vdash \mathbf{foo.select}\ false{\leftarrow}\mathbf{y}=\varsigma(s)1:[\mathbf{x}:int,\mathbf{y}:int,\mathbf{col}:colors\diamond].$$

Both programs produce an extendible bidimensional colored point.

*Example 3 (Object Subtyping).* Let point as in the Example 1 and let c_point be obtained by extending point with a col field. By an inspection of the typing rules we derive

$$\vdash \text{point} : P_\diamond, \qquad \vdash \text{c\_point} : CP_\diamond,$$

where

$$P \triangleq [\mathbf{x} : int] \qquad CP \triangleq [\mathbf{x} : int, \text{col} : colors]$$
$$P_\diamond \triangleq [\mathbf{x} : int \diamond] \qquad CP_\diamond \triangleq [\mathbf{x} : int, \text{col} : colors \diamond].$$

Now consider the following programs and related (derivable) types:

$$\begin{aligned}
f_1 &\triangleq \lambda s{:}P.s.\mathbf{x} &&: P{\to}int \\
f_2 &\triangleq \lambda s{:}P.s{\leftarrow}\mathbf{x} = \varsigma(s'{:}[\,])2 &&: P{\to}P \\
f_3 &\triangleq \lambda s{:}P_\diamond.s{\leftarrow}\text{col} = \varsigma(s'{:}[\,])red &&: P_\diamond{\to}CP_\diamond.
\end{aligned}$$

Again, by inspecting the typing rules, we get that the following judgments are derivable:

$$\begin{aligned}
&\vdash & f_1\,\text{point} &: int & &\vdash & f_1\,\text{c\_point} &: int \\
&\vdash & f_2\,\text{point} &: P & &\vdash & f_2\,\text{c\_point} &: P \\
&\vdash & f_3\,\text{point} &: CP_\diamond & &\nvdash & f_3\,\text{c\_point} &: CP_\diamond.
\end{aligned}$$

The last judgment is correctly false since $CP_\diamond \nless :P_\diamond$.

# 6   Classes-as-Objects

In this section, we show how the functional object calculus $\mathcal{O}bj1^+_{\lt:}$ can easily codify classes as objects; here we give a simple first-order encoding of classes, metaclasses, and instances, that share a lot of similarities with the object-oriented language *Smalltalk-80* [15]. This encoding shares both the class- and the delegation-based object-oriented styles of programming, because it allows to build classes and instances (and assign a type in presence of a "width" subtyping relation) and to extend and override dynamically some object methods. In the object-oriented jargon, creating an instance of a given class can be viewed as an activity that must be *delegated* to some object. Then the following question arises: which object should have the responsibility for this activity? One solution places a layer of management between the user, who desires the creation of a new object, and the code that performs the allocation of the memory. It follows that, for each class, say A, to be defined, we have a corresponding proper object, that has the responsibility of creating instances of A. We call that object (the *metaclass*) A_Class; it must have all the information about the size of the class it represents, the methods to which instances of this class will respond and a method New, that performs the creation of the class A. As such, the class A is an instance of the (meta)class A_Class. The class A, in turn contains a method, called new, that performs the creation of instances of the class A. Figure 8 depicts the class and subclass hierarchy.

In the next subsections, we present the encoding of the metaclasses, classes and instances of Figure 8. In particular, we present the encoding of the classes

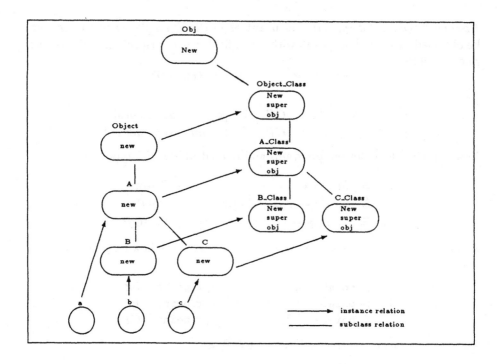

**Fig. 8.** The Class-Subclass Hierarchy

and metaclasses of points and colored points. Then, we present the typing of those objects in the $\mathcal{O}bj1^+_{\leq}$ type system. It is worth noting that the only objects that need to be built are the objects representing metaclasses and the top level object **Obj**: objects representing classes and instances are generated via message sending and successive reductions.

## 6.1 Metaclasses

Let the following types:

$$\sigma_1 \triangleq [\mathbf{New} : [\diamond]] \qquad \sigma_5 \triangleq [\mathbf{New} : \sigma_2, \mathbf{super} : \sigma_1, \mathbf{obj} : [\diamond]]$$
$$\sigma_2 \triangleq [\mathbf{new} : [\diamond]] \qquad \sigma_6 \triangleq [\mathbf{New} : \sigma_3, \mathbf{super} : \sigma_5, \mathbf{obj} : P_\diamond]$$
$$\sigma_3 \triangleq [\mathbf{new} : P_\diamond] \qquad \sigma_7 \triangleq [\mathbf{New} : \sigma_4, \mathbf{super} : \sigma_6, \mathbf{obj} : CP_\diamond]$$
$$\sigma_4 \triangleq [\mathbf{new} : CP_\diamond].$$

The metaclasses **Obj_Class**, **Point_Class**, and **C_Point_Class**, together with the top-level object of the hierarchy **Obj**, are encoded as follows:

$$\mathbf{Obj} \triangleq [\mathbf{New} = \varsigma(s{:}[\,])[\,]]$$
$$\mathbf{Obj\_Class} \triangleq [\mathbf{New} = \varsigma(s{:}[\mathbf{obj}{:}[\diamond]])[\mathbf{new} = \varsigma(s'{:}[\,])s.\mathbf{obj}],$$
$$\mathbf{super} = \varsigma(s{:}[\,])\mathbf{Obj},$$
$$\mathbf{obj} = \varsigma(s{:}[\mathbf{super}{:}\sigma_1])s.\mathbf{super}.\mathbf{New}]$$

$$\text{Point\_Class} \triangleq [\text{New} = \varsigma(s:[\text{obj}:P_o])[\text{new} = \varsigma(s':[\,])]s.\text{obj}],$$
$$\text{super} = \varsigma(s:[\,])\text{Obj\_Class},$$
$$\text{obj} = \varsigma(s:[\text{super}:\sigma_5])s.\text{super}.\text{obj} \twoheadleftarrow x = \varsigma(s':[\,])1]$$
$$\text{C\_Point\_Class} \triangleq [\text{New} = \varsigma(s:[\text{obj}:CP_o])[\text{new} = \varsigma(s':[\,])]s.\text{obj}],$$
$$\text{super} = \varsigma(s:[\,])\text{Point\_Class},$$
$$\text{obj} = \varsigma(s:[\text{super}:\sigma_6])s.\text{super}.\text{obj} \twoheadleftarrow \text{col} = \varsigma(s':[\,])red].$$

The meaning of the methods of the above metaclasses is as follows. When the method **New** is invoked on the metaclasses[2] (i.e **Point\_Class** and **C\_Point\_Class**), it produces as result another object, which is the class representing all the objects instances (e.g. points and colored points, respectively). The **super** method contains a pointer of the direct super(meta)class of the class to be defined. Finally, the method **obj** contains a copy of the object instance of the class; that object will be cloned when an instance of the class is created (by sending the message **new** to the class).

It is easy to verify that the above objects can be typed in $Obj1^+_{\prec:}$ by the following derivable types:

$$\varepsilon \vdash \text{Obj} \quad : \sigma_1 \qquad \varepsilon \vdash \text{Point\_Class} \quad : \sigma_6$$
$$\varepsilon \vdash \text{Obj\_Class} : \sigma_5 \qquad \varepsilon \vdash \text{C\_Point\_Class} : \sigma_7.$$

## 6.2 Classes

The classes **Object**, **Point**, and **C\_Point**, are encoded in $Obj1^+_{\prec:}$ as follows:

$$\text{Object} \triangleq [\text{new} = \varsigma(s:[\,])[\,]]$$
$$\text{Point} \triangleq [\text{new} = \varsigma(s:[\,])[\,] \twoheadleftarrow x = \varsigma(s':[\,])1]$$
$$\text{C\_Point} \triangleq [\text{new} = \varsigma(s:[\,])[\,] \twoheadleftarrow x = \varsigma(s':[\,])1 \twoheadleftarrow \text{col} = \varsigma(s':[\,])red]],$$

with the following derivable judgments in the equational theory

$$\varepsilon \vdash \text{Object} \stackrel{ev}{=} [\text{new} = \varsigma(s:[\,])[\,]] \qquad\qquad : \sigma_2$$
$$\varepsilon \vdash \text{Point} \stackrel{ev}{=} [\text{new} = \varsigma(s:[\,])[x = \varsigma(s':[\,])1]] \qquad : \sigma_3$$
$$\varepsilon \vdash \text{C\_Point} \stackrel{ev}{=} [\text{new} = \varsigma(s:[\,])[x = \varsigma(s':[\,])1, \text{col} = \varsigma(s':[\,])red]] : \sigma_4,$$

and it holds

$$\text{Obj\_Class.New} \stackrel{ev}{\twoheadrightarrow} \text{Object}$$
$$\text{Point\_Class.New} \stackrel{ev}{\twoheadrightarrow} \text{Point}$$
$$\text{C\_Point\_Class.New} \stackrel{ev}{\twoheadrightarrow} \text{C\_Point}.$$

---

[2] The **New** method should be "fired" automatically and only once on all defined metaclasses.

## 6.3   Instances

When the method **new** is invoked on the classes **Point** and **C_Point**, it produces as results points and colored points objects instances, respectively. This means that

$$\texttt{Object.new} \xrightarrow{ev} [\,]$$

$$\texttt{Point.new} \xrightarrow{ev} [\mathbf{x} = \varsigma(s':[\,])1]$$

$$\texttt{C\_Point.new} \xrightarrow{ev} [\mathbf{x} = \varsigma(s':[\,])1, \mathtt{col} = \varsigma(s':[\,])red],$$

and

$$\varepsilon \vdash [\,] \; : \; [\diamond]$$
$$\varepsilon \vdash [\mathbf{x} = \varsigma(s':[\,])1] \; : \; P_\diamond$$
$$\varepsilon \vdash [\mathbf{x} = \varsigma(s':[\,])1, \mathtt{col} = \varsigma(s':[\,])red] \; : \; CP_\diamond.$$

## 6.4   Discussion

We have presented a functional encoding of classes and metaclasses in terms of typable objects of our Extended Calculus of Primitive Objects. The objects of this encoding are typable in the first-order system $\mathcal{O}bj1^+_{\preceq:}$, provided that no method will return the object itself or an update of *self*. This encoding agrees with both the class- and the delegation-based object-oriented styles of programming. The soundness of the type system guarantees that every program will not go into the *message-not-understood* run-time error. The class-subclass hierarchy shares a lot of similarities with the one of *Smalltalk-80*. Although not treated here, it is not difficult to complete this encoding with *class* and *instance* methods and fields (we recall that a field is a methods that does not make use of *self*).

We point out that color points and points metaclasses *cannot* be obtained by object override from point and object metaclasses, respectively, since we do not have "depth" subtyping. For the same reason, color points and points classes *cannot* be obtained by object override from point and object classes. Moreover, we observe that color points and points instances *can* be obtained by inheritance (i.e. by successive object extensions) from the point and object instances, respectively, i.e:

$$[\,] \!\leftarrow\! \mathbf{x} = \varsigma(s':[\,])1 \xrightarrow{ev} [\mathbf{x} = \varsigma(s':[\,])1]$$

$$[\mathbf{x} = \varsigma(s':[\,])1] \!\leftarrow\! \mathtt{col} = \varsigma(s':[\,])red \xrightarrow{ev} [\mathbf{x} = \varsigma(s':[\,])1, \mathtt{col} = \varsigma(s':[\,])red],$$

even if $[\diamond] \not\preceq: P_\diamond \not\preceq: CP_\diamond$, thanks to our subtyping rules. Finally, note that this encoding will assign diamond-types to class-instances; as such, class instances can be extended and overridden in pure delegation object-oriented style.

The above encoding is not the only possible one; as an example, if we want to turn into a simple class-based style of programming, then we can drop the possibility of dynamically extending and overriding class instances. Then, we could design a type system for $\mathcal{O}bj1^+_{\preceq:}$, where we can distinguish between two kinds of objects:

- objects (contained inside the methods of the classes and metaclasses) which can be extended and overridden (but not subsumed);
- objects (representing class instances) which can be only used via message sending, with saturated object-types and whose object-types agrees with a "depth-width" subtyping relation.

The resulting type system will have, although not in details but in the spirit, some similarities with [14] (see the related work). Our experience says that the above presented mixed "class-delegation" style of programming is more flexible and powerful than the "class-only" one. The following simple example show how classes, objects, and object extensions can be easily integrated thanks to our subtyping relation among object-types.

*Example 4.* Let the `Point` and `C_Point` classes be defined as in Subsection 6.2, and consider the following program (let $P_{col} \triangleq [\mathbf{x} : int \diamond \mathbf{col} : colors]$):

$$f \triangleq \lambda s{:}P_{col}.(s{\leftarrow}\mathbf{col}{:}\varsigma(s{:}[\,])red).\mathbf{x} : P_{col}{\rightarrow}int.$$

This function will accept as input both an instance of the `Point` and `C_Point` classes, and as a consequence the following judgments are derivable: $f$ `Point.new` : *int*, and $f$ `C_Point.new` : *int*.

## 7 Related Work

Among the many object-based languages we find in the literature, we recall the following ones.

M.Abadi, in [1], presents a small functional language which include the main features of Modula-3. This language allows object override, a small form of object extension and "width" subtyping. The soundness of the typing system is guaranteed by a denotational semantics.

The *Lambda Calculus of Objects* of [12] is an untyped $\lambda$-calculus enriched with object primitives. Objects are built up from an *empty object* by adding new methods or overriding existing ones. A primitive call to the methods of the objects is provided. The calculus supports a simple inheritance mechanism, a straightforward *mytype* method specialization, and dynamic lookup of methods. Its operational semantics deals with the special symbol *self* of object-oriented languages directly by lambda abstraction. This calculus, however: (*i*) lacks of a subtyping relation on objects; (*ii*) consider the objects as *ordered sequences* of methods instead of *sets* of methods (apart from making difficult to write mutually recursive methods, this constraint leads to a somewhat complicated formulation of the operational semantics which makes use of a *bookeeping* reduction to extract the appropriate method upon the evaluation of a message); (*iii*) does not have an equational theory on objects.

[14] extends [12] with a the new **pro**-type, denoted by $\mathbf{pro}\,t.\langle\!\langle \mathbf{m}_i : \sigma_i \rangle\!\rangle^{i \in I}$, in order to add subtyping. If we can assign a **pro**-type to an object, then we can add new methods or override existing ones. At this level, only trivial subtyping is

possible. Then we can "change" the object into a different kind of object where methods cannot be altered (i.e. the only operation on objects is message sending), by "sealing" a **pro**-type into a real object-type denoted by $\mathbf{obj}\, t.\langle\!\langle \mathbf{m}_i : \sigma_i \rangle\!\rangle^{i \in I}$. Even if from the outside of the object the only operation is message sending, the internal methods can override other methods of their host object. Preventing from the outside extension and override gives (*self-covariant*) "width-depth" subtyping.

The [14] calculus and the $\mathcal{O}bj1_{\prec:}^{+}$ calculus are closely related. In fact, both calculi have two kinds of object-types. The **pro**-types can be compared with our diamond-types: the former does not allows subtyping, whereas the latter it does. Objects assigned to both types can be extended and overridden. Moreover the **obj**-types of [14] can be like our saturated object-types; the former agrees with a "width-depth" subtyping relation, whereas the latter allows only "width" subtyping. Objects assigned to **obj**-types cannot be extended nor overridden, whereas objects assigned to saturated types can be overridden. The next table compares the two calculi.

| | **pro**-types | **obj**-types | diamond-types | saturated-types |
|---|:---:|:---:|:---:|:---:|
| Self-types | √ | √ | | |
| Method extension | √ | | √ | |
| Method override | √ | | √ | √ |
| Width-<: | | √ | √ | √ |
| Depth-<: | | √ | | |

In [10], an orthogonal solution was taken in order to add subtyping to the Lambda Calculus of Objects: a subtyping relation "compatible" with method extension was introduced. Subtyping is subject to the restriction that a method can be forgotten only if the remaining methods in the object do not refer to it. This is obtained by *labeling* the type of a method **m** by the names of the methods of the object that **m** uses. For example, we can derive for the (diagonal) **point** of Section 3 the type $\vdash \mathbf{point} : [\mathbf{x} : nat, \mathbf{y} : int_x]$, but we cannot derive for **point** the type $\vdash \mathbf{point} : [\mathbf{y} : int_x]$, since the method **y** uses **x**. As pointed out in [8, 17], there are programs which can be typed in [10] and cannot be typed in [14] and vice-versa.

[18] presents an "explicitly typed" version of the Lambda Calculus of Objects, by making use of *dynamic typing*. This calculus has a sound and decidable type system, "width" subtyping on labeled object-types, and it allows for *first-class* method bodies that can be passed as function arguments. This increase the expressiveness of the language, since it allows to write "portable methods".

In [9], a more flexible typing system for the Lambda Calculus of Objects is given, by allowing objects to be typed independently from the order of their method additions. This extension also gives provision for method invocation when the receiver of the message is an *incomplete object*, i.e. an object whose implementation is only partially specified. A permutation rewriting rule between methods is sound but no subtyping is provided for this calculus.

[8] contains a very clear and simple encoding of object-types, by combining bounded quantification with labeled-types; in fact, labels record not only the useful methods which are sent to or overridden in *self*, but also the transitive closure of (the dependencies of) the method used by *self* in the method body. This calculus features "width" subtyping on labeled object-types.

[7] shows that the *matching* relation [11] can be fruitfully be employed in the Lambda Calculus of Objects, by making a substantially simplification of the typing rules of [12].

Another related paper is [21], which combines row-variables and refined subtyping in presence of extensible objects. There are similarities with our proposal, in particular diamond-types behave like **Pre-** and **Maybe**-types of [21]. But the subtyping of [21] is weaker than ours, since, for example, one cannot derive that the type of "colored point" is less than the type of "point", i.e. using our notation, that $[\mathbf{x}:int, \mathbf{col}:colors]<:[\mathbf{x}:int]$. The reason of this weakness is due to the fact that, in [21] the only subtyping rules are $(Shift_o)$ (that convert a **Pre**-type into a **Maybe**-type), and $(Extend_o)$ (that introduces a **Maybe**-type). Other differences are that we do not require object types to be total functions from names to types, and that we avoid row-variables by taking advantage of subtyping.

## 7.1 Conclusions

We presented an extension of the Calculus of Primitive Objects of [5], called $\mathcal{O}bj1^+_{<:}$, which allows one to dynamically add methods, and we introduced a static type system for this calculus that makes provision both for objects extension and for a "width" subtyping relation between object-types. The new features are obtained by extending the object-types of [5] with subsumption-parts, which convey information about methods that are subsumed. The $\mathcal{O}bj1^+_{<:}$ calculus allows a considerable number of programs to be typed, whereas they are not typable in $\mathcal{O}bj1_{<:}$, i.e. the original first-order system. The type systems allow for static detection of run-time errors such as *message-not-understood*.

A final remark concerns method encapsulation via variance annotations, a feature that is not accounted in our system and it is instead provided in [3]. However, the solution proposed in [3] could be accomplished as well as in the $\mathcal{O}bj1^+_{<:}$ calculus.

Moreover, the $\mathcal{O}bj1^+_{<:}$ type system can be easily extended with self-types by modeling the self-application semantics via *bounded universal polymorphism*. This conservative (w.r.t. $\mathcal{O}bj1^+_{<:}$) extension can be easily obtained with a very little cost with respect to the rules of $\mathcal{O}bj1^+_{<:}$, and it is presented in [16].

We conclude this paper with some open problems which will be subjects of future work:

1. Recently, M.Abadi has studied the possibility of extending the $\mathcal{O}bj1_{<:}$ calculus in an orthogonal way with respect to our $\mathcal{O}bj1^+_{<:}$ one. In this work-in-progress, a more flexible typing rule for method addition is given, by allowing incomplete objects to be typed independently from the order of their method additions. We believe this idea can be adopted and adapted with

labeled-types of [10]. This flexibility appears to be highly desirable for prototyping languages, such as delegation-based languages, where prototypes may reasonably be defined, and operated with as well, while part of their implementation (i.e. their methods) are yet to be defined. We also conjecture that our extension and Abadi's extension can be easily integrated, in order to build a calculus which allows for both features.

2. J. Palsberg [19] has described a (P-complete) type inference algorithm for an untyped version of the $Obj1_{<:}$ calculus. Does this result holds also for the type inference version of $Obj1^+_{<:}$?.

3. The type inference version of the Extended Primitive Calculus of Objects and the Lambda Calculus of Objects [12] share a lot of similarities. It seems reasonable to find a suitable encoding of one calculus into the other and a sound type system which fits both calculi.

**Acknowledgments** We wish to thank Martin Abadi and Luca Cardelli for their precious @-discussions, and the anonymous referees for their comments and suggestions.

# References

1. M. Abadi. Baby Modula-3 and a Theory of Objects. *Journal of Functional Programming*, 1(2):249-283, 1994.

2. M. Abadi and L. Cardelli. A Theory of Primitive Objects: Second-Order Systems. *Science of Computer Programming*, 25(2-3):81-116, 1995.

3. M. Abadi and L. Cardelli. An Imperative Object Calculus. *Theory and Practice of Objects Systems*, 1(3):151-166, 1996.

4. M. Abadi and L. Cardelli. *A Theory of Objects*. Springer-Verlag, 1996.

5. M. Abadi and L. Cardelli. A Theory of Primitive Objects: Untyped and First Order System. *Information and Computation*, 125(2):78-102, 1996.

6. H. P. Barendregt. *The Lambda Calculus: Its Syntax and Semantics*, volume 103 of *Studies in Logic and the Foundations of Mathematics*. North-Holland, Amsterdam, revised edition, 1984.

7. V. Bono and M. Bugliesi. Matching Constraint for the Lambda Calculus of Objects. In *Proc. of TLCA-97*, LNCS. Springer-Verlag, 1997. To appear.

8. V. Bono, M. Bugliesi, M. Dezani-Ciancaglini, and L. Liquori. Subtyping Constraint for Incomplete Objects. In *Proc. of CAAP-97*, LNCS. Springer-Verlag, 1997. To appear.

9. V. Bono, M. Bugliesi, and L. Liquori. A Lambda Calculus of Incomplete Objects. In *Proc. of MFCS-96*, volume 1113 of *LNCS*, pages 218-229. Springer-Verlag, 1996.

10. V. Bono and L. Liquori. A Subtyping for the Fisher-Honsell-Mitchell Lambda Calculus of Objects. In *Proc. of CSL-94*, volume 933 of *LNCS*, pages 16-30. Springer-Verlag, 1995.

11. K.B. Bruce, A. Shuett, and R. van Gent. Polytoil: a Type-safe Polymorphic Object-Oriented Language. In *Proc. of ECOOP-95*, volume 952 of *LNCS*, pages 16-30, 1995.

12. K. Fisher, F. Honsell, and J. C. Mitchell. A Lambda Calculus of Objects and Method Specialization. *Nordic Journal of Computing*, 1(1):3-37, 1994.

13. K. Fisher and J. C. Michell. The Development of Type Systems for Object Oriented Languages. *Theory and Practice of Objects Systems*, 1(3):189-220, 1995.

14. K. Fisher and J. C. Mitchell. A Delegation-based Object Calculus with Subtyping. In *Proc. of FCT-95*, volume 965 of *LNCS*, pages 42–61. Springer-Verlag, 1995.

15. A. Goldberg and D. Robson. *Smalltalk-80: The Language and its Implementation*. Addison-Wesley, 1983.

16. L. Liquori. An Extended Theory of Primitive Objects. Technical Report CS-23-96, Computer Science Department, University of Turin, Italy, 1996.

17. L. Liquori. *Type Assigment Systems for Lambda Calculi and for the Lambda Calculus of Objects*. PhD thesis, University of Turin, February 1996.

18. L. Liquori and G. Castagna. A Typed Lambda Calculus of Objects. In *Proc. of Asian-96*, volume 1212 of *LNCS*, pages 129–141. Springer-Verlag, 1996.

19. J. Palsberg. Efficient Inference of Object Types. *Information and Computation*, 123:198–209, 1995.

20. G. Plotkin. A Structural Approach to Operational Semantics. Technical Report DAIMI FN-19, Aarhus University, Denmark, 1981.

21. D. Remy. Refined Subtyping and Row Variables for Record Types. Draft, 1995.

# A   The Typing Rules of $\mathcal{O}bj1^+_{<:}$

**Type Rules**

$$\frac{}{\varepsilon \vdash ok} \; (Empty) \qquad \frac{\Gamma \vdash \sigma \quad s \notin dom(\Gamma)}{\Gamma, s : \sigma \vdash ok} \; (Weak) \qquad \frac{\Gamma \vdash ok}{\Gamma \vdash \omega} \; (Type - \Omega)$$

$$\frac{\begin{array}{c}\Gamma \vdash \sigma_i \quad \forall i \in I \\ \Gamma \vdash \sigma_j \quad \forall j \in J \quad I \cap J = \emptyset\end{array}}{\Gamma \vdash [\mathtt{m}_i : \sigma_i \diamond \mathtt{m}_j : \sigma_j]_{j \in J}^{i \in I}} \; (Diamond-Type) \qquad \frac{\Gamma \vdash \sigma_i \quad \forall i \in I}{\Gamma \vdash [\mathtt{m}_i : \sigma_i]^{i \in I}} \; (Sat-Type)$$

$$\frac{\Gamma, s : \sigma, \Gamma' \vdash ok}{\Gamma, s : \sigma, \Gamma' \vdash s : \sigma} \; (Proj) \qquad \frac{\Gamma \vdash o : \sigma \quad \Gamma \vdash \sigma <: \tau}{\Gamma \vdash o : \tau} \; (<:)$$

$(\text{Let } \tau_i \triangleq [\mathtt{m}_h : \sigma_h]^{h \in H_i}).$

$$\frac{\Gamma, s_i : \tau_i \vdash o_i : \sigma_i \quad \forall i \in I \quad H_i \subseteq I}{\Gamma \vdash [\mathtt{m}_i = \varsigma(s_i{:}\tau_i)o_i]^{i \in I} : [\mathtt{m}_i : \sigma_i \diamond]^{i \in I}} \; (Object) \qquad \frac{\Gamma \vdash o : [\mathtt{m}_k : \sigma_k]}{\Gamma \vdash o.\mathtt{m}_k : \sigma_k} \; (Select)$$

$$\frac{\Gamma \vdash o : \tau \quad \Gamma \vdash \tau <: [\mathtt{m}_i : \sigma_i]^{i \in I} \quad \Gamma, s_k : [\mathtt{m}_i : \sigma_i]^{i \in I} \vdash o' : \sigma_k \quad k \in I}{\Gamma \vdash o \leftarrow \mathtt{m}_k = \varsigma(s_k{:}[\mathtt{m}_i : \sigma_i]^{i \in I})o' : \tau} \; (Over)$$

$(\text{Let } \tau_k \triangleq [\mathtt{m}_h : \sigma_h]^{h \in H}).$

$$\frac{\Gamma \vdash o : [\mathtt{m}_i : \sigma_i \diamond \mathtt{m}_j : \sigma_j]_{j \in J}^{i \in I} \quad \Gamma, s_k : \tau_k \vdash o' : \sigma_k \quad H \subseteq I \quad k \in J}{\Gamma \vdash o \leftarrow \mathtt{m}_k = \varsigma(s_k{:}\tau_k)o' : [\mathtt{m}_i : \sigma_i \diamond \mathtt{m}_j : \sigma_j]_{j \in J-\{k\}}^{i \in I+\{k\}}} \; (Ext)$$

## Subtype Rules

$$\frac{\Gamma \vdash \sigma}{\Gamma \vdash \sigma <: \sigma} \ (Refl) \qquad \frac{\Gamma \vdash \sigma <: \tau \quad \Gamma \vdash \tau <: \rho}{\Gamma \vdash \sigma <: \rho} \ (Trans) \qquad \frac{\Gamma \vdash \sigma}{\Gamma \vdash \sigma <: \omega} \ (\Omega)$$

$$\frac{\Gamma \vdash [\mathtt{m}_i : \sigma_i \diamond \mathtt{m}_j : \sigma_j]_{j \in J}^{i \in I+K}}{\Gamma \vdash [\mathtt{m}_i : \sigma_i \diamond \mathtt{m}_j : \sigma_j]_{j \in J}^{i \in I+K} <: [\mathtt{m}_i : \sigma_i \diamond \mathtt{m}_j : \sigma_j]_{j \in J+K}^{i \in I}} \ (Shift_\diamond)$$

$$\frac{\Gamma \vdash [\mathtt{m}_i : \sigma_i \diamond \mathtt{m}_j : \sigma_j]_{j \in J+K}^{i \in I}}{\Gamma \vdash [\mathtt{m}_i : \sigma_i \diamond \mathtt{m}_j : \sigma_j]_{j \in J}^{i \in I} <: [\mathtt{m}_i : \sigma_i \diamond \mathtt{m}_j : \sigma_j]_{j \in J+K}^{i \in I}} \ (Extend_\diamond)$$

$$\frac{\Gamma \vdash [\mathtt{m}_i : \sigma_i \diamond \mathtt{m}_j : \sigma_j]_{j \in J}^{i \in I}}{\Gamma \vdash [\mathtt{m}_i : \sigma_i \diamond \mathtt{m}_j : \sigma_j]_{j \in J}^{i \in I} <: [\mathtt{m}_i : \sigma_i]^{i \in I}} \ (Sat_\diamond)$$

$$\frac{\Gamma \vdash [\mathtt{m}_i : \sigma_i]^{i \in I+J}}{\Gamma \vdash [\mathtt{m}_i : \sigma_i]^{i \in I+J} <: [\mathtt{m}_i : \sigma_i]^{i \in I}} \ (Width)$$

## Typed Equational Theory

$$\frac{\Gamma \vdash \mathtt{o}_2 \stackrel{ev}{=} \mathtt{o}_1 : \tau}{\Gamma \vdash \mathtt{o}_1 \stackrel{ev}{=} \mathtt{o}_2 : \tau} \ (Eq\text{--}Symm) \qquad \frac{\Gamma \vdash \mathtt{o}_1 \stackrel{ev}{=} \mathtt{o}_2 : \tau \quad \Gamma \vdash \mathtt{o}_2 \stackrel{ev}{=} \mathtt{o}_3 : \tau}{\Gamma \vdash \mathtt{o}_1 \stackrel{ev}{=} \mathtt{o}_3 : \tau} \ (Eq\text{--}Trans)$$

$$\frac{\Gamma \vdash \mathtt{o}_1 \stackrel{ev}{=} \mathtt{o}_2 : \sigma \quad \Gamma \vdash \sigma <: \tau}{\Gamma \vdash \mathtt{o}_1 \stackrel{ev}{=} \mathtt{o}_2 : \tau} \ (Eq\text{--}<:) \qquad \frac{\Gamma \vdash \mathtt{o}_1 : \sigma \quad \Gamma \vdash \mathtt{o}_2 : \tau}{\Gamma \vdash \mathtt{o}_1 \stackrel{ev}{=} \mathtt{o}_2 : \omega} \ (Eq\text{--}\Omega)$$

$$\frac{\Gamma, s : \tau, \Gamma' \vdash ok}{\Gamma, s : \tau, \Gamma' \vdash s \stackrel{ev}{=} s : \tau} \ (Eq\text{--}Var) \qquad \frac{\Gamma \vdash \mathtt{o}_1 \stackrel{ev}{=} \mathtt{o}_2 : [\mathtt{m}_k : \sigma_k]}{\mathtt{o}_1.\mathtt{m}_k \stackrel{ev}{=} \mathtt{o}_2.\mathtt{m}_k : \sigma_k} \ (Eq\text{--}Select)$$

$$\frac{\begin{array}{c} \Gamma \vdash \mathtt{o}_1 \stackrel{ev}{=} \mathtt{o}_2 : \tau \quad \Gamma \vdash \tau <: [\mathtt{m}_i : \sigma_i]^{i \in I} \\ \Gamma, s_k : [\mathtt{m}_i : \sigma_i]^{i \in I} \vdash \mathtt{o}' \stackrel{ev}{=} \mathtt{o}'' : \sigma_k \qquad k \in I \end{array}}{\Gamma \vdash \mathtt{o}_1 \!\leftarrow\! \mathtt{m}_k = \varsigma(s_k : [\mathtt{m}_i : \sigma_i]^{i \in I})\mathtt{o}' \stackrel{ev}{=} \mathtt{o}_2 \!\leftarrow\! \mathtt{m}_k = \varsigma(s_k : [\mathtt{m}_i : \sigma_i]^{i \in I})\mathtt{o}'' : \tau} \ (Eq\text{--}Over)$$

(Let $\tau_k \triangleq [\mathtt{m}_h : \sigma_h]^{h \in H}$, and $\tau \triangleq [\mathtt{m}_i : \sigma_i \diamond \mathtt{m}_j : \sigma_j]_{j \in J-\{k\}}^{i \in I+\{k\}}$.)

$$\frac{\begin{array}{c} \Gamma \vdash \mathtt{o}_1 \stackrel{ev}{=} \mathtt{o}_2 : [\mathtt{m}_i : \sigma_i \diamond \mathtt{m}_j : \sigma_j]_{j \in J}^{i \in I} \quad H \subseteq I \\ \Gamma, s_k : \tau_k \vdash \mathtt{o}' \stackrel{ev}{=} \mathtt{o}'' : \sigma_k \qquad k \in J \end{array}}{\Gamma \vdash \mathtt{o}_1 \!\leftarrow\! \mathtt{m}_k = \varsigma(s_k : \tau_k)\mathtt{o}' \stackrel{ev}{=} \mathtt{o}_2 \!\leftarrow\! \mathtt{m}_k = \varsigma(s_k : \tau_k)\mathtt{o}'' : \tau} \ (Eq\text{--}Ext)$$

**Typed Equational Theory** (continue)

(Let $\tau_i \triangleq [\mathbf{m}_h : \sigma_h]^{h\in H_i}$, and $\tau_j \triangleq [\mathbf{m}_k : \sigma_k]^{k\in K_j}$, and $\tau \triangleq [\mathbf{m}_i : \sigma_i \diamond \mathbf{m}_j : \sigma_j]_{j\in J}^{i\in I}$).

$$\dfrac{\begin{array}{ll} \Gamma, s_i : \tau_i \vdash o_i : \sigma_i & \forall i \in I \quad H_i \subseteq I \\ \Gamma, s_j : \tau_j \vdash o_j : \sigma_j & \forall j \in J \quad K_j \subseteq I+J \end{array}}{\Gamma \vdash [\mathbf{m}_i = \varsigma(s_i{:}\tau_i)o_i]^{i\in I} \overset{ev}{=} [\mathbf{m}_i = \varsigma(s_i{:}\tau_i)o_i, \mathbf{m}_j = \varsigma(s_j{:}\tau_j)o_j,]_{j\in J}^{i\in I} : \tau} \quad (Eq\text{--}Obj\text{--}{<}{:})$$

(In the next rules, let $o \triangleq [\mathbf{m}_z = \varsigma(s_z{:}\tau_z)o_z]^{z\in Z}$).

$$\dfrac{\Gamma \vdash o : [\mathbf{m}_k : \sigma_k]}{\Gamma \vdash o.\mathbf{m}_k \overset{ev}{=} o_k\{s_k \leftarrow o\} : \sigma_k} \quad (Eq\text{--}Select_{ev})$$

(Let $\rho \triangleq [\mathbf{m}_i : \sigma_i]^{i\in I}$).

$$\dfrac{\Gamma \vdash o : \tau \quad \Gamma \vdash \tau{<}{:}\rho \quad \Gamma, s_k : \rho \vdash o' : \sigma_k \quad k \in I}{\Gamma \vdash o{\leftarrow}\mathbf{m}_k = \varsigma(s_k{:}\rho)o' \overset{ev}{=} [\mathbf{m}_z = \varsigma(s_z{:}\tau_z)o_z, \mathbf{m}_k = \varsigma(s_k{:}\rho)o']^{z\in Z-\{k\}} : \tau} \quad (Eq\text{--}Over_{ev})$$

(In the next rules, let $\tau_k \triangleq [\mathbf{m}_h : \sigma_h]^{h\in H}$, and $\tau \triangleq [\mathbf{m}_i : \sigma_i \diamond \mathbf{m}_j : \sigma_j]_{j\in J-\{k\}}^{i\in I+\{k\}}$).

$$\dfrac{\Gamma \vdash o : [\mathbf{m}_i : \sigma_i \diamond \mathbf{m}_j : \sigma_j]_{j\in J}^{i\in I} \quad \Gamma, s_k : \tau_k \vdash o' : \sigma_k \quad H \subseteq I \quad k \in Z-I}{\Gamma \vdash o{\leftarrow}\mathbf{m}_k = \varsigma(s_k{:}\tau_k)o' \overset{ev}{=} [\mathbf{m}_z = \varsigma(s_z{:}\tau_z)o_z, \mathbf{m}_k = \varsigma(s_k{:}\tau_k)o']^{z\in Z-\{k\}} : \tau} \quad (Eq\text{--}Ext_{ev}^1)$$

$$\dfrac{\Gamma \vdash o : [\mathbf{m}_i : \sigma_i \diamond \mathbf{m}_j : \sigma_j]_{j\in J}^{i\in I} \quad \Gamma, s_k : \tau_k \vdash o' : \sigma_k \quad H \subseteq I \quad k \in J-Z}{\Gamma \vdash o{\leftarrow}\mathbf{m}_k = \varsigma(s_k{:}\tau_k)o' \overset{ev}{=} [\mathbf{m}_z = \varsigma(s_z{:}\tau_z)o_z, \mathbf{m}_k = \varsigma(s_k{:}\tau_k)o']^{z\in Z} : \tau} \quad (Eq\text{--}Ext_{ev}^2)$$

# A Reflective Architecture for Process Control Applications

*Charlotte Pii Lunau*

*Department of Computer Science, Aalborg University*
*Fredrik Bajers vej 7E, 9220 Aalborg, Denmark*
*lunau@cs.auc.dk*

## ABSTRACT

This paper presents a reflective architecture for process control applications with composition of metaobjects. Reflection is used to separate a model of physical entities from the monitoring and controlling part of the application and to exchange metaobjects dynamically. Dynamic exchange of metaobjects is used to implement context sensitive monitoring. Being able to program a monitoring strategy in a single metaobject, and to exchange a metaobject depending on plant state, significantly ease the programming of the monitoring and controlling part. Composition of metaobjects makes the architecture extensible and avoids to program metaobjects for all possible combinations of behaviour. A diagnosis system based on the proposed architecture has been implemented.

**Topics:** Reflection, Composability, Adaptability

## 1 INTRODUCTION

This paper presents an architecture for process control applications which makes it easier to develop applications and to adapt the applications to changing environments. The architecture is based on computational reflection and composition of metaobjects. Computational reflection separates the base level of a computation from the metalevel. The metalevel is monitoring and influencing the base level. This separation is used to obtain a structured architecture where a model of the physical system is located at the base level and the monitoring and controlling part constitutes the metalevel. A model of a physical system is relatively static, it only requires changes when new hardware, in form of sensors are added or removed. The monitoring and controlling part of a process control application must detect and react to state changes and faults in the process. In complex systems, the number of state changes and the combination of faults are large. In traditional architectures, the monitoring and controlling part is programmed as one module containing a number of large case statement. It is difficult to ensure that all cases and combinations of faults are covered and it is difficult to extend and maintain the software. By placing the monitoring and controlling part at the metalevel, this part can be divided into a number a independent metaobjects. Each metaobject is responsible for one fault or for a combination of faults. The metaobjects are dynamically exchanged at run time dependent on developments in the monitored process.

Main contributions of the paper include definition of requirements to reflection in process control applications and a definition of a reflective architecture with composition of metaobjects, suitable for process control applications.

The proposed architecture has been evaluated by implemented a diagnosis system, which handles fire and damages to the hull onboard ships. The diagnosis system is a prototype which has been demonstrated to ship owners and to classification societies.

Experience from implementing the prototype demonstrated the following main advantages of using a reflective architecture:

- The physical layer is separated from the monitoring and controlling part

- Monitoring strategies are separated into metaobjects

- Metaobjects are dynamically exchanged as faults are occurring

- Adaptability is obtained by adding new metaobjects

The advantages lead to a modular design with a clear separation of issues. This separation makes it easier to implement, maintain, and adapt process control applications.

To build an application with a reflective architecture, we need a reflective programming language. Commercial available object-oriented languages, such as Smalltalk-80 [Goldberg and Robson 83], Objective-C [Cox 86],[Next 92], and Clos [Kiczales et al. 91] contain structural reflection, where changes are applied at compile time. Our analysis of the requirements to reflection for process control applications, presented in Section 4, require computational reflection, where changes take place at run time. We therefore had to extend the object-oriented language Objective-C with computational reflection and composition of metaobjects. Computation reflection is obtained by intercepting all messages to objects, which has a metaobject attached. The message is redirected to the metaobject either before or after the method is invoked in the base level object. Extension of Objective-C with computational reflection is described in Appendix A.

## 1.1 RELATED WORK

A number of papers discuss reflection seen from a programming language point of view. Computational reflection is discussed in [Smith 82], [Maes 87] and [Ferber 89]. Structural reflection is discussed in [Kiczales et al. 91] and [Cointe 87]. However, only few papers address the advantages of applications based on a reflective architecture. [Rao 91] reports on the design and implementation of a window system, called Silica. Silica's design separates parts of the basic functionality of window systems into independent objects called contracts. The contracts are reified through a protocol and constitute the reflective level. The contracts can be selected for each window independently and they can be specialized by a user. Silica's design is radically different from ours. Silica's reflective level is obtained by reifying implementation details through an interface, without the use of neither metaclasses nor computational reflection.

[Agha and Sturman 94] use computational reflection to dynamically install dependable protocols in distributed system using an Actor based language. We do share the goals of dependability, modularity, and composition with [Agha and Sturman 94], but our application areas and programming language environments differ significantly. [Agha and Sturman 94] focus on dependable services in a distributed system, while our focus is on context sensitive monitoring driven by requirements from an industrial application.

[Aksit et. al 93] proposes composition filters to extend a language and to allow independent extensions to be composed. Composition filters are implemented using message interception and come in two variants input filters and output filters. All input filters are invoked before the method on the object. Output filters deal with messages sent from an object. Input filters and our composition of metaobjects are similar in that they both compose behaviour. However, input filters are allowed to reject the method invocation on the object, while our metaobjects always invoke the method. Input filters are always invoked before the method, while our metaobjects can be invoked before or after method invocation. Our metaobjects does not support the equivalence of output filters. The main focus of composition filters is language extensions, while our focus is to build an architecture for a reflective application.

## 1.2 OUTLINE OF THE PAPER

The paper starts the background for advocating new architectures for software development. Next, the application area is described and a set of requirements to reflection in process control applications is identified. Based on the requirements, a reflective architecture with dynamic exchange of metaobjects and composition of metaobjects is defined. The next section presents a diagnosis system which handles fires and damages onboard a ship. The diagnosis system is implemented using the reflective architecture. Finally, the conclusions are presented. The extensions to

Objective-C are described in Appendix A. Appendix B contains the metaobject class hierarchy used by the diagnosis system.


## 2 BACKGROUND

The production of adaptable software systems has become an important goal of software engineering. In general, adaptability ensures that systems can evolve over time by adding new functionality and changing existing services.

At present a number of mechanisms for obtaining adaptability coexist. One such mechanism is design patterns [Gamma et. al. 94] where each pattern defines aspects that vary over time. Examples of aspects are:

| Pattern | Aspect that vary |
|---------|------------------|
| Adapter | interface to an object |
| Bridge | implementation of an object |
| Composite | structure and composition of an object |
| Observer | objects that depend on another object |
| Strategy | an algorithm |

Table 1 Design patterns and their variations

Besides design reuse, a goal of design patterns is to obtain a more flexible and dynamic design with greater potential for reuse. Many design patterns emphasises object composition, where an object can be substituted by another object, at run-time, if they have identical interfaces.

Another mechanism for obtaining adaptability is reflection. In object-oriented programming two kinds of reflection exist with different purposes: Structural and computational.

Structural reflection is obtained by metaclasses where a metaclass defines the behaviour and structure of it class. Changes to a metaclass influences its class and all objects of the class. Using structural reflection it is not possible to make adaptations to individual objects; adaptations apply to all objects of a class. Using structural reflection adaptations take place at compile time because a class needs to be defined and compiled before objects can be created.

Computational reflection has a close relation between an object and its metaobject. Each individual object can have a metaobject attached and objects of the same class can be attached to metaobjects of different classes. Furthermore it is possible to dynamically remove or attach metaobjects. A metaobject monitors and affects its base level object, dependent on the base level object's state. A base level object and its metaobject are co-ordinated through a causal connection. A causal connection implies that any changes made in a metaobject are immediately reflected in the base level object's state and behaviour.

In our implementation of computational reflection all messages sent to an object, with an attached metaobject, are intercepted and redirected to the metaobject. The same behaviour can be obtained using an event/notification mechanism, such as the Observer design pattern [Gamma et.al.95] or the Observable/Observer classes in Java [Chan and Lee 96]. However, computational reflection has a number of advantages over event/notification mechanisms.

In event/notification mechanisms all objects reside at the same level and therefore no division of an application into separate levels exist. Furthermore, all observable or subject objects must share a common superclass, which maintains a list of current observers and implements a notification method. Each observable/subject object must explicitly invoke the notification method, whenever a change has taken place. This implies that monitoring cannot be extended to include new objects without changing the objects, so they inherit from the common superclass and explicit invoke the notification method.

Using computational reflection, there is a clear separation between monitored and monitoring objects, because they reside at different levels. Any object can, at any time, have a metaobject attached or detached and notification is implicit for all objects with an attached metaobject. Thus, computational reflection provides better support for adaptive software than the simpler event/notification mechanism.

## 3 PROCESS CONTROL APPLICATIONS

A process control application monitors and controls a physical system and it must be able to react to changes and faults in the physical system. Changes and faults occur randomly and in bursts. The software must be able to react to the changed situation dynamically. This implies that the process control software should be able to change its structure and behaviour while it is running.

A physical system can be anything from a fairly simple thermostat regulating the temperature to complex production lines in a factory. Monitoring is performed by collecting input from sensors and evaluating it against an expected behaviour. Sensors are connected to physical entities and can be either binary, measuring an on/off state or analogue, measuring a continuos value. For instance, a sensor connected to the outlet of a pump measures the pressure in the connected tube. Interpretation of the pressure informs about the state of the pump; states may include pump running, pump stopped, pump running at half speed. Advanced diagnosis systems use development of sensor values to predict whether a failure is about to occur. This requires that value and time are logged, statistical signal processing is used, and fault detection techniques applied. Detection and isolation of state changes in a plant usually require fusion of data from several sensors and a mathematical model of the physics involved. Output from such detectors can be considered as virtual sensor signals which must be treated along with the physical signals.

Control actions are performed to prevent faults from occurring or to remedy the situation when a fault has occurred. Control is performed by actuators, which for instance turn a valve or start/stop a pump. Connection to sensors and actuators is obtained through a real time local area network.

Process control applications are usually designed as closed-loop systems. Closed-loop implies that sensor measurements are used to control the physical process by changing the settings of entities, such as valves and pumps via actuators. A traditional architecture for a process control application is shown in Figure 1.

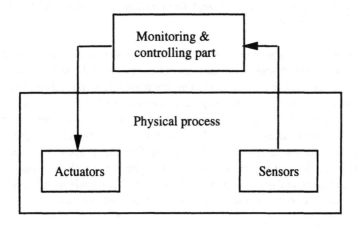

Figure 1 A traditional architecture for a process control application

In traditional architectures, the controller can be rather complex to design and implement, due to a large set of possible faults and the complexity of the underlying physical system. It is difficult to ensure that all combinations of faults are covered and such systems are difficult to extend and adopt to changes in an industrial plant.

## 4 REQUIREMENTS TO REFLECTION IN PROCESS CONTROL APPLICATIONS

In this section, we identify a number of requirements to reflection in process control applications. The requirements are identified based on our experience designing and implementing a number of alarm and diagnosis systems for use onboard ships and we believe the requirements are applicable to sensor based process control applications in general.

In process control applications, the same type of sensors are measuring on a variety of different physical entities. For instance, analogue sensors measure pressures and temperatures. They are connected to units, such as water tanks, outlet from pumps, accommodation areas, and refrigerators. The monitored entities have different functions and behaviour and need individual monitoring strategies. A monitoring strategy is related to the monitored entity and not to the type of sensor used to perform the monitoring. This implies that sensor objects of the same type need different monitoring strategies, i.e. different metaobjects attached.

In case of a failure in one of the monitored entities, it must be possible to exchange the monitoring strategy for the failed entity. This implies that sensors of the same type measuring on the same type of entities need individual monitoring strategies and it must be possible to dynamically exchange the monitoring strategy, when changes occur in the physical process.

In many cases, it is insufficient to look at one sensor value at a time. Instead it is necessary to look at a set of sensor values to get an overview of the state of a process. One example is a fire onboard a ship. Here the monitoring and controlling part needs to know all compartments on fire, to propose a suitable fire fighting strategy. A fire fighting strategy typically includes decreasing the temperature in a compartment by cooling the boundaries using water. The monitoring and controlling part must determine the boundaries of all compartments on fire and propose to cool those boundaries. This is obtained by letting all compartments on fire share a single meta object, which monitors the fire compartments' sensors. This leads to a requirement that a single meta object must be able to monitor several sensor objects.

Another example, where more than one sensor value is needed, is when a sensor value is not available, either because the sensor has failed or because a sensor is not attached to a physical entity. Here the process control application needs to collect values from other sensors to calculate the state of a physical entity or a process. This leads to a requirement that monitoring strategy metaobjects know each other and must be able to communicate.

A common requirement is to log the values of sensors. Logging is a reflective activity and is naturally done in a logging meta object. But most sensors already have a monitoring meta object attached. Although the number of monitoring strategies is known it is impractical to predict all possible needed combinations. Furthermore, it is desirable to be able to extend the meta level with new functionalities without having to incorporate this functionality in all existing metaobjects. A general solution to the problem is to compose metaobjects. Fortunately, metaobjects implement independent behaviour and composition is possible and easy. Thus, it is a requirement to compose metaobjects attached to a base object.

The following list summarises the requirements, identified above:

- Sensor objects of the same type must be able to attach different metaobjects .

- Each sensor object may need an individual metaobject

- Metaobjects must be changed dynamically when changes in the process occur.

- A metaobject must be able to monitor more than one base object

- Metaobjects must be able to communicate with each other

- It must be possible to compose metaobjects attached to a base object

The next section presents a reflective architecture, which fulfils these requirements.


## 5 A REFLECTIVE ARCHITECTURE

Based on the requirements from the previous section, a reflective architecture for process control applications is presented. The architecture is implemented in Objective-C extended with computational reflection and composition of metaobjects. A reflective architecture separates an application into a base-level and a reflective-level. First, we discuss the objects at the two levels.

The base-level objects are all the physical entities, such as pumps, valves, tubes, tanks etc., depending on the actual application. Sensors and actuators are also part of the base-level. Objects at the base-level need to be connected using relations, because we need to be able to deduce which physical entities a sensor object actually is measuring. For instance, measuring if a pump is running is usually done by attaching a flow sensor to the outlet tube of the pump. Changes in the physical entities are reflected in the sensor objects only. The actuators are used to influence the process in critical situations by operating on the physical entities, such as opening a valve.

The reflective-level consists of metaobjects performing a number of different functions. One set of metaobjects is responsible for monitoring the physical process. Monitoring is performed by attaching metaobjects to sensor objects. With the possibility of dynamically exchanging metaobjects, the monitoring part can be divided into a number of independent metaobjects, each performing a specific and limited part of the overall monitoring. Typically, the monitoring will be divided into three major areas: Monitoring during normal operation, monitoring when there is a suspicion that a fault is about to happen, and monitoring when a fault has occurred.

During normal operation simple checks of the values of the sensor objects are performed. As soon as there is a suspicion that a fault is about to happen, because some values are exceeding their normal operation range, the monitoring metaobject exchanges itself with a fault detection metaobject. A fault detection metaobject decides if a fault is about to happen or if it was a false alarm. This decision can be made by calculating increase/decrease rates for the values of a sensor object and by attaching metaobjects to an extended set of sensor objects. A fault detection metaobject can issue control commands to prevent a fault from occurring. If a fault occurs the fault detection metaobject exchanges itself with a fault handling metaobject. A fault handling metaobject has two responsibilities: To remedy the fault by issuing control commands in co-operation with the control part and to monitor the effects of the remedy actions. To fulfil the last responsibility, the fault handling metaobject may need to add metaobjects to an extended set of sensor objects. When a fault has been circumvented the fault handling metaobject exchanges itself with a monitoring metaobject. The set of state changes for the monitoring metaobjects is shown in Figure 2.

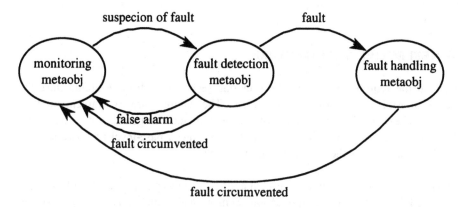

Figure 2  Exchange of monitoring metaobjects.

Another set of objects residing at the reflective level is responsible for controlling the physical process. The controlling objects are not attached to sensor objects, but are invoked from the monitoring metaobjects. The controlling objects perform control actions by communication with actuators at the base-level. A control action can be to move a specified amount of water from one tank to another. This requires starting of a pump and calculating which valves to open and which to close. Tanks are connected through a common tube system and a connection between two tanks requires opening/closing of a set of valves.

## 5.1 COMPOSITION OF METAOBJECTS

Traditional reflective architectures allow each base object to have one metaobject attached. In process control applications, several independent aspects of behaviour need to be monitored simultaneously, as discussed in Section 4. The monitoring can be performed by having a large set of metaobjects which contain combinations of the different aspects to be monitored. However, this will soon be incomprehensible. Composing metaobjects are a much more structured approach, where each metaobject is responsible for one aspect. Composition of metaobjects is obtained by attaching one system metaobject to a base object. The system metaobject administrates the composed metaobjects, and invoke them in turn. The system metaobject contains two lists. On the pre list are all metaobjects that should be notified before the method is performed in the base object. The post list contains the metaobjects that need to be notified after the performance of the method in the base object. A meta object may be in both lists at the same time. The architecture is shown in Figure 3.

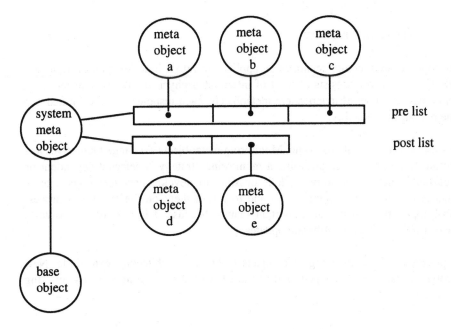

Figure 3  A meta architecture with composition of metaobjects

The system metaobject is invisible to the application. Meta objects are attached and removed using the following statements:

```
[aBaseObject insertPreMetaObject: aMetaObject]
[aBaseObject insertPostMetaObject: aMetaObject]
[aBaseObject withdrawPreMetaObject: aMetaObject]
[aBaseObject withdrawPostMetaObject: aMetaObject]
```

When a metaobject is attached to a base level object, all messages send to the base object are intercepted. A metaobject decides which messages to handle and metaobjects attached to the same base object can handle different messages.

## 5.2 CAUSAL CONNECTION

In process control applications, it does not make sense to talk about a causal connection between a base-level object and a metaobject. The directly monitored base-level objects are sensor objects and their is no way to dynamically change their behaviour. However, if we look at a physical system in a greater perspective, we are monitoring the entire process by selecting a set of sensor objects and we are affecting its behaviour through actuators. The way the physical process is affected is dependent on the metaobjects. However, instead of changing a metaobject, we exchange it with another metaobject, which has a different affect on the physical process.

### 5.3 ARCHITECTURE SUMMARY

The proposed architecture separates an application into a base level and a reflective level. The base level consists of a set of interrelated physical entities. The reflective level consists of a set of independent metaobjects, each responsible for a limited part of the overall functionality.

The architecture is highly dynamic. Monitoring metaobjects exchange themselves as a situation develops. This implies that a monitoring strategy is selected dependent on the current context. Furthermore, it is possible to develop new metaobjects or to correct errors in existing metaobjects and to install them on the fly. For a process control application, this is an important feature because it is usually expensive to close down the system for software updates.

The possibility for composing metaobjects makes the architecture extendible. New metaobjects can be developed and installed without affecting already existing metaobjects.

## 6 A DIAGNOSIS SYSTEM WITH A REFLECTIVE ARCHITECTURE

This section describes a diagnosis system which we have implemented using the reflective architecture proposed in Section 5.

The specific diagnosis system is an emergency management system for use on board ships. The system detects fires and damages to the hull, based on around 500 sensors and provides decision support for handling of emergencies. On board a ship, the master is responsible for safety and for the operation of the ship. The diagnosis system must not automatically control the ship for reasons of legal responsibility. Instead, the system proposes which actions to take. The actions are carried out when they have been acknowledged at a graphical user interface, so the diagnosis system is carrying out control through the actuators although it does not do it automatically.

The diagnosis system is described by its base level objects and by objects at the reflective level, which handle the two kinds of emergencies.

## 6.1 THE BASE LEVEL

The base level models the ship and consists of a variety of ship objects, such as decks, compartments, tanks, fire equipment, pumps, sensors, and actuators. All together 49 different ship objects are defined. All ships consists of the same type of objects, but they differ in the number and placement of the objects. To model a specific ship, a set of ship objects are connected using relations. In a shipmodel, it is possible, given one ship object, to get to any other ship object via the relations. A shipmodel expresses the static structure of the ship including the location of sensor objects. Two different types of sensor objects exist, analogue sensors which measure a value and binary sensors which measure an on/off state. Analogue sensors are measuring contents in tanks, pressures in tubes, and temperatures in compartments. Binary sensors are measuring the state of valves, smoke detectors, fire doors, and watertight doors. When physical entities, such as fire doors or valves, change their states, the changes are reflected by a change of state in their corresponding sensor objects.

To demonstrate the diagnosis system on land a sensor simulator was developed. The simulator constantly update all sensor objects and it can be used to generate faults. When faults are simulated mathematical models are used to calculate the changes of sensor values. On board a ship the diagnosis system will be connected to a process net, which collects values from the physical sensors and updates the sensor objects in the diagnosis system.

## 6.2 THE REFLECTIVE LEVEL

The reflective level consists of 10 different metaobject classes, whose objects are dynamically attached, replaced, and removed from sensor objects depending on the development of an emergency. Composition of metaobjects is used to attach a number of metaobjects to sensor objects. It is a requirement to log all sensor values and logging is performed by attaching an event logging metaobject. The event logging metaobject is usually attached permanently to all sensor objects. The class hierarchy for the metaobjects are shown in Appendix B. The diagnosis system handles two types of emergencies: fire and damages to the hull. These are described below.

### 6.2.1 FIRES

A fire emergency goes through three steps: monitoring, detection, and fire fighting. During the monitoring phase one metaobject, called the FireMonitoringMetaObject is monitoring all temperature sensors in accommodation compartments. If one sensor is exceeding its normal operation value, individual monitoring of that sensor is performed and the shared FireMonitoringMetaObject exchanges itself with a FireDetectionMetaObject.

To give an example of a metaobject, we will present the simple FireMonitoringMetaObject. All sensor objects in accommodation compartments share one FireMonitoringMetaObject. Each time one of the sensor objects is updated, by a SetValue:atTime message, the FireMonitoringMetaObject is invoked. A metaobject is invoked by the message handleMsg: aReceiver selector: (SEL)aSelector args: arguments, where aReciever is the base level object. The FireMonitoringMetaObject make a simple check to test whether the sensor value, i.e. the temperature is greater than an upperlimit. If the upperlimit is exceeded the FireMonitoringMetaObject exchanges itself with a FireDetectionMetaobject. Here is the code:

```
-handleMsg: aReceiver selector: (SEL)aSelector
                                  args: arguments
{
   id    fireDetectionMetaObject;


   struct sensorObjectDef {
      @defs (SensorObject);
   } *public;

if (aSelector == @selector(setValue:atTime:)){
   public = (struct sensorObjectDef *) aReceiver;

   if (public->value > upperLimit) {
    fireDetectionMetaObject =[[FireDetectionMetaObject
                              alloc] init: aReciever];
     [aReceiver withdrawPostMetaObject:self];
     [aReceiver insertPostMetaObject:
                           fireDetectionMetaObject];
   }


}
return self;

}
```

Figure 4 The code of the FireMonitoringMetaObject.

The FireDetectionMetaObject is responsible for intensified monitoring in a possible fire situation, for issuing a fire warning, and to continue monitoring the situation until a fire is detected or until it has been determined that it was a false alarm. A fire warning is issued, when it is suspected that a fire will burst out. Issuing of fire warnings are based on interpretation of sensor values from smoke detectors, current temperature, and a temperature increase rate in the compartment. The FireDetectionMetaObject calculates the temperature increase rate and attach a metaobject to the smoke detector in the compartment.

When a fire is detected, the FireDetectionMetaobject on the sensor object in the compartment on fire is exchanged with a FireHandlingMetaObject. The exchange is done by the FireDetectionMetaObject. One FireHandlingMetaObject monitors and controls all compartments on fire, so the FireDetectionMetaObject checks if a FireHandlingMetaObject already exists. If it does not exist, it is created and the exchange takes place. Figure 5 shows a situation where the temperature is normal in eleven compartments, temperature is increasing in three compartments, and one compartment is on fire.

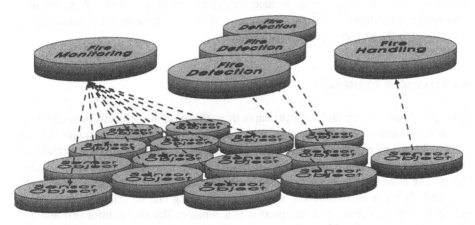

Figure 5    Eleven normal compartments, three compartments with increasing temperature, and one compartment on fire.

The FireHandlingMetaObject is responsible for issuing a fire alarm at the graphical user interface and for monitoring the development and the spreading of the fire. Furthermore, the FireHandlingMetaObject communicates with a mathematical fire model, which predicts how the fire will spread throughout the ship. This information is presented at the graphical user interface together with a strategy for fire fighting.

When the fire is spreading and adjacent compartments catch fire, their metaobjects are exchanged with the FireHandlingMetaObject. The FireHandlingMetaObject is complex, it   monitors more than one object and has knowledge of which compartments are on fire. This situation is shown in Figure. 6.

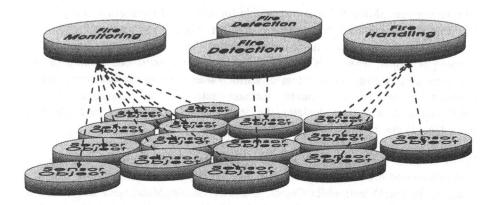

Figure 6 Nine normal compartments, two compartments with increasing temperature, and four compartments on fire.

When a fire is detected all relevant state changes are shown at the graphical user interface. Relevant state changes include sprinklers, valves, fire doors, dampers, and ventilation. Monitoring of state changes is done by dynamically connecting a metaobject to the relevant binary sensor objects.

### 6.2.2 DAMAGES TO THE HULL

Damages to the hull use the same principle of exchanging metaobjects, depending on the development of the emergency. A difference is that individual monitoring of sensor objects measuring contents in tanks takes place from the beginning. Individual monitoring is needed because tanks do not have the same size and their contents differ. The attached DamageMonitoringMetaObjects monitor increase/decrease rates in a tank. If the level is suddenly increasing/decreasing and no pumping operations take place, the reflective level interprets it as a damage. The user is informed and the DamageMonitoringMetaObject is exchanged with a DamageHandlingMetaObject. The DamageHandlingMetaObject communicates with a mathematical stability module, which calculates the stability of the ship and proposes pumping of ballast water into or out of tanks. When the user starts a pumping operation moving a specified amount of ballast water from one tank to another, this operation is also monitored by an AutomaticPumpTransferMetaObject. The metaobject monitors when the specified amount of water has been moved and stops the pumping operation automatically Starting and stopping an operation is done by sending control commands to actuators.

The handling of a fire emergency and a damage to the hull follow the same basic principle of dynamically exchanging metaobjects depending on the development of the emergency. Furthermore, the set of entities that are monitored is changing dynamically, depending on the situation. The reflective level is also able to monitor operations and to stop them automatically when they are finished.

# 7 CONCLUSION

To obtain dynamically adaptable process control applications, we have suggested a reflective architecture which is implemented using computational reflection. The architecture fulfils the requirements we have identified based on our experience developing several diagnosis and alarm systems and the architecture should thus be useful for a range of process control applications. We have implemented one specific diagnosis system based on the proposed architecture and a number of important benefits were achieved.

The benefits include: Separation of a model of a physical process and the monitoring and controlling part. This allows the two parts to be programmed and maintained independently. Dynamic exchange of metaobjects allows monitoring strategies to be programmed as single comprehensible entities. The entities are dynamically exchanged to obtain the equivalence of an overall monitoring strategy. Composition of metaobjects avoids to program numerous metaobjects with all possible combinations of behaviour. Instead each behaviour is programmed in one metaobject and the metaobjects are composed by attaching a number of metaobjects to the same base level object.

Using the proposed reflective architecture, we have obtained a highly modular system which was easy to implement and test.

# 8 ACKNOWLEDGEMENTS

The definition of the reflective architecture and the implementation of the diagnosis system were developed as part of the EEC project ATOMOS under the EURET programme. The functional specification of the system was developed in co-operation with The Danish Maritime Institute and Lloyds Register of Shipping, London. The research was also supported by the Danish Research Council under grant number 9500756. This support is gratefully acknowledged.

# REFERENCES

[Agha and Sturman 94]    Gul Agha, Daniel Sturman:
                         A Methodology for Adapting to Patterns of Faults
                         To appear in G.Koob(ed):
                         *Foundations of Ultradependability*
                         Vol. 1, Kluwer Academic 1994

186

[Aksit et.al 93]               M. Aksit; K. Wakita; j. Bosch, L. Bergmans; A. Yonezawa:
Abstracting object-interactions using composition-filters.
*Object-based Distributed Processing*
Lecture Notes in Computer Science Vol. 791.
Springer-Verlag 1993.

[Chan and Lee 96]         P. Chan; R. Lee:
*The Java Class Libraries: An Annotated Reference.*
Addison-Wesley, Reading, Massachusetts, 1996

[Christensen et al. 94]     Kim Harding Christensen, Charlotte Pii Lunau, Jeppe Sommer:
*Design Specification for the Emergency Management System Emma*
Technical Report Atomos Task 2304
Aalborg University 1994

[Cointe 87]                 Pierre Cointe:
Metaclasses are First Class: the ObjVlisp Model
*Proc. of Object-Oriented Programming: Systems, Languages and Applications*
October 1987

[Cox 86]                    Brad J. Cox:
*Object-Oriented Programming An Evolutionary Approach*
Addison-Wesley, Reading, Massachusetts, 1986

[Ferber 89]                 Jacques Ferber:
Computational Reflection in Class Based Object Oriented Languages.
*Proc. of Object-Oriented Programming: Systems, Languages and Applications*
p 317 - 326, October 1989

[Gamma et. al. 94]         E. Gamma; R. Helm; R. Johnson; J. Vlissides:
*Design Patterns Elements of Reusable Object-Oriented Software*
Addison-Wesley, Reading, Massachusetts, 1994

[Goldberg and Robson 83]   Adele Goldberg, David Robson:
*Smalltalk-80 the language and its implementation*
Addison-Wesley, Reading, Massachusetts, 1983

| | |
|---|---|
| [Kiczales et al. 91] | Gregor Kiczales, Jim des Rivieres, Daniel Bobrow: *The Art of the Metaobject Protocol.* MIT Press, Cambridge, Massachusetts, 1991 |
| [Lunau and Nielsen 95] | Charlotte Pii Lunau and John Koch Nielsen: Emma: An Emergency Management System for use onboard Ships *Proceedings of IFAC Workshop on Control Applications in Marine Systems* p. 164-173 Trondheim May 1995. |
| [Maes 87] | Pattie Maes: *Computational Reflection* Ph D. Thesis Technical Report 87-2 Artificial Intelligence Laboratory Vrije University Brussel, 1987 |
| [NeXT 92] | NeXTSTEP Object-Oriented Programming and the Objective C Language: Release 3 Addison-Wesley Publishing Company Readings, 1992. |
| [Rao 91] | Ramano Rao: Implementation Reflection in Silica Proceedings of ECOOP '91 p. 251-267 *Lecture Notes in Computer Science,* Springer-Verlag 1991 |
| [Smith 82] | Brian C. Smith: *Reflection and Semantics in a Procedural Language* Technical Report TR-272, MIT 1982 |

# APPENDIX A: COMPUTATIONAL REFLECTION IN OBJECTIVE-C

This Appendix describes how Objective-C is extended to allow computational reflection.

## IMPLEMENTATION OF COMPUTATIONAL REFLECTION

To extend a class based language with computational reflection, messages need to be reified and reflected upon.

In Objective-C, a message sent is translated into a call of the function objc_msgSend(receiver, selector, arguments). This function need to be changed so that it first checks if the receiver has a metaobject. If the receiver has a metaobject the function must sent a handleMsg to the metaobject, as shown in Figure A.1

```
objc_msgSend(receiver, selector, arguments)
    if [receiver hasMetaObject]
      [objc_msgSend(metaObject(receiver),
          "handleMsg:receiver:args",
                 receiver,selector,arguments)]
```

Figure A.1 Changed *Objc_msgSend* function

Unfortunately, it is not possible to change the *objc_msgSend(receiver, selector, arguments)* function because it is part of Objective-C's runtime system. Instead the functionality is obtained by changing class pointers dynamically. In Objective-C each object has a *isa* pointer to its class. The class has a *isa* pointer to its metaclass and a list of methods used by the runtime system when resolving message sending. When an object is sent a message and the runtime system cannot find an implementation of the method the receiving object is sent a *-forward::* message. In order to provoke a *-forward::* message for each message sent to an object with a metaobject we change the *isa* pointer of the object. Instead of pointing at the object's class the *isa* pointer points to a class MessageIntercept that implements the *-forward::* method as it's only method. MessageIntercept's implementation of *-forward::* first have to find the metaobject of the object causing the intercept and then sends it the *-handleMsg:receiver:args:* message.

Because Objective-C is class based, metaobjects are instances of classes. The only responsibility that metaobjects need to fulfil is the ability to respond to the *-handleMsg:receiver:args:* message. This implies that new metaobjects are easy to define and they can be defined using inheritance.

Metaobjects need to be attached and removed dynamically to objects. In order to do this, Object has been extended with a new category. A category is a mechanism for extending the set of methods defined on a class, without having access to the source code of the class. The new category contains the following three methods:

```
@interface Object(metakit)
    -insertPreMetaObject: (id <MetaObject> aMetaObject
    -insertPostMetaObject: (id <MetaObject> aMetaObject
    -withdrawPreMetaObject: (id <MetaObject> aMetaObject
    -withdrawPostMetaObject: (id <MetaObject> aMetaObject
    -(BOOL)hasMetaObject;
    -(id<metaObject>)metaObject;
@end
```

The *-insertPreMetaObject* and *-insertPostMetaObject* methods make the argument object the metaobject of the receiver. The *-withdrawPreMetaObject* and *-*

*withdrawPostMetaObject* methods remove the argument object from the list of metaobjects. *-hasMetaObject* returns YES if the receiver has a metaobject. *-metaObject* returns the metaobject of the receiver.

## APPENDIX B: THE METAOBJECT CLASS HIERARCHY

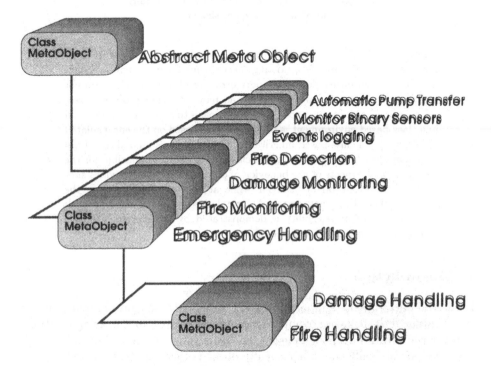

# Dynamic Object Evolution without Name Collisions

Mira Mezini

Department of Electrical Engineering and Computer Science (FB 12),
University of Siegen, D-57068 Siegen, Germany
mira@informatik.uni-siegen.de

**Abstract.** Support for modular evolution of objects is required in many application areas. However, existing mechanisms for incremental behavior composition either do not support evolving objects at all, or do not satisfactorily solve the encapsulation and name collision problems associated with them. In this paper, a new approach to behavior composition in a class-based environment is presented. It is based on the encapsulated object model of class-based inheritance, but introduces an additional abstraction layer between objects and classes. By being responsible for the compositional aspects of the behavior of objects, this layer provides support for the evolution of behavior while at the same time solving the name conflicts that may occur. A formal description of the approach is provided and its feasibility is demonstrated by implementing it as a metalevel extension of Smalltalk-80.

## 1 Introduction

In several object-oriented application areas, support for dynamic and incremental evolution of the behavior of objects is required. For example, in an application containing entities that model persons, an entity may acquire and abandon several roles, dynamically and independently of each other (e.g. being a student, an employee, a project manager, or a sportsman). These different roles may share some common structure and behavior (e.g. the name of the person), but they may exhibit role-specific behavior which is visible only within a particular context of the respective role (e.g. the identification numbers in the student and sportsman roles of a person). The need for evolving objects in order to adequately model roles has been pointed out in [11].

The subject-oriented approach to software development [12] goes even further: it requires the same objects to be shared by suites of cooperating applications called *subjects*. The goal is to enable the incremental enhancement of already existing systems through new functionality such that the present persistent objects not only remain valid, but are also automatically extended to support the new functionality. Similar to roles, some state and behavior may be shared between different subjects, while others may only be visible in the context of specific subjects. Although supporting subjectivity is a more general problem that is beyond the scope of this paper, support for evolvable objects is definitely one of the basic requirements to be satisfied.

A third area where support for evolvable objects is required are systems that adapt their behavior to run-time conditions and/or application requirements for achieving better performance and/or effectiveness [2, 3, 16]. The components of such systems should ideally have a range of implementations from which the most appropriate one is chosen in a particular situation. Furthermore, for better reusability, the range of supported implementations should be extensible. For example, a toolkit for multimedia application design should be able to support clients in computing environments ranging from hand-held PDA devices to powerful workstations, and communication environments ranging from telephone lines to high-speed and wireless networks. It should also be able to handle a variety of compression standards, rather than become obsolete as new ones emerge. Since multimedia processing is sensitive to variations in resource availability, replaceable presentation processing algorithms that can be dynamically configured according to the run-time environment should be supported.

As indicated by the application areas presented above and illustrated by an example in the next section, two main issues need to be considered by an incremental composition mechanism providing support for evolving objects. First, *dynamic composition* should be supported in the sense that (a) behavior modifications may happen after the object has become operational, and (b) once accomplished, a modification may remain valid only under certain conditions. Second, the mechanism should provide for *internal encapsulation*. In general, objects being considered here are composed of several aspects (roles, subjects, implementations). These aspects may at the same time be coupled to and disjoint from each other in the sense that they may (a) cooperate by sharing state or by jointly performing operations, but (b) nevertheless need to hide parts of their implementation from the others. An incremental composition mechanism that provides for internal encapsulation is able to cope with these conflicting interests. The internal encapsulation issue also manifests itself as the name collisions issue in multiple inheritance hierarchies, as indicated by Knudsen in [18]. However, in the case of evolving objects the situation gets worse, since the conflicts cannot be detected at compile time.

Unfortunately, none of the existing object-oriented incremental composition mechanisms provides a general framework to handle these issues in a uniform manner. The class-based inheritance models do not support dynamic composition, as argued in [11, 22, 24, 30, 32, 35]. The object-based [38] and hybrid [33] inheritance models do provide support for dynamic composition of object behavior, but at the price of violating the encapsulation of the client interface [35] and losing valuable sharing and structuring mechanisms [32]. The approaches that model real-world entities by a set of role [11] or exemplar [19] objects lack object identity semantics and therefore do not support a general form of object evolution. The mixin-methods approach [34] rectifies the encapsulation problem of the object-based model by enclosing possible modifications within an object itself, but the problem is that an object is required to know all its possible modifications in advance [35]. Moreover, neither the mixin-methods approach, nor more advanced approaches to behavior composition, such as *composition filters*

[1] or the *context relation* [30], adequately support internal encapsulation.

With respect to internal encapsulation, most of existing inheritance models either declare name collisions as invalid, i.e. they do not support internal encapsulation at all (like single inheritance and linear approaches to multiple inheritance [14, 26]), or exploit ad-hoc solutions mostly based on renaming and class qualification of message selectors (like graph-based approaches [4, 21, 31]). The latter are criticized in [6, 7, 39] because they violate late binding and consequently restrain reusability, even in a static environment. While being considered as remedies for the static case, more advanced solutions proposed in [6, 7, 39] still exhibit flexibility problems especially in dynamic environments.

We claim that the inability of the existing approaches to uniformly handle dynamic composition and internal encapsulation is due to the lack of sufficient abstraction levels in their design, which are needed to distinguish between defining, composing and supplying behavior. Based on this observation, a mechanism for incremental composition of object behavior is presented in this paper which uniformly deals with both issues, by an explicit combination layer, introduced between an object and the software components that define its behavior(s). A *combiner-metaobject* is associated with each evolving object, responsible for the compositional aspects of the object's behavior. The behavior definition of an evolving object is dispersed between a class that provides the standard behavior of the object and a set of mixin-like [5] software modules, called *adjustments*, that provide different modifications of the standard behavior in specific contexts. However, there is no static inheritance relationship between the class and the adjustments involved in the definition of an object. The information about how these cooperate with each other to yield a full behavior is managed by the combiner-metaobject in a way that provides internal encapsulation. From this information the combiner-metaobject derives the environment where to evaluate the messages sent to the object. Modifying the behavior of the object is a matter of requesting the combiner-metaobject to update the information it encapsulates, and can thus be performed dynamically.

Instead of designing a new language from scratch for demonstrating the viability of our proposal, a prototype of the mechanism has been implemented as an extension of Smalltalk-80 [10]. Smalltalk-80 has been chosen because of its existing metalevel facilities that enable the implementation of the mechanism as an extension of the standard image, without changes in the virtual machine. Other metalevel facilities of Smalltalk-80 also allow us to keep the overhead related to the additional metalevel indirection to a minimum.

The paper is organized as follows. In section 2 we illustrate the issues associated with dynamic object composition and internal encapsulation. In section 3, the proposed model for solving them is presented. A formal description of the model follows in section 4, and implementation issues are briefly discussed in section 5. A discussion of the features of the proposed model and related work follows in section 6. Section 7 concludes the paper and outlines topics for future research.

## 2 An Example

In this section, the issues that need to be solved by a behavior composition mechanism are illustrated by means of an example. Consider an atomic data type [40] representing a bank account within a database system. Its simplified functional aspect, i.e. the externally observable functionality it provides, is specified in the *Account* module in Fig. 1. The non-functional aspects of the *Account* object, concerned with local synchronization and recovery such as *begin-transaction*, *commit-transaction* and *abort-transaction*, are specified in the *AtomicObject* module in Fig. 1. Suppose that the database system supports object-based concurrency control [37], i.e. the concurrency semantics are defined at the level of object operations and not at the level of elementary read and write operations, taking into account the application semantics in order to increase the level of concurrency[1]. Then, the application semantics to be used by the concurrency controller are represented by the *conflictRelationStructure* data structure in *AtomicObject*. In the presence of an object-based concurrency control, when an operation on an account object is called, information about the transaction making the call should be recorded in order to later use it at transaction commit time for deciding whether to make the effects of a transaction permanent or not. The default information recording functionality is implemented by *recordTransactionInfo* in *AtomicObject* (Fig. 1) which exploits the *infoStruct* for storing the information. The definition of an account object, as seen by the concurrency controller is given by *RecordAccount* in Fig. 1.

Furthermore, suppose that our hypothetical database system is adaptive in terms of both the functional and non-functional aspects. For example, the *debit* functionality of an account may dynamically change depending on some conditions, e.g. depending on who attempts to withdraw how much money if the account is shared by a group of people, or the amount of money already withdrawn from an automatic teller machine within the last 24 hours. These two special withdrawing behaviors are schematically modeled by the *SharedAccount*, respectively *ATMAccount* modules in Fig. 1. A special action, represented by the *specialAction* method, should be performed in both cases before the withdrawal takes place. Additionally, assume that the system supports adaptable concurrency control [2], i.e. a multiplicity of optimistic, pessimistic, or hybrid concurrency control strategies are provided, each valid under certain conditions. For example, the strategy may be switched between pessimistic and optimistic depending on the conflict level in the system, or from one optimistic strategy to another depending on some heuristics based on the state of an object. This implies the presence of multiple modules implementing variations of *AtomicObject*. The behavioral landscape becomes much more complicated when replication and persistency issues are concerned.

The above example system illustrates the issues that a mechanism for incremental object composition should deal with. Obviously, an atomic account

---

[1] An object-based strategy allows, for example, that two credit operations from two different transactions may be scheduled concurrently.

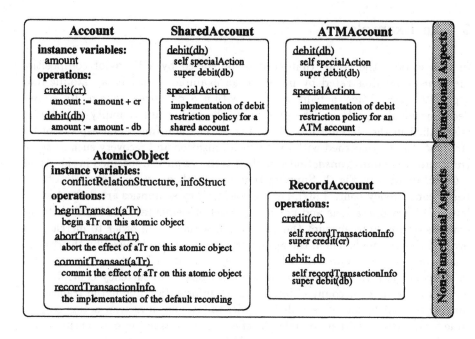

**Fig. 1.** The specification of an account object

object in this system should be able to change its behavior, becoming a shared account when required by its owner, changing to a shared and ATM-account, when a withdrawal attempt from an automatic teller machine occurs, and then switching to an optimistic atomic account due to a low level of conflicts detected. All of the above behavior alterations may happen after the account object has become operational. Additionally, a particular acquired behavior might remain valid only under certain conditions.

For illustrating the internal encapsulation issue, consider a shared account and its *debit* operation. The complete definition of *debit* is a combination of the definition in *SharedAccount* with that in *Account*, where the former incrementally modifies the latter, i.e. the *super* parameter in *SharedAccount* is the method in *Account*. Now suppose that the account becomes additionally an *ATMAccount*. The definition of *debit* should be further refined by the *debit* operation in *ATMAccount* to perform both special actions before really accomplishing the withdrawal, i.e. there is no conflict here. The situation is, however, different with regard to the *specialAction* operations. Each of the special *debit* operations has it own *specialAction*, which should be invisible to the other. The mechanism for incremental composition of object behavior should provide some kind of internal encapsulation between different subparts of the shared and ATM-account object, in addition to enabling them to jointly contribute to the full debit behavior by being incremental modifications of each other.

# 3   General Overview of the Model

There are trade-offs related to both issues illustrated above. As pointed out in [35], there is a trade-off between dynamic composition and the encapsulation of the client interface. Taking the object-based approach would allow dynamic modification, but by merging specialization and usage entities into a single unit, all encapsulation problems inherent to specialization [31] now concern the object's client interface as well. Thus, the choice of a class-based approach is obvious, but even the two-layered design of the latter seems to be insufficient for two reasons. First, while the objects are relieved from the burden of generating behavior, i.e. the client and composition interfaces are separated, no abstraction is provided for behavior alteration at the object level. While it is possible to have explicit conditionals in an object's code to alter its behavior to reflect changes in it state, the idea of object-oriented programming is to lift such dispatch at the language level. Avoiding the "case"-like style of procedural programming is an essential factor for the qualitative progress in reusability attributed to the object-oriented paradigm. Furthermore, state-related alterations do not cover all kinds of behavior alterations desired.

Second, there is a trade-off between incremental behavior modification, dynamic or not, and internal encapsulation between the subparts of an object, also called class encapsulation in [27], as identified by [33, 39]. The implementations of different aspects involved in the behavior of an object should be mutually visible to enable incremental modification, and at the same time certain parts of them should be hidden. This trade-off is the source of the name collisions problem. As pointed out by Nierstrasz et al. [27] and Bracha et al. [6], the class-based approach to incremental behavior composition fails to properly solve this trade-off because classes are overloaded to serve both as templates for defining object behavior and as software components responsible for behavior composition by means of inheritance. The separation of these roles by providing explicit components for each of the two different kinds of interfaces supported by classes is the key to uniformly solve the issues of dynamic composition and internal encapsulation in the model proposed in this paper. The model, presented in Fig. 2, has a three layered design consisting of the *behavior definition*, *behavior combination*, and *behavior provision* layer.

The behavior definition layer is responsible for the specification of behavior as a set of independent software modules, and the provision layer is responsible to provide clients with functionality. The known abstractions existing in the standard class-based model, classes and objects, are elements of the definition and the provision layer, respectively. The behavior combination layer represents the additional abstraction between an object and its behavior definition. Its elements, called *metaCombiners*, are responsible for the structural aspects of the behavior of the underlying object and its evolution. Since objects remain the same as in the class-based model, only the first two layers will be the subject of the informal discussion in this section.

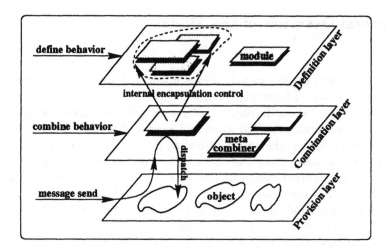

**Fig. 2.** The structure of the model

### 3.1 Behavior Definition Layer

Because of the highly complex and dynamic nature of the behavioral landscape of the objects we are concerned with, an approach to behavior definition should provide total expressiveness of the object's behavioral structure. In the proposed model the behavior definition of an object is in general dispersed among the class the object is initially generated from and a set of independent software modules, called *adjustments*. The class specifies the default (intrinsic) functionality of an object. In contrast, adjustments specify modifications of the default definition of an object, valid under special conditions. While there is always a class involved in the behavior definition of an object, the set of involved adjustments may be empty.

Adjustments are similar to mixins [5], in that the methods modeling the special behavior may refer to a parent behavior, which need not be known at the adjustment definition time and can be bound later. In order to support the special behavior, an adjustment may also declare state that is accessible only within the adjustment methods. Generally, there are three kinds of adjustments. *Specialization adjustments* specialize a class, or generally a full combined behavior definition, in a similar way to mixins. *Connection adjustments* connect two other modules by specifying how their methods are interrelated. *Class-like adjustments* are very similar to classes in that they provide full functionality (do not refer to any *super* parameter), which however does not make sense when standing alone. For illustration let us consider the following definitions for the account example presented above, written in the language *DOORS* being currently under development as a higher-level language on top of the *metaCombiner* mechanism for supporting the construction of adaptable object-oriented systems [25].

*class* Account *inherits* Object *def* {amount} *in*

   { credit(cr){amount := amount+cr}; debit(db){amount := amount-db; ...; }

*adjustment* SharedAccount *def* {} *in*

   { debit(db){self specialAction(cr); super debit(cr)}; specialAction(db){ ...}; }

*adjustment* ATMAccount *def* {} *in*

   { debit(db){self specialAction(cr); super debit(cr)}; specialAction(db){ ...}; }

*adjustment* AtomicObject *def* {conflictRelationStructure, infoStruct} *in*

   { beginTransaction(aTr){ ... }; abortTransaction(aTr){ ... } ...; }

*adjustment* RecordAccount *def* {} *in*

   { debit(db) {self recordTransactionInfo; super debit(db);}; ...; }

ATMAccount *specializes* Account *when* {"ATM account condition"}

SharedAccount *specializes* Account *when* {"shared account condition"}

*replicas* {{SharedAccount, ATMAccount} ↦ {specialAction}}

RecordAccount *connects* {Account, AtomicObject} *when* {"atomicity condition"}

   *alsoActivate* AtomicObject

In addition to the syntactic constructs for specifying classes and adjustments, the language also provides the following expressions.

- The *specializes* and *connects* expressions specify the type of adjustments. In the example above, *SharedAccount* and *ATMAccount* are specified to be specialization adjustments for the class *Account*. *AccountRecord* is a connection adjustment for *Account* and *AtomicObject*: its redefinition e.g. for *debit* simply specifies the interconnection between *debit* in *Account* and *recordTransactionInfo* in *AtomicObject*. Finally, *AtomicObject* is a class-like adjustment: it defines full functionality in the sense that no *super* call is made. However, the synchronization and recovery functionality it provides is meaningful only in conjunction with some application functionality, e.g. that defined in *Account*.

- The *when* expression specifies the event that causes the activation of an adjustment. An adjustment is said to be activated when it becomes part of the behavior definition of an object. The activation event may be a conditional on an object's state, a certain application-level declaration, or another external event, e.g. the activation of another adjustment.

- The *alsoActivate* expression specifies adjustments to be simultaneously activated. In the example above, the activation of *RecordAccount* should be accompanied by the activation of *AtomicObject*. Thus, the behavior definition of an atomic account object is always a combination of *Account*, *RecordAccount* and *AtomicObject*.

- The *replicas* expression specifies the interaction between methods for messages with the same name in different modules. When two methods are defined for the same message by two modules that may get involved in the definition of the same object, either one incrementally modifies the other, or they represent two different meanings of the message with different validity scopes and should be handled independently. The latter are explicitly annotated as *replicas*. A method that is not explicitly specified as being a replica but contains no *super* call, overwrites an existing method for the same message.

As the result of translating the class and adjustment specifications, class and adjustment metaobjects are created to internally represent the respective definitions. Additionally, so-called *Manager* metaobjects are automatically created and associated with each class for internally managing the information provided by the expressions above. The resulting infrastructure of the definition layer of *DOORS* is presented in detail in [24]. Since the emphasis in this paper is on the composition semantics of *DOORS* realized by the *metaCombiner* mechanism, further details about the definition layer are left out of this paper. This is also reflected by the denotational semantics in the following section, where *metaCombiner* operations are exposed at the syntactic level as metaexpressions. The following discussion assumes that class and adjustment modules, corresponding entities that contain specifications of replica-methods, and other higher-level constructs responsible for adjustment activation that avoid exposing the *metaCombiner* mechanism to the user exist. The discussion focuses only on how this mechanism handles requests for dynamic behavior combination.

## 3.2 Combination Layer

Despite the similarity between adjustments and mixins, there is an important semantic difference in the way the behavior they define is "bound" to that of their parent: there is no "physical" inheritance relationship between the class of an object and the adjustment that may get involved in its behavior definition over time. Dynamically "assembling" together default and special behavior is the responsibility of *metaCombiners* belonging to the combination layer. A metaCombiner is associated with each evolvable object, at instantiation time, taking responsibility for the compositional aspects of the object's behavior. Staying between an object and its dispersed behavior definition, a metaCombiner realizes some kind of connecting bridge between both, by taking over two responsibilities. First, it manages the information about how behavior definitions from different modules cooperate to yield a full behavior, in a way that provides internal encapsulation. Second, from this information it derives the environment where to evaluate the messages sent to the object. Modifying the behavior of the object is a matter of requesting the metaCombiner to update the information it encapsulates, and can thus be performed dynamically. This double role is also reflected by the definition of a *metaCombiner*, schematically shown in Fig. 3.

The *methodEnvironment* data structure encapsulated by a metacombiner plays a central role in the realization of its double functionality. Similar to method dictionaries in Smalltalk, or virtual tables in C++, this has the structure of a table with an entry for each message supported by the object. But in contrast to a class, a *metaCombiner* does not provide any behavior definition. Instead of containing the code corresponding to a message name, the method environment of the metaCombiner simply contains information about the behavioral structure of the message, as follows.

```
instance variables:
    methodEnvironment
operations:
  insert: anAdj combination: aComb
      integrate the definitions of anAdj according to aComb

  insert: adj1 after: adj2 combination: aComb
      integrate the adj1 definitions after those of aj2 according to aComb

  remove: anAdj
      cancel the definitions of anAdj

  next
      if more than one following definition for the current message then call
      executeReplicas, otherwise execute the sole definition

  executeReplicas: aReplicaSet
      check the validity of aReplicaSet and execute the valid definition
```

**Fig. 3.** The definition of a metaCombiner

In order to support internal encapsulation, the modules involved in the definition of an object are virtually – through the information stored in the method environment – grouped in *visibility scopes* individually for each message. Each replica definition, *rd*, of a message *m* has its individual visibility scope, defined as the set of modules having visibility for it, i.e. the set of modules for which *x* has the definition *rd*. Each scope has a unique identifier that is constructed successively along the alterations of the object's behavior, as discussed later. For messages with several scope-specific definitions the corresponding entry in the method environment contains one sub-entry for each scope-specific definition. This sub-entry is indexed by the corresponding scope identifier and encodes information about the set of modules jointly contributing to this scope-specific method definition, in the order in which these contributions should be executed. Messages with a single definition are a special case of those with multiple scope-specific definitions: their corresponding entry in *methodEnvironment* has a single sub-entry.

Consider, for example, the double restricted atomic account, *anAccount*, in Fig. 4. There are two sub-entries for the *specialAction* message, indexed by the scope identifiers *B*, respectively *C*. The sole elements of the order structures associated with these scope identifiers point to *SharedAccount* and *ATMAccount*, respectively. These adjustments have been marked with the labels *B*, respectively *C* in order to identify them within scope identifiers. The distribution of marks and the construction of scope identifiers will be discussed below. The scope identifier of the first sub-entry implies that only methods in *SharedAccount* have visibility for the *specialAction* definition encoded in the corresponding order structure: only the label assigned to *SharedAccount*, *B*, is included in the scope identifier. In contrast, the entries for *debit* and *recordTransactionInfo* have only one sub-entry, i.e. for both these messages there is a unique definition visible within the

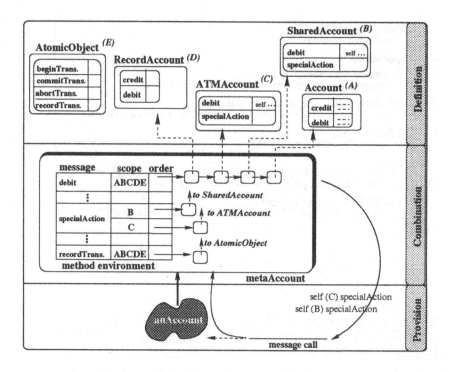

**Fig. 4.** The definition of an evolvable account object

scope of the entire object, as it is also reflected in the content of the respective scope identifiers.

The information in the method environment is exploited by the *dispatching functionality* (the *next* and *executeReplicas:* operations in Fig. 3). According to the information in the order structure of the *debit* entry, the information needed for the transaction validation time is gathered first by executing the implementation of *debit* in *RecordAccount*. Then, the *debit* implementations of *ATMAccount*, *SharedAccount*, and *Account* are successively executed. Additionally, *methodEnvironment* provides the information needed for deciding which of the multiple definitions of a message is valid in the context where the invocation of the message happens. When *self* invocations from the code of the adjustments already involved in the behavior definition of the object happen, only those definitions are valid whose associated scope identifier is "compatible" with (includes) the label assigned to the caller adjustment.

For illustration, let us follow the execution of *debit:* sent to *anAccount* in Fig. 4, after the implementation in *RecordAccount* has been executed. During the execution of the *SharedAccount* implementation, *specialAction* gets invoked. Although there are two different definitions for this message, only the one found in *SharedAccount* is valid in the context of the current *self* invocation. The adjustment *ATMAccount* is not in the same scope identifier as *SharedAccount*, which is the origin of the invocation. The execution continues with the implementation for *debit* provided by *ATMAccount*, which in turn calls the *specialAction* message again. This time, the implementation of *ATMAccount* will be executed. The process ends with the execution of the implementation for *debit* in *Account*.

Intuitively, this selective execution is equivalent to equipping each *self* invocation within an evolvable object with an implicit parameter informing the dispatching process about the specific flavor, i.e. the internally encapsulated subpart of the object which the current *self* invocation stems from. In Fig. 4, this is illustrated by putting the label of the caller adjustment in brackets after the *self* variable in calls from within the *debit:* method. A precise description of how these internal encapsulation boundaries are established and taken into consideration during message dispatching is given in the denotational semantics in the next section. Currently, only methods that are not visible to clients are allowed to have multiple scope-specific definitions. However, this is not because the mechanism is principally unable to deal with other cases. It simply reflects the fact that the mechanism presented here should be considered as a framework for supporting evolving objects in a range of areas, which may have different semantics for dealing with multiple scope-specific definitions. For example, the subject making the invocation may be used as a criteria for chosing the valid scope-specific definition(s) of an interface message in a subjective environment, while "as-"constructs may be used for modeling role-specific behavior. Being modeled in an object-oriented way, the mechanism can be specialized to serve several concrete areas.

The second responsibility of a *metaCombiner* is the initialization and maintenance of the methodEnvironment information. This is initialized when the object is initially created. All entries have a single scope identifier: a special label marking class definitions, and all order structures have a single element pointing to the class. For more details about the initialization consider the instantiation semantics in the next section. Passing an adjustment component together with the request to integrate or cancel its definitions from the current behavior definition of the object corresponds to an object evolution. This is supported by *insert* and *remove* operations on a metaCombiner (the *insert:combination:*, *insert: after: combination:*, and *remove:* operations in Fig. 3), which appropriately update the method environment. Thus, the evaluation of future messages to the underlying object, accomplished by the dispatching functionality, will occur in the context of the updated behavior definition.

When an adjustment has to be integrated, an additional parameter, called a *combination rule*, is passed to the metaCombiner. A combination rule contains the messages whose corresponding methods in the adjustment should be considered as *replicas*[1]. For example, suppose that the modules in Fig. 4 are inserted

---

[1] While currently supporting only method combination, the mechanism can be extended to support more complex combination rules used for composing subjects [12].

in the following order: *Account, RecordAccount, AtomicObject, SharedAccount*. Now, in order to insert *ATMAccount*, the *insertAdj: after: combination:* message should be sent to *metaAccount* with the following parameters: *ATMAccount, SharedAccount* and a combination rule that annotates *specialAction* as *replica*. Based on the combination rules, the metaCombiner successively constructs the visibility scope identifiers, such that the internal encapsulation of the replica-methods is ensured, as described in the following summary of the functionality of the *insert:combination:* operation.

- First, the adjustment to be inserted is marked with a label that identifies the behavior alteration related to the current insertion within the structures of the method environment. An adjustment which is inserted more than once will have as many different labels as the number of its insertions. This allows to achieve a similar effect as the so-called *repeated inheritance* [11]. Labels are released by the remove functionality. A new element of the order structure is created for the adjustment.
- For each replica-message defined in the adjustment to be inserted, a new scope is created with the label of the adjustment as its identifier. A new sub-entry is created for the message in the method environment, associating the new scope identifier with the new order element.
- For each *refinement* definition, i.e. a non-replica definition for a message that already exists in the method environment, the label assigned to the adjustment is added into all currently existing scope identifiers which makes the method visible within all currently existing scopes. In this way the late binding of *self* is emulated. The new ordering element is added at the beginning of the order structure, thus incrementally modifying the current combined definition of the message.
- For each new method definition, i.e. a definition for a message that did not exist in the method environment, a new scope identifier is created, containing all currently distributed labels – the definition is visible within the scope of the entire object. A new entry is added into the method environment for the new message associating the created scope identifier to its definition.

The *insert: combination:* operation models the modification of the entire combined behavior of an object. The *insert: after: combination:* operation serves to modify a subpart of the combined behavior. Its functionality and that of the *remove:* operation are defined similarly. For a precise description of these operations, consider their denotational semantics in the next section.

# 4 Formal Description

In this section a formal description of the model will be presented, as an extension of the denotational semantics of an object-oriented language with state proposed by Hense in [13]. The language defined in [13], called *O'Small*, can be considered as a simplified Smalltalk, in that complicated constructs are eliminated, while preserving the intuitiveness of its inheritance mechanism. We prefer to formally describe the result of integrating the *metaCombiner* mechanism into *O'Small* rather than describe its prototype implementation as an extension of Smalltalk-80, which is outlined in the next section. In this way, the comprehensive denotational semantics available for *O'Small* can be partly reused. However, concerning the composition semantics, the extended *O'Small* and the prototype implementation in the next section are essentially equivalent to each other and to the informal semantics described in the previous section.

For the definition of syntactic and semantic domains the following notation is used. The name of the domain is given on the left side of a line. The metavariable on the right side designates a member of the domain, while the text between the name and the metavariable informally describes the domain. The structure of compound domains is given between the name and the informal description, as a composition of operations on other domains. For the sake of simplicity, the following formal description focuses on the new syntactic constructs and those that have a modified semantics in the extension. The semantic of the syntactic clauses that are not affected by the extension, such as the program clause $(P)$, the clauses for compound expressions $(C)$, variable definitions $(V)$, as well as some of the expression clauses $(E)$, is left out of this description. However, since these are standard constructs that are supported by (almost) any object-oriented language, we assume that the intuitive understanding of their semantics should suffice to read the semantics of the new and modified constructs; refer to [13] for an exact definition.

*Syntactic domains*

| | | |
|---|---|---|
| Ide | the domain of identifiers | I |
| Bas | the domain of basic constants | B |
| Pro | the domain of programs | P |
| Exp | the domain of expressions | E |
| CExp | the domain of compound expressions (commands) | C |
| MExp | the domain of metaexpressions | ME |
| Var | the domain of variable declarations | V |
| Meth | the domain of method declarations | M |
| Cls | the domain of class definitions | K |
| Adj | the domain of adjustment definitions | A |
| BDef | the domain of behavior definition modules | BD |

*Syntactic clauses*

| | | |
|---|---|---|
| P | ::= | BD C |
| BD | ::= | K $\mid$ A $\mid$ BD$_1$ BD$_2$ $\mid$ $\varepsilon$ |
| K | ::= | class I$_1$ inherits I$_2$ def V in M $\mid$ I$_1$ combine I$_2$ I$_3$ rep I$_4$ |
| A | ::= | adjustment I def V in M |
| ME | ::= | evolve E $\mid$ I$_1$ insert A rep I$_2$ $\mid$ I$_1$ insert A$_1$ after A$_2$ rep I$_2$ $\mid$ I remove A |
| E | ::= | ME $\mid$ B $\mid$ true $\mid$ false $\mid$ I $\mid$ E.I(E$_1$,...,E$_n$) $\mid$ new E $\mid$ newEvol E |
| C | ::= | E $\mid$ I := E $\mid$ if E then C$_1$ else C$_2$ $\mid$ while E do C $\mid$ C$_1$;C$_2$ |
| V | ::= | var I := E $\mid$ V$_1$ V$_2$ $\mid$ $\varepsilon$ |
| M | ::= | meth I(I$_1$,...,I$_n$) C $\mid$ M$_1$M$_2$ $\mid$ $\varepsilon$ |

## Semantic domains

| | | | |
|---|---|---|---|
| Lab | | adjustment labels | lb |
| Unit | | the one-point-domain | u |
| Bool | | the domain of booleans | b |
| Loc | | the domain of locations | l |
| Bv | | the domain of basic values | e |
| Scope | $= \mathcal{P}(\text{Lab})$ | method scopes | sc |
| $\text{Record}_{\alpha,\beta}$ | $= \alpha \mapsto [\beta + \bot]$ | records | |
| Env | $= \text{Record}_{Ide,Dv}$ | environments | r |
| CombEnv | $= \text{Record}_{\{se,gen\},Dv}$ | combiner environments | $r_{mc}$ |
| Object | $= \text{Record}_{Ide,Dv}$ | objects | o |
| $\text{ST}_{\alpha}$ | $= \text{Store} \rightarrow [\alpha \times \text{Store}]$ | state transformer values | x |
| Store | $= \text{Record}_{Loc,Sv}$ | stores | s |
| Dv | $= \text{Loc} + \text{Rv} + \text{Method}_n + \text{Class}$ | denotable values | d |
| | $+ \text{GenList} + \text{SMethod}_n + \text{Adjust}$ | | |
| Sv | $= \text{File} + \text{Rv}$ | storable values | v |
| Rv | $= \text{Unit} + \text{Bool} + \text{Bv} + \text{Object}$ | R-values | v |
| File | $= \text{Rv}^*$ | files | i |
| $\text{Method}_n$ | $= \text{Dv}^n \mapsto \text{ST}_{Dv}$ | method values | m |
| $\text{SMethod}_n$ | $= \text{Dv} \rightarrow [\text{Dv}^n \rightarrow \text{Record}_{Scope,ST_{Dv}}]$ | scoped method values | sm |
| Class | $= \text{ST}_{Object} \rightarrow \text{ST}_{Object}$ | class values | c |
| Adjust | $= \text{ST}_{Object} \rightarrow \text{Class}$ | adjustment values | a |
| Comb | $= \text{ST}_{CombEnv} \rightarrow \text{ST}_{CombEnv}$ | metacombiner values | mc |
| GenList | $= \text{Adjust}^* \times \text{Class}$ | generator lists | g |

## Semantic functions

$$[\![\,]\!]_K: \quad \text{Cls} \rightarrow \text{Env} \rightarrow \text{ST}_{Env}$$
$$[\![\,]\!]_A: \quad \text{Adj} \rightarrow \text{Env} \rightarrow \text{ST}_{Env}$$
$$[\![\,]\!]_{SM}, [\![\,]\!]_M: \quad \text{Meth} \rightarrow \text{Env} \rightarrow \text{Env}$$
$$[\![\,]\!]_E \; [\![\,]\!]_R: \quad \text{Exp} \rightarrow \text{Env} \rightarrow \text{ST}_{Dv}$$
$$[\![\,]\!]_{ME}: \quad \text{MExp} \rightarrow \text{Env} \rightarrow \text{ST}_{Dv}$$

Consider the class declaration function in Fig. 5. Similar to the standard semantics as defined in [13], the $x_{super}$ parameter is bound at the class declaration time. However, in contrast to the standard semantics, the evaluation of a class declaration is performed by two different functions in Fig. 5, depending on the value of $b$. This parameter is bound at the object creation time, as indicated by the functions for instance creation in Fig. 9. It is true when evolvable objects have to be created, and false otherwise. When $b$ is false, the semantic definition remains the same as the standard one in [13] (the second choice of the conditional). The $x_{self}$ parameter is the state transformer returned by applying the fix-point operator to the class, as indicated by the function for *"new E"* in Fig. 9. Applying $x_{self}$ to the creation time store, $s_{create}$, returns the method environment to which the *self* parameter of the object being created (referred to within $M$) is definitively bound, leaving the store unchanged.

If $b$ is true, however, the state transformer passed as parameter, $x_{mc}$, returns a combiner-environment after being applied to the store ($r_{mc}$). As indicated by

$[\![$class $I_1$ inherits $I_2$ defines V in $M]\!]_K r = [\![I_2]\!]_E$ * Class? * $\lambda c.\text{result}[I_1 \mapsto w \boxed{\triangleright} c],$

$$w = \lambda x_{super}.\lambda b.\text{cond}(\lambda x_{mc}.\lambda s_{create}.[\![M]\!]_M(\begin{bmatrix} self & \mapsto (r_{mc}\ se) \\ super & \mapsto r_{super} \end{bmatrix} \oplus r_{local} \oplus r),$$

$$\lambda x_{self}.\lambda s_{create}.[\![M]\!]_M(\begin{bmatrix} self & \mapsto r_{self} \\ super & \mapsto r_{super} \end{bmatrix} \oplus r_{local} \oplus r))$$

$(r_{super}, s_{super}) = (x_{super}\ s_{create})$  $(r_{self}, -) = (x_{self}\ s_{create})$
$(r_{local}, s_{new}) = ([\![V]\!]_V r\ s_{super})$  $(r_{mc}, -) = (x_{mc}\ s_{create})$

The auxiliary functions used above are defined as follows:

The generic function * is defined by Hense for the composition of commands and declarations, as follows. Let $f$ and $g$ be two functions with the following types:

$$f : \left\langle \begin{array}{c} \text{Store} \\ D_1 \mapsto \text{Store} \end{array} \right\rangle \to [D_2 \times \text{Store}], \qquad g : D_2 \to \text{Store} \to [D_3 \times \text{Store}]$$

The lines in braces represent alternatives. The alternatives below depend on the choices of the alternatives above. If the upper/lower alternative of a brace above has been chosen, the upper/lower alternative in every brace below has to be chosen, as well. The composition of $f$ and $g$ is defined, as follows:

$$f*g : \left\langle \begin{array}{c} \text{Store} \\ D_1 \mapsto \text{Store} \end{array} \right\rangle \to [D_3 \times \text{Store}], \qquad f*g = \left\langle \begin{array}{c} \lambda s_1 \\ \lambda d_1.\lambda s_1 \end{array} \right\rangle \cdot \begin{cases} (\bot, s_2), & \text{if } s_2 \text{ err} \\ g\ d_2\ s_2, & \text{otherwise} \end{cases}$$

where $(d_2, s_2) = \left\langle \begin{array}{c} f\ s_1 \\ f\ d_1 s_1 \end{array} \right\rangle$

result: $D \to \text{Store} \to [D \times \text{Store}]$,  result $d = \lambda s.(d, s)\cdot$

cond: $[D \times D] \to \text{Bool} \to D$, $\text{cond}(d1, d2) = \lambda b.b \mapsto d1, d2$

$D? : D' \to \text{Store} \to [D' \times \text{Store}], D \subseteq D', D? = \lambda d.\begin{cases} \text{result } d\ d \in D \\ \text{error} \quad \text{otherwise} \end{cases}$

$\oplus, \boxed{\triangleright}$ are the left-preferential record combination operator, respectively the inheritance operator as defined in [9]

**Fig. 5.** Class declaration

the semantic function for creating evolvable objects ( *"newEvol E"* in Fig. 9), $x_{mc}$ is the result of evaluating an implicit *"evolve E"* metaexpression. The function for this metaexpression, given in Fig. 6, creates a new combiner-environment as follows. First, the fix-point operator is applied to the non-evolvable version of the class to be instantiated, $(c')$ and a binding for the pseudo-variable *flav* is appended to the result. The method environment gained in this way is bound as the value of *se* in the combiner-environment being created. When present in a method environment, the pseudo-variable *flav* designates the module which methods in the environment belong to. As it can be also noticed in the adjustment declaration function in Fig. 7, all environments used to bind *self* within methods of an evolvable object do contain a binding for *flav*. This models the implicit parametrization of *self*-calls used to indicate the internal "encapsulated subobject" which a certain (*self*) call stems from. As discussed in the previous section and indicated by the semantic function for method invocation below, this information is used to dispatch the invocation. The *gen* entry of the created combiner-environment is bound to a transformation of *se* accomplished by the *scoped* function. This function stamps all methods in *se* as being visible within the default scope (the special label *def*).

$$
\begin{array}{l}
[\![ \text{evolve E} ]\!]_{ME}r = [\![ \text{E} ]\!]_E r \ * \ \lambda c.(c \text{ false}) \ * \ \text{Class?} \ * \ \lambda c'.(\text{result comb}), \\[4pt]
\quad \text{comb} = \lambda x.\lambda s.
\begin{bmatrix}
gen & \mapsto & \lambda x.\text{result(scoped(se, } def)) \\
se & \mapsto & [flav \mapsto def] \oplus r_{self}
\end{bmatrix},\ (r_{self}, \text{-}) = \text{Fix}(c')s \\[8pt]
\quad \text{scoped: Env} \times \text{Lab} \to \text{Env}, \qquad \text{scoped(r, lb)(x)} = [\text{lb} \mapsto (r\ x)] \\[4pt]
\quad def \text{ is a special label used to mark the default definition}
\end{array}
$$

**Fig. 6.** Metaexpressions (1)

The combiner-environment constructed in this way is passed (indirectly through "*newEvol*") as a parameter to the class declaration function ($r_{mc}$ in Fig. 5). As it can be seen in Fig. 5, when an evolvable object is created ($b = true$), instead of binding the *self* parameter within $M$ definitively to a particular method environment, as in the non-evolvable case, it is bound to the *se* variable within the combiner environment. This indirection, which is the key to dynamic behavior evolution, is schematically presented in Fig.11. Before going on with the semantic function for adjustment declaration, notice that the semantic function for the "$I_1$ *combine* $I_2$ *with* $I_3$ *rep* $I_4$" clause, which enables the use of the metaCombiner mechanism to statically compose behavior definition modules, is omitted in Fig. 5, since this clause is equivalent to the sequence: $I_1 := evolve\ I_2;\ I_1\ insert$ $I_3\ rep\ I_4$.

Similar to wrappers used to model mixins in [13], the evaluation of adjustment declarations in Fig.7 results in a function of the *super* and *self* parameters. However, it differs from wrapper functions, as follows. There are two additional parameters: the label *lb*, and the combination rule *cr*, both to be bound at insertion time, as indicated by the functions in Fig. 10. *lb* is further passed as a parameter to $[\![ M ]\!]_{SM}$, where it will be used to construct scope identifiers. The function $[\![ ]\!]_{SM}$ (Fig. 8) creates so-called scoped method environments encapsulated by a metaCombiner, as informally described in the previous section. Scoped method environments differ from standard ones created by $M[\![ ]\!]$ in that they expect an additional parameter: the *super* scoped method environment, $r_{superMeth}$. The new scoped environment for a message $I$ is created as follows. For each association ($sc_i$, $m_i$) in $r_{superMeth}$, (a) the new scope identifier is created by appending *lb* to $sc_i$, and (b) $C$ is evaluated with the *super* parameter (that may appear free in it) bound to $m_i$.

$$[\![\text{adjustment I defines V in M}]\!]_A r = \text{result}[I \mapsto a], \text{ where:}$$

$$a = \lambda lb.\lambda cr.\lambda x_{super}.\lambda x_{self}.\lambda s_{insert}.((a_{ref} \oplus a_{rep}) \boxed{\oplus} r_{super}, lb)$$

$$a_{ref}(\text{x}) = \begin{cases} r_{meth}(x) \,\boxdot\, r_{super}(x) & x \in \text{dom}(r_{meth}) \cap \text{dom}(r_{super}) \cap \overline{\text{dom}}(cr) \\ \bot & \text{otherwise} \end{cases}$$

$$a_{rep}(\text{x}) = \begin{cases} r_{meth}(x) \,\boxed{\oplus}\, r_{super}(x) & x \in \text{dom}(r_{meth}) \cap \text{dom}(r_{super}) \cap \text{dom}(cr) \\ \bot & \text{otherwise} \end{cases}$$

$$r_{meth} = [\![M]\!]_{SM}([\text{self} \mapsto ([flav \mapsto lb] \oplus r_{self})] \oplus r_{loc} \oplus r) \, lb$$
$$(r_{loc}, \text{-}) = ([\![V]\!]r \, s_{insert}), \, (r_{self}, \text{-}) = (x_{self} \, s_{insert}), \, (r_{super}, \text{-}) = (x_{super}, s_{insert})$$

$\boxdot$, $\boxed{\oplus}$ are the application operation, respectively the distributive version of the left-preferential record combination operator as defined in [9]

**Fig. 7.** Adjustment definition functions

$$[\![\text{meth } I(I_1, ..., I_n) \, C]\!]_{SM} r =$$
$$\lambda lb. \left[ I \mapsto \lambda r_{supMeth}.\lambda d_1. \ ... \ \lambda d_n. \begin{bmatrix} sc'_1 \mapsto [\![C]\!] \, (r_{arg} \oplus [super \mapsto m_1] \oplus r) \\ ... \\ sc'_k \mapsto [\![C]\!] \, (r_{arg} \oplus [super \mapsto m_k] \oplus r) \end{bmatrix} \right],$$

$$r_{arg} = \begin{bmatrix} I_1 \mapsto d_1 \\ ... \\ I_n \mapsto d_n \end{bmatrix}, \, sc'_i = lb \cup sc_i, \, sc_i \in \text{dom}(r_{supMeth}), \, m_i = (r_{supMeth} \, sc_i)$$

$$[\![M_1 \, M_2]\!]_{SM} r = ([\![M_2]\!]_{SM} r) \oplus ([\![M_1]\!]_{SM} r)$$
$$[\![\epsilon]\!]_{SM} r = [\,]$$

$$[\![\text{meth } I(I_1, ..., I_n) \, C]\!]_M r = \left[ I \mapsto \lambda d_1. \ ... \ \lambda d_n. [\![C]\!] \, \left( \begin{bmatrix} I_1 \mapsto d_1 \\ ... \\ I_n \mapsto d_n \end{bmatrix} \oplus r \right) \right]$$

$$[\![M_1 M_2]\!]_M r = ([\![M_2]\!]r) \oplus ([\![M_1]\!]r)$$

$$[\![\epsilon]\!]_M r = [\,]$$

**Fig. 8.** Method definition functions

The $cr$ parameter (Fig. 7) controls the integration of the method environment resulting from $[\![M]\!]_{SM}$ with $r_{super}$. For non-replica methods, i.e. $x \in \overline{dom}(cr)$, the $super$ method, $r_{super}(x)$, is applied to the function bound to $x$ in the environment returned by $[\![M]\!]_{SM}$. In contrast, no $super$ parameter is applied to the replica-methods ($x \in dom(cr)$). Thus, in contrast to mixin-wrappers the application of the *super* parameter has been shifted to the method level. Notice that the *self* environment of adjustment methods (see the binding for *self* in the environment where $[\![M]\!]_{SM}$ is evaluated, in Fig 7) binds the pseudo-variable *flav* to the adjustment label *lb*, marking the methods with the label of the adjustment they belong to. The rest of the *self* environment consists of $r_{self}$. This results from applying the fix-point operator to the generator entry (*gen*) of a metaCombiner after the adjustment get inserted into it, as indicated by the functions in Fig. 10.

After all its parameters are bound, the adjustment declaration function returns a pair consisting of a scoped method environment and the assigned label. The method environment is a combination of the new method environment derived from the adjustment definitions, $a_{ref} \oplus a_{rep}$, with the *super* method environment, $r_{super}$, whereby the former overwrites the latter. Before leaving the semantics of the behavior definition constructs ($K,A$), let us briefly consider the evaluation of variable definitions. Both definitions for class and adjustment declarations in Fig. 5 and 7 share the non-recursive allocation of the instance variable environment. With respect to the visibility of instance variables, strong encapsulation is exploited: in both cases only $r_{local}$ is used for the evaluation of method definitions.

$[\![\text{new } E]\!]_E r = [\![E]\!]r * \lambda c.(c \text{ false}) * \text{Class?} * \lambda c'.\lambda s.(\text{Fix}(c'))s$

$[\![\text{newEvol } E]\!]_E r = [\![E]\!] * \lambda c.(c \text{ true}) * \text{Class?} * \lambda c'.\lambda s.(c' \ x_{mc} \ s),$
$\quad x_{mc} = \text{Fix}([\![\text{evolve } E]\!]_{ME} r)$

$[\![E.I(E_1,...,E_n)]\!]_E r = [\![E]\!]_R r * \text{Object?} * \lambda o.(\text{EObj } o) * \text{cond}((\text{match d } flavor), d)$
$\quad * \text{Method?} * \lambda m.[\![E_1]\!]_R r * \lambda d_1. \, .... [\![E_n]\!]_R r * \lambda d_n.m(d_1, ...,d_n),$

$\quad\quad flavor = (o \ flav), \quad d = (o \ I), \quad \text{EObj} = \lambda o.\begin{cases} false \ (o \ flav) = \bot \\ true \ \text{otherwise} \end{cases}$

$\quad\quad \text{match: Env} \times \text{Lab} \to \text{Method}_n, \ \text{match} = \lambda r.\lambda lb.(r \ sc), \exists \ sc \in dom(r), \ lb \in sc$

$[\![E]\!]_R r = [\![E]\!]_E r * \text{deref} * \text{Rv?},$

$\quad\quad \text{deref: Dv} \to \text{Store} \to [\text{Dv} \times \text{Store}], \quad \text{deref} = \lambda e.\begin{cases} cont \ e \ e \in \text{Loc} \\ error \ \text{otherwise} \end{cases}$

**Fig. 9.** Semantics of instantiation and message invocation

As shown in Fig. 9, the creation of non-evolvable objects (*"new E"*) remains essentially the same, except that the boolean parameter of the class function is first bound to false. In the case of evolvable objects (*"newEvol E"*), a new combiner environment ($x_{mc}$) is created, as already discussed above, and passed as a parameter to the class function. As already discussed above and illustrated in Fig. 11, the *self* parameter within the class declaration function (Fig. 5) will be bound to the *se* entry of the combiner parameter, i.e. *self* is not directly bound to a method environment, but instead to a variable that contains a method environment. The content of this variable is modified as adjustments are inserted or removed, as shown by the semantic functions for metaexpressions in Fig. 10.

$$[\![I_1 \text{ insert A rep } I_2]\!]_{ME}r = [\![I_1]\!]_E * \text{Comb?} * \lambda mc.[\![A]\!]_A * \lambda a.[\![I_2]\!]_E * \lambda cr.\text{newLabel}$$
$$* \lambda lb.(\lambda x.\lambda s.(\begin{bmatrix} gen \mapsto gen_1 \\ se \mapsto rs_1 \end{bmatrix} \oplus r_{mc}))$$

$$[\![I_1 \text{ insert } A_1 \text{ after } A_2 \text{ rep } I_2]\!]_{ME}r = [\![I_1]\!]_E * \text{Comb?} * \lambda mc.[\![A_1]\!]_A * \lambda a_1.$$
$$[\![A_2]\!]_A * \lambda a_2.[\![I_2]\!]_E * \lambda cr.\text{newLabel} * \lambda lb.(\lambda x.\lambda s.(\begin{bmatrix} gen \mapsto gen_2 \\ se \mapsto rs_2 \end{bmatrix} \oplus r_{mc}))$$

$$[\![I \text{ remove } A]\!]_{ME}r = [\![I]\!]_E * \text{Comb?} * \lambda mc.[\![A]\!]_A * \lambda a_3.(\lambda x.\lambda s.(\begin{bmatrix} gen \mapsto gen_3 \\ se \mapsto rs_3 \end{bmatrix} \oplus r_{mc}))$$

$(r_{mc}, \text{-}) = (\text{Fix}(mc))s, \quad gen_0 = (r_{mc} \ gen),$

$gen_1 = \text{Extend}(gen_0, (a \ lb \ cr)) \quad gen_2 = \text{AfterExtend}(gen_0, (a_1 \ lb \ cr), a_2),$

$gen_3 = \text{Extract}(gen_0, \pi_2(a_3)), \quad rs_i = \text{Fix}(\text{GenComp } gen_i)s \ (i = 1,2,3),$

Extend: GenList $\rightarrow$ Adjust $\rightarrow$ GenList, $\quad$ Extend = $\lambda gen.\lambda a.(a, gen)$,

GenComp: GenList $\rightarrow$ Class,

$$\text{GenComp} = \lambda gen. \begin{cases} gen & \text{if } (sz \ gen) = 1 \\ comp(\pi_1(hd \ gen), GenComp(tl \ gen)), & \text{otherwise} \end{cases}$$

comp: Adjust $\times$ Class $\rightarrow$ Class, $\quad$ comp = $\lambda a.\lambda c.(a \ \Box \ \text{result}(c))$

The auxilairy functions *sz*, *hd*, and *tl* return the size, the head, and the tail of a list, respectively. $\pi_i$ $(i = 1,2)$ are the projection functions

**Fig. 10.** Meta-expression functions (2)

Let us consider the function for the first insert clause in Fig. 10. First, the current generator list, $gen_0$, is updated by *Extend*. Within *Extend*, the label generated by the auxiliary function *newLabel* (*lb*) along with the combination rule (*cr*) are passed as parameters to the result of evaluating the adjustment to be inserted, *a*. This results in a pair, containing the scoped method environment of the adjustment – a function of *super* and *self* – and the generated label, as already shown in Fig.7. The *Extend* function adds this pair into the current generator list, yielding the new generator list $gen_1$ to be bound to *gen*. The generator entity of the combiner has been modeled as a list, in order to keep the function for the remove clause simple. After the binding for *gen* is modified, the *GenComp* function recursively bounds the *super* parameters of the adjustments in the list. The fix-point application binds the *self* parameter of the resulting chain yielding the method environment ($rs_i$) which becomes the new value of *se*. The semantic functions for the other two clauses are defined in a similar way: *AfterExtend* adds the adjustment method environment at a certain position into the list, while *Extract* removes it from the list.

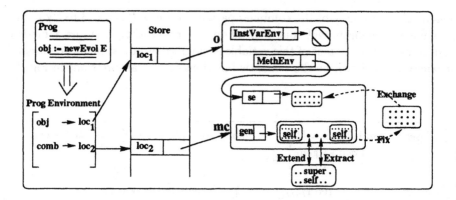

**Fig. 11.** Indirect binding of self

## 5 Implementation Issues

The proposed model has been prototypically implemented as a metaextension of the standard Smalltalk image. In this section we will briefly present how the mechanism is integrated into the standard Smalltalk system. Additionally, we will show how the metalevel facilities of Smalltalk are exploited to keep the overhead related to the metalevel indirection to a minimum.

The functionality of the *metaCombiner* is implemented as a subclass of *Class*, which models the behavior of class objects in Smalltalk-80 [10]. Thus, a *meta-Combiner* is a class which additionally supplies combination and explicit dispatching functionality. A new method for creating evolvable objects is added on the instance creation functionality of classes. Instead of creating an instance of the receiver class, this new method creates an empty *metaCombiner*, makes this a subclass of the receiver class, and finally instantiates the created *meta-Combiner*. Fig. 12 illustrates the result of creating a new object *Cl-object* as an instance of the class *CL*.

By making the *metaCombiner* the class of the object, it automatically becomes the default place where the dispatching of the messages to the object starts. However, its explicit dispatcher functionality remains inactivated as long as no adjustment is inserted into it. Since the automatically created *metaCombiner* is an empty subclass of the original class, all messages are further dispatched to the original class. This remains valid for the unmodified messages also after adjustments are inserted into the *metaCombiner*, since only modified messages are inserted into its method dictionary, which plays the method environment role. It is evident that there is no extra overhead for these messages. Adjustments are implemented as a special kind of of classes which provide only instance-template functionality. Instead of using the pseudo-variable *super* to

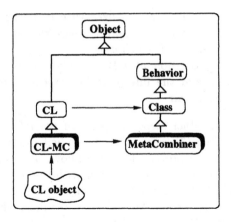

**Fig. 12.** Creating a new object

invoke the method they refine, adjustment methods make a special call, *self class next*. This invokes the dispatching functionality (*next* operation) of the *metaCombiner* – the class of *self* in this call – instead of the implicit dispatching functionality. The lookup part of the dispatching functionality makes use of the order structure associated with each message in the method dictionary of a *metaCombiner*. Since this is implemented as a list of pointers to those inserted modules that contain a method for the message in the order of their execution, there is no additional overhead related to method lookup. In order to keep the potential overhead related to the execution of the method returned by the lookup part small, we make use of the reflective facilities of Smalltalk-80 [10], which allow the reification of the interpretation context chain by means of the pseudo-variable *thisContext*.

From the discussion above, the execution of a modified message $m$ results in a sequence of pairs, $EP_i$, of the form: *(application-code, dispatch-code)*, where application-code denotes the implementation of the message provided by the module $i$ in the order structure and dispatch-code is the code for the explicit dispatch operation, *next*, which may get invoked within application-code. In order to illustrate the use of the context reification facility, consider the execution of a certain pair, $EP_i$. Let *code-context* and *dispatch-context* be the context where the execution of $EP_i.$*application-code*, and $EP_i.$*dispatch-code* occurs, respectively. The interpretation steps of $m$ are given below.

1. The $EP_i.$*application-code* is executed in *code-context*.
2. This execution may invoke the dispatch operation *next*; in this case the interpreter opens a new context, the *dispatch-context*.
3. The execution of $EP_i.$*dispatch-code* will be performed in *dispatch-context*, as follows. First, the sub-definition of the message following the current application-code will be found in the order structure, and the sender context

(*thisContext sender*) will be reinitialized with it. It should be noticed that the sender of *thisContext* is *code-context*, where the interpretation continues after the execution of $EP_i.dispatch\text{-}code$.

4. At this point, the execution of $EP_i.dispatch\text{-}code$ has finished, *dispatch-context* gets closed, and the interpretation process continues with step 1 for the next execution pair.

Except for step (3), all other steps are parts of the interpretation process of the virtual machine. Step (3) represents our explicit intervention point in this process. The interpretation process described above ends with the execution of a method which does not invoke *next* calls, or with the method provided by the class of the object. The latter does not invoke any explicit dispatching operation. Instead, it may invoke *super* calls. At this point, the dispatching of the modified part is finished and the dispatching of the *super* call follows the original class inheritance chain; consequently, it cannot be the source of additional overhead. In the discussion above we have implicitly assumed that the lookup part of the dispatching returns only one successor method at each execution step. The execution of the replicas-methods is realized in a similar way.

# 6  Discussion and Related Work

In this section we discuss the properties of the proposed model and show how the additional abstraction provided by the explicit combination layer enables the orthogonalization of the conflicting issues: dynamicity versus encapsulation of the client interface, and incremental modification versus internal data encapsulation. In both cases, related work is presented, too.

## 6.1  Encapsulated Object Modification

The object composition provided by the *metaCombiner* mechanism satisfies the requirement for dynamic composition. An object's behavior can be modified quite naturally after it has been created, by sending an insert/remove request to the object's metaCombiner. In this way, our model is superior to other approaches providing a restricted form of object modification, like the mixin-methods approach [35]. By allowing both the insertion and cancellation of adjustments, our solution satisfies the requirement for behavior alterations that may remain valid under certain conditions. The dispatcher role of the meta-Combiner enables modifications to be performed transparently, but nevertheless they immediately affect an object's future behavior.

Despite object modification, the encapsulation of the client interface is preserved in our proposal. In [35], Steyaert et al. have formulated the *immaculate client interface* design principle, which states that an object should expose only the client interface to its message passing clients, and hide knowledge about how the object can be modified from them. Objects in our model satisfy the immaculate client interface principle. They remain records just like in the class-based model and expose only the client interface to their clients. As it can be verified by the semantic functions of the previous section, modifications of the *self* environment happen in conjunction with the creation of the object and adjustment insertion/removal. In contrast to object-based inheritance, message passing involves neither wrapping nor fixing.

In [35] Steyaert et al. identify the provision of explicit constructs for behavior generators, like classes in Smalltalk, as a potential source for violating encapsulation. We only partly agree with them in this point. Their assertion certainly holds for object-based systems, where such explicit generator constructs are the only existing abstraction. In our model, *metaCombiners* are explicit entities responsible for modifying the behavior of the underlying object. The increased power provided by such explicit constructs is indeed related to a certain danger if their availability is not restricted. As already mentioned, the main motivation behind the design of our approach is to support the design of metaarchitectures for adaptable systems. Since it is the system itself that controls its own adaptability, it is also the only client that uses metaCombiners in order to dynamically adapt the behavior of the objects it is composed of. Additionally, the functionality of the *metaCombiners* can be orthogonally enhanced by supplying suitable tools for enhancing the reliability, by restricting the availability of their explicit combination functionality only to certain "privileged" users. Another extension could be concerned with providing explicit tools for controlling which kind of modifications are allowed.

The *predicate objects* approach proposed by Chambers [8] is similar to our approach in that it provides language support to allow the modification of an object's behavior to reflect changes in the object's state. In this approach the implementation of an object is factored into a group of state-specific prototypes. The choice of a particular prototype behavior is based on predicates over the state of the object. In this way, predicate objects avoid the drawbacks of representing state (a) as data, resulting in the case-like style of programming, or (b) through subclasses, resulting in the combinatorial explosion problem. While serving a similar purpose, our proposal is more general. The *metaCombiner* approach can emulate the state-specific behavior modeled by the predicate objects. However, except for internal state conditioned modifications, it is able to deal with changing the implementation of an object because of some external conditions in the environment this object operates on, as it is required by adaptive systems, or for extending the functionality of already existing persistent objects. Furthermore, in contrast to the predicate objects approach, in our approach automatic method combination is provided, and the set of supported behavior modifications need not be fixed at the object's creation time. With respect to the last aspect, predicate objects are more similar to the *mixin-methods* approach. Last but not least, predicate objects support state-related object modification in the prototype-based language *Cecil*. In contrast, our model is intended to enable object behavior modification in class-based languages.

The *metaCombiner* model is also related to the *composition filters* model of the language *Sina* [1]. Both models aim at a modular extension of the conventional object model to facilitate the construction of large-scale complex systems which support multiple application requirements in an extensible way. The *meta-Combiner* approach seems to simulate the same data abstraction techniques as those supported by composition filters, however with a simpler object model. The roles played by different elements of composition filters, such as *internals*, and *filters*, are uniformly modeled by adjustments in our proposal. The inheritance data abstraction supported by the *dispatch filter* in Sina is an object-based one. An object encapsulates an internal object for each of its behavioral flavors. This results in an increased number of objects in the system, and more importantly may cause the duplication of the attributes of "parent" objects that are inherited through two different internals. Sina requires the programmer to avoid inconsistencies related to this duplication. Since the internals participating in the behavior of an object should be fixed at the class definition time, it is not possible to extend the behavior of existing persistent objects. Additionally, the *metaCombiner* approach provides a richer semantics for method combination. The composition filters object model does not support incremental combination of the implementations of a single message provided by different internals. The default strategy for solving name collisions is an explicit ordering of the involved internal objects in the dispatch filter which very much resembles the linearization approaches to multiple inheritance.

*Metaobject protocols* [15], also support some kind of object modification. The main idea underlying these systems is that certain aspects of an object's behavior are put under the control of metaobjects which communicate among each other by means of message passing. When a certain aspect becomes "activated", a request is sent to the corresponding (handler) metaobject to take care of it. Modification of a behavioral aspect is provided by exchanging the corresponding metaobject. For example, two different object models for concurrent and distributed objects are modeled in the CodA architecture [20]. An object can become concurrent by attaching a concurrent model as its meta. However, combining two overlapping object models (containing metaobjects for the same aspect), such as the concurrent and distributed object model, requires programmer intervention [20]. This is due to the modeling of behavioral aspects by means of objects. Modifying a behavioral aspect now requires modification of the metaobject. The problem is thus simply shifted to the metaobject level, but not eliminated.

In contrast, in our model different aspects are modeled by software modules which are descriptive entities that can be combined more easily than objects. The single metaobject associated with an object does not deal with a specific aspect, but instead with the combination of aspect descriptions. In this respect, our model can be considered as a special case of the *aspect-oriented programming* paradigm [17]. An aspect is a self-contained subprogram that describes a global property of a program. Each application domain might have a different set of aspects, such as synchronization and distribution aspects of client/server applications. Aspects are automatically combined into executable code by a new kind of compiler called *Aspect Weaver*. Thus, our model can be seen as applying the aspect-oriented decomposition principle to the design of object-oriented systems. Our model is a special case in that all aspects are described in the same language, while one of the goals of the aspect-oriented approach is to allow different aspects to be described in different languages. In contrast to aspect-oriented programming which emphasizes the separation of concerns beyond the functional modularization boundary, the emphasis of our approach is on dynamic (re)weaving.

Recently, Seiter et al. [30] proposed the context relationship between classes in order to achieve evolution of object behavior in class-based systems. The basic idea is that if class $C$ is context-related to a base class $B$, then B-objects can get their functionality dynamically altered by the presence of C-objects. In general, a context class contains method updates for several base classes. A context object may be explicitly attached to a base object, or it may be attached to a method invocation, in which case it is implicitly attached to a set of base objects involved in the method invocation. The context relation supports behavior evolution because the C-object attached to the B-object may vary at run-time. More importantly, the evolution is not based on aggregation as with metaobject protocols, but on method environment update. This is similar to our approach. However, the evolution achieved by the context attachment is more restricted as compared to our approach. Although there is some evidence in the paper about the advantage of supporting incremental attachement to allow multiple implementations to be executed for the same method, only overriding is supported at the semantic level [29]. Consequently, there is no support for more general modifications, as illustrated by a shared and ATM-account.

## 6.2 Internal Encapsulation

While the emphasis of this paper has been on the dynamic behavior alteration, it is obvious that the *metaCombiner* mechanism can be applied to static behavior composition as well, in this case being a more expressive alternative to the conventional static inheritance. This is also reflected in the denotational semantics presented earlier in this paper where the syntactic clause $I_1 combine\ I_2\ I_3\ rep\ I_4$ is provided for static composition. In this use, the *metaCombiner* approach to behavior composition is related to other more expressive and modular alternatives to static inheritance, such as *mixin-based* inheritance [6], its derivative proposed in [39], and *feature-oriented programming* [28]. However, the static *metaCombiner* model is more general than these approaches with respect to dealing with the trade-off between internal encapsulation and incremental modification.

In the *metaCombiner* composition model, incremental modification and internal encapsulation are treated separately. While internal encapsulation is realized by means of visibility scopes, incremental modification happens independently of these scopes, individually for each method. Adjustments are separated in visibility scopes according to their replicated methods. This ensures that a module in one scope of a replicated method cannot invoke the definition of this method from another scope. Nevertheless, definitions from adjustments in different scopes can flexibly be arranged in an incremental modification relationship by means of their individual execution ordering, or they can invoke shared attributes from each other by means of *self* calls. This different kind of treatment is made possible due to the additional abstraction level separating the inheritance structure from behavior definition. In order to emphasize the importance of this separation, we will show in the following how the flexibility problems of advanced approaches to the name collision problem, such as [6, 7, 39], can be traced down to its absence.

In the absence of the combination layer, a single kind of relationship between modules is supposed to globally regulate both the internal encapsulation and the incremental modification relation between their corresponding methods. This leads to the following possible situations. The first possibility is to use the replicated methods as the basis for the relationship between modules. Two modules defining replicas of the same message are made globally invisible for each other. The consequence is that methods which represent incremental modifications of each other are automatically considered as replicas. Dummy subclasses are needed, simply for reestablishing the incremental modification relationship between the latter. This situation is typical for the graph oriented multiple inheritance approaches [4, 7, 21, 36]. For illustration, the hierarchy in Fig. 13 a) represents the definition of a shared and ATM-account, modeled in the *point of view notion of multiple inheritance* [7] approach. The single role of the class *ASAccount* is to reimplement *debit:*, merely because otherwise it would be impossible to connect both versions of *debit:*, defined in *SharedAccount* and in *ATMAccount*, respectively, such that they are executed one after the other. With the explicit as-expressions, explicit inheritance structure information is unnecessarily hard-coded into the implementation of classes, which damages the flexibility especially in dynamic environments.

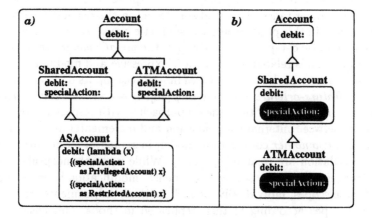

**Fig. 13.** Double restricted account in graph and linear models

A second alternative is to use the refinement methods as the basis of the relationship between modules. All modules are put into a total order, which results in a single visibility scope. This corresponds to linear approaches such as [6, 39]. Inflexible fixing and renaming is needed in order to provide individual scopes for the replicated methods, which are otherwise impossible when the modules are totally ordered. The definition of a shared and ATM-account in the linear approach presented in [39] is shown in Fig. 13 b). Black boxes within the definitions for *debit:* are used to show that *specialAction:* has been fixed in these definitions and then removed from the domain of both modules. This results in a kind of class qualification. In order to refine the *specialAction:* attribute of the *SharedAccount*, say by means of a class *SpecialShared* reimplementing *specialAction:* to provide a special sharing strategy, the hierarchy of modules must be rebuilt and the fix-point operator must be reapplied. Obviously, the problem related to message qualification is here less severe than in graph oriented approaches [4, 21], due to the total expressiveness on the inheritance structure provided by the mixin-based approach. Nevertheless, this is true only for static environments; any kind of class qualification is not practicable in a dynamic environment.

# 7 Conclusions

In this paper, a new approach to dynamic evolution of object behavior in a class-based environment has been proposed. The approach is based on introducing an additional abstraction layer between objects and classes in order to control the compositional aspects of the behavior of evolving objects. The metaobjects on this explicit combination layer provide support for dynamic behavior alterations in specific contexts without violating the encapsulation of the client interface and support for internal encapsulation. A formal description of the approach was presented and its feasibility was demonstrated by implementing it as a metalevel extension of Smalltalk-80. There are several areas for future research. First, it is interesting to study the usefulness of the proposed model in various applications areas where dynamic object modification is required. Second, an interesting area is to investigate how the *metaCombiner* mechanism can be utilized to provide object behavior evolution in a static typed language like C++.

**Acknowledgements**

The author is grateful to Wolfgang Merzenich for promoting this research, and to Bernd Freisleben for encouraging the work on this paper and for useful suggestions on earlier versions of it. Many thanks to the anonymous referees for their useful comments.

# References

1. Aksit M., Wakita K., Bosch J., Bergmans L., and Yonezawa A. Abstracting object interactions using composition-filters. In Guerraoui R., Nierstrasz O. and Riveill

M., eds., *Object-based Distributed Processing*, LNCS 791, pp 152-184, Springer-Verlag, 1993.

2. Atkins M.S. and Coady M.Y. Adaptable concurrency control for atomic data types. In *ACM Transactions on Computer Systems*, vol. 10, no. 3, pp. 190–225, 1992.

3. Black A, Consel C., Pu C., Walpole J., Cowan C., Autrey T., Inouye J, Kethana L., Zhang K.. Dream and reality: incremental specialization in a commercial operating system. Technical Report TR-95-001, Oregon Graduate Institute of Science and Technology, 1995.

4. Borning A. H. and Ingalls D. H. H.. Multiple inheritance in Smalltalk-80. In *Proceedings at the National Conference on AI*, Pittsburgh, 1982.

5. Bracha G, and Cook W.. Mixin-based inheritance. In *Proceedings OOP-SLA/ECOOP '90, ACM SIGPLAN Notices*, vol. 25, no. 10, pp. 303–311, 1990.

6. Bracha G. and Lindstrom G. Modularity meets inheritance. Technical Report UUCS-91-017, University of Utah, 1991.

7. Carré B. and Geib J. M. The point of view notion for multiple inheritance. In *Proceedings OOPSLA/ECOOP '90, ACM SIGPLAN Notices*, vol. 25, no. 10, pp. 312–321, 1990.

8. Chambers C. Predicate classes. In W.Olthoff, ed., *Proceedings ECOOP '93*, LNCS 707, pp. 268–297, Springer-Verlag, 1993.

9. Cook W. and Palsberg J. A denotational semantics of inheritance and its correctness. In *Proceedings OOPSLA '89, ACM SIGPLAN Notices*, vol. 24, no. 10, pp. 433–443, 1989.

10. Goldberg A. and Robson D. *Smalltalk 80: the Language and its implementation*. Addison-Wesley, 1983.

11. Gottlob G., Schrefl M., Roeck B. Extending object-oriented systems with roles. In *ACM Transactions on Information Systems*, vol.14, no.3, pp 268–296, 1996.

12. Harrison W. and Ossher H. Subject-oriented programming: (A critique of pure objects). In *Proceedings OOPSLA '93*, ACM SIGPLAN Notices, vol. 28, no. 10, pp. 411–428, 1993.

13. Hense A. V. Denotational semantics of an object oriented programming language with explicit wrappers. In *Theoretical Aspects of Computer Software 1991*, LNCS 526, pp. 548–567, Springer-Verlag, 1991.

14. Keene S. Object-oriented programming in Common Lisp: a programmer's guide to CLOS, Addison-Wesley, 1989.

15. Kiczales G., des Rivières J., Bobrow D. G. *The art of the metaobject protocol*, MIT Press, 1991

16. Kiczales G. Towards a new model of abstraction for the engineering of software. Invited Talk in OOPSLA '94, (http://www.xerox.com/PARC/spl/eca/oi.html).

17. Kiczales G., Irwin J., Lamping J., Loingtier J. M., Lopes C. V., Maeda C., Mendhekar A. A position paper on aspect-oriented programming. (http://www.parc.xerox.com/spl/projects/aop/position.html).

18. Knudsen J. L. Name collision in multiple classification hierarchies. In S. Gjessing and K. Nygaard, eds., *Proceedings ECOOP '88*, LNCS 322, pp. 93–109, Springer-Verlag, 1988.

19. LaLonde W. R., Thomas D. A., Pugh J. R. An exemplar based Smalltalk. In *Proceedings OOPSLA '86, ACM SIGPLAN Notices*, vol. 21, no. 11, pp. 322–330, 1986.

20. McAffer J. Meta-level programming with CodA. In W. Olthoff, ed., *Proceedings of the ECOOP '95*, LNCS 952, pp. 190–214. Springer-Verlag, 1995.

21. Meyer B. *Object-oriented software construction*. Prentice Hall, 1988.
22. Mezini M. Supporting evolving objects without giving up classes. In B. Meyer C. Minings and R. Duke, eds., *Proceedings of the 18th TOOLS Conference*, pp. 183–197, Prentice Hall, 1995.
23. Mezini M. Dynamic metaclass construction for an explicit specialization interface. In *Proceedings of the Reflection '96 Conference*, pp. 203–219, 1996.
24. Mezini M. Incremental redefinition of open implementations. In Ch. Zimmermann, ed., *Advances in object-oriented metalevel architectures and reflection*, pp. 265-290, CRC Press Inc., 1996.
25. Mezini M. Ph.D. Thesis (in preparation)
26. Moon D. A. Object-oriented programming with Flavors. In *Proceedings OOPSLA '86, ACM SIGPLAN Notices*, vol. 21, no. 11, pp. 1–8, 1986.
27. Nierstrasz O and Tsichritzis D. Object-oriented software composition. Prentice Hall, 1995
28. Prehofer C. Feature-oriented programming. To appear in *Proceedings of ECOOP '97*.
29. Seiter L. M. Design Patterns for Managing Evolution. Ph.D. Thesis, Northeastern University, 1996.
30. Seiter L. M., Palsberg J, Lieberherr K. Evolution of object behavior using context relations. In Garlan D., ed., *Proceedings of the 4th ACM SIFSOFT Symposium on Foundations of Software Engineering*, Software Engineering Notes, vol. 21, no. 6, pp. 46–56, ACM Press, 1996.
31. Snyder A. Inheritance and development of encapsulated software components. In B. Shriver and P. Wegner, ed., *Research Directions in Object-Oriented Programming*, pp. 165–188, MIT Press, 1987.
32. Stein L. A., Lieberman H., Ungar D. The treaty of Orlando. In W. Kim and F. Lochovsky (Eds.), *Object-Oriented Concepts, Databases and Applications*, pp. 31–48. ACM Press and Addison-Wesley.
33. Stein L. A. Delegation is inheritance. In *Proceedings OOPSLA '87, ACM SIGPLAN Notices*, vol. 22, no. 12, pp. 138–146, 1987.
34. Steyaert P., Codenie W., D'Hondt T., D'Hondt K., Lucas C., Van Limberghen M. Nested Mixin-Methods in Agora. In O. Nierstrasz, ed., *Proceedings ECOOP '93*, LNCS 707, pp. 197–219. Springer-Verlag, 1993.
35. Steyaert P. and De Meuter W. A marriage of class-based and object-based inheritance without unwanted children. In W. Olthoff, ed., *Proceedings ECOOP '95*, LNCS 952, pp. 127–145, Springer-Verlag, 1995.
36. Stroustrup B. *The C++ programming language*. Addison-Wesley, 1986.
37. Stroud, R.J. and Wu Z. Using metaobject protocols to implement atomic data types. In W. Olthoff, ed., *Proceedings ECOOP '95*, LNCS 952, pp. 168–189, Springer-Verlag, 1995.
38. Ungar D. and Smith R. B.. Self: the power of simplicity. In *Proceedings OOPSLA '87, ACM SIGPLAN notices*, vol. 22, no. 12, pp. 227–242, 1987.
39. Van Limberghen M. and Mens T. Encapsulation and composition as orthogonal operations on mixins: A solution to multiple inheritance problems. In *Object-Oriented Systems*, 3(1), 1996.
40. Weihl, W.E. and Liskow, B. Implementation of resilient, atomic data types. *ACM Transactions on Programming Languages and Systems*, 7(2), pp. 244–269, 1985.

# Aspect-Oriented Programming

Gregor Kiczales, John Lamping, Anurag Mendhekar, Chris Maeda,
Cristina Lopes, Jean-Marc Loingtier and John Irwin

Xerox Palo Alto Research Center[*]

We have found many programming problems for which neither procedural
nor object-oriented programming techniques are sufficient to clearly capture
some of the important design decisions the program must implement. This
forces the implementation of those design decisions to be scattered throughout
the code, resulting in "tangled" code that is excessively difficult to develop
and maintain. We present an analysis of why certain design decisions have
been so difficult to clearly capture in actual code. We call the properties
these decisions address *aspects*, and show that the reason they have been hard
to capture is that they *cross-cut* the system's basic functionality. We present
the basis for a new programming technique, called aspect-oriented programming, that makes it possible to clearly express programs involving such aspects, including appropriate isolation, composition and reuse of the aspect
code. The discussion is rooted in systems we have built using aspect-oriented
programming.

## 1. Introduction

Object-oriented programming (OOP) has been presented as a technology that can
fundamentally aid software engineering, because the underlying object model
provides a better fit with real domain problems. But we have found many programming problems where OOP techniques are not sufficient to clearly capture
all the important design decisions the program must implement. Instead, it
seems that there are some programming problems that fit neither the OOP approach nor the procedural approach it replaces.

This paper reports on our work developing programming techniques that
make it possible to clearly express those programs that OOP (and POP) fail to
support. We present an analysis of why some design decisions have been so
difficult to cleanly capture in actual code. We call the issues these decisions
address *aspects*, and show that the reason they have been hard to capture is that
they *cross-cut* the system's basic functionality. We present the basis for a new
programming technique, called aspect-oriented programming (AOP), that makes

---

[*] 3333 Coyote Hill Road, Palo Alto, CA 94304, USA.  gregor@parc.xerox.com

it possible to clearly express programs involving such aspects, including appropriate isolation, composition and reuse of the aspect code.

We think of the current state of AOP research as analogous to that of OOP 20 years ago. The basic concepts are beginning to take form, and an expanding group of researchers are using them in their work [1, 4, 13, 28]. Furthermore, while AOP qua AOP is a new idea, there are existing systems that have AOP-like properties. The contribution of this paper is an analysis of the problems AOP is intended to solve, as well as an initial set of terms and concepts that support explicit AOP-based system design.

The paper presents AOP in an example-driven way—the generalizations and definitions are all derived from examples, rather than presented in advance. Section 3 uses a medium-scale example to present the aspect-tangling problem AOP solves; the section culminates with a definition of the term aspect. Section 4 presents several more small examples of aspects. Sections 5 and 6 each provide an example of a complete AOP system. The remaining sections present future work, related work and conclusions.

## 2. Background Assumptions

This section outlines important assumptions about the relationship between programming languages and software design processes that underlie the rest of the paper.

Software design processes and programming languages exist in a mutually supporting relationship. Design processes break a system down into smaller and smaller units. Programming languages provide mechanisms that allow the programmer to define abstractions of system sub-units, and then compose those abstractions in different ways to produce the overall system. A design process and a programming language work well together when the programming language provides abstraction and composition mechanisms that cleanly support the kinds of units the design process breaks the system into.

From this perspective, many existing programming languages, including object-oriented languages, procedural languages and functional languages, can be seen as having a common root in that their key abstraction and composition mechanisms are all rooted in some form of generalized procedure. For the purpose of this paper we will refer to these as generalized-procedure (GP) languages. (This is not to say that we are ignorant of the many important advantages of OOP languages! It is only to say that for the purposes of the discussion in this paper, it is simpler to focus on what is common across all GP languages.)

The design methods that have evolved to work with GP languages tend to break systems down into units of behavior or function. This style has been called functional decomposition [25-27].[1] The exact nature of the decomposition differs between the language paradigms of course, but each unit is encapsulated in a procedure/function/object, and in each case, it feels comfortable to talk about what is encapsulated as a *functional* unit of the overall system. This last point may be so familiar that it feels somewhat redundant. But it is important that we give it explicit attention now, because in the course of this paper will be considering units of system decomposition that are not functional.

# 3. What Are Aspects?

To better understand the origins of tangling problems, and how AOP works to solve them, this section is organized around a detailed example, that is based on a real application we have been working with [18, 22]. There are three implementations of the real application: easy to understand but inefficient, efficient but difficult to understand, and an AOP-based implementation that is both easy to understand and efficient. The presentation here will be based on three analogous but simplified implementations.

Consider the implementation of a black-and-white image processing system, in which the desired domain model is one of images passing through a series of filters to produce some desired output. Assume that important goals for the system are that it be easy to develop and maintain, and that it make efficient use of memory. The former because of the need to quickly develop bug-free enhancements to the system. The latter because the images are large, so that in order for the system to be efficient, it must minimize both memory references and overall storage requirements.

## 3.1 Basic Functionality

Achieving the first goal is relatively easy. Good old-fashioned procedural programming can be used to implement the system clearly, concisely, and in good alignment with the domain model. In such an approach the filters can be defined as procedures that take several input images and produce a single output image. A set of primitive procedures would implement the basic filters, and higher level filters would be defined in terms of the primitive ones. For example, a primitive or! filter, which takes two images and returns their pixelwise logical or, might be implemented as:[2]

---

[1] In some communities this term connotes the use of functional programming languages (i.e. side-effect free functions), but we do not use the term in that sense.

[2] We have chosen Common Lisp syntax for this presentation, but this could be written fairly easily in any other Algol-like language.

```
(defun or! (a b)
   (let ((result (new-image)))
      (loop for i from 1 to width do
         (loop for j from 1 to height do
            (set-pixel result i j
               (or (get-pixel a i j)
                   (get-pixel b i j)))))
      result))
```

*loop over all the pixels in the input images*

*the operation to perform on the pixels*

*storing pixels in the result image*

Starting from or! and other primitive filters, the programmer could work up to the definition of a filter that selects just those black pixels on a horizontal edge, returning a new image consisting of just those boundary pixels.

| functionality | implementation |
|---|---|
| pixelwise logical operations | written using loop primitive as above |
| shift image up, down | written using loop primitive; slightly different loop structure |
| difference of two images | `(defun remove! (a b)` `(and! a (not! b)))` |
| pixels at top edge of a region | `(defun top-edge! (a)` `(remove! a (down! a)))` |
| pixels at bottom edge of a region | `(defun bottom-edge! (a)` `(remove! a (up! a)))` |
| horizontal edge pixels | `(defun horizontal-edge! (a)` `(or! (top-edge! a)` `(bottom-edge! a)))` |

Note that only the primitive filters deal explicitly with looping over the pixels in the images. The higher level filters, such as horizontal-edge!, are expressed clearly in terms of primitive ones. The resulting code is easy to read, reason about, debug, and extend—in short, it meets the first goal.

## 3.2 Optimizing Memory Usage

But this simple implementation doesn't address the second goal of optimizing memory usage. When each procedure is called, it loops over a number of input images and produces a new output image. Output images are created frequently, often existing only briefly before they are consumed by some other loop. This results in excessively frequent memory references and storage allocation, which in turn leads to cache misses, page faults, and terrible performance.

The familiar solution to the problem is to take a more global perspective of the program, map out what intermediate results end up being inputs to what other filters, and then code up a version of the program that fuses loops appropriately to implement the original functionality while creating as few intermediate images as possible. The revised code for `horizontal-edge!` would look something like:

```
(defun horizontal-edge! (a)
   (let ((result (new-image))          only three result
         (a-up (up! a))                images are created
         (a-down (down! a)))
      (loop for i from 1 to width do        one loop structure
         (loop for j from 1 to height do      shared by many
            (set-pixel result i j              component filters
               (or (and (get-pixel a i j)
      operations            (not (get-pixel a-up i j)))
      from many             (and (get-pixel a i j)
      sub-filters           (not (get-pixel a-down i j)))))))
      result))
```

Compared to the original, this code is all tangled up. It incorporates all the different filters that `horizontal-edge!` is defined in terms of, and fuses many, but not all, of their loops together. (The loops for `up!` and `down!` are not fused because those operations have a different looping structure.)[3] In short, revising the code to make more efficient use of memory has destroyed the original clean component structure.

Of course, this is a very simple example, and it is not so difficult to deal with such a small amount of tangled code. But in real programs the complexity due to such tangling quickly expands to become a major obstacle to ease of code development and maintenance. The real system this example was drawn from is an important sub-component of an optical character recognition system. The clean implementation of the real system, similar to the first code shown above, is only 768 lines of code; but the tangled implementation, which does the fusion optimization as well as memoization of intermediate results, compile-time memory allocation and specialized intermediate datastructures, is 35213 lines. The tangled code is extremely difficult to maintain, since small changes to the functionality require mentally untangling and then re-tangling it.

---

[3] Our AOP-based re-implementation of the full application fuses these other loops as well. We chose not to show that code here because it is so tangled that it is distractingly difficult to understand.

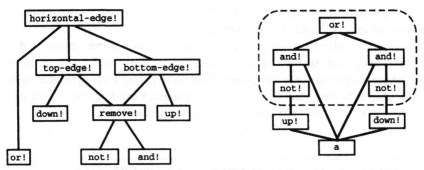

Figure 1: Two different diagrams of the un-optimized horizontal-edge! filter. On the left is the functional decomposition, which aligns so directly with the domain model. On the right is a data flow diagram, in which the boxes are the primitive filters and the edges are the data flows between them at runtime. The box labeled a at the bottom is the input image.

## 3.3 Cross-Cutting

Returning to the example code, Figure 1 provides a different basis for understanding the tangling in it. On the left there is the hierarchical structure of the filtering functionality. On the right there is a data flow diagram for the original, un-optimized version of horizontal-edge!. In this diagram, the boxes and lines show the primitive filters and data flow between them. The dashed oval shows the boundary of what is fused into a single loop in the optimized version of horizontal-edge!.

Notice that the fusion oval does not incorporate all of horizontal-edge! In fact, it doesn't align with any of the hierarchical units on the left. While the two properties being implemented—the functionality and the loop fusion—both originate in the same primitive filters, they must compose differently as filters are composed. The functionality composes hierarchically in the traditional way. But the loop fusion composes by fusing the loops of those primitive filters that have the same loop structure and that are direct neighbors in the data flow graph. Each of these composition rules is easy to understand when looking at its own appropriate picture. But the two composition relationships cut each other so fundamentally that each is very difficult to see in the other's picture.

This cross-cutting phenomena is directly responsible for the tangling in the code. The single composition mechanism the language provides us—procedure calling—is very well suited to building up the un-optimized functional units. But it can't help us compose the functional units and the loop fusion simultaneously, because they follow such different composition rules and yet must co-compose.

This breakdown forces us to combine the properties entirely by hand—that's what happening in the tangled code above.

In general, whenever two properties being programmed must compose differently and yet be coordinated, we say that they *cross-cut* each other. Because GP languages provide only one composition mechanism, the programmer must do the co-composition manually, leading to complexity and tangling in the code.

We can now define two important terms more precisely:

---

With respect to a system and its implementation using a GP-based language, a property that must be implemented is:

**A component, if it can be cleanly encapsulated in a generalized procedure** (i.e. object, method, procedure, API). By cleanly, we mean well-localized, and easily accessed and composed as necessary. Components tend to be units of the system's functional decomposition, such as image filters, bank accounts and GUI widgets.

**An aspect, if it can not be cleanly encapsulated in a generalized procedure.** Aspects tend not to be units of the system's functional decomposition, but rather to be properties that affect the performance or semantics of the components in systemic ways. Examples of aspects include memory access patterns and synchronization of concurrent objects. (Section 4 provides more examples of aspects.)

---

Using these terms it is now possible to clearly state the goal of AOP: To support the programmer in cleanly separating components and aspects from each other,[4] by providing mechanisms that make it possible to abstract and compose them to produce the overall system. This is in contrast to GP-based programming, which supports programmers in separating only components from each other by providing mechanisms that make it possible to abstract and compose them to produce the overall system.[5]

---

[4] Components from each other, aspects from each other, and components from aspects.

[5] Our analysis of aspects as system properties that cross-cut components helps explain the persistent popularity of mechanisms like dynamic scoping, catch and throw in otherwise purely GP languages. These mechanisms provide a different composition mechanism, that helps programmers implement certain aspects in their systems.

# 4. Other Examples of How Aspects Cross-Cut Components

Before going on to the presentation of AOP, and how it solves the problem of aspect tangling in code, this section briefly presents several more examples of aspects and components. For each example in the table below we list an application, a kind of GP language that would do a good job of capturing the component structure of the application, a likely component structure for the application if programmed using that kind of language, and the aspects that would cross-cut that component structure.

| application | GP language | components | aspects |
|---|---|---|---|
| image processing | procedural | filters | loop fusion |
| | | | result sharing |
| | | | compile-time memory allocation |
| digital library | object-oriented | repositories, printers, services | minimizing network traffic |
| | | | synchronization constraints |
| | | | failure handling |
| matrix algorithms | procedural | linear algebra operations | matrix representation |
| | | | permutation |
| | | | floating point error |

Some aspects are so common that they can easily be thought about without reference to any particular domain. One of the best examples is error and failure handling. We are all familiar with the phenomenon that adding good support for failure handling to a simple system prototype ends up requiring many little additions and changes throughout the system. This is because the different dynamic contexts that can lead to a failure, or that bear upon how a failure should be handled, cross-cut the functionality of systems.

Many performance-related issues are aspects, because performance optimizations often exploit information about the execution context that spans components.

# 5. First Example of AOP

In this section we return to the image processing example, and use it to sketch an AOP-based re-implementation of that application. The presentation is based on a system we have developed, but is simplified somewhat. The complete system is discussed in [22]. The goal of this section is to quickly get the complete structure of an AOP-based implementation on the table, not to fully explain that structure. Section 6 will provide that explanation.

The structure of the AOP-based implementation of an application is analogous to the structure of a GP-based implementation of an application. Whereas a GP-based implementation of an application consists of: (i) a language, (ii) a compiler (or interpreter) for that language, and (iii) a program written in the language that implements the application; the AOP-based implementation of an application consists of: (i.a) a *component language* with which to program the components, (i.b) one or more *aspect languages* with which to program the aspects, (ii) an a*spect weaver* for the combined languages, (iii.a) A *component program*, that implements the components using the component language, and (iii.b) one or more *aspect programs* that implement the aspects using the aspect languages. Just as with GP-based languages, AOP languages and weavers can be designed so that weaving work is delayed until runtime (RT weaving), or done at compile-time (CT weaving).

## 5.1 The Component Language & Program

In the current example we use one component language and one aspect language. The component language is similar to the procedural language used above, with only minor changes. First, filters are no longer explicitly procedures. Second, the primitive loops are written in a way that makes their loop structure as explicit as possible. Using the new component language the or! filter is written as follows:

```
(define-filter or! (a a)
  (pixelwise (a b) (aa bb) (or aa bb)))
```

The pixelwise construct is an iterator, which in this case walks through images a and b in lockstep, binding aa and bb to the pixel values, and returning a image comprised of the results. Four similar constructs provide the different cases of aggregation, distribution, shifting and combining of pixel values that are needed in this system. Introducing these high-level looping constructs is a critical change that enables the aspect languages to be able to detect, analyze and fuse loops much more easily.

## 5.2 The Aspect Language & Program

The design of the aspect language used for this application is based on the observation that the dataflow graph in Figure 1 makes it easy to understand the loop fusion required. The aspect language is a simple procedural language that provides simple operations on nodes in the dataflow graph. The aspect program can then straightforwardly look for loops that should be fused, and carry out the fusion required. The following code fragment is part of the core of that aspect program—it handles the fusion case discussed in Section 5. It checks whether two nodes connected by a data flow edge both have a pixelwise loop structure, and if so it fuses them into a single loop that also has a pixelwise structure, and that has the appropriate merging of the inputs, loop variables and body of the two original loops.

```
(cond ((and (eq (loop-shape node) 'pointwise)
            (eq (loop-shape input) 'pointwise))
       (fuse loop input 'pointwise
             :inputs (splice …)
             :loop-vars (splice …)
             :body (subst …)))))
```

Describing the composition rules and fusion structure for the five kinds of loops in the real system requires about a dozen similar clauses about when and how to fuse. This is part of why this system could not be handled by relying on an optimizing compiler to do the appropriate fusion—the program analysis and understanding involved is so significant that compilers cannot be counted upon to do so reliably. (Although many compilers might be able to optimize this particular simple example.) Another complication is the other aspects the real system handles, including sharing of intermediate results and keeping total runtime memory allocation to a fixed limit.

## 5.3 Weaving

The aspect weaver accepts the component and aspect programs as input, and emits a C program as output. This work proceeds in three distinct phases, as illustrated in Figure 2.

In phase 1 the weaver uses unfolding as a technique for generating a data flow graph from the component program. In this graph, the nodes represent primitive filters, and the edges represent an image flowing from one primitive filter to another. Each node contains a single loop construct. So, for example, the node labeled A contains the following loop construct, where the #<...> refer to the edges coming into the node:

```
(pointwise (#<edge1> #<edge2>) (i1 i2) (or i1 i2))
```

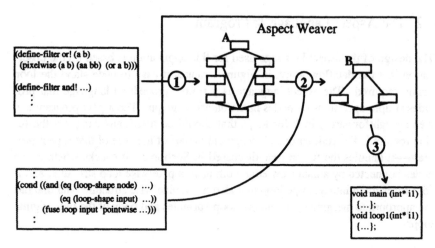

Figure 2: The aspect weaver for image processing applications works in three phases.

In phase 2 the aspect program is run, to edit the graph by collapsing nodes together and adjusting their bodies accordingly. The result is a graph in which some of the loop structures have more primitive pixel operations in them than before phase 2. For example, the node labeled **B**, which corresponds to the fusion of 5 loops from the original graph, has the following as its body:

```
(pointwise (#<edge1> #<edge2> #<edge3>) (i1 i2 i3)
  (or (and (not i1) i2) (and (not i3) i2))))
```

Finally, in phase 3, a simple code generator walks over the fused graph, generating one C function for each loop node, and generating a main function that calls the loop functions in the appropriate order, passing them the appropriate results from prior loops. The code generation is simple because each node contains a single loop construct with a body composed entirely of primitive operations on pixels.

A crucial feature of this system is that the weaver is not a "smart" compiler, which can be so difficult to design and build. By using AOP, we have arranged for all the significant implementation strategy decisions—all the actual smarts—to be provided by the programmer, using the appropriate aspect languages. The weaver's job is integration, rather than inspiration.[6]

---

[6] While asking the programmer to explicitly address implementation aspects sounds like it might be a step backwards, our experience with work on open implementation suggests that in fact it isn't [9, 10, 12, 17] While the programmer is addressing implementation in the memory aspect, proper use of AOP means that they are expressing implementation strategy at an appropriately abstract level, through an appropriate aspect language, with appropriate locality. They are not addressing implementation details, and they are not working directly with the tangled implementation. In evaluating the AOP-based implementation it is important to compare it with both the naïve inefficient implementation and the complex efficient implementation.

## 5.4 Results

The real system is somewhat more complex of course. For one thing, there are two additional aspect programs, one of which handles sharing of common sub-computations, and one of which ensures that the minimum possible number of images are allocated at any one time. In this system, all three of the aspect programs are written in the same aspect language.

In this example, the AOP based re-implementation has met the original design goals—the application code is easy to reason about, develop and maintain, while at the same time being highly efficient. It is easy for the programmer to understand the components and how they compose. It is easy for the programmer to understand the aspects, and how they compose. It is easy for the programmer to understand the effect of the aspect programs on the total output code. Changes in either the filter components or the fusion aspect are easily propagated to the whole system by simply re-weaving. What isn't easy is for the programmer to generate the details of the output code. The power of the AOP approach is that the weaver handles these details, instead of the programmer having to do the tangling manually.

Our AOP based re-implementation of the application is 1039 lines of code, including the component program and all three aspect programs. The aspect weaver itself, including a reusable code generation component is 3520 lines (the true kernel of the weaver is 1959 lines). The performance of the re-implementation is comparable to a 35213 line manually tangled version (the time efficiency is worse and the space efficiency is better).[7]

As with many other software engineering projects, it is extremely difficult to quantify the benefits of using AOP without a large experimental study, involving multiple programmers using both AOP and traditional techniques to develop and maintain different applications [6, 21, 36]. Such a study has been beyond the scope of our work to date, although we hope to do one in the future. In the meantime, we have developed one initial measure of the degree to which applying AOP techniques can simplify an application. This measure compares a GP-based implementation of an application to an AOP-based implementation of the same application. It measures the degree to which the aspects are more concisely coded in the AOP-based implementation than in a non-AOP based implementation. The general equation for this measure, as well as the numbers for this particular application are as follows:

---

[7] Our current code generator doesn't use packed datastructures, this results in a factor of 4 performance penalty between the hand-optimized implementation and the aspect-oriented implementation. The aspect-oriented implementation is nonetheless over 100 times faster than the naive implementation.

$$\text{reduction in bloat due to tangling} = \frac{\text{tangled code size - component program size}}{\text{sum of aspect program sizes}} = \frac{35213 - 756}{352} = 98$$

In this metric, any number greater than 1 indicates a positive outcome of applying AOP. This application represents an extremely large gain from using AOP, in other applications we have developed the gain ranges from 2 to this number [8, 14, 22]. It could be said that the size of the weaver itself should be included in the sum in the denominator. The point is debatable, since the weaver is usable by any number of similar image processing applications, not just the table recognizer. But we note that even with the entire weaver included, this metric evaluates to 9.

Any single metric has somewhat limited utility. We believe that this one is useful in this case because on the other important grounds of performance, the AOP-based implementation of the application is comparable to the non-AOP based implementation. Section 7 presents some of the requirements we have identified for quantitative measures of AOP utility.

# 6. Second Example of AOP

This section uses a second example of an AOP-based system to elaborate on component language design, aspect language design and weaving. Once again, the example is a simplified version of a real system we are developing, which is described in [14]. The example comes from the document processing domain where we wanted to implement a distributed digital library that stores documents in many forms and provides a wide range of operations on those documents. The component language, aspect languages and aspect weaver presented in this section are more general-purpose in nature than the highly domain-specific example in the previous section.

The functionality of this system is well captured using an object-oriented model. In such an approach the objects are documents, repositories, different printable forms for the documents (pdf, ps, rip...), printers, servers etc. There are several aspects of concern, including:

- Communication, by which we mean controlling the amount of network bandwith the application uses by being careful about which objects and sub-objects get copied in remote method calls. For example, we want to be sure that when a book object is included in a remote method invocation, the different printed representations of the book aren't sent across the wire unless they will be needed by the receiving method.
- Coordination constraints, by which we mean the synchronization rules required to ensure that the component program behaves correctly in the face of multiple threads of control.

- Failure handling, by which we mean handling the many different forms of failure that can arise in a distributed system in an appropriately context-sensitive way.

For now, we will continue with just the communication aspect. Handling both communication and coordination using AOP is discussed in [14]. Failure handling using AOP is a future research goal.

## 6.1 The Component Language & Program

Designing an AOP system involves understanding what must go into the component language, what must go into the aspect languages, and what must be shared among the languages. The component language must allow the programmer to write component programs that implement the system's functionality, while at the same time ensuring that those programs don't pre-empt anything the aspect programs need to control. The aspect languages must support implementation of the desired aspects, in a natural and concise way. The component and aspect languages will have different abstraction and composition mechanisms, but they must also have some common terms, these are what makes it possible for the weaver to co-compose the different kinds of programs.

To keep the common terms from becoming points of contention, the aspect languages must address different issues than the component languages. In the image processing system, replacing low-level loops with the higher-level looping primitives is an example of ensuring that component programs don't pre-empt aspect programs. This change makes it easier for the aspect programs to detect and implement opportunities for loop fusion.

In this example, component programs must implement elements such as books, repositories, and printers. In order to allow the communication aspect program to handle communication, component programs must avoid doing so. In this case Java™ serves quite well as the component language. It provides an object model that implements the appropriate components, and avoids addressing the communication aspect.[8] So, using Java as our component language, the definition of two simple classes, books and repositories of books, look like:

---

[8] [14] explains that in order to support the coordination aspect language, some lower-level synchronization features must be removed from Java before it can be used as the component language. These are the keyword `synchronized`, and the methods `wait`, `notify` and `notifyAll`.

```
public class Book {                 public class Repository {
  String title, author;               private Book      books[];
  int isbn;                           private int       nbooks = 0;
  OCR ocr;
  PDF pdf;                            public Repository (int dbsize)
  Postscript ps;                      {
  RIP rip;                              books = new Book[dbsize];
                                      }
  public String get_title()         public void register (Book b)
  {                                   {
    return title;                       books[nbooks++] = b;
  }                                   }
  public String get_author()        public void unregister(Book b)
  {                                   {  ...  }
    return author;                   public Book lookup (String s)
  }                                   {  ...  }
  public int get_isbn() {           }
    return isbn;
  }
}
```

## 6.2  The Aspect Language & Program

Communication aspect programs would like to be able to control the amount of copying of arguments that takes place when there is a remote method invocation. To do this, the aspect language must effectively allow them to step into the implementation of method invocation, to detect whether it is local or remote, and to implement the appropriate amount of copying in each case.

One way to do this is to provide runtime reflective access to method invocation. As has been shown in [7, 23, 35, 37] such reflective access can be used to control the communication aspect of a distributed object system. But this kind of reflective access is so powerful that it can be dangerous or difficult to use. So in this case we have chosen to provide a higher-level aspect language, that is more tailored to the specific aspect of controlling copying in remote method invocations.

The communication aspect language we have designed allows the programmer to explicitly describe how much of an object should be copied when it is passed as an argument in a remote method invocation. Using this language, the following fragment of the communication aspect program says that when books are registered with a repository, all of their sub-objects should be copied; when they are de-registered or returned as the result of a lookup, only the ISBN number is copied. The rest of the book, including large sub-objects such as the printable representations, is not copied unless it is needed at some later time.

```
remote Repository {
  void register (Book);
  void unregister (Book: copy isbn);
  Book: copy isbn lookup(String);
}
```

## 6.3  Aspect Weaver

Aspect weavers must process the component and aspect languages, co-composing them properly to produce the desired total system operation. Essential to the function of the aspect weaver is the concept of *join points*, which are those elements of the component language semantics that the aspect programs coordinate with.

In the image processing example, the join points are the data flows of the component program. In this distributed objects example, the join points are the runtime method invocations in the component program. These two examples serve to illustrate an important point about join points—they are not necessarily explicit constructs in the component language. Rather, like nodes in the dataflow graph and runtime method invocations they are clear, but perhaps implicit, elements of the component program's semantics.

Aspect weavers work by generating a *join point representation* of the component program, and then executing (or compiling) the aspect programs with respect to it. In the digital library example, the join-point representation includes information about dynamic method invocations such as the concrete classes of the arguments and their location. The join point representation can be generated at runtime using a reflective runtime for the component language. In this approach, the aspect language is implemented as a meta-program, called at each method invocation, which uses the join point information and the aspect program, to know how to appropriately marshal the arguments.[9] Thus the higher-level aspect language we have designed is implemented on top of a lower level one, as often happens in GP languages.

In the image processing application, the join point representation is quite simple. It is just the data flow graph, operations to access the body of nodes, and operations to edit the graph.

---

[9] In our actual system we use compile-time reflective techniques, so that no interpretive overhead is incurred at runtime.

# 7. Open Issues

As an *explicit* approach to programming, AOP is a young idea. Our work to date has been primarily focused on designing and implementing aspect-oriented programming languages, and using those languages to develop prototype applications. This programming-centric initial focus has been natural, and it parallels the early development of OOP. But there is a great deal of work still to be done to assess the overall utility of AOP, to better understand its relation to existing ideas, and to further develop it so that it can be useful for a wide range of users.

One important goal is quantitative assessment of the utility of AOP. How much does it help in the development of real-world applications? How much does it help with maintenance? Can we develop measures of which applications it will be more or less useful for? This is a difficult problem, for all the same reasons that quantitative assessment of the value of OOP has been difficult, but we believe that it is important to begin work on this, given that it will take time to get solid results.

We also believe it is important to begin a systematic study to find existing systems that have AOP-like elements in their design. We see this as a way to quickly accelerate development of the AOP ideas, by providing a way to get rough empirical evidence without having to build large new systems from the ground up.

Another important area for exploration is the space of different kinds of component and aspect language designs. Can we develop a collection of component and aspect languages that can be plugged together in different ways for different applications? Can we use meta-level frameworks [2, 3, 20, 38] to build such a collection?

What theoretical support can be developed for AOP? What kinds of theories can best describe the interaction between aspects and components and how they must be woven? Can such theories support development of a practical weaving toolkit?

What about the analysis and design process? What are good design principles for aspectual decomposition? What are good "module" structures for aspect programs? How can we train people to identify aspects? Clearly separate them? Write aspect programs? Debug AOP systems? Document AOP systems?

Another important area of exploration is the integration of AOP with existing approaches, methods, tools and development processes. As the examples in this paper show, AOP can be used as an improvement to existing techniques. To fulfill this promise it must developed it a way that integrates well with those techniques.

# 8. Related Work

In this section we give a brief survey of work related to ours. We start with work that is more closely related and proceed out to work that is less closely related.

## 8.1 Work Explicitly Connected to AOP

Several other groups have begun to explicitly consider their work in AOP terms. These include:

- Mehmet Aksit et. al., at the University of Twente, have developed the composition filters object model, which provides control over messages received and sent by an object [1]. In their work, the component language is a traditional OOP, the composition filters mechanism provides an aspect language that can be used to control a number of aspects including synchronization and communication. Most of the weaving happens at runtime; the join points are the dynamic message sends and receives arriving at an object.

- Calton Pu et. al. at the Oregon Graduate Institute, in their work on Synthetix, are developing high performance, high portability and high adaptiveness OS kernels [19, 28]. In their work, the components are familiar functional elements of OS kernels. The aspects are primarily optimizations based on invariants that relate to how a service is being used. Their weaver technology uses partial evaluation to effectively specialize the kernel code for particular use cases. Their code is structured to expose as join points those places where an invariant becomes or ceases to be true.

- Karl Lieberherr et. al., at Northeastern University are developing techniques that make object-oriented programs more reusable and less brittle in the face of common program evolution tasks [13, 15, 31]. In their work, the component languages are existing OOPs like C++ and Java. Succinct traversal specifications [13] and context objects [31] provide aspect languages that can be used to address a variety of cross-cutting issues. Weaving of aspect programs that use succinct traversal specification is compile-time oriented, the join point representation is, roughly speaking, the class graph. Weaving of aspect programs that use context objects is more runtime oriented, the join points are the dynamic method and function calls.

## 8.2 Reflection and Metaobject Protocols

Aspect-oriented programming has a deep connection with work in computational reflection and metaobject protocols [11, 20, 24, 32, 34, 38]. A reflective system provides a base language and (one or more) meta-languages that provide control over the base language's semantics and implementation. The meta languages provide views of the computation that no one base language component could ever see, such as the entire execution stack, or all calls to objects of a given class. Thus, they cross-cut the base level computation. In AOP terms, meta-languages are lower-level aspect languages whose join points are the "hooks" that the reflective system provides. AOP is a goal, for which reflection is one powerful tool.

We have exploited this connection to great advantage in our work on AOP. When prototyping AOP systems we often start by developing simple metaobject protocols for the component language, and then prototype imperative aspect programs using them. Later, once we have a good sense of what the aspect programs need to do, we develop more explicit aspect language support for them.

The connection is particularly evident in section 6, where the aspect languages we provided could have been layered on top of a reflective architecture. Similarly, the loop fusion aspect described in Section 5 can be implemented, with some degree of efficiency, using the method combination facility in the CLOS metaobject protocol [11, 33]. This connection is also evident in the work mentioned in Section 8.1; both the Demeter work and the composition filters work have been described as being reflective facilities [16].

## 8.3 Program Transformation

The goal of work in program transformation is similar to that of AOP. They want to be able to write correct programs in a higher-level language, and then mechanically transform those program into ones with identical behavior, but more efficient performance. In this style of programming, some of the properties the programmer wants to implement are written in an initial program. Other properties are added by passing that initial program through various transformation programs. This separation is similar in spirit to the component/aspect program separation.

But the notion of component and aspect are new to AOP. These terms provide additional value in system design. Also, while some transformations are aspectual in nature, others are not. Transformation programs tend to operate in terms of the syntax of the program being transformed. If other join points are desired, it is the responsibility of the transformation program to somehow manifest them. Thus, while it is possible to layer some kinds of aspect programs on top of a program transformation substrate, that is a separate piece of implementation work.

We would like to do a systematic analysis of the transformations developed by this community, to see which of them can be used for providing different kinds of aspect languages.

## 8.4 Subjective Programming

A natural question to ask is whether subjective programming [5] is AOP or vice versa. We believe that AOP and subjective programming are different in important ways. Analogously to the way object-oriented programming supports automatic selection among methods for the same message from different classes, subjective programming supports automatic combination of methods for a given message from different subjects. In both cases, the methods involved are components in the AOP sense, since they can be well localized in a generalized procedure. It is even possible to program in either an object-oriented style or a subjective style on top of an ordinary procedural language, without significant tangling. The same is not true of AOP. Thus, while the aspects of AOP tend to be about properties that affect the performance or semantics of components, the subjects of subjective programming tend to be additional features added onto other subjects. We believe that subjective programming is complementary to, and compatible with, AOP.

## 8.5 Other Engineering Disciplines

Many other engineering disciplines are based on well-established aspectual decompositions. For example, mechanical engineers use static, dynamic and thermal models of the same system as part of designing it. The differing models cross-cut each other in that the different properties of a system compose differently. Similarly, some software development tools explicitly support particular aspectual decomposition: tools for OMT [29, 30] methods let programmers draw different pictures of how objects should work.

# 9. Conclusions

We have traced the complexity in some existing code to a fundamental difference in the kinds of properties that are being implemented. Components are properties of a system, for which the implementation can be cleanly encapsulated in a generalized procedure. Aspects are properties for which the implementation cannot be cleanly encapsulated in a generalized procedure. Aspects and cross-cut components cross-cut each other in a system's implementation.

Based on this analysis, we have been able to develop aspect-oriented programming technology that supports clean abstraction and composition of both components and aspects. The key difference between AOP and other approaches is that AOP provides component and aspect languages with different abstraction and composition mechanisms. A special language processor called an aspect weaver is used to coordinate the co-composition of the aspects and components.

We have had good success working with AOP in several testbed applications. The AOP conceptual framework has helped us to design the systems, and the AOP-based implementations have proven to be easier to develop and maintain, while being comparably efficient to much more complex code written using traditional techniques.

# Acknowledgments

Thanks to Karl Lieberherr, Carine Lucas, Gail Murphy and Bedir Tekinerdogan who generously provided extensive comments on earlier drafts of the paper, and to Andy Berlin, Geoff Chase, Patrick Cheung, John Gilbert, Arthur Lee, Calton Pu, Alex Silverman, Marvin Theimer and Mark Yim with whom we have had many discussions about AOP.

Thanks also to all the attendees of the AOP Friends Meetings, with whom we spent an enjoyable two days discussing AOP and related ideas: Mehmet Aksit, Lodewick Bergmans, Pierre Cointe, William Harrison, Jacques Malenfant, Satoshi Matsuoka, Kim Mens, Harold Ossher, Calton Pu, Ian Simmonds, Perri Tarr, Bedir Tekinerdogan, Mark Skipper, and Patrick Steyaert

# Bibliography

1. Aksit M., Wakita K., et al., *Abstracting object interactions using composition filters*, in proc. *ECOOP'93 Workshop on Object-Based Distributed Programming*, pp. 152-184, 1993.
2. Bobrow D. G., DeMichiel L. G., et al., *Common Lisp Object System Specification*, in *SIGPLAN Notices*, vol. 23, 1988.
3. Chiba S., *A Metaobject Protocol for C++*, in proc. *Conference on Object-Oriented Programming Systems, Languages, and Applications (OOPSLA 95)*, Austin, 1995.
4. Consel C., *Program Adaptation based on Program Transformation*, in proc. *ACM Workshop on Strategic Directions in Computing Research*, 1996.
5. Harrison W. and Ossher H., *Subject-oriented programming (a critique of pure objects)*, in proc. *Conference on Object-Oriented Programming: Systems, Languages, and Applications*, pp. 411--428, Washington D.C., 1993.
6. Henry S. and Kafura D., *Software Structure Metrics Based on Information Flow*, in *IEEE Transactions on Software Engineering*, vol. SE-7: 509--518, 1981.
7. Ichisugi Y., Matsuoka S., et al., *Rbcl: A reflective object-oriented concurrrent language without a run-time kernel*, in proc. *International Workshop on New Models for Software Architecture '92; Reflection and Meta-Level Architecture*, pp. 24--35, 1992.
8. Irwin J., Loingtier J.-M., et al., *Aspect-Oriented Programming of Sparse Matrix Code*, Xerox PARC, Palo Alto, CA. Technical report SPL97-007 P9710045, February, 1997.
9. Kiczales G., *Foil for the Workshop on Open Implementation*, Xerox PARC, Web pages, http://www.parc.xerox.com/spl/eca/oi/workshop-94/foil/main.html
10. Kiczales G., *Why are Black Boxes so Hard to Reuse?*, Invited Talk, OOPSLA'94, Video tape, Web pages, http://www.parc.xerox.com/spl/eca/oi/gregor-invite.html

11. Kiczales G., des Rivères J., et al., *The Art of the Metaobject Protocol*. Book published by MIT Press, 1991.
12. Kiczales G., Lamping J., et al., *Open Implementation Design Guidelines*, in proc. *International Conference on Software Engineering*, (Forthcoming), 1997.
13. Lieberherr K. J., Silva-Lepe I., et al., *Adaptive Object-Oriented Programming Using Graph-Based Customization*, in *Communications of the ACM*, vol. 37(5): 94-101, 1994.
14. Lopes C. V. and Kiczales G., *D: A Language Framework for Distributed Programming*, Xerox PARC, Palo Alto, CA. Technical report SPL97-010 P9710047, February, 1997.
15. Lopes C. V. and Lieberherr K., *Abstracting Process-to-Function Relations in Concurrent Object-Oriented Applications*, in proc. *European Conference on Object-Oriented Programming*, pp. 81-99, Bologna, Italy, 1994.
16. Lopes C. V. and Lieberherr K., *AP/S++: Case-Study of a MOP for Purposes of Software Evolution*, in proc. *Reflection'96*, pp. 167-184, S. Francisco, CA, 1996.
17. Maeda C., Lee A., et al., *Open Implementation Analysis and Design*, in proc. *Symposium on Software Reuse (To Appear, May 1997)*, 1997.
18. Mahoney J. V., *Functional Visual Routines*, Xerox Palo Alto Research Center, Palo Alto SPL95-069, July 30, 1995, 1995.
19. Massalin H. and Pu C., *Threads and Input/Output in the Synthesis Kernel*, in *Proceedings of the 12th ACM Symposium on Operating Systems Principles* :pp 191-201, 1989.
20. Matsuoka S., Watanabe T., et al., *Hybrid Group Reflective Architecture for Object-Oriented Concurrent Reflective Programming*, in *European Conference on Object Oriented Programming* :pp 231-250, 1991.
21. McClure C., *A Model for Program Complexity Analysis*, in proc. *3rd International Conference on Software Engineering*, Los Alamitos, CA, 1978.
22. Mendhekar A., Kiczales G., et al., *RG: A Case-Study for Aspect-Oriented Programming*, Xerox PARC, Palo Alto, CA. Technical report SPL97-009 P9710044, February, 1997.
23. Okamura H., Ishikawa Y., et al., *Al-1/d: A distributed programming system with multi-model reflection framework*, in proc. *International Workshop on New Models for Software Architecture '92; Reflection and Meta-Level Architecture*, pp. 36--47, 1992.
24. Okamura H., Ishikawa Y., et al., *Metalevel Decomposition in AL-1/D*, in proc. *International Symposium on Object Technologies for Advanced Software*, pp. 110-127, 1993.
25. Parnas D. L., *Designing Software for Extension and Contraction*, in proc. *3rd International Conference on Software Engineering*, pp. 264-277, 1978.
26. Parnas D. L., *On a 'Buzzword': Hierarchical Structure*, in proc. *IFIP Congress 74*, pp. 336-339, 1974.
27. Parnas D. L., *On the Criteria to be Used in decomposing Systems into Modules*, in *Communications of the ACM*, vol. 15(2), 1972.

28. Pu C., Autrey T., et al., *Optimistic Incremental Specialization: Streamlining a Commercial Operating System*, in proc. *15th ACM Symposium on Operating Systems Principles (SOSP'95)*, 1995.
29. Rational, *Rational Web pages*, Rational Software Corporation, Web pages, http://www.rational.com
30. Rumbaugh J., Blaha M., et al., *Object-Oriented Modeling and Design*. Book published by Prentice Hall, 1991.
31. Seiter L. M., Palsberg J., et al., *Evolution of Object Behavior Using Context Relations*, in proc. *Fourth ACM SIGSOFT Symposium on the Foundations of Software Engineering*, pp. 46--57, San Francisco, 1996.
32. Smith B. C., *Reflection and Semantics in a Procedural Language LCS Technical Report*, M.I.T., Cambridge, MA, 1982.
33. Steele G. L., *Common LISP: The Language, 2nd Edition*. Book published by Digital Press, 1990.
34. Wand M. and Friedman D. P., *The Mystery of the Tower Revealed: A Non-Reflective Description of the Reflective Tower*, in *Proceedings of the ACM Conference on LISP and Functional Programming* :pp 298-307. ACM, 1986.
35. Watanabe T. and Yonezawa A., *Reflection in an object-oriented concurrent language*, in proc. *ACM Conference on Object-Oriented Programming Systems, Languages, and Applications (OOPSLA 88)*, pp. 306--315, San Diego, CA, 1988.
36. Yau S. and Collofello J., *Some Stability Measures for Software Maintenance*, in *tse*, vol. SE-6: 545--552, 1980.
37. Yokote Y., *The Apertos Reflective Operating System: The Concept and its Implementation*, in proc. *Conference on Object-Oriented Programming: Systems, Languages, and Applications*, 1992.
38. Yonezawa A. and Watanabe T., *An Introduction to Object-Based Reflective Concurrent Computation*, in *Proceedings of the ACM SIGPLAN Workshop on Object-Based Concurrent Programming, SIGPLAN Notices, 24(4)*, Agha G., Wegner P., et al., Eds., 1989.

# DRASTIC:
# A Run-Time Architecture for
# Evolving, Distributed, Persistent Systems

Huw Evans and Peter Dickman
{huw,pd}@dcs.gla.ac.uk
http://www.dcs.gla.ac.uk/~drastic

Department of Computing Science
University of Glasgow
Glasgow, G12 8RZ, UK

**Abstract.** Modern systems must be adaptable — to changing requirements, bug-fixes, new technologies and reconfiguration. For critical applications this must be possible at run-time; for complex applications it
should be limitable to major sub-divisions of the system. The DRAS-
TIC architecture addresses these goals by exploiting object persistence
and distributed systems implementation techniques. It enables run-time
changes of types, implementations, and the system configuration. This
is based on a novel architectural abstraction of locality for evolution,
called the 'zone'. Contracts between zones automatically limit the visibility of such changes between zones. We present work in progress on
DRASTIC's computational model and run-time system, illustrating support for software evolution and highlighting key features of our current
implementation.

## 1 Introduction

Existing platforms offer little or no support for the management of change in,
and evolution of, enterprise-critical applications. Furthermore, the facilities for
the management (garbage collection, recovery, reorganisation and so on) of large
distributed datasets rarely meet the needs of modern information systems. For
example, CORBA [Obj95a] provides the software engineer with little support for
managing the complexities involved when changing object interface definitions.
CORBA also does not provide abstractions to constrain the effects of a change
in a software component, making such a change visible throughout the entire
system.

Software starts to evolve almost as soon as it is written: users require new
features and ask for amendments. To compound the problem, within large systems, initially identical software components can evolve in different directions.
In addition, large systems cannot always be shut down in their entirety because
they may be too complex or mission critical, for example airline seat reservation
systems and on-line banking systems.

As systems are becoming more complex and ever larger, maintaining them
will become more of a problem. The DRASTIC project recognises this difficulty

and proposes tackling it by providing the programmer with a run-time system where the focus is placed on describing and controlling the effects of software evolution. Four key points underpin our approach.

Firstly, a DRASTIC system is subdivided into smaller, more easily managed sub-domains called zones. The organization of zones can follow the structure of the business using them, although this is not enforced. Zones encapsulate change; if a software component is changed in one zone, that change is not visible outside it. Zones are introduced at design time, subsequently becoming explicit components in the run-time system.

Secondly, the software in each zone is evolved as a coherent whole, largely autonomously from software in other zones, even though the source code may originally have been shared by components in many zones.

Thirdly, the evolution of the entire system is made explicit at the level of a zone by defining 'zone contracts' between them. These contracts specify which program types can be exchanged between zones and the transformations that are required should an object move from one zone to another or if a method invocation is made that crosses a zone boundary.

Lastly, zone autonomy is supported by inserting code supplied by the software engineer at the zone boundary. These software fragments, called change absorbers, handle the transformations indicated above and enforce the zone contract.

The DRASTIC run-time platform provides a distributed systems programming environment with support for orthogonally persistent processes. The run-time environment contains a number of repositories that hold information regarding the current configuration of the system. This information can be queried by processes and the software engineer to dynamically reconfigure the system at run-time. In addition, at run-time, DRASTIC intercepts all inter-process application-level object references. The ability to do this is the key to our approach to supporting run-time software evolution.

## 1.1 Project Goals

The DRASTIC project aims to provide support for large, evolving and integrated information systems. This support is being demonstrated by building a series of prototype systems. These systems explore different ways that distributed reference management, zones and zone contracts can be implemented and presented to the software engineer. Software evolution is supported by providing a platform that allows program types to be changed at run-time.

## 1.2 Overview of Paper

The first half of this paper presents DRASTIC's design: our model is presented in §2, an extended example is elaborated in §3 and DRASTIC's architecture is discussed in §4. With reference to the example, the second part of the paper details how software evolution is supported: §5 shows how the architecture performs computation within an evolving system and §6 provides some preliminary performance measurements. Section 7 describes related work, with §8 and §9 detailing the project's current status and areas of further work.

# 2  DRASTIC's Model

This section describes the key models and critical decisions that underpin the DRASTIC approach. The zone model and contract model, described in sections 2.2 and 2.3, are concerned with how to sub-divide and describe a complex system so that it can be effectively evolved and maintained. Section 2.4 describes the model of evolution assumed. In an evolving system the potential for changing types, and corresponding modification of objects, means that questions of identity must be addressed; sections 2.5, 2.6 and 2.7 present the approach taken to naming types, objects and processes respectively. This section is concluded with a description of the distributed object model (§2.8) and persistence model (§2.9) which are concerned with access to objects over space and time respectively.

Since evolution of a complex system requires deep understanding of the application semantics, evolution cannot be fully automated. Therefore, our goal is to minimise the effort required by the software architect and we present their rôle in using the DRASTIC system in §3.1.

## 2.1  Motivating Example

Organisations tend to be divided into smaller groups or subdomains, for example, departments such as finance and payroll. Each subdomain should be as autonomous as possible, so they can effectively manage their rôle in the organisation.

The design, installation and maintenance of software in an organisation should also reflect this subdivision for reasons of autonomy. Updating all of the software in an organisation in one go will often be prohibitively expensive, but may be affordable on a per-department basis. Therefore, it is much more realistic for a particular sub-domain to be able to manage its own software independently of others. Changes made in one sub-domain may not make sense in another and should a change be made that does affect another, ideally we would like to limit the effect of that change to only the two sub-domains concerned. DRASTIC allows a system to be decomposed into such sub-domains, which are called zones.

One such organisation that can be clearly divided into zones is a hospital. Hospitals are usually decomposed along the lines of medical speciality — such as pathology, X-Ray, gynaecology and geriatrics — and administrative boundaries, finance, hospital catering, management information systems and so on. Imagine a simplified hospital consisting of just two zones, the X-Ray zone and the morgue zone, which has a computerised patient management system. When the system was first installed, the software in both zones agreed on the data making up a patient record. However, over the life of the hospital, the software will need to be updated many times. This can create disparities between the system's software components and such changes may affect the definition of the patient record.

If the X-Ray department chooses to amend its patient record type, to capture a patient's X-Ray history, this change should not necessarily affect any other department in the hospital. The change could instead be encapsulated within the zone changing the type. But, departments may wish to exchange information, which may require a patient record object to move from the X-Ray zone to the morgue zone. The morgue department's software, however, has no concept of a patient record with an X-Ray history. The object needs to be transformed in some way when it crosses the boundary between zones and simply discarding the additional data may not be an acceptable solution. DRASTIC supports such transformations by inserting software components, provided by the software engineer, between zones. These transformers are called change absorbers and are more fully described in section 2.4.

Whenever a change is made to the software in one zone that will affect the software in another, both zones need to be aware of the kind of change being made. In a complex system, such as the hospital, some way of agreeing what can pass from one zone to another needs to be defined. This is to ensure that zones can be used to encapsulate change and so that change management becomes an explicit part of the maintenance of the system. DRASTIC supports this by defining a pair-wise agreement between zones which specifies the types that two zones are prepared to exchange. We refer to this as the zone contract.

## 2.2 Zone Model

A DRASTIC system is decomposed into a number of largely autonomous spaces called zones. This decomposition is made at design time, and remains explicit throughout the software life-cycle. At run-time a zone is a named, logical collection of processes distributed over a number of hosts. Zones support the recognition and exploitation of the almost-disjoint application subdomains which are known to developers and users, but which cannot be cogently described and supported at the system level on current platforms. In our example, one zone might contain all the hosts in the X-Ray department of the hospital. However, zones do not have to follow such a rigid physical organisation. It is possible both to have a zone containing processes that are physically separated by large distances, eg. with hosts in Scotland, Finland and the United States, and for processes on the same host to belong to different zones.

All the objects in a zone evolve as a single unit, thus the zone is the unit of evolution in the DRASTIC system. A DRASTIC process combines an optional store, the DRASTIC support platform and the language run-time. A process is considered to be a single address space that encapsulates objects and supports their execution. DRASTIC processes contain application objects. Objects hold references to other, potentially remote, objects and the DRASTIC platform intercepts these references at the process and zone boundaries to support software evolution. Zones exist from design time through to becoming explicit system components in the run-time system. When a reference traverses a zone boundary it passes through processes that bridge two zones. The zone boundary processes (ZBPs) handle any transformations that are required when objects migrate between two zones or when invocations are performed along a reference that crosses a zone boundary.

Zones constrain the effects of evolution. Without them, a change to a software component might be visible throughout the entire system. Allowing a change to propagate throughout an entire system usually requires that each software component be recompiled, or if not recompiled, at least examined to ascertain the impact of the change. This creates a lot of work for the software engineer. Encapsulating change allows collections of software components to evolve largely autonomously, reducing component recompilation requirements and the need to check code.

Within DRASTIC, a process is required to reside in precisely one zone. To ensure a process can only be in one zone at any one time, DRASTIC zones do not overlap and it is not possible to nest one inside another. This requirement makes the design of the system much easier. If a process were allowed to reside in two zones simultaneously, a possible ambiguity could arise when evolving objects of a particular type. Consider two zones, A and B, and a process P which consists of a single object of type t. Assume that P is allowed to reside simultaneously in both zones. If zone A and zone B evolve type t, but evolve it differently, two different types now exist, $t_A$ and $t_B$. Without adding considerable complexity to the model and run-time architecture there is no way of deciding how P's object of type t should evolve.

## 2.3   Contract Model

The zone contract is a pair-wise agreement between two distinct zones. It describes which types can flow between zones, the permitted invocations and what needs to be done to transform objects at the zone boundary. For the purposes of implementation the contract is a description of the transformations to be applied to objects and references that are exported from one zone and imported into another (figure 1a). When viewed by a software engineer, a contract between any two zones, for example A and B (figure 1b), is seen from the point of view of what a zone imports and exports. Zone A exports objects of type X and Y to zone B and imports from it objects of type X and Z.

In figure 1a, zone A's contract specifies it will export to zone B objects of type X and Y and zone B will import from zone A objects of type X' and Y'. Transformations between the two zones protect the software in one zone from changes made to the software in the other zone.

Zone B exports objects of type Z which zone A imports; no transformation is applied. It is necessary to specify this in the contract because the two zones exchange this data and because, over time, one zone's definition of Z may change. Without explicitly capturing this information in the contract, the knowledge required to permit change to either Z is easily lost. By specifying a seemingly redundant transformation greater control can be exercised over subsequent changes made to the system.

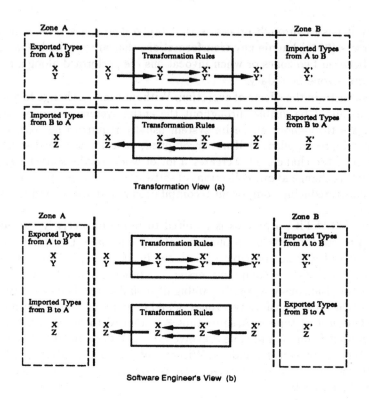

**Fig. 1.** Zone A and B's Contract

A zone contract allows the software architect to describe the interactions between two zones. As a complex system evolves, these contracts will need to be reviewed and periodically updated. For example, the contract between the X-ray zone and the morgue zone described in section 2.1 would allow a patient record object to move between the two zones. The contract therefore provides the software engineer with greater control over the consistency of their system. For example, if one zone exports a type to another zone, that second zone should import it. Perhaps, as a result of evolution, that type should no longer be exported. However, the importing zone may still rely on it. Capturing this kind of information is important in managing large systems and can provide valuable feedback to the software engineer when a system is being modified.

It is possible to extend the idea of contracts to be more than just pair-wise, capturing information for a set of zones; however such a description seems to get extremely complex very quickly. It may be possible to take a global view of the entire system, checking for consistency in a way that is not possible with our pair-wise approach, but this, also, seems to be difficult to realise at run-time. Pair-wise agreements appear to capture sufficient information in a manageable way to allow realistic systems to be modelled using them. Extensions to this approach, with global consistency checking of contracts, are an area for future work.

## 2.4 Evolution Model

To effectively maintain modern systems, support for evolution is essential. Critical applications need to be capable of being evolved at run-time. For complex applications, evolution should be limitable to major sub-divisions of the system. DRASTIC's zones divide the application into more manageable parts, such that one zone can be evolved independently of others. The transformation rules contained within a contract are realised at run-time in software components called change absorbers. A change absorber is code provided by the software engineer which can transform objects of one type into objects of another type. DRASTIC allows processes in one zone to be evolved while allowing other processes in other zones to continue execution, even when these processes hold references to each other. This is done by intercepting application-level object references and placing change absorbers along the reference chain between the invoking object and the object being invoked.

The DRASTIC zone is the unit of evolution. In the current DRASTIC design, all software and data in a zone must be evolved at the same time. If some instances of a type in one zone were allowed to evolve while others remained at the previous version, this would make the run-time platform much more complicated. In future DRASTIC prototypes, this issue of selective evolution may be considered. When evolving a zone in its entirety, any databases the zone may contain may require some form of schema modification to take place. The DRASTIC project does not directly address this issue, instead providing an appropriate framework within which schemata can be changed.

## 2.5 Type Identity

Types are named entities in the DRASTIC system, to permit them to be referred to in contracts and during evolution. Within a single zone each type is uniquely identified, with the type name-spaces being zone-specific. The same identifier may be used for distinct types in two different zones, and identical types may be given distinct names in different zones. The zone contracts are written using the names from the two participating zones, with the type names being implicitly extended by their zone names. Furthermore, the association of names to types within a zone can change over time. When a type is evolved, changing its definition, it may, but is not required to, retain the same name.

## 2.6 Object Identity

Objects have identity in the DRASTIC system, and within the DRASTIC platform object identifiers are used. Again, the object name spaces are zone specific, with objects being uniquely identified within their zone. Implicit extension of the object name by the zone name provides unique names for objects within a persistent application system, since zones have distinct names within a given complex application.

Since objects may be transformed during evolution, and can be migrated, it is not necessarily possible to rely on the implementation language object naming mechanisms. In our current implementation, for example, migration of an object relies on the construction of a new proxy and actual object in the recipient process. The Java run-time views these as new language-level objects. However, within the DRASTIC system the object is the same, it has just moved location. Any code the programmer has that depends upon the language-level identity remaining unchanged would now fail.

To solve the object identity problem, the DRASTIC pre-processor ensures that all migratable objects support an identity checking operation. This operation relies on an identity field in the object which is not affected by migration. It is safe to do this as the original actual object will be removed from the system if the migration is successful, so only one object with that identity is visible at any one time.

## 2.7 Process Identity

Processes in a distributed system contain objects that need to refer to other objects which are potentially in other processes. Within a DRASTIC process, objects refer to each other using language-level object references. Within a single persistent application system (PAS), globally available services used by DRASTIC, such as name servers to allow the system to boot, are at well known locations. Each persistent application system within DRASTIC is given a unique name which does not change over its lifetime. Each zone within a persistent application system is represented by a name which is unique within that PAS. Processes within a particular zone are also uniquely named within that zone by attaching the name to the store that the process is booted over (processes with no store are given new names when they are started). In the current implementation, DRASTIC uses simple strings to represent names. These names are part of a process' persistent state and different instantiations of the same process over time are distinguished by a monotonically increasing value. Using the persistent application, zone and process name together, a process can be uniquely identified in a DRASTIC system. More compact and richer name representations may be explored in future versions of the platform.

## 2.8 Distributed Object Model

Distribution is central to building modern software systems. Many modern systems have to be distributed as the people involved in the enterprise are themselves spread over large geographic distances. The underlying distribution model adopted by DRASTIC is similar to that provided by the Emerald [BHJ+87] system. Objects in DRASTIC are described by classes, containing an interface and an implementation either of which may evolve in any way. For example, a method's implementation may change or a method signature may evolve (expand or contract) over time.

Information describing the current system configuration, such as initialisation files and program source code, also tends to be geographically distributed. Managing these repositories of information requires a distributed system support layer in which the current system description can be modified and the system subsequently reconfigured. The relationship between DRASTIC and other systems which focus solely on this reconfiguration problem is addressed in §7.

**Failure Model** Distributed systems exhibit partial failure. At any one time, some subset of a distributed system's components may be faulty and these faults can be visible at the application programming level. For example, processes may suddenly crash and inter-process messages may be lost or duplicated. DRASTIC's process failure model assumes any process may crash at any time but that when a process crashes it does so without exhibiting Byzantine behaviour. Message delivery is assumed to be at most once.

The DRASTIC run-time system offers the system architect some assistance with failure (eg. the ability to restart a crashed process) but it does not attempt to mask all errors related to distribution as, in the general case, this is not possible. For example, consider a non-replicated server: if the server is actually down when a client wishes to use it, due to hardware modification, there is no alternative but to report an error at the client side. DRASTIC allows failures at the granularity of an object, as an invocation through an object reference may fail due to a network error. Such partial failures may lead to method call failure, but within DRASTIC it is never possible to invoke the wrong object as a result of failures. This gives programmers a form of referential integrity that is compatible with a distributed system's failure semantics.

## 2.9 Persistence Model

It is a common requirement when building such large, long-lived, distributed systems that objects need to out-live the process that created them, typically by being written to hard disk. DRASTIC supports this using the concept of orthogonal persistence by reachability [AM95]. This is implemented by transitive reachability from a distinguished object, a persistent root, that is known to the persistence mechanism. Thus, any object in a DRASTIC process that is reachable, either directly or indirectly, from the persistent root is periodically made persistent automatically. In our current implementation orthogonal persistence is provided by Persistent Java [AJDS96].

Without support for orthogonal persistence, the programmer would be required to explicitly transfer to and from stable storage data-structures that should out-live the process that manipulates them. This means that programmers spend a lot of time flattening their complex data-structures into other data-structures, such as streams of bytes, that are easily written to and read from disk. Orthogonal persistence makes this explicit conversion unnecessary, allowing the software engineer to concentrate on the semantics of their application.

# 3 Extended Example

This section describes the example that will be used throughout the rest of the paper. Before the example is introduced, the view of the system as seen by the software architect is presented together with how they could decompose a system into zones. The programmer's view of the DRASTIC system is then described.

## 3.1 The Software Architect's View

System decomposition is a powerful tool in the design of complex systems. Using zones, DRASTIC allows the software architect to capture this decomposition and explicitly express it in a uniform manner from design time through to run-time. Zones also allow the software architect to encapsulate components, such as legacy systems. Contracts allow the software architect to explicitly describe which objects can flow across zone boundaries, increasing system modularity. They also specify which object transformations are required at zone boundaries, increasing system autonomy.

The software architect using DRASTIC will describe their distributed system as a collection of zones. Each zone will have contracts with a number of other zones. The software architect will provide change absorbers which are placed between zones to protect one zone's software from changes in other zones. It is the goal of DRASTIC to provide as much automation for this as possible. For example, once the change absorbers have been defined, DRASTIC automatically inserts them where necessary in the zone boundaries.

**Choosing an Appropriate Decomposition** So far, how the software engineer chooses an appropriate system decomposition has not been described. The goal of the DRASTIC project is not to define a methodology for the development of a zoned system, rather it is to build a prototypical run-time system that supports the construction of systems that can evolve dynamically. Within our research group a related project called ZEST is underway. The ZEST project focusses on the software engineering issues raised by the idea of decomposing a system into a collection of zones. DRASTIC is intended to be one possible run-time support for systems designed using approaches like that being developed within ZEST.

## 3.2 Programmer's Model

The programmer using DRASTIC uses the programming model provided by their chosen implementation language. If more than one language is used in an application, other problems may arise, for example, when comparing two object references for equality. These problems must be addressed and DRASTIC is intended, in principle, to support language heterogeneity, although in the current implementation only Java [GM96] is supported. Supporting multiple implementation languages is not the main focus of this work and the implications for the run-time system are not discussed in this paper.

## 3.3 The Example

The example system used in this paper is that of a hospital. A hospital can be divided into a number of zones where, for example, one zone would be responsible for dealing with X-rays, another the hospital catering, a third the morgue and so on.

The software in each of these zones will tend to evolve independently of the software in other zones. Two zones may have originally shared the source code for a given type, but when the type is evolved in one zone, a copy of the source code may be taken and updated.

Imagine a simple hospital system that has been decomposed by the software engineer into two zones, the X-ray zone and the morgue zone (figure 2).

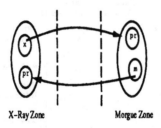

X-Ray Zone        Morgue Zone

**Fig. 2.** The Initial System Architecture

The software engineer has defined one main type, the patient record (PR), that both zones understand. Two objects of this type exist in processes that are executing in the zones, one object (pr) per process. Both processes also contain one other object with a single reference to the patient record in the other zone, x in the X-Ray zone and m in the Morgue zone. Figure 3 contains the initial definition of the patient record type and the original contract between the two zones. It is assumed that each field has two associated methods (not shown) that get and set the particular field. For example, the id field will have methods int getId() and void setId(int i) defined.

A variety of changes are possible, such as modifying an existing method's signature, adding or removing a field from the class' state and reorganising the class inheritance hierarchy. The software architect is free to make such changes to a zone whenever they feel it is appropriate. Therefore, at some point in the future, the X-Ray zone may have its PR type updated, creating a new type PR_X. At some other time, the PR type in the morgue zone may also be updated, to

```
class PR
{
    int      id;
    Name     name;
    Address address;
}
```

| Direction of Transfer | Exported Types | Transformations Required | Imported Types |
|---|---|---|---|
| X–Ray to Morgue | PR | None | PR |
| Morgue to X–Ray | PR | None | PR |

**Fig. 3.** Initial Definition of the Patient Record and X-Ray and Morgue Zones Contract

another type, different to both the PR and the PR_X types, resulting in another type, PR_M.

The changes that will be considered in this paper are illustrated on figure 4. In this new configuration, the PR type has been changed in both zones, leading to PR_X and PR_M (note that neither PR_X nor PR_M is a subtype of PR). Any of these objects moving between zones will now need to be transformed, as will any method invocations. The zone contract will also have to be changed.

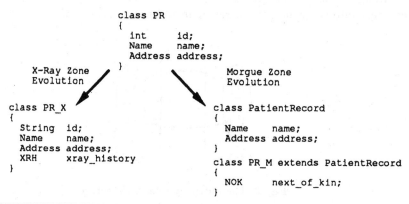

| Direction of Transfer | Exported Types | Transformations Required | Imported Types |
|---|---|---|---|
| X–Ray to Morgue | PR_X | PR_X to PR_M | PR_M |
| Morgue to X–Ray | PR_M | PR_M to PR_X | PR_X |

**Fig. 4.** Updated Definition of the Patient Record X-Ray and Morgue Zones Contract

The new type in the X-Ray zone, PR_X, uses a new representation for the patients record's identifier. It has been changed from an integer to a String. A new field to capture a patient's X-Ray history has also been added. The PR type in the morgue zone has undergone a more extensive change. A patient in the morgue zone is now identified by a combination of their name and address and this has been abstracted out into a class PatientRecord. PR_M extends PatientRecord, which itself supports fewer methods and holds less state than PR, providing an extra field to capture a patient's next of kin.

# 4 DRASTIC's Architecture

This section describes in detail the DRASTIC platform's high-level support data-structures. Firstly, the architecture of an application process is described. This is followed by a top-down description of the rest of the DRASTIC architecture, starting at the system-wide level, moving down through the multi-zone architecture, ending with the architecture of a single zone.

## 4.1 Within an Application Process

When a process boots over the DRASTIC platform, the process acquires several additional objects (figure 5). The two objects that handle incoming references are the InHandler and the incoming reference table (IRT). The InHandler handles incoming migrating objects and invocations to objects in this process that are remotely accessible. The InHandler has a reference to the IRT which contains references to application-level objects as well as a weighted reference count for distributed garbage collection.[1] The outgoing reference table and RemoteStoreDescriptors handle out-going object references. Application level objects logically hold references to the target object. In practise the reference is pointing at a slot in the ORT. The ORT handles the indirection of references from this process and this usually involves referring to the RemoteStoreDescriptor object. The RemoteStoreDescriptor is responsible for packaging up outgoing object migrations and method invocations into a format suitable for transfer across a network. The IRT and ORT tables allow DRASTIC to construct chains of references that, logically, lead from one application object to another application object.

All inter-process references that an application level process creates are indirected through the DRASTIC platform. This is so the DRASTIC platform can, by inserting other objects along these references, implement run-time software evolution by intercepting application level method invocations. A process' InHandler also provides a way for other processes to contact it.

DRASTIC evolves sets of processes as a unit. Working at a finer granularity would require intercepting intra-process invocations. This is expensive, slowing down local invocations which are much more numerous than remote calls. Intercepting intra-process invocations would also involve changing the language run-time system or the compiler.

CallHandlers are objects that are provided automatically by the DRASTIC platform, after pre-processing the application's source code. A CallHandler contains code to call a particular type's methods should an object of that type be remotely invokable. For example, if the pr object was to migrate from its process in the morgue zone to the process in the X-Ray zone, a mechanism would be required so that methods of the migrated object could be invoked. This is provided by the CallHandler. It is not enough to use a conventional RPC mechanism at this level, as a remote method invocation would pass straight through

---

[1] The distributed garbage collection algorithm used in DRASTIC is outside the scope of this paper. The interested reader is referred to [Dic92].

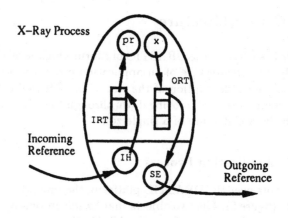

X–Ray Process

Incoming
Reference

Outgoing
Reference

IRT : Incoming Reference Table    IH : InHandler
ORT : Outgoing Reference Table    SE : StoreExemplar

**Fig. 5.** A Process' Main Data-Structures

from caller to callee, bypassing DRASTIC and, in particular, the zone boundaries. The ability to intercept remote invocations is the key to our approach to supporting run-time software evolution.

Most DRASTIC processes are booted over their own persistent store. All objects that are transitively reachable from a persistent root are regularly checkpointed (stabilised) and placed on disk, thus the store becomes a snapshot of a process' state. DRASTIC processes are normally defined to be either running over their store or not running, and a store can have either zero or one process running over it. If one process requires access to another store that does not currently have a process running over it, DRASTIC's daemon processes will attempt to boot a process over that store. However, not all processes require the services of a persistent store, for example, the client in a client/server architecture. DRASTIC, therefore, allows a process to boot without a persistent store.

Should a process crash, when another process is started over the store all persistent objects are reinitialised to contain their last saved state. Orthogonally persistent systems aid in the construction of such fault tolerant systems. Crashed processes can be restarted and will fault in their objects during the normal course of execution. No special code has to be written to retrieve the last known process state and execution can be rapidly resumed because objects are faulted-in as needed rather than requiring all of the previously saved state to be read before resuming execution.

Having a snapshot of a process on disk facilitates the simple evolution of a process. When a change is made to a type that is contained in a particular process, that process can be terminated, causing its state to be written to the store. The store can then be traversed, changing old objects for objects instantiated from the new type. A new process, containing code that understands the new type can then be booted over the manipulated store.[2]

## 4.2 System Wide

A DRASTIC system consists of many zones and, within a zone, processes need to contact each other. DRASTIC provides two levels of name server. The "Name Server" in figure 6 allows application level objects to contact each other. The zone specific process manager (ZSPMdaemon) allows DRASTIC platforms to contact each other (see §4.4). At the system wide level, daemons within zones need to find out about other processes in other zones. This is done through the zone boundary name servers (see figure 7).

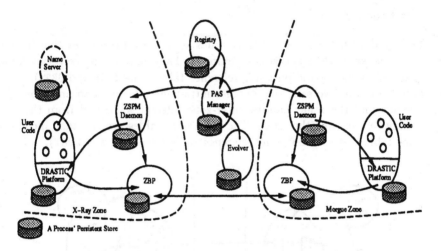

**Fig. 6.** System Wide Process

A multi-zone application description is contained in a persistent application systems manager (PASManager). The PASManager contains information on the persistent application system's contracts as well as references to each ZSPMdaemon. When booted, the PASManager is used by each ZBP process to initialise its transformation rules, which are embodied in code provided by the software engineers. When the software architect wants to evolve zones, an **evolver** process causes changes to take place in the PASManager. The **evolver** manages and checks the contract information, deriving change absorber code when possible. It then informs the affected zones that they are to be evolved, using an API present at the ZSPMdaemons.

Ideally, the PASManager would be replicated for protection against faults and there could be many **evolver** processes running over a DRASTIC platform. In

---

[2] Booting a process over a store and reinitialising a process after a crash both have implications for DRASTIC's fault tolerant remote method invocation protocol. A discussion of this protocol is outside the scope of this paper.

our current implementation, the **PASManager** is a centralized server and there is at most one **evolver** process at any given time.

The registry process is the lowest-level name server in the DRASTIC platform and it is at a well known location. The **PASManager** registers with it and each **ZSPMdaemon** gets a reference to the **PASManager** from the registry.

The **PASManager** and the **evolver** are separate processes as they capture distinct roles within an evolving system. The **PASManager** stores the contracts and is a name server for the **ZSPMdaemons**, whereas the **evolver** contains information about what needs to be done when evolution is required. The **evolver** calculates which zones need to be amended for a given change and how the **ZBPs** and contracts are affected. This information is passed to the **PASManager** for execution.

### 4.3 Between Zones

At the boundary between two distinct zones are a pair of processes that handle references between these two zones (figure 7). They contain tables very similar to a process' incoming and outgoing reference tables (the **IRTs** and **ORTs**). Now, however, there are two sets, one handles intra-zone references to and from the **ZBP** process and the other handles inter-zone references, to and from the corresponding **ZBP** in the other zone. The additional tables are the zone incoming reference table and zone outgoing reference table (the **ZIRT** and **ZORT**).

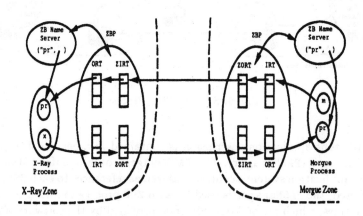

**Fig. 7.** Handling Inter-Zone References

When a **ZBP** is started for a given zone it is started in the context of a pair of zones, requiring another **ZBP** in the target zone. In a system with a large number of zone contracts this may result in a large number of **ZBP** processes per zone. However, it is important in such a system to be able to effectively manage the references that cross zone boundaries. This is facilitated by having one **ZBP** process per contract on either side of the zone boundary.

The ZBP process at one side of a pair enforces the contract on that side of the pair. If an application program tries to pass an object, or a reference to an object, from one zone to another, without the appropriate type being described in the contract, an exception is raised in the invoking code.

Over time it is possible for many change absorbers to be inserted along an individual inter-zone reference. The series of change absorbers can be contained in either, or both, ZBP processes. DRASTIC implements a stacking discipline for the management of the change absorbers, so that it is always possible to transform an object from its exported type to its imported type, through a series of (possibly zero) transformations. If a change absorber is removed because, for example, the type it transforms to no longer exists in the system, new change absorbers may be necessary to ensure a complete transformation.

A separate zone boundary name server (ZBNS) is provided so that application level objects in one zone can be made visible to application level objects in other zones. A process wishing to advertise an object to other processes outside its zone places a named reference to that object in its local ZBNS. For example, both the X-Ray process and the morgue process have advertised their pr objects with their respective ZBNSs in figure 7. If another process in the morgue zone wanted a reference to the pr object in the X-Ray zone, without obtaining it from the local process, it would contact the ZBNS in its local zone passing the name ("pr") to a method provided by the ZBNS for querying the remote ZBNS. The morgue zone ZBNS then contacts the X-Ray zone's ZBNS, via the ZBPs, asking for a reference to an object with that name. The query between the two ZBNSs is conducted through the two ZBPs so any reference that is passed back is subject to the necessary transformations. Within the context of the contract between the two zones, such a reference is guaranteed to be legal.

## 4.4 Within a Zone

When creating a zone, several daemon processes are started. The ZSPMdaemon is used by the DRASTIC platforms, which are created when starting application level processes over them. The ZSPMdaemon is a name server that contains a mapping from a process' name to the process' InHandler. When a DRASTIC process is booted it registers itself with the ZSPMdaemon, allowing other processes in that zone to obtain references to it.

Providing name servers for use within a zone decreases the amount of dependency one zone has on another, increasing its autonomy. It would be possible to have name servers directly accessible from outside their zone. For the current implementation and development of the architecture, however, strict separation of concerns is proving very helpful, hence the provision of the zone boundary name servers, corresponding to each contract, in each zone.

Five sorts of name server are used in the current implementation of DRASTIC: the Registry, PASManager, evolver, ZSPMDaemon and ZBNS. It would be possible to simplify the system by combining the Registry, PASManager and evolver into one service and the ZSPMDaemon and ZBNS into another and in-

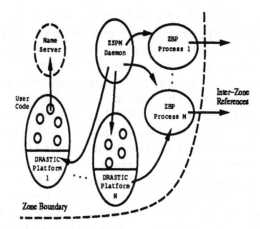

**Fig. 8.** Processes Booted within a Zone

creasing their functionality. This would make the services more like traders, capable of supporting sophisticated queries.

All of the DRASTIC platform's daemons and name servers can be restarted, providing a simple form of fault tolerance. Processes with references to these servers need to rebind, although within the DRASTIC platform this is done automatically by the code used to access such servers.

### 4.5  Implementation Details

Space limitations prevent a discussion of some of the implementation details of the DRASTIC platform. The interested reader is referred to [ED97tr] which is a more detailed version of this paper.

## 5  Evolution within DRASTIC

This section describes in detail how the DRASTIC platform supports computation within a system that undergoes evolution. The description is broken into four sections: firstly, the computation before evolution is described; then what occurs during system evolution is presented; how computation is performed after the change is described next; with a discussion of the differences in the system before and after evolution concluding this section.

### 5.1  Computation Before Evolution

The physical architecture of the example system before any evolution occurs is given in figure 9, which is a more detailed version of figure 2.

Assume that object m in the morgue zone wants to set the id number of the pr object in the X-Ray zone:

```
pr.setId(946);
```

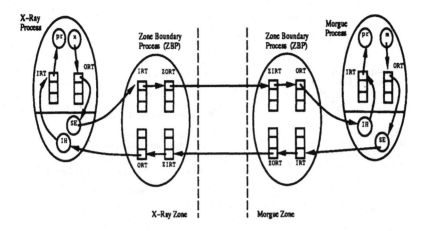

**Fig. 9.** Physical Architecture Before Evolution

The application-level invocation on `pr` is intercepted by the DRASTIC platform as the object being invoked is remote to this process. The `StoreExemplar` for this process pickles[3] the `int` value of 946 and forwards the call request with the pickled arguments to the `ZBP` process from the morgue zone to the X-Ray zone. The morgue `ZBP` looks up the necessary transformations for calls to PR objects invoking the `setId` method. Before evolution takes place, no conversions are necessary (see figure 3) and the morgue zone's `ZBP` just passes the call through to the `ZBP` process at the X-Ray zone where the lookup is done again. No conversion is required at this side so the call is passed to the `InHandler` associated with the process that contains the `pr` object. The `InHandler` passes the pickled arguments to the object's `CallHandler` which unpickles them and executes the `setId` method, passing the integer as an argument. If there were any results from this method call, the `CallHandler` would pickle them and pass this pickle to the `InHandler` for returning to the invoking object.

## 5.2 Evolving the System

The software engineer plays an integral role in the evolution of the software in a DRASTIC system. Figure 10 shows how the PR type has been evolved by both zones, leading to three new types, PR_X, PatientRecord and PR_M.

After evolution, when both processes have had their PR typed object evolved to their new type, the example application looks like figure 11.

---

[3] Pickling takes an object and converts it into a form suitable for transfer across a network. The pickled object contains enough information for the object to be unpickled into its original form. Pickling is also referred to as "serialization" or "marshalling".

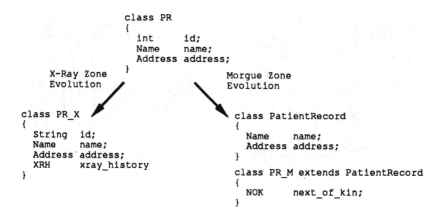

**Fig. 10.** The Updated Patient Record

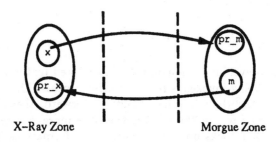

X–Ray Zone          Morgue Zone

**Fig. 11.** The System Architecture After Evolution

To evolve both zones in this way, the software architect will have changed the zones' contents and the code as above. This change triggers changes to the zone contract and requires that new or amended change absorbers be provided.

The software engineer has to provide change absorbers to handle the disparity that has come about because of the evolution. After evolution, the **m** object in the morgue zone has a reference to an object of type PR_M as all **pr** typed objects in the morgue zone have been evolved to be objects instantiated from type PR_M. However, the object it actually refers to is of type PR_X (figure 11). The code in the morgue zone will not be able to call the new methods to get and set the X-Ray history. However, it does have the ability to call the **get** and **set** methods on the name and address fields, which the morgue zone is using to identify a PatientRecord. As the morgue zone is now using two fields to identify a patient's record, it makes sense for the software engineer to provide two methods to abstract over this implementation detail. Therefore, the PatientRecord class is assumed to also support these methods:

The **x** object experiences a similar disparity. After evolution, it holds a reference to a PR_X typed object as all PR typed objects in the X-Ray zone have been evolved to be instantiated from PR_X. However, the object it actually refers to is

| Direction of Transfer | Exported Types | Transformations Required | Imported Types |
|---|---|---|---|
| X–Ray to Morgue | PR | None | PR |
| Morgue to X–Ray | PR | None | PR |

| Direction of Transfer | Exported Types | Transformations Required | Imported Types |
|---|---|---|---|
| X–Ray to Morgue | PR_X | PR_X to PR_M | PR_M |
| Morgue to X–Ray | PR_M | PR_M to PR_X | PR_X |

**Fig. 12.** The X-Ray Morgue Zone Contract Before and After Evolution

```
String getId();
void setId(String name, String addr);
```

**Fig. 13.** Extra PatientRecord Methods to Hide Implementation Details

of type PR_M (figure 11). PR_X objects identify a patient using a single `String` id. Therefore, x can attempt to call `String getId()` and `void setId(String id)`. It is the rôle of the change absorbers at the zone boundary to handle the transformations between the PR_X and PR_M typed objects.

Inserting the change absorbers into the run-time system is handled automatically by DRASTIC. The system wide **evolver** process (figure 6) is aware of which zone boundary processes contain sets of change absorbers that need to be updated. The update is handled automatically through an API presented by each zone boundary process.

## 5.3 Evolving the Zone

In the current implementation, a zone is evolved in four stages. The four stages are executed automatically by the DRASTIC system once the software engineer has provided all the necessary updated and new software components.

1. Freezing the zone
2. Updating the objects
3. Updating the change absorbers
4. Thawing the zone

In a more sophisticated system these changes would be performed incrementally, rather than freezing the entire zone until all objects have been evolved.

**Freezing the Zone** Freezing the evolving zone will temporarily prevent objects in other zones from contacting objects in the evolving zone. To freeze a zone, a message is sent by the `ZSPMDaemon` to all the processes executing in that zone. On receipt of this message a process executes an identified piece of code, supplied by the software engineer, which executes the necessary actions to safely terminate this process. References from objects in other zones to objects in this zone are still allowed. Terminating a process does not imply that any references to objects it embodied will fail, but if method invocations were forced to prematurely return, the software engineer would have to add code to handle methods failing due to evolution. This is clearly undesirable and one of the goals of this architecture is to ensure that references into the evolving zone from external zones are only temporarily blocked; the invocation should only be delayed, rather than responding with an error due to ongoing evolution. If an object external to the currently evolving zone tries to invoke a method belonging to an object that temporarily now no longer exists due to evolution, the invocation will not be rejected, it will be noted by the DRASTIC system and blocked. Once the evolution of the zone has completed and the process that contains the evolved object has been restarted, the invocation will be allowed to proceed.

All objects in the evolving zone will also be prevented from contacting objects outside of their zone.

The piece of code that terminates the process safely is required as only the software engineer knows how to safely terminate a process. It is possible for some methods to be executing infinite loops, eg. servers continually waiting on incoming requests. If the DRASTIC system merely waited for all currently executing methods to finish before attempting evolution, processes that had methods with infinite loops would never become available. Where such a loop is necessary, the software engineer is required to add code to allow termination of the loop when required for evolution.

**Updating the Objects** All objects in the X-Ray and morgue zones are updated to be of their respective types. This is realised in the current DRASTIC implementation by terminating each process, so that an up-to-date copy of its persistent data is residing on disk (as described above). Each affected object in the persistent store is then converted to be an instance of the new type. This may require writing code that takes the state of a PR object and loads it into a PR_X object, for example. A similar conversion is done in the morgue zone to produce PR_M objects. If a process which has been booted without a persistent store is terminated and brought back it is assumed to be capable of resuming from where it left off; in effect we assume such processes are stateless.

**Updating Change Absorbers** Both ZBP processes need to have change absorbers added to convert objects and method invocations from the incoming type to the type used locally. During the lifetime of a complex system, many change absorbers may be inserted along a given reference. For example, the patient record may go through several amendments, requiring one change absorber per change. These are placed in the ZBP in a stack, ensuring that the transformation is coherent.

**Thawing the Zone** Once all the change absorbers are in place and all the conversions have been completed, the zone is thawed and invocations can proceed to objects of the new type.

## 5.4  Computation After Evolution

This section is divided in two: first we describe a method invocation from the morgue zone to the X-Ray zone and then a method invocation in the opposite direction.

**Morgue Zone to X-Ray Zone Method Invocation**  After the system has been evolved, the system's physical architecture is as in figure 14. The two processes contain objects of the new type and the ZBPs contain the necessary change absorbers.

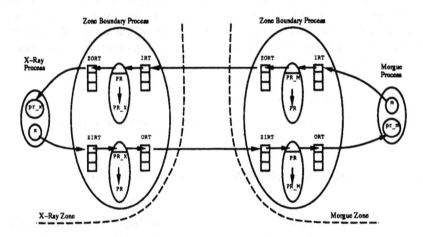

**Fig. 14.** Physical Architecture After Evolution

The code in the morgue process has been changed to make use of the PR_M type. Therefore, the call made by the m object to set the identifier of the pr_x object could become:

> Name    name  = new Name("Joe", "Bloggs");
> Address addr  = new Address("17", "Lilybank Gardens");
>
> m.setId(name, addr);

The actions performed at the morgue zone require the setId() call on the PR_M typed object to be transformed into a call on to a PR typed object. This is handled by the PR_M to PR change absorber in the ZBP in the morgue zone. This change absorber could look something like that in figure 15.

```
class PR_M_to_PR          void setId(Name name, Address addr)
{                         {
  PR pr;                    int trans_id = transformId(name, addr);
}
                            pr.setId(trans_id);
                          }
```

**Fig. 15.** Simplified PR_M to PR Change Absorber

The **setId()** method of the change absorber is the same as the **PR_M** typed object. The **name** and **addr** objects are used by the **transformId** method to generate an integer used in the call forward on **pr.setId(trans_id)**.

When this forwarded call is received by the X-Ray zone's **ZBP** the call is found to be following a reference containing one or more change absorbers. This requires that the method invocation is passed through the PR to PR_X change absorber.

The PR to PR_X change absorber in the X-Ray zone takes the incoming method invocation on **setId(int id)** which was called from the PR_M to PR change absorber above and the unpickled argument, which is the value generated from the above **transformId**. The argument was unpickled by a **CallHandler** contained in the **ZBP**.

```
class PR_to_PR_X          void setId(int id)
{                         {
  PR_X pr_x;                String s = transformId(id);
}                          pr_x.setId(s);
                          }
```

**Fig. 16.** Simplified PR to PR_X Change Absorber

The class that handles the change from PR to PR_X typed objects (figure 16) will have a method that has the same signature as the PR **setId** method. In that method the integer is converted to a String and then the **setId** method on the **pr_x** object is called. The call to **pr_x.setId(s)** would then be a call through to the **pr_x** object in the X-Ray zone and would be handled as any other incoming invocation through the process' **InHandler**, **CallHandler** and IRT.

The **transformId** methods in both of these change absorbers are more than just conversions from one representation to another as they may depend on the semantics of the invoked object. This understanding is provided by the software engineer, who is the only one who knows the desired semantics of the application.

**X-Ray to Morgue Zone Method Invocation** The **x** object in the X-Ray zone invokes the **String getId()** method on its reference. On the X-Ray zone side the PR_X to PR change absorber is invoked to convert the String to an integer. The change absorber for this will look similar to that in figure 17.

The call **pr.getId()** in figure 17 is forwarded to the **ZBP** in the morgue zone which has a PR to PR_M change absorber. This change absorber has a method

```
class PR_X_to_PR          String getId()
{                         {
  PR pr;                    int id = pr.getId();
}
                            return transformId(id);
                          }
```

**Fig. 17.** Simplified PR_X to PR Change Absorber

that matches the **int getId()** method signature and it calls on to the **pr_m** object. This could be implemented in the PR to PR_M change absorber given in figure 18.

```
class PR_TO_PR_M          int getId()
{                         {
  Map        id_map;        Name name    = pr_m.getName();
                            Address addr = pr_m.getAddress();
  PR_M       pr_m;
}                           // '+' is overloaded to produce a suitable
                            // argument for the get method

                            return id_map.get(name + addr);
                          }
```

**Fig. 18.** Simplified PR to PR_M Change Absorber

As the change in the morgue zone has caused the **int id** field to be removed from PR_M typed objects, some form of conversion is required between the integer value that has to be returned and the name and address fields used by PR_M typed objects.

The software architect has decided to do this by defining a map from the patient's name and address to the integer value that should be returned. Using a map is purely an implementation decision on the part of the software architect. They have decided that the semantics embodied in the system are such that this mapping will always result in the same **int id** value being returned for a given **name** and **address** pair.

It must be stressed that the conversion from the **name** and **address** pairs to integers in this way is an application-level issue. There are many other ways of converting between the two patient record identifiers. The software architect must ensure two things: that there is an object in the change absorber list in the morgue zone with a method that has the same signature as was called by code in the change absorber in the X-Ray zone[4], and that for a given **name** and **address** pair the same **int id** will always be returned. How the conversion is performed to protect the change in one zone from the change in the other is something that only the software engineer can know. The same argument applies to the two kinds of **transformId** methods used in the other change absorbers.

Adding the **setId()** and **getId()** methods to the PatientRecord class is more

---

[4] The DRASTIC platform provides some support to allow this to be checked.

than just an abstraction over the implementation of that type. The identifier for a PatientRecord in the morgue zone consists of a name and address field. Both of these fields are required to identify a particular patient record. If setId() was not defined, a call to **getName()**, for example, would only return the name of the patient. As the identifier for a patient record in the morgue zone is defined using both fields, a method is required so both fields are used when retrieving the patient's id. The need to define this method is a semantic issue as only the software engineer knows that both fields must be used to identify a particular patient record.

**Semantic Change Absorbers** When an object passes across a zone boundary it undergoes a series of transformations. During these transformations, data may be lost or gained as the intermediate objects could contain differing numbers of fields, as in the example in section 5.4. The software engineer could define a change absorber that provided default values for object fields that are added when transforming an object.

A more sophisticated change absorber could save and restore some of an object's data during its outward and return journeys. This requires that the change absorber has access to the ZBP's persistent store. If state saved on the outward journey is required on the object's return journey then two or more change absorbers may need to share state. If the software engineer wants to do this, they must write code that can identify particular objects as they travel across the change absorber in either direction, hence the need for DRASTIC object identifiers to be exposed to the application programmer.

This assumes that the object travels through the change absorber in the same ZBP pair on the outward and return journeys. It is possible for an object to leave a zone via one pair of ZBPs and return via a different pair, eg. by moving from zone A to zone B and then from B to zone C before returning to zone A. If this were to happen, any object state that was stored on the outward journey would be present in the A to B pair of ZBPs. The object is, however, travelling back to zone A from zone C and so will pass through the pair of ZBPs for the zone C to zone A contract, missing any state saved on the outward journey. This is an extremely complex problem to solve at the application-level. The DRASTIC platform allows the application programmer to do this, although it is not recommended. Building support into the platform to solve this problem requires taking a higher-level view than the current pair-wise view of zones and this is not an area that the current DRASTIC platform and design addresses.

## 5.5 Architectural Differences after Evolution

The main architectural difference after evolution is the addition of the change absorbers. When a method invocation is performed along this reference, the method argument has to be unpickled and transformed, potentially using other change absorbers. This argument is then passed to a method on the change absorber which has the same signature as the method being called at the invoking process. The change absorber's method will then call on to the **pr_x** object in the X-Ray process. When the PR_X object's method returns, it passes any results back to the calling change absorber. The change absorber will then pass the result back to the invoking process.

Another difference is the inheritance hierarchy in the morgue zone consists of two classes, the PatientRecord and PR_M class. The change absorber in the **ZBP** at the morgue zone protects the software in the X-Ray zone from being aware of this change. The change absorber presents a method that has the same signature as called by the **x** object. Inside this method was the call onto the evolved object, thus hiding the change from the X-Ray zone.

The system's configuration repositories are now different. For example, the **PASManager**'s contents have changed because the X-Ray and morgue zone contract has been updated.

Other processes in other zones may have experienced a delay while the X-Ray zone was changed. Objects migrating into the X-Ray zone and requests to invoke object methods were temporarily delayed during evolution. An object migration that was started but not completed by the end of evolution may be rejected as the new contract may not allow transfer of the object's type between the two zones. The information that an attempted object migration has failed will be returned in the same way as errors are reported due to communication failure. It is up to the software engineer to decide whether or not to distinguish between these two sorts of problem.

The **m** object and **x** objects are not aware there has been a change in the other zone, only that communication with that zone was temporarily delayed.

# 6 Performance Measurements

This section presents some preliminary performance measurements of our unoptimised DRASTIC system. Section 6.1 gives timings for a null method invocation within a single Java virtual machine and between two processes using RMI, section 6.2 gives figures for a null method invocation within the DRASTIC system.

The measurements were conducted using a 10Mbit/s Ethernet and lightly loaded Sun SPARCstation 20 workstations running Sparc Solaris. The Java virtual machine used was version 1.0.2 of Sun Microsystem's JDK which does not use any just in time (JIT) compiler technology. Two mechanisms were used for the timings. One, incurring an overhead of $4\mu s$, permitted the measurement of events known to take less than one second. An alternative approach for longer timers introduced an overhead of $34\mu s$, but allocated memory and could therefore introduce occasional delays of $340\mu s$ due to extension of the Java heap.

All measurements were conducted repeatedly, and in every case the variance in measurements was negligible. The timer overheads above have been subtracted from the figures presented below. Values exceeding 1ms have been rounded to two significant figures or 1ms, whichever is the greater accuracy.

## 6.1 Timing Java

A null method invocation was executed in a single Java virtual machine and in the context of RMI to establish a base from which to compare the other timings.

Java executed a null method invocation in $2\mu s$, however the first call took approximately $70\mu s$. The decrease is due to the optimisations that are performed by the Java virtual machine on the first invocation of an object's method. Subsequent calls are much faster as the virtual machine has an optimised path to finding the method to execute.

A null method invocation between two different processes was conducted using RMI. The first test was from an object in one process to a different object in another process with both processes running on the same machine. The average elapsed time was $6200\mu s$. When the processes were run on two different machines, the cost increased to $8200\mu s$.

## 6.2 Timing DRASTIC

The timings for DRASTIC are divided into two sections. First figures for communication between processes in the same zone are presented, then for processes in two different zones.

**Intra-Zone Measurements** The time taken to invoke the null method on a local object that exists in a process booted over the DRASTIC platform is $2\mu s$. This is the same as the local Java case as objects in a DRASTIC process that are not capable of being migrated are the same as conventional Java objects i.e. DRASTIC adds no overhead in this case.

If the software engineer requires an object to be migratable the source code for that object's class must be preprocessed to add a proxy object which is called by the software engineer's code. The proxy then forwards the call to the actual object. In the local case where both the proxy and the actual object are in the same process the null method invocation takes $32\mu s$. The majority of this cost, $28\mu s$, is because the proxy is synchronizing on an object before and after the call is forwarded. These synchronizations are done to ensure the proxy's state is consistent, as a concurrently executed **migrate** method call to move the object elsewhere could invalidate the object's state if no synchronization was used. Without the overhead of the synchronization, the forwarded call would cost about $4\mu s$, which is to be expected as two method invocations are required: one to the proxy and one from the proxy to the actual object.

The next two tests involve DRASTIC remote method invocations through proxies to objects in other processes which are running on the same or different hosts in the same zone. To conduct this test a number of DRASTIC name servers need to be running. This is so objects in different processes can gain references to other objects placed in the name servers under well known names. Running the name servers contributes some load to the machines, but this is not appreciable in the figures.

The first DRASTIC remote method invocation is performed between two objects residing in different processes running on the same machine. This invocation takes 128,000$\mu$s. In this case, the reference that the invoking side is using was retrieved from its local zone boundary name server (ZBNS) and therefore the invocation chain leads from the caller to the callee through the ZBNS. This means the call has to be forwarded using two RMI calls. An optimised case with the call going directly from caller to callee reduces the cost to 55,000$\mu$s. When running the two processes on different machines the unoptimised cost is 146,000$\mu$s, reducing to 84,000$\mu$s for the optimised case. If these figures are compared to the RMI values given earlier it can be seen that the added functionality provided by DRASTIC, the ability to migrate objects and evolve objects, adds a factor of approximately twelve over a conventional RMI call. However, the DRASTIC platform has not been optimised; in particular, several strings are passed as arguments even in a notionally null remote call. Profiling suggests that the marshalling costs of handling these strings may dominate the DRASTIC remote call costs, so we are now investigating more efficient representations for type and method names.

**Inter-Zone Measurements** The final test performed was between two processes running on different machines which are placed in different DRASTIC zones. This requires that a zone boundary process (ZBP) and a zone boundary name server (ZBNS) be run in each zone. A reference to the object to be invoked is placed in its local ZBNS. A different object in a process running in the other zone obtains a copy of that reference by querying its local ZBNS. The local ZBNS contacts the remote ZBNS via the ZBPs for that reference. It is then returned through both ZBPs and ZBNSs. In the unoptimised case, this generates a reference similar to the case above, that leads from one process to another via four other processes. The optimised case misses out each ZBNS on either side, reducing the number of other processes involved to two, the two ZBPs. An unrestricted zone contract was active during this test. The ZBP, ZBNS and the process being measured in each zone were run on the same machine.

To invoke the null method in one process from another process running in a different zone on a different machine, using the unoptimised path of four intermediate processes cost 382,000$\mu$s. Using the optimised path, the cost is reduced to 241,000$\mu$s.

The optimised intra-zone call takes 84,000$\mu$s and the optimised call across the zone boundary costs 241,000$\mu$s. The factor of three increase is to be expected as the inter-zone call has to travel through the two ZBP processes. The cost of calling across the zone boundary is 236,000$\mu$s (382,000$\mu$s−146,000$\mu$s) in the unoptimised case and 157,000$\mu$s (241,000$\mu$s−84,000$\mu$s) in the optimised case.

**Timing with Java JDK1.1** The DRASTIC system has recently been ported to version 1.1 of Sun's JDK, with an encouraging increase in performance. For example, in the case of a Java RMI from two different processes running on the same machine the mean elapsed time has reduced from 6200$\mu$s to 5400$\mu$s. When the processes are running on two different machines the elapsed time reduces from $8200\mu s$ to $7100\mu s$. Under JDK1.1 the cost of a DRASTIC inter-zone call that leads through the two ZBPs has reduced from $241,000\mu s$ to $136,000\mu s$.

This increase in speed can largely be attributed to the use of assembler code in the main interpreter loop of JDK1.1.

# 7 Related Work

It is not possible to give a comprehensive treatment of other work due to space limitations. The interested reader is referred to [ED97tr].

## 7.1 CORBA

CORBA does not directly address the issue of evolution. CORBA separates an object's interface and implementation and provides two repositories where object interfaces and implementations may be stored. The primary role of the interface repository (the implementation repository is similar) is to manage and provide access to a collection of object definitions specified in OMG IDL. A CORBA ORB provides the means by which client processes make requests and receive responses to and from servers. A critical use of the interface repository is for connecting ORBs together. When an object is passed from one ORB to another, it may be necessary to create a new object to represent the passed object in the receiving ORB. This may require locating the interface information in an interface repository in the receiving ORB. By getting the object's repository id from a repository in the sending ORB, it is possible to look up the interface in a repository in the receiving ORB. To succeed, however, the interface for that object must be installed in both repositories with the same repository id [Obj95b]. If the remote interface is evolved it may be given a new repository id and CORBA does not provide a means of tracking such an evolution, leaving the programmer to manage this complexity.

When adding a new interface to a repository it is possible that external processes may see an incoherent repository. A coherent repository is one whose contents can be expressed as a valid collection of OMG IDL definitions [Obj95c]. The repository does not ensure that it contains coherent information and it is possible to enter information that does not make sense, although those errors that are detected are reported. The expectation in [Obj95c] is that a combination of conventions, administrative controls and tools that add information to the repository will work to create a coherent view of the repository information. The programmer has to manage this and there is no means of bounding the effects of evolution as the contents of a repository are visible throughout the system.

# 8 Current Status

The DRASTIC project is half-way through its initial funding and this paper has, therefore, presented work in progress.

The basic DRASTIC architecture was first implemented with Modula-3 [CDJ⁺89]
using Network Objects [ABW95] for distribution. The current implementation
uses PJava [AJDS96] and Java's [GM96] remote method invocation package,
RMI [WRD96]. Porting from one language to another was relatively easy, suggesting that DRASTIC's architecture and design may indeed be somewhat language independent.

Object migration and distributed reference management were completed during the Modula-3 prototype. The current implementation has built on this architecture and it now supports multiple zones and persistence.

# 9 Further Work

Much work remains to be done in the DRASTIC project, including providing
a more general framework in which object migration can take place. We are
currently experimenting with several different object migration APIs, one of
which will allow groups of objects to migrate atomically.

Extension and optimisation of the DRASTIC platform is an ongoing effort
to support more efficient run-time type evolution and to allow us to conduct
additional experiments.

More tools are required to support the software engineer. For example, a
more complete pre-processor for the generation of migratable objects is needed.
A tool to assist the software engineer in checking the coherency of a series of
change absorbers may prove useful.

Manipulations of the Java virtual machine to provide basic support for class
evolution at a level below the DRASTIC platform is also being investigated, to
permit the construction of more challenging demonstrations.

## 9.1 Freezing a Zone

The most significant area for future work is in dealing with currently executing
object migrations when freezing a zone. Freezing an entire zone before it can
be evolved is inefficient and potentially problematical as it unnecessarily keeps
objects frozen after their evolution. A more incremental approach must be taken
where objects are thawed immediately after they have been evolved. The process
of freezing a zone causes all the currently executing processes to terminate to
ensure a consistent version of their state is on disk. This problem is illustrated
below with an example.

**Invocations that do not Return** Consider a zone called P with a single
process in it called p. Process p contains an object o with a method m1 which
executes an infinite loop. Another process, q, which is in another zone, has a
reference to o and it is currently executing m1.

When zone P is evolved the ZSPMDaemon will send process p the **evolve**
message. On receipt of this message, process p will terminate. However, process

q is executing the m1 method. When the evolved process p is started again, m1 must be restarted at the point where it left off to ensure correct behaviour. The current DRASTIC platform does not support this and it is left up to the programmer to start m1 running again for all references to object o from outside the evolved zone.

**Involving the Software Engineer** The above example illustrates why a more sophisticated approach to freezing a zone is required. The simplistic freezing of an entire zone is only being used at the moment to gain experience in this area. We do not believe that this problem can be solved automatically, in the general case. We are therefore seeking to find clean models which permit the software architect to apply their knowledge of the application's semantics to this issue.

### 9.2  Minimising Zone Evolution Time

Evolving a zone is a costly operation as the store for each process has to be manipulated to transform objects from one type to another. In a distributed, persistent environment the services that processes provide need to be highly available. It will not always be possible to terminate a process, evolve the contents of its store and restart it as evolving the store will cause the process to be unavailable for an unacceptably long period of time. To minimise the amount of time a process is not available can be accomplished by doing as much of the evolution as possible off-line, but this raises other difficult questions.

## 10  Summary

In this paper we have presented DRASTIC's model and run-time architecture. DRASTIC uses zones to decompose a system into collections of processes that evolve as a single unit. Zones are concepts at design time which are realised as explicit system components at run-time. Contracts are pair-wise agreements between zones that describe which types can and cannot flow between any two zones, what needs to be done to transform objects as they move from one zone to another and how to transform inter-zone method invocations. It has been shown, through an extended example, how zones increase system modularity by encapsulating software and how contracts increase autonomy by explicitly describing the degree of coupling between zones. Change absorbers, provided by the software engineer, are automatically inserted at the zone boundary to protect one zone's software from changes made to software in other zones. How the software architect would build a system using DRASTIC has been described in some detail.

At run-time the DRASTIC platform intercepts all inter-process application-level object references. The ability to do this is the key to our approach to supporting run-time software evolution.

# Acknowledgements

The DRASTIC project is supported by the UK Engineering and Physical Sciences Research Council (EPSRC) under its Architectures for Integrated Knowledge-Manipulation Systems programme (AIKMS). The project also receives support from Digital and ICL.

The authors thank the referees for their helpful comments.

# References

[ABW95]  S. Owicki A. Birrell, G. Nelson and E. Wobber. Network objects. Technical Report 115, DEC SRC, December 1995.

[AJDS96]  M. Atkinson, M. Jordan, L. Daynès, and S. Spence. Design issues for persistent Java: a type-safe, object-oriented, orthogonally persistent system. In *Proceedings of The Seventh International Workshop on Persistent Obje ct Systems*, Cape May, New Jersey, USA, May 1996.

[AM95]  M. Atkinson and R. Morrison. Orthogonal persistent object systems. *VLDB Journal*, 4(3):319–401, 1995.

[BHJ+87]  A. Black, N. Hutchinson, E. Jul, H. Levy, and L. Carter. Distribution and abstract data types in Emerald. *IEEE Transactions on Software Engineering*, SE-13(1):65–76, January 1987.

[CDJ+89]  L. Cardelli, J. Donahue, M. Jordan, B. Kalsow, and G. Nelson. The Modula-3 type system. In *Conference Record of the Sixteenth Annual ACM Symposium on Principles of Programming Languages, Austin, Texas*, pages 202–212. ACM, January 1989.

[Dic92]  P. Dickman. *Distributed Object Management in a Non-Small Graph of Autonomous Networks With Few Failures*. PhD thesis, University of Cambridge, September 1992.

[ED97tr]  Huw Evans and Peter Dickman. Drastic: A run-time architecture for evolving, distributed, persistent systems. Technical report, Department of Computing Science, Glasgow University, 1997.

[GM96]  J. Gosling and H. McGilton. The Java language environment: A white paper. Technical report, Sun Microsystems, 2550 Garcia Avenue, Mountain View, CA 94043, USA, October 1996.

[Obj95a]  Object Management Group. *The Common Object Request Broker: Architecture and Specification*, July 1995. Version 2.0.

[Obj95b]  Object Management Group. *The Common Object Request Broker: Architecture and Specification*, July 1995. Version 2.0, page 6-3.

[Obj95c]  Object Management Group. *The Common Object Request Broker: Architecture and Specification*, July 1995. Version 2.0, page 6-4.

[WRD96]  A. Wollrath, R. Riggs, and C. Darke. Java(tm) remote method invocation specification: Prebeta draft, version 1.1. Technical report, Sun Microsystems, Inc, 2550 Garcia Avenue, Mountain View, CA 94043, USA, November (C) 1996.

# A General Framework for Inheritance Management and Method Dispatch in Object-Oriented Languages

Wade Holst and Duane Szafron
{wade,duane}@cs.ualberta.ca

Department of Computing Science
University of Alberta
Edmonton, Canada

**Abstract.** This paper presents the DT Framework, a collection of object-oriented classes representing a generalized framework for inheritance management and table-based method dispatch. It demonstrates how most existing table-based dispatch techniques can be generalized and made incremental, so that relevant entries in the dispatch table are modified each time a selector or class hierarchy link is added or removed. The incremental nature makes the framework highly efficient, with low millisecond average modification time, and supports table-based dispatch even in schema-evolving languages. During table maintenance, the framework detects and records inheritance conflicts, and maintains information useful during compile-time optimizations.

## 1 Introduction

Object-oriented programming languages have become popular due to the abstraction and information hiding provided by inheritance and polymorphism. However, these same properties pose difficulties for efficient implementation, necessitating (among others) algorithms for inheritance management and method dispatch. In this paper, we present an object-oriented solution to an object-oriented problem.

Object-oriented languages provide code-reuse at two levels. At the first level are generic libraries of basic data structures like sets and growable arrays. Rich libraries for collections, graphics and other specialized areas provide object-oriented languages with much of their power. At a second level, *application frameworks* capture the collaborations of a group of objects, leaving the specific details to be implemented ([GHJV95]). These details are implemented by framework clients, who subclass on the classes provided by the framework. These subclasses provide implementations of the abstract functionality to represent client-specific behavior. In other cases, the user merely chooses between concrete leaf classes to obtain the desired functionality. Thus, in the same way that *templates* generalize the implementation of a particular class, *frameworks* generalize the implementation of an entire group of interacting classes. Templates are instantiated by providing parameters to the template class. Frameworks are instantiated by providing concrete implementations of abstract functions.

This paper presents the DT Framework; a general framework for both compile-time and run-time inheritance management and method dispatch that applies to a broad class of object-oriented languages: schema-evolving, dynamically typed, single-receiver languages with type/implementation-paired multiple inheritance. A *schema-evolving* language is one with the ability to define new methods and classes at run-time. A *dynamically typed* language is one in which some (or all) variables and method return values are unconstrained, in that they can be bound to instances of any class in the entire environment. A *single-receiver* language is one in which a single class, together with a selector, uniquely establishes a method to invoke (as opposed to multi-method languages, discussed in Section 7). *Type/implementation-paired inheritance* refers to the traditional form of inheritance used in most object-oriented languages, in which both the definition and implementation of inherited selectors are propagated together (as opposed to inheritance in which these two concepts are separated, as discussed in Section 7). Finally, *multiple inheritance* refers to the ability of a class to inherit selectors from more than one direct superclass. Within this paper, we will refer to this collection of languages as $\Psi$.

The primary benefit of the DT Framework is its ability to incrementally modify dispatch table information. Table-based dispatch techniques have traditionally been static, and efficient implementations usually rely on a complete knowledge of the environment before the dispatch table is created. However, dispatch techniques that rely on complete knowledge of the environment have two disavantages: 1) they cannot be used by schema-evolving languages that can modify the environment at run-time, and 2) they preclude the ability of the language to perform separate compilation of source code. One of the fundamental contributions of the DT Framework is a collection of algorithms that provide incremental dispatch table updating in all table-based dispatch techniques. An implementation of the DT Framework exists, and detailed run-time measurements of the algorithms are presented in Section 6.

Any compiler or run-time system for a language in $\Psi$ can obtain a substantial amount of code-reuse by being a client of the DT Framework, since the framework provides functionality that such compilers and run-time systems must implement. In this paper, we will refer to compilers and run-time systems as DT Framework clients. For our purposes, a language that can be compiled is inherently non-schema-evolving, and *compilers* can be used on such languages (i.e. C++). By *run-time system* we mean support existing at run-time to allow schema-evolution in the language (i.e. Smalltalk).

The DT Framework makes a variety of research contributions besides the identification of the framework itself. It extends research in each of these areas:

1. *Data Structures*: The framework identifies the *method-set* data structure, a critical structure that allows inheritance management to be made incremental, allows detection and recording of inheritance conflicts, and maintains information useful in compile-time optimizations.

2. *Algorithms*: The framework demonstrates how inheritance management and maintenance of dispatch information can be made incremental. A critical recursive algorithm is designed that handles both of these issues and recomputes only the information necessary for a particular environment modification. As well, the similarities and differences between adding information to the environment and removing information from the environment are identified, and the algorithms are optimized for each.

3. *Table-Based Dispatch*: The framework identifies the similarities and differences between the various table-based dispatch techniques. It shows how the method-set data-structure and inheritance management algorithms can be used to allow incremental modification of the underlying table in any table-based dispatch technique. It also introduces a new hybrid dispatch technique that combines the best aspects of two existing techniques.

The method-set data structure, the incremental algorithms, and their ability to be used in conjunction with any table-based dispatch technique results in a complete framework for inheritance management and maintenance of dispatch information that is usable by both compilers and run-time systems. The algorithms provided by the framework are incremental at the level of individual *environment modifications*, consisting of any of the following:

1. Adding a selector to a class.

2. Adding one or more class inheritance links, including the adding of a class *between* two or more existing classes.

3. Removing a selector from a class

4. Removing one or more class inheritance links.

The following capabilities are provided by the framework:

1. *Inheritance Conflict Detection*: In multiple inheritance, it is possible for inheritance conflicts to occur when a selector is visible in a class from two or more superclasses. The Framework detects and records such conflicts as they occur.

2. *Dispatch Technique Independence*: Clients of the framework provide to end-users the capability to choose at compile-time or run-time the dispatch technique to use. Thus, an end-user could compile a C++ program using virtual function tables, or selector coloring, or any other table-based dispatch technique.

3. *Schema-Evolving Languages*: Dispatch tables have traditionally been created by compilers and are usually not extendable at run-time. This implies that schema-evolving languages can not use such table-based dispatch techniques. By making dispatch table modification incremental, the DT Framework allows schema-evolving languages to use any table-based dispatch technique, maintaining the dispatch table at run-time as the environment is dynamically altered.

4. *Dynamic Schema Evolution*: The DT Framework provides efficient algorithms for arbitrary environment modification, including adding a class between classes already in an inheritance hierarchy. Even more important, the algorithms handle both additions to the environment *and* deletions from the environment.

5. *Separate Compilation*: Of the five table-based dispatch techniques discussed in Section 2, three of them require knowledge of the complete environment. In situations where library developers provide object files, but not source code, these techniques are unusable. Incremental dispatch table modification allows the DT Framework to provide separate compilation in all five dispatch techniques.

6. *Compile-time Method Determination* : It is often possible (especially in statically typed languages) for a compiler to uniquely determine a method address for a specific message send. The more refined the static typing of a particular variable, the more limited is the set of applicable selectors when a message is sent to that variable. If only one method applies, the compiler can generate a function call or inline the method, avoiding runtime dispatch. The method-set data structure maintains information to allow efficient determination of such uniqueness.

The rest of this paper is organized as follows. Section 2 summarizes the various method dispatch techniques. Section 3 presents the DT Framework. Section 4 discusses how the table-based method dispatch techniques can be implemented using the DT Framework. Section 5 discusses details specific to compilers and details specific to runtime systems. Section 6 reports execution performance results when the DT Framework is applied to various real-world class hierarchies. Section 7 discusses related and future work, and Section 8 summarizes the results. Acknowledgements and references complete the paper.

## 2 Method Dispatch Techniques

In object-oriented languages, it is often necessary to compute the method address to be executed for a class/selector pair, $< C, \sigma >$, at run-time. Since message sends are so prevalent in object-oriented languages, the dispatch mechanism has a profound effect on implementation efficiency. Two general dispatch classifications exist: dynamic techniques, which compute (and cache) dispatched messages at runtime, and static techniques, which precompute all addresses before execution so that dispatch becomes a simple table access. In the discussion that follows, $C$ is the receiver class and $\sigma$ is the selector at a particular call-site. The notation $< C, \sigma >$ is shorthand for the class/selector pair. It is assumed that each class in the environment maintains a dictionary mapping native selectors to their method addresses, as well as a set of immediate superclasses. We give a very brief summary of the dispatch techniques. For detailed descriptions, see [Dri93], and for a comparison of relative dispatch performance, see [DHV95].

### 2.1 Dynamic Dispatch Techniques

1. *ML: Method Lookup*[1] (Smalltalk-80 [GR83]). Method dictionaries are searched for selector $\sigma$ starting at class $C$, going up the inheritance chain, until a method for $\sigma$ is found or no more parents exist (in which case a *messageNotUnderstood* method is invoked to warn the user). This technique is space efficient but time inefficient.

2. *LC: Global Lookup Cache* ([GR83, Kra83]) uses $< C, \sigma >$ as a hash into a global cache, whose entries store a class $C$, selector $\sigma$, and address A. During a dispatch, if the entry hashed to by $< C, \sigma >$ contains a method for the class/selector pair, it can be executed immediately, avoiding ML. Otherwise, ML is called to obtain an address and the resulting class, selector and address are stored in the global cache.

---

[1] In [DHV95, Dri93], and others, this is referred to as Dispatch Table Search (DTS). However, to avoid confusion with our dispatch tables, we refer to it as Method Lookup

3. *IC: Inline Cache* ([DS94]) stores addresses at each call-site. The initial address at each call-site invokes ML, which modifies the call-site once an address is obtained. Subsequent executions of the call-site invoke the previously computed method. Within each method, a *method prologue* exists to ensure that the receiver class matches the expected class (if not, ML is called to recompute and modify the call-site address).

4. *PIC: Polymorphic Inline Caches* ([HCU91]) store multiple addresses, modifying a special call-site specific stub-routine. On the first invocation of a stub-routine, ML is called. However, each time ML is called, the stub is extended by adding code to compare subsequent receiver classes against the current class, providing a direct function call (or even code inlining) if the test succeeds.

## 2.2 Static Dispatch Techniques

The static dispatch techniques are all table-based, in that a mapping from every legal class/selector pair to the appropriate executable address is precomputed before dispatch occurs. These techniques have traditionally been used at compile-time, but the DT Framework shows how they can be supported at run-time. In all of these techniques, classes and selectors are assigned numbers which serve as indices into the dispatch table. Whether these indices are unique or not depends on the dispatch technique.

1. *STI: Selector Table Indexing* ([Cox87]) uses a a two-dimensional table in which both class and selector indices are unique. This technique is not practical from a space perspective and is never used in implementations.

2. *SC: Selector Coloring* ([DMSV89, AR92]) compresses the two-dimensional STI table by allowing selector indices to be non-unique. Two selectors can share the same index as long as no class recognizes both selectors. The amount of compression is limited by the largest complete behavior (the largest set of selectors recognized by a single class).

3. *RD: Row Displacement* ([DH95]) compresses the two-dimensional STI table into a one-dimensional master array. Selectors are assigned unique indices in such a way that when all selector rows are shifted to the right by the index amount, the two-dimensional table has only one method in each column.

4. *VTBL: Virtual Function Tables* ([ES90]) have a different dispatch table for each class, so selector indices are class-specific. However, indices are constrained to be equal across inheritance subgraphs. Such uniqueness is not possible in multiple inheritance, in which case multiple tables are stored in each multi-derived class.

5. *CT: Compact Selector-Indexed Dispatch Tables* ([VH96]) separate selectors into one of two groups: *standard selectors* have one main definition and are only overridden in subclasses, and any selector that is not standard is a *conflict selector*. Two different tables are maintained, one for standard selectors, the other for conflict selectors. The standard table can be compressed by *selector aliasing* and *class sharing*, and the conflict table by class sharing alone. *Class partitioning* is used to allow class sharing to work effectively.

# 3 The DT Framework

The DT Framework provides a collection of abstract classes that define the data and functionality necessary to modify dispatch information incrementally during environment modification. Recall that, from the perspective of the DT Framework, *environment modification* occurs when selectors or class hierarchy links are added or removed.

The DT Framework consists of a variety of special purposes classes [2]. Figure 1 shows the class hierarchies. We describe the data and functionality that each class hierarchy needs from the perspective of inheritance management and dispatch table modification. Clients of the framework can specify additional data and functionality by subclassing some or all of the classes provided by the framework.

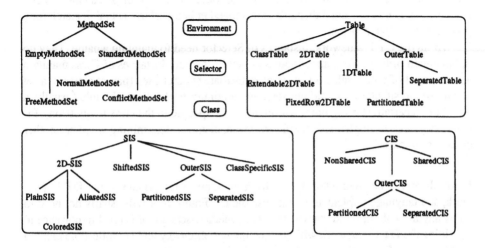

**Fig. 1.** The DT Framework Class Hierarchy

The MethodSet hierarchy represents the different kinds of address that can be associated with a class/selector pair (i.e. messageNotUnderStood, inheritanceConflict, or user-specified method). The Table hierarchy describes the data-structure used to represent the dispatch table, and provides the functionality needed to access, modify and add entries. The SIS and CIS hierarchies implement methods for determining selector and class indices. Although these concepts are components of Tables, they have been separated out into classes in their own right so as to allow the same table to use different indexing strategies.

## 3.1 The DT Classes

The Environment, Class and Selector classes are not subclassed within the DT Framework itself, but the MethodSet, Table, SIS and CIS classes are subclassed (clients of the Framework are free to subclass any DT class they choose). A detailed figure of

---

[2] In this discussion, we present the conceptual names of the classes, rather than the exact class names used in the C++ implementation

the internal state of the fundamental DT classes is provided in Section 6.2: *Effects on Dispatch Performance*.

**Environment, Class and Selector:** The DT Environment class acts as an interface between the DT Framework client and the framework itself. However, since the client can subclass the DT Framework, the interface is a white box, not a black one. Each client creates a unique instance of the DT Environment and as class and method declarations are parsed (or evaluated at run-time), the client informs the Environment instance of these environment modifications by invoking its interface operations. These interface operations are: *Add Selector*, *Remove Selector*, *Add Class Links*, and *Remove Class Links*. The environment also provides functionality to register selectors and classes with the environment, save extended dispatch tables, convert extended dispatch tables to dispatch tables, merge extended dispatch tables together and perform actual dispatch for a particular class/selector pair.

Within the DT Framework, instances of Selector need to maintain a name. They do not maintain indices, since such indices are table-specific. Instances of Class maintain a name, a set of native selectors, a set of immediate superclasses (parent classes), a set of immediate subclasses (child classes), and a pointer to the dispatch table (usually, a pointer to a certain starting point within the table, specific to the class in question). Finally, they need to implement an efficient mechanism for determining whether another class is a subclass.

**Method-sets:** The MethodSet hierarchy is in some ways private to the DT Framework, and language implementors that use the DT Framework will usually not need to know anything about these classes. However, method-sets are of critical importance in providing the DT Framework with its incremental efficiency and compile-time method determination. For a given selector, a method-set implicitly represents the set of all classes that share the same method for that selector. Only one class in each of these sets natively defines the selector, and this class is referred to as the *defining class* of the method-set.

The Table class and its subclasses represent extended dispatch tables, which store *MethodSet* pointers instead of addresses. By storing method-sets in the tables, rather than simple addresses, the following capabilities become possible:

1. Localized modification of the dispatch table during environment modification so that only those entries that need to be will be recomputed.

2. Efficient inheritance propagation and inheritance conflict detection.

3. Detection of simple recompilations (replacing a method for a selector by a different method) and avoidance of unnecessary computation in such situations.

4. Compile-time method determination.

Every entry of an extended dispatch table represents a unique class/selector pair, and contains a MethodSet instance, even if no user-specified method exists for the class/selector pair in question. Such empty entries usually contain a unique instance of *EmptyMethodSet*, but one indexing strategy uses *FreeMethodSet* instances, which represent contiguous blocks of unused table entries. Instances of both of these classes have a special *methodNotUnderstood* address associated with them. Non-empty table entries are *StandardMethodSets*, and contain a *defining class, selector, address* and a set of child method-sets. The *NormalMethodSet* subclass represents a user-specified method address, and the *ConflictMethodSet* subclass represents an inheritance conflict that occurred due to multiple inheritance.

Associated with each standard MethodSet is the concept of its dependent classes. For a method-set $M$ representing class/selector pair $< C, \sigma >$, the *dependent classes* of $M$ consist of all classes which inherit selector $\sigma$ from class $C$. Furthermore, each selector $\sigma$ defined in the environment generates a *method-set inheritance graph*, which is an induced subgraph of the class inheritance hierarchy, formed by removing all classes which do not natively define $\sigma$. Method-set hierarchy graphs are what allow the DT Framework to perform compile-time method determination. These graphs can be maintained by having each method-set store a set of child method-sets. For a method-set $M$ with defining class $C$ and selector $\sigma$, the child method-sets of $M$ are the method-sets for selector $\sigma$ and classes $C_i$ immediately below $C$ in the method-set inheritance graph for $\sigma$. Figure 2 shows a small inheritance hierarchy and the method-set hierarchies obtained from it for selectors $\alpha$ and $\beta$.

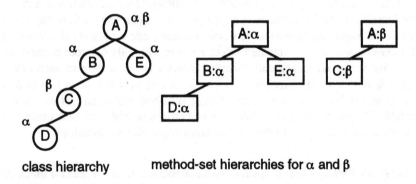

class hierarchy          method-set hierarchies for $\alpha$ and $\beta$

**Fig. 2.** An inheritance hierarchy and its associated method-set hierarchies

The concept of dependent classes is what decided us to name our fundamental datastructure a *method-set*, since the inheritance hierarchy can be divided into a set of mutually exclusive classes (where these sets are selector-dependent). However, note that a method-set does not explicitly store its dependent classes; instead, the defining class and selector stored in the method-set provide enough information to compute the dependent classes by looking at appropriate entries in the dispatch table.

**Tables:** Each Table class provides a fundamental structure for storing method-sets, and maps the indices associated with a class/selector pair to a particular entry in the table structure. Each of the concrete table classes in the DT Framework provides a different underlying table structure. The only functionality that subclasses need to provide is that which is dependent on the structure. This includes table access, table modification, and dynamic extension of the selector and class dimensions of the table.

The 2DTable class is an abstract superclass for tables with orthogonal class and selector dimensions. Rows represent the selector dimension, and columns represent the class dimension. The Extendable2DTable class can dynamically grow in both selector and class dimensions as additional elements are added to the dimensions. The FixedRow2DTable dynamically grows in the class dimension, but the size of the selector dimension is established at time of table creation, and cannot grow larger.

The concrete 1DTable class represents tables in which selectors and classes share the same dimension. Selector and class indices are added together to establish an entry within this one dimensional table.

The OuterTable class is an abstract superclass for tables which contain subtables. Most of the functionality of these classes involves requesting the same functionality from a particular subtable. For example, requesting the entry for a class/selector pair involves determining (based on selector index) which subtable is needed, and requesting table access from that subtable. Individual selectors exist in at most one subtable, but the same class can exist in multiple subtables. For this reason, class indices for these tables are dependent on selector indices (because the subtable is determined by selector index). For efficiency, selector indices are *encoded* so as to maintain both the subtable to which they belong, as well as the actual index within that subtable. The PartitionedTable class has a dynamic number of FixedRow2DTable instances as subtables. A new FixedRow2DTable instance is added when a selector cannot fit in any existing subtable. The SeparatedTable class has two subtables, one for *standard selectors* and one for *conflict selectors*. A standard selector is one with only one root method-set (a new selector is also standard), and a conflict selector is one with more than one root method-set. A *root method-set* for $< C, \sigma >$ is one in which class $C$ has no superclasses that define selector $\sigma$. Each of these subtables can be an instance of either Extendable2DTable or PartitionedTable. Since PartitionedTables are also outer tables, such implementations express tables as subtables containing subsubtables.

**Selector Index Strategy (SIS):** Each table has associated with it a selector index strategy, which is represented as an instance of some subclass of SIS. The OuterTable and 1DTable classes have one particular selector index strategy that they must use, but the 2DTable classes can choose from any of the 2D-SIS subclasses.

Each subclass of SIS implements Algorithm *Determine Selector Index*, which provides a mechanism for determining the index to associate with a selector. Each SIS class maintains the current index for each selector, and is responsible for detecting selector index conflicts. When such conflicts are detected, a new index must be determined that does not conflict with existing indices. Algorithm *Determine Selector Index* is responsible for detecting conflicts, determining a new index, storing the index, ensuring that space exists in the table for the new index, moving method-sets from the old table locations to new table locations, and returning the selector index to the caller.

The abstract 2D-SIS class represents selector index strategies for use with 2D-Tables. These strategies are interchangeable, so any 2D-Table subclass can use any concrete subclass of 2D-SIS in order to provide selector index determination. The PlainSIS class is a naive strategy that assigns a unique index to each selector. The ColoredSIS and AliasedSIS classes allow two selectors to share the same index as long as no class in the environment recognizes both selectors. They differ in how they determine which selectors can share indices. AliasedSIS is only applicable to languages with single inheritance.

The ShiftedSIS class provides selector index determination for tables in which selectors and classes share the same dimension. This strategy implements a variety of auxiliary functions which maintain doubly-linked freelists of unused entries in the one-dimensional table. These freelists are used to efficiently determine a new selector index. The selector index is interpreted as a shift offset within the table, to which class indices are added in order to obtain a table entry for a class/selector pair.

The ClassSpecificSIS assigns selector indices that depend on the class. Unlike in the other strategies, selector indices do not need to be the same across all classes, although two classes that are related in the inheritance hierarchy *are* required to share the index for selectors understood by both classes.

The PartitionedSIS class implements selector index determination for Partitioned-Table instances. When selector index conflicts are detected, a new index is obtained by asking a subtable to determine an index. Since FixedRow2D subtables of PartitionedTable instances are not guaranteed to be able to assign an index, all subtables are asked for an index until a subtable is found that can assign an index. If no subtable can assign an index, a new subtable is dynamically created.

The SeparatedSIS class implements selector index determination for SeparatedTable instances. A new index needs to be assigned when a selector index conflict is detected or when a selector changes status from standard to conflicting, or vice-versa. Such index determination involves asking either the standard or conflict subtable to find a selector index.

**Class Index Strategy (CIS):** Each table has associated with it a class index strategy, which is represented as an instance of some subclass of CIS. The OuterTable and 1DTable classes have one particular class index strategy that they must use, but the 2DTable classes can choose from either of the 2D-CIS subclasses.

Each subclass of CIS implements Algorithm *Determine Class Index*, which provides a mechanism for determining the index to associate with a class. Each CIS class maintains the current index for each class, and is responsible for detecting class index conflicts. When such conflicts are detected, a new index must be determined that does not conflict with existing indices. Algorithm *Determine Class Index* is responsible for detecting conflicts, determining a new index, storing the index, ensuring that space exists in the table for the new index, moving method-sets from old table locations to new table locations, and returning the class index to the caller.

The NonSharedCIS class implements the standard class index strategy, in which each class is assigned a unique index as it is added to the table. The SharedCIS class allows two or more classes to share the same index if all classes sharing the index have exactly the same method-set for every selector in the table.

The PartitionedCIS and SeparatedCIS classes implement class index determination for PartitionedTable and SeparatedTable respectively. In both cases, this involves establishing a subtable based on the selector index and asking that subtable to find a class index.

## 3.2 The DT Algorithms

Although the class hierarchies are what provide the DT Framework with its flexibility and the ability to switch between different dispatch techniques at will, it is the high-level algorithms implemented by the framework which are of greatest importance. Each of these algorithms is a *template method* describing the overall mechanism for using inheritance management to incrementally maintain a dispatch table, detect and record inheritance conflicts, and maintain class hierarchy information useful for compile-time optimizations. They call low-level, technique-specific functions in order to perform fundamental operations like table access, table modification and table dimension extension. In this paper, we provide a high-level description of the algorithms. A detailed discussion of the algorithms and how they interact can be found in [HS96].

**The Interface Algorithms:** Framework clients do not need to know anything about the implementation details of the framework. Instead, they create an instance of the DT Environment class and send messages to this instance each time an environment modification occurs. Four fundamental *interface* algorithms for maintaining inheritance changes exist in the Environment class: Algorithms *Add Selector*, *Remove Selector*, *Add Class Links*, and *Remove Class Links*. In all four cases, calling the algorithm results in a modification of all (and only) those table entries that need to be updated. Inheritance conflict recording, index conflict resolution and method-set hierarchy modification are performed as the table is updated. Most of this functionality is not provided directly by the interface algorithms; instead these algorithms establish how two fundamental inheritance management algorithms (Algorithms *Manage Inheritance* and *Manage Inheritance Removal*) should be invoked.

Algorithm *Add Selector* is invoked each time a selector $\sigma$ is defined in a particular class $C$, and Algorithm *Remove Selector* is invoked each time a selector is removed from a class[3]. Algorithm *Add Class Links* could be implemented as a simple algorithm that adds a single inheritance link between two classes, but a more efficient implementation is possible when it is extended to allow the adding of an arbitrary number of parent and child class links at the same time. Algorithm *Remove Class Links* is equally general with respect to removing class hierarchy links.

In addition to the four interface routines for modifying the inheritance hierarchy, there are also registration routines for creating or finding instances of classes and selectors. Each time the language parser encounters a syntactic specification for a class or selector, it sends a *Register Class* or *Register Selector* message to the DT environment, passing the name of the class or selector. The environment maintains a mapping from name to instance, returning the desired instance if already created, and creating a new

---

[3] We assume that inheritance exceptions are handled as special method declarations. Removing a selector from a class without a native definition for that class can be interpreted as a request for an inheritance exception.

instance if no such instance exists. Note that the existence of a selector or class does not in itself affect the inheritance hierarchy; in order for the dispatch tables to be affected, a selector must be associated with a class (Algorithm *Add Selector*) or a class must be added to the inheritance hierarchy (Algorithm *Add Class Links*).

**Algorithms for Inheritance Management:** Algorithm *Manage Inheritance*, and its interaction with Algorithms *Add Selector* and *Add Class Links*, form the most important part of the DT Framework. Algorithm *Manage Inheritance* is responsible for propogating a MethodSet instance provided to it from Algorithms *Add Selector* or *Add Class Links* to all dependent classes of the method-set. During this propagation, the algorithm is also responsible for maintaining inheritance conflict information and managing selector index conflicts. Algorithm *Manage Inheritance Removal* plays a similar role with respect to Algorithms *Remove Selector* and *Remove Class Links*.

Algorithms *Manage Inheritance* and *Manage Inheritance Removal* are recursive algorithms that are applied to a class, then invoked on each child class of that class. Recursion terminates when a class with a native definition is encountered, or no child classes exist. During each invocation, tests are performed to determine which of three possible scenarios is to be executed: *method-set insertion*, *method-set child updating*, or *conflict creation* (*conflict removal*, in *Manage Inheritance Removal*). Each scenario either identifies a method-set to propagate to children of the current class, or establishes that recursion should terminate. Due to inheritance conflicts, a recursive call may not necessarily propagate the incoming method-set.

These algorithms have gone through many refinements, and the current implementations provide extremely efficient inheritance management, inheritance conflict detection, index conflict resolution and method-set hierarchy maintenance. An indepth discussion of how these algorithms are implemented, the optimal tests used to establish scenarios, and how the method-set data structure provides these tests, is available in [HS96].

These algorithms are implemented in the abstract Table class, and do not need to be reimplemented in subclasses. However, these algorithms do invoke a variety of operations which do need to be overridden in subclasses. Thus, Algorithms *Manage Inheritance* and *Manage Inheritance Removal* act as *template methods* ([GHJV95]), providing the overall structure of the algorithms, but deferring some steps to subclasses. Subclasses are responsible for implementing functionality for determining selector and class indices, accessing and modifying the table structure, and modifying method-set hierarchies.

**Algorithms for Selector and Class Index Determination:** Each selector and class instance is assigned an index by the DT Framework. The indices associated with a class/selector pair are used to establish an entry within the table for that class/selector pair. An *index strategy* is a technique for incrementally assigning indices so that the new index does not cause index conflicts. An *index conflict* occurs when two class/selector pairs with differing method-sets access the same entry in the table. Since it is undesirable for an entry to contain more than one method-set (see [VH94, VH96]), we want to resolve the conflict by assigning new indices to one of the class/selector pairs. Note that since indices are table specific, and each table has a single selector index strategy and class index strategy, it is the index strategy instances that maintain the currently assigned indices for each selector and class, rather than having each selector and class instance maintain multiple indices (one for each table they participate in).

Given a class/selector pair, Algorithm *Determine Selector Index* returns the index associated with the selector. However, before returning the index, the algorithm ensures that no selector index conflict exists for the selector in question. If such a conflict does exist, a new selector index is computed that does not conflict with any other existing selector index, the new index is recorded, the selector dimension of the associated table is extended (if necessary), and all method-sets representing selector $\sigma$ are moved from the old index to the new index, within the table. Algorithm *Determine Class Index* performs a similar task for class indices. Algorithm *Determine Selector Index* is provided by classes in the SIS inheritance hierarchy, and Algorithm *Determine Class Index* by classes in the CIS inheritance hierarchy.

## 4   Incremental Table-based Method Dispatch

All of the table-based techniques can be implemented using the DT Framework. However, due to the non-incremental nature of the virtual function table technique (VTBL), an incremental implementation of VTBL would be quite inefficient, so the current implementation of the framework does not support VTBL dispatch. All other techniques are provided, and the exact dispatch mechanism is controlled by parameters passed to the DT Environment constructor. The parameters indicate which table(s) to use, and specify the selector and class index strategies to be associated with each of these tables.

1. *STI*: uses Extendable2DTable, PlainSIS, and NonSharedCIS.

2. *SC*: uses Extendable2DTable, ColoredSIS, and NonSharedCIS.

3. *RD*: uses 1DTable, ShiftedSIS and NonSharedCIS.

4. *VTBL*: uses ClassTable, ClassSpecificSIS and NonSharedCIS.

5. *CT*: uses a SeparatedTable with two PartitionedTable subtables, each with Fixed-Row2DTable subsubtables. The selector index strategy for all subsubtables of the standard subtable is AliasedSIS, and the strategy for all subsubtables of the conflict subtable is PlainSIS. All subsubtables use SharedCIS.

6. *ICT*: identical to CT, except that the standard subtable uses ColoredSIS instead of AliasedSIS.

7. *SCCT*: identical to CT, except that both standard and conflict subtables used ColoredSIS (instead of AliasedSIS and PlainSIS respectively).

The last two techniques are examples of what the DT Framework can do to combine existing techniques into new hybrid techniques. For example, ICT dispatch uses selector coloring instead of selector aliasing to determine selector indices in the standard table, and is thus applicable to languages with multiple inheritance. Even better, SCCT uses selector coloring in both standard and conflict tables (remember that the CT dispatch effectively uses STI-style selector indexing in the conflict table).

In addition to providing each of the above dispatch techniques, the framework can be used to analyze the various compression strategies introduced by CT dispatch in isolation from the others. For example, a dispatch table consisting of a PartitionedTable, whose FixedRow2DTable subtables each use PlainSIS and SharedCIS indexing strategies, allows us to determine how much table compression is obtained by class sharing alone. Many variations based on SeparatedTable and PartitionedTable, their subtables, and the associated index strategies, are possible.

# 5   Efficiency issues within Compilers and Run-time Systems

Both compilers and run-time systems benefit equally from the dispatch technique independence provided by the DT Framework. In addition, the framework provides each of them with additional useful functionality.

## 5.1   Compilers

The DT Framework provides compilers with the following advantages: 1) maintenance of inheritance conflicts, 2) compile-time method determination, and 3) the ability to perform separate compilation.

In languages with multiple inheritance, it is possible for inheritance conflicts to occur, when a class with no native definition for a selector inherits two distinct methods for the selector from two or more superclasses. For the purposes of both efficiency and software verification, compile-time detection of such conflicts is highly desirable.

The most substantial benefit that the DT Framework provides to compilers is the recording of information needed to efficiently determine whether a particular class/selector pair is uniquely determined at compile-time. In such cases, the compiler can avoid run-time method dispatch entirely, and generate an immediate function call or even inline the code.

Another powerful capability provided to compilers by the DT Framework is separate compilation. Each library or collection of related classes can be compiled, and an extended dispatch table stored with the associated object code. At link-time, a separate DT Environment for each library or module can be created from the stored dispatch tables. The linker can then pick one such environment (usually the largest) and ask that environment to merge each of the other environments into itself. This facility is critical in situations where a library is being used for which source code is not provided. Since certain dispatch table techniques require the full environment in order to maintain accurate tables (i.e. SC, RD and CT) library providers who do not want to share their source code need only provide the inheritance hierarchy and selector definition information needed by the DT Framework.

Finally, note that although it is necessary to use the extended dispatch tabl to incrementally modify the inheritance information, it is not necessary to maintain the extended dispatch table at run-time in non-schema-evolving compiled languages. Once linking is finished, the linker can ask the DT Environment to create a simple dispatch table from the extended dispatch table, and this dispatch table can be stored in the executable for static use at run-time.

## 5.2 Run-time Systems

The DT Framework provides run-time systems with: 1) table-based dispatch in schema-evolving languages, 2) dynamic schema evolution, and 3) inheritance conflict detection.

The utility of the DT Framework is fully revealed when it is used by run-time systems. Because of the efficiency of incremental inheritance propagation and dispatch table modification, it can be used even in heavily schema-evolving languages like Smalltalk ([GR83]) and Tigukat ([OPS+95]). However, this functionality is provided at the cost of additional space, because an extended dispatch table must be maintained at run-time, rather than a traditional dispatch table containing only addresses. Note also that without additional space utilization, dispatch using an extended dispatch table is more expensive than normal table dispatch because of the indirection through the method-set stored at a dispatch table entry in order to obtain an address. By doubling the table size, this can be avoided by having the extended dispatch table store both a MethodSet pointer and an address. In dispatch techniques like RD and CT that are space-efficient, this doubling of size may be worth the improvements in dispatch performance.

Some mechanism to support dynamic schema evolution is necessary to provide languages with full-fledged schema-evolution. The DT Framework allows arbitrary class hierarchy links to be added and removed no matter what the current state of the classes.

Finally, the framework allows inheritance conflicts to be detected at the time they are produced, rather than during dispatch. This allows schema-evolving languages to return error indicators immediately after a run-time environment modification. A common complaint with schema-evolving languages is a lack of software verification; the DT Framework provides a partial solution to this.

# 6  Performance Results

In the previous sections, we have described a framework for the incremental maintenance of an extended dispatch table, using any table-based dispatch technique. In this section, we summarize the results of using the DT Framework to implement STI, SC, RD, ICT and SCCT dispatch and generate extended dispatch tables for a variety of object-oriented class libraries.

In order to test the algorithms, we can model a compiler or run-time interpreter with a simple parsing program that reads input from a file. Each line of the file is either a selector definition (consisting of a selector name and class name), or a class definition (consisiting) of a class name and a list of zero or more parent class names. The order in which the class and selector definitions appear in this file represent the order in which a compiler or run-time system would encounter the same declarations.

[DH95] demonstrated the effectiveness of the non-incremental RD technique on twelve real-world class libraries. We have executed the DT algorithms on this same set of libraries in order to determine what effects dispatch technique, input order and library size have on per-invocation algorithm execution times and on the time and memory needed to create a complete extended dispatch table for the library in question. The cross-product of technique, library and possible input ordering generates far too much data to present here, so we have choosen two representative libraries from [DH95], Parcplace1 and Geode, as well as the change log from a commercial Smalltalk programmer in a local company called Biotools. Table 1 summarizes some useful statistics for these classes.

| Library | C | S | M | m | P | B |
|---|---|---|---|---|---|---|
| Biotools | 493 | 4052 | 11802 | 5931 | 1.0 | 132 |
| Parcplace1 | 774 | 5086 | 178230 | 8540 | 1.0 | 401 |
| Geode | 1318 | 6549 | 302709 | 14194 | 2.1 | 795 |

**Table 1.** Statistics for various object-oriented environments

In the table, $C$ is the total number of classes, $S$ is the total number of selectors, $M$ is the total number of legitimate class-selector combinations, $m$ is the total number of defined methods, $P$ is the average number of parents per class, and $B$ is the size of the largest complete behavior, (c.f. [DH95]).

Of the 15 different input orderings we analyzed, we present three, a non-random ordering that is usually best for all techniques and libraries, a non-random ordering that is the worst of all non-random orderings, and our best approximation of a natural ordering. By *natural ordering*, we mean the ordering of class and selector definitions that would occur during the development of the hierarchy in question. In the case of the Biotools hierarchy, the natural ordering is easily obtained, since Smalltalk maintains a change log of every class and selector defined, in the order they are defined. For the ParcPlace and Geode libraries, we assume that a completely random ordering of the classes and selectors is representative of the natural ordering.

Table 2 presents the total time and memory requirements for each of these data samples, applied to each of the techniques on the best, worst and natural (real) input orderings. The DT code is implemented in C++, was compiled with g++ -O2, and executed on a Sparc-Station 20/50. This code is publicly available from ftp://ftp.cs.ualberta.ca/pub/Dtf.

Overall execution time, memory usage and table fill-rates for the published non-incremental versions are provided for comparision. We define *fill-rate* as the percentage of total table entries having user-defined method addresses (including addresses that indicate inheritance conflicts). Note that in the case of CT, this definition of fill-rate is misleading, since class-sharing allows many classes to share the same column in the table[4].

In [AR92], the incremental algorithm for SC took 12 minutes on a Sun 3/80 when applied to the Smalltalk-80 Version 2.5 hierarchy (which is slightly smaller than the Parcplace1 library presented in Table 2), where this time excludes the processing of

---

[4] A more accurate measure of fill-rate is possible, but is not relevant to this paper. So as not to misrepresent data, we do not describe CT fill-rates here.

| Library | Order | Timings (seconds) | | | | | Memory (MBytes) | | | | |
|---------|-------|-----|------|--------|-------|------|------|-----|------|-----|------|
| | | STI | SC | RD | ICT | SCCT | STI | SC | RD | ICT | SCCT |
| Biotools | best | 5.7 | 3.5 | 5.7 | 6.7 | 10.7 | 10.6 | 1.2 | 1.0 | 1.3 | 1.0 |
| | worst | 11.4 | 7.0 | 10.9 | 11.4 | 11.6 | 11.3 | 1.2 | 1.2 | 1.3 | 1.0 |
| | natural | 18.3 | 13.8 | 20.2 | 21.9 | 22.5 | 10.7 | 1.1 | 1.1 | 1.8 | 1.0 |
| Parc1 | best | 8.6 | 7.2 | 9.3 | 16.9 | 18.3 | 20.1 | 2.7 | 2.6 | 1.9 | 1.6 |
| | worst | 23.4 | 30.5 | 126.0 | 37.2 | 34.9 | 20.6 | 3.0 | 4.2 | 2.2 | 1.8 |
| | natural | 24.2 | 28.0 | 1064.0 | 73.2 | 77.3 | 20.1 | 3.1 | 5.6 | 2.6 | 2.1 |
| Geode | best | 25.3 | 27.1 | 133.1 | 61.4 | 68.4 | 44.5 | 8.7 | 7.0 | 4.8 | 4.3 |
| | worst | 59.9 | 84.3 | 937.0 | 125.7 | 133.4 | 44.8 | 8.9 | 11.8 | 5.6 | 5.0 |
| | natural | 67.4 | 75.7 | 6032.0 | 157.7 | 174.1 | 44.3 | 9.0 | 13.9 | 8.3 | 6.8 |

**Table 2.** General Time and Space Results for the DT Framework

certain special classes. The DT Framework, applied to all classes in this library, on a Sun 3/80, took 113 seconds to complete. No overall memory results were reported in [AR92] (DT uses 2.5 Mb), but their algorithm had a fill-rate within 3% of optimal (the maximum total number of selectors understood by one class is a minimum on the number of rows to which SC can compress the STI table). Using the best input ordering, the DT algorithms have a fill-rate within 1% of optimal.

In [DH95], non-incremental RD is presented, and the effects of different implementation strategies on execution time and memory usage are analyzed. Our current DT implementation of RD is roughly equivalent to the implementation strategies DIO and SI as described in that paper. Implementing strategies DRO and MI, which give better fill-rates and performance for static RD, requires complete knowledge of the environment. Their results were ran on a SPARCstation-20/60, and were 4.3 seconds for Parcplace1, and 9.6 seconds for Geode. Total memory was not presented, but detailed fill-rates were. They achieved a 99.6% fill-rate for Parcplace1 and 57.9% for Geode (using SI). Using the input ordering that matches their ordering as closely as possible, our algorithms gave fill-rates of 99.6% and 58.3%. However, fill-rates for the random ordering were 32.0% and 20.6% respectively.

In [VH96], non-incremental CT is presented, with timing results given for a SPARC-station-5. A timing of about 2 seconds for Parcplace1 can be interpolated from their data, and a memory consumption of 1.5 Mb. Results for Geode were not possible because Geode uses multiple inheritance. In the DT Framework, we use selector coloring instead of selector aliasing, which removes the restriction to languages with single inheritance. On a SPARCstation-5, the DT algorithms run in 21.1 seconds using 1.9 Mb when applied to Parcplace1, and run in 70.5 seconds using 4.8 Mb when applied to Geode.

We have also estimated the memory overhead incurred by the incremental nature of the DT Framework. The data maintained by the Environment, Class and Selector classes is needed in both static and incremental versions, and only a small amount of the memory taken by Tables is overhead, so the primary contributor to incremental overhead is the collection of MethodSet instances. The total memory overhead varies with the memory efficiency of the dispatch technique, from a low of 15% for STI, to a high of 50% for RD and SCCT.

## 6.1 Per-invocation costs of the DT algorithms

Since we are stressing the incremental nature of the DT Framework, the per-invocation cost of our fundamental algorithms, *Add Selector*, *Add Class Links* and *Inheritance Manager*, are of interest. Rather than reporting the timings for every recursive call of IMA, we report the sum over all recursive calls from a single invocation from Algorithm *Add Selector* or Algorithm *Add Class Links*. The per-invocation results for the *Parcplace1* library are representative, so we will summarize them. Furthermore, SC, ICT and SCCT techniques have similar distributions, so we will present only the results for SC and RD dispatch. In Parcplace1, Algorithm *Add Selector* is always called 8540 times, and Algorithm *Add Class Links* is called 774 times, but the number of times Algorithm *Manage Inheritance* is invoked from these routines depends on the input ordering. Per-invocation timings were obtained using the getrusage() system call and taking the sum of system and user time. Note that since Sun 4 machines have a clock interval of 1/100 seconds, the granularity of the results is 10ms.

Table 3 shows six histograms for SC dispatch. Each histogram indicates how many invocations of each algorithm fell within a particular millisecond interval. The first row represents per-invocation timings for the optimal ordering, and the second row for the random ordering. In all libraries, for all orderings, all algorithms execute in less than 10 milliseconds for more than 95% of their invocations. Thus, without limiting the y-axis of the histograms, the initial partition would dominate all others so much that no data would be visible. For this reason, we have limited the y-axis and labelled the first partition with its number of occurences. For Algorithm *Add Selector*, maximum (average) per-invocation times were 30 ms (0.7 ms) for optimal order, and 120 ms (0.6 ms) for random order. For Algorithm *Add Class Links*, they were 10 ms (0.1 ms) and 4100 ms (27.3 ms), and for Algorithm *Manage Inheritance*, 30 ms (0.2 ms) and 120 ms (0.25 ms).

Table 4 shows similar timings for RD dispatch. The variation in timing results between different random orderings can be as much as 100% (the maximum time is twice the minimum time). For Algorithm *Add Selector*, maximum (average) per-invocation times were 80 ms (0.9 ms) for optimal order, and 1970 ms (6.7 ms) for random order. For Algorithm *Add Class Links*, they were 10 ms (0.1 ms) and 52740 ms (12763 ms), and for Algorithm *Manage Inheritance*, 70 ms (0.2 ms) and 3010 ms (24.5 ms).

## 6.2 Effects on Dispatch Performance

In [DHV95], the dispatch costs of most of the published dispatch techniques are presented. The costs are expressed as formulae involving processor-specific constants like load latency (L) and branch miss penalty (B), which vary with the type of processor being modeled. In this section, we observe how the incremental nature of our algorithms affects this dispatch speed.

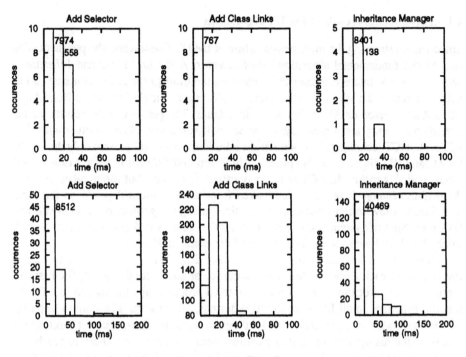

**Table 3.** Per-invocation timing results for SC dispatch

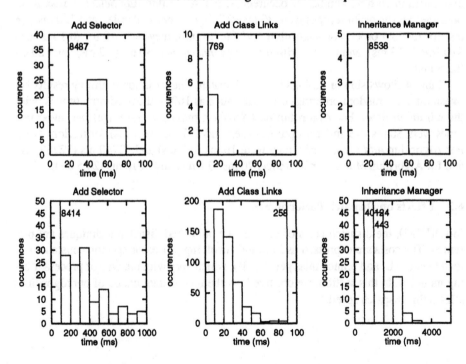

**Table 4.** Per-invocation timing results for RD dispatch

At a particular call-site, the selector in the method send and the class of the receiver object together uniquely determine which method to invoke. Conceptually, in object-oriented languages, each object knows its (dynamic) class, so we can obtain a class index for a given object. This index, along with the index of the selector (which is usually known at compile-time), uniquely establishes an entry within a global dispatch table. In this scheme, we do a fair amount of work to obtain an address: get the class of the receiver object, access the class index, get the global table, get the class-specific part of the table (based on class index), and get the appropriate entry within this subtable (based on selector index).

The above dispatch sequence can be improved by making a simple observation: if each class explicitly stored its portion of the global dispatch table, we could avoid the need to obtain a class index. In fact, we would no longer need to maintain a class index at all (the table replaces the index). In languages where the size of the dispatch table is known at compile-time it is even more efficient to assume that each class *is* a table, rather than assuming that each class contains a table. This avoids an indirection, since we no longer need to ask for the class of an object, then obtain the table from the class: we now ask for the class and immediately have access to its table (which starts at some constant offset from the beginning of the class itself). Thus, all of the table-based dispatch techniques must do at least the following (they may also need to do more): 1) get table from receiver object, 2) get method address from table (based on selector index), 3) call method.

So, now we want to determine how much dispatch performance degrades when using the DT Framework, with its incremental nature, dynamic growing of tables as necessary, and the use of extended dispatch tables instead of simple dispatch tables. Note that during dispatch, indirections may incur a penalty beyond just the operation itself due to load latency (in pipelined processors, the result of a load started in cycle $i$ is not available until cycle $i+L$). In the analysis of [DHV95], it is assumed that the load latency, L, is 2 (non-pipelined processors can assume L = 1). This implies that each extra indirection incurred by the DTF algorithms will slow down dispatch by at least one cycle (for the load itself) and by at most L cycles (if there are not other operations that can be performed while waiting for the load).

Figure 3 shows a conceptual version of the internal state of the fundamental DT classes. In the figure, rather than showing the layout of all of the Table subclasses, we have chosen Extendable2DTable as a representative instance. The only difference between this table and any of the other tables is the nature of the *Data* field. This field (like most fields in the figure) is of type *Array*, a simple C++ class that represents a dynamically growable array. The *Data* field of the Array class is a pointer to a contiguous block of words (usually containing indices or pointers to other DT class instances). Usually, such Arrays have more space allocated than is actually used (hence the *Alloc* and *Size* fields), but this overhead is a necessary part of dynamic growth.

From Figure 3, it can be seen that the Extendable2DTable class has a *Data* field which is an Array class. This Array class handles dynamic growth as new elements are added, and also has a *Data* field, which points to a dynamically allocated block of contiguous words in memory. Each word in this block is a pointer to a DT Class object. In the figure, each Class object also has a *Data* field (another growable array),

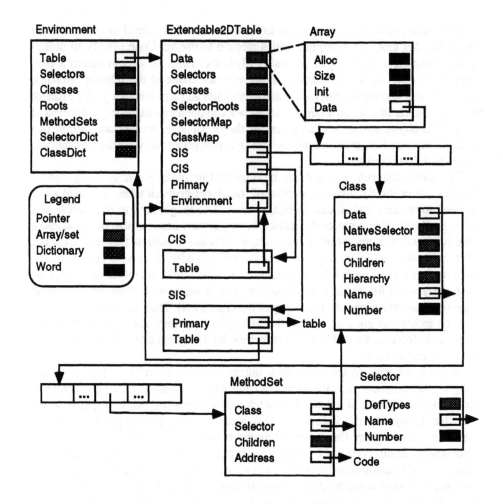

**Fig. 3.** C++ Class Layouts for DT Classes

which in turn points to a block of dynamically allocated memory. Each entry in this block is a pointer to a MethodSet instance, which contains a pointer to the method to execute. Note that in Figure 3 Class instances are not considered to *be* dispatch tables, and instead contain a growable array representing the class-specific portion of the global dispatch table.

Given this layout, two extra indirections are incurred, one to get the table from the class, and one to get the method-set from the table. Thus, dispatch speeds in all table-based techniques will be increased by at most $2 \times L$ cycles. Depending on the branch miss penalty (B) of the processor in question (the dominating variable in dispatch costs in [DHV95]), this results in a dispatch slow-down of between 50% (B=1) and 30%(B=6) when L=2.

Given these performance penalties, the DT Framework would not be desirable for use in production systems. However, it is relatively easy to remove both of the indirections mentioned, one by using a modest amount of additional memory, and the other by relying on implementations of object-oriented languages that do not use object-tables. By removing these indirections, the DT Framework has exactly the same dispatch performance as non-incremental implementations.

We can remove the extra indirection needed to extract the address from the method-set by using some extra space. As is shown in Figure 4, each table entry is no longer just a pointer to a MethodSet instance; it is instead a two-field record containing both the address and the MethodSet instance (the address field within the method-set itself becomes redundant). This does slightly decrease the efficiency of incremental modification (it is no longer possible to change a single MethodSet address and have it be reflected in multiple table entries), but optimizing dispatch is more important than optimizing table maintenance. Furthermore, the amount of inefficiency is minimal, given how quickly Algorithm *Add Selector* executes. Finally, the extra space added by effectively doubling the number of table entries is not necessarily that expensive, especially in techniques like RD and CT. For example, in RD, the space for the table is about 25% of the total memory used, so doubling this table space increases the overall space used by 25%.

The other extra indirection exists because in Figure 3 classes *contain* tables instead of *being* tables. In the non-incremental world, the size of each class-specific dispatch table is known at compile-time, so at run-time it is possible to allocate exactly enough space in each class instance to store its table directly. At first glance, this does not seem possible in the DT Framework because the incremental addition of selectors requires that tables (and thus classes) be able to grow dynamically. The reason this is difficult is because dynamic growth necessitates the allocation of new memory (and the copying of data). Either we provide an extra indirection, or provide some mechanism for updating every variable pointing to the original class object, so that it points to the new class object. Fortunately, this last issue is something that object-oriented language implementations that do not use object tables already support, so we can take advantage of the underlying capabilities of the language implementation to help provide efficient dispatch for the language. For example, in Smalltalk, indexed instance variables exist (Array is an example), which can be grown as needed. We therefore treat classes as *being* tables, rather than *containing* tables, and avoid the second indirection. Figure 4 shows the object, class and table layouts that allow the DT Framework to operate without incuring penalties during dispatch.

# 7 Related and Future Work

## 7.1 Related Work

[DHV95] presents an analysis of the various dispatch techniques and indicates that in most cases, IC and PIC are more efficient than STI, SC and RD, especially on highly pipelined processors, because IC and PIC do not cause pipeline stalls that the table indirections of STI, SC and RD do. However, even if the primary dispatch technique is IC or PIC, it may still be useful to maintain a dispatch table for cases were a miss occurs, as a much faster alternative to using ML (method lookup) or LC (global cache)

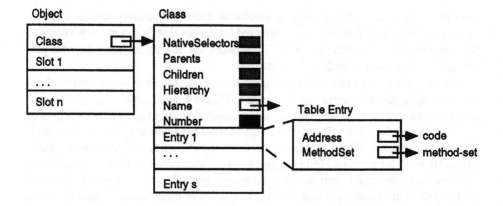

**Fig. 4.** Improved Table Layout to Optimize Dispatch

and ML together. Especially in schema-evolving languages with substantial multiple inheritance, ML is extremely inefficient, since each inheritance path must be searched (in order to detect inheritance conflicts).

[DGC95] discusses static class hierarchy analysis and its utility in optimizing object-oriented programs. They introduce an *applies-to* set representing the set of classes that share the same method for a particular selector. These sets are represented by our concept of dependent classes. Since each method-set implicitly maintains its set of dependent classes, the DT algorithms have access to such sets, and to the compile-time optimizations provided by them.

[AR92] presents an incremental approach to selector coloring. However, the algorithm proposed often performs redundant work by checking the validity of selector colors each time a new selector is added. The DT algorithms demonstrates how to perform selector color determination only when absolutely necessary (i.e. only when a selector color conflict occurs), and has generalized the approach to a variety of table-based approaches. [DH95] presents selector-based row displacement (RD) and discusses how to obtain optimal compression results. [VH96] presents the compact selector indexed table (CT), expanding on previous work in [VH94].

Predicate classes, as implemented in Cecil ([Cha93]), allow a class to change its set of superclasses, at run-time. The DT Framework provides an efficient mechanism for implementing predicate classes using table-based dispatch.

### 7.2  Future Work

The DT Framework provides a general description of all work that needs to be performed to handle inheritance management and method dispatch in schema-evolving, dynamically typed, single-receiver languages with multiple inheritance. A variety of extensions are possible.

First, the framework as presented handles methods, but not internal state. A mechanism to incrementally modify object layout is a logical, and necessary, extension. Second, multi-method languages such as Tigukat [OPS+95] and Cecil [Cha92] have the ability to dispatch a method based not only on the dynamic type of a receiver, but also on the dynamic types of all arguments to the selector. Multi-methods extend the expressive power of a language, but efficient method dispatch and inheritance management is an even more difficult issue in such languages. Extending the DT Framework to handle multi-method dispatch is part of our continued research in this area. Third, the framework currently assumes that inheriting the interface of parents classes implies that the implementation associated with the interface is inherited also. A more general mechanism for inheritance management that separates these concepts is desirable. The DT Framework is planned to be used to implement all three of these concepts in Tigukat, an object-oriented database language with massive schema-evolution, multi-method dispatch, multiple implementation types, and many other extensions to the object-oriented paradigm.

Fourth, although the DT Framework provides a general mechanism for handling table-based method dispatch, it is really only one component of a much larger framework that handles all method dispatch techniques. The DT Framework can be extended so that framework clients call interface algorithms each time a call-site is encountered, similar to the manner in which the environment is currently called, when class and selector definitions are encountered. This would extend the DT Framework to encompass all known method dispatch techniques.

Fifth, the DT Framework allows various compression techniques, like selector aliasing, selector coloring, and class sharing, to be analyzed both in isolation, and in interaction with one another. More research about how these techniques interact, and about how SCCT dispatch can be optimized, is necessary.

# 8 Conclusion

We have presented a framework that is usable by both compilers and run-time systems to provide table-based method dispatch, inheritance conflict detection, and compile-time method determination. The framework relies on a collection of technique independent algorithms for environment modification, which call technique-dependent algorithms to perform fundamental operations like table access and index determination. The framework unifies all table-based method dispatch techniques into a cohesive whole, allowing a language implementor to change between techniques by changing the manner in which the DT Environment is instantiated. Incremental versions of all table-based techniques except VTBL have been implemented, all of which have low milli-second per-invocation execution times.

The framework provides a variety of new capabilities. The various table-based dispatch techniques have differing dispatch execution times and memory requirements. Since the framework allows any table-based dispatch technique to be used, a particular application can be optimized for either space or dispatch performance. Furthermore, the DT Framework allows table-based dispatch techniques to be used in schema-evolving languages. In the past, schema-evolving languages necessitated the use of a non-table-based technique. One reason that C++ uses virtual function tables is that they allow for separate compilation, unlike other table-based dispatch techniques. The DT Framework now allows all table-based dispatch techniques to work with separate compilation. Finally, the framework introduces a new level of software verification in schema-evolving languages by allowing inheritance conflicts to be detected immediately when they occur, rather than during dispatch.

The framework has been used to merge SC and CT method dispatch into a hybrid dispatch technique with the advantages of both. The CT dispatch technique is limited by its restriction to single-inheritance. By replacing selector aliasing by selector coloring, we obtain a dispatch technique that works with multiple inheritance and that benefits from the class sharing made possible by CT class partitioning. Furthermore, SCCT dispatch provides slightly better compression because the conflict table can be colored, unlike in CT dispatch, where it remains uncompressed.

The DT Framework currently consists of 36 classes, 208 selectors, 494 methods, and 1081 meaningful class/selector pairs. When the DT Framework is applied to a completely random ordering of itself, a SCCT-based dispatch table is generated in 0.436 seconds. Since compiling the framework requires 390 seconds, even the slowest dispatch technique and input ordering produce a dispatch table in a negligible amount of time, relative to overall compilation time.

# 9  Acknowledgements

The authors would like to thank both Karel Driesen and Jan Vitek for several discussions during the compilation of this paper. As well, the ECOOP Program Committee provided several useful suggestions that improved the paper. This research was supported in part by the NSERC research grant OGP8191.

# References

[AR92]     P. Andre and J.C. Royer. Optimizing method search with lookup caches and incremental coloring. In *OOPSLA'92 Conference Proceedings*, 1992.

[Cha92]    Craig Chambers. Object-oriented multi-methods in cecil. In *ECOOP'92 Conference Proceedings*, 1992.

[Cha93]    Craig Chambers. Predicate classes. In *ECOOP'93 Conference Proceedings*, 1993.

[Cox87]    Brad Cox. *Object-Oriented Programming, An Evolutionary Approach*. Addison-Wesley, 1987.

[DGC95]    Jeffrey Dean, David Grove, and Craig Chambers. Optimzation of object-oriented programs using static class hierarchy analysis. In *ECOOP'95 Conference Proceedings*, 1995.

[DH95]     K. Driesen and U. Holzle. Minimizing row displacement dispatch tables. In *OOPSLA'95 Conference Proceedings*, 1995.

[DHV95]    K. Driesen, U. Holzle, and J. Vitek. Message dispatch on pipelined processors. In *ECOOP'95 Conference Proceedings*, 1995.

[DMSV89]   R. Dixon, T. McKee, P. Schweizer, and M. Vaughan. A fast method dispatcher for compiled languages with multiple inheritance. In *OOPSLA'89 Conference Proceedings*, 1989.

[Dri93]    Karel Driesen. Method lookup strategies in dynamically typed object-oriented programming languages. Master's thesis, Vrije Universiteit Brussel, 1993.

[DS94]   L. Peter Deutsch and Alan Schiffman. Efficient implementation of the smalltalk-80 system. In *Principles of Programming Languages*, Salt Lake City, UT, 1994.

[ES90]   M.A. Ellis and B. Stroustrup. *The Annotated C++ Reference Manual*. Addison-Wesley, 1990.

[GHJV95] Erich Gamma, Richard Helm, Ralph Johnson, and John Vlissides. *Design Patterns: Elements of Reusable Object-Oriented Software*. Addison-Wesley, 1995.

[GR83]   A. Goldberge and David Robson. *Smalltalk-80: The Language and its Implementation*. Addison-Wesley, 1983.

[HCU91]  Urs Holzle, Craig Chambers, and David Ungar. Optimizing dynamically-typed object oriented languages with polymorphic inline caches. In *ECOOP'91 Conference Proceedings*, 1991.

[HS96]   Wade Holst and Duane Szafron. Inheritance management and method dispatch in reflexive object-oriented languages. Technical Report TR-96-27, University of Alberta, Edmonton, Canada, 1996.

[Kra83]  Glenn Krasner. *Smalltalk-80: Bits of History, Words of Advice*. Addison-Wesley, Reading, MA, 1983.

[OPS⁺95] M.T. Ozsu, R.J. Peters, D. Szafron, B. Irani, A. Lipka, , and A. Munoz. Tigukat: A uniform behavioral objectbase management system. In *The VLDB Journal*, pages 100–147, 1995.

[VH94]   Jan Vitek and R. Nigel Horspool. Taming message passing: Efficient method lookup for dynamically typed languages. In *ECOOP'94 Conference Proceedings*, 1994.

[VH96]   Jan Vitek and R. Nigel Horspool. Compact dispatch tables for dynamically typed programming languages. In *Proceedings of the Intl. Conference on Compiler Construction*, 1996.

# Optimizing Smalltalk by Selector Code Indexing Can Be Practical

Tamiya Onodera and Hiroaki Nakamura*

IBM Research, Tokyo Research Laboratory
1623-14, Shimo-tsuruma, Yamato-shi, Kanagawa-ken 242 Japan
{onodera, nakamura}@trl.ibm.com

**Abstract.** Selector code indexing is a simple and effective way of optimizing method lookups. However, it has not been considered practically applicable in Smalltalk, because the space overhead is prohibitive. We propose a new technique called "dispatch caches indexed by selector codes" (CISCO), which maintains a small number of dispatch tables indexed by a small number of selector codes. The space overhead is thus a small constant, however many classes and selectors there are in a system, while it almost maintains the runtime efficiency of selector code indexing. The simulation results show that, when carefully applied, optimization by CISCO is very promising, with cache miss ratios of less than 1.0% in real programs.

## 1 Introduction

Message sends are abundant in object-oriented computation. Unlike in a procedure call, the method actually invoked at a message send varies depending on the class of the receiver. Executing a message send consists of two steps: *method lookup* and *method invocation*. When compared to a procedure call, the first step of method lookup simply creates an extra runtime overhead. Even worse, this overhead is exaggerated, since message sends tend to be denser than procedure calls in imperative languages.

The naive implementation of method lookup in Smalltalk is as follows. Given a pair of a selector and a receiver class, the system first searches the *method dictionary* of the class for a method of the selector. If no such method is found, it continues searching the method dictionaries of the superclasses along the superclass chain.

Obviously, this naive implementation is prohibitively expensive. Therefore, even early implementations of Smalltalk-80 applied a kind of optimization, which was the beginning of numerous efforts to reduce the overhead of message sends. When we look at the optimization techniques of this kind that have been invented

---

* Current address: University of Illinois at Urbana-Champaign, Department of Computer Science, 1304 W.Springfield Ave. Urbana, IL 61801 USA; hnakamur@uiuc.edu

so far, either in Smalltalk or in other dynamic object-oriented languages,[2] we find three different basic ideas — *caching, static binding,* and *selector code indexing.*

The purpose of caching is to accelerate method lookup. For instance, a hash table *per system* was used to cache lookup results in early Smalltalk-80 systems. The remarkable techniques of inline caches [6] and polymorphic inline cache (PIC) [13] are variants of caching *per send,* although these are also considered to be applications of static binding, as explained below. Between the two we can also find a cache *per method* [10] and a cache *per class* [16].

The primary aim of static binding is to eliminate the overhead of method lookup by using type information.[3] As a result, the cost of a message send is reduced to that of a procedure call. More importantly, the cost can be completely eliminated by inlining smaller methods. In short, static binding attempts to bring the performance of Smalltalk closer to that of C.

A variety of techniques along these lines have been proposed; they differ mainly in the way that type information is obtained. Here we mention only recent works. *Static hierarchy analysis* [5] performs static analysis in order to detect those methods understood by a class that are not overridden by any subclasses of the class. *Customization* obtains information about receiver types from the system lookup routine, and generates a tailored version of a method for each of the receiver types [2]. *Type feedback* collects type information accumulated in *polymorphic inline caches,* and adaptively optimizes methods [15]. The Cecil language uses execution profiles off-line to selectively specialize methods [4], and to predict receiver types [12].

Selector code indexing reduces the cost of method lookup to that of array indexing. The approach assigns integers to selectors and constructs a *dispatch table* for each class. Given a pair of a selector and a receiver class, the method to be invoked is retrieved by referencing the dispatch table of the receiver class at the index assigned to the selector. This technique is commonly used in C++ implementations, but has not been considered a choice in the Smalltalk arena. The main reason, as we will explain in detail later, is that the space overhead created by dispatch tables is prohibitively high.

Research has therefore been done on how to compress dispatch tables. Some techniques use *selector coloring* [9, 1], while others use *row displacement compression* [7, 8]. However, when applied to commercial Smalltalk systems, even the best existing algorithm increases the sizes of the virtual images by more than 1.5 times.

What we propose here is a *dispatch cache indexed by selector code* (CISCO). The approach is based on the observation that most Smalltalk programs only use dozens of classes and selectors for a short period of time in execution. Specifically, we use a small number (for instance, 128) of dispatch tables with a small number (for instance, 64) of entries. The space overhead is thus a small constant, however many classes and selectors there are in a Smalltalk system.

---

[2] Actually, many important techniques have been developed in a pure object-oriented language, Self, and will hopefully also be applied in optimizing Smalltalk.

[3] We use type and class interchangeably here.

The remainder of the paper is organized as follows. Section 2 describes previous work based on selector code indexing. Section 3 explains our CISCO approach in detail, and Section 4 shows the simulation results using trace data of real Smalltalk programs. Section 5 describes our approach to previous work. Finally, Section 6 presents our conclusions and future directions.

## 2 Optimizations by Selector Code Indexing

Optimization by selector code indexing constructs a dispatch table for each class, and compiles a message send into something like the following pseudo-C code:

```
(*receiver->dispatchTable[code(selector)]])(receiver,arg1,arg2,...);
```

Here the code function maps a given selector to an integer value, and its choice is the key to applying selector code indexing.

Simply numbering all the selectors uniquely is totally prohibitive. For instance, Digitalk VisualSmalltalk Version 3.0 contains 1,596 classes and 10,025 different selectors. This implies that each class has a dispatch table of 10,025 words, and that the total memory consumption amounts to over 63 MB.

However, naively constructed dispatch tables contain a lot of empty entries. In VisualSmalltalk, for instance, a class understands only 240 selectors on average. Therefore, in optimizations using dispatch tables, strenuous efforts have been made to compress dispatch tables and to fill them as densely as possible. Two different techniques have been proposed: *selector coloring* and *row displacement compression*. We will describe them below, focusing on improvements in space overheads. In doing so, we will use a small class hierarchy, shown in Figure 1.

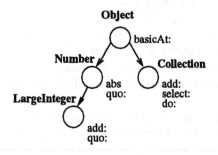

**Fig. 1.** A small class hierarchy

## 2.1 Selector Coloring

Selector coloring attempts to compress dispatch tables by sharing a code among selectors. Two selectors can be given the same code if and only if no class understands both. Finding a valid numbering is reduced to the problem of graph coloring, where nodes are selectors and arcs are drawn between two selectors if a class understands both of them. Figure 2 shows a coloring for the small class hierarchy. Actually, the coloring is optimal, giving the minimal number of colors.

| Colors | Selectors | |
|--------|-----------|---------|
| 1 | basicAt: | |
| 2 | abs | select: |
| 3 | quo: | do: |
| 4 | add: | |

**Fig. 2.** A coloring of selectors

When applied to commercial Smalltalk systems, selector coloring still produces empty entries at a rate of 40% to 60% in dispatch tables [8]. Besides, the incremental algorithm proposed in Andre and Roger [1] takes 9 hours on a Sun-3/80 to color 45,000 selectors of 766 classes in a Smalltalk system.

## 2.2 Row Displacement Compression

Row displacement compression attempts to fold naively constructed dispatch tables into a single long array by shifting each an appropriate amount [7]. The technique was originally proposed for compressing parse tables. See Figure 3.

The algorithm is also partially successful in reducing the space overhead. When applied to commercial Smalltalk systems, it still generates the same order of empty entries as selector coloring [8].

However, a variation can eliminate almost all the empty entries [8]. It builds a dispatch table not for each class but for each selector, and applies row displacement compression to these selector-based tables. The main reason for this amazing result is that the algorithm used prefers a large number of short tables to a small number of long tables.

Though the reduction is almost optimal, we could argue that it is not practically applicable. Table 1 compares optimal space overheads and virtual images in commercial Smalltalk systems. We estimate optimal space overheads by squeezing all the empty entries out of naively constructed dispatch tables. As the table shows, even the optimal algorithm makes virtual images more than 1.5 times larger; the overhead is too large for the algorithm to be used in a commercial system.

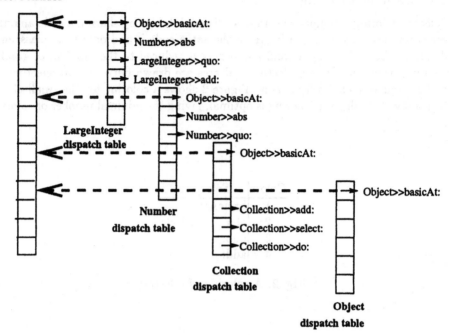

**Fig. 3.** A row displacement compression

| System | No. of Classes | No. of Selectors | Sizes of Virtual Images (MB) | Optimal Space Overhead (MB) |
|---|---|---|---|---|
| VisualSmalltalk 3.0 | 1,596 | 10,025 | 3.81 | 3.10 |
| VisualAge 2.0 | 3,241 | 17,509 | 7.12 | 7.69 |
| VisualWorks 2.0 | 1,910 | 12,196 | 4.77 | 2.47 |

**Table 1.** Comparing the sizes of virtual images and optimal space overheads in three commercial Smalltalk systems.

## 2.3 Selector Mismatch

Before we conclude this section, we discuss an important problem or event called a *selector mismatch*. As we will see in the next section, selector mismatches play a significant role in CISCO. A selector mismatch occurs when we compress dispatch tables, whether by selector coloring or by row displacement compression. Here we explain it in the context of selector coloring. Let us consider a message send such as aNumber quo: 7. Given the coloring in Figure 2, this message send is compiled into something like the following pseudo-C code:

```
(*aNumber->dispatchTable[3])(aNumber,7)
```

A problem occurs when aNumber erroneously holds an instance of Collection. Since a Collection is being sent to the message with quo:, the DoesNotUnderstand exception must be raised. However, the compiled code totally overlooks this, and causes the do: method of Collection to be invoked.

Dixon et al. [9] suggest assigning selectors unique numbers to detect and recover from a selector mismatch; here we call such unique numbers *selector cards*. When a method is created, the card of the selector is also stored in the method. Just before we attempt to make an indirect call through a dispatch table, we match the card of the message selector and that stored in the method looked up. The above pseudo-C code is now as follows, where we assume that the selector quo: is assigned the card 26.

```
method = aNumber->dispatchTable[3];
if (method->selectorCard == 26/* card of quo:*/)
  (*method)(aNumber,7)
else
  SelectorMismatchHandler(...);
```

In this example, the handler will simply raise the DoesNotUnderstand exception

Maintaining selector cards is not expensive. For instance, we can simply augment the existing symbol table to include the task of maintaining the card.

## 3 Dispatch Cache Indexed By Selector Code

The main reason for the prohibitive cost of space and time in conventional approaches is that a code is assigned to every selector and a dispatch table is built for every class. However, as the theory of locality suggests, it is very likely that, in most Smalltalk programs, a small number of selectors and classes are involved in message sends for each short period of time in execution.

This observation leads to our basic idea of *dispatch caches indexed by selector codes* (CISCO). We assign codes to a limited number of selectors at each point of time in execution. Accordingly, the size of a CISCO is limited to that number. Furthermore, we construct dispatch caches for a limited number of classes at each point of time in execution. The space overhead is therefore a small constant, however many classes and selectors exist in a Smalltalk system. Obviously, both the set of selectors with codes and the set of classes having dispatch caches are dynamically changed; we maintain dispatch caches for *hot* classes, and fill entries for *hot* selectors.

The rest of the section describes the details of the approach. We assume that the base Smalltalk system is implemented as a bytecode interpreter, as described in Goldberg and Robson [11]. However, the overall discussion is applicable to other Smalltalk systems such as those based on dynamic compilation.

## 3.1 Data Structures in Virtual Image

We define two additional instance variables, `card` for the `CompiledMethod` class and `dispatchCache` for the `Behavior` class. The former is initialized to hold the card of the selector of a method, when the method is created. The latter is used to store a dispatch cache, and initially points to the default dispatch cache. The entries of the default dispatch cache are all filled with a special method, named `selectorMismatchRaiser` (see Figure 4). The intention is to make any initial attempt to invoke a method through the default dispatch cache end up with a selector mismatch. Note that the card stored in the special method is not equal to the one in any normal method.

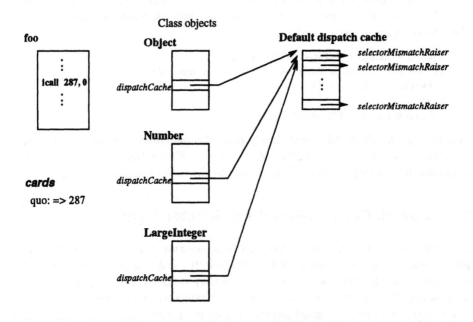

**Fig. 4.** Initial Virtual Image

Each message send is compiled into a new bytecode named `icall`. The instruction takes two arguments, the card and the code of the message selector.

Though the code is not yet assigned at code generation, any valid index in a dispatch cache can be used as the selector code. In addition, since we do not use the **send** bytecodes any more, we can simply reuse the **send** bytecode ranges for our purpose. In addition, we can define short forms of **icall** instructions for arithmetics and heavily used selectors, just like the **send** bytecodes in Goldberg and Robson [11], thereby minimizing their impact on the existing code generation scheme.

## 3.2 Caching Activities

The execution of message sends is realized by two functions in the virtual machine, **vmicall** and **selectorMismatchHandler**. In executing message sends, the functions control both caching activities and cache consistency management. We leave the latter until the next subsection, and focus on the former, namely, how dispatch cache entries are incrementally filled in the course of execution.

As an example, let us consider the **icall** instruction of the method **foo** in Figure 4; the selector is **quo:**, and the card is 287. Assume that the instruction is about to be executed against an instance of the class **LargeInteger**. The **vmicall** function attempts to execute it by making an indirect invocation through the dispatch cache of **LargeInteger**. However, since the dispatch cache is simply the default cache, a selector mismatch occurs, and control is transferred to the **selectorMismatchHandler**. See also Figure 3.2, which shows the details of what **vmicall** does.

```
void vmicall(OOP card, Byte code){
    // Get the receiver from the stack
    OOP receiver=....;
    // Perform a quick method lookup by array indexing.
    Method method=receiver->klass->dispatchCache[code];

    // Check cards if a selector mismatch does not happen.
    if (method->card != card)
        method=selectorMismatchHandler(receiver->klass,card, code);

    // Invoke the method.
    invoke(method);
}
```

**Fig. 5.** Execution of an **icall** instruction

The handler first allocates a dispatch cache for the class **LargeInteger**, and obtains a code for the selector **quo**. It then performs a general lookup, and stores the method found in the dispatch cache at the selector code. Finally, before it returns, it backpatches the code portion of the **icall** instruction. Figure 6 shows the result; we assume that the code 2 was assigned to the selector.

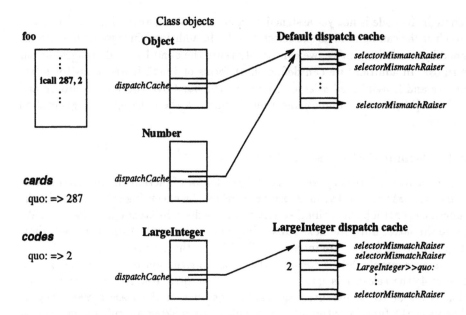

**Fig. 6.** Virtual image just after the **icall** instruction has been executed against a **LargeInteger**.

Let us continue the example and consider the subsequent executions of the same instruction. Thanks to backpatching, if the receiver class is the same, a fast lookup with array indexing in the **vmicall** function always produces a correct method. If the receiver class is different, the execution nicely results in a selector mismatch, followed by almost the same caching activities as described above. Figure 7 shows the virtual image after the same instruction has been executed again, but this time against an instance of **Number**.

The selector mismatch handler is described in more detail in Figure 3.2. The handler first checks whether the class currently has its own dispatch cache. If not, the handler calls the **allocDispatchCache** function, which manages a memory region for dispatch caches. The function looks for a free dispatch cache from the region, and initializes all the entries with **selectorMismatchRaiser**. When the region is full, the function makes room by choosing a victim class. In this case, it reinitializes **dispatchCache** of the victim class to the default dispatch cache.

The handler obtains the selector code by calling the **getSelectorCode** function, which manages the assignment of codes to selectors. If a code is currently assigned to the selector, the function returns the code. Otherwise, it searches for a free code, and records the assignment of the code to the selector. This may require that the function first makes a code free by choosing a victim selector and canceling the assignment to the victim.

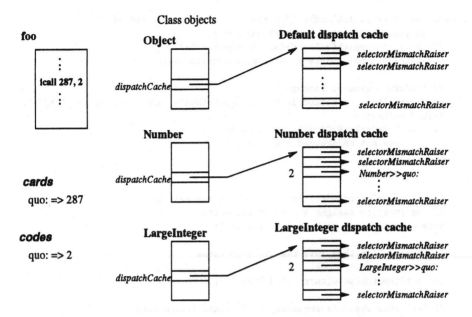

**Fig. 7.** Virtual image just after the `icall` instruction has been executed again, but this time against a **Number**.

## 3.3  Consistency Management

During the course of execution, as we have seen, dispatch caches are removed from classes and code assignments are taken away from selectors. The removal of a class's dispatch cache causes no serious problem, since at the time of removal the dispatch cache manager resets the instance variable `dispatchCache` to point to the default dispatch cache. Thus, executing a `icall` instruction against the class later results in a selector mismatch; in this case, the handler reallocates a dispatch cache for the class.

On the other hand, canceling a code assignment to a selector creates inconsistencies in the virtual image that are severe at first glance, since the handler has backpatched some of the `icall` instructions by using the code assignment. If we had to undo such backpatches each time a code assignment was canceled, it would introduce an additional cost for managing dependencies or performing an exhaustive scan of all the methods in a system. Either way, it might completely offset the performance gains achieved by our approach.

Fortunately, we do not have to eagerly fix inconsistencies at all. Actually, we do not have to do anything. The selector mismatch handler, as defined in Figure 3.2, detects and fixes inconsistencies *incrementally*. As an example, see Figure 9. The `icall` instruction in the method **goo** has just been executed; the selector is **add:**, and the message was sent to a **LargeInteger**. We also assume

```
Method selectorMismatchHandler(OOP klass, OOP card, Byte code){
    // Allocate a dispatch cache if necessary.
    if (klass->dispatchCache==defaultDispatchCache)
        klass->dispatchCache=allocDispatchCache(klass);

    // Perform a general lookup.
    // Obviously, if a method is found, the method's card is equal to ''card''.
    Method method;
    if ((method=lookupByCard(klass, card))==0){
        // Does not understand the message.
        ...;
    }

    // Ask getSelectorCode() for the code of the selector.
    // The function assigns a code if necessary.
    Byte currentCode = getSelectorCode(card);

    // Stores the method into the dispatch cache
    // at the selector code.
    klass->dispatchCache[currentCode]=method;

    // Backpatch the code argument of the icall instruction
    // if necessary.
    if (currentCode!=code){
        instructionPointer[-1]=currentCode.
    }
    return method;
}
```

**Fig. 8.** Handling of a selector mismatch

that the assignment to the selector quo: was canceled, and that the code freed was assigned to the selector add:. Thus, the method of LargeInteger>>add: is stored at the index 2 in the dispatch cache of LargeInteger.

The icall instruction in the method foo depends on the canceled assignment. Let us consider what happens if the instruction is executed against a LargeInteger. The vmicall function retrieves the method at the index 2 from the dispatch cache. Since the card in the instruction is different from that in the method, it results in a selector mismatch. In the handler, a code is reassigned to the selector quo:, the method LargeInteger>>quo: is stored at the new code, and the instruction being executed is backpatched again according to the new code. Figure 10 shows the result.

Finally, notice not only that inconsistencies are incrementally fixed, but also that they are fixed only for the instructions actually executed; we do not have to waste time by dealing with instructions that are never executed.

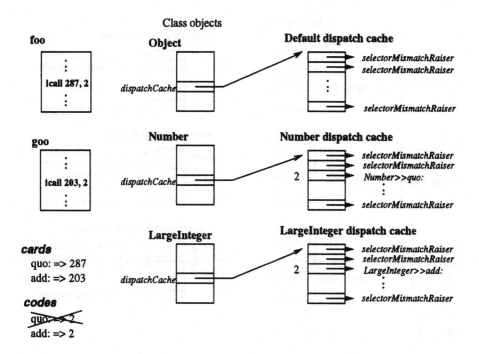

**Fig. 9.** An inconsistency has been created by cancelling a code assignment. The assignment to the selector quo: was canceled, and the code freed was assigned to the selector add:.

## 3.4 Invariants

So far, we have described the system behavior rather informally. Here we put it into a more formal perspective. First, we show the invariant that each entry $e$ in the dispatch cache of class $C$ stratifies.

- The entry $e$ contains a normal method $m$ and $m = lookupByCard(C, m->card)$.
- Otherwise, $e$ contains a special method such as **selectorMismatchRaiser**.

The invariant holds, since a dispatch cache entry is filled only in the selector mismatch handler, as in Figure 3.2.

Let us consider the execution of the following **icall** instruction against the class $C$, and ensure that the **vmicall** function always invokes the correct method.

    icall card, code

Let $m$ be $C-> dispatchCache[code]$. Whether $m$ is a normal method or the special method, if a selector mismatch is detected, the handler finds a correct method at any rate. Otherwise, $m-> card$ must be equal to $card$. Together

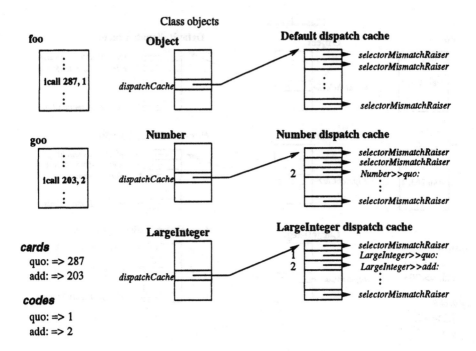

**Fig. 10.** The inconsistency has been fixed lazily. The instruction in the method foo had been executed. The inconsistency was detected as a selector mismatch, and a new code has been assigned to the selector add:.

with the invariant, this shows that $m = lookupByCard(C, card)$. That is, $m$ is the correct method to be invoked.

Notice that the invariant does not specify that the card of $m$ must have any particular relationship with the index at which $m$ is stored. Surprisingly, this means that, whatever the current code assignments are, and whatever the past code assignments were, the system behaves correctly. The selector mismatch handler actually uses the code assignment to a selector both as an index for storing a method in a dispatchCache, and as a code for backpatching an icall instruction with. However, it does so for efficiency but not for correctness.

### 3.5 Responsiveness to Smalltalk Dynamics

A system based on CISCO can respond to any change to a program quickly enough for use in an interactive environment. First, it is obvious that, when a new class is added, we do not need any special treatment.

When a method is deleted, all we have to do is to overwrite the card of the method as that of a special method. The above invariant is thus still maintained, and calling the deleted method ends up with a selector mismatch. The handler will perform a general lookup, but will not be able to find an appropriate method. As for the deletion of a class, we can treat this as equivalent to deleting the methods of the class.

When a new method is defined in a class, more work is required, since the addition may affect the lookup results, and some entries can no longer satisfy the above invariant. Therefore, we have to remove all such entries from the dispatch caches. A complication is that we do not know the exact indices of such invalid entries in dispatch caches; such an entry is not necessarily at the code currently assigned to the selector of the newly defined method.

The simplest solution is to reset all the dispatch caches of the subclasses of $C$ to the default dispatch cache. We can keep the system responsive, at the cost of selector mismatches in a later execution.

### 3.6 Variations

CISCO can be combined with selector coloring, where the `getSelectorCode` function maintains code assignments so that it assigns a code to more than one selector as long as every class understands at most one of them. The more selectors are simultaneously assigned codes, the fewer code assignments are canceled. The number of selectors is reduced accordingly, and the performance is expected to be further improved.

Obviously, the cost of the coloring must be taken into account. We think that it is small enough, since only hot selectors must be colored, and their conflicts have to be determined solely on the basis of hot classes.

Notice that the discussion about the invariant shows that the correct behavior does not depend on the code assignments, and thus does not depend on the code assignment algorithm; the system still also behaves correctly under selector coloring.

Before concluding the section, let us consider briefly the application of CISCO to a system using dynamic compilation. We can apply the overall framework discussed so far with the following minor modifications. First, a message send is compiled into a sequence of machine code that loads the address of the dispatch cache and makes an indirect call through an entry; any valid index can be used as an initial value. Second, each machine code version of a method contains the preamble, which checks two cards, one passed as a parameter and the other stored in itself. Third, the entries in the default dispatch cache and a new dispatch cache are initialized to the address of the selector mismatch handler. Finally, the handler stores in the dispatch cache the address of the method looked up, and backpatches the indirect call instruction by using the selector code.

## 4 Performance Estimations

We have estimated the effectiveness of CISCO by first tracing message sends in real programs, and then running a simulator against the data obtained. We used a UNIX port of Squeak [17] as the base system. Squeak is a rapid prototyping environment from Apple Research Laboratory, based on a full-fledged implementation of Smalltalk with more than 650 classes. We built the system under AIX 4.1 after making a few modifications so that we could trace each message send. Each line of trace data consists of the caller method, the current instruction point, the receiver class, the message selector, and the callee method.

Tables 2 and 3 summarize the programs we traced and their runtime statistics, respectively. Notice that primitive message sends are counted only when they fail. The reason for this is that, unless they fail, primitive message sends have already been optimized by methods such as "type prediction," and should not be the target of optimization by CISCO.

| Program | Description |
|---|---|
| browser | Opened up a new browser window for the class *Browser*, and visited four methods of two categories. |
| fileIn | Filed in 1,184 lines of source file generated below. This exercised the Smalltalk compiler. |
| fileOut | Filed out the class *CCodeGenerator*. |
| senders | Computed all the senders of *#open*, which resulted in 29 methods. |
| implementors | Computed all the implementors of: *#at : put :*, which resulted in 15 methods. |

**Table 2.** Description of programs measured

| Program | No. of message sends | No. of receiver classes | No. of selectors | No. of methods | No. of call sites |
|---|---|---|---|---|---|
| browser | 1,213,525 | 161 | 652 | 904 | 2,223 |
| fileIn | 384,846 | 129 | 519 | 669 | 1,528 |
| fileOut | 9,495 | 49 | 170 | 213 | 393 |
| senders | 37,347 | 341 | 44 | 56 | 64 |
| implementors | 3,783 | 343 | 43 | 52 | 59 |

**Table 3.** Runtime statistics of programs studied

The CISCO simulator processes trace data obtained in the abovementioned way and reports the number of major events, including selector mismatches, code assignment cancels, and backpatches. It uses a simple FIFO-based eviction rule to manage both dispatch caches (in the `allocDispatchCache` function) and selector codes (in the `getSelectorCode` function), while it can vary the number of available dispatch caches and selector codes. It consists of about 600 lines of Java code.

For each program, we simulated the mismatch ratios, varying the numbers of dispatch caches and selector codes. Notice that all the simulations were cold-started. The results are shown in Figures 11 to 15. For the *browser* and *fileIn* programs, performance improvements are almost saturated at the combination of 128 caches and 64 codes, where the mismatch ratios are less than 1.0%.

The *fileOut* program shows relatively high ratios that are not significantly changed by increasing the numbers of available caches and codes. Because of cold starts, every call site raises a mismatch when the send instruction there is first executed. This leads to 393 mismatches in the *fileOut* program, which account for most of the mismatches in each simulation. This is not the case in warm-started simulations whose results are also shown in Figure 13. For each set of trace data, the simulator was fed the date twice, and mismatches were collected only from the second run.

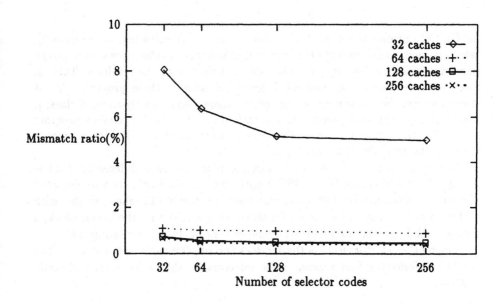

**Fig. 11.** Selector mismatch ratio in the *browser* program

The *senders* and *implementors* programs have characteristics unsuitable

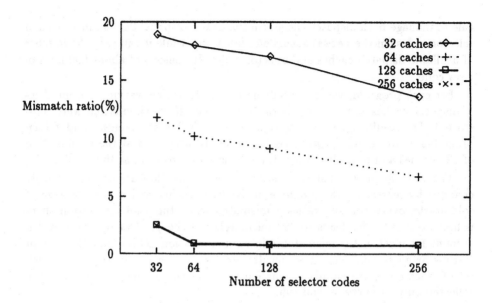

**Fig. 12.** Selector mismatch ratio in the *fileIn* program

for CISCO optimizations. Each contains *megamorphic* call sites, where message selectors, such as `includesSelector:` and `allSubclassesDo:`, are sent to all the `Behavior` classes in the system. This also coincides with the results in Table 3; more receiver classes are involved in fewer call sites in these programs. What is even worse, the *implementors* program "stays" very shortly at each class; it sends 5.97 messages on average during each stay, whereas the *senders* program sends 53.7 messages on average. This accounts for the extremely high mismatch ratios in the *implementors* program.

Our solution is to handle such megamorphic call sites differently; that is to say, we exclude them from CISCO optimization. Such sites can be detected statically or dynamically. For instance, a message send of `allBehaviorsDo:` with a literal block is a good candidate for static analysis. Within the literal block, a message send against the block argument is very likely to be megamorphic.

Among the selectors used in the *senders* and *implementors* programs, we can detect the following four megamorphic selectors by the abovementioned static analysis.

```
allSubclassesDo: subclassesDo: includesSelector:
whichSelectorsReferTo:special:byte:
```

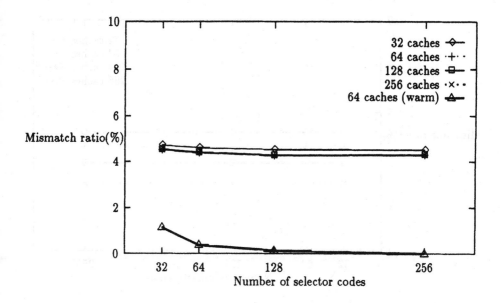

**Fig. 13.** Selector mismatch ratio in the *fileOut* program

| Program | No. of message sends | No. of receiver classes | No. of selectors | No. of methods | No. of call sites |
|---------|--------|--------|--------|--------|--------|
| senders | 35,051 | 40 | 41 | 54 | 58 |
| implementors | 1,497 | 32 | 40 | 50 | 53 |

**Table 4.** Runtime statistics of the *senders* and *implementors* after megamorphic call sites have been removed.

Table 4 shows the two programs' runtime statistics obtained by excluding these megamorphic selectors. The simulations against these new trace data show that, even with the minimal configuration of 32 caches and 32 selectors, the mismatch ratio in the *senders* program is improved to less than 0.5%. On the other hand, the mismatch ratio in the *implementors* program is improved to 4.61% with the same configuration, and to 0.13% if the simulation is warm-started.

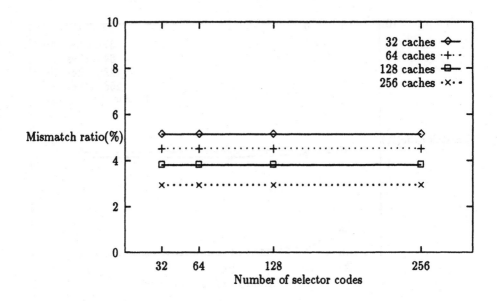

**Fig. 14.** Selector mismatch ratio in the *senders* program

## 5 Related Work and Discussion

A lookup cache also speeds up method lookup, and is consulted by using a hash value computed from a selector and/or a receiver class [11]. On the other hand, a CISCO is referenced in exactly the same way as array indexing, and as a result the successful lookup is much faster. Furthermore, upon dynamic compilation, a system using a lookup cache usually compiles a message send into a call to the lookup routine. On the other hand, a system using CISCO generates for each send a short sequence of machine code for indexing into a dispatch table.

As mentioned in Section 2, a major concern in optimizations based on dispatch tables has been the space overhead of dispatch tables. Selector coloring compresses dispatch tables by sharing a code with more than one selector [9, 1]. Row displacement compression reduces the size of dispatch tables by fitting them into a single long array [7, 8]. However, even the best existing algorithm [8] makes virtual images more than 1.5 times larger when applied in commercial Smalltalk systems. On the other hand, CISCO simply involves a constant space overhead of as little as 32K bytes, regardless of how many classes and selectors exist in a Smalltalk system, while it preserves a constant lookup time in most method lookups.

Furthermore, all the existing techniques require a global reorganization when

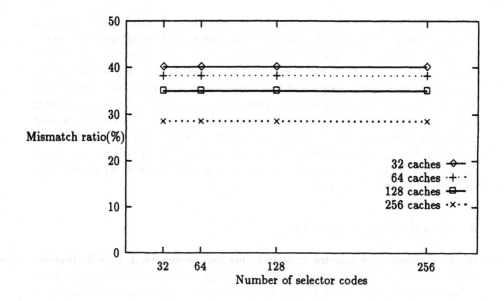

**Fig. 15.** Selector mismatch ratio in the *implementors* program

some change is made to a program. For instance, addition of a new class to a system using selector-based row displacement compression [8] necessitates a refitting of all the dispatch tables. CISCO does not depend on any global view, and is able to keep the system responsive all the time. As explained in Section 3.5, even in the worst case, the system only has to reset a small constant number of instance variables for dispatch caches to the default dispatch cache.

Static binding brings a greater performance improvement, especially when combined with inlining. The major concern here is the implementation effort. First, the system needs to keep track of dependency relationships between source code and optimized code, since a program change invalidates information that has been used to statically bind a method at a message send site; if such a change is made, the static binding has to be undone. Second, the system needs to *deoptimize* code on demand in order to provide the semantics explicitly described in the source code, even if the code is optimized [14].

These issues are not necessarily still open, and good solutions have been proposed and implemented [3, 14]. However, they require substantial implementation efforts, especially if they are implemented in existing Smalltalk systems. We have heard that most Smalltalk vendors are interested in applying Self-like optimizations, but, as far as we know, no vendor has completed an implementation yet. This is evidence of how tough the implementation is. On the other hand,

CISCO is as easy to implement as the method using dispatch tables, and can thus be considered as a good short-term solution in optimizing message sends.

As revealed in Section 4, megamorphic message sends do not fit into CISCO optimization. Notice that their runtime behaviors are also very unsuitable for optimizations by inline caches and PIC; at any rate, they must be optimized differently. The best way to optimize megamorphic message sends is to use dispatch tables that only accommodate those megamorphic selectors. For each class, such a dispatch table can be built statically for a predefined set of megamorphic selectors or filled dynamically for "hot" megamorphic selectors. When the latter approach is taken, it is regarded as a variation of CISCO in which only the number of selectors is limited.

# 6 Concluding Remarks

We have shown that selector code indexing can be practical. CISCO imposes a small constant space overhead, however many classes and selectors there are in Smalltalk systems, while by and large maintaining the runtime efficiency of dispatch tables. In addition, it is very easy to implement.

An interesting possible future direction is to apply CISCO to statically typed object-oriented languages, such as C++ and Java. Message sends are usually implemented in these languages by using dispatch tables. However, the more large class libraries applications reply on, the more space the dispatch tables consume. CISCO can be used to improve the space efficiency while keeping applications almost as efficient as in dispatch tables. Furthermore, it matches Java's capabilities for loading classes over networks by allowing for a selective loading of methods, without wasting space by allocating complete method tables.

# Acknowledgments

We would like to thank Mikio Takeuchi and Kevin O'Brien for their helpful discussions. We are also grateful to anonymous reviewers for their valuable comments.

# References

1. Pascal Andre and Jean-Claude Royer. Optimizing Method Search with Lookup Caches and Incremental Coloring. *OOPSLA '92 Conference Proceedings* pp. 110-126.
2. Craig Chambers and David Ungar. Customization: Optimizing Compiler Technology for SELF, a Dynamically-Typed Object-Oriented Programming Language. *Proceedings of the SIGPLAN '89 Conference on Programming Language Design and Implementation* pp. 146-180.
3. Craig Chambers, Jeffrey Dean, and David Grove. A Framework for Selective Recompilation in the Presence of Complex Intermodule Dependencies. *17th International Conference on Software Engineering* 1995.

4. Jeffrey Dean, Craig Chambers, and David Grove. Selective Specialization for Object-Oriented Languages. *Proceedings of the SIGPLAN '95 Conference on Programming Language Design and Implementation* pp. 93-102.

5. Jeffrey Dean, David Grove, and Craig Chambers. Optimization of Object-Oriented Programs Using Static Hierarchy Analysis. *Proceeding of ECOOP '95*

6. L. Peter Deutsch and Alan Schiffman. Efficient Implementation of the Smalltalk-80 System. *Proceeding of the 11th Symposium on the Principles of Programming Languages* 1984, pp. 297-302.

7. Karel Driesen. Selector Table Indexing & Sparse Arrays. *OOPSLA '93 Conference Proceedings* pp. 259-270.

8. Karel Driesen and Urs Hölzle. Minimizing Row Displacement Dispatch Tables. *OOPSLA '95 Conference Proceedings* pp. 141-155.

9. R. Dixon, T. McKee, P. Schweizer, and M. Vaughan. A Fast Method Dispatcher for Compiled Languages with Multiple Inheritance. *OOPSLA '89 Conference Proceedings* pp. 211-214.

10. Patrick H. Dussud. TICLOS: An Implementation of CLOS for the Explore Family. *OOPSLA '89 Conference Proceedings* pp. 215-219.

11. Adele Goldberg and David Robson. *Smalltalk-80: The Language and Its Implementation.* Addison-Wesley, 1983.

12. David Grove, Jeffrey Dean, Charles Garrett, and Craig Chambers. Profile-Guided Receiver Class Prediction. *OOPSLA '95 Conference Proceedings* pp. 107-122.

13. Urs Hölzle, Craig Chambers, and David Ungar. Optimizing Dynamically Typed Object-Oriented languages With Polymorphic Inline Caches. *ECOOP '91 Conference Proceedings*

14. Urs Hölzle, Craig Chambers, and David Ungar. Debugging Optimized Code with Dynamic Deoptimization. *Proceedings of the SIGPLAN '92 Conference on Programming Language Design and Implementation* pp. 32-43.

15. Urs Hölzle and David Ungar. Optimizing Dynamically-Dispatched Calls with Run-Time Type Feedback. *Proceedings of the SIGPLAN '94 Conference on Programming Language Design and Implementation* pp. 146-180.

16. Next. *Concepts: Objective-C Release 3.1.* Next Computer Inc., 1993.

17. Ted Kaehler. *Apple Research Labs Releases Prototype of "Squeak".* http://www.research.apple.com/research/proj/Learning_Concepts/squeak/intro.html

# Objects, Associations and Subsystems: A Hierarchical Approach to Encapsulation

J.C. Bicarregui, K.C. Lano, T.S.E. Maibaum

Imperial College, London

**Abstract.** We describe a compositional approach to the formal interpretation of type view diagrams and statecharts. We define theories for object instances and classes, and theories for associations between them. These theories are combined with categorical constructions to yield a formalisation of the entire system.

We observe that some notations require the identification of theories intermediate between the theories of the constituent classes and associations and that of the entire system. This leads us to propose a notion of subsystem which generalises the concept of object and yields an approach to system specification employing object-like encapsulation in a nested hierachy of components[1].

## 1 Introduction

The combination of data encapsulation through the aggregation of related attributes, and instance identity to distinguish separate occurrences of that encapsulated data is a powerful feature of the object oriented paradigm. Objects provide a convenient way to group related attributes (eg: a table has a length, a width and a height), Object Identifiers (OIds) give us the ability to model the distinct existence of two or more instances with exactly the same characteristics (two tables may have the same attributes but still be different tables).

The indirection implicit in the use of OIds is then exploited to distinguish attributes which are themselves objects from attributes which are (pure) values. We will use the terms "reference attributes" and "value attributes" for these respectively. An example of the use of reference attributes is in structural decomposition of an object. For example if a table has four legs and a top, then a particular table object, *table23*, may comprise of four particular leg objects, *leg12*, *leg13*, *leg14*, *leg15*, and a top, *top27*. Examples of pure attributes are the height, length and width of the table given above.

Properties of objects can relate both pure attributes and reference attributes indiscriminately. For example a long table might be one that is more than twice as long as it is wide, a level table must have the four legs of the same length, and the height of the table is the length of the legs plus the depth of the top, etc.

---

[1] This work is being undertaken by the UK EPSRC project "Formal Underpinnings of Object Technology".

In most Object Oriented Analysis and Design notations value attributes are considered to be part of the object itself, whereas reference attributes are given via associations between objects. Associations are therefore a separate modelling tool in the Object Oriented designers toolbox. Opinions differ as to whether associations should themselves be objects with their own object identities, whether associations are a separate primitive concept which should have identities (AIds), or whether associations should be *pure* constructions without identities.

Associations-as-objects yield an economy of form and a uniform approach to modelling but may be confusing two separate purposes. Associations with AIds enable the distinction of two copies of the same association between the same objects. Pure associations enable a value-based approach to equality and do not require the overhead of indirection in construction.

More generally, the same issues arise when we collect objects together in larger aggregations. The concept of "subsystem" can be adopted as a means to provide coarse grained modularity in OO design. Subsystems can be defined using the class-instance approach as for objects, they can be managed by coordinating objects and they can be units of encapsulation in the same way as objects. Subsystems can provide a structure in which properties of collections of objects can be defined at the appropriate level without complete globalisation (as in Fusion operation schemas [4]) or over localisation (as in Syntropy statecharts [5]). If subsystems are considered to be first class objects, then they yield the possibility of developing a nested hierarchy of levels of granularity and hence a compositional approach to vertical structuring.

An open question is whether there is merit in attributing identifiers to instances of subsystems (SIds) in the way that Oids are given to object instances. In this paper we adopt the position that a hierarchical approach to structuring designs is essential if large designs are not to be subject to an exponential increase in complexity. We therefore separate the concerns of aggregation (as embodied in objects and associations) and instance identity (as embodied in OIds) and formally define the concept of subsystem as a first class construction and argue that it is a generalisation of the familiar concept of both object and association.

The ideas presented here have arisen out of the formalisation of the "Syntropy" approach to object oriented analysis and design which has shown that many existing notations, although sometimes attributed to object classes, need to be formalised at a level in between objects and systems. In structuring the formal interpretation of system diagrams to formalise these notations, it becomes clear that their representation as part of an object class is inappropriate and that their interpretation at a higher level is more justified.

Two examples we will examine in this paper are the **RadioButton** example of [5], and an example of multiple constraints between associations. The radio button example of [5] highlights the lack of clarity which can arise as a result of enforced local (to objects) behaviour specification. The Syntropy statechart in this case is shown in Figure 1. The **true** filter in the event list indicates that *every* existing object of **RadioButton** may react to the **turn_on** event. The way in which they react depends upon whether they are the button being pressed (**x** = **self**) and what their current state is. It is not immediately evident from

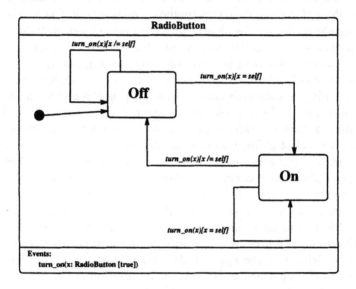

**Fig. 1.** Statechart of Radio Button

this diagram that in fact, after a **turn_on(x)** event, that *only* **x** will be in the **On** state, and all other existing radio buttons will be in the **Off** state. Nor is it clear that actually the final state of an object depends only on whether it is **x**, and not on its starting state. We examine more abstract and design-free versions of this specification in Section 3.

Similarly, because Syntropy, OMT or Fusion defines no level of structuring between individual classes and entire systems (or domains), constraints between associations and between attributes of different classes are expressed via navigation expressions and invariants which are local to particular classes. Such localisation may be arbitrary (the expressions and invariants could just as well be written in other classes) and may therefore reduce the clarity and abstraction of the specifications concerned.

For example, consider Figure 2. Here there are two alternative ways of expressing the constraint that every student taught by a college is either an external student or lives at the college. As an invariant of **College** we could write:

**teaches ⊆ accomodates ∪ external_students**

As an invariant of **Student** we could alternatively express it as:

**external_at = taught_at ∨ lives_at = taught_at**

Subset constraints could alternatively be used between associations. Again, we will give a more abstract presentation of this situation using subsystems in Section 3.

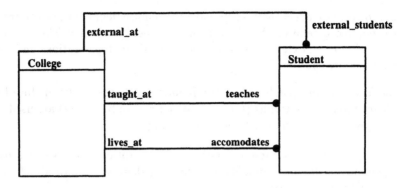

**Fig. 2.** Subsystem Example

## Overview

In Section 2, the major part of this work, we describe a hierarchical formalisation of the Syntropy diagrammatic notations where each diagrammatic component is interpreted separately and the system description is built in a compositional way from these separate interpretations. We observe how many of the constructions are naturally interpreted in theories which correspond to identified parts of the overall system. In Section 3 we propose the notion of subsystem as a "first class object" which generalises the concept of object and yields a hierarchical approach to encapsulation where subsystems are nested one inside the other. Section 4 concludes with a summary of the achievements so far and discusses further work required.

## 2 Formalising Syntropy

### 2.1 Syntropy

Syntropy [5] is a methodology for object-oriented analysis and design similar to OMT [14] with additional formal specification elements derived from Z[15]. It represents a significant advance over previous object-oriented methods in giving mathematical specifications of data models and dynamic behaviour.

Three distinct levels of modelling are used in Syntropy. At each of these three levels, type view diagrams depict the structure of object classes. Objects have attributes of non-object types. Associations between classes are depicted by connecting lines. Statecharts [10] are also used at each of the three levels. However, different models of communication are used at each level of abstraction.

- *Essential models* describe the problem domain of the application. They describe the system as a whole including the proposed software solution and its environment. They use events to abstract from the localisation of methods in classes.

- *Specification models* abstractly model the requirements of the software application, hence defining the software/environment boundary. They decompose a reaction to an external event into a series of event generations and internal reactions by specific classes.

- *implementation models* model the required software in detail. In addition, object interaction graphs (termed *mechanisms* in Syntropy) are used at this level, with object to object message passing.

Syntropy adopts a number of mathematical notations, however, a semantics is only indicated for data models. In addition, there is no formal definition of refinement between models.

## 2.2 The Object Calculus

The Object Calculus [7] is a formalism based on structured first order theories composed by morphisms between them.

An object calculus theory models a component of a system. It consists of a set $S$ of constant symbols, a set $A$ of *attribute symbols* (denoting time-varying data) and a set $G$ of *action symbols* (denoting atomic operations). Axioms describe the types of the attributes and dynamic properties of the actions.

A global, discrete linear model of time is adopted (eg. [12]) and axioms are specified using temporal logic operators including: $\bigcirc$ (in the next state), $\bullet$ (in the previous state), $\mathcal{U}$ (strong until), $\mathcal{S}$ (strong since), $\square$ (always in the future), $\blacksquare$ (always in the past), $\diamond$ (sometime in the future) and $\blacklozenge$ (sometime in the past). The predicate **BEG** is true exactly at the first moment. For the purposes of this paper only the "next" temporal operator will be required.

The temporal operators are also expression constructors. If e is an expression, $\bigcirc$e denotes the value of e in the next time interval, etc.

In the style of [9], theories are composed by morphisms to yield a modular definition of a whole system. The Object Calculus defines a notion of locality which ensures that only actions local to a particular theory can effect the value of the local attributes. For each theory we have a logical axiom

$$\bigvee_{g_i \in G} g_i \quad \vee \quad \bigwedge_{a \in A} a = \bigcirc a$$

"Either some action $g_i$ of the theory executes in the current interval, or every attribute a of the theory remains unchanged in value over the interval."

## 2.3 Interpreting Object Types

Figure 3 depicts a fragment of a Syntropy type view diagram. A single class, **A**, is defined with two attributes, **f** and **g**, of (non-object) types $T_1$ and $T_2$ respectively[2].

---

[2] Note object-typed attributes are given via associations, see Section 2.4.

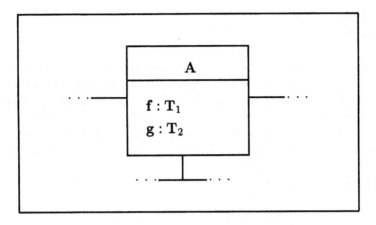

**Fig. 3.** Part of a type view diagram

Such a diagram can be understood as a view of a typical object of the type, or it can be interpreted as depicting the entire class of such objects. To interpret this diagram, we define two Object Calculus theories. The first gives the theory of a single instance of the type, the second manages the collection of currently existing instances. A number of the former are then combined with the latter to form the theory of the class.

*The signature of a generic instance* We define a theory, $\mathbf{A_i}$ for a typical object of this class. The theory of the instance introduces a sort for the type of each attribute, there are no constant (or function) symbols and, for each attribute, there is an attribute symbol for each attribute. For the present, there are no actions, we will later use information in the statechart to define the actions.

$$\mathcal{S} = \{\mathbf{T_1, T_2}\}$$
$$\mathcal{A} = \{\mathbf{f : T_1, g : T_2}\}$$
$$\mathcal{G} = \{\ldots\}$$

*self* A key technique used in OO notations is that an individual object can refer to itself as **self** whilst it's external identity (its object identifier) is given by the class. As in [8], we interpret **self** using **A**-morphisms which add the object identifier as an extra parameter when attributes and actions are globalised (see Section 2.3).

*The signature of the class* The creation and deletion of instances is accomplished through a class manager. Class manager and class instances are then combined to form the theory of the class. The definition of the class manager is independent of the structure of **A** and so is defined in terms of a general class type **X**.

The class manager theory, **M**, introduces a sort for identifiers of objects, @**X** and no constant symbols. It is convenient to define an attribute, $\overline{\mathbf{X}}$, to record the finite set of currently existing instances. In terms of [16], @**C** is $\mathbf{ext(C)}$ and the value of $\overline{\mathbf{C}}$ at time $\pi$ is $\mathbf{ext_\pi(C)}$. There are actions of **M** to create and kill objects of **X**.

$$\mathcal{S} = \{\, @\mathbf{X} \,\}$$
$$\mathcal{A} = \{\, \overline{\mathbf{X}} : \mathbb{F}@\mathbf{X} \,\}$$
$$\mathcal{G} = \{\, \mathbf{create} : @\mathbf{X}, \mathbf{kill} : @\mathbf{X} \,\}$$

Note that creating an instance does not initialise it. Creation and initialisation can be brought together via an action **new** which synchronises them.

We cannot create an existing object nor delete a non-existent one[3] (*pre-create* and *pre-kill*). Creation adds an object to the set of existing objects and deletion removes it (*post-create* and *post-kill*). We require that objects are only added or removed from the set of existing objects by creation and deletion. These six conditions can be condensed to:

$$\mathbf{create}(\mathbf{x}) \;\Leftrightarrow\; \mathbf{x} \notin \overline{\mathbf{X}} \wedge \mathbf{x} \in \bigcirc\overline{\mathbf{X}}$$
$$\mathbf{kill}(\mathbf{x}) \;\Leftrightarrow\; \mathbf{x} \in \overline{\mathbf{X}} \wedge \mathbf{x} \notin \bigcirc\overline{\mathbf{X}}$$

which concisely characterise the two actions.

We may wish to give an initialisation stating, for example, that the set of existing objects is initially empty (*initialisation*)

$$\mathbf{BEG} \;\Rightarrow\; \overline{\mathbf{X}} = \varnothing$$

*Embedding instances in the class* At any point in time, there are a finite number of living instances. The theories of these are combined with the theory of the class manager via morphisms which name each instance according to the identifier given when it is created (Figure 4).

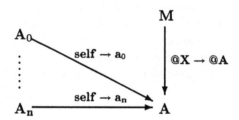

**Fig. 4.** Instance and class manager theories are embedded in the theory of the class

We combine the theory of each instance with the theory of the class via an @**A**-morphism which adds an extra parameter of type @**A** to each attribute and action symbol [8][4]. This is equivalent to defining **self** as a constant in the

---

[3] In a deontic setting one could use the notion of "permitted" here.

[4] A morphism, $\sigma$, of object signatures from $\theta_1 = (\Sigma_1, \mathbf{A}_1, \Gamma_1)$ to $\theta_2 = (\Sigma_2, \mathbf{A}_2, \Gamma_2)$ is a triple comprising: a morphism of algebraic signatures $\sigma_\nu : \Sigma_1 \to \Sigma_2$; for each $\mathbf{f} : \mathbf{s}_1, \ldots, \mathbf{s}_n \to \mathbf{s}$ in $\mathbf{A}_1$, an attribute symbol $\sigma_\alpha(\mathbf{f}) : \sigma_\nu(\mathbf{s}_1), \ldots, \sigma_\nu(\mathbf{s}_n) \to \sigma_\nu(\mathbf{s})$ in $\mathbf{A}_2$; and, for each $\mathbf{g} : \mathbf{s}_1, \ldots, \mathbf{s}_n$ in $\Gamma_1$, an action symbol $\sigma_\gamma(\mathbf{g}) : \sigma_\nu(\mathbf{s}_1), \ldots, \sigma_\nu(\mathbf{s}_n)$ in $\Gamma_2$.

Given a signature morphism, the translation of formulae is defined according to their structure in the usual way, and given two object descriptions, $(\theta_1, \Phi_1)$ and $(\theta_2, \Phi_2)$, a morphism, $(\theta_1, \Phi_1) \to (\theta_2, \Phi_2)$, is a signature morphism which preserves

instance theory which acts as a (dummy) placeholder for later identification with the object identifiers in the class theory.

The resultant theory, **A**, has an attribute **att(a)** for each attribute **att** of each existing instance **a**. For example, for instance $a_i$ and attribute **f**, there is an attribute $\sigma_i(\mathbf{f})$ in the class theory. In effect **f** is a (finite) partial function from @**A** to $\mathbf{T}_1$. We define a syntactic sugar which names the $\sigma_i(\mathbf{f})$ conveniently

$\mathbf{f} : @\mathbf{A} \rightarrow \mathbf{T}_1$

$a_i.\mathbf{f} = \sigma_i(\mathbf{f})$

So, in **A**, **f** is a partial function from @**A** to $\mathbf{T}_1$ which is written in the right. A similar approach is taken to the naming of instance actions.

*History and the state* Note that we have, up to this point, avoided the use of any temporal operator other than "next". This is because all behaviour determining history has been explicitly stored in the attributes. However, for example, we may wish to require that it is not possible for an object to be "reborn". This can be given using temporal operators or can be given in the above style by augmenting the state with a "memory" of past objects. $\overline{\mathbf{X}}$ would then distinguish between objects that have lived and those which have not.

$\overline{\mathbf{X}} : @\mathbf{X} \rightarrow \{ \text{ unborn}, \text{alive}, \text{dead} \}$

Axioms would chart the evolution of objects from unborn, through alive, to dead.

## 2.4 Interpreting Associations

We now formalise the notion of an association as depicted in Figure 5. We will interpret the association without any knowledge of the structure of the objects it associates[5]. Thus we have a generic theory of associations. We then use a renamed copy of this theory for each particular association in the model.

We begin with the most general case, a many-many association depicted by the black "blobs" at each end of the connecting line. The same approach will also work for other cardinalities of association by requiring further axioms for the constrained cases. For this section we consider only how to interpret associations at the level of the classes. In some circumstances, such as when the association has attributes of its own, it may be desirable to make a two level construction as was done for object classes.

---

validity and locality, ie. for which we have: $\Phi_2 \Rightarrow_{\theta_2} \sigma(\mathbf{p})$ is valid for each valid $\mathbf{p} \in \theta_1$; and $\Phi_2 \Rightarrow_{\theta_2} (\theta_1 \rightarrow_\sigma \theta_2)$, where $\Rightarrow_{\theta_2}$ is entailment in $\theta_2$, and $(\theta_1 \rightarrow_\sigma \theta_2)$ is the $\theta_2$ formula which is the translation of the locality axiom of $\theta_1$.

Given a sort **A**, and a morphism of object signatures, $\sigma$, the **A**-morphism, $\sigma_\mathbf{A}$, is the same as $\sigma$ except that it adds an extra parameter of sort **A** to each attribute and action symbol. Thus for example, for given $a : \mathbf{A}$, for each attribute symbol **f** and $e_i : s_i$, $\sigma_\mathbf{A}(\mathbf{f}(e_1, \ldots, e_n)) = \sigma_\mathbf{A}(\mathbf{f})(a, \sigma_\mathbf{A}(e_1), \ldots, \sigma_\mathbf{A}(e_n))$.

[5] We do however assume each class theory has been constructed from instance theories and class manager theory as defined above.

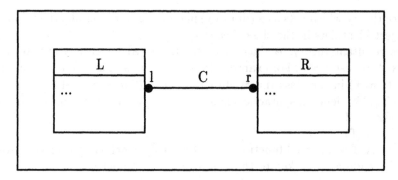

**Fig. 5.** A simple association

The association is interpreted as a many-many relation **lr** between object identifiers for the class on the left, @**L** and the class on the right, @**R**[6]. Note that **lr** plays the same role as $\overline{X}$, it is the set of existing links in the association. The theory signature is:

$\mathcal{S} = \{\ @\mathbf{L}, @\mathbf{R}\ \}$

$\mathcal{A} = \{\ \mathbf{lr} : \mathbb{F}(@\mathbf{L} \times @\mathbf{R})\ \}$

$\mathcal{G} = \{\ \mathbf{link} : @\mathbf{L} \times @\mathbf{R}, \mathbf{unlink} : @\mathbf{L} \times @\mathbf{R}\ \}$

As for object classes, we require axioms for adding and removing pairs from the relation and again have an "instance-by-instance" locality requirement which yields a characterisation of the two actions

$\mathbf{link}(l, r) \Leftrightarrow (l, r) \notin \mathbf{lr} \wedge (l, r) \in \bigcirc \mathbf{lr}$

$\mathbf{unlink}(l, r) \Leftrightarrow (l, r) \in \mathbf{lr} \wedge (l, r) \notin \bigcirc \mathbf{lr}$

In this case, as there are no identifiers for links, we do not require no-rebirth.

Again, it may be appropriate to add an axiom concerning the initialisation such as

$\mathrm{BEG} \Rightarrow \mathbf{lr} = \varnothing$

There is no axiomatic constraint between **link** for the association and **create** for the object classes here. Such constraints are given when the theories of objects and association are brought together. In keeping with encapsulation, there are no actions to update or inspect the associated object instances directly.

*Bringing association and objects together* Now assume that **A** and **B** are associated by **C** in a diagram **D**. **D** is interpreted as the co-limit of the theories for **A**, **B** and **C**. The class manager theories for **A** and **B** provide the "glue" which brings theories of objects and associations together. **C** is "glued" to each of **A** and **B** by identifying @**L** and @**R** with @**A** and @**B** respectively. Where names would otherwise clash, they are subscripted by the name of the theory from which they emanate. Purely for convenience, **lr** is renamed to **ab** in **D**.

---

[6] This turns out to be considerably more convenient than having a pair of primitive functions $\mathbf{r} : @\mathbf{L} \to \mathbb{F}@\mathbf{R}$ and $\mathbf{l} : @\mathbf{R} \to \mathbb{F}@\mathbf{L}$, such functions can be defined from the relation if required.

Figure 6 shows the hierarchical construction of the theories involved, and how these relate (dashed arrows) to the object model. Notice that **D** corresponds to a theory of a "subsystem" which includes all of the items in the object model.

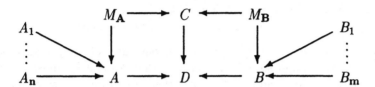

**Fig. 6.** The type view diagram is interpreted as the colimit of the object and association theories.

We now add axioms to **D** or to **C** which interpret the particular kind of association required.

**Cardinality Constraints.** Firstly, whatever kind of association is required, it can only link existing objects. This can be formalised by stating that the relation only relates the existing objects.

$$\mathbf{ab} \subseteq \overline{\mathbf{A}} \times \overline{\mathbf{B}}$$

This property relates the symbols of the association theory with those of the two class manager theories (but not those of the instance theories). These symbols are all available in the colimit of the association theory and manager theories and it is therefore meaningful to give it as an axiom of the theory "C" in the above diagram.

The axiom can be written as an extra, trans-theory, postcondition for **link**

$$\mathbf{link}(\mathbf{a}, \mathbf{b}) \Rightarrow \mathbf{a} \in \bigcirc\overline{\mathbf{A}} \wedge \mathbf{b} \in \bigcirc\overline{\mathbf{B}}$$

which, due to locality, yields a synchronisation between **link** and **create**

$$\mathbf{link}(\mathbf{a}, \mathbf{b}) \Rightarrow \mathbf{a} \in \overline{\mathbf{A}} \vee \mathbf{a}.\mathbf{create_A}$$
$$\mathbf{link}(\mathbf{a}, \mathbf{b}) \Rightarrow \mathbf{b} \in \overline{\mathbf{B}} \vee \mathbf{b}.\mathbf{create_B}$$

*Optional unary associations* ( ▭━▭ ) If the "blob" on the right is white, that is each $\overline{\mathbf{A}}$ is associated with at most one $\overline{\mathbf{B}}$, then the relation is a (partial) map from @**A** to @**B**.

$$\forall \mathbf{a}, \mathbf{b_1}, \mathbf{b_2} \cdot (\mathbf{a}, \mathbf{b_1}) \in \mathbf{ab} \wedge (\mathbf{a}, \mathbf{b_1}) \in \mathbf{ab} \Rightarrow \mathbf{b_1} = \mathbf{b_2}$$

This can be interpreted purely in the theory of the association by strengthening the constraints on **link**

$$\mathbf{link}(\mathbf{a}, \mathbf{b}) \Rightarrow \mathbf{a} \notin \mathrm{dom}\,\mathbf{ab}$$
$$\mathbf{link}(\mathbf{a}, \mathbf{b}) \wedge \mathbf{link}(\mathbf{a}, \mathbf{b'}) \Rightarrow \mathbf{b} = \mathbf{b'}$$

Thus this constraint is truly a specialisation of the concept of association, independent of all other constructions.

*Compulsory unary associations* ( ▭━▭ ) If the blob on the right is missing altogether, that is each $\overline{\mathbf{A}}$ is associated with exactly one $\overline{\mathbf{B}}$, then the map is total on $\overline{\mathbf{A}}$. Again this is a constraint between association and class manager theories

$$\mathrm{dom}\,\mathbf{ab} = \overline{\mathbf{A}}$$

Note that we do not require the map to be surjective since an @**B** can be associated with an empty set of @**A**s.

Again this can be ensured by conditions relating **create** and **kill** from the class manager for **A** with the relation **ab** from the association theory

$\quad$ a.create$_\mathbf{A}$ $\Leftrightarrow$ a $\notin$ dom ab $\wedge$ a $\in$ dom $\bigcirc$ab

$\quad$ a.kill$_\mathbf{A}$ $\Leftrightarrow$ a $\in$ dom ab $\wedge$ a $\notin$ dom $\bigcirc$ab

Conversely, for the one-many case, we have conditions on $\mathbf{ab}^{-1}$.

*One-one associations* ( ⊟—⊟ ) In the one-one case, we simply have both of these sets of axioms and so we can conclude that **As** and **Bs** must be created and deleted in lock-step and therefore that there are always the same number of $\overline{\mathbf{A}}$s as $\overline{\mathbf{B}}$s.

**Lifetime Constraints** ( ⊟—◇⊟ ) A "diamond" on the association is a constraint concerning the lifetimes of the associated objects. Diamonds can be interpreted independently of multiplicities.

A diamond at the right hand end of the association, indicates that **As** can only exist if linked with some (set of) **Bs** and that this set must be constant throughout the **A**'s lifetime[7]. This is ensured if **As** can be linked to **Bs** only when they are created, and unlinked only when deleted

$\quad$ link(a, b) $\Rightarrow$ a $\notin$ $\overline{\mathbf{A}}$ $\wedge$ a $\in$ $\bigcirc\overline{\mathbf{A}}$

$\quad$ unlink(a, b) $\Rightarrow$ a $\in$ $\overline{\mathbf{A}}$ $\wedge$ a $\notin$ $\bigcirc\overline{\mathbf{A}}$

There are similar rules for a diamond on the left of an association.

**Subtypes** ( ⊟—◅⊟ ) In the semantics, we interpret subtyping as a particular form of association with particular cardinality and lifetime constraints and where the object identifiers are drawn from the same set of tokens. This interpretation can then be used to show the validity of all the subtyping transformations of Chapter 8 of [5] with the exception of target splitting[13] in case that the target state is already nested. From the perspective of system structuring, however, which is the focus of this work, details of this are not relevant but can be found in [3].

We have seen how the interpretation of components of a type view diagram can be interpreted in a hierarchy of theories each corresponding to the separate diagram elements. We note that the formalisation of some particular constraints available in the diagrammatic notation are interpreted in the theories resulting from the composition of the theories of the separate diagram elements. This trend will be continued in the interpretation of statecharts which follows and will lead us to identify the concept of subsystem described in Section 3. In general the set of attributes of a subsystem theory will be the union of the sets of attributes of its constituent class and association theories, and similarly for actions.

---

[7] It is not clear whether Syntropy requires the set associated in an aggregation to be non-empty. We assume it is not.

## 2.5 Interpreting Statecharts

Statecharts are the most complex and semantically rich notation employed by Syntropy. Based on [10], they depict the state space of an object, partitioned according to "those states which distinguish the possible orderings of events" ([5], p.91). Statecharts have distinct interpretations at the essential, specification and implementation modelling levels. We focus on the essential level, but many of the semantic interpretations also apply to the specification and implementation levels[8].

State classes, depicted by boxes with a diagonal line in their top left hand corner, represent varying subsets of the objects of the superclass where an individual instance can move between the subtypes. Statecharts define the transitions which take instances from one state class to another.

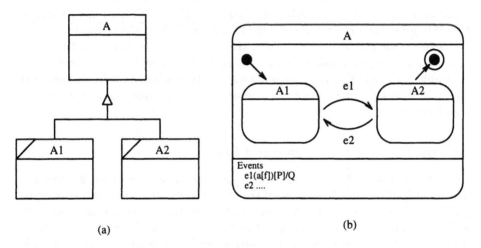

(a)            (b)

**Fig. 7.** State types and statechart for class **A**

For example, Figure 7 depicts a class with two state subtypes. $A_1$ and $A_2$. The subtypes in Figure 7(a) correspond to the states in Figure 7(b). The arrow from the solid blob indicates that the object is created in state $A_1$ and the arrow to the ringed blob represents object deletion from state $A_2$. The other arrows indicate state transitions $e_1$ and $e_2$ which take the object from state $A_1$ to state $A_2$ and back respectively. In the essential model, the lack of further arrows indicates that, for example, $e_1$ "cannot happen" when the object is in state $A_2$.

In Syntropy, the effect of transitions is specified by preconditions and postconditions similar to those used in Z or VDM. For example, $e_1[\mathbf{P}]/\mathbf{Q}$, indicates

---

[8] Note that statecharts in Syntropy correspond only loosely to those of Harel [10, 11]. The semantics given here is intended to formalise statecharts as used in Syntropy and does not correspond to the semantics of Harel.

that transition $e_1$ can only occur if the predicate $\mathbf{P}$ holds and that the two-state predicate $\mathbf{Q}$ must hold between the before and after states when $e_1$ occurs.

Further semantics is given by **Events** listed in the textual part at the bottom of the statechart. Events are system-wide, but can be targeted at particular objects by the use of parameters and filters. Typically, events effect a state transition in a single object of the class and have the same name as a state transition in the diagrammatic part of the statechart. The instance targeted by the event is passed as an extra parameter, $\mathbf{a}$, of the object type (c.f. the extra parameter introduced in the $\mathbf{A}$-morphism). In this case, the default filter, $\mathbf{a} =$ **self**, is assumed to indicate that only the object passed as parameter responds to the event. More complex situations can be modelled using this mechanism where the filter, $\mathbf{f}$, is a predicate identifying which events the **self** object should react to.

The same event can correspond to more than one transition in the diagrammatic part of the statechart. Where the sources of the arrows are different states, the state gives the precondition for the transition. Where the same event name labels two arrows from the same state, the choice between them is indicated by separate explicit preconditions which are annotated directly on the arrows.

Unlike the use in Syntropy, we make a syntactic distinction between the event and its associated transitions by capitalising the event name and indexing the transition names.

## 2.6 Interpreting State Types and Events

The information in the class diagram is interpreted as in Sections 2.3 and 2.4. The statechart defines the actions of the classes and instances which were omitted in Section 2.3. Each arrow in the statechart represents a state transition and is interpreted as an action $e_i$ of the instance theory. Several arrows can be used to describe different cases of a particular system event. The event itself is interpreted as an action $\mathbf{E}$ in the theory of the subtype/supertype subsystem and is synchronised with the instance actions that correspond to the required state changes. For example, in the above diagram, if $e_1$ and $e_2$ are different transitions for the event $\mathbf{E(a)}$ then $e_1$ and $e_2$ are interpreted as separate actions in the instance theory of $\mathbf{A}$ whereas $\mathbf{E(a)}$ is interpreted in the theory of the $\{\mathbf{A}, \mathbf{A}_1, \mathbf{A}_2\}$ subsystem and then synchronised with $e_1$ and $e_2$ via an axiom of the form

$$\mathbf{E(a)} \Rightarrow \mathbf{a}.e_1 \vee \mathbf{a}.e_2$$

*Filters.* More generally, events are of the form $\mathbf{E(p[F])}$, where the parameter $\mathbf{p}$ is a list of object or value parameters and the filter $\mathbf{F}$ is a predicate involving the parameters, **self** and the class constants. Object instances that satisfy the filter will undergo the corresponding transition (depending on their state and precondition), whereas objects for which a filter fails to hold ignore the associated event

$$\mathbf{E(p[F])} \Rightarrow \forall \mathbf{a} \in @\mathbf{A} \cdot \mathbf{a}.\mathbf{F} \Rightarrow \mathbf{a}.e_1 \vee \mathbf{a}.e_2$$

Here $\mathbf{a.F}$ is $\mathbf{F}$ with $\mathbf{a}$ substituted for self. For example, in the default case, where $\mathbf{F}$ is $\mathbf{p} = $ self, then $\mathbf{a.F}$ is $\mathbf{p} = \mathbf{a}$ and we regain the simpler condition above.

Note that when an event is not listed for a statechart, we require the event to go undetected by the object (rather than be blocked). In order to ensure this, we interpret unlisted events as having a filter of **false**.

*Interpreting preconditions* Preconditions in the essential model are intended to specify that certain transitions "cannot occur" in given circumstances. Thus we interpret preconditions as (blocking) guards which prevent execution of the transition they annotate. Consider the transition $e_1[\mathbf{P}]/\mathbf{Q}$ from state $\mathbf{A}_1$ to state $\mathbf{A}_2$. We define a *permission axiom* in the instance theory which expresses that $e_1$ can only occur when $\mathbf{P}$ holds.

$$e_1 \Rightarrow \mathbf{P}$$

Note, that this interpretation prevents preconditions from being weakened in refinement, that is, such transformations do not yield theory extensions. Thus subtyping form 5 of Chapter 8 of [5] (weakening preconditions) is not valid in essential models[9].

At the class level, each transition is also guarded by the state from which it occurs, for example, we have

$$\mathbf{a}.e_1 \Rightarrow \mathbf{a} \in \overline{\mathbf{A}_1}$$

*Postconditions* Postconditions are expressed in terms of the change between attribute values of the current state and those after the transition. Modifications to associations which result from postconditions defining a change to one end only are assumed to be made explicit in the postcondition.

For the above transition with postcondition, $\mathbf{Q}$, we have the *state-transition* axiom

$$e_1 \Rightarrow \mathbf{Q}$$

where $\mathbf{Q}$ is a predicate in attribute symbols $\mathbf{f}_i$ and $\mathbf{f}_i'$ and we replace $\mathbf{f}_i'$ with $\bigcirc\mathbf{f}_i$ in $\mathbf{Q}$.

At the class level, the event additionally moves the targeted instances to state $\mathbf{A}_2$

$$\mathbf{a}.e_1 \Rightarrow \mathbf{a} \in \bigcirc\overline{\mathbf{A}_2}$$

*Orthogonal state machines* Syntropy allows non-interfering concurrency to be specified via orthogonal statecharts although multiple simultaneous events are not supported. The state space is now the cartesian product of the spaces indicated by the two statechart components. The above approach supports a simple interpretation of orthogonal statecharts in terms of their components. Again the reader is referred to [3] for details.

The above interpretation of filters, preconditions and postconditions assumes only local attributes are used in the defining expressions. However, Syntropy

---

[9] In specification models, on the other hand, preconditions are to be interpreted as assumptions: any behaviour is valid if a transition is executed when its precondition is false. So preconditions *can* be weakened in specification models.

allows "navigation expressions" in which the conditions depend on the attributes of associated objects.

In such cases the relevant permission and state-transition axioms have to be "lifted" to an appropriate theory. Where the expression simply refers to an attribute of an associated object, the theory built for the association (**D** in the above diagram) suffices. Where the expression "navigates" further afield, a larger theory must be used. In this case, the theory required is that including all the visited theories. (The order of inclusion is not important as the co-limit construction is independent of the order in which the theories are combined.)

These larger theories are in any case part of the construction of the interpretation of the system as a whole, but until now their construction has been completely implicit. Therefore, in making explicit which theory interprets each navigation expression we add considerable complexity to the interpretation of the general system since each navigation expression potentially visits a collection of objects from different classes and hence identifies a new theory in its interpretation.

For this reason, we here advocate that a hierarchical approach is adopted when constructing system descriptions where predefined subsystems are employed and navigation expressions are confined as far as possible to the enclosing subsystem. (The same effect can be achieved by post-processing a system description to identify which collections of classes are linked by navigation expressions.) In the next section we discuss the use of subsystems as "first class" constructions in system description which leads to a definition of subsystem which is a generalisation of the concept of object and yields a hierarchical form of object orientation.

An example of application of the above semantics to the radio button statechart of Section 1 yields instance actions

1. $\mathbf{turn\_on_1(x)}$ representing the transition from **On** to itself in the case that $\mathbf{x = self}$;

2. $\mathbf{turn\_on_2(x)}$ representing the transition from **On** to **Off** in the case that $\mathbf{x \neq self}$;

3. $\mathbf{turn\_on_3(x)}$ representing the transition from **Off** to **On** in the case that $\mathbf{x = self}$;

4. $\mathbf{turn\_on_4(x)}$ representing the transition from **Off** to **Off** in the case that $\mathbf{x \neq self}$.

The class action $\mathbf{Turn\_on(x)}$ then has the axiom:

$$\mathbf{Turn\_on(x)} \Rightarrow$$
$$\forall \mathbf{a} : @\mathbf{RadioButton} \cdot \mathbf{a.turn\_on_1(x)} \vee \mathbf{a.turn\_on_2(x)} \vee$$
$$\mathbf{a.turn\_on_3(x)} \vee \mathbf{a.turn\_on_4(x)}$$

because the filter is **true** (ie, every object **a** may potentially react to the event). But we know that

$$\mathbf{a.turn\_on_1(x)} \Rightarrow \mathbf{a} \in \overline{\mathbf{On}} \wedge \mathbf{x = a} \wedge \mathbf{a} \in \bigcirc\overline{\mathbf{On}}$$

by the axioms for this transition, and similarly for the other transitions, so that:

$$\textbf{Turn\_on(x)} \Rightarrow$$
$$\forall \, a : @\textbf{RadioButton} \cdot$$
$$a \in \overline{\textbf{On}} \, \wedge \, x = a \, \wedge \, a \in \bigcirc\overline{\textbf{On}} \ \vee$$
$$a \in \overline{\textbf{On}} \, \wedge \, x \neq a \, \wedge \, a \in \bigcirc\overline{\textbf{Off}} \ \vee$$
$$a \in \overline{\textbf{Off}} \, \wedge \, x = a \, \wedge \, a \in \bigcirc\overline{\textbf{On}} \ \vee$$
$$a \in \overline{\textbf{Off}} \, \wedge \, x \neq a \, \wedge \, a \in \bigcirc\overline{\textbf{Off}}$$

From this we can, after some work, deduce that $\bigcirc\overline{\textbf{On}}$ must be $\{x\}$ and $\bigcirc\overline{\textbf{Off}}$ must be the complement of this set.

## 3  Subsystems

In the introduction we identified two key aspects of object orientation. Firstly, Objects aggregate related attributes, and secondly, Object Identifiers globally identify particular instances of one of these aggregations. In Section 2 we have seen how the formal interpretation of objects, classes and associations leads us to consider the concept of subsystem as a means of interpreting the constraints between related objects. From this perspective, subsystems provide aggregation, just as did objects, but at a coarser level of granularity. In this section we discuss whether other aspects of object orientation, in particular instance identity, can also usefully be applied to subsystems.

Although the concept of subsystem is not defined in Syntropy, we have seen how some notations implicitly assume it. We considered examples such as cardinality and lifetime constraints which must be interpreted in the subsystem comprising the association and the associated objects. In this respect, associations provide the simplest form of subsystem. Constraints on associations define particular properties of the subsystem. Navigation expressions which are interpreted in the theory including all visited constructs (objects and associations) are another example of a notation which requires the identification of a subsystem that encompasses the navigated path. Relationships between associations (Syntropy allows us to state that one association is a sub-relation of another) are also subsystem properties.

The above are particular cases of conditions we might give concerning the structures defined in a type hierarchy. Other, more general constraints might be:

- arbitrary properties for association,

- arbitrary properties relating associations,

- arbitrary properties inter-relating associated classes.

Subsystems provide the construction at the correct level of granularity to allow us to formalise such descriptions.

In the case of the **RadioButton** example, for instance, we can specify the effect of the **Turn\_on(x)** event at the level of the subsystem which includes **RadioButton** and the two subtypes **On** and **Off**:

$$\textbf{Turn\_on(x)} \;\Rightarrow\; \bigcirc\overline{\textbf{On}} = \{\; \textbf{x}\; \} \;\land\; \bigcirc\overline{\textbf{Off}} = \overline{\textbf{RadioButton}} \setminus \{\; \textbf{x}\; \}$$

Likewise, the student teaching example of Section 1 can be expressed via a subsystem which includes the two classes and the three associations (Figure 8). **Tuition** can be regarded as a class with attributes $\overline{\textbf{Student}}$ and $\overline{\textbf{College}}$, the

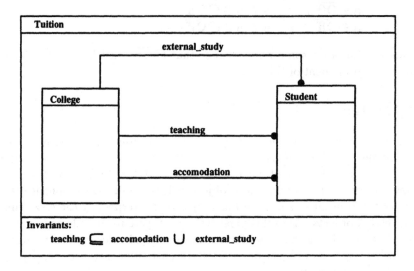

**Fig. 8.** Subsystem Example – Extended Notation

sets of existing students and colleges, and attributes

$$\textbf{external\_study}: \overline{\textbf{College}} \;\leftrightarrow\; \overline{\textbf{Student}}$$
$$\textbf{teaching}: \overline{\textbf{College}} \;\leftrightarrow\; \overline{\textbf{Student}}$$
$$\textbf{accomodation}: \overline{\textbf{College}} \;\leftrightarrow\; \overline{\textbf{Student}}$$

representing the current value of the associations concerned. The local invariants of the classes can be deduced from this more global model. Operations that change associations would also be most naturally specified at the level of a subsystem which includes the association and the classes it connects.

The concept of subsystem exists in a restricted form in Fusion or in Octopus [2]. An aggregate in Fusion is a group of classes, associations and attributes (but not operations, at the analysis level). In Octopus it is used to partition an application into functional sub-applications, rather like the domain concept of Syntropy [6]. The concept of subsystem we are proposing is more general in that it is hierarchical construct which can be used to define more than two levels of structure, and allows properties and operations to be localised at an appropriate level.

Subsystems therefore support the principle that we should specify operations and properties as *locally as possible*, without compromising comprehensibility, but not more locally.

We propose the concept of subsystems as a generalisation of objects and associations. Subsystems should include the fundamental aspects of objects (aggregation and identity) and associations (relationships between objects) and should be usable as "first class objects" to give a nested hierarchy with encapsulation at each level (ie. vertical and horizontal structuring). We discuss each aspect in turn.

## 3.1 Aggregation - The class-instance approach

We advocate that the class-instance approach, as employed for objects, is also used for subsystems. A subsystem class is a collection of object classes (or subsystem classes when subsystems are nested) which are related by associations and which collect together related objects at the next lower level of granularity. To formally interpret a subsystem we would therefore define a manager theory and instance theories as was done for objects in Section 2.

A subsystem can be identified from an existing (one level) type view diagram by encircling those object classes which are to be included in the subsystem class. The included object classes must be linked by associations also within the subsystem.

The interface which encapsulates the subsystem is simply those associations of the constituent components which link to components outside the subsystem. For specification and implementation models, where a set of operations define the interface to an object (its protocol in Smalltalk terms), we identify a distinguished set of the lower level operations to act as subsystem operations.

## 3.2 Identity - The root object

Syntropy employs a useful convention by which every system description should have a root object class to which every class is associated (either directly or via other classes). The root class must have precisely a single instance in any particular instantiation of the system. All instances in the system must also be associated to the root instance (either directly or indirectly) at all times.

We propose that the concept of root object can usefully be employed at the level of subsystems as well as for the entire system. The identity of the root instance can then be used as the identity of the subsystem instance or a new indexing of subsystem instances by subsystem identifiers can be provided. It is of little consequence whether subsystem identifiers are globally unique or whether they are unique within the enclosing subsystem instance at the next higher level. In the latter case, tuples of subsystem identifiers (corresponding to the nested levels of subsystem) can be used to identify subsystem instances.

## 3.3 Open issues

Two important open issues remain in the definition of the concept of subsystem. Firstly, it is not clear whether enclosed subsystems can be shared between enclosing ones and secondly, it remains to be defined how notions of subclass and inheritance should be applied to subsystems.

# 4   Conclusions and further work

We have formalised some aspects of class diagrams and statecharts as used in the "Syntropy" method of Object Oriented Analysis and Design. This interpretation has been axiomatic as opposed to others which are primarily denotational such as [1].

We have shown that a formal and modular semantics can be given to Syntropy essential models where separate theories are defined for instances, class managers and associations. Statecharts are interpreted with their diagrammatic part defined in the instance theory, and textual part in the class theory. We employed a style of axiomatisation where preconditions and postconditions of actions are defined in terms of the attributes so giving a style of specification very similar to that of model-oriented formalisms such as VDM and Z.

This formalisation could form the basis for a system supporting reasoning about the models developed enabling the use of proof for the validation and verification of designs. The same approach could be taken to the interpretation of other notations such as UML and therefore improve usefulness of these methods and also the process of the definition of the methods themselves.

In interpreting Statecharts, we distinguished between local actions for instance state transitions and system actions for events. We adopted a style of axiomatisation where the local effect of actions is interpreted directly in terms of the local attributes and synchronisation between actions in different theories is given implicitly by trans-theory constraints on attributes. Were theories to be executable, these implicit constraints would require implementation to ensure the synchronisations between actions of different classes.

The formalisation has brought to the fore some features of the langauge which might otherwise be unclear. For example it distinguishes between preconditions and guards, shows the orthogonality of cardinality and lifetime constraints, and seperates concepts of the generic instance from those of the class manager.

This formalisation of Syntropy has indicated some areas where notations are non-modular. We observed that the formalisation of associations has to be undertaken in the theory which incorporates the object and association primitives and that the formalisation of navigation expressions requires an amalgamation of an arbitrary collection of theories. We proposed the concept of subsystems as a coarser grained generalisation of objects and suggested that they can then be used in a hierarchical description of systems employing nested subsystems. We advocate that the class-instance approach can be usefully employed for subsystems just as it is for objects. The use of instance identity is also proposed for subsystems.

The treatment of unborn and dead instances requires infinite colimit diagrams. It is believed that these infinite colimits are well behaved because the morphisms are almost everywhere trivial, however, the underlying mathematics for this does need to be rehearsed.

Significantly, we have only interpreted essential models, some aspects of Specification and Implementation models are similar, others would require further work. Within essential models, we have not attempted to formalise nested statecharts nor associations with attributes. We believe that the concept of subsystem will also be of use here. Demonstrating the correctness of refinements between levels of model is not even addressed informally in Syntropy.

# References

1. M Abadi and L Cardelli, *An Imperative Object Calulus*, TAPSOFT '95, Mosses, Nielsen and Schwartzbach (Eds), Springer-Verlag, LNCS 915, 1995.
2. Maher Awad, Juha Kuusela and Jurgen Ziegler. *Object-Oriented Technology for Real-Time Systems: A Practical Approach Using OMT and Fusion.* Prentice Hall, Upper Saddle River, NJ, March 1996.
3. Towards a Compositional Interpretation of Object Diagrams. J.C. Bicarregui, K.C. Lano and T.S.E. Maibaum. To appear: Proc. of IFIP TC2 Working Conference on Algorithmic Languages and Calculi, Strasbourg, February, 1997.
4. Coleman D. *et al.*, *Object-oriented Development: The FUSION Method.* Prentice Hall Object-oriented Series, 1994.
5. Cook and Daniels, *Designing Object Systems with Syntropy*, Prentice Hall, 1994.
6. S Cook and J Daniels. Syntropy Case Study: The Petrol Station. Technical report, Object Designers Ltd., 1996.
7. J. Fiadeiro and T. Maibaum, *Temporal Theories and Modularisation Units for Concurrent System Specification*, Formal Aspects of Computing, Vol.4, No. 3, 1992. Springer-Verlag.
8. J. Fiadeiro and T. Maibaum *Describing, Structuring and Implementing Objects*, in de Bakker *et al.*, *Foundations of Object Oriented languages*, LNCS 489, Springer-Verlag, 1991.
9. Goguen, J. and Burstall, R. Introducing Institutions. In Clarke and Kozen, eds. Logics of Programs, pp. 221-256, Springer-Verlag, 1984.
10. D. Harel, *Statecharts: A Visual Formalism for Complex Systems*, Sci. Comput. Prog. **8** pp. 231-274 (1987).
11. D. Harel and E. Gery, *Executable Object Modelling with Statecharts* Proc. 18th Int. Conf. Soft. Eng., IEEE Press, 1996, pp. 246-257.
12. L. Lamport, The Temporal Logic of Actions, Digital Technical Report 79, 130 Lytton Avenue, Palo Alto, Califiornia 94301. December 25th, 1991.
13. K. Lano, Enhancing Object-Oriented Methods with Formal Notations, TAPOS, to appear, 1997.
14. Rumbaugh, J. et al. Object-Oriented Modelling and Design, Prentice-Hall, Englewoods Cliffs, New jersey, 1991.
15. M. Spivey, The Z Notation: a reference manual, Prentice-Hall, 1992.
16. Wieringa R., de Jonge W., Spruit P., *Roles and Dynamic Subclasses: A Model Logic Approach*, IS-CORE report, Faculty of Mathematics and Computer Science, Vrije Universiteit, Amsterdam, 1993.

# Towards a Formalization of the Unified Modeling Language*

Ruth Breu, Ursula Hinkel, Christoph Hofmann, Cornel Klein,
Barbara Paech, Bernhard Rumpe, Veronika Thurner

Institut für Informatik
Technische Universität München
D-80290 München
http://www4.informatik.tu-muenchen.de/

**Abstract.** The Unified Modeling Language UML is a language for specifying, visualizing and documenting object-oriented systems. UML combines the concepts of OOA/OOD, OMT and OOSE and is intended as a standard in the domain of object-oriented analysis and design. Due to the missing formal, mathematical foundation of UML the syntax and the semantics of a number of UML constructs are not precisely defined. This paper outlines a proposal for the formal foundation of UML that is based on a mathematical system model.

## 1 Introduction

The Unified Modeling Language [2] is a set of description techniques suited for specifying, visualizing and documenting object-oriented systems. The language has been developed by G. Booch, J. Rumbaugh and I. Jacobson since October 1994 and combines the concepts of OOA/OOD [1], OMT [24], and OOSE [17], as well as a number of ideas from other methods and description techniques like Harel's statecharts [14].

In January 1997 UML has been submitted to OMG as a proposal for a standard notation of object-oriented analysis and design techniques [2]. Currently, UML focuses only on notation. Method and process issues are outlined, but not dealt with in detail. However, it is stated that the process is to be use-case driven, architecture centric, iterative and incremental (Summary of [2], p. 7). In our work, we refer to the most recent UML version 1.0.

Like other software engineering methods UML provides a set of "intuitive" graphical and textual description techniques that are supposed to be easily understandable for both system developers and expert users working in the application domain. However, often the exact meaning of such description techniques

---

* This paper partly originates from a cooperation of the DFG project Bellevue and the SysLab project, which is supported by the DFG under the Leibniz program, by Siemens-Nixdorf and Siemens Corporate Research.

is not clearly defined. As a consequence, the usage of those techniques and, correspondingly, the interpretation of models developed may differ considerably. Furthermore, without exact semantics, checks for completeness and consistency cannot be precisely defined, let alone supported by a tool. Quite often, the models emerging during system development have severe shortcomings, which inevitably lead to erroneous software systems. Therefore, the high effort spent on modeling not always yields software systems of high quality.

In order to ensure the correct usage of description techniques in modeling, and to enable tool supported consistency checks, the definition of a precise semantics of the notations involved is crucial. The semantics defines the exact meaning of description techniques in an unambiguous way. Furthermore, the formal framework serves as a basis for defining the interconnections between different notational concepts and different stages of design. Last but not least a semantic foundation checks the soundness of the description technique and thus may lead to an improvement of the description technique itself.

Having recognized the importance of a formal foundation, the UML developers already have made first attempts at a formal semantics definition. In the language documentation a metamodel for UML concepts is presented. The metamodel itself is given in UML notation by a class diagram and annotations in prose. This approach to a formal semantics of UML brings about several difficulties.

First, the semantics of class diagrams is not precisely defined itself. For example, the usage of aggregation is a frequently discussed topic. Consequently, class diagrams provide a very weak basis for defining a formal semantics.

Second, the use of class diagrams limits the semantics definition to a description of static relationships between UML concepts. As a documentation of the structure of diagrams, the UML metamodel contains valuable information for tool developers who have to handle storage and retrieval of diagrams. However, there exists no interpretation that models the dynamic aspects of system behavior in an appropriate way. Thus, the metamodel is not sufficient as a formal semantics definition of UML concepts. As far as we know, also the novel approaches to a semantics definition pursued by the UML developers [20] do not overcome this deficiency.

Our approach to the formal foundation of UML is based on the well-studied and established mathematical theory of streams and stream processing functions [5]. Streams have proved to be an adequate setting for the formalization of the semantics of concurrent systems. In order to model the static and dynamic properties of an object-oriented system in a structured way, we augment the mathematical framework by the notion of *system models*. A system model characterizes an abstract view of the systems under development. A system model both describes the static structure of objects and their behavior over time. The idea of a system model is advantageous for several reasons.

First, a system model provides an integrated view of a system. This is particularly important as the UML description techniques allow us to define only partial views of a system. The semantic mapping of partial syntactical system views to an overall mathematical system view has the advantage that relationships between different description techniques can be studied in a homogeneous setting.

Second, the concept of system models establishes an auxiliary layer on top of the basic mathematical theory. In this semantic layer object-oriented notions like objects, object identities and object states have a direct correspondence to mathematical concepts in the system model. Thus, the use of a system model helps us to increase the readability and understandability of the semantics definition considerably.

For the semantics definition we employ our experience gained during the SYS-LAB project. In SYSLAB a formally founded design method has been developed covering description techniques similar to those of UML [18, 13, 12, 15, 21, 29].

The intention of this paper is to outline the basic ideas and the overall structure of the formal foundation of UML. Through the semantic definition of UML concepts, we detected a number of language features which are not yet fully clear. We discuss some of these aspects in the respective sections.

The paper is organized as follows: In Section 2 we give a short overview of the basic modeling concepts of UML. In Section 3 we present a proposal for the formal foundation of UML. The subsections of Section 3 focus on the overall mathematical system view and on the different description techniques UML offers. Section 4 contains a summary and our conclusions.

## 2  A Short Overview of UML

In the following we give a short sketch of the basic UML description techniques:

- class and object diagrams,
- use case diagrams,
- sequence diagrams,
- collaboration diagrams,
- state diagrams and
- activity diagrams.

Note that we concentrate on those models and description techniques that are relevant for describing the structure and behavior of systems. Therefore, we omit the implementation diagrams (component and deployment diagrams), which are helpful for modeling the physical structure of a system only. Furthermore, we focus on basic concepts, but omit some more advanced modeling features which are beyond the scope of this work. For a detailed description of UML we refer to [2].

**Class and object diagrams:** A class diagram describes the static structure of a system, consisting of a number of classes and their relationships. A class is a description of a set of objects and contains attributes and operations. An object diagram is a graph of instances. A static object diagram shows the detailed state of a system at a certain point in time, whereas a dynamic object diagram, also called collaboration diagram, models the state of a system over some period of time.

Structural relationships between objects of different classes are represented by associations (the instances of associations are called links). The definition of associations may be enhanced by attributes, association classes, role names and cardinality (multiplicity). Generalization represents the relationship between superclasses and subclasses, i.e. between a more general class and a more specific class. Thus, the specific class is fully consistent with the superclass and adds additional information. Aggregation, which is a concept of OMT, is a special form of binary association representing the whole-part relationship. Composition is a form of aggregation for n-ary associations, which implies strong ownership and coincident lifetime of a part with the whole. For structuring complex systems, class packages are introduced, which are groupings of class model elements and may be nested.

The **use case diagram** captures Jacobson's use cases. A use case diagram shows a collection of use cases and external actors that interact with the system. A use case describes the interactions and the behavior of a system during an entire transaction that involves several objects and actors. Within a use case model, relationships between use cases can be modeled, i.e. a use case can include other use cases as part of its behavior description. The specification of the external behaviour of a use case may be given by a state diagram. The implementation of a use case can be described by a collaboration diagram.

Since the use case diagram is strongly connected with the development process, we omit it in the current stage of our semantics definition.

**Sequence diagrams**, called interaction diagrams in OOSE, show patterns of interactions (i.e. the sending of messages) among a set of objects in a temporal order. In addition, a sequence diagram may show the lifelines of the objects involved in the interactions.

**Collaboration diagrams** are similar to object diagrams in OOA/OOD and describe the collaboration between objects. Collaboration diagrams depict objects and links between them. Links visualize the message flow between the corresponding objects. Messages may have an argument list and a return value. Message ordering in the overall transaction is described by a modified Dewey decimal numbering, specifying the sequential position of a message within its corresponding thread. A composite object is an instance of a composite class which implies the composition aggregation betweeen the class and its part. Parameterized collaborations represent design patterns that can be used repeatedly in different designs.

**State diagrams**, based on the statecharts by Harel [14], are similar to the state-machine diagrams used in OOA/OOD and OMT. They describe the reaction of an object, in reply to events received, in form of responses and actions.

State diagrams basically consist of states and state transitions. A state represents a condition during the existence of an object in which it waits for an event to be received, performs some action or satifies some condition.

An event is an occurrence that may trigger a state transition. Examples for events are the receipt of an explicit signal, and the call upon an object's method. State transitions describe which events an object can receive in a particular state and which state the object adopts after the reception of the event. The sending of events to other objects is part of the transition.

An additional concept in state diagrams are atomic and non-interruptible actions, which are connected to a transition. An action is executed when the corresponding transition fires. It is also possible to invoke internal "do" actions that are carried out within a state and take time to complete. An internal action is initiated when the state is entered and can be interrupted by an event that triggers a state transition.

Timing conditions on the behavior of an object can be introduced by transition times that are associated with a transition to specify the time at which the transition is to fire. Like in statecharts, nesting of states is specified by introducing concurrent or mutually exclusive disjoint substates.

**Activity diagrams** are a special case of state diagrams that are to be used in situations where most of the events represent the completion of internally-generated actions. Thus, the behavior is dominated by internal processing. In contrast, state diagrams are to be used for situations where mainly asynchronous events occur.

An essential feature of UML is the concept of **stereotypes**. Stereotypes are used for classifying modeling elements, thus allowing the user of UML to extend the semantics of the metamodel and to adapt the predefined notational concepts of UML to specific needs. For the evolution of a design the **refinement** relationship associates two descriptions of the same thing at different levels of abstraction. Refinement includes, among others, the relation between an analysis class and a design class.

# 3 A Proposal for the Formal Foundation of UML

This section represents a proposal for a formal foundation of UML. First, we describe our approach to a formalization and introduce the mathematical system model that is used to give an integrated underlying formal semantics for all description techniques of UML. Then, we describe how the semantics of the description techniques of UML can be formalized with respect to the system model.

## 3.1 Roadmap to Formalization

In the introduction we have motivated, *why* a formalization of UML description techniques is useful. We argued that a precise semantics is important not only for the developer, but also for tool vendors, methodologists (people that create the method) and method experts (people that use the method and know it in detail).

Thus, we get the following requirements for a formalization:

1. A formalization must be complete, but as abstract and understandable as possible.
2. The formalization of a heterogeneous set of description techniques has to be integrated to allow the definition of dependencies between them.

This does not mean that every syntactical statement must have a formal meaning. Annotations or descriptions in prose are always necessary for documentation, although they do not have a formal translation. They may eventually be translated into a formal description or even into code during software development when the system model is further refined.

To manage the complexity of formalization, a layer between syntactic description techniques and pure mathematics is introduced, as depicted in Figure 1. The pure mathematics is only used to define the *system model*. This system model is then used as an integrated underlying semantics for all description techniques.

As a further advantage, the system model explicitly defines notions of software systems in terms of mathematical concepts, e.g. object identifiers and messages. In contrast to the more implicit semantics of many other approaches, this leads to a better understanding of the developed systems.

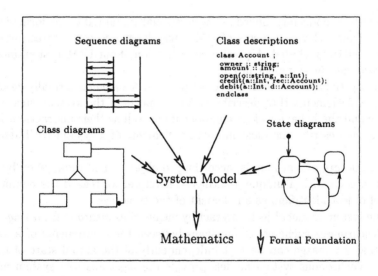

**Fig. 1.** Layered formalization of description techniques

The system model formally defines a notion of a system that obeys the properties defined in Section 3.2. A document of a given description technique is defined by relating its syntactic elements to elements of a system, such as the existing set of classes, or other structural or behavioral entities. The semantics of a document is then given by a subset of the system model. This subset of the system model consists exactly of all systems that are correct implementations of the document.

To use a set of systems and not a single one as the basis of the proposed semantics has several advantages. For example, refinement of documents corresponds to set inclusion. Furthermore, we get the meaning of different documents modeling different aspects of the system by intersection of their respective semantics. But the main reason is that, in contrast to fully executable programming languages, description techniques allow *underspecification* of system properties in many different ways. A proper semantics thus cannot be captured by a single system. For the same reason, it is not possible to give an operational semantics in the sense that a document specifies a single abstract machine that "executes" it.

## 3.2  System Model

The system model described below is a refinement of the SYSLAB system model as presented in [18], [27] and [11]. Each document, for instance an object diagram, is regarded as a constraint on the system model. The system model provides a common basis to define an integrated semantics of all description techniques. On this basis, notions like *consistency* and *refinement* of documents can be precisely defined.

The system model introduced below is especially adapted to the formalization of UML. Thus, relevant aspects of UML like classes, objects, states, messages etc. are explicitly included. A precise formalization of our UML system model is currently under development in [16].

Formally, the *system model* is a set of systems. A *system* is formally described by a tuple of elements that describe various aspects of the system, such as the structure and the behavior of its components as well as their interaction. In the following, we describe the most important elements of a system with identifier *sys*.

The structure of a system is, according to object-orientation, given by a set of objects, each with a unique identifier. Therefore, we regard the enumerable set *ID* of object identifiers as an element of the tuple *sys*.

In the system model objects interact by means of *asynchronous message passing*. Asynchronous exchange of messages between the components of a system means that a message can be sent independently of the actual state of the receiver. Asynchronous system models provide the most abstract system models for systems with message exchange, since deadlock problems as in synchronous systems do not occur. Note that synchronous message passing can be modeled by using two asynchronous messages, a "call" and a "return". To model communication between objects we use the theory of timed communication histories as given in [6]. The notion of explicit time in the system model allows us to deal with real time, as proposed in UML.

We regard our objects as spatially or logically distributed and as interacting in parallel. As described in UML, sequential systems are just a special case, where always exactly one object is "active".

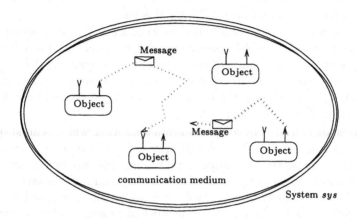

**Fig. 2.** Objects in the UML system model

Interaction between objects occurs through the exchange of messages, as shown in Figure 2. Let $MSG$ be an element of $sys$, denoting the set of all possible messages in a system. Each object with identifier $id \in ID$ has a unique set of messages it accepts. Its input interface is defined by

$msg_{id} \subseteq MSG$

The *behavior* of an object is the relationship between the sequences of messages it receives and the sequences of messages it emits as a reaction to incoming messages. We allow our objects to be nondeterministic, such that more than one reaction to an input sequence is possible.

According to [5, 9], the set of timed communication histories over $M$ is denoted by $M^{\bar{\omega}}$. Each communication history contains as information the time unit in which a message occurs, as well as a linear order on the messages it contains. A communication history thus models the observable sequence of incoming or outgoing messages of one object. The behavior of a nondeterministic object $id$ is then given by the mapping of its input stream to the set of possible ouput streams. Thus, the behavior of an object $id$ is given by the relation between its input and output streams

$behavior_{id} \subseteq msg_{id}^{\bar{\omega}} \times MSG^{\bar{\omega}}$

Objects encapsulate data as well as processes. *Encapsulation of data* means that the state of an object is not directly visible to the environment, but can be accessed using explicit communication. *Encapsulation of process* means that the exchange of a message does not (necessarily) imply the exchange of control: each object can be regarded as a separate process. Given the set of possible states $STATE$ of objects in a system, the function *states* assigns a subset of possible states to every object:

$$states_{id} \subseteq STATE$$

Furthermore, a state transition system is associated with each object, modeling the connection between the behavior and the internal state of an object. We use a special kind of automata [13] for this purpose.

Such an automaton of an object *id* consists of a set of input messages $msg_{id}$, a set of output messages $MSG$, a set of states $states_{id}$, and a set of initial states $states_{id}^0 \subseteq states_{id}$. The nondeterministic transition relation $\delta_{id}$ defines the behavior of the automaton. From the state-box behavior, given for the automaton in terms of state transitions, the black-box behavior in terms of the *behavior*-relation can be derived (cf. [13]).

Messages are delivered by a *communication medium*, which is an abstraction of message passing as it is done in real systems by the runtime system of the programming language or by the operating system. The communication medium buffers messages as long as necessary. Each message contains the receiver's identifier, so that the communication medium is essentially composed of a set of message buffers, one for each object. The order of messages between two particular objects is always preserved by the communication medium. The contents of messages are not modified. Messages cannot be duplicated or lost. No new messages are generated by the communication medium. This is formalized in [11].

Objects are grouped into classes. We assume that each system owns a set $CN$ of class names. $CN$ may, for instance, be derived from UML class diagrams. In object-oriented systems, each object identifier denotes an object that belongs to exactly one class. This is represented by the function

$$class : ID \to CN.$$

Classes are structured by an inheritance relation, which we denote by $. \sqsubseteq .$ (read: "subclass of"). The inheritance relation is transitive, antisymmetric and reflexive, as usual. With every class $c \in CN$ a signature $\Sigma_c$ is associated, containing all attributes and methods together with their argument and result types. The signature induces a set of input messages for each object of the class. One impact of inheritance is that signatures are only extended: $c \sqsubseteq d \Rightarrow \Sigma_d \subseteq \Sigma_c$.

Another distinguishing feature of object-orientation is the dynamic creation of objects. Deletion need not be modeled, as we assume that our objects are garbage collected in the usual way. However, we may define a special *finalize()*-method that may be used to clean up objects, as, for instance, in Java. Initially, a finite subset of objects (usually containing one element) exists and is active. We regard objects to be created and to be active after having received a first message. Thus, the creation of a new object essentially consists of a message transmission from the creator to the created object. To allow this, each object is equipped with a sufficiently large (usually infinite) set of object identifiers denoting the set of all object identifiers the object may create:

$$creatables : ID \rightarrow \mathcal{P}(ID)$$

To prevent multiple creation, these sets of identifiers have to be pairwise disjoint, and objects that are initially active are not creatable at all.

## 3.3 Class and Object Model

Class and object diagrams describe the static structure of a system. The origin of class diagrams are E/R diagrams, which have been successfully applied for years in database design. Although class diagrams are widely accepted in practice, the straightforward adaptation of E/R diagrams to an object-oriented context (through the correspondence *entity = object*) leads to deep semantic problems, since a number of features in E/R diagrams have no exact interpretation in the object-oriented setting. Below, the main concepts and problems of class and object diagrams in UML are summarized, and their mapping to the system model is sketched.

**Classes and Objects** Intuitively, a class $c$ in an UML class diagram describes a set of objects. This is reflected in our system model by three aspects. First, the methods and attributes of class $c$ describe the syntactical interface of all objects belonging to that class. This syntactical interface defines the signature $\Sigma_c$ as given in the system model. Second, the state space of the objects of class $c$ is determined. The state of an object is structurally determined by the attributes of the class and may contain both basic values (like integers or strings) and identifiers of other objects. The set of all states of objects of class $c$ is denoted by $states_{id}$. Third, a subset $ID_c$ of the set $ID$ of all identifiers is defined, although only implicitly by stating $|ID_c| = \emptyset$ for abstract classes, resp. $|ID_c| = \infty$ for others. The set $ID_c$ is the set of all identifiers of objects of class $c$, subclasses not included.

A class diagram describes the object structure of the system to be developed. In this respect, the semantics of the whole class diagram is the set of possible *system states*. A system state consists of the state of all objects that exist at some point in time. Formally, we describe a system state by an indexed family $\{s_{id} : id \in ID, s_{id} \in states_{id}\}$.

**Associations** Associations between classes in UML are supported in various other object-oriented analysis methods and originally come from the notion of relationship types in the entity/relationship approach.

The system view of E/R modeling is based on a global system state and global transactions on the system state. In this setting, relationship types are modeled by entities (set theoretic relations or tables) with the property of bidirectionality and symmetry.

It is obvious that in the object-oriented framework associations have to be interpreted in a different way: both dynamic behavior and states are localized in the objects. There are several alternatives to interpret associations and links in the context of classes and objects. In order to clarify these alternatives, we use the simple example of Figure 3, where we model the distributed structure of a warehouse by two classes *Branch* and *Central Office* connected by an association *coordinates*.

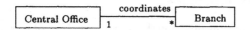

**Fig. 3.** A class diagram modeling a distributed warehouse

- One possibility is to interpret an association as a set of *data links*. In the example this means that a central office object "knows about" branch objects and vice versa. Associations therefore pose additional requirements on the object states. Inherently, associations in this interpretation are not bidirectional relations but correspond to two (semantically independent) unidirectional relations. See for example [25]. The consistency of the two relations is an integrity constraint imposed on linked objects. Another feature related with associations, the specification of their multiplicity, is also an integrity constraint between linked objects and is discussed below.
- A second possibility is to model any association by a separate class, a so-called *association class*. At first sight, this solution seems to be close to the interpretation of relationship types in the E/R approach. However, the paradigm of local object states requires every tuple of linked objects to be connected via an object of the association class. Thus, in this interpretation bidirectionality has to be modeled explicitly and the consistency problem sketched above remains. Thus, this modeling alternative is less abstract in the object-oriented setting than the first alternative and should be limited to the case in which associations are equipped with additional attributes.
- A third solution is to interpret associations as *communication links*. In the example the association *coordinates* then means that a central office object is able to communicate with branch objects and vice versa. Communication links in most cases induce data links, since a prerequisite for communication with other objects is to know about their existence.

In the sense of underspecification, we define the semantics of an association as one of these solutions. The actual choice is left to the developer, e.g. when it becomes clear which objects will send messages along the association. However, in this paper we only talk about the first and simplest solution. In our system model, an association between two classes is modeled within the set of states of the respective objects.

**Object Diagrams** Conceptually, an object icon in an object diagram depicts a single object at a certain point of time (with fixed attribute values). An object diagram thus describes a snapshot of the system and corresponds to a set of system states in our system model. However, the use of an object icon together with class icons usually means that an appropriate object is present in all system states, from beginning to termination. This is formalized by adding an appropriate identifier to the set of initially active objects in the system model.

UML allows some relaxations and extensions of the notations of objects. Among these extensions are the definition of anonymous objects (i.e. objects specified solely by their class without an object identifier), objects without associated attribute values and the stack icon denoting multiple objects.

Anonymous objects stand for "an object" of the given class. Rather than single system states, object diagrams with anonymous objects describe structural properties of system states in a similar way as class diagrams do.

**Aggregation and Composites** UML supports two kinds of aggregation: Shared aggregation and composite aggregation (composition). In a composition, the lifetime of the parts is closely related with the lifetime of the whole. Therefore, "the multiplicity of the aggregate may not exceed 1" ([2], Notation Guide, p. 47), i.e. the parts are not shared among several aggregates. In contrast, shared aggregation puts less constraints on the association, since it allows for sharing, and decouples the lifetimes of the parts from the lifetime of the whole.

This differentiates the current version of UML from Version 0.91, where both concepts have been inconsistently mixed into one. Like constraints, aggregations and compositions are conditions on the system state, and, therefore, can easily be mapped into the system model.

**Constraints** Constraints are conditions on the system state. Constraints can refer to single objects (e.g. for specifying dependencies between attributes) or to several (linked) objects. In UML, constraints are specified as informal text. In order to enable a formal modeling we consider constraints to be predicates over the system states consisting of objects. As already discussed, further types of constraints are induced by other features of class diagrams, e.g. by the multiplicity indicators and by dependencies between associations.

Because there are a lot of different kinds of constraints, a general solution for constraint formalization is not possible. However, the definition of new types of precisely expressible constraints would considerably improve UML. This would allow design decisions regarding static properties of a system to be captured in a more precise and compact way.

**Generalization** Inheritance is the generalization relation between classes. In our system model, inheritance is modeled by . $\sqsubseteq$ . and induces the following three relations:

- Subclasses extend the interface of their superclasses. In our system model this means that the signature of the superclass is a subset of the signature of any of its subclasses.

- A second relation relates the state spaces of super- and subclasses. This structural relation models the property that objects of subclasses have the attributes of their superclasses and participate in associations belonging to their superclasses.
- A third effect of inheritance concerns the sets of object identifiers. For a given class $c$, the set of associated objects is given by $\{id \in ID \mid class(id) \sqsubseteq c\}$. The inheritance relation induces a subset relation between the sets of object identifiers associated with the subclass and the superclass. This subset relation models *(subtype) polymorphism*, i.e. the property that each object of a subtype is also an object of the supertype.

The above relations describe the static properties of super- and subclasses. In the UML documentation nothing is stated about the dynamic properties of inheritance, i.e. how the behaviors of super- and subclasses are related. In fact, inheritance of dynamic behavior is an issue that has been neglected in object-oriented analysis methods so far.

Behavioral inheritance is a well-studied notion at the level of formal specifications (subclasses inherit the abstract properties of their superclasses, see for example [19], [22]) and at the level of programming languages (subclasses may inherit the code of methods of their superclasses). In contrast, only first attempts have been made to relate state diagrams of superclasses and state diagrams of subclasses. One approach to this problem has been presented in [25] and [26].

**Class Packages** Class packages group parts of a class diagram. They define a syntactical name space and, therefore, need no semantic counterpart in the system model.

Class packages may contain classes of other packages that are assumed to be imported. The dependency between class packages can be interpreted as the visualization of such an import of classes. Aggregation of class packages can be seen as the alternative presentation of hierarchically nested packages.

### 3.4 Sequence and Collaboration Diagrams

In contrast to state diagrams, which describe local behavior of objects, sequence diagrams describe global behavior, i.e. interaction sequences between objects. However, the methodological use of sequence diagrams has to be precisely investigated, because sequence diagrams do not provide a complete specification of behavior, but only describe exemplary scenarios. Since collaboration diagrams and sequence diagrams express similar information, but show it in different ways, all propositions made about sequence diagrams in this section apply to collaboration diagrams as well (see [2], Notation Guide, p. 66).

**Exemplary Behavior** The goal of sequence diagrams is to model typical interaction sequences between a set of objects. In Figure 4 a sequence diagram, similar to the one in the UML Notation Guide, is given. The sequence diagram depicts a typical scenario of interaction between the three objects named Caller, Exchange and Receiver.

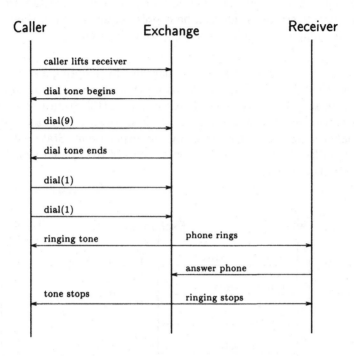

**Fig. 4.** A sequence diagram modeling a phone call

While the concentration on standard cases leads to an easy-to-use notation that is understandable by both software engineers and application experts, it has to be stressed that a sequence diagram does not describe a necessary, but only a possible (or exemplary) interaction sequence between the involved objects. This leads to a semantic problem if sequence diagrams should be considered as a *specification technique.*

In particular, a sequence diagram does not specify in which states the objects have to be in order for the described interaction sequence to occur. For instance, in the above example the phone would not ring if the receiver was busy. Moreover, even if these states had been specified (for instance by giving an interaction sequence leading to the state), the sequence diagram would still leave open whether the described interaction sequence is the only possible one to occur or whether there are other possible interaction sequences. Therefore, from a strictly formal point of view, a sequence diagram not really makes a proposition about the executions of a system.

Note that this is a principal problem that stems from the fact that the objective of sequence diagrams is to describe exemplary behavior. This problem can be relaxed by using additional language constructs such as repetition and choice, thus providing a means for the description of complete sets of alternative sequence diagrams.

We are currently developing a method for a seamless transition from exemplary behavior descriptions that can be expressed, for instance, using sequence diagrams, to complete specifications using state diagrams.

**Formalization** We formalize sequence diagrams by adopting a state box view. For each vertical line in a sequence diagram that corresponds to an object an abstract state automaton is defined along the lines of [12]. State automata consist of a set of states, an initial state, and a set of transitions. In our case, a transition is either labeled by an input event or by an output event. State automata can easily be translated into state transition systems of the system model [12], but this is not exploited here.

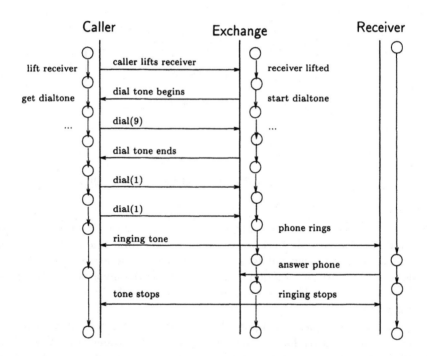

**Fig. 5.** Sequence diagram with abstract state automata

In contrast to the concrete state transition systems that are given by the state diagrams of the involved objects and that describe the complete behavior of the objects, the abstract state automata, which are derived from the sequence diagram, only describe part of the behavior of the objects. These state automata can be derived from the sequence diagram as follows:

- Between any two interactions, and before the first and after the last interaction, a state is introduced. Each abstract state $s_i^a$ of the state automaton corresponds to the set of concrete states $S_i^c$, which is a subset of the state space $states_{id}$ of the object. Note that the state sets corresponding to different abstract states do *not* have to be disjoint.
- With each interaction of the object in the sequence diagram, denoted by the $i$th arrow ending or beginning at the vertical line, an abstract transition between the states $s_i^a$ and $s_{i+1}^a$ is associated. This abstract transition corresponds to a nonempty set of concrete transitions of $\delta_{id}$, i.e. of the transition relation of the state transition system of the object (see Section 3.5).

The idea of using states between interactions is taken from [28]. In [28] "extended event traces" (EETs) are formalized. EETs are a notation similar to sequence diagrams; they are used with the objective to give a complete behavior description. Moreover, [8] shows how EETs can be used for describing complete interaction behavior in software architectures.

By using a state box view, our formalization makes it more apparent what is missing in sequence diagrams in order to be a specification technique:

- They leave completely open the relationship between abstract states in the sequence diagram and concrete states in the state diagrams of the involved objects.
- They only describe which concrete transitions may occur, but they do not forbid other concrete transitions.

To sum up, a sequence diagram describes the behavior of an object only partially, because it corresponds only to a subset of all paths in the state diagram of the object, and because it does not make this correspondence explicit. In contrast, a state diagram describes all paths, and, therefore, the complete behavior of the object.

## 3.5   State Diagrams

State diagrams serve as the connection between the structure of an object-oriented system and its behavior. Thus, state diagrams play a central role in the development of object-oriented systems. UML state diagrams look similar to Harel's statecharts [14]. However, several modifications and extensions make it difficult to define a precise semantics. In the following we sketch a semantic foundation based on the system model. The formalization is based on a semantic definition of similar state diagrams, which can be found in [12].

A state diagram can be attached either to a class or to the implementation of an operation ([2], Notation Guide, p.89). Their semantics differs accordingly. First we treat the semantics of class state diagrams. Class state diagrams are associated with the class names in $CN$ and describe the lifecycles as well as the behavior of objects. The description is based on the actual state, which changes during the lifecycle.

**Class State Diagrams** In the following, we discuss the semantics of a state diagram associated with a class $c \in CN$ by transforming it into a state transition system (see Section 3.2).

**States** A class state diagram $c$ consists of a finite set $STDStates_c$ of possibly nested *diagram states* and a finite set $STDTrans_c$ of *diagram transitions*. Diagram states are (optionally) labeled by names that are taken from the set $STDNames_c$. A diagram state denotes an equivalence class of object states $states_{id}$ of the corresponding object. The semantics of elementary diagram states is, therefore, given by a function $st$ associating with each diagram state $S \in STDStates_c$ and each object identifier $id \in ID_c$ a corresponding set of object states $st(S, id) \subset states_{id}$.

The above requirement that each diagram state denotes exactly one equivalence class of object states can easily be achieved by assuming the name of the diagram state as an additional attribute of class $c$ (and introducing internal names for anonymous states).

The semantics of compound diagram states is defined as follows:

– The semantics of a composite diagram state (a so-called "OR-state") is given by the union of the state sets denoted by the subdiagram states.
– The semantics of a concurrently nested diagram state (a so-called "AND-state") is given by building the Cartesian product of its component diagram states.

Note that, although AND-states give a notion of concurrency, they can also be used to give a modular description of independent behavioral units of one sequential object. We do not allow feedback-composition of statecharts in order to simplify the semantic definition of state diagrams, as well as their understandability by the UML user. A similar comment was made in ([3], Metamodel, p.12).

As described above, the states of a state diagram are mapped to the states $states_{id}$ of the state transition system, which is already given by the semantics of a class diagram. The subset of initial states $states_c^0(id)$ is given by the states reachable by the initial event.

**Events** "An *event* is a significant occurrence. It has a location in time and space ..." ([2], Glossary, p.7). Therefore, we model events as simple transmissions of messages, occurring at some point in time. Each event $ev$ gives rise to a set of messages $msg(ev)$. Input events of class $c$ are modeled by the set $msg(ev) \subseteq msg_c$ of accepted messages. Similarly, output events are given as a subset of $MSG$.

UML distinguishes four different cases of events: receipt of a signal, receipt of an operation call, satisfaction of a condition and passage of a period of time ([2], Notation Guide, p.94). The first three are modeled as transitions, which are described in the next section. The semantics of the last is explained in [7] and not treated here.

**Transitions** "A ... *transition* is a relationship between two states ... when a specified event occurs ..." ([2], Notátion Guide, p.96).

Each transition $(s, d, ev, out, C) \in STDTrans_c$ in the state diagram consists of a *source diagram state s*, a *destination diagram state d*, an input *event-signature ev*, a possibly empty output *send-clause out* and a guard condition $C$. UML also allows action-expressions, which are "... written in terms of operations, attributes, and links of the owning object ..." and "... must be an atomic operation." ([2], Notation Guide, p. 96). If the action expression does not contain calls or signals to other objects, it just restricts the resulting object states (and is, in this respect, similar to postconditions as allowed in Syntropy [10]). This can be easily incorporated into the semantics given below. However, when other objects are involved within an atomic action expression, communication with other objects is hidden in the action expression. As discussed below, in Section 3.5 on operation state diagrams, in a concurrent setting the semantics of communications not shown in the class state diagrams is not clear.

A transition in the diagram $(s, d, ev, out, C)$ is mapped to a set of transitions in the state transition system of the system model. Each transition in this set fulfills the following conditions:

- The transition starts in some state of the equivalence class $st_c(s)$ of the source diagram state and ends in some state of the equivalence class $st_c(d)$ of the destination diagram state.
- It is labeled with an input message from the set $msg(ev)$. This set may be empty.
- In addition, it is labeled with the set of output messages $msg(out)$. This set may be empty.
- It fulfills condition $C$.

The transition relation $\delta_c(id)$ of a state transition system of an object $id$ of class $c$ contains all transitions of these sets for all transitions in the state diagram.

UML distinguishes between simple transitions, complex transitions and transitions to nested states. We do not consider these details here, since composite states can always be expanded to simple states. We assume that the semantics of transitions is determined only after this expansion.

In addition to transitions, behavior can also be specified in UML state diagrams as internal activity, in particular entry, exit, and do actions. The latter can be treated similarly to general action expressions.

"If an event does not trigger any transitions, it is simply ignored." ([2], Notation Guide, p. 96). This is modeled by an extension of $\delta_c(id)$ with default transitions that leave the state unchanged. We remark, however, that another possibility is to model such events as chaotic behavior in the sense of *underspecification*. This allows for a refinement calculus on state diagrams as given in [26].

**Operation State Diagrams** It is difficult to define the semantics of a state diagram "... attached to a method (operation implementation) ..." ([2], Notation Guide, pp. 89), since none of the examples and only very little text in the UML documentation are devoted to this use. There are two major possiblities of how to associate a notion of state to an operation: either only the states of one object are shown such that the operation state diagram only describes the effect of the operation on one object, or the state covers several objects. In the latter case the diagram states must refer to a combination of the participating objects' states, thus modeling the "... condition during ... an interaction" ([2], Notation Guide, pp.90) this method is involved in. Furthermore, interactions between the participating objects are internal activities with respect to this operation state diagram.

In both cases the question arises, how several operation state diagrams and class diagrams should be combined and integrated. In a concurrent setting operation execution may be intertwined, such that not all states of each operation are visible in the object behavior. For example, the effect of a transfer operation between two bank accounts might not be visible in the object state after execution of the transfer operation, since concurrent deposits and withdrawals might have changed the accounts already.

Therefore, the simplest solution of combining class and operation state diagrams, namely, to view the operation state diagram just as as a complex action expression attached to the operation calls in the class state diagrams, is not always adequate. As an action expression, execution of operation state diagrams must be atomic (non-interruptible), which is not true for the transfer example above. In [4] a solution is discussed that attaches virtual objects to operation state diagrams, which can be called concurrently. This requires explicit synchronization of the access of the virtual operation objects to the object state. In [23] a solution is discussed that determines the semantics as the interleaving of the operation state diagrams based on a stack handling the operation calls. A thorough discussion of the different solutions is outside the scope of the paper. We just conclude that the combination of object behavior descriptions and operation behavior descriptions is an unsolved problem in the area of object-oriented modeling methods.

**General Remarks on State Diagrams** In the following, we suggest some improvements for state diagrams:

- In addition to *guard conditions*, postconditions should also be allowed. As mentioned above, this is a more abstract way of expressing the local effect of action expressions.
- There are several object-oriented approaches that implicitly use pattern matching, as used in functional programming languages, to relate input events and their argument values to the event triggers and their expressions. The use of these pattern matching techniques should be stated explicitly as a description mechanism in UML and be defined more precisely.

### 3.6  Activity Diagrams

Activity diagrams are a special case of state diagrams where all states have an internal action and no transition has an input event. They can be "... attached ... to a class or to the implementation of an operation and to a use case" ([2], Notation Guide, p.106). The first two cases have already been discussed for state diagrams in general (see section 3.5). In this section we discuss activity diagrams with swimlanes and action-object flow. These features seem to be particularly relevant for use case description. Another possible use would be to specify some operation of a composed object.

In the presence of swimlanes, the semantics of activity diagrams needs to be changed considerably. The main reason is that now several objects are involved and operate on their own object state. Thus, there is no notion of global state within one activity diagram and the transitions explicitly depict data and object flow between single activities. Hence, it is not adequate to give activity diagrams a semantics in terms of one state transition system.

As mentioned in ([2], Notation Guide, p.111), in some cases activity diagrams with action-object flow should be substituted by sequence diagrams. Also in our view, activity diagrams with swimlanes are more similar to sequence diagrams than to state diagrams. However, it is not clear from the UML documentation, whether they should only be used as a notational variant of sequence diagrams (where, for instance, action states correspond to named parts of the object life-line) or whether some semantic differences are intended. Since they have not been included in earlier versions of UML [3], it seems likely that a more detailed explanation will be given in the next version.

## 4  Conclusion

In the preceding sections we have presented a proposal for the formal foundation of the Unified Modeling Language. As a direct result of our work, we detected a number of concepts that are not precisely defined, like the meaning of constraints in a concurrent setting of objects or the way how operations are specified and integrated in the overall object behavior. We also suggested enhancements of the UML descriptions, and we have argued that it is possible to map the UML language constructs to a coherent and sound semantic model.

A main idea of the semantics is to represent an overall system view in the semantic domain. This overall system view has been called system model. A system model describes both static and dynamic behavior of objects, including, for instance, dynamic object creation, concurrent behavior of objects with asynchronous message sending and inheritance relations.

The semantic domain of streams, on which our approach is based, has proved to be powerful enough to model specific properties of application domains like real-time systems and information systems. This is important, since UML claims to be an application independent analysis and design language.

There is still a lot of work to be done. Besides the precise elaboration of the semantics, there are several directions for future work.

A first main direction focuses on the benefits of the system model. As stated in the introduction, a formal semantics is the prerequisite for studying refinement steps, relationships between different description techniques, and for giving conditions that ensure the consistency of a system specification. In a second step, such properties have to be studied in the semantic domain, and, what is crucial, have to be formulated at the syntactical level of UML. Only if, for instance, consistency conditions can be formulated at the level of the description techniques, they can be integrated into a tool and support a sound system development. First work in this area has been presented, for instance in [26], where refinement steps for state diagrams are elaborated.

A second main direction for future work concerns aspects of the design process. Like UML itself, our semantic framework has been defined independently of a design methodology. Issues that still have to be addressed in more detail are, for instance, operation specifications and use case specifications. In the current stage of development, it is not clear what techniques effectively support the designer to specify operations and use cases and how they are integrated in the system specification. A first approach clarifying the relationships between the notions of messages, events and methods (operations) has been presented in [4]. These studies provide guidelines and schemes for integrating partial views of a system (like operation behavior) into an overall system view and assist the developer to gain a structured and sound system specification.

### Acknowledgments

We thank Grady Booch, Ivar Jacobson and Gunnar Övergaard for interesting discussions regarding UML. We also thank Manfred Broy and Ingolf Krüger for stimulating discussions and comments on earlier versions of this paper.

# References

1. G. Booch. *Object-Oriented Analysis and Design with Applications*. Benjamin Cummings, 1994.
2. G. Booch, J. Rumbaugh, and I. Jacobson. The Unified Modeling Language for Object-Oriented Development, Version 1.0, 1996.
3. G. Booch, J. Rumbaugh, and I. Jacobson. The Unified Modeling Language for Object-Oriented Development, Version 0.9, 1996.
4. R. Breu and R. Grosu. Modeling the dynamic behaviour of objects - about events, messages and methods. submitted to publication, 1997.
5. M. Broy, F. Dederichs, C. Dendorfer, M. Fuchs, T. F. Gritzner, and R. Weber. The Design of Distributed Systems — An Introduction to FOCUS – revised version –. SFB-Bericht 342/2-2/92 A, Technische Universität München, January 1993.
6. M. Broy, F. Dederichs, C. Dendorfer, M. Fuchs, T.F. Gritzner, and R. Weber. The Design of Distributed Systems - An Introduction to FOCUS. Technical Report SFB 342/2/92 A, Technische Universität München, 1993. http://www4.informatik.tu-muenchen.de/reports/TUM-I9202.ps.gz.
7. M. Broy, R. Grosu, and C. Klein. Timed State Transition Diagrams. submitted to publication, 1997.

8. M. Broy, C. Hofmann, I. Krüger, and M. Schmidt. A graphical description technique for communication in software architectures. Technical Report TUM-I9705, Technische Universität München, 1997.

9. M. Broy and K. Stølen. Specification and Refinement of Finite Dataflow Networks — a Relational Approach. In *Proc. FTRTFT'94*, LNCS 863, pages 247–267. Springer-Verlag, Berlin, 1994.

10. S. Cook and J. Daniels. *Designing Object Systems*. Prentice Hall, 1994.

11. R. Grosu, C. Klein, and B. Rumpe. Enhancing the syslab system model with state. TUM-I 9631, Technische Universität München, 1996. http://www4.informatik.tu-muenchen.de/reports/TUM-I9631.html.

12. R. Grosu, C. Klein, B. Rumpe, and M. Broy. State transition diagrams. TUM-I 9630, Technische Universität München, 1996. http://www4.informatik.tu-muenchen.de/reports/TUM-I9630.html.

13. R. Grosu and B. Rumpe. Concurrent timed port automata. TUM-I 9533, Technische Universität München, 1995. http://www4.informatik.tu-muenchen.de/reports/TUM-I9533.html.

14. D. Harel. Statecharts: a visual formalism for complex systems. *Science of Computer Programming*, 8:231–274, 1987.

15. R. Hettler. Description techniques for data in the SYSLAB method. Technical Report TUM-I9632, Technische Universität München, 1996. http://www4.informatik.tu-muenchen.de/reports/TUM-I9632.html.

16. C. Hofmann, C. Klein, and B. Rumpe. The object oriented system model. internal report, to appear as technical report, Technische Universität München, 1997.

17. I. Jacobson. *Object-Oriented Software Engineering - A Use Case Driven Approach*. Addison-Wesley, 1992.

18. C. Klein, B. Rumpe, and M. Broy. A stream-based mathematical model for distributed information processing systems - SysLab system model -. In Elie Naijm and Jean-Bernard Stefani, editors, *FMOODS'96 Formal Methods for Open Object-based Distributed Systems*, pages 323–338. ENST France Telecom, 1996.

19. B. Liskov and J.M. Wing. A new definition of the subtype relation. In *ECOOP,LNCS 707*, pages 118–141. Springer Verlag, 1993.

20. G. Övergaard. *The Semantics of the Unified Modeling Language - Tutorial at OOPSLA'96*. ACM, San Jose, October 1996.

21. B. Paech. A framework for interaction description with roles. submitted to publication, 1997.

22. B. Paech and B. Rumpe. A new Concept of Refinement used for Behaviour Modelling with Automata. In *FME'94, Formal Methods Europe, Symposium '94*, LNCS 873. Springer-Verlag, Berlin, October 1994.

23. B. Paech and B. Rumpe. The state based description of services. submitted to publication, 1997.

24. J. Rumbaugh. *Object-Oriented Modelling and Design*. Prentice Hall, 1991.

25. B. Rumpe. *Formale Methodik des Entwurfs verteilter objektorientierter Systeme*. Herbert Utz Verlag Wissenschaft, 1996. PhD thesis, Technische Universität München.

26. B. Rumpe and C. Klein. Automata with output as description of object behavior. In H. Kilov and W. Harvey, editors, *Specification of Behavioral Semantics in Object-Oriented Information Modeling*, pages 265–286, Norwell, Massachusetts, 1996. Kluwer Academic Publishers. http://www4.informatik.tu-muenchen.de/papers/RumpeKlein_SoBS1996.html.

27. B. Rumpe, C. Klein, and M. Broy. Ein strombasiertes mathematisches Modell verteilter informationsverarbeitender Systeme - Syslab Systemmodell -. Technical Report TUM-I9510, Technische Universität München, Institut für Informatik, March 1995. http://www4.informatik.tu-muenchen.de/reports/TUM-I9510.ps.gz.

28. B. Schätz, H. Hußmann, and M. Broy. Graphical Development of Consistent System Specifications. In J. Woodcock M.-C. Gaudel, editor, *FME'96: Industrial Benefit and Advances In Formal Methods*, pages 248–267. Springer, Lecture Notes in Computer Science 1051, 1996.

29. V. Thurner. A description technique for business process modelling. internal report, to appear, 1997.

# Coordination Requirements Expressed in Types for Active Objects

Franz Puntigam

Technische Universität Wien, Institut für Computersprachen
Argentinierstraße 8, 1040 Vienna, Austria. E-mail: franz@complang.tuwien.ac.at

**Abstract.** An object's type is usually regarded as a contract between the object and each of its users. However, in concurrent (and sometimes also in sequential) systems it is more useful to regard a type as a contract between an object and the unity of all users: The users must be coordinated before sending messages to the object. Types in the proposed model express requirements on the coordination of users; objects must accept messages only in pre-specified orders. The model ensures statically that objects behave as specified by their types, and users are coordinated appropriately.

*Keywords:* Type model, concurrency, active objects.

## 1 Introduction

Each expression written in a statically typed programming language has a unique type specified explicitly or derivable at compile-time. Strong typing ensures that violations of type constraints (type errors) cannot occur during program execution [4]. Static and strong typing can increase the readability and reliability of programs and support optimizations. In the object-oriented paradigm, types specify contracts between objects (servers) and their users (clients) [14]. These contracts play an important role in the maintenance and reuse of software.

An object's type is usually viewed as the object's signature, often associated with a name or another entity used as (informal) description of the object's behavior. In some languages, programmers can formally express their expectations on the input and result parameters and give partial specifications of the behavior using assertions (preconditions, postconditions and invariants). Users get the promised results if they call the object's methods when the preconditions are satisfied. This type concept is quite useful for a large class of applications.

### 1.1 The Problem

Sometimes, methods shall be called only in certain circumstances depending on the object's current state and history. For example, let "iconify" be a method that replaces a window on a screen with an icon. Preconditions seem to be appropriate for specifying that "iconify" shall be called only when the window is displayed [13]. However, preconditions have limitations: They are not "history sensitive" [12] and cannot always be checked statically, loosing the advantages of strongly typed languages.

In concurrent and distributed systems it is difficult for a user to know an object's state even at run-time; other users may cause unpredictable state changes. Unexpected effects may occur even if all preconditions are satisfied: For example, two concurrent users send "iconify" at about the same time to a displayed window. The window is replaced with an icon when the first message is handled. A further user sees the new state and sends a message causing the window to be displayed again. Then, the window is immediately replaced by an icon again when the second iconify-message is handled. This behavior is probably unexpected because one of the iconify-messages is dealt with in a context different from the one in which the message was sent.

There are several ways to prevent that messages are dealt with in wrong contexts. For example, the programmer implements a protocol ensuring that only one client can send "iconify" to a displayed window. But there is no support from the type system. A type in current type models is a contract between each individual user and an object, but not between the whole set of users and the object. It is not possible to express in the type that users must be coordinated before sending messages like "iconify". There is the implicit assumption that each object must be able to handle all supported messages from all users in arbitrary interleaving. As the windows example shows, this assumption can be too restrictive in practice.

## 1.2 The Proposal

A type model addressing this problem is proposed in the present paper. The type model is based on a process calculus in which each object has a unique identifier (mail address), a behavior and a queue of received messages, as in the actor model [1, 7]. Objects communicate by asynchronous message passing. Some actions in the calculus are annotated with type information. A type specifies all possible sequences of messages accepted by an object as well as type constraints on the messages' parameters. A type checker (or compiler) shall be able to ensure statically that

- objects can deal with all message sequences specified by the objects' types;
- users of an object are coordinated so that only messages specified by the object's type are sent to the object in an expected order.

In a type-consistent program, all objects can deal properly with all received messages. There are no "message-not-understood-errors", unintended behaviors or deadlocks caused by wrong messages or wrong message orders. (The type model cannot prevent all kinds of deadlocks. But it can prevent that an object blocks with a nonempty message queue, waiting for messages not in the queue.)

The messages each user can send to an object are controlled by *type marks*. A type mark allows a user to send some messages. Sometimes, the combination of several type marks allows a user to send a message, while one of these type marks alone is not sufficient for that. Type marks are passed to other users as side-effects of sending messages. The programmer must provide code for coordinating the users by passing messages; the compiler checks if the users actually have all type marks they need.

The proposed type model supports subtyping and genericity. According to the principle of substitutability, an instance of a subtype can be used wherever an instance of a supertype is expected [11, 29]. A subtype extends a supertype by supporting additional messages and message orders so that each message accepted by an object of a supertype is also accepted by an object of a subtype.

In Sect. 2 we describe the kind of object systems considered in this paper and work out important requirements on types in these systems. In Sect. 3 we introduce types that can express coordination requirements and discuss some of their properties. In Sect. 4 we outline a type checking algorithm. An example in Sect. 5 shows how the type model can be used. A comparison with related work follows in Sect. 6. An extended version of this paper is available as a technical report [24].

## 2 Active Objects and Type Consistency

We consider systems composed of active objects that communicate through asynchronous message passing. An active object has its own (single) thread of execution, a behavior, a unique identifier (used as mail address), and an unlimited buffer of received messages. According to its behavior, an object can accept messages from its buffer, send messages to other objects, and create new objects. All messages are received and accepted in the same (logical) order they were sent; message buffers operate in a first-in-first-out manner. These restrictive assumptions make it easier to show how the type model works.

A program specifies the behavior of all objects in an object system. We assume that programs are written in a language based on a process calculus like those explored by Hoare [8], Milner [15, 16, 17] and others [2, 6, 9]. These calculi provide a theoretically well-founded and expressive basis for specifying the behavior of active objects. But they have to be adapted so that all messages sent to some address are handled sequentially by a single object, and atomic actions carry type information. The used calculus shall be simple enough to show static type checking, and expressive enough to support all important language concepts.

### 2.1 The Process Calculus

A *process* specifies the behavior of an object. Fig. 1 shows the syntax of processes denoted by $\theta$. An object with behavior 0, the zero process, does nothing. There are three atomic actions for sending messages, accepting messages and creating new objects. Semicolons separate actions from the processes which shall be executed after the actions. A message consists of a constant name $c$ (the message selector) and a list of arguments $a_1, \ldots, a_n$. (We write a line over an expression as

$$\theta ::= 0 \qquad \text{(zero process; no action)}$$

$$\mid x.c[\bar{a}]; \theta \qquad \text{(send message } c \text{ with arguments } \bar{a} \text{ to } x; \text{ then execute } \theta)$$

$$\mid c(\bar{x})^{\bar{\varphi}}; \theta \qquad \text{(accept message } c \text{ with parameters } \bar{x} \text{ of types } \bar{\varphi}; \text{ then } \theta)$$

$$\mid (x)\$a^{[\bar{\sigma}]}[\bar{a}']; \theta \qquad \text{(create new object } x \text{ that executes } a^{[\bar{\sigma}]}[\bar{a}']; \text{ then } \theta)$$

$$\mid a{=}a' ? \theta : \theta' \qquad \text{(execute } \theta \text{ if } a = a'; \text{ otherwise execute } \theta')$$

$$\mid \theta + \theta' \qquad \text{(alternatives; execute either } \theta \text{ or } \theta')$$

$$\mid a^{[\bar{\sigma}]}[\bar{a}'] \qquad \text{(call } a \text{ with type arguments } \bar{\sigma} \text{ and arguments } \bar{a}')$$

$$a ::= x \qquad \text{(parameter or object identifier)}$$

$$\mid {}^{(\bar{s})}(\bar{x})^{\bar{\varphi}}\theta^{\sigma} \qquad \text{(closed process; does not contain free variable names)}$$

**Fig. 1.** Syntax of Processes

an abbreviation of an indexed list of expressions; e.g., $\bar{a}$ stands for $a_1, \ldots, a_n$. Superscripts represent type annotations.) An accepting action $c(x_1, \ldots, x_n)^{\varphi_1, \ldots, \varphi_n}$ is executable only if the first message in the buffer of received messages has the selector $c$ and arguments $a_1, \ldots, a_n$, where each $a_i$ satisfies the type constraints of $\varphi_i$. The arguments are substituted for the parameters $x_1, \ldots, x_n$. All parameters will be replaced with arguments. Arguments are either object identifiers or *closed processes* which specify object behavior.

A closed process ${}^{(\bar{s})}(\bar{x})^{\bar{\varphi}}\theta^{\sigma}$ consists of

- type parameters $\bar{s}$ (to be substituted by object types),
- parameters $\bar{x}$ of types $\bar{\varphi}$ (standing for object identifiers and closed processes),
- and a process $\theta$ (specifying the behavior) which conforms to the type $\sigma$.

We differentiate between object types (denoted by $\sigma, \tau, \ldots$) and arbitrary types (i.e. types of closed processes or objects, denoted by $\varphi, \psi, \ldots$). Type parameters always stand for object types. (An extended version of this work [24] differentiates between object type parameters, closed process type parameters and general type parameters.)

Closed processes (that resemble generic procedures in imperative languages) can be called by providing types as substitutions for type parameters, and arguments of appropriate types as substitutions for parameters. New objects created by an atomic action get a closed-process call as behavior specification.

Conditional execution is provided in two forms: $a{=}a' ? \theta : \theta'$ corresponds to an if-then-else-statement, where the condition is true if $a$ and $a'$ are equal object identifiers or equivalent closed processes. $\theta + \theta'$ specifies two alternatives; one of them is selected nondeterministically for execution. If $\theta$ and $\theta'$ are headed by incompatible message accepting actions, the first message in the buffer determines the alternative to be executed. Special syntax was selected for equality (and equivalence) comparisons because type checking is easier if if-paths and else-paths occur pairwise.

As in the polyadic $\pi$-calculus [17] pairwise different names enclosed in round brackets represent parameters. They bind further occurrences of these names. An occurrence of a name $n$ in a process is free if it is not bound, i.e., not preceded by a name abstraction $(\ldots, n, \ldots)$. Constant names like those used as message selectors always are free. All free names in closed processes must be constant. Because of this restriction it is possible to pass closed processes as arguments between objects. Arguments enclosed in square brackets are substituted for parameters. We write $\theta\{\bar{a}/\bar{x}\}$ for a process constructed from $\theta$ by simultaneously substituting $\bar{a}$ for all free occurrences of $\bar{x}$, respectively. (Of course, the lists $\bar{a}$ and $\bar{x}$ must have the same length.)

In general, we allow closed processes to be defined recursively. In a closed process $p = {}^{(\bar{s})}(\bar{x})^{\overline{\varphi}}\theta^\sigma$, the name $p$ can occur in $\theta$. This name is silently replaced with the closed process wherever needed.

## 2.2   Examples

A set of simple running examples is used throughout this paper. The examples describe several kinds of data stores (buffers). The closed process S is called within the definition of S:

$$S = {}^{(s)}()\text{put}(x)^s; \text{get}(y)^{\sigma_B}; y.\text{back}[x]; S^{[s]}[]^{\sigma_S}$$

S specifies the behavior of a data store with a capacity of at most one element of an object type given by the type parameter $s$. The closed process has no parameters. A data store first accepts a message "put" with a single argument of type $s$. This message inserts an element into the data store. Then, it accepts a message "get" with an argument of object type $\sigma_B$ (which will be specified later). The argument is supposed to be the identifier of an object that wants to receive the element in the data store as an argument of a message "back". The next action sends this message. Finally, S is called recursively. An object behaving according to S accepts "put" and "get" in alternation, beginning with "put". Other sequences of messages are not acceptable.

The closed process Sd resembles S, but supports the additional message "del" when the buffer is empty. The execution terminates after accepting this message:

$$Sd = {}^{(s)}()(\text{put}(x)^s; \text{get}(y)^{\sigma_B}; y.\text{back}[x]; Sd^{[s]}[] + \text{del}(); 0)^{\sigma_{Sd}}$$

Data stores able to hold arbitrary numbers of elements can behave as Si:

$$Si = {}^{(s)}(x)^{\sigma_{Si}}(\text{put}(y)^s; Sf^{[s]}[x, y] + \text{get}(y)^{\sigma_B}; x.\text{get}[y]; Si^{[s]}[x])^{\sigma_{Si}}$$
$$Sf = {}^{(s)}(x, y)^{\sigma_{Si}, s}(\text{get}(z)^{\sigma_B}; z.\text{back}[y]; Si^{[s]}[x] + \text{put}(z)^s; x.\text{put}[z]; Sf^{[s]}[x, y])^{\sigma_{Si}}$$

Objects with this behavior accept "put" and "get" in arbitrary order. Since the used process calculus does not support dynamic memory management, arrays, etc., the elements in the data stores are simply stored as messages in the objects' buffers. The messages are inspected; all get-messages are written back into the buffer by sending them to the self-reference $x$, until a put-message is accepted. Then, put-messages are written back into the buffer, and after accepting a get-message, "back" is sent, and this cycle is repeated. This implementation is not very efficient, but it is useful as an example for type checking.

## 2.3  Execution and Type Errors

An object system is essentially a set of active objects. Each object executes its thread according to its process as follows:

- If the process is 0, the object's execution halts.
- If the process is of the form $x.c[\bar{a}]; \theta$, a message with selector $c$ and arguments $\bar{a}$ is appended to the end of the buffer belonging to the object identified by $x$. Then, the process becomes $\theta$.
- For a process of the form $c(\bar{x})^{\bar{\varphi}}; \theta$, if the object's buffer is not empty and the first message has the selector $c$ and arguments $\bar{a}$ satisfying the type constraints of $\bar{\varphi}$ (where $\bar{x}$, $\bar{\varphi}$ and $\bar{a}$ are lists of the same length), this message is removed from the buffer, and the process becomes $\theta\{\bar{a}/\bar{x}\}$. Otherwise the execution blocks until the condition is satisfied.
- For a process of the form $(x)\$a^{[\bar{\sigma}]}[\bar{a}']; \theta$, a new object with a new buffer and a new identifier $y$ is constructed. The new object behaves according to $a^{[\bar{\sigma}]}[\bar{a}']\{y/x\}$, and the process of the creating object becomes $\theta\{y/x\}$. (The new object identifier is substituted for the parameter $x$.)
- A process $^{(\bar{s})}(\bar{x})^{\bar{\varphi}}\theta^{\sigma[\bar{\tau}]}[\bar{a}]$ (i.e. a call, where the called expression is a closed process) is executed as $\theta\{\bar{\tau}/\bar{s}\}\{\bar{a}/\bar{x}\}$ provided that the lists $\bar{s}$ and $\bar{\tau}$ as well as $\bar{x}$, $\bar{\varphi}$ and $\bar{a}$ have the same lengths, and the arguments $\bar{a}$ satisfy the type constraints $\bar{\varphi}$. (Types are substituted for type parameters, and arguments for parameters.)
- A conditional expression $a=a'\,?\,\theta:\theta'$ is executed as $\theta$ if $a = a'$. Otherwise it is executed as $\theta'$.
- For a process $\theta + \theta'$, either $\theta$ or $\theta'$ is selected for execution. The selected alternative must be executable, i.e. neither blocked nor equal to 0. If no alternative is executable, the selection is deferred until an alternative becomes executable.

If the execution of an object cannot proceed for some unintended reason, a type error has been detected. These type errors can occur:

- In a call $a^{[\bar{\tau}]}[\bar{a}']$, the called expression $a$ is not a closed process, or $a$ is of the desired form $^{(\bar{s})}(\bar{x})^{\bar{\varphi}}\theta^{\sigma}$, but the lengths of the lists $\bar{s}$ and $\bar{\tau}$ or $\bar{x}$, $\bar{\varphi}$ and $\bar{a}'$ are different, or the arguments $\bar{a}'$ do not satisfy the type constraints $\bar{\varphi}$.
- There is at least one message in the buffer, but the execution still is blocked because no message accepting action in any alternative can deal with the message. The object does not understand the first message in the buffer because a message of this selector and number of arguments is not supported, or the arguments do not satisfy the parameters' type constraints.
- The process is 0, although there are messages in the buffer.

A program assigns a process (not containing free variables) to each initial object. All buffers are initially empty. Objects created later at run-time get their processes (as closed processes and argument lists) from the creating objects. Since closed processes cannot be created at run-time, programs contain all information needed for static type checking.

## 2.4 Type Consistency

Strong, static typing ensures that a system never gets into a state where type errors show up. A type error occurring in some system state already exists in the program specifying the system behavior. An intuitive definition of type consistency is:

**Definition 1.** A program $P$ is weakly type-consistent if and only if no system with behavior $P$ gets into a state where type errors show up.

Unfortunately, this definition is not strong enough: It does not support incremental software development processes and separate type checking. In practice, software components shall be compiled separately. And parts of a program—especially closed processes—shall be replaceable with new parts of compatible types without affecting the whole program's type consistency. The following definition seems to be more appropriate:

**Definition 2.** For a compatibility relation $C$ on closed processes, a program $P$ is type-consistent w.r.t. $C$ if and only if $P$ and each program $Q$ are weakly type-consistent, where $Q$ is constructed from $P$ by substituting arbitrary closed processes $p_1, \ldots, p_n$ by closed processes $q_1, \ldots, q_n$ with $q_i \, C \, p_i$ ($1 \leq i \leq n$).

The less restrictive the compatibility relation $C$, the more freedom has the programmer in replacing software components without affecting type consistency, but the smaller is the set of type-consistent programs. A compromise between freedom in replacing components type-safely and freedom in programming (which influences the simplicity of developing components) must be found. An appropriate compromise is a compatibility relation defined just as restrictive as needed for separate compilation. Separate compilation is possible if

- all parameters are associated with static type constraints;
- no further assumptions than expressed in type constraints are made;
- arguments must satisfy the parameters' type constraints.

If these conditions hold (as in the proposed model), a closed process that satisfies some constraints can be replaced without further type checking by closed processes satisfying at least the same constraints. These constraints are expressed in the closed processes' (and the corresponding objects') types. In the rest of this work we use the compatibility relation $\sqsubseteq$:

**Definition 3.** Two closed processes $p$ and $q$ of types $\varphi$ and $\psi$, respectively, are related by $p \sqsubseteq q$ if and only if $\varphi$ is a subtype of $\psi$.

For example, it shall be possible to replace the closed process S (as defined in Sect. 2.2) with Sd or Si; Sd $\sqsubseteq$ S and Si $\sqsubseteq$ S shall hold because both, Sd and Si, accept all message sequences accepted by S.

When replacing a closed process, it is sufficient to check the type consistency of the new closed process, provided that the new closed process' type is a subtype of the replaced one's type.

$$\varphi ::= @(\overline{s})\langle\overline{\varphi}\rangle\sigma \qquad \text{(closed process type; without free type parameters)}$$
$$\quad | \; \sigma \qquad\qquad \text{(object type)}$$

$$\sigma ::= \{\overline{u}\}|b \qquad \text{(descriptive object type)}$$
$$\quad | \; \sigma \times \sigma' \qquad \text{(combination of object types)}$$
$$\quad | \; s \qquad\qquad \text{(type parameter)}$$

$$u ::= c \qquad\qquad \text{(simple state descriptor)}$$
$$\quad | \; c^* \qquad\qquad \text{(replicated state descriptor)}$$

$$b ::= 0 \qquad\qquad \text{(empty behavior descriptor)}$$
$$\quad | \; c\langle\overline{\varphi}\rangle\{\overline{c}\}{\rightarrow}\{\overline{u}\} \quad \text{(message descriptor)}$$
$$\quad | \; b + b' \qquad\quad \text{(combined behavior descriptor)}$$

**Fig. 2.** Syntax of Types

## 3 Message Sequences Expressed in Types

### 3.1 Syntax and (Informal) Semantics of Types

The proposed model supports types of two kinds: Types of objects and types of closed processes. This distinction is reflected in the syntax of types as defined in Fig. 2, where $\varphi, \psi, \ldots$ denote types of any kind, and $\sigma, \tau, \ldots$ object types.

*Descriptive object types* partially specify the behavior of these types' instances (objects). They describe the acceptable messages as well as restrictions on their orders. During computation, an object's type may change in the same way as the object's process. Hence, types shall contain variable components. A type $\{\overline{u}\}|b$ consists of two parts: The *activating set* $\{\overline{u}\}$ represents an abstract state of the type's instances. The *behavior descriptor* $b$ describes a set of messages; their acceptability depends on the activating set. (Alternative message descriptors in behavior descriptors are combined by +; 0 denotes a behavior descriptor not supporting any message.) When an object's process changes, the activating set can also change, but the behavior descriptor remains unchanged.

An activating set $\{\overline{u}\}$ is a multi-set of *state descriptors*, each denoted by $u, v, w, \ldots$. Different states are distinguished by the presence or absence of state descriptors. Some of the constant names used as state descriptors are marked with an asterisk indicating that an infinite number of the name's duplicates are contained in the multi-set.

For each supported message, the behavior descriptor contains a *message descriptor* $d\langle\overline{\varphi}\rangle\{\overline{c}\}\{\overline{v}\}$, where $d$ is the message selector, $\overline{\varphi}$ the list of parameter types, $\{\overline{c}\}$ the *in-set* and $\{\overline{v}\}$ the *out-set*. The message descriptor is *active* if all names in the multi-set $\{\overline{c}\}$ are contained in the activating set. (A name $c$ is regarded as being contained in the multi-set if $c^*$ or $c$ is in the multi-set.) An active message descriptor specifies an acceptable message. When a corresponding message is accepted, the names in $\{\overline{c}\}$ are removed from the activating set (but not state descriptors of the form $c^*$), and the state descriptors in the multi-set $\{\overline{v}\}$ are added.

A closed process type $@(\bar{s})\langle\bar{\varphi}\rangle\sigma$ specifies the type parameters $\bar{s}$ and the parameter types $\bar{\varphi}$ of its instances (closed processes), as well as the initial types of objects behaving according to these closed processes. The (most concrete) type of a closed process $p = {}^{(\bar{s})}(\bar{x})^{\bar{\varphi}}\theta^{\sigma}$ is $@(\bar{s})\langle\bar{\varphi}\rangle\sigma$, where $\sigma$ (or more completely $\sigma\{\bar{\tau}/\bar{s}\}$) is a type of an object with behavior $p^{[\bar{\tau}]}[\bar{a}]$, i.e. a call of $p$.

For example, the object type $\sigma_S$ of an empty simple data store with behavior S (as introduced in Sect. 2.2) can be:

$$\sigma_S = \{\text{empty}\} \mid \text{put}\langle s\rangle\{\text{empty}\}\to\{\text{full}\} + \text{get}\langle\sigma_B\rangle\{\text{full}\}\to\{\text{empty}\}$$

Only "put" is acceptable. After accepting "put", the activating set becomes $\{\text{full}\}$, and only "get" becomes acceptable. The parameter type of "get" may be the object type

$$\sigma_B = \{\text{once}\} \mid \text{back}\langle s\rangle\{\text{once}\}\to\{\}$$

i.e., the object accepts "back" with an argument of type $s$ only once. ($\{\}$ denotes an empty multi-set.)

The types $\sigma_{Sd}$ and $\sigma_{Si}$ of empty data stores with behavior Sd and Si (as introduced in Sect. 2.2), respectively, can be:

$$\sigma_{Sd} = \{\text{empty}\} \mid \text{put}\langle s\rangle\{\text{empty}\}\to\{\text{full}\} + \text{get}\langle\sigma_B\rangle\{\text{full}\}\to\{\text{empty}\}$$
$$+ \text{del}\langle\rangle\{\text{empty}\}\to\{\}$$
$$\sigma_{Si} = \{\} \mid \text{put}\langle s\rangle\{\}\to\{\} + \text{get}\langle\sigma_B\rangle\{\}\to\{\}$$

An instance of a combination of object types $\sigma \times \tau$ accepts all messages specified by $\sigma$ as well as those specified by $\tau$ in arbitrary interleaving. When accepting messages specified by $\sigma$, only $\sigma$ is updated, and when accepting messages specified by $\tau$, only $\tau$ is updated. Combinations of object types play an important role in subtyping, static type checking, and together with type parameters.

A type parameter $s$ does not give any information about the messages acceptable by instances of $s$. Sometimes we need type parameters, but still want to have some information about acceptable messages. In object-oriented languages like Eiffel, bounded type parameters (where types substituted for type parameters must be subtypes of some type constants) can provide this type information. Unfortunately, bounded type parameters are not directly applicable in our model: If a message is sent to an instance of a type represented by a type parameter, the type may change; we have no representation of the changed type. Combinations of object types of the form $\{\bar{u}\}|b \times s_1 \times \cdots \times s_n$ provide a solution: Instances of these types are known to accept messages according to $\{\bar{u}\}|b$; the activating sets in the first parts of the types can be updated, while the type parameters remain unchanged.

## 3.2 Normalizable Object Types

If a user of an object knows that the object's type is $\{\bar{u}\}|b$, the user can safely send an acceptable message to the object. Then, the user updates his knowledge of the object's type, and the object updates its type after accepting the message.

Of course it is necessary that the object and its user update the type in the same way so that the user's knowledge remains valid. However, object types as described so far do not necessarily specify deterministically, how types shall be updated after sending or accepting a message: For example, if the type is of the form $\{c_1, c_2\} \mid d\langle\overline{\varphi}\rangle\{c_1\}\rightarrow\{c_3\} + d\langle\overline{\varphi}\rangle\{c_2\}\rightarrow\{c_4\} + \cdots$, the updated activating set is $\{c_2, c_3\}$ or $\{c_1, c_4\}$, depending on the considered message descriptor. In the rest of this paper we deal only with deterministic object types, where for each supported message there is only one possibility of updating the activating set. A sufficient (but not necessary) condition for deterministic object types is that all message descriptors have pairwise different message selectors.

State descriptors in activating sets and out-sets are useful only if there are message descriptors depending on these state descriptors. If a state descriptor does not occur in any in-set, it has no meaning. State descriptors without meaning are undesirable, especially when combining object types. Therefore, we define object types in normal form by:

**Definition 4.** An object type $\{\overline{u}\}\mid b \times s_1 \times \cdots \times s_m$ (where $m \geq 0$ and $b$ is 0 or of the form $d_1\langle\overline{\varphi}_1\rangle\{\overline{c}_1\}\rightarrow\{\overline{v}_1\} + \cdots + d_n\langle\overline{\varphi}_n\rangle\{\overline{c}_n\}\rightarrow\{\overline{v}_n\}$) is in normal form if and only if all message selectors $d_1, \ldots, d_n$ are pairwise different and there exists a $c \in \bigcup_{1 \leq i \leq n}\{\overline{c}_i\}$ for each $c, c^* \in \bigcup_{1 \leq i \leq n}\{\overline{v}_i\} \cup \{\overline{u}\}$, and all object types occurring in $\overline{\varphi}_1, \ldots, \overline{\varphi}_n$ are in normal form.

The specific form of object types in normal form is not always useful. For example, the types $\sigma_S$, $\sigma_{Sd}$, $\sigma_{Si}$ and $\sigma_B$ (shown in Sect. 3.1) are not in normal form because $s$ is not in normal form. Sometimes we need object types only semantically equivalent to object types in normal form. The type parameter $s$ is semantically equivalent to the object type $\{\}\mid 0 \times s$ in normal form:

**Definition 5.** An object type $\sigma$ is normalizable if and only if $\sigma$ can be reduced to an object type in normal form by

- using associativity, commutativity and 0 as neutral element of +,
- using associativity, commutativity and $\{\}\mid0$ as neutral element of $\times$,
- and repeatedly applying the rules R1 to R4:

R1 For a type $\{\overline{u}\}\mid b$: Remove a state descriptor $c$ or $c^*$ from the activating set or an out-set in $b$ if $c$ does not occur in any in-set.

R2 For a multi-set of state descriptors: Remove all duplicates of state descriptors of the form $c^*$; if the multi-set contains $c^*$, remove all $c$.
   This rule is sound because $c^*$ stands for an infinite number of copies of $c$.

R3 For a type $\{\overline{u}\}\mid b$: Simultaneously remove message descriptors of the form $d\langle\varphi_1, \ldots, \varphi_n\rangle\{\overline{c}\}\rightarrow\{\overline{v}\}$ from $b$ and then apply R1 to the remaining rules if (for each removed message descriptor) $b$ contains a further message descriptor $d\langle\psi_1, \ldots, \psi_n\rangle\{\overline{c}'\}\rightarrow\{\overline{v}'\}$, where each $\varphi_i$ is a subtype of $\psi_i$ ($1 \leq i \leq n$), $\{\overline{c}'\}$ is a sub-multi-set of $\{\overline{c}\}$, and (with $w$ and $w'$ constructed from $v$ and $v'$, respectively, by applying R1) $\{\overline{w}\}$ is a sub-multi-set of $\{\overline{w}'\}$.
   This rule removes unnecessary message descriptors dealing with messages also dealt with by other message descriptors:

- Each argument type conforming to a parameter type of a removed message descriptor also conforms to the corresponding parameter type of a remaining message descriptor.
- A remaining message descriptor always is active when a removed message descriptor was active.
- When corresponding messages are accepted, the remaining message descriptors add all state descriptors added by the removed ones.

R4 For a type $\{\overline{u}\}|b \times \{\overline{v}\}|b'$, where $\{\overline{u}\}|b$ and $\{\overline{v}\}|b'$ are in normal form: Replace this type with $\{\overline{u}, \overline{v}\} \mid b + b'$.

This rule reflects the informal semantics: Instances of $\sigma \times \tau$ accept at least all messages acceptable by $\sigma$ and those acceptable by $\tau$ in arbitrary interleaving. ($\{\overline{u}\}|b \times \{\overline{v}\}|b'$ specifies more acceptable messages than interleavings of $\{\overline{u}\}|b$ and $\{\overline{v}\}|b'$ if message descriptors in $b+b'$ depend on state descriptors in both, $\{\overline{u}\}$ and $\{\overline{v}\}$.) Since $\{\overline{u}\}|b$ and $\{\overline{v}\}|b'$ are in normal form, $\{\overline{u}\}$ and $\{\overline{v}\}$ cannot contain state descriptors useful in $b + b'$ but not in $b$ and $b'$, respectively.

All object types that can be reduced to the same object type using the algebraic properties and R1 to R4 are regarded as equivalent. We write $\sigma \equiv \tau$ if $\sigma$ and $\tau$ are equivalent. It is easy to see that the rules are terminating and confluent. Hence, there exists an effective algorithm for deciding whether or not two object types are equivalent.

Rule R4 expresses an equivalence between combinations of object types and descriptive object types. An important equivalence for all behavior descriptors $b$ and activating sets $\{\overline{u}_1\}, \ldots, \{\overline{u}_n\}$ is $\{\overline{u}_1\}|b \times \cdots \times \{\overline{u}_n\}|b \equiv \{\overline{u}_1, \ldots, \overline{u}_n\}|b$. (Since all combined object types have the same behavior descriptor, the same set of state descriptors is useful for them. Replicated message descriptors in $b+\cdots+b$ can be removed by applying R3.) Type checking is based on this equivalence. In the specific case of activating sets $\{\overline{u}\}$ containing only replicated state descriptors of the form $c^*$, the equivalence $\{\overline{u}\}b \times \{\overline{u}\}b \equiv \{\overline{u}\}b$ holds. Combinations of object types with different behavior descriptors are used in subtyping.

Object type equivalence is easily extended to closed process types: Two closed process types are equivalent if they have the same numbers of type parameters, and the parameter types as well as the types specifying the initial object behavior are pairwise equivalent (after renaming type parameters). The notions of normal forms and normalizable types also can easily be adapted to closed process types: A closed process type $\varphi$ is normalizable (or in normal form) if all object types occurring in $\varphi$ are normalizable (in normal form).

We assume that object types and closed process types can be defined recursively: For a type $\sigma = \{\overline{u}\}|b$, the type name $\sigma$ can occur as parameter type in $b$; and for a type $\psi = @(\overline{s})\langle\overline{\varphi}\rangle\sigma$, the name $\psi$ can occur in $\overline{\varphi}$. These names are silently replaced with the corresponding type expressions wherever needed. Type equivalence is decidable even when using recursive types. (The corresponding rules are not shown here because of their rather involved technicalities.)

The normalizability property of object types is preserved when types are updated: After accepting a message, only useful state descriptors are added to activating sets; behavior descriptors and type parameters remain unchanged.

## 3.3 Subtyping

According to the principle of substitutability, an instance of a subtype can be used wherever an instance of a supertype is expected [11, 29]. Especially, an instance of a subtype must accept all message sequences as promised by a supertype. This consideration immediately leads to the definition:

**Definition 6.** An object type $\sigma$ is a subtype of an object type $\tau$ (formally $\sigma \leq \tau$) if and only if there exists an object type $\sigma'$ such that $\sigma \equiv \tau \times \sigma'$.

A closed process type $@(\bar{s})\langle\varphi_1,\ldots,\varphi_n\rangle\sigma$ is a subtype of a closed process type $\psi$ if and only if $\psi$ (after renaming bound type parameters) is of the form $@(\bar{s})\langle\psi_1,\ldots,\psi_n\rangle\tau$ and $\psi_i \leq \varphi_i$ (for all $1 \leq i \leq n$) and $\sigma \leq \tau$.

The subtype relation on object types directly reflects the following property: A subtype $\sigma$ extends a supertype $\tau$ by supporting additional messages and message orders (as specified by $\sigma'$). Each message accepted by an instance of $\tau$ is also accepted by an instance of $\tau \times \sigma'$ (and equivalently $\sigma$).

Types of closed processes have contravariant parameter types: If an instance $p$ of a type $@(\bar{s})\langle\bar{\varphi}\rangle\sigma$ is expected in a call $p^{[\bar{\tau}]}[\bar{a}]$, each instance of a subtype $\psi$ can be used instead of $p$ and must be able to deal with all arguments $\bar{a}$. An object executing this call must accept all messages specified by $\sigma$.

It is easy to verify that subtyping is an antisymmetric, reflexive and transitive relation on equivalence classes of types.

An important step in deciding whether or not an object type $\sigma$ is a subtype of a type $\tau$ is to find an appropriate type $\sigma'$ such that $\sigma \equiv \tau \times \sigma'$. Fortunately, $\sigma'$ can easily be found for object types in normal form: If $\sigma$ is of the form $\{\bar{u}\}|b \times s_1 \times \cdots \times s_m \times \cdots \times s_n$, and $\tau$ of the form $\{\bar{v}\}|b' \times s_1 \times \cdots \times s_m$, then $\sigma'$ is $\{\bar{w}\}|b \times s_{m+1} \times \cdots \times s_n$, where $\{\bar{w}\}$ contains all state descriptors in $\{\bar{u}\}$ except those in $\{\bar{v}\}$. Under these conditions, $\sigma \leq \tau$ can be decided by deciding whether or not $\{\bar{u}\}|b \equiv \{\bar{v},\bar{w}\} | b + b'$. If $\sigma$ and $\tau$ cannot be brought into these forms using commutativity of $\times$, $\sigma$ is not a subtype of $\tau$.

Intuitively, the object types $\sigma_S$, $\sigma_{Sd}$ and $\sigma_{Si}$ (defined in Sect. 3.1) shall be related by $\sigma_{Si} \leq \sigma_S$ and $\sigma_{Sd} \leq \sigma_S$, but $\sigma_{Si}$ and $\sigma_{Sd}$ shall not be related by subtyping. These types are (after replacing $s$ with $\{\}|0 \times s$) in normal form. We show $\sigma_{Si} \leq \sigma_S$ by showing $\sigma_{Si} \equiv \sigma_S \times \sigma'_{Si}$, where $\sigma'_{Si} = \sigma_{Si}$:

$$
\begin{aligned}
\sigma_S \times \sigma_{Si} &\equiv \{\text{empty}\} \,|\, \text{put}\langle s\rangle\{\text{empty}\}{\to}\{\text{full}\} + \text{put}\langle s\rangle\{\}{\to}\{\} \\
&\quad + \text{get}\langle\sigma_B\rangle\{\text{full}\}{\to}\{\text{empty}\} + \text{get}\langle\sigma_B\rangle\{\}{\to}\{\} \\
&\equiv \{\} \,|\, \text{put}\langle s\rangle\{\}{\to}\{\} + \text{get}\langle\sigma_B\rangle\{\}{\to}\{\} = \sigma_{Si}
\end{aligned}
$$

First, the type combination is resolved by using R4. Then, a message descriptor for "put" and one for get are removed simultaneously by applying R3. (The two message descriptors cannot be removed sequentially because the out-sets would not be appropriate.) The proof of $\sigma_{Sd} \leq \sigma_S$ is equally simple:

$$
\begin{aligned}
\sigma_S \times \sigma_{Sd} &\equiv \{\text{empty}\} \,|\, \text{put}\langle s\rangle\{\text{empty}\}{\to}\{\text{full}\} + \text{put}\langle s\rangle\{\text{empty}\}{\to}\{\text{full}\} \\
&\quad + \text{get}\langle\sigma_B\rangle\{\text{full}\}{\to}\{\text{empty}\} + \text{get}\langle\sigma_B\rangle\{\text{full}\}{\to}\{\text{empty}\} \\
&\quad + \text{del}\langle\rangle\{\text{empty}\}{\to}\{\} \\
&\equiv \sigma_{Sd}
\end{aligned}
$$

# 4 Type Checking

Static type checking is divided into two logical parts. One part checks whether objects (regarded as servers) are actually able to accept all messages as promised by the object's type. The other part checks whether objects (regarded as users) send only type-conforming messages. Before we can give a type checking algorithm, we have to state which messages users can safely send to an object.

## 4.1 Type Marks

As mentioned in Sect. 1.2, the messages each user can send to an object are controlled by type marks. In a process, the initial type mark for an object is the type annotation of the parameter standing for the object. (We will usually say "type mark of a parameter" instead of "type mark for an object represented by a parameter".) Type annotations of parameters bound in message receiving actions or closed processes (parameter types) are specified explicitly. The type annotation of the parameter bound in an object creating action is the annotation of the closed process specifying the new object's behavior. If a parameter of type $@(\overline{s})\langle\overline{\varphi}\rangle\sigma$ is used for this closed process, the initial type mark for the created object is $\sigma$.

A type mark of $x$ always reflects the user's knowledge about the type of the object represented by $x$. A process $x.c[\overline{a}];\theta$ is type-conforming only if the type mark of $x$ specifies an acceptable message with selector $c$ and an appropriate number of parameters with appropriate types. The type mark of $x$ in $\theta$ can be different: The type mark must be updated by removing the state descriptors in the corresponding message descriptor's in-set from the activating set and adding the state descriptors in the out-set.

An object can have several users who send messages concurrently. The object must be able to accept all messages from concurrent users in arbitrary interleaving. Combinations of object types have the required properties: If there are $n$ parameters $x_1,\ldots,x_n$ (standing for the same object) with type marks $\sigma_1,\ldots,\sigma_n$, respectively, the object must understand all messages according to $\sigma_1 \times \cdots \times \sigma_n$. Especially, if the object is of type $\{\overline{u}_1,\ldots,\overline{u}_n\}|b$, each parameter $x_i$ can have a type mark $\sigma_i$ with $\{\overline{u}_i\}|b \leq \sigma_i$.

An object creating action $(x)\$a^{[\overline{\tau}]}[\overline{a}']$ binds a single parameter $x$; no other parameter stands for the new object. Hence, the type mark $\sigma$ of $x$ can be equal to the new object's type. When an alias of $x$ (i.e. a further parameter standing for the same object as $x$) is introduced by using $x$ as an argument, $x$'s type mark $\sigma$ must be split into $\sigma_1$ and $\sigma_2$, where $\sigma \equiv \sigma_1 \times \sigma_2$; $x$ gets the new type mark $\sigma_2$, and the new parameter's initial type mark is $\sigma_1$. So, the condition stated in the previous paragraph remains satisfied. In general, type splitting has to be applied whenever a new alias is introduced, i.e. for each use of a parameter of an object type as an argument. The original type mark $\sigma$ of a parameter $x$ used as argument is known as well as the explicitly specified type mark $\sigma_1$ (parameter type) of the new alias. The new type mark $\sigma_2$ of $x$ can be computed from the equivalence $\sigma \equiv \sigma_1 \times \sigma_2$ in the same way as the object type needed in proving

$\sigma \leq \sigma_1$ (see Sect. 3.3). If $\sigma \leq \sigma_1$ does not hold, the types of $x$ and its new alias are incompatible and the program is not type-consistent.

A type $\sigma \times \tau$ can specify more acceptable messages than all interleavings of acceptable messages specified by $\sigma$ and $\tau$. A single parameter with a type mark $\sigma \times \tau$ can allow a user to send more messages than two parameters with type marks $\sigma$ and $\tau$. Therefore, the process calculus contains conditional expressions of the form $x{=}y\,?\,\theta:\theta'$ (where $x$'s type mark is $\sigma$, and $y$'s type mark is $\tau$). In the if-path $\theta$, $x$ and $y$ are regarded as equal with the combined type mark $\sigma \times \tau$, whereas in the else-path $\theta'$, $x$ and $y$ still have separate type marks.

No updating and splitting of types is necessary for closed process types. Closed process types are handled in the same way as types in conventional object-oriented languages.

For a human reader it is rather easy to understand the type annotations of the closed processes S, Sd and Si (as introduced in Sect. 2.2 with types defined in Sect. 3.1). Directly after accepting a message $get(y)^{\sigma_B}$, $y$ has the type mark $\{once\} \mid back\langle s\rangle\{once\}{\rightarrow}\{\}$, and $x$ has the type mark $s$. After an action $y.back[x]$, $y$'s type mark is updated to $\{\} \mid back\langle s\rangle\{once\}{\rightarrow}\{\}$, and $x$'s type mark is split such that $x$'s new type mark is $\{\}|0$. Neither $x$ nor $y$ accept any further message. The type mark $\sigma_{Si}$ resembles a type in a conventional object-oriented language: It remains unchanged after sending messages to its instances, and it can be split into $\sigma_{Si}$ and $\sigma_{Si}$ because $\sigma_{Si} \equiv \sigma_{Si} \times \sigma_{Si}$.

## 4.2 Checking Type Marks

Since each occurrence of a parameter is associated with a type mark, it is not difficult for a compiler to ensure that users send only messages as specified in the type marks to an object. A checker of type marks walks (from left to right) through each (closed) process in a program. Thereby it has to

- initialize the type mark of each parameter where it is bound; free parameters must not occur in a program;
- for each message sending action $x.d[a_1, \ldots, a_n]$:
  1. ensure that $x$'s type mark specifies an active message descriptor of the form $d\langle\varphi_1, \ldots, \varphi_n\rangle\{\bar{c}\}{\rightarrow}\{\bar{u}\}$, and update $x$'s type mark;
  2. for each $1 \leq i \leq n$: if $a_i$ is a parameter, ensure that $a_i$'s type mark is a subtype of $\varphi_i$ and (if $\varphi_i$ is an object type) split $a_i$'s type mark; otherwise ($a_i$ is a closed process $^{(\bar{s})}(\bar{x})^{\bar{\psi}}\theta^{\sigma}$) check the type marks and the object behavior of $a_i$ and ensure $@(\bar{s})\langle\bar{\psi}\rangle\sigma \leq \varphi_i$;
- for each action $a^{[\sigma_1, \ldots, \sigma_m]}[a_1, \ldots, a_n]$ or $(x)\$a^{[\sigma_1, \ldots, \sigma_m]}[a_1, \ldots, a_n]$ (after initializing $x$'s type mark):
  1. ensure that $a$ is a closed process $^{(s_1, \ldots, s_m)}(\bar{x})^{\varphi_1, \ldots, \varphi_n}\theta^{\sigma}$ for which a check of the type marks and the object behavior succeeds, or $a$ is a parameter with a type mark $@(s_1, \ldots, s_m)\langle\varphi_1, \ldots, \varphi_n\rangle\sigma$;
  2. for each $1 \leq i \leq n$: if $a_i$ is a parameter, ensure that $a_i$'s type mark is a subtype of $\varphi_i$ and (if $\varphi_i$ is an object type) split $a_i$'s type mark;

otherwise ($a_i$ is a closed process $^{(\bar{s}')}(\bar{x}')^{\bar{\psi}}\theta^\tau$) check the type marks and the object behavior of $a_i$ and ensure $@(\bar{s}')\langle\bar{\psi}\rangle\tau \le \varphi_i$;

- for each expression $\theta + \theta'$: check $\theta$ and $\theta'$ independently (with the same type marks at the beginning);
- for each expression $a=a' ? \theta : \theta'$: if both, $a$ and $a'$ are parameters standing for object types, check $\theta'$ with the current type marks, and check $\theta\{a/a'\}$ independently with updated type marks, where $a$'s updated type mark is a combination of $a$'s and $a'$'s current type marks;

  otherwise ($a$ or $a'$ is a closed process or a parameter standing for a closed process) check $\theta$ and $\theta'$ independently.

**Proposition 7.** *Let $P$ be a program passing the above checks. Then, no system with behavior $P$ can get into a state where an object's type does not contain an active message descriptor corresponding to the first message in the object's buffer. Furthermore, the checks ensure that each called expression is an appropriate closed process.*

This proposition holds because each object's type is a subtype of the combination of the type marks of all parameters standing for this object. Checking type marks ensures that type marks are actually used as described in Sect. 4.1.

## 4.3   Checking Object Behavior

A type checker also has to ensure that each object always can deal with all messages corresponding to an active message descriptor in the object's type. A checker of object behavior walks (from left to right) through each closed process $^{(\bar{s})}(\bar{x})^{\bar{\psi}}\theta^\sigma$ in a program. Thereby it has to ensure for $\theta$ with $\sigma$ that

- $\sigma$ is a normalizable object type $\{\bar{u}\}|b$; then, $\sigma$ is reduced to normal form;
- if $\theta$ is 0, no message descriptor in $\sigma$ is active;
- if $\theta$ is $d_1(\bar{x}_1)^{\bar{\varphi}_1}; \theta_1 + \cdots + d_n(\bar{x}_n)^{\bar{\varphi}_n}; \theta_n$ ($n \ge 1$), $\sigma$ contains no active message descriptor $d\langle\bar{\varphi}'\rangle\{\bar{c}\}\to\{\bar{v}\}$ with $d \notin \{d_1,\ldots,d_n\}$ (i.e., there is at least one message accepting action for each active message descriptor), and checking succeeds for each $d_i(\bar{x}_i)^{\bar{\varphi}_i}; \theta_i$ with $\sigma$ ($1 \le i \le n$);
- if $\theta$ is $\theta_1 + \cdots + \theta_n$ ($n \ge 1$), where at least one $\theta_i \ne 0$ has no message receiving action in the head, checking succeeds for each $\theta_i$ with $\sigma$ ($1 \le i \le n$);
- (in addition to the above two items) if $\theta$ is $d(\bar{x})^{\varphi_1,\ldots,\varphi_n}; \theta'$ and $\sigma$ contains an active message descriptor $d\langle\varphi'_1,\ldots,\varphi'_n\rangle\{\bar{c}\}\to\{\bar{v}\}$, each $\varphi'_i \le \varphi_i$ ($1 \le i \le n$) and checking succeeds for $\theta'$ with $\sigma'$, where $\sigma'$ is constructed by updating $\sigma$;
- if $\theta$ is $d(\bar{x})^{\bar{\varphi}}; \theta'$ and $\sigma$ contains no appropriate active message descriptor, this dead code ($\theta$) is eliminated (replaced with 0);
- if $\theta$ is $x.d[\bar{a}]; \theta'$ or $(x)\$a^{[\bar{\tau}]}[\bar{a}']; \theta'$, checking succeeds for $\theta'$ with $\sigma$;
- if $\theta$ is $a=a' ? \theta' : \theta''$, checking succeeds for $\theta'$ with $\sigma$ and for $\theta''$ with $\sigma$;
- if $\theta$ is $a^{[\bar{\tau}]}[\bar{a}']$ and $a$ is a closed process $^{(\bar{s}')}(\bar{x}')^{\bar{\psi}'}\theta'^\tau$ or a parameter of type $@(\bar{s}')\langle\bar{\psi}'\rangle\tau$, then $\tau\{\bar{\psi}'/\bar{s}'\} \le \sigma$.

**Proposition 8.** *Let P be a program passing the above checks. Then, each object in a system with behavior P accepts all messages specified by the object's type.*

The checks ensure that there is a message accepting action for each active message descriptor.

The main result of this paper directly follows from the definition of $\sqsubseteq$ (given in Sect. 2.4), Proposition 7 and Proposition 8:

**Theorem 9.** *A program passing the above checks of type marks and object behavior is type-consistent w.r.t. $\sqsubseteq$.*

For each $q \sqsubseteq p$, the closed process $q$ substituted for $p$ is checked in the same way as $p$. Since $q$'s type is a subtype of $p$'s type, $q$ satisfies all constraints promised by $p$'s type.

Programs accepted by our type checker do not suffer from an important kind of deadlocks:

**Theorem 10.** *Let P be a program passing the above checks of type marks and object behavior. Then, in a system with behavior P, the execution of an object with a nonempty message buffer cannot be blocked.*

Deadlocks can occur only if a user does not send a message needed by an object.

We shall estimate the complexity of type checking: A type checker runs through each process once for checking object behavior and once for checking type marks. (Of course, these phases can be combined.) No part of a process must be checked several times in each phase. The type checker always knows which checks must be applied to show type consistency. Thus, the type checker runs through the code at most twice. Assuming an appropriate type representation and considering type comparisons with a worst case time complexity of at most quadratic order, the worst case time complexity of the whole type checker is of at most quadratic order.

# 5 Discussion

## 5.1 Coordination with Type Marks

The solution of the dining philosophers problem in Fig. 3 shall demonstrate how synchronization restrictions can be expressed in the proposed type model. Philosophers sit around a table and spend their time with thinking and eating. Each philosopher has a plate of spaghetti and a fork. However, two forks are needed for eating this kind of spaghetti. When a philosopher becomes hungry, he has to borough a fork from his neighbor. All philosophers shall get a fair chance to eat. The dining philosophers problem is a well-known example from a class of problems, where several concurrent users (philosophers) need exclusive access to limited, shared resources (forks).

The behavior descriptor $b_P$ specifies the messages each philosopher can deal with. A philosopher always is in one of four abstract states: thinking, asking his

$$b_P = \text{eat}\langle\{\}|b_P, \{\text{down}\}|b_F\rangle\{\text{thinking}\}\rightarrow\{\text{asking}\} +$$
$$\text{ask}\langle\{\text{asking}\}|b_P\rangle\{\}\rightarrow\{\} +$$
$$\text{yes}\langle\{\text{eating}\}|b_P, \{\text{nice}\}|b_P, \{\text{down}\}|b_F\rangle\{\text{asking}\}\rightarrow\{\text{eating}\} +$$
$$\text{no}\langle\{\text{thinking}\}|b_P\rangle\{\text{asking}\}\rightarrow\{\text{thinking}\} +$$
$$\text{think}\langle\rangle\{\text{eating}\}\rightarrow\{\text{thinking}\} +$$
$$\text{grant}\langle\{\}|b_P\rangle\{\text{thinking}\}\rightarrow\{\text{nice}\} +$$
$$\text{back}\langle\{\text{thinking}\}|b_P, \{\text{down}\}|b_F\rangle\{\text{nice}\}\rightarrow\{\text{thinking}\}$$

$$b_F = \text{get}\langle\rangle\{\text{down}\}\rightarrow\{\text{up}\} +$$
$$\text{put}\langle\rangle\{\text{up}\}\rightarrow\{\text{down}\}$$

$$\text{Pth} = {}^{()}(x,y,z)^{\{\text{thinking}\}|b_P,\{\}|b_P,\{\text{down}\}|b_F}($$
$$\text{ask}(y')^{\{\text{asking}\}|b_P}; x.\text{grant}[y]; x'.\text{yes}[x',x,z]; \text{Pf}^{[]}[] +$$
$$x.\text{eat}[y,z]; y.\text{ask}[x]; \text{Pf}^{[]}[])^{\{\text{thinking}\}|b_P}$$

$$\text{Pf} = {}^{()}(\text{ask}(y)^{\{\text{asking}\}|b_P}; y.\text{no}[y]; \text{Pf}^{[]}[] +$$
$$\text{grant}(y)^{\{\}|b_P}; \text{Pn}^{[]}[y] +$$
$$\text{eat}(y,z)^{\{\}|b_P,\{\text{down}\}|b_F}; \text{Pa}^{[]}[y,z])^{\{\text{thinking}\}|b_P}$$

$$\text{Pn} = {}^{()}(y)^{\{\}|b_P}(\text{ask}(y')^{\{\text{asking}\}|b_P}; y'.\text{no}[y']; \text{Pn}^{[]}[y] +$$
$$\text{back}(x,z)^{\{\text{thinking}\}|b_P,\{\text{down}\}|b_F}; \text{Pth}^{[]}[x,y,z])^{\{\text{nice}\}|b_P}$$

$$\text{Pa} = {}^{()}(y,z)^{\{\}|b_P,\{\text{down}\}|b_F}(\text{ask}(y')^{\{\text{asking}\}|b_P}; y'.\text{no}[y'], \text{Pa}^{[]}[y,z] +$$
$$\text{yes}(x,y,z')^{\{\text{eating}\}|b_P,\{\text{nice}\}|b_P,\{\text{down}\}|b_F}; z.\text{get}[]; z'.\text{get}[]; \text{Pe}^{[]}[x,y,z,z'] +$$
$$\text{no}(x)^{\{\text{thinking}\}|b_P}; \text{Pth}^{[]}[x,y,z])^{\{\text{asking}\}|b_P}$$

$$\text{Pe} = {}^{()}(x,y,z,z')^{\{\text{eating}\}|b_P,\{\}|b_P,\{\text{up}\}|b_F,\{\text{up}\}|b_F}($$
$$\text{ask}(y')^{\{\text{asking}\}|b_P}; y'.\text{no}[y']; \text{Pe}^{[]}[x,y,z,z'] +$$
$$x.\text{think}[]; z.\text{put}[]; z'.\text{put}[]; y.\text{back}[y,z']; \text{Pg}^{[]}[x,y,z])^{\{\text{eating}\}|b_P}$$

$$\text{Pg} = {}^{()}(x,y,z)^{\{\text{thinking}\}|b_P,\{\}|b_P,\{\text{down}\}|b_F}($$
$$\text{ask}(y')^{\{\text{asking}\}|b_P}; y'.\text{no}[y']; \text{Pg}^{[]}[x,y,z] +$$
$$\text{think}(); \text{Pth}^{[]}[x,y,z])^{\{\text{eating}\}|b_P}$$

**Fig. 3.** Closed Processes for Dining Philosophers

right neighbor for a fork, being nice by giving his fork to his left neighbor, and eating with two forks. The acceptable messages depend on the abstract state. As the behavior descriptor $b_F$ shows, a fork can be in two states: down on the table or up in a philosopher's hand. The abstract states of philosophers and forks as well as the acceptable messages for each abstract state and the corresponding state changes are shown graphically in Fig. 4.

When asked for a fork, a philosopher with behavior Pth gives his fork to a neighbor by sending "grant" to himself and "yes" to the philosopher who asked. (Parameter $x$ stands for the philosopher itself, $y$ for his right neighbor, $y'$ for his left neighbor who asks for the fork, and $z$ for the own fork.) When a philosopher becomes hungry, he sends "eat" to himself and "ask" to his right neighbor. All further requests for a fork are answered with "no". When receiving "grant", the (nice) philosopher waits for the message "back" from his left neighbor who returns the fork, and then continues with thinking. When receiving "eat", the

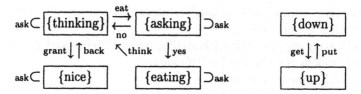

**Fig. 4.** The Abstract States of a Dining Philosopher and a Fork

(asking) philosopher waits for an answer from his right neighbor. If the answer is "no", he continues with thinking. Otherwise he takes his and his neighbor's fork and begins to eat. When he is no longer hungry, he puts the forks on the table, returns one of them to his neighbor and sends himself a message "think". When receiving this message, he begins to think again.

As the example shows, the proposed model can actually deal with rather difficult synchronization problems in a type-safe manner. Types express in which circumstances messages are supported, and a type checker ensures that only supported messages are received and each object can handle all supported messages. For example, each philosopher can be sure that he does not receive a message "eat" while he is "nice".

The type model cannot ensure that the solution of this problem is free of deadlocks because there is no way to ensure that all users send messages as expected. For example, a philosopher always remains in state "nice" if his neighbor does not return his fork. The type model also cannot prevent live-locks. But with this type model it is impossible that an object does not understand a message in its buffer.

The example in Fig. 3 also shows that synchronization sometimes requires additional messages and message arguments. A message "ask" contains a reference to the sending philosopher as a parameter; the answer shall be returned to this parameter. The answer also contains this parameter, although the receiver of the answer knows it. But it is still necessary to have this parameter: The parameter of "ask" is associated with a type mark which allows the receiver to send a reply. In order to avoid uncontrolled aliasing (since appropriate type splitting is impossible), the philosopher cannot keep the type mark describing his own abstract state. The answer returns the (updated) type mark so that the philosopher can continue to send messages to himself.

## 5.2 Object Types as Automata

Usually, descriptive object types correspond to finite automata: Activating sets represent states, acceptable messages represent state transitions. Fig. 4 shows the automata corresponding to the types of philosophers and forks.

It is not possible to represent all protocols as finite automata. Even if possible, it may not be desirable to represent an involved protocol as an object type because it can be difficult for a programmer to handle many different type marks. But, it is always possible to use arbitrary approximations to such protocols: A type of the form $\{\} \mid d_1\langle\overline{\varphi}_1\rangle\{\}\to\{\} + \cdots + d_n\langle\overline{\varphi}_n\rangle\{\}\to\{\}$ is a simple first approximation of a protocol supporting the messages $d_1,\ldots,d_n$; the corresponding automaton has only one state. The type model ensures that an object of this type always accepts each supported message. If the object accepts a message that should not be received because of a constraint on message orders not expressed in the type, the object can raise an exception. A constraint on message orders expressed in a type is checked statically, while one not expressed in the type is checked dynamically. The first approximation can be improved by adding further abstract states (and constraints on message orders) to the type.

Since activating sets can hold an unlimited number of state descriptors, an automaton corresponding to an object type can, in principle, have an unlimited number of states. However, without some extensions of the model, we cannot make much use of this flexibility. If we extend the model with integer variables (over given ranges) as generic parameters and allow the corresponding integers to specify the number of occurrences of state descriptors in activating sets and be used in conditions of if-then-else-expressions, we can actually use object types that correspond to automata with an unlimited number of states. For example, $\sigma_{Su}$ is the type of a data store that always accepts put-messages, but only as many get-messages as there are elements in the store:

$$\sigma_{Su} = \{\} \mid \mathrm{put}\langle s\rangle\{\}\to\{\mathrm{full}\} + \mathrm{get}\langle\sigma_B\rangle\{\mathrm{full}\}\to\{\}$$

This type corresponds to an automaton with an unlimited number of states. It is no more difficult to deal with $\sigma_{Su}$ than with types corresponding to finite automata. For example, it is easy to show $\sigma_{Si} \leq \sigma_{Su} \leq \sigma_{S}$. But integer variables as generic parameters are needed, for example, to specify a closed process that performs different actions on such data stores, depending on the number of elements.

## 6 Related Work

Much work on types for concurrent languages and models has been done. The majority of this work is based on Milner's $\pi$-calculus [15, 17] and similar calculi. Especially, the problem of inferring most general types was considered by Gay [5] and Vasconcelos and Honda [28]. Nierstrasz [19], Pierce and Sangiorgi [20], Vasconcelos [27] and Kobayashi and Yonezawa [10] deal with subtyping in such calculi. But their type models differ in an important aspect from the one presented in this work: They cannot represent constraints on the order of messages and ensure statically that all sent messages will be processed.

Several proposals [10, 20, 27] support subtyping in a similar way as sequential object-oriented languages based on the typed $\lambda$-calculus: A type of an active object specifies the set of messages that will be accepted by all instances; a subtype specifies an extended set of messages. Some of these proposals [20, 27] ensure that all sent messages will be processed, but do not support constraints on the sequence of messages. The proposal of Kobayashi and Yonezawa [10] ensures neither message processing nor constraints on message sequences.

A large amount of work based on "path expressions" [3, 26] and, more recently, process algebra [2, 15] shows that reasoning about the order of messages in concurrent systems is quite difficult. Not much work was done on type models able to deal with constraints on message sequences because of the difficulty of this problem. Nierstrasz [19] argues that it is essential for a type model to regard an object as a process in a process calculus. He proposes "regular types" and "request substitutability" as foundations of subtyping. However, his very general results are not concrete enough to develop a static type system from them, especially because his approach does not consider aliases.

The proposal of Nielson and Nielson [18] can deal with constraints on message sequences. As in the type model proposed in this paper, types in their proposal are based on a process algebra, and a type checker updates type information while walking through a process expression. However, their proposal does not control aliases; types are regarded as contracts between an object and a single user, not as a contract between an object and the whole set of its users. Thus, their type model cannot ensure that all sent messages are understood. But subtyping is supported so that instances of subtypes preserve the properties expressed in supertypes; if a program corresponding to a supertype sends only understood messages, also a program corresponding to a subtype does so. Because types in their model specify the communication between processes completely, subtyping is rather restricted.

The present work improves earlier work on the process type model [21, 22, 23]. These earlier type models also support subtyping and ensure statically that all sent messages are understood, although constraints on message sequences are considered. The type model in the present work uses a new type representation that has several advantages over the old one:

- It provides better support for the coordination of users. In the earlier models, a user sometimes had to ask the object if some messages were acceptable. In the present model, users coordinate themselves without asking the object.
- The present model supports more efficient type checking. In some versions of the process type model, type checking was exponential in time, or even undecidable. Now, type checking time is quadratic in the worst case.
- The earlier models did not support genericity.

A type representation slightly similar to the one used in this work was proposed in [25]. But that proposal does not deal with subtyping and genericity and does not provide a formal analysis. A more thorough and formal treatment of the present work can be found in [24].

*Future work.* The work on this type model is not yet finished. Currently, it is not possible to specify in types which response is expected from the receiver of a message. There is ongoing work to make it possible for a type checker to ensure statically that the receiver of a message sends an appropriate reply. More expressive behavior descriptions as in [11] shall also be considered. Furthermore, the type model shall be adapted for different kinds of communication, including synchronous message passing, restricted buffer sizes, and reordering of messages in message buffers. Several kinds of "fine tuning", especially considering explicit self-references, shall help to reduce the necessary syntactical overhead of using this type model.

## 7  Conclusions

The results of this work show that it is indeed feasible to regard a type as a contract between an (active) object and the unity of all users. Types specify constraints on the expected sequences of messages. A type checker can ensure statically that concurrent users are actually coordinated so that all sequences of messages sent to an object conform to the object's type, and the object accepts all type-conforming messages. Subtyping, genericity and separate compilation can be supported.

## References

1. Gul Agha. *Actors: A Model of Concurrent Computation in Distributed Systems.* The MIT Press, 1986.
2. J. C. M. Baeten and W. P. Weijland. *Process Algebra*, volume 18 of *Cambridge Tracts in Theoretical Computer Science.* Cambridge University Press, 1990.
3. R. H. Campbell and A. N. Habermann. The specification of process synchronization by path expressions. In E. Gelenbe, editor, *Proceedings of the International Symposium on Operating Systems*, volume 16 of *Lecture Notes in Computer Science*, pages 89–102. Springer-Verlag, 1974.
4. Luca Cardelli and Peter Wegner. On understanding types, data abstraction, and polymorphism. *ACM Computing Surveys*, 17(4):471–522, 1985.
5. Simon J. Gay. A sort inference algorithm for the polyadic $\pi$-calculus. In *Conference Record of the 20th Symposium on Principles of Programming Languages*, January 1993.
6. Matthew Hennessy. *Algebraic Theory of Processes.* The MIT Press, 1988.
7. Carl Hewitt. Viewing control structures as patterns of passing messages. *Journal of Artificial Intelligence*, 8(3), 1977.
8. C. A. R. Hoare. Communicating sequential processes. *Communications of the ACM*, 21(8):666–677, August 1978.
9. Kohei Honda and Mario Tokoro. An object calculus for asynchronous communication. In Pierre America, editor, *Proceedings ECOOP'91*, volume 512 of *Lecture Notes in Computer Science*, pages 141–162, Geneva, Switzerland, July 1991. Springer-Verlag.
10. Naoki Kobayashi and Akinori Yonezawa. Type-theoretic foundations for concurrent object-oriented programming. *ACM SIGPLAN Notices*, 29(10):31–45, October 1994. Proceedings OOPSLA'94.
11. Barbara H. Liskov and Jeannette M. Wing. A behavioral notion of subtyping. *ACM Transactions on Programming Languages and Systems*, 16(6):1811–1841, November 1994.

12. Satoshi Matsuoka and Akinori Yonezawa. Analysis of inheritance anomaly in object-oriented concurrent programming languages. In Gul Agha, Peter Wegner, and Akinori Yonezawa, editors, *Research Directions in Concurrent Object-Oriented Programming*. The MIT Press, 1993.

13. Bertrand Meyer. Systematic concurrent object-oriented programming. *Communications of the ACM*, 36(9):56–80, September 1993.

14. Bertrand Meyer. *Reusable Software: The Base Object-Oriented Component Libraries*. Prentice-Hall, Englewood Cliffs, NJ, 1994.

15. R. Milner, J. Parrow, and D. Walker. A calculus of mobile processes (parts I and II). *Information and Computation*, 100:1–77, 1992.

16. Robin Milner. *Communication and Concurrency*. Prentice-Hall, New York, 1989.

17. Robin Milner. The polyadic $\pi$-calculus: A tutorial. Technical Report ECS-LFCS-91-180, Dept. of Comp. Sci., Edinburgh University, 1991.

18. Flemming Nielson and Hanne Riis Nielson. From CML to process algebras. In *Proceedings CONCUR'93*, volume 715 of *Lecture Notes in Computer Science*, pages 493–508. Springer-Verlag, 1993.

19. Oscar Nierstrasz. Regular types for active objects. *ACM SIGPLAN Notices*, 28(10):1–15, October 1993. Proceedings OOPSLA'93.

20. Benjamin Pierce and Davide Sangiorgi. Typing and subtyping for mobile processes. In *Proceedings LICS'93*, 1993.

21. Franz Puntigam. Flexible types for a concurrent model. In *Proceedings of the Workshop on Object-Oriented Programming and Models of Concurrency*, Torino, June 1995.

22. Franz Puntigam. Type specifications with processes. In *Proceedings FORTE'95*. IFIP WG 6.1, October 1995.

23. Franz Puntigam. Types for active objects based on trace semantics. In Elie Najm et al., editor, *Proceedings of the 1st IFIP Workshop on Formal Methods for Open Object-based Distributed Systems*, Paris, France, March 1996. IFIP WG 6.1, Chapman & Hall.

24. Franz Puntigam. Coordination requirements expressed in types for active objects. Technical report, Institut für Computersprachen, Technische Universität Wien, Vienna, Austria, 1997. Electronically available under http://www.complang.tuwien.ac.at/franz/papers/ecoop97tr.ps.gz.

25. Franz Puntigam. Types that reflect changes of object usability. In *Proceedings of the Joint Modular Languages Conference*, volume 1204 of *Lecture Notes in Computer Science*, Linz, Austria, March 1997. Springer-Verlag.

26. Jan van den Bos, Rinus Plasmeijer, and Jan Stroet. Process communication based on input specifications. *ACM Transactions on Programming Languages and Systems*, 3(3):224–250, July 1981.

27. Vasco T. Vasconcelos. Typed concurrent objects. In *Proceedings ECOOP'94*, volume 821 of *Lecture Notes in Computer Science*, pages 100–117. Springer-Verlag, 1994.

28. Vasco T. Vasconcelos and Kohei Honda. Principal typing schemes in a polyadic pi-calculus. In *Proceedings CONCUR'93*, July 1993.

29. Peter Wegner and Stanley B. Zdonik. Inheritance as an incremental modification mechanism or what like is and isn't like. In S. Gjessing and K. Nygaard, editors, *Proceedings ECOOP'88*, volume 322 of *Lecture Notes in Computer Science*, pages 55–77. Springer-Verlag, 1988.

# Java is Type Safe — Probably

Sophia Drossopoulou and Susan Eisenbach

Department of Computing
Imperial College of Science, Technology and Medicine
email: sd and se @doc.ic.ac.uk

**Abstract.** Amidst rocketing numbers of enthusiastic Java programmers and internet applet users, there is growing concern about the security of executing Java code produced by external, unknown sources. Rather than waiting to find out empirically what damage Java programs do, we aim to examine first the language and then the environment looking for points of weakness. A proof of the soundness of the Java type system is a first, necessary step towards demonstrating which Java programs won't compromise computer security.

We consider a type safe subset of Java describing primitive types, classes, inheritance, instance variables and methods, interfaces, shadowing, dynamic method binding, object creation, null and arrays. We argue that for this subset the type system is sound, by proving that program execution preserves the types, up to subclasses/subinterfaces.

## 1 Introduction

Before the first complete Java language description was available [13] use of the language was extremely widespread and the rate of increase in usage is steep. The language may not have reached a stable point in its development yet: there exist differences between the language descriptions [16, 17, 13], and there are many suggestions for additional features [19, 2]. Several studies have uncovered flaws in the security of the Java system [11], and have pointed out the need for a formal semantics.

Java combines the experience from the development of several object oriented languages, such as C++, Smalltalk and CLOS. The main features of the language are primitive types (character, integer, boolean, float), classes with inheritance, instance/class variables and methods, interfaces for class signatures, shadowing of instance variables, dynamic method binding, exceptions, arrays, strings, class modifiers (private, protected, public *etc*), final/abstract classes and methods, nested scopes, separate compilation, constructors and finalizers. The philosophy of the language designers was to include only features with already known semantics, and to provide a small and simple language.

Nevertheless, we feel that the introduction of some new features in Java, as well as the specific combination of features, justifies a study of the Java formal semantics. The use of interfaces, reminiscent of [9, 5] is a simplification of the signatures extension for C++ [3] and is – to the best of our knowledge – novel. The mechanism for dynamic method binding is that of C++, but we know of no formal definition. Java adopts the Smalltalk approach whereby all object variables are implicitly pointers.

Furthermore, although there are a large number of studies of the semantics of isolated programming language features or of minimal programming languages [1], there have not been many studies of the formal semantics of *actual* programming languages . In addition, the interplay of features which are very well understood in isolation, might introduce unexpected effects.

Experience confirms the importance of formal studies of type systems early on during language development. Eiffel, a language first introduced in 1985, was discovered to have a loophole in its type system in 1990 [8, 18]. Given the growing usage of Java, it seems important that if there are loopholes in the type system they be discovered early on.

We aim to argue that the type system of Java is sound, in the sense that unless an exception is raised, the evaluation of any expression will produce a value of a type "compatible" with the type assigned to it by the type system.

We were initially attracted to Java, because of its elegant combination of several tried language features. For this work we were guided by the language descriptions, [17], [13]. We found the language description complete and unambiguous, in the sense that any question relating to semantics could be answered unambiguously by [13]. However, we discovered some rules to be more restrictive than necessary, and the reasons for some design decisions were not obvious. We hope that the language authors will publish a language design rationale soon.

## 1.1 The Java subset considered so far

In this paper we consider the following parts of the Java language: primitive types, classes and inheritance, instance variables and instance methods, interfaces, shadowing of instance variables, dynamic method binding, object creation with new, the null value, arrays, and some exceptions[12].

We chose this Java subset because we consider the Java way of combining classes, interfaces and dynamic method binding to be both novel and interesting. Furthermore, we chose an imperative subset right from the start, because the extension of type systems to the imperative case has sometimes uncovered new problems, (*e.g.* multi-methods for functional languages [7], and for imperative languages in[4], the Damas and Milner polymorphic type systems for functional languages [10], and for the imperative extension [21]). We considered arrays, because of the known requirement for run time type checking.

We describe the language as in the [13] definition with the exception of method binding, which we model as described in [17], because it imposes a weaker requirement. Namely, [17] requires methods that hide methods from superclasses or superinterfaces to have a return type that can be widened to the return type of the hidden method, whereas [13] requires them to have the same type. Because the first requirement is weaker, our soundness result automatically applies to the new, stricter version of Java as in [13].

## 1.2 Our approach

We define Java$_s$, a safe subset of Java containing the features listed previously, a term rewrite system to describe the Java$_s$ operational semantics and a type inference system to describe compile-time type checking. We prove that program execution preserves the types up to the subclass/subinterface relationship.

We aimed to keep the description straightforward, and so we have removed some of the syntactic sugar in Java, *e.g.* we require instance variable access to have the form this.var as opposed to var, and we require the last statement in a method to be a return statement. These restrictions simplify the type inference and term rewriting systems.

The type system is described in terms of an inference system. In contrast with many type systems for object oriented languages, it does not have a subsumption rule, a crucial property when type checking message expressions, *c.f.* 3.2. Contrary to Java, Java$_s$ statements have a type – and thus we can type check the return values of method bodies.

The execution of Java programs requires some type information at run-time (*e.g.* method descriptors as in ch. 15.11 in [13]). For this reason, we define Java$_{se}$, an enriched version of Java$_s$ containing compile-time type information to be used for method call and field access. Interestingly, it turns out, that in contrast to Java and Java$_s$, Java$_{se}$ *does* enjoy a "substitution property". Hence in Java$_{se}$ the replacement of a subexpression of type T by another subexpression of a subtype of T, does not affect the type of the overall expression – up to the subclass/subinterface relationship. This should not be surprising, since the lack of a substitution property in Java was probably the reason for the introduction of method descriptors in the first place.

The operational semantics is defined for Java$_{se}$ as a ternary rewrite relationship between configurations, terms and configurations. Configurations are tuples of terms and states. The terms represent the part of the original program remaining to be executed. We describe method calls through textual substitution.

We have been able to avoid additional structures such as program counters and higher order functions. The Java$_s$ simplifications of eliminating block structure and local variables allow the definition of the state as a flat structure, where addresses are mapped to objects and global variables are mapped to primitive values or addresses. Objects carry their classes (similar to the Smalltalk abstract machine [15], thus we do not need store types [1], or location typings [14]). Objects are labelled tuples, where each label contains the class in which it was declared. Array values are tuples too, and they are annotated by their type and their dimension.

This paper is organized as follows: In section 2 we give the syntax of Java$_s$. In section 3 we define the static types for Java$_s$, and the mapping from Java$_s$ to Java$_{se}$. In section 4 we describe states, configurations and the operational semantics for Java$_{se}$. In section 5 we prove the Subject Reduction Theorem. In section 6 we give an example. Finally, in section 7 we outline further work and draw some conclusions.

# 2 The language Java$_s$

Java$_s$ describes a subset of Java, including classes, instance variables, instance methods, inheritance of instance methods and variables, shadowing of instance variables, interfaces, widening, method calls, assignments, object creation and access, the null value, instance variable access and the exception NullPointExc, arrays, array creation and the exceptions ArrStoreExc, NegSzeExc and IndOutBndExc. We have not yet considered initializers, constructors, finalizers, class variables and class methods, local variables, class modifiers, final/abstract classes and methods, **super**, strings, numeric promotions and widenings, concurrency, the handling of exceptions, packages and separate compilation.

There are slight differences between the syntax of Java$_s$ and Java which were introduced to simplify the formal description. A Java program contains both type and evaluation information. The type information consists of variable declarations, parameter and result types for methods, and interfaces of classes. The evaluation information consistent statements in method bodies. In Java$_s$ this information is split into two: type information is contained in the environment (usually represented by a $\Gamma$), whereas evaluation information is reflected in the program (usually represented by a $p$). An example can be seen in section 6.

We follow the convention that Java$_s$ keywords appear as keyword, identifiers as **identifier**, nonterminals appear in italics as *Nonterminal*, and the metalanguage symbols appear in roman (*e.g.* ::=, ( ,*, )). Identifiers with the suffix Id (*e.g.* VarId) indicate the identifiers of newly declared entities, whereas identifiers with the suffix Name (*e.g.* VarName) indicate a previously declared entity.

## 2.1 Programs

A program consists of a sequence of class bodies. Class bodies consist of a sequence of method bodies.

Method bodies consist of the method identifier, the names and types of the arguments, and a statement sequence. We require that there is exactly one return statement in each method body, and that it is the last statement. This simplifies the Java$_s$ operational semantics without restricting the expressiveness, since it requires at most a minor transformation to enable any Java method body to satisfy this property.

We need only consider conditional statements, assignments and method calls. This is because loop, break, continue and case statements can be coded in terms of conditionals and loops; try and throw statements belong to exceptions which are outside the scope of the current state of our investigations.

We consider values, method calls, and instance variable access. Java values are primitive (*e.g.* literals such as true, false, 3, $'c'$ *etc*), references or arrays. References are null, or pointers to objects. The expression new C creates a new object of class C, whereas the expression new $T[m_1]...[m_n][]_1...[]_k$, $n \geq 1, k \geq 0$ creates a $n+k$-dimensional array value. Pointers to objects are implicit. We distinguish variable types (sets of possible run-time values for variables) and method types, as can be seen in figure 1.

$$
\begin{array}{ll}
\textit{Program} & ::= \{ \; ( \; \textit{ClassBody} \; )^* \; \} \\
\textit{ClassBody} & ::= \texttt{ClassId ext ClassName} \; \{ \; ( \; \textit{MethodBody} \; )^* \; \} \\
\textit{MethodBody} & ::= \texttt{MethId is} \; (\lambda \; \texttt{ParId} : \textit{VarType}.)^* \; \{ \; \textit{Stmts} \; ; \; \texttt{return} \; [\textit{Expr}] \; \} \\
\textit{Stmts} & ::= \epsilon \; | \; \textit{Stmts} \; ; \; \textit{Stmt} \\
\textit{Stmt} & ::= \texttt{if} \; \textit{Expr} \; \texttt{then} \; \textit{Stmts} \; \texttt{else} \; \textit{Stmts} \\
& \quad | \quad \textit{Var} := \textit{Expr} \\
& \quad | \quad \textit{Expr} \\
\textit{Expr} & ::= \textit{Value} \\
& \quad | \quad \textit{Var} \\
& \quad | \quad \textit{Expr}.\texttt{MethName} \; ( \; \textit{Expr}^* ) \\
& \quad | \quad \texttt{new ClassName} \\
& \quad | \quad \texttt{new} \; \textit{SimpleType} \; (([\; \textit{Expr} \;])^+ ([\;])^*) \; | ([\;])^+) \\
\textit{Var} & ::= \texttt{Name} \\
& \quad | \quad \textit{Var}.\texttt{VarName} \\
& \quad | \quad \textit{Var}[\textit{Expr}] \\
& \quad | \quad \texttt{this} \\
\textit{Value} & ::= \textit{PrimValue} \; | \; \texttt{null} \\
\textit{PrimValue} & ::= \textit{intValue} \; | \; \textit{charValue} \; | \; \textit{byteValue} \; | \; \dots \\
\textit{VarType} & ::= \textit{SimpleVarType} \; | \; \textit{ArrayType} \\
\textit{SimpleType} & ::= \textit{PrimType} \; | \; \texttt{ClassName} \; | \; \texttt{InterfaceName} \\
\textit{ArrayType} & ::= \textit{SimpleType}[\;] \; | \; \textit{ArrayType}[\;] \\
\textit{PrimType} & ::= \texttt{bool} \; | \; \texttt{char} \; | \; \texttt{int} \; | \; \dots \\
\textit{MethType} & ::= \textit{ArgType} \rightarrow (\textit{VarType} \; | \; \textit{void}) \\
\textit{ArgType} & ::= (\textit{VarType} \; (\times \textit{VarType})^*)
\end{array}
$$

**Fig. 1.** $\text{Java}_s$ programs

## 2.2 The environment

The environment, usually denoted by a $\Gamma$, contains both the subclass and interface hierarchies and variable type declarations. It also contains the type definitions of all variables and methods of a class and its interface. *StandardEnv* should include all the predefined classes, *e.g.* **Object** and all the classes described in chapters 20-22 of [13], but at the moment it is empty. Declarations consist of class declarations, interface declarations and identifier declarations.

A class declaration introduces a new class as a subclass of another class (if no explicit superclass is given, then **Object** will be assumed), a sequence of component declarations, and optionally, interfaces implemented by the class. Component declarations consist of field identifiers and their types, and method identifiers and their signatures. Method bodies are not declarations; they are found in the program part rather than the environment.

An interface declaration introduces a new interface as a subinterface of several other interfaces and a sequence of components. The only interface components in $\text{Java}_s$ are methods, because interface variables are implicitly static, and we have

$$
\begin{array}{lll}
\mathit{Env} & ::= & \mathit{StandardEnv} \mid \mathit{Env}\ ;\ \mathit{Decl} \\
\mathit{StandardEnv} & ::= & \epsilon \\
\mathit{Decl} & ::= & \texttt{ClassId}\ \mathsf{ext}\ \texttt{ClassName}\ \mathsf{impl}\ (\texttt{InterfName})^* \\
 & & \quad \{\ (\texttt{VarId} : \mathit{VarType})^*\ (\texttt{MethId} : \mathit{MethType})^*\ \} \\
 & \mid & \texttt{InterfId}\ \mathsf{ext}\ \texttt{InterfName}^* \{\ (\texttt{MethId} : \mathit{MethType})^*\ \} \\
 & \mid & \texttt{VarId} : \mathit{VarType}
\end{array}
$$

**Fig. 2.** Java$_s$ environments

not yet considered static variables. Variable declarations introduce variables of a given type.

$$
\frac{\Gamma = \Gamma',\ \mathtt{C}\ \ \mathsf{ext}\ \ \mathtt{C}'\ \mathsf{impl}\ \ldots\{\ldots\}, \Gamma''}{\begin{array}{l}\Gamma \vdash \mathtt{C} \sqsubseteq \mathtt{C} \\ \Gamma \vdash \mathtt{C} \sqsubseteq \mathtt{C}'\end{array}}
\qquad
\frac{\begin{array}{l}\Gamma \vdash \mathtt{C} \sqsubseteq \mathtt{C}' \\ \Gamma \vdash \mathtt{C}' \sqsubseteq \mathtt{C}''\end{array}}{\Gamma \vdash \mathtt{C} \sqsubseteq \mathtt{C}''}
$$

$$
\frac{\Gamma = \Gamma',\ \mathtt{C}\ \ \mathsf{ext}\ \ \mathtt{C}'\ \mathsf{impl}\ \ldots\mathtt{I}\ldots\{\ \ldots\ \}, \Gamma''}{\Gamma \vdash \mathtt{C} :_{imp} \mathtt{I}}
\qquad
\frac{}{\vdash \mathtt{Object} \sqsubseteq \mathtt{Object}}
$$

$$
\frac{\Gamma = \Gamma',\ \mathtt{I}\ \ \mathsf{ext}\ \ldots,\ \mathtt{I}'\ ,\ldots\{\ \ldots\ \}, \Gamma''}{\begin{array}{l}\Gamma \vdash \mathtt{I} \leq \mathtt{I} \\ \Gamma \vdash \mathtt{I} \leq \mathtt{I}'\end{array}}
\qquad
\frac{\begin{array}{l}\Gamma \vdash \mathtt{I} \leq \mathtt{I}' \\ \Gamma \vdash \mathtt{I}' \leq \mathtt{I}''\end{array}}{\Gamma \vdash \mathtt{I} \leq \mathtt{I}''}
$$

**Fig. 3.** subclass and subinterface relationships

The subclass $\sqsubseteq$ and the implements $:_{imp}$ relations are defined by the inference rules in figure 3. Every class introduced in $\Gamma$ is its own subclass, and the assertion $\Gamma \vdash \mathtt{C} \sqsubseteq \mathtt{C}$ indicates that `C` is defined in the environment $\Gamma$ as a class. The direct superclass of a class is indicated in its declaration. `Object` is a predefined class. The assertion $\Gamma \vdash \mathtt{C} :_{imp} \mathtt{I}$ indicates that the class `C` was declared in $\Gamma$ as providing an implementation for interface `I`. The subclass relationship is transitive. Every interface is its own subinterface and the assertion $\Gamma \vdash \mathtt{I} \leq \mathtt{I}$ indicates that `I` is defined in the environment $\Gamma$ as an interface. The superinterface of an interface is indicated in its declaration. The subinterface relationship is transitive.

**Definition 1** *For a method type* $\mathtt{MT}= \mathtt{T}_1 \times \ldots \times \mathtt{T}_n \rightarrow \mathtt{T}$, *we define the* argument types *and the* result type*:*

- $Args(\mathtt{MT}) = \mathtt{T_1} \times \ldots \times \mathtt{T_n}$
- $Res(\mathtt{MT}) = \mathtt{T}$

Variable types (*i.e.* primitive types, interfaces, classes and arrays) are required in type declarations; method types (*i.e.* $\mathtt{n}$ argument types, and a result type, with $\mathtt{n} \geq 0$) are required in method declarations. The assertion $\Gamma \vdash \mathtt{T} \diamond_{VarType}$ means that $\mathtt{T}$ is a variable type, $\Gamma \vdash \mathtt{AT} \diamond_{ArgType}$ means that $\mathtt{AT}$ is a method argument type, and $\Gamma \vdash \mathtt{MT} \diamond_{MethType}$ means that $\mathtt{MT}$ is a method type.

$$\frac{\Gamma \vdash \mathtt{C} \sqsubseteq \mathtt{C}}{\Gamma \vdash \mathtt{C} \diamond_{VarType}} \qquad \frac{\Gamma \vdash \mathtt{I} \leq \mathtt{I}}{\Gamma \vdash \mathtt{I} \diamond_{VarType}} \qquad \frac{\Gamma \vdash \mathtt{T} \diamond_{VarType}}{\Gamma \vdash \mathtt{T[]} \diamond_{VarType}}$$

$$\frac{}{\begin{array}{l}\vdash \mathtt{int} \diamond_{VarType} \\ \vdash \mathtt{char} \diamond_{VarType} \\ \vdash \mathtt{bool} \diamond_{VarType}\end{array}} \qquad \frac{\begin{array}{l}\Gamma \vdash \mathtt{T} \diamond_{VarType} \\ \Gamma \vdash \mathtt{T_i} \diamond_{VarType} \quad \mathtt{i} \in \{\mathtt{1}, \ldots \mathtt{n}\}, \mathtt{n} \geq 0\end{array}}{\begin{array}{l}\Gamma \vdash \mathtt{T_1} \times \ldots \times \mathtt{T_n} \diamond_{ArgType} \\ \Gamma \vdash \mathtt{T_1} \times \ldots \times \mathtt{T_n} \rightarrow \mathtt{T} \diamond_{MethType}\end{array}}$$

**Fig. 4.** method and variable types

The widening relationship, described in figure 5, exists between variable types. If a type $\mathtt{T}$ can be widened to a type $\mathtt{T'}$ (expressed as $\Gamma \vdash \mathtt{T} <_{wdn} \mathtt{T'}$), then a value of type $\mathtt{T}$ can be assigned to a variable of type $\mathtt{T'}$ without any run-time casting or checking taking place. This is defined in chapter 5.1.4 [17]; chapter 5.1.2 in [17] defines widening of primitive types, but here we shall only be concerned with widening of references. Furthermore, for the null value, we introduce the type $\mathtt{nil}$ which can be widened to any array, class or interface.

$$\frac{\Gamma \vdash \mathtt{T} \diamond_{VarType}}{\Gamma \vdash \mathtt{T} <_{wdn} \mathtt{T}} \qquad \frac{\Gamma \vdash \mathtt{T} \sqsubseteq \mathtt{T'}}{\Gamma \vdash \mathtt{T} <_{wdn} \mathtt{T'}} \qquad \frac{\Gamma \vdash \mathtt{T} \leq \mathtt{T'}}{\Gamma \vdash \mathtt{T} <_{wdn} \mathtt{T'}} \qquad \frac{\Gamma \vdash \mathtt{T} <_{wdn} \mathtt{Object}}{\Gamma \vdash \mathtt{nil} <_{wdn} \mathtt{T}}$$

$$\frac{\begin{array}{l}\Gamma \vdash \mathtt{T} \leq \mathtt{T} \\ \textit{or } \Gamma(\mathtt{T}) = \mathtt{T'[]}\end{array}}{\Gamma \vdash \mathtt{T} <_{wdn} \mathtt{Object}} \qquad \frac{\Gamma \vdash \mathtt{T} <_{wdn} \mathtt{T'}}{\Gamma \vdash \mathtt{T[]} <_{wdn} \mathtt{T'[]}} \qquad \frac{\begin{array}{l}\Gamma \vdash \mathtt{T} \sqsubseteq \mathtt{T'} \\ \Gamma \vdash \mathtt{T'} :_{imp} \mathtt{T''} \\ \Gamma \vdash \mathtt{T''} \leq \mathtt{T'''}\end{array}}{\Gamma \vdash \mathtt{T} <_{wdn} \mathtt{T'''}} \qquad \frac{}{\Gamma \vdash \mathtt{nil} <_{wdn} \mathtt{nil}}$$

**Fig. 5.** widening relationship

## 2.3 Well-formed declarations and environments

It is easy to see that the relations $\sqsubseteq$, $:_{imp}$, $\leq$ and $<_{wdn}$ are computable for any environment. In this section we describe the Java requirements for variable, class and interface declarations to be well-formed. We indicate by $\Gamma \vdash \Gamma' \diamond$, that the declarations in environment $\Gamma'$ are well-formed, under the declarations of the larger environment $\Gamma$. We need to consider a larger environment $\Gamma$ because Java allows forward declarations (*e.g.* in section 6 the class Phil uses the class FrPhil whose declaration follows that of Phil). We shall call $\Gamma$ well-formed, iff $\Gamma \vdash \Gamma \diamond$. Therefore, the assertion $\Gamma \vdash \Gamma' \diamond$ is checked in two stages: The first stage establishes the relations $\sqsubseteq$, $:_{imp}$, $\leq$ and $<_{wdn}$ for the complete environment $\Gamma$, and the second stage establishes that the declarations in $\Gamma'$ are well-formed one by one, according to the rules in this section. Not surprisingly, the empty environment is well-formed. We need the notion of definition table lookup, *i.e.* $\Gamma(\text{Id})$,

$$\Gamma \vdash \epsilon \diamond \qquad \qquad \frac{\Gamma \vdash \Gamma' \diamond \qquad \Gamma \vdash T \diamond_{VarType} \qquad \Gamma'(\mathbf{x}) = \mathsf{Undef}}{\Gamma \vdash \Gamma', \mathbf{x} : T \diamond}$$

**Fig. 6.** well-formed declarations

which returns the definition of the identifier Id in $\Gamma$, if it has one.

**Definition 2** *For an environment $\Gamma$, with unique definitions for every identifier, we define $\Gamma(\text{id})$ as follows:*

- $\Gamma(\mathbf{x}) = T$ *iff* $\Gamma = \Gamma', \mathbf{x} : T, \Gamma''$
- $\Gamma(\mathbf{C}) = \mathbf{C}$ ext $\mathbf{C}'$ impl $\mathbf{I}_1, \ldots \mathbf{I}_n\{v_1 : T_1, \ldots v_m : T_m, m_1 : MT_1, \ldots m_k : MT_k\}$
  *iff*
  $\Gamma = \Gamma', \mathbf{C}$ ext $\mathbf{C}'$ impl $\mathbf{I}_1, \ldots \mathbf{I}_n\{v_1 : T_1, \ldots v_m : T_m, m_1 : MT_1, \ldots m_k : MT_k\}, \Gamma''$
- $\Gamma(\mathbf{I}) = \mathbf{I}$ ext $\mathbf{I}_1, \ldots \mathbf{I}_n\{m_1 : MT_1, \ldots m_k : MT_k\}$ *iff*
  $\Gamma = \Gamma'', \mathbf{I}$ ext $\mathbf{I}_1, \ldots \mathbf{I}_n\{m_1 : MT_1, \ldots m_k : MT_k\}, \Gamma'''$
- $\Gamma(\mathbf{I}) = \mathsf{Undef}$ *otherwise*

The chapters 8.2 and 9 in [13] describe restrictions imposed on component (*i.e.* variable or method) definitions in a class or interface. We first introduce some functions to find the class components:

- $FDec(\Gamma, \mathbf{C}, \mathbf{v})$ indicates the nearest superclass of C (possibly C itself) which contains a declaration of the instance variable v and its declared type;
- $FDecs(\Gamma, \mathbf{C}, \mathbf{v})$ indicates all the field declarations for v, which were declared in a superclass of C, and possibly hidden by C, or another superclass.

- $MDecs(\Gamma, C, m)$ indicates all method declarations (*i.e.* both the class of the declaration and the signature) for method $m$ in class $C$, or inherited from one of its superclasses, and not hidden by any of its superclasses;
- $MSigs(\Gamma, C, m)$ returns all signatures for method $m$ in class $C$, or inherited and not hidden by any of its superclasses.

An example can be found in section 6.

**Definition 3** *For an environment* $\Gamma$, *containing a class declaration for* $C$, *i.e.* $\Gamma = \Gamma', C \text{ ext } C' \text{ impl } I_1, \ldots I_n \{v_1 : T_1, \ldots v_k : T_k, m_1 : MT_1, \ldots m_1 : MT_1\}, \Gamma''$, *and where* $\sqsubseteq$ *is acyclic, we define:*

- $FDec(\Gamma, \text{Object}, v) = \text{Undef}$ *for any* $v$
  $FDec(\Gamma, C, v) = (C, T_j)$ *iff* $v = v_j$
  $FDec(\Gamma, C, v) = FDec(\Gamma, C', v)$ *iff* $v \neq v_j \; \forall j \in \{1, \ldots k\}$
- $FDecs(\Gamma, C, v) = \{(C', T) \mid \Gamma \vdash C \sqsubseteq C', (C', T) = FDec(\Gamma, C', v)\}$
- $MDecs(\Gamma, \text{Object}, m) = \emptyset$
  $MDecs(\Gamma, C, m) = \{ (C, MT_j) \mid m = m_j \}$
  $\cup \{ (C'', MT'') \mid (C'', MT'') \in MDecs(\Gamma, C', m), \quad and$
  $\forall j \in \{1, \ldots 1\} : \; if \; m = m_j \; then \; Args(MT_j) \neq Args(MT'') \}$
- $MSigs(\Gamma, C, m) = \{ MT \mid \exists C'' \; with \; (C'', MT) \in MDecs(\Gamma, C, m) \}$

Similar to classes, we introduce the following functions to look up the interface components: $MDecs(\Gamma, I, m)$ is all the method declarations (*i.e.* the interface of the declaration and the signature) for method $m$ in interface $I$, or inherited – and not hidden – from any of its superinterfaces; $MSigs(\Gamma, I, m)$ returns all signatures for method $m$ in interface $I$, or inherited – and not hidden – from a superinterface.

**Definition 4** *For an environment* $\Gamma$, *containing an interface declaration for* $I$, *i.e.* $\Gamma = \Gamma', I \text{ ext } I_1, \ldots I_n \{m_1 : MT_1, \ldots m_k : MT_k\}, \Gamma''$, *and where* $\leq$ *is acyclic, we define:*

- $MDecs(\Gamma, I, m) = \{ (I, MT_j) \mid m = m_j \} \cup \{ (I', MT') \mid$
  $\exists j \in \{1, \ldots n\} \; with \; (I', MT') \in MDecs(\Gamma, I_j, m)$
  $and \; \forall i \in \{1, \ldots k\} \; if \; m = m_i \; then \; Args(MT') \neq Args(MT_i) \}$
- $MSigs(\Gamma, I, m) = \{ MT' \mid \exists I' : (I', MT') \in MDecs(\Gamma, I, m) \}$

The following lemma says that if a type $T$ inherits a method signature from another type $T'$ *i.e.* if $(T', MT) \in MDecs(\Gamma, T, m)$, then $T'$ is either a class or an interface exporting that method, and no other superclass of $T$, which is a subclass of $T'$ exports a method with the same identifier and argument types. Also, if a class $C$ inherits a field declaration for $v$, then there exists a $C'$, a superclass of $C$ which contains the declaration of $v$.

**Lemma 1.** *For any environment* $\Gamma$, *type* $T$, $T'$ *and identifiers* $v$ *and* $m$:

- $(T', MT) \in MDecs(\Gamma, T, m) \implies$

- $\Gamma \vdash \mathtt{T} \sqsubseteq \mathtt{T}'$ *and* $\Gamma(\mathtt{T}') = \mathtt{T}'$ ext $\dots$impl $\dots\{\dots\mathtt{m} : \mathtt{MT}\dots\}$ *and*
  $\forall \mathtt{C} \neq \mathtt{T}', \mathtt{T}''$ *with:* $\Gamma \vdash \mathtt{C} \sqsubseteq \mathtt{T}'$, $\Gamma \vdash \mathtt{T} \sqsubseteq \mathtt{C}$ :
  $\Gamma(\mathtt{C}) \neq \mathtt{C}$ ext $\dots$impl$\dots\{\dots\mathtt{m} : Args(\mathtt{MT}) \rightarrow \mathtt{T}''\}$
  *or*
- $\Gamma \vdash \mathtt{T} \leq \mathtt{T}'$ *and* $\Gamma(\mathtt{T}') = \mathtt{T}'$ ext $\dots\{\dots\mathtt{m} : \mathtt{MT}\dots\}$ *and*
  $\forall \mathtt{I} \neq \mathtt{I}', \mathtt{T}''$ : *with* $\Gamma \vdash \mathtt{I} \leq \mathtt{T}', \Gamma \vdash \mathtt{T} \leq \mathtt{I}$ :
  $\Gamma(\mathtt{I}) \neq \mathtt{I}$ ext $\dots\{\dots\mathtt{m} : Args(\mathtt{MT}) \rightarrow \mathtt{T}''\}$
- $FDec(\Gamma, \mathtt{C}, \mathtt{v}) = (\mathtt{C}', \mathtt{T}') \implies \Gamma(\mathtt{C}') = \mathtt{C}'\dots\{\dots\mathtt{v} : \mathtt{T}\dots\}$ *and* $\Gamma \vdash \mathtt{C} \sqsubseteq \mathtt{C}'$
  *and* $\forall \mathtt{C}'', \mathtt{T}''$ *with* $\Gamma \vdash \mathtt{C} \sqsubseteq \mathtt{C}'', \Gamma \vdash \mathtt{C}'' \sqsubseteq \mathtt{C}'$ : $\Gamma(\mathtt{C}'') \neq \mathtt{C}''$ ext $\dots$impl$\dots\{\dots\mathtt{v} : \mathtt{T}''\}$

When a new class is declared as $\mathtt{C}$ ext $\mathtt{C}'$ impl $\mathtt{I}_1, \dots \mathtt{I}_n\{\mathtt{v}_1 : \mathtt{T}_1, \dots \mathtt{v}_k : \mathtt{T}_k, \mathtt{m}_1 : \mathtt{MT}_1, \dots \mathtt{m}_l : \mathtt{T}_l\}$, [13] imposes the following requirements:

- there can be sequences of superinterfaces, instance variable declarations, and instance method declarations;
- the previous declarations are well-formed;
- there is no prior declaration of $\mathtt{C}$
- there are no cyclic subclass dependencies between $\mathtt{C}'$ and $\mathtt{C}$
- the declarations of the class $\mathtt{C}'$, interfaces $\mathtt{I}_j$ and variable types $\mathtt{T}_j$ may precede or *follow* the declaration for $\mathtt{C}$ – this is why we require $\Gamma \vdash \mathtt{C}' \sqsubseteq \mathtt{C}'$, rather than $\Gamma' \vdash \mathtt{C}' \sqsubseteq \mathtt{C}'$;
- the $\mathtt{MT}_j$ are method types;
- instance variable identifiers are unique;
- instance methods with the same identifier must have different argument types;
- a method overriding an inherited method must have a result type that *widens* to the result type of the overridden method – here we follow [17] instead of [13] which requires the result types to be identical; we prefer the former because it is a more general definition;
- "unless a class is abstract, the declarations of methods defined in each direct superinterface must be implemented either by a declaration in this class, or by an existing method declaration inherited from a superclass" - again we follow [17] instead of [13], and we require the implementing method to have a result type that *widens* to the result type of the interfaces method, instead of requiring them to be identical.

When a new interface $\mathtt{I}$ is introduced as $\mathtt{I}$ ext $\mathtt{I}_1, \dots \mathtt{I}_n\{\mathtt{m}_1 : \mathtt{MT}_1, \dots \mathtt{m}_l : \mathtt{T}_l\}$, the following requirements must be satisfied:

- there may be sequences of superinterfaces and instance method declarations;
- the previous declarations are well-formed;
- there is no prior declaration of $\mathtt{I}$;
- there are no cyclic subinterface dependencies between $\mathtt{I}$ and $\mathtt{I}_j$;
- the $\mathtt{I}_j$ are interfaces – whose declaration may precede or *follow* that of $\mathtt{I}$;
- the $\mathtt{MT}_j$ are method types;
- instance methods with the same identifier must have different argument types;

$n \geq 0,\ k \geq 0,\ l \geq 0$
$\Gamma \vdash \Gamma' \diamond$
$\Gamma'(\mathtt{C}) = \mathsf{Undef}$
$NOT\ \ \Gamma \vdash \mathtt{C'} \sqsubseteq \mathtt{C}$
$\Gamma \vdash \mathtt{C'} \sqsubseteq \mathtt{C'}$
$\Gamma \vdash \mathtt{I_j} \leq \mathtt{I_j}\ \ j \in \{1, ...n\}$
$\Gamma \vdash \mathtt{T_j}\ \diamond_{VarType}\ \ j \in \{1, ...k\}$
$\Gamma \vdash \mathtt{MT_j}\ \diamond_{MethType}\ \ j \in \{1, ...l\}$
$\mathtt{v_i} = \mathtt{v_j}\ \ \Longrightarrow\ \ i = j\ \ j, i \in \{1, ...k\}$
$\mathtt{m_i} = \mathtt{m_j}\ \ \Longrightarrow\ \ i = j\ \ or\ \ Args(\mathtt{MT_i}) \neq Args(\mathtt{MT_j})\ \ j, i \in \{1, ...l\}$
$\forall j \in \{1, ...l\}\ \ \mathtt{MT} \in MSigs(\Gamma, \mathtt{C'}, \mathtt{m_j}), Args(\mathtt{MT}) = Args(\mathtt{MT_j})\ \ \Longrightarrow$
$\quad \Gamma \vdash Res(\mathtt{MT_j}) <_{wdn} Res(\mathtt{MT})$
$\forall m, \forall j \in \{1, ...k\}\ \ \mathtt{AT} \to \mathtt{T} \in MSigs(\Gamma, \mathtt{I_j}, m)\ \ \Longrightarrow$
$\quad \exists \mathtt{T'}\ \ with\ \ \mathtt{AT} \to \mathtt{T'} \in MSigs(\Gamma, \mathtt{C}, m),\ \Gamma \vdash \mathtt{T'} <_{wdn} \mathtt{T}$
$\overline{\Gamma \vdash \Gamma', \mathtt{C\ ext\ C'\ impl\ I_1}, ... \mathtt{I_n}\{\mathtt{v_1} : \mathtt{T_1}, ... \mathtt{v_k} : \mathtt{T_k}, \mathtt{m_1} : \mathtt{MT_1}, ... \mathtt{m_l} : \mathtt{MT_l}\}\ \diamond}$

$n \geq 0, l \geq 0$
$\Gamma \vdash \Gamma' \diamond$
$\Gamma'(\mathtt{I}) = \mathsf{Undef}$
$NOT\ \ \Gamma \vdash \mathtt{I_i} \leq \mathtt{I}\ \ j \in \{1, ...n\}$
$\Gamma \vdash \mathtt{I_j} \leq \mathtt{I_j}\ \ j \in \{1, ...n\}$
$\Gamma \vdash \mathtt{MT_j}\ \diamond_{MethType}\ \ j \in \{1, ...l\}$
$\mathtt{m_i} = \mathtt{m_j}\ \ \Longrightarrow\ \ i = j\ \ or\ \ Args(\mathtt{MT_i}) \neq Args(\mathtt{MT_j})$
$\mathtt{MT} \in MSigs(\Gamma, \mathtt{I_i}, \mathtt{m_j}), Args(\mathtt{MT}) = Args(\mathtt{MT_j})\ \ \Longrightarrow$
$\quad \Gamma \vdash Res(\mathtt{MT_j}) <_{wdn} Res(\mathtt{MT})\ \ \ \ \forall j \in \{1, ...k\}, i \in \{1, ...n\}$
$\overline{\Gamma \vdash \Gamma', \mathtt{I\ ext\ I_1}, ... \mathtt{I_n}\{\ \mathtt{m_1} : \mathtt{MT_1}, ... \mathtt{m_l} : \mathtt{MT_l}\}\ \diamond}$

**Fig. 7.** class and interface declarations

- a method overriding an inherited method (a method is inherited if defined
  in one of the superinterfaces, and it is overridden if it has the same identifier
  and same argument types) must have a result type that widens to the result
  type of the overridden method – as for classes, here too we follow [17] instead
  of [13].

### 2.4 Properties of well-formed environments

**Lemma 2.** *If $\Gamma \vdash \Gamma \diamond$, then $\Gamma$ contains at most one declaration for any identifier, and there are no cycles in the $\sqsubseteq$ and $\leq$ relationship.*

In the following lemma we show that two types that are in the subclass relationship are classes, that $\sqsubseteq$ is reflexive, transitive and antisymmetric, that the

subclass hierarchy forms a tree, that two types that are in the subinterface relationship are interfaces, and that $\leq$ is transitive, reflexive and antisymmetric. Note, that unlike $\sqsubseteq$, $\leq$ does not form a tree:

**Lemma 3.** *If $\Gamma \vdash \Gamma \diamond$, then:*

- $\Gamma \vdash \mathtt{C} \sqsubseteq \mathtt{C}' \implies \Gamma \vdash \mathtt{C} \sqsubseteq \mathtt{C}$ *and* $\Gamma \vdash \mathtt{C}' \sqsubseteq \mathtt{C}'$
- $\Gamma \vdash \mathtt{C} \sqsubseteq \mathtt{C}'$ *and* $\Gamma \vdash \mathtt{C} \sqsubseteq \mathtt{C}'' \implies \Gamma \vdash \mathtt{C}' \sqsubseteq \mathtt{C}''$ *or* $\Gamma \vdash \mathtt{C}'' \sqsubseteq \mathtt{C}'$
- *The $\sqsubseteq$ relationship is a partial order.*
- $\Gamma \vdash \mathtt{I} \leq \mathtt{I}' \implies \Gamma \vdash \mathtt{I}' \leq \mathtt{I}'$ *and* $\Gamma \vdash \mathtt{I} \leq \mathtt{I}$
- *The $\leq$ relationship is a partial order.*

The following lemma says that widening is reflexive, transitive and antisymmetric; that if an interface widens to another type, then the second type is a superinterface of the first; that if a type widens to a class, then the type is a subclass of that class; that if a class widens to an interface $\mathtt{I}$, then the class implements a subinterface of $\mathtt{I}$; that if an interface widens to another type, then the interface is identical to the type, or one of its immediate superinterfaces is a subinterface of that type.

**Lemma 4.** *If $\Gamma \vdash \Gamma \diamond$, then:*

- $\Gamma \vdash \mathtt{I} \leq \mathtt{I}$ *and* $\Gamma \vdash \mathtt{I} <_{wdn} \mathtt{T} \implies \Gamma \vdash \mathtt{I} \leq \mathtt{T}$
- $\Gamma \vdash \mathtt{C} \sqsubseteq \mathtt{C}$ *and* $\Gamma \vdash \mathtt{T} <_{wdn} \mathtt{C} \implies \Gamma \vdash \mathtt{T} \sqsubseteq \mathtt{C}$
- $\Gamma \vdash \mathtt{C} \sqsubseteq \mathtt{C}$ *and* $\Gamma \vdash \mathtt{C} <_{wdn} \mathtt{I}$ *and* $\Gamma \vdash \mathtt{I} \leq \mathtt{I} \implies$
  $\exists \mathtt{C}', \mathtt{I}': \quad \Gamma \vdash \mathtt{C} \sqsubseteq \mathtt{C}', \ \Gamma \vdash \mathtt{C}' :_{imp} \mathtt{I}'$ *and* $\Gamma \vdash \mathtt{I}' \leq \mathtt{I}$
- $\Gamma = \Gamma', \ \mathtt{I} \ \mathtt{ext} \ \mathtt{I}_1 \ldots \mathtt{I}_n\{\ldots\}, \Gamma''', \ and \ \Gamma \vdash \mathtt{I} <_{wdn} \mathtt{T} \implies$
  $\mathtt{I} = \mathtt{T}$ *or* $\Gamma \vdash \mathtt{I}_k \leq \mathtt{T}$ *for a* $\mathtt{k} \in \{1, \ldots \mathtt{n}\}$
- *The $<_{wdn}$ relationship is a partial order.*

If a type $\mathtt{T}$ widens to another type $\mathtt{T}'$, and $\mathtt{T}'$ has a method $\mathtt{m}$, then there exists in $\mathtt{T}$ a unique method $\mathtt{m}$ with the same argument types, and whose return type can be widened to that of $\mathtt{T}'$. Note that we follow the more general rule from [17] as opposed to [13].

**Lemma 5.** *If $\Gamma \vdash \Gamma \diamond$, for types $\mathtt{T}$ and $\mathtt{T}'$, with $\Gamma \vdash \mathtt{T} <_{wdn} \mathtt{T}'$, and $\mathtt{MT}' \in MSigs(\Gamma, \mathtt{T}', \mathtt{m})$ :*

$\exists_1 \mathtt{MT} \in MSigs(\Gamma, \mathtt{T}, \mathtt{m})$ *with* $Args(\mathtt{MT}) = Args(\mathtt{MT}')$.
*Furthermore,* $\Gamma \vdash Res(\mathtt{MT}) <_{wdn} Res(\mathtt{MT}')$

From now on we assume implicitly that all environments are well-formed.

## 3  The type rules

Type checking is described in terms of a type inference system. In parallel with type checking the program is slightly modified, and enriched with type information. The $\text{Java}_s$-program is turned into a $\text{Java}_{se}$-program. The enriching of the program by type information is described by the mapping *Comp*:

$$Comp : \text{Java}_s \longrightarrow \text{Java}_{se}$$

## 3.1 Java$_{se}$, enriching Java$_s$

Some compile-time type information is necessary for the execution of Java method calls and of instance variable access. This information is calculated when type checking, and needs to be available during execution.

Therefore, we defined Java$_{se}$, an extended version of Java$_s$, which includes the appropriate type information. Furthermore, terms like $\alpha_i$ represent references to objects, which will be necessary for describing the operational semantics. Also, in order to describe method evaluation without using closures, in Java$_s$ we allow an expression to consist of a sequence of statements. Finally, execution of Java$_{se}$ programs may raise the exceptions NullPointExc, indicating an attempt to access an instance variable of the null pointer, ArrStoreExc indicating an attempt to assign a value of the wrong class to an array component, IndOutBndExc indicating an index out of the array bounds, and NegSzeExc, when attempting to create a new array value of a negative size. The syntax of Java$_{se}$ may be obtained from the syntax of Java$_s$ by applying the modifications and additions in figure 8:

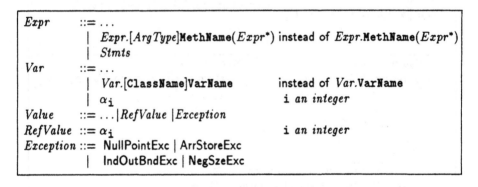

**Fig. 8.** type rules for Java$_{se}$

## 3.2 Types for Java$_s$

The types for variables, primitive values and null are described in figure 9.

The type rules for assignments, return statements, statement sequences and conditionals are given in figure 10. An expression of type T$'$ can be assigned to a variable of a type T, if T$'$ can be widened to T. A statement sequence has the same type as its last statement. A return statement has **void** type, or the same type as the expression it returns. A conditional consists of two statement sequences of the same type.

$$\vdash \textbf{null} \; : \; \textbf{nil}$$
$$Comp\{\!|\textbf{null}, \Gamma|\!\} = \textbf{null}$$

$$\vdash \textbf{true} \; : \; \textbf{bool}$$
$$Comp\{\!|\textbf{true}, \Gamma|\!\} = \textbf{true}$$

$$\vdash \textbf{false} \; : \; \textbf{bool}$$
$$Comp\{\!|\textbf{false}, \Gamma|\!\} = \textbf{false}$$

$$\dfrac{\textbf{i} \text{ is an integer}}{\vdash \textbf{i} \; : \; \textbf{int}}$$
$$Comp\{\!|\textbf{i}, \Gamma|\!\} = \textbf{i}$$

$$\dfrac{\textbf{c} \text{ is a character}}{\vdash \textbf{c} \; : \; \textbf{char}}$$
$$Comp\{\!|\textbf{c}, \Gamma|\!\} = \textbf{c}$$

$$\Gamma \vdash \textbf{x} \; : \; \Gamma(\textbf{x})$$
$$Comp\{\!|\textbf{x}, \Gamma|\!\} = \textbf{x}$$

**Fig. 9.** types of primitive values and variables

$$\dfrac{\Gamma \vdash \textbf{v} \; : \; \textbf{T} \quad \Gamma \vdash \textbf{e} \; : \; \textbf{T}' \quad \Gamma \vdash \textbf{T}' <_{wdn} \textbf{T}}{\Gamma \vdash \textbf{v} := \textbf{e} \; : \; \textbf{void}}$$
$$Comp\{\!|\textbf{v} := \textbf{e}, \Gamma|\!\} =$$
$$Comp\{\!|\textbf{v}, \Gamma|\!\} := Comp\{\!|\textbf{e}, \Gamma|\!\}$$

$$\dfrac{\Gamma \vdash \textbf{stmts} \; : \; \textbf{T} \quad \Gamma \vdash \textbf{stmt} \; : \; \textbf{T}'}{\Gamma \vdash \textbf{stmts}; \textbf{stmt} \; : \; \textbf{T}'}$$
$$Comp\{\!|\textbf{stmts} \; ; \; \textbf{stmt}, \Gamma|\!\} =$$
$$Comp\{\!|\textbf{stmts}, \Gamma|\!\} \; ; \; Comp\{\!|\textbf{stmt}, \Gamma|\!\}$$

$$\Gamma \vdash \textbf{return} \; : \; \textbf{void}$$
$$Comp\{\!|\textbf{return}, \Gamma|\!\} = \textbf{return}$$

$$\dfrac{\Gamma \vdash \textbf{e} \; : \; \textbf{T}}{\Gamma \vdash \textbf{return e} \; : \; \textbf{T}}$$
$$Comp\{\!|\textbf{return e}, \Gamma|\!\} = \textbf{return} \; Comp\{\!|\textbf{e}, \Gamma|\!\}$$

$$\dfrac{\Gamma \vdash \textbf{stmts} \; : \; \textbf{T} \quad \Gamma \vdash \textbf{stmts}' \; : \; \textbf{T} \quad \Gamma \vdash \textbf{e} \; : \; \textbf{bool}}{\Gamma \vdash (\textbf{if e then stmts else stmts}') \; : \; \textbf{T}}$$
$$Comp\{\!|\textbf{if e then stmts else stmts}', \Gamma|\!\} =$$
$$\text{if } Comp\{\!|\textbf{e}, \Gamma|\!\} \text{ then } Comp\{\!|\textbf{stmts}, \Gamma|\!\} \text{ else } Comp\{\!|\textbf{stmts}', \Gamma|\!\}$$

**Fig. 10.** types of statements

Figure 11 contains the type rules for newly created objects or arrays. For a class C, the expression new C has type C. For a simple type T, the expression new T[$e_1$]...[$e_n$][]$_1$...[]$_k$ is a n+k-dimensional array of elements of type T.

Figure 12 contains the type rules for array and field accesses. The possibility of a runtime exception is described with the operational semantics in figures 20 and 18. Only classes have fields.

Figure 13 contains the type rules for method bodies and method calls, as in ch. 15.11, [17]: A method is *applicable* if the actual parameter types can be widened to the corresponding formal parameter types. A signature is *more special* than another signature, if and only if it is defined in a subclass or subinterface and all argument types can be widened to from the argument types of the second

$$\frac{\Gamma \vdash C \sqsubseteq C}{\Gamma \vdash \text{new } C \;:\; C} \\ Comp \llbracket \text{new } C, \Gamma \rrbracket = \text{new } C$$

$$\frac{\begin{array}{l} n \geq 1, k \geq 0 \\ \Gamma \vdash T \diamond_{VarType}, \quad \text{a simple type} \\ \Gamma \vdash e_i \;:\; \text{int} \quad i \in \{1, ...n\} \end{array}}{\begin{array}{l} \Gamma \vdash \text{new } T[e_1]...[e_n][]_1 \cdots []_k \;:\; T[]_1 \cdots []_{n+k} \\ Comp \llbracket \text{new } T[e_1]...[e_n][]_1 \cdots []_k, \Gamma \rrbracket = \\ \quad \text{new } T[Comp \llbracket e_1, \Gamma \rrbracket]...[Comp \llbracket e_n, \Gamma \rrbracket][]_1 \cdots []_k \end{array}}$$

**Fig. 11.** object and array creation type rules

$$\frac{\begin{array}{l} \Gamma \vdash v \;:\; T[] \\ \Gamma \vdash e \;:\; \text{int} \end{array}}{\begin{array}{l} \Gamma \vdash v[e] \;:\; T \\ Comp \llbracket v[e], \Gamma \rrbracket = \\ \quad Comp \llbracket v, \Gamma \rrbracket [Comp \llbracket exp, \Gamma \rrbracket] \end{array}}$$

$$\frac{\begin{array}{l} \Gamma \vdash v \;:\; T \\ FDec(\Gamma, T, f) = (C, T') \end{array}}{\begin{array}{l} \Gamma \vdash v.f \;:\; T' \\ Comp \llbracket v.f, \Gamma \rrbracket = Comp \llbracket v, \Gamma \rrbracket.[C]f \end{array}}$$

**Fig. 12.** array and field access type rules

signature; this defines a partial order. The most special signatures are the minima of the "more special" partial order.

**Definition 5** *For an environment* $\Gamma$*, variable types* $T$ *and* $T_i$*,* $i \in \{1, ...n+1\}$*, and identifier* $m$*, the* most special declarations *are defined as follows:*

- $ApplMeths(\Gamma, m, T, T_1 \times ... \times T_n) = \{(T', MT') \mid (T', MT') \in MDecs(\Gamma, T, m)$
  *and* $MT' = T'_1 \times ... \times T'_n \rightarrow T'_{n+1}$ *and* $\Gamma \vdash T_i <_{wdn} T'_i$ *for* $i \in \{1, ...n\}\}$
- $(T, T_1 \times ... \times T_n \rightarrow T_{n+1})$ *is* more special than $(T', T'_1 \times ... \times T'_n \rightarrow T'_{n+1})$ *iff*
  $\Gamma \vdash T <_{wdn} T'$ *and* $\Gamma \vdash T_i <_{wdn} T'_i$ *for all* $i \in \{1, ...n\}$
- $MostSpec(\Gamma, m, T, T_1 \times ... \times T_n) =$
  $\{(T', MT') \mid (T', MT') \in ApplMeths(\Gamma, m, T, T_1 \times ... \times T_n)$ *and*
  *if* $(T'', MT'') \in ApplMeths(\Gamma, m, T, T_1 \times ... \times T_n)$ *and* $(T'', MT'')$ *is* more
  special than $(T', MT')$ *then* $T'' = T'$ *and* $MT' = MT''\}$

The signatures of the more specific applicable methods are contained in the set $MostSpec(,,,)$. A message expression is type correct when this set contains exactly one pair. The argument types of the signature of this pair is stored as the *method descriptor*, c.f. ch.15.11 in [13], and the result type of the signature is the type of the message expression.

$$\frac{\begin{array}{l} \Gamma \vdash e_i \ : \ T_i \quad i \in \{1, ...n\}, n \geq 1 \\ MostSpec(\Gamma, m, T_1, T_2 \times ... \times T_n) \ = \ \{(T, MT)\} \end{array}}{\begin{array}{l} \Gamma \vdash e_1.m(e_2 ... e_n) \ : \ Res(MT) \\ Comp\{\!\!\{e_1.m(e_2 ... e_n), \Gamma\}\!\!\} = \\ \quad Comp\{\!\!\{e_1, \Gamma\}\!\!\}.[Args(MT)]m(Comp\{\!\!\{e_2, \Gamma\}\!\!\} ... Comp\{\!\!\{e_n, \Gamma\}\!\!\}) \end{array}}$$

$$\frac{\begin{array}{l} mBody = m \ \text{is} \ \lambda x_1 : T_1 ... \lambda x_n : T_n.\{ \ stmts \ \} \\ x_i \neq this \quad i \in \{1, ...n\} \\ z_1, ..., z_n \ \text{are new variables in} \ \Gamma \\ stmts' = stmts[z_1/x_1, ..., z_n/x_n] \\ \Gamma, z_1 : T_1 ... z_n : T_n \vdash stmts' \ : \ T' \\ \Gamma \vdash T' <_{wdn} T \end{array}}{\begin{array}{l} \Gamma \vdash mbody \ : \ T_1 \times ... \times T_n \rightarrow T \\ Comp\{\!\!\{mBody, \Gamma\}\!\!\} = m \ \text{is} \ \lambda x_1 : T_1 ... \lambda x_n : T_n.\{ Comp\{\!\!\{stmts, \Gamma\}\!\!\} \} \end{array}}$$

**Fig. 13.** types of method calls and bodies

The renaming of the variables in the method body (*i.e.* $stmts[z_1/x_1, ..., z_n/x_n]$) is necessary in order to avoid name clashes and also, in order for the lemma 9 to hold – as pointed out in [20]. Furthermore, it is worth noticing, that the rules describing method bodies do not determine $T$, the return type of the method; this is taken from the environment $\Gamma$, when applying the rule describing class bodies, as in figure 14.

Figure 14 contains the type rules for class bodies and programs. A class body cBody satisfies its declaration, $\Gamma(C)$, if it provides a method body for each of the method declarations contained in $\Gamma(C)$ .

Note, that the method bodies $mBody_i$ are type checked in the environment $\Gamma$, this : C, which does not contain the instance variable declarations $v_1 : T_1$ ..., $v_k : T_k$. Thus, by the type system, we force the use of the expression this.$v_j$ as opposed to $v_j$.

A program $p = \{ cBody_1, ... cBody_n \}$ is well-typed, if it contains a class body for each declared class, and if all class bodies, $cBody_i$, are well-typed and satisfy their declarations. Furthermore, each class is transformed by *Comp*.

The following two functions will be needed for the operational semantics. The function $MethBody(m, AT, cBody)$ finds the method body with identifier m and argument types AT, in the class body cBody – if any exists. It can easily be seen that because of the requirements for classes in 2.3, if the environment $\Gamma$ is well-formed, the function $MethBody(m, AT, cBody)$ returns either an empty set or a set with one element.

**Definition 6** *For a class body* cBody = C ext C' { $mBody_1, ... mBody_n$ }, *declared in* $\Gamma$ *as* $\Gamma(C) = $ C ext C' impl ...{ $m_1 : MT_1 ... m_n : MT_n$ }, *we define:*
$MethBody(m, AT, cBody) = \{mPS_j \mid mBody_j = m \ \text{is} \ mPS_j \ and \ Args(MT_j) = AT\}$

$$\frac{\begin{array}{l}\mathtt{n} \geq 0, \mathtt{k} \geq 0, \mathtt{m} \geq 0\\ \Gamma \vdash \Gamma \diamond\\ \Gamma(\mathtt{C}) = \mathsf{C\ ext\ C'\ impl\ } \mathtt{I}_1 \ldots \mathtt{I}_n \{\ \mathtt{v}_1 : \mathtt{T}_1 \ldots \mathtt{v}_k : \mathtt{T}_k, \mathtt{m}_1 : \mathtt{MT}_1 \ldots \mathtt{m}_l : \mathtt{MT}_l\ \}\\ \mathsf{cBody} = \mathsf{C\ ext\ C'}\ \{\ \mathtt{mBody}_1, \ldots \mathtt{mBody}_l\ \}\\ \Gamma(\mathtt{this}) = \mathsf{Undef}\\ \mathtt{mBody}_i = \mathtt{m}_i \text{ is } \mathtt{mPrsSts}_i \quad \mathtt{i} \in \{1, \ldots l\}\\ \Gamma, \mathtt{this} : \mathsf{C} \vdash \mathtt{mBody}_i\ :\ \mathtt{MT}_i \quad \mathtt{i} \in \{1, \ldots l\}\end{array}}{\begin{array}{l}\Gamma \vdash \mathsf{cBody}\ :\ \Gamma(\mathsf{C})\\ \mathit{Comp}\{\![\mathsf{cBody}, \Gamma]\!\} = \mathsf{C\ ext\ C'}\ \{\mathit{Comp}\{\![\mathtt{mBody}_1, \Gamma]\!\} \ldots \mathit{Comp}\{\![\mathtt{mBody}_l, \Gamma]\!\}\}\end{array}}$$

$$\frac{\begin{array}{l}\mathtt{C}_1 \ldots \mathtt{C}_n \text{ are all the classes defined in } \Gamma \quad \mathtt{n} \geq 0\\ \mathtt{p} = \{\ \mathsf{cBody}_1, \ldots \mathsf{cBody}_n\ \}\\ \mathsf{cBody}_i = \mathtt{C}_i \text{ ext } \ldots \{\ \ldots\ \} \quad \text{for } \mathtt{i} \in \{1, \ldots n\}\\ \Gamma \vdash \mathsf{cBody}_i\ :\ \Gamma(\mathtt{C}_i) \quad \mathtt{i} \in \{1, \ldots n\}\end{array}}{\begin{array}{l}\Gamma \vdash \mathtt{p}\ :\ \Gamma\\ \mathit{Comp}\{\![\mathtt{p}, \Gamma]\!\} = \{\ \mathit{Comp}\{\![\mathsf{cBody}_1, \Gamma]\!\} \ldots \mathit{Comp}\{\![\mathsf{cBody}_n, \Gamma]\!\}\ \}\end{array}}$$

**Fig. 14.** type rules for class bodies and programs

The function $\mathit{MethBody}(\mathtt{m}, \mathtt{AT}, \mathtt{C}, \mathtt{p})$ finds the method body with identifier $\mathtt{m}$ and argument types $\mathtt{AT}$, in the nearest superclass of class $\mathtt{C}$ – if any exists. It returns a single pair consisting of the class containing the appropriate method body, and the method body itself or the empty set if none exists.

**Definition 7** *For a program* $\mathtt{p} = \{\ \mathsf{cBody}_1, \ldots \mathsf{cBody}_n\ \}$, *we define:*

$\mathit{MethBody}(\mathtt{m}, \mathtt{AT}, \mathtt{C}, \mathtt{p}) =$
  *let* $\mathsf{cBody}_j = \mathsf{C\ ext\ C'}\ \{\ \ldots\ \}$ *in* (*for appropriate* $\mathtt{j} \in \{1, \ldots n\}$)
  *let* $\mathtt{mBody} = \mathit{MethBody}(\mathtt{m}, \mathtt{AT}, \mathsf{cBody}_j)$ *in*
  *if* $\mathtt{mBody} = \emptyset$ *then*
    *if* $\mathtt{C'} = \mathtt{Object}$ *then* $\emptyset$
    *else* $\mathit{MethBody}(\mathtt{m}, \mathtt{AT}, \mathtt{C'}, \mathtt{p})$
  *else* $(\mathtt{C}, \mathtt{mBody})$

### 3.3 Properties of the Java$_s$ type system

The following lemma says, that in a well-typed Java$_s$ program any class that widens to a superclass or superinterface provides an implementation for each method exported by the superclass or superinterface.

**Lemma 6.** *For any well-formed environment* $\Gamma$, *variable types* $\mathtt{T}$, $\mathtt{T}_1$, ..., $\mathtt{T}_n$, $\mathtt{T}_{n+1}$, *class* $\mathtt{C}$ *and a Java$_s$ program* $\mathtt{p}$, *if:*

- $\Gamma \vdash \mathtt{p}\ :\ \Gamma$
- $\Gamma \vdash \mathtt{C} <_{wdn} \mathtt{T}$

- $T_1 \times \ldots T_n \to T_{n+1} \in MSigs(\Gamma, T, m)$

*then*

- $\exists T'_{n+1}, C' : (C', T_1 \times \ldots T_n \to T'_{n+1}) \in MDecs(\Gamma, C, m),$   *and*
  $\Gamma \vdash T'_{n+1} <_{wdn} T_{n+1}$   *and*   $\Gamma \vdash C \sqsubseteq C'$   *and*
- $MethBody(m, T_1 \times \ldots T_n, p, C) = (C', \lambda x_1 : T_1, \ldots \lambda x_n : T_n.\{\ \text{stmts}\ \})$   *and*
  $\Gamma, \text{this} : C', x_1 : T_1, \ldots x_n : T_n \vdash \text{stmts} : T''_{n+1}$   *and*   $\Gamma \vdash T''_{n+1} <_{wdn} T'_{n+1}$

## 3.4 Absence of the subsumption rule

The type inference system described in the previous sections does not have a subsumption rule. The *subsumption rule* says, that any expression of type T, also has type T' if T is a subtype of T'. In the case of Java, where subtypes are expressed by the $<_{wdn}$ relation, it would have had the form:

$$\frac{\Gamma \vdash e : T \qquad \Gamma \vdash T <_{wdn} T'}{\Gamma \vdash e : T'}$$

For example, in section 6, the type of `aPhil.like` is `Phil`, but the type of `pascal.like` is `Food`, although $\Gamma_0 \vdash$ `aPhil` : `Phil`, $\Gamma_0 \vdash$ `pascal` : `FrPhil`, and $\Gamma_0 \vdash$ `FrPhil` $<_{wdn}$ `Phil`. In fact, introduction of the subsumption rule would make this type system non-deterministic – although [6] develops a system for Java which has a subsumption rule, and in which the types of method call and field access are determined by using the *minimal types* of the expressions.

## 3.5 Extending the type rules to Java$_{se}$

The Java$_{se}$ syntax is in most parts identical to that of Java$_s$. For these cases the type rules are identical. The only cases where the syntax differs are method call, field access, and the object references $\alpha_i$. These are shown in figure 15.

The type of a reference depends on the class of the object pointed at in the current state $\sigma$ (states will be introduced in section 4), therefore, the type of a Java$_{se}$ term depends on both the environment *and* the state, and type assertions for Java$_{se}$ terms t have the form $\Gamma, \sigma \vdash t : T$.

If an object is stored at address $\alpha_i$, then its class is the type of the reference $\alpha_i$. If a k-dimensional array of T is stored at $\alpha_i$, then the k-dimensional array of T, $T[]_1 \ldots []_k$ is the type of this reference. Objects and array values are defined in section 4.

The difference between the type of a field access expression in Java$_s$ and Java$_{se}$ is, that in Java$_{se}$ the type depends on the descriptor (*i.e.* C) instead of the type of the variable at the left of the field access (*i.e.* T).

In Java$_{se}$ method calls we search for appropriate methods, using the descriptor signature $(T_2 \times \ldots \times T_n)$, instead of the types of the actual expressions $(T'_2, \ldots T'_n)$. For this search we first examine the class of the receiver expression for a method body with appropriate argument types, and then *its* superclasses:

$$\frac{\sigma(\alpha_i) = << \ldots >>^C}{\Gamma, \sigma \vdash \alpha_i \; : \; C} \qquad \frac{\sigma(\alpha_i) = << \ldots >>^{T[]_1 \cdots []_k}}{\Gamma, \sigma \vdash \alpha_i \; : \; T[]_1 \cdots []_k}$$

$$\frac{\begin{array}{l} \Gamma, \sigma \vdash v \; : \; T \\ \Gamma, \sigma \vdash T <_{wdn} C \\ FDec(\Gamma, C, f) = (\, C, T') \end{array}}{\Gamma, \sigma \vdash v.[C]f \; : \; T'} \qquad \frac{\begin{array}{l} \Gamma, \sigma \vdash e_i \; : \; T'_i \quad i \in \{1, \ldots n\}, n \geq 0 \\ \Gamma, \sigma \vdash T'_i <_{wdn} T_i \quad i \in \{2, \ldots n\} \\ FirstFit(\Gamma, m, T'_1, T_2 \times \ldots \times T_n) = \{(T, MT)\} \end{array}}{\Gamma, \sigma \vdash e_1.[T_2 \times \ldots \times T_n]m(e_2 \ldots e_n) \; : \; Res(MT)}$$

**Fig. 15.** types for Java$_{se}$

**Definition 8** *Given environment* $\Gamma$, *types* $T_1, \ldots T_n$, *argument types* $AT = T_2 \times \ldots \times T_n$ *and an identifier* m, *we define:*

$$FirstFit(\Gamma, m, T_1, AT) = \{(T, MT) \mid (T, MT) \in MDecs(\Gamma, T_1, m) \text{ and } Args(MT) = AT\}$$

**Lemma 7.** *For a well-formed environment* $\Gamma$, *types* $T'_1, T_1 \ldots T_n$, *argument types,* $AT = T_2 \times \ldots \times T_n$, *where* $\Gamma \vdash T_1 <_{wdn} T'_1$:

- *the set* $FirstFit(\Gamma, m, T_1, AT)$ *contains up to one element*
- $\exists T', MT' : FirstFit(\Gamma, m, T'_1, AT) = (T', MT') \implies$
  $\exists T, MT : FirstFit(\Gamma, m, T_1, AT) = (T, MT)$ *and*
  $\Gamma \vdash T <_{wdn} T'$ *and* $\Gamma \vdash Res(MT) <_{wdn} Res(MT')$

### 3.6 Properties of the Java$_{se}$ type system

We expect the type of a Java$_{se}$-expression to be related to the type of the original Java$_s$-expression. In fact, they are identical. The type system assigns unique types to any well-typed Java$_s$ or Java$_{se}$ term.

**Lemma 8.** *For types* T, T', *state* $\sigma$, *environment* $\Gamma$, *Java$_s$ term* t, *and Java$_{se}$ term* t':

- $\Gamma \vdash t \; : \; T \implies \Gamma, \sigma \vdash Comp\{t, \Gamma\} \; : \; T$
- $\Gamma \vdash t \; : \; T$ *and* $\Gamma \vdash t \; : \; T' \implies T = T'$.
- $\Gamma, \sigma \vdash t' \; : \; T$ *and* $\Gamma, \sigma \vdash t' \; : \; T' \implies T = T'$.
- *Expressions containing exceptions are not type correct.*

## 4 The operational semantics

Figure 16 describes the run time model for the operational semantics.

Firstly, the state is flat; it consists of mappings from identifiers to primitive values or to references, and from references to objects or arrays.

Every object is annotated by its class. An object consists of a sequence of labels and values. Each label also carries the class in which it was defined; this is needed for labels shadowing labels from superclasses, cf [13] ch. 9.5. For example, as in section 6, $\ll$ `like Phil:` $\alpha_5$, `like FrPhil: croissant` $\gg^{\text{FrPhil}}$ is an object of class `FrPhil`. It inherits the field `like` from `Phil`, and has the field `like` from `FrPhil`.

Arrays carry their dimension and type information, and they consist of a sequence of values for the first dimension. For example $\ll 3, 5, 8, 11 \gg^{\text{int}[]}$, is a one dimensional array of integers.

Configurations are tuples of Java$_{se}$ terms and states, or just states. The operational semantics is a mapping from programs and configurations to configurations. For a given program p, the operational semantics maps configurations to new configurations.

$$
\begin{array}{lll}
\textit{State} & ::= (\textbf{Ident} \longrightarrow (\ \textit{Value}\ ))^* \cup (\ \textit{RefValue} \longrightarrow \textit{ObjectOrArray}\ )^* \\
\textit{ObjectOrArray} & ::= \textit{Object}\ |\ \textit{Array} \\
\textit{Object} & ::= \ll(\textbf{LabelName ClassName}: \textit{Value}\ )^* \gg^{\textbf{ClassName}} \\
\textit{Array} & ::= \ll(\ \textit{Value}\ )^* \gg^{\textit{ArrayType}} \\
\textit{Configuration} & ::= <\ \text{Java}_{se}\text{-term},\ \textit{state}\ > \cup <\ \textit{state}\ > \\
\leadsto & :\quad \text{Java}_{se}\text{program} \longrightarrow \textit{Configuration} \longrightarrow \textit{Configuration} \\
\leadsto_{\text{p}} & :\quad \textit{Configuration} \longrightarrow \textit{Configuration}
\end{array}
$$

**Fig. 16.** Java$_{se}$ runtime model

Next, we define some operations on states and objects.

### 4.1 State and object modifications, ground terms

We require objects to be constructed according to their class, array values to conform to their dimension and to consist of values of appropriate types, and variables to contain values of the appropriate type.

**Definition 9** *A value* **val** *weakly conforms to a type* **T** *in an environment* $\Gamma$ *and a state* $\sigma$ *iff:*

- *if* **val** *is a primitive value, then* **T** *is a primitive type, and* **val**$\in$**T**;
- *if* **val**=null, *then* **T** *is a class, interface or array type;*
- *if* **val**=$\alpha_j$ *and* $\sigma(\alpha_j) = \ll...\gg^{\textbf{C}}$, *then* **C** *is a class,* **T** *is a class or interface, and* $\Gamma \vdash \textbf{C} <_{wdn} \textbf{T}$;
- *if* **val**=$\alpha_j$ *and* $\sigma(\alpha_j) = \ll$**val**$_0$,...**val**$_{n-1}\gg^{\textbf{T}'[]_1\cdots[]_k}$ *for a simple type* **T**' *and integers* $n \geq 0$, $k \geq 1$, *then* $\Gamma \vdash \textbf{T}'[]_1\cdots[]_k <_{wdn} \textbf{T}$.

*A value* **val** *conforms to a type* **T** *in an environment* $\Gamma$ *and a state* $\sigma$ *iff* **val** *weakly conforms to* **T** *in* $\Gamma$ *and* $\sigma$ *and*

- if $val = \alpha_j$ and $\sigma(\alpha_j) = \ll v_1 \, C_1 : val_1, \ldots v_n \, C_n : val_n \gg^C$, then for all labels $v$, classes $C'$, types $T'$ with $(C', T') \in FDecs(\Gamma, C, v)$, there exists a $k \in \{1, \ldots n\}$ such that $v_k = v$, $C_k = C'$, and $val_k$ weakly conforms to $T'$ in $\Gamma$ and $\sigma$;

- if $val = \alpha_j$ and $\sigma(\alpha_j) = \ll val_0, \ldots val_{n-1} \gg^{T'[]_1 \cdots []_k}$, then $\forall i \in \{0, \ldots n-1\} :$ $val_i$ weakly conforms to $T'[]_2 \cdots []_k$.

Furthermore, a state $\sigma$ conforms to an environment $\Gamma$ iff for all identifiers $x$, and integers $i$

- if $\Gamma(x) \neq \mathbf{Undef}$ then $\sigma(x)$ conforms to $\Gamma(x)$ in $\Gamma$ and $\sigma$;
- if $\sigma(\alpha_i) = \ll \ldots \gg^C$, then $\alpha_i$ conforms to $C$ in $\Gamma$ and $\sigma$;
- if $\sigma(\alpha_i) = \ll \ldots \gg^{T[]_1 \cdots []_n}$, then $\alpha_i$ conforms to $T[]_1 \ldots []_n$ in $\Gamma$ and $\sigma$.

Also, an environment $\Gamma$ conforms to environment $\Gamma'$ iff

- for any identifier $x$, if $\Gamma'(x) \neq \mathbf{Undef}$, then $\Gamma(x) = \Gamma'(x)$;
- for any identifier $x$, if $\Gamma'(x) = \mathbf{Undef} \neq \Gamma(x)$, then $x$ is declared in $\Gamma$ as a variable.

**Lemma 9.** *Given two environments* $\Gamma$, $\Gamma'$, *where* $\Gamma$ *conforms to* $\Gamma'$,

- $\Gamma \vdash \Gamma \diamond \implies \Gamma' \vdash \Gamma' \diamond$;
- for any program $p$: $\Gamma' \vdash p : \Gamma' \implies \Gamma \vdash p : \Gamma$;
- for any term $t$, and type $T$: $\Gamma' \vdash t : T \implies \Gamma \vdash t : T$;
- $\Gamma \vdash T <_{wdn} T' \iff \Gamma' \vdash T <_{wdn} T'$;
- for $T_1 \ldots T_n : FirstFit(\Gamma, m, T_1, T_2 \times \ldots \times T_n) = FirstFit(\Gamma', m, T_1, T_2 \times \ldots \times T_n)$.

**Definition 10** *For object* $obj = \ll l_1 \, C_1 : val_1, l_2 \, C_2 : val_2, \ldots l_n \, C_n : val_n \gg^{C'}$, *state* $\sigma$, *value* $val$, *identifier or reference* $z$, *class* $C$, *field identifier* $f$, *an* $m \geq 0$, *array* $arr = \ll val_0, \ldots val_{n-1} \gg^{T[]_1 \cdots []_m}$ *and integer value* $k$ *we define:*

- the access to field $f$ declared in class $C$ as $obj(f, C)$:
  $obj(f, C) = val_i$ where $f = l_i$ and $C = C_i$
- the access to component $f$, $C$ of an object stored at a reference $z$ in state $\sigma$ :
  $\sigma(z, f, C) = \sigma(z)(f, C)$
- the access to the $k^{th}$ component of arr, $arr[k]$ :
  $arr[k] = val_k$ $\qquad$ if $0 \leq k \leq n - 1$
  $arr[k] = \mathsf{IndOutBndExc}$ otherwise
- a new state, $\sigma' = \sigma[z \mapsto val]$, such that:
  $\sigma'(z) = val$
  $\sigma'(z') = \sigma(z')$ for $z' \neq z$ :
- a new object, $obj' = obj[f, C \mapsto val]$, and a new state, $\sigma' = \sigma[z, f, C \mapsto val]$ :
  $obj'(f, C) = val$
  $obj'(f', C') = obj(f', C')$ $\qquad$ if $f \neq f'$ or $C \neq C'$
  $\sigma' = \sigma[z \mapsto \sigma(z)[f, C \mapsto val]]$
- a new array, $arr' = arr[k \mapsto val]$, and a new state, $\sigma' = \sigma[arr, k \mapsto val]$ :

$$\begin{array}{ll} \mathtt{arr'[k] = val} \\ \mathtt{arr'[j] = arr[j]} & \textit{if } \mathtt{j \neq k} \\ \sigma' \quad\;\; = \sigma[\mathtt{arr \mapsto arr[k \mapsto val]}] \end{array}$$

$$\frac{< \mathtt{stmts}, \sigma > \leadsto_p < \sigma' >}{< \mathtt{stmts; stmt}, \sigma > \leadsto_p < \mathtt{stmt}, \sigma' >}$$

$$\frac{< \mathtt{stmts}, \sigma > \leadsto_p < \mathtt{stmts'}, \sigma' >}{\begin{array}{l} < \mathtt{stmts; stmt}, \sigma > \\ \leadsto_p < \mathtt{stmts'; stmt}, \sigma' > \end{array}}$$

$$\frac{< \mathtt{e}, \sigma > \leadsto_p < \mathtt{e'}, \sigma' >}{\begin{array}{l} < \mathtt{if \ e \ then \ stmts \ else \ stmts'}, \sigma > \\ \leadsto_p < \mathtt{if \ e' \ then \ stmts \ else \ stmts'}, \sigma' > \end{array}}$$

$$\frac{}{\begin{array}{l} < \mathtt{if \ true \ then \ stmts \ else \ stmts'}, \sigma > \\ \leadsto_p < \mathtt{stmts}, \sigma > \end{array}}$$

$$\frac{< \mathtt{if \ false \ then \ stmts \ else \ stmts'}, \sigma >}{\leadsto_p < \mathtt{stmts'}, \sigma >}$$

$$\frac{}{< \mathtt{return}, \sigma > \leadsto_p < \sigma >}$$

$$\frac{< \mathtt{e}, \sigma > \leadsto_p < \mathtt{e'}, \sigma' >}{< \mathtt{return \ e}, \sigma > \leadsto_p < \mathtt{return \ e'}, \sigma' >}$$

$$\frac{\mathtt{val \ is \ ground}}{< \mathtt{return \ val}, \sigma > \leadsto_p < \mathtt{val}, \sigma >}$$

**Fig. 17.** statements

We distinguish ground terms which cannot be further rewritten, and l-ground terms, which are "almost ground", since they may not be further rewritten if they appear on the left hand side of an assignment:

**Definition 11** *A Java$_{se}$ term* t *is*

- ground *iff* t *is a primitive value, or if* t=$\alpha_i$ *for some i;*
- l-ground *iff* t *is ground, or* t=id *for some identifier* id, *or* t= $\alpha_i$.[C]f *for a class* C *and a field* f *and integer value* i, *or* t = $\alpha_i$[k] *for some integer values* i *and* k.

## 4.2 Program execution

Figures 17-20 describe the operational semantics of Java$_{se}$.

Figure 17 describes the execution of statements. Statement sequences are evaluated from left to right. In conditional statements the condition is evaluated first; if it evaluates to true, then the first branch is executed, otherwise the second. A return statement terminates execution. A statement returning an expression evaluates this expression until ground and replaces itself by this ground value – thus modelling methods returning values.

$$\frac{}{< \mathtt{id}, \sigma > \leadsto_p < \sigma(\mathtt{id}), \sigma >} \qquad \frac{\sigma(\alpha_i) \neq \mathsf{null}}{< \alpha_i.[\mathtt{C}]\mathtt{f}, \sigma > \leadsto_p < \sigma(\alpha_i, \mathtt{f}, \mathtt{C}), \sigma >}$$

$$\frac{< \mathtt{v}, \sigma > \leadsto_p < \mathtt{v}', \sigma' >}{< \mathtt{v}.[\mathtt{C}]\mathtt{f}, \sigma > \leadsto_p < \mathtt{v}'.[\mathtt{C}]\mathtt{f}, \sigma' >} \qquad \frac{< \mathtt{v}, \sigma > \leadsto_p < \mathtt{v}', \sigma' >}{< \mathtt{v}[\mathtt{e}], \sigma > \leadsto_p < \mathtt{v}'[\mathtt{e}], \sigma' >}$$

$$\frac{< \mathtt{e}, \sigma > \leadsto_p < \mathtt{e}', \sigma' >}{< \alpha_i[\mathtt{e}], \sigma > \leadsto_p < \alpha_i[\mathtt{e}'], \sigma' >} \qquad \frac{\begin{array}{c}\sigma(\alpha_i) \neq \mathsf{null} \\ \mathtt{k} \text{ an integer value}\end{array}}{< \alpha_i[\mathtt{k}], \sigma > \leadsto_p < \sigma(\alpha_i)[\mathtt{k}], \sigma >}$$

$$\frac{\sigma(\alpha_i) = \mathsf{null}}{< \alpha_i.[\mathtt{C}]\mathtt{f}, \sigma > \leadsto_p < \mathsf{NullPointExc}, \sigma >} \qquad \frac{\begin{array}{c}\sigma(\alpha_i) = \mathsf{null} \\ \mathtt{k} \text{ an integer value}\end{array}}{< \alpha_i[\mathtt{k}], \sigma > \leadsto_p < \mathsf{NullPointExc}, \sigma >}$$

**Fig. 18.** variables

In figure 18 we describe the evaluation of variables, field access and array access. Variables (*i.e.* identifiers, instance variable access or array access) are evaluated from left to right. The rules about assignment in 20 will prevent an expression like $\mathtt{x}$ or $\alpha_i.[\mathtt{C}]\mathtt{v}$ from being rewritten any further if it is the left hand side of an assignment. They would allow an expression of the form $\mathtt{u[C1].w[C2].x[C3].y}$ to be rewritten to an expression of the form $\alpha_j[\mathtt{C3}].\mathtt{y}$ for some j. Furthermore, there is *no* rule of the form $< \alpha_j, \sigma > \leadsto_p < \sigma(\alpha_j), \sigma >$. This is because there is no explicit dereferencing operator in Java. Objects are passed as references, and they are dereferenced only implicitly, when their fields are accessed.

Array access as described here adheres to the rules in ch. 15.12 of [13], which require full evaluation of the expression to the left of the brackets. Thus, with our operational semantics, $\mathtt{a}[(\mathtt{a} = \mathtt{b})[3]]$ corresponds to $\mathtt{a}[\mathtt{b}[3]]; \mathtt{a} = \mathtt{b}$.

In figure 19 we describe the creation of new objects or arrays, cf. ch. 15.8-15.9 of [13]. Essentially, a new value of the appropriate array or class type is created, and its address is returned. The fields of the array, and the components the object are assigned initial values (as defined in ch. 4.5.5. of [13]) of the type to which *they* belong.

**Definition 12** *The* initial value *of a simple type is defined as follows*:

- 0 *is the initial value of* int
- *' '* *is the initial value of* char
- false *is the initial value of* bool
- null *is the initial value of any class or interface*

Figure 20 describes the evaluation of assignments. The left hand side is evaluated

$$\frac{\begin{array}{l} \alpha_i \text{ is new in } \sigma \\ v' = \ll f_1\, C_1 : v_1, ... f_n\, C_n : v_n \gg^C \\ \forall (C', T') \in FDecs(\Gamma, C, f) \\ \quad \exists k : f_k = f, C_k = C' \\ \quad v_k \text{ initial value for } T' \end{array}}{< \text{new } C, \sigma > \leadsto_p < \alpha_i, \sigma[\alpha_i \mapsto v'] >} \qquad \frac{\begin{array}{l} n \geq 0 \\ T \text{ is a simple type} \\ \alpha_i \text{ is new in } \sigma \\ v_0 = v_1 ... = v_{n-1} \text{ is initial for } T \\ \sigma' = \sigma[\alpha_i \mapsto \ll v_0, ... v_{n-1} \gg^{T[]}] \end{array}}{< \text{new } T[n], \sigma > \leadsto_p < \alpha_i, \sigma' >}$$

$$\frac{\begin{array}{l} 1 \leq j \leq k, \ k \geq 1, \ m \geq 0 \\ n_i \text{ ground for } i \in \{1, ... j-1\} \\ < n_j, \sigma > \leadsto_p < n'_j, \sigma' > \end{array}}{\begin{array}{l} < \text{new } T[n_1]...[n_k][]_1...[]_m, \sigma > \leadsto_p \\ < \text{new } T[n_1]...[n'_j]...[n_k][]_1...[]_m, \sigma' > \end{array}} \qquad \frac{\begin{array}{l} m \geq 1, n \geq 0, k \geq 1 \\ \alpha_i \text{ new in } \sigma \\ \sigma' = \sigma[\alpha_i \mapsto \ll null_0, ... null_{n-1} \gg^{T[]_1...[]_k}] \end{array}}{< \text{new } T[n][]_2...[]_k, \sigma > \leadsto_p < \alpha_i, \sigma' >}$$

$$\frac{\begin{array}{l} k \geq 1, m \geq 0 \\ n_i \text{ ground for } i \in \{1, ... k\} \\ n_j < 0 \text{ for some } j \in \{1, ... k\} \end{array}}{< \text{new } T[n_1]...[n_k][]_1..[]_m, \sigma > \leadsto_p < \text{NegSzeExc}, \sigma >}$$

$$\frac{\begin{array}{l} n_1 \geq 0, \ k \geq 2, \ m \geq 0, \ \sigma_0 = \sigma, n_i \text{ ground } i \in \{1, ... k\} \\ T \text{ is a simple type} \\ < \text{new } T[n_2]...[n_k][]_1...[]_m, \sigma_i > \leadsto_p < \alpha_{j_i}, \sigma_{i+1} > \qquad i \in \{0, ... n_1 - 1\} \\ \alpha_{j_i} \text{ is new in } \sigma_{n_i} \qquad i \in \{0, ... n_1\} \\ \sigma' = \sigma_{n_1}[\alpha_{j_{n_1}} \mapsto \ll \alpha_{j_0}, ..., \alpha_{j_{n_1-1}} \gg^{T[]_1...[]_{k+m}}] \end{array}}{< \text{new } T[n_1]...[n_k][]_1...[]_m, \sigma > \leadsto_p < \alpha_{j_{n_1}}, \sigma' >}$$

**Fig. 19.** object and array creation

first, until it becomes l-ground. Then the right hand side is evaluated, up to the point of obtaining a ground term. Then the state is modified accordingly. Note that we have *no* rule of the form $< \alpha_j := \text{value}, \sigma > \leadsto_p ....$ This is because in Java overwriting of objects is not possible – only sending messages to them, or overwriting selected instance variables.

Figure 21 describes the evaluation of method calls. Expressions are evaluated left to right, cf ch. 9.3 in [17]. The first rule describes rewriting the $k^{th}$ expression, where all the previous expressions (*i.e.* $e_i, i \in \{1, ... k-1\}$) are ground. The second rule describes dynamic method look up, taking into account the argument types, and the statically calculated method descriptor AT, and where $t[t'/x]$ has the usual meaning of replacing the variable $x$ by the term $t'$ in the term $t$.

$$\frac{\text{v is not l-ground}}{< v, \sigma > \leadsto_p < v', \sigma' >}{< v := e, \sigma > \leadsto_p < v' := e, \sigma' >} \qquad \frac{\text{v is l-ground}}{< e, \sigma > \leadsto_p < e', \sigma' >}{< v := e, \sigma > \leadsto_p < v := e', \sigma' >}$$

$$\frac{\begin{array}{l}\text{val is ground}\\ \text{id is an identifier}\end{array}}{\begin{array}{l}< id := val, \ \sigma > \leadsto_p\\ < \sigma[id \mapsto val] >\end{array}} \qquad \frac{\begin{array}{l}\sigma(\alpha_i) \neq null\\ \text{val is ground}\end{array}}{\begin{array}{l}< \alpha_i.[C]v := val, \sigma > \leadsto_p\\ < \sigma[\alpha_i, v, C \mapsto val] >\end{array}}$$

$$\frac{\begin{array}{l}\sigma(\alpha_i) = null\\ \text{val is ground}\end{array}}{\begin{array}{l}< \alpha_i.[C]v := val, \sigma > \leadsto_p\\ < NullPointExc, \sigma >\end{array}} \qquad \frac{\begin{array}{l}\sigma(\alpha_i) = null\\ \text{val, k ground}\end{array}}{\begin{array}{l}< \sigma(\alpha_i)[k] := val, \sigma > \leadsto_p\\ < NullPointExc, \sigma >\end{array}}$$

$$\frac{\begin{array}{l}\text{val is ground}\\ \sigma(\alpha_i)[k] = IndOutBndExc\end{array}}{\begin{array}{l}< \alpha_i[k] := val, \sigma > \leadsto_p\\ < IndOutBndExc, \sigma >\end{array}}$$

$$\frac{\begin{array}{l}\text{val is ground}\\ \sigma(\alpha_i)[k] \neq IndOutBndExc\\ \sigma(\alpha_i) = \ll...\gg^{T[]_1 \cdots []_m}\\ \text{val conforms weakly to T in } \sigma\end{array}}{\begin{array}{l}< \alpha_i[k] := val, \sigma > \leadsto_p\\ < \sigma[\sigma(\alpha_i), k \mapsto val] >\end{array}} \qquad \frac{\begin{array}{l}\text{val is ground}\\ \sigma(\alpha_i)[k] \neq IndOutBndExc\\ \sigma(\alpha_i) = \ll...\gg^{T[]_1 \cdots []_m}\\ \text{val does not conform weakly to T, } \sigma\end{array}}{\begin{array}{l}< \alpha_i[k] := val, \sigma > \leadsto_p\\ < ArrStoreExc, \sigma >\end{array}}$$

**Fig. 20.** assignment

### 4.3 Properties of the operational semantics

The operational semantics is deterministic:

**Lemma 10.** *For any configuration with a state that conforms to the environment, and any Java$_{se}$ term, the relation $\leadsto_p$ determines at most one step.*

**Lemma 11.** *For any Java$_{se}$ term t, state $\sigma$ and environment $\Gamma$, if t does not contain an assignment to $\alpha_i$ as a subterm, and $< Comp\{t, \Gamma\}, \sigma > \leadsto_p < t', \sigma >$, then t' does not contain an assignment to $\alpha_i$ as a subterm.*

## 5 Soundness of the Java$_s$ type system

The subject reduction theorem says, that any well-typed Java$_{se}$ term either rewrites to a term which will lead to an exception or rewrites to another well-typed term of a type that can be widened to the type of the original term.

$$\frac{\begin{array}{l}\mathtt{e_i} \text{ is ground, for all } \mathtt{i} \in \{\mathtt{1}, ...\mathtt{k}-\mathtt{1}\}, \mathtt{n} \geq \mathtt{k} \geq 1 \\ <\mathtt{e_k}, \sigma> \rightsquigarrow_{\mathtt{p}} <\mathtt{e'_k}, \sigma'>\end{array}}{<\mathtt{e_1}.[\mathtt{AT}]\mathtt{m}(\mathtt{e_2}, \ldots, \mathtt{e_k}, \ldots \mathtt{e_n}), \sigma> \rightsquigarrow_{\mathtt{p}} <\mathtt{e_1}.[\mathtt{AT}]\mathtt{m}(\mathtt{e_2}, \ldots, \mathtt{e'_k}, \ldots \mathtt{e_n}), \sigma'>}$$

$$\frac{\begin{array}{l}\mathtt{val_i} \text{ is ground } \mathtt{i} \in \{\mathtt{1}, ...\mathtt{n}\}, \mathtt{n} \geq 1 \\ \sigma(\mathtt{val_1}) = \ll \ldots \gg^{\mathtt{C}} \\ \mathtt{AT} = \mathtt{T_2} \times \ldots \times \mathtt{T_n} \\ \mathit{MethBody}(\mathtt{m}, \mathtt{AT}, \mathtt{C}, \mathtt{p}) = (\mathtt{C'}, \lambda \mathtt{x_2} : \mathtt{T_2} \ldots \lambda \mathtt{x_n} : \mathtt{T_n}.\{\ \mathtt{stmts}\ \}) \\ \mathtt{z_i} \text{ are new identifiers in } \sigma \\ \sigma' = \sigma[\mathtt{z_1} \mapsto \mathtt{val_1}] \ldots [\mathtt{z_n} \mapsto \mathtt{val_n}] \\ \mathtt{stmts'} = \mathtt{stmts}[\mathtt{z_1}/\mathtt{this}, \mathtt{z_2}/\mathtt{x_2}, \ldots \mathtt{z_n}/\mathtt{x_n}]\end{array}}{<\mathtt{val_1}.[\mathtt{AT}]\mathtt{m}(\mathtt{val_2}, \ldots \mathtt{val_n}), \sigma> \rightsquigarrow_{\mathtt{p}} <\mathtt{stmts'}, \sigma'>}$$

**Fig. 21.** method calls

**Theorem 1 Subject Reduction** *For a state $\sigma$ that conforms to an environment $\Gamma$, a $Java_{se}$ program* p *with $\Gamma \vdash \mathtt{p} : \Gamma$, a non-ground $Java_{se}$ term* t *that contains no assignments of the form $\alpha_{\mathtt{i}} := \ldots$, and type* T *with $\Gamma, \sigma \vdash \mathtt{t} : \mathtt{T}$, there exist $\sigma'$, $\mathtt{t'}$ such that:*

- $<\mathtt{t}, \sigma> \rightsquigarrow_{\mathtt{p}} <\mathtt{t'}, \sigma'>$, *and*
  - $\exists \mathtt{t''}, \sigma'' : <\mathtt{t'}, \sigma'> \rightsquigarrow_{\mathtt{p}}^* <\mathtt{t''}, \sigma''>$ *and* $\mathtt{t''}$ *contains an exception*

    *or*
  - $\exists \Gamma', \mathtt{T'} :$ *$\Gamma'$ conforms to $\Gamma$, $\sigma'$ conforms to $\Gamma'$, and $\Gamma', \sigma' \vdash \mathtt{t'} : \mathtt{T'}$, and $\Gamma \vdash \mathtt{T'} <_{wdn} \mathtt{T}$*

  *or*
- $<\mathtt{t}, \sigma> \rightsquigarrow_{\mathtt{p}} <\sigma'>$ *and $\sigma'$ conforms to $\Gamma$*

*Furthermore, if* t *is a variable, and not l-ground, then $<\mathtt{t}, \sigma> \rightsquigarrow_{\mathtt{p}} <\mathtt{t'}, \sigma'>$ and $\mathtt{t'}$ is not ground. Also, if* t *is not l-ground and not an array access, then $\mathtt{T} = \mathtt{T'}$.*

**Theorem 2 Soundness** *Take any $Java_s$ term* t*, a well-formed environment $\Gamma$, a type* T *with $\Gamma \vdash \mathtt{t} : \mathtt{T}$ a $Java_s$ program* p *with $\Gamma \vdash \mathtt{p} : \Gamma$, and a state $\sigma$ that conforms to $\Gamma$. Then there exists a $Java_{se}$ program $\mathtt{p'}$, $\mathtt{p'} = Comp\{\![\mathtt{p}, \Gamma]\!\}$, a $Java_{se}$ term term $\mathtt{t'}$, and a state $\sigma'$, such that:*

- *The execution of $< Comp\{\![\mathtt{t}, \Gamma]\!\}, \sigma > \rightsquigarrow_{\mathtt{p'}}^*$ does not terminate*

  *or*
- $< Comp\{\![\mathtt{t}, \Gamma]\!\}, \sigma > \rightsquigarrow_{\mathtt{p'}}^* <\mathtt{t'}, \sigma'>$ *and $\mathtt{t'}$ contains an exception as a subterm*

  *or*

- $\mathbf{T} \neq \mathbf{void}$, *and* $< Comp\{\![t, \Gamma]\!\}, \sigma > \leadsto_{\mathbf{p'}}^* < t', \sigma' >$ *and* $t'$ *is ground,*
  *and* $\exists \mathbf{T'} : \ \Gamma, \sigma' \vdash t' : \mathbf{T'}, \ \Gamma \vdash \mathbf{T'} <_{wdn} \mathbf{T}$ *and* $\sigma'$ *conforms to* $\Gamma$
  *or*
- $\mathbf{T} = \mathbf{void}$, *and* $< Comp\{\![t, \Gamma]\!\}, \sigma > \leadsto_{\mathbf{p'}}^* < \sigma' >$ *and* $\sigma'$ *conforms to* $\Gamma$

## 6  An example

The following, admittedly contrived, Java program serves to demonstrate the concepts introduced in the previous sections, and can have the following interpretation: Philosophers like philosophers. When a philosopher thinks about a problem together with another philosopher, then, after some deliberation they refer the problem to a third philosopher. When a philosopher thinks together with a French philosopher, they produce a book. French philosophers like food; when they think together with another philosopher, they finally refer the question to a French philosopher (such method overriding was allowed in [17]).

```
class Phil {
        Phil like ;
        Phil think(Phil y){ ... }
        Book think(FrPhil y){ ... }
}
class FrPhil extends Phil {
        Food like ;
        FrPhil think(Phil y){ like = oyster ; ... }
}
Phil aPhil ; FrPhil pascal ;
... pascal.like ; pascal.think(pascal) ; pascal.think(aPhil) ;
... aPhil.like ; aPhil.think(pascal) ; aPhil.think(aPhil) ;
aPhil = pascal ;
... aPhil.like ; aPhil.think(pascal) ; aPhil.think(aPhil) ;
```

The functions $FDec(,,)$, $FDecs(,,)$, $MSigs(,,)$, and $MDecs(,,)$ are as follows:

$FDec(\Gamma_0, \mathbf{Phil}, \mathbf{like}) \quad = ( \ \mathbf{Phil}, \ \mathbf{Phil} \ )$
$FDec(\Gamma_0, \mathbf{FrPhil}, \mathbf{like}) \quad = ( \ \mathbf{FrPhil}, \ \mathbf{Food} \ )$

$FDecs(\Gamma_0, \mathbf{Phil}, \mathbf{like}) \quad = \{ \ ( \ \mathbf{Phil}, \ \mathbf{Phil} \ ) \ \}$
$FDecs(\Gamma_0, \mathbf{FrPhil}, \mathbf{like}) \quad = \{ \ ( \ \mathbf{Phil}, \ \mathbf{Phil} \ ),$
$\qquad\qquad\qquad\qquad\qquad\quad ( \ \mathbf{FrPhil}, \ \mathbf{Food} \ ) \ \}$

$MDecs(\Gamma_0, \mathbf{Phil}, \mathbf{think}) \quad = \{ \ ( \ \mathbf{Phil}, \ \mathbf{Phil} \rightarrow \mathbf{Phil} \ ),$
$\qquad\qquad\qquad\qquad\qquad\qquad ( \ \mathbf{Phil}, \ \mathbf{FrPhil} \rightarrow \mathbf{Book} \ ) \ \}$
$MDecs(\Gamma_0, \mathbf{FrPhil}, \mathbf{think}) = \{ \ ( \ \mathbf{FrPhil}, \ \mathbf{Phil} \rightarrow \mathbf{FrPhil} \ ),$
$\qquad\qquad\qquad\qquad\qquad\qquad ( \ \mathbf{Phil}, \ \mathbf{FrPhil} \rightarrow \mathbf{Book} \ ) \ \}$

$MSigs(\Gamma_0, \mathbf{Phil}, \mathbf{think}) \quad = \{ \ \mathbf{Phil} \rightarrow \mathbf{Phil}, \ \mathbf{FrPhil} \rightarrow \mathbf{Book} \ \}$
$MSigs(\Gamma_0, \mathbf{FrPhil}, \mathbf{think}) = \{ \ \mathbf{Phil} \rightarrow \mathbf{FrPhil}, \ \mathbf{FrPhil} \rightarrow \mathbf{Book} \ \}$

The corresponding Java$_s$ environment $\Gamma_0$ is:

```
Γ₀ = Phil ext Object { like : Phil, think : Phil → Phil,
                       think : FrPhil → Book, },
     FrPhil ext Phil { like: Food, think : Phil → FrPhil },
     aPhil : Phil, pascal : FrPhil
```

The corresponding Java$_s$ program is p:

```
p = {Phil ext Object { think is λ y:Phil.{ ... },
             think is λ y:FrPhil.{ ... } },
     FrPhil ext Phil { think is
             λ y:Phil.{ this.like := oyster ; ... } } }
... }
```

The program p would be mapped to p′, the following Java$_{se}$ program:

```
p′ = Comp{|p, Γ₀|} = {
     Phil ext Object { think is λ y:Phil. { ... },
             think is λ y:FrPhil. { ... } }
     FrPhil ext Phil { think is λ y:FrPhil.
             { this.[FrPhil]like := oyster ; ... } }
pascal.[FrPhil]like ; pascal.[FrPhil]think (pascal) ;
        pascal.think(aPhil) - ambiguous method call!
aPhil.[Phil]like ; aPhil.[FrPhil]think (pascal) ;
        aPhil.[Phil]think (aPhil) ;
aPhil = pascal ;
aPhil.[Phil]like ; aPhil.[FrPhil]think (pascal) ;
        aPhil.[Phil]think (aPhil) ;
}
```

The state $\sigma_0$ conforms to the environment $\Gamma_0$:
$\sigma_0(\text{aPhil}) = \alpha_2$
$\sigma_0(\alpha_2) \quad = \ll\text{like Phil: } \alpha_4\text{, like FrPhil: croissant }\gg^{\text{FrPhil}}$
$\sigma_0(\alpha_4) \quad = \ll\text{like Phil: null }\gg^{\text{Phil}}$

Execution of the method call aPhil.[Phil]think (aPhil) results in the following rewrites

$< \text{aPhil.[Phil]think(aPhil)}, \sigma_0 > \leadsto_{p′} < \alpha_2\text{.[Phil]think(aPhil)}, \sigma_0 > \qquad \leadsto_{p′}$
$< \alpha_2\text{.[Phil]think}(\alpha_2), \sigma_0 > \qquad \leadsto_{p′} < (\text{w.[FrPhil]like:=oyster;}\ldots), \sigma_1 > \leadsto_{p′}$
$< (\ldots), \sigma_2 >$

where $\sigma_1$, $\sigma_2$ are:

$\sigma_1(\texttt{aPhil}) = \sigma_0(\texttt{aPhil}) = \alpha_2$

$\sigma_1(\texttt{w}) \quad = \qquad\quad = \alpha_2$

$\sigma_1(\texttt{w}') \quad = \qquad\quad = \alpha_2$

$\sigma_1(\alpha_2) \quad = \sigma_0(\alpha_2) \quad = \ll\texttt{like Phil}:\alpha_4, \texttt{ like FrPhil}:\texttt{croissant}\gg^{\texttt{FrPhil}}$

$\sigma_1(\alpha_4) \quad = \sigma_1(\alpha_4) \quad = \ll\texttt{like Phil}:\texttt{null}\gg^{\texttt{Phil}}$

$\sigma_2(\texttt{aPhil}) = \sigma_1(\texttt{aPhil}) = \alpha_2$

$\sigma_2(\texttt{w}) \quad = \sigma_1(\texttt{w}) \quad = \alpha_2$

$\sigma_2(\texttt{w}') \quad = \sigma_1(\texttt{w}') \quad = \alpha_2$

$\sigma_2(\alpha_2) \quad = \qquad\quad = \ll\texttt{like Phil}:\alpha_4, \texttt{ like FrPhil}:\texttt{oyster }\gg^{\texttt{FrPhil}}$

$\sigma_2(\alpha_4) \quad = \sigma_1(\alpha_4) \quad = \ll\texttt{like Phil}: \texttt{null }\gg^{\texttt{Phil}}$

If we consider the "environment extension" as in theorem 1, then in the third step of the reductions, we would have the environment $\Gamma' = \Gamma_0, \texttt{w}:\texttt{FrPhil}, \texttt{w}':\texttt{FrPhil}$. The states $\sigma_1$, $\sigma_2$ conform to $\Gamma'$.

Execution of an array creation expression $\texttt{new int}[2][3][][]$, for the state $\sigma_0$:
$< \texttt{new int}[2][3][][], \sigma_0 > \leadsto_{p'} < \alpha_7, \sigma_5 >$ where $\alpha_5$ and $\alpha_6$ are new in $\sigma_0$, and have the following contents in $\sigma_5$:

$\sigma_5(\alpha_5) = \ll\texttt{null}, \texttt{null}, \texttt{null}\gg^{\texttt{int}[][]}$

$\sigma_5(\alpha_6) = \ll\texttt{null}, \texttt{null}, \texttt{null}\gg\gg\texttt{int}[][]$

$\sigma_5(\alpha_7) = \ll\alpha_5, \alpha_6\gg^{\texttt{int}[][][]}$

# 7 Conclusions and future work

We have given a formal description of the operational semantics and type system for a substantial subset of Java. We consider this subset to contain many of the features which together might have led to difficulties in the Java type system. By applying some simplifications we obtained a straightforward system which we believe does not diminish the application of our results.

We aim to extend the language subset to describe a larger part of Java, and we also hope that our approach may serve as the basis for other studies on the language and possible extensions.

# 8 Acknowledgments

We are greatly indebted to several people, who read previous versions of this work and gave us valuable feedback and uncovered flaws: Donald Syme, Sarfraz Khurshid, Peter Sellinger, David von Oheimb, Yao Feng, Steve Vickers, Guiseppe Castagna and an anonymous FOOL4 referee for feedback.

We would also like to express our appreciation to Bernie Cohen for awakening our interest in the application of formal methods to Java and especially to all our students whose overwhelming interest in Java convinced us that this work needed to be undertaken.

# References

1. M. Abadi and L. Cardelli. A semantics of object types. In *LICS'94 Proceedings*, 1994.
2. Joseph A. Bank, Barbara Liskov, and Andrew C. Myers. Parameterized types and Java. In *POPL'97 Proceedings*, January 1997.
3. Gerald Baumgartner and Vincent F. Russo. Signatures: A language extension for improving type abstraction and subtype polymorphism in C++. *Software–Practice & Experience*, 25(8):863–889, August 1995.
4. John Boyland and Giuseppe Castagna. Type-safe compilation of covariant specialization: A practical case. In *ECOOP'96 Proceedings*, July 1996.
5. P. Canning, William Cook, and William Olthoff. Interfaces for object-oriented programming. In *OOPLSA'89*, pages 457–467, 1989.
6. Giuseppe Castagna. Parasitic Methods: Implementation of Multimethods for Java. Technical report, C.N.R.S, November 1996.
7. Giuseppe Castagna, Giorgio Ghelli, and Giuseppe Longo. A calculus for overloaded functions with subtyping. *Information and Computation*, 117(1):115–135, 15 February 1995.
8. William Cook. A Proposal for making Eiffel Type-safe. In S. Cook, editor, *ECOOP'87 Proceedings*, pages 57–70. Cambridge University Press, July 1989.
9. William Cook, Walter Hill, and Peter Canning. Inheritance is not subtyping. In *POPL'90 Proceedings*, January 1990.
10. Luis Damas and Robin Milner. Principal Type Schemes for Functional Languages. In *POPL'82 Proceedings*, 1982.
11. Drew Dean, Edward W. Felten, and Dan S. Wallach. Java security: From HotJava to Netscape and beyond. In *Proceedings of the 1996 IEEE Symposium on Security and Privacy*, pages 190–200, May 1996.
12. Sophia Drossopoulou and Susan Eisenbach. Is the Java type system sound? In *Proceedings of the Fourth International Workshop on Foundations of Object-Oriented Languages*, January 1997.
13. James Gosling, Bill Joy, and Guy Steele. *The Java Language Specification*. Addison-Wesley, August 1996.
14. R. Harper. A simplified account of polymorphic references. Technical Report CMU-CS-93-169, Carnegie Mellon University, 1993.
15. Daniel Ingalls. The smalltalk-76 programming system design and implementation. In *POPL'78 Proceedings*, pages 9–15, January 1978.
16. The Java language specification, October 1995.
17. The Java language specification, May 1996.
18. Bertrand Meyer. Static typing and other mysteries of life, December 1995.
19. Martin Odersky and Philip Wadler. Pizza into Java: Translating theory into practice. In *POPL'97 Proceedings*, January 1997.
20. Peter Sellinger. private communication, October 1996.
21. Mads Tofte. Type Inference for Polymorphic References. In *Information and Computation'80 Conference Proceedings*, pages 1–34, November 1980.

# Feature-Oriented Programming: A Fresh Look at Objects

Christian Prehofer

Institut für Informatik, Technische Universität München,
80290 München, Germany, prehofer@informatik.tu-muenchen.de

**Abstract.** We propose a new model for flexible composition of objects from a set of features. Features are similar to (abstract) subclasses, but only provide the core functionality of a (sub)class. Overwriting other methods is viewed as resolving feature interactions and is specified separately for two features at a time. This programming model allows to compose features (almost) freely in a way which generalizes inheritance and aggregation. For a set of $n$ features, an exponential number of different feature combinations is possible, assuming a quadratic number of interaction resolutions. We present the feature model as an extension of Java and give two translations to Java, one via inheritance and the other via aggregation. We further discuss parameterized features, which work nicely with our feature model and can be translated into Pizza, an extension of Java.

## 1 Introduction

A major contribution of object-oriented programming is reuse by inheritance or subclassing. Its success and its extensive use have led to several approaches to increase flexibility (mix-ins [18, 2], around-messages in Lisp [8], class refactoring methods [12]) and to approaches using different composition techniques, such as aggregation and (abstract) subclasses.

In this paper we propose a new model for object-oriented programming which nicely generalizes inheritance and includes the above mentioned extensions and new concepts. Instead of a rigid class structure, we propose writing features which are composed appropriately when creating objects. Features are similar to abstract subclasses or mixins [2]. The main difference is that we separate the core functionality of a subclass from overwriting methods of the superclass. We view overwriting more generally as a mechanism to resolve dependencies or interactions between features, i.e. some feature must behave differently in the presence of another one.

We resolve feature interactions by lifting functions of one feature to the context of the other. Similar to inheritance, this is accomplished by method overwriting, but lifters depend on two features and are separate entities used for composition. In contrast, inheritance just overwrites methods of the superclass.

Our new model allows to compose objects from individual features (or abstract subclasses) in a fully flexible and modular way. Its main advantage is that

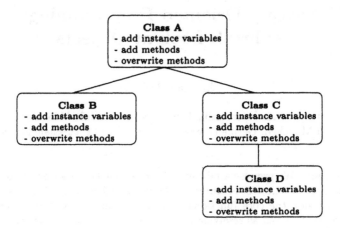

**Fig. 1.** Typical Class Hierarchies

objects with individual services can be created just by selecting the desired features, unlike object-oriented programming. Hence feature-oriented programming is particularly useful in applications where a large variety of similar objects is needed. The main novelty of this approach is a modular architecture for composing features with the required interaction handling, yielding a full object.

Consider for instance an example modeling stacks with the following features:

**Stack,** providing push and pop operations on a stack.
**Counter,** which adds a local counter (used for the size of the stack).
**Lock,** adding a switch to allow/disallow modifications of an object (here used for the stack).
**Bound,** which implements a range check, used for the stack elements.
**Undo,** adding an undo function, which restores the state as it was before the last access to the object.

In an object-oriented language, one would extend a class of stacks by a counter and similarly with the other features. Usually, a concrete class is added onto another concrete class. We generalize this to independent features which can be added to any object. For instance, we can run a counter object with or without lock. Furthermore, it is easy to imagine variations of the features, for instance different counters or a lock which not even permits read access. With our approach, we show that it is easy to provide such a set of features with interaction handling for simple reuse.

With feature-oriented programming, a feature repository replaces the rigid structure of conventional class hierarchies. Both are illustrated in Figures 1 and 2. The composition of features in Figure 2 uses an architecture for adding interaction resolution code (via overwriting) which is similar to constructing a concrete class hierarchy. To construct an object, features are added one after another in a particular order. (As we only compose objects, there is no real notion

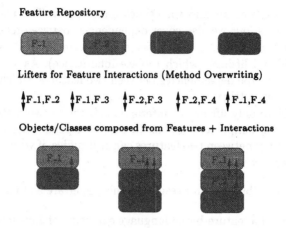

**Fig. 2.** Composing Objects in the Feature Model

of a class, which is hence often confused with the (type of) objects.) If a feature is added to a combination of $n$ features, we have to apply $n$ lifters in order to adapt the inner features. As we consider interactions of two features at a time, there is only a quadratic number $\binom{n}{2} = \frac{n^2 - n}{2}$ of lifters, but an exponential number $\binom{n}{k}, k = 1, \ldots, n$ of different feature combinations can be created. For instance, in the above example, we have 5 features with 10 interactions and about 30 sensible feature combinations. This number grows if different implementations or variations of features are considered (e.g. single- or multi-step undo). The observation that most, but not all, interactions can be handled for two features at a time is a major premise of this approach.

We show that feature-oriented programming generalizes object-oriented techniques and gives a new conceptual model of objects and object composition. To support this, we will show how to create Java [6] code for concrete feature selections, first using inheritance and then using aggregation and delegation. This shows the relations with known techniques and compares both techniques. In fact, we will show two cases where aggregation is more expressive than inheritance, refining earlier results [17].

To summarize, feature-oriented programming is advantageous for the following reasons:

– It yields more flexibility, as objects with individual services can be composed from a set of features. This is clearly desirable, if many different variations of one software component are needed or if new functionality has to be incorporated frequently.
– As the core functionality is separated from interaction handling, it provides more structure and clarifies dependencies between features. Hence it encourages to write independent, reusable code, as in many cases subclasses should be an independent entity, and not a subclass. This also makes class refac-

toring [12] much easier and sometimes unnecessary. The idea is similar to abstract classes, but we also cover dependencies between features.

- We show that parameterized features (similar to templates) work nicely with interactions and liftings (which replace inheritance). As we will see, there can also occur type dependencies between two features, which can be clearly specified in our setting.
- As we consider only liftings or interactions between two features at a time, the model is as simple as possible. In case of dependencies between several features, liftings between two features can still suffice, if we consider auxiliary features (see Sec. 4.2).

The technical contributions and results in this paper are as follows:

- Translations of a feature-based language extension of Java into Java, one via inheritance and one via aggregation and delegation.
- An analysis of parameterized features and type dependencies between features, followed by a translation into Pizza [11], an extension of Java.
- The translations lead to a detailed comparison of aggregation and inheritance. This unveils two cases where aggregation is more powerful than inheritance due to typing problems.

The origin of this idea of features in fact goes back to applications of monad theory in functional programming, as discussed in [13, 14]. In this earlier paper, composition of state monads was compared to inheritance and extended to other monads in functional programming. The motivation for this work was the recent development in telecommunication and multimedia software, where feature interactions have recently attracted great attention [21, 3]. Examples for feature-oriented programming in this area are discussed in [13, 15].

In the following section, we discuss the first three features of the stack example. We define the feature-oriented extension of Java via translations in Section 3, followed by an extension to parameterized features in Section 4. This section also discusses the remaining two features, undo and bound. Examples in Section 5 and discussions of the approach in Section 6 and Section 7 conclude the paper.

## 2    A First Example for Feature-Oriented Programming

In this section, we introduce feature-oriented programming with the above example modeling variations of stacks. (The undo and bound features are shown later in Section 4.) For this purpose, we present an extension of Java in the following.

Note that we only treat stacks over characters; parametric stacks will be considered later. We first define interfaces for features. Although not strictly needed for our ideas, they are useful if there are several implementations for one interface. Furthermore, they ease translation into Java, as a class can implement several interfaces in Java.

```
interface Stack {
  void empty();
  void push(char a);
  void push2(char a);
  void pop();
  char top();
}
interface Counter {
  void reset();
  void inc();
  void dec();
  int size();
}
interface Lock {
  void lock();
  void unlock();
}
```

The code below provides base implementations of the individual features. The notation **feature** SF defines a new feature named SF, which implements stacks. Similar to class names in Java, SF is used as a new constructor. Using the other two feature implementations, CF and LF,

```
new LF (CF (SF))
```

creates an object with all three features. For interaction handling, it is important that features are composed in a particular order, e.g. the above first adds CF to SF and then adds LF.

```
feature SF implements Stack {
    String s = new String();
    void empty() {s = ""; }  // Use Java Strings ...
    void push(char a) {s = String.valueOf(a).concat(s); };
    void pop() {s = s.substring(1); } ;
    char top() { return (s.charAt(0) ); } ;
    void push2(char a) {this.push(a) ; this.push(a); };
}
feature CF implements Counter {
    int i = 0;
    void reset() {i = 0; };
    void inc() {i = i+1; };
    void dec() {i = i-1; };
    int size() {return i; };
}
feature LF implements Lock {
    boolean l = true;
    void lock() {l = false;};
```

```
    void unlock() {l = true;};
    boolean is_unlocked() {return l;};
}
```

In addition to the base implementations, we need to provide lifters, which replace method overwriting in subclasses. Such lifters are separate entities and always handle two features at a time. In the following code, features (via interfaces) are lifted over concrete feature implementations. For instance, the code below feature CF lifts Stack adapts the functions of Stack to the context of CF, i.e. the counter has to be updated accordingly. When composing features, this lifter is used if CF is added to an object (type) with a feature with interface Stack, and not just directly to a stack implementation. This is important for flexible composition, as shown below.

```
feature CF lifts Stack {
  void empty() {this.reset(); super.empty() ;};
  void push(char a) {this.inc(); super.push(a) ;};
  void pop() { this.dec(); super.pop() ;};
}
feature LF lifts Stack {
  void empty() {if (this.is_unlocked()) {super.empty();}};
  void push(char a) {if (this.is_unlocked()) {super.push(a);}};
  void pop() { if (this.is_unlocked()) {super.pop();}};
}
feature LF lifts Counter {
  void reset() {if (this.is_unlocked()) {super.reset();}};
  void inc() {if (this.is_unlocked()) {super.inc();}};
  void dec() {if (this.is_unlocked()) {super.dec();}};
}
```

Methods which are unaffected by interactions are not explicitly lifted, e.g. top and size. Note that the lifting to the lock feature is schematic. Hence it is tempting to allow default lifters, as discussed in Section 7.

The modular specification of the three features, separated from their interactions, allows the following object compositions:

- Stack with counter
- Stack with lock
- Stack with counter and lock
- Counter with lock

For all these combinations, the three lifters shown above adapt the features to the combinations. The resulting objects behave as desired. In addition, we can of course use each feature individually (even lock). With the remaining two features, bound and undo (shown later), many more combinations are possible in the same way.

The composition of lifters and features is shown in Figure 3 for an example with three features. To compose stack, counter, and lock, we first add the counter

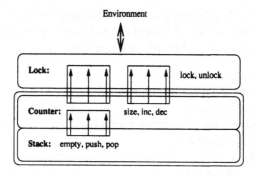

**Fig. 3.** Composing features (rounded boxes) by lifters (boxes with arrows)

to the stack and lift the stack to the counter. Then the lock feature is added and the inner two are lifted to lock. Hence the methods of the stack are adapted again, using the lifter from stack to lock.

The composed object provides the functionality of all selected features to the outside, but for composition we need an additional ordering. In particular, the outermost feature is not lifted, similar to the lowest class in a class hierarchy, whose functions are not overwritten.

Although inheritance can be used for such feature combinations, all needed combinations, including feature interactions, have to be assembled manually. In contrast, we can (re)use features by simply selecting the desired ones when creating an object.

In the above example, each feature can be run independently. In other examples it is often needed to write a feature assuming that some other feature is available. For this, a feature declaration may require other features, e.g. in the following example:

```
feature DisplayAdapter assumes AsciiPrintable  {
  void show_window(...) { ... }
  ...  }
```

Consequently, an implementation may use the operations provided by the feature AsciiPrintable in order to produce output on a window system.

In general, the base functionality of a new feature can rely on the functionality of the required ones. This idea of assuming other features is a further difference to usual abstract subclass concepts. (Note that the extended object can obviously have more than just the required features.)

## 3  Translation to Java

To provide a precise definition of our Java extension, we show two translations into Java. The first translation uses inheritance, while the second uses aggregation with delegation. Hence this also serves to compare the feature model with both of these approaches and will highlight two cases where both differ.

We assume the following abstract program with

- $I_i$ feature interfaces
- $I_i.t_{k_i}$ methods declared for interface $I_i$
- $F_i$ corresponding features
- $F_i.vardecls$ declaration of instance variables
- $F_i.f_{k_i}$ code for methods $I_i.t_{k_i}$
- $F_{i,j}$ lifter for $F_j$ to $I_i$
- $F_{i,j}.f_{k_j}$ code for lifting $I_j.t_{k_j}$

```
interface I₁ {
    I₁.t₁;                          // method declarations
    ⋮
    I₁.tₖ₁;
}

    ⋮

interface Iₘ {
    Iₘ.t₁;
    ⋮
    Iₘ.tₖₘ;
}
feature F₁ implements I₁ assumes I₁^l₁,...,I₁^lₙ {
    F₁.vardecls                     // variable declarations
    I₁.t₁ F₁.f₁;                     // method implementations
    ⋮
    I₁.tₖ₁ F₁.fₖ₁;
}

    ⋮

    // lifters
feature Fᵢ lifts Iⱼ {
    Iⱼ.t₁ Fᵢ,ⱼ.f₁;                   // function redefinitions
    ⋮
    Iⱼ.tₖⱼ Fᵢ,ⱼ.fₖⱼ;
}
```

For this schematic program, concrete object creations can be translated into Java in two ways, reflecting two object-oriented programming techniques: aggregation and inheritance. For both translations, the feature interfaces are preserved, while the feature code is merged into concrete classes, as shown below.

For sake of presentation, the translation is simplified in order to make the obtained code as explicit as possible. Therefore, we assume the following:

1. The names of (instance) variables as well as method names are distinct for all features.
2. Assume that method calls to *this* are explicit, i.e. always *this.fct*(...) instead of *fct*(...).
3. Variable declarations have no initializations.

## 3.1 Translation via Inheritance

For this translation, we create a concrete set of classes, one extending the other, for each used feature combination $F_1(F_2(F_3(\ldots(F_n)\ldots)))$. First a new class $F_1\_F_2\_F_3\_\ldots$ is introduced, which extends $F_2\_F_3\_\ldots$, followed by a class $F_3\_\ldots$. The class $F_1\_F_2\_F_3\_\ldots$ adds the functionality for interface $I_1$ and lifters for all others.

Formally, an object creation

**new** $F_1(F_2\ldots(F_n)\ldots)$

translates to

**new** $F_1\_F_2\_\ldots\_F_n$

Furthermore, we need the following Java classes for $i = 1, \ldots, n$:

**class** $F_i\_F_{i+1}\_\ldots\_F_n$ **extends** $F_{i+1}\_\ldots\_F_{n-1}$ **implements** $I_i, \ldots, I_n$ {
                                         // Feature i implementation
    $F_i.vardecls$                // variable declarations
    $I_i.t_1\ F_i.f_1;$           // function implementations
    $\vdots$

    $I_i.t_{k_i}\ F_i.f_{k_i};$
                                       // Lift Feature i+1 to i
    $I_{i+1}.t_1\ F_{i,i+1}.f_1;$  // function redefinitions
    $\vdots$

    $I_{i+1}.t_{k_{i+1}}\ F_{i,i+1}.f_{k_{i+1}};$
    $\vdots$                                 // Lift Feature n to i
    $I_n.t_1\ F_{i,n}.f_1;$       // function redefinitions
    $\vdots$

    $I_n.t_{k_n}\ F_{i,n}.f_{k_n};$
}

Observe that $n - i$ lifters are needed, which may call methods of the super class. The translation assumes that the features required for $F_i$ via **assumes** are present in the extended class. Otherwise, undeclared identifies occur in the translated code, which would only be allowed in a dynamically typed language. This assumption is not needed for aggregation, which accounts for a small difference between the two translations. Another difference will be examined in the following section on parameterized features.

For instance, our three features from the introduction translate into the following class hierarchy, if an object of type LF (CF (SF)) is used.

```
class SF implements Stack {
  String s = new String();
  void empty() { s = "";}
  void push( char a) {s = String.valueOf(a).concat(s);};
  void pop() {s = s.substring(1); } ;
  char top() { return (s.charAt(0) ); } ;
  void push2( char a) {this.push(a) ; this.push(a); };
}
class CF_on_SF extends SF implements Counter, Stack {
  int i = 0;
  void reset() {i = 0; };
  void inc() {i = i+1; };
  void dec() {i = i-1; };
  // lift SF to CF
  void empty() {this.reset(); super.empty() ;};
  void push( char a) {this.inc(); super.push(a) ;};
  void pop() { this.dec(); super.pop() ;};
}
class LF_on_CF_on_SF extends CF_on_SF
                     implements Lock, Counter, Stack {
  boolean l = true;
  void lock() {l = false;};
  void unlock() {l = true;};
  boolean is_unlocked() {return l ;};
  // lift CF to LF
  void reset() {if (this.is_unlocked()) {  super.reset(); }};
  void inc() {if (this.is_unlocked()) { super.inc(); }};
  void dec() {if (this.is_unlocked()) {  super.dec(); }};
  // lift SF to LF
  void empty() {if (this.is_unlocked()) {super.empty(); }};
  void push( char a) {if (this.is_unlocked()) {super.push(a);}}
  void pop() { if (this.is_unlocked()) {super.pop();}};
}
```

In this example, the above code provides for most sensible combinations, except for stack with lock only or counter with lock. In general, this translation introduces intermediate classes, which may be reused for other feature combinations.

## 3.2 Translation via Aggregation

Aggregation is a common technique for composing objects from different classes to a larger object. It is used in some object-based systems as a replacement for inheritance.

This translation requires a set of base implementations and one new class for each feature combination. The idea of the translation is to create a class, where, for each selected feature, one instance variable of this type is used to delegate the services, similar to [7]. We have to be careful with delegation and calls to **this**, which should not be sent to the local object. Hence we have to supply the delegate object with the right pointer to the enclosing object, which "replaces" **this**. For this purpose, we create a base class for each feature implementation with an extra variable which will point to the composed object. This construction enables us to check the **assumes** clauses globally, i.e. wrt the newly created set of features. With the inheritance translation we had to check these assumptions for each newly added class wrt its superclass.

Unlike the first translation, we need a few further technical assumptions. For all lifters, all methods are lifted explicitly, e.g.

```
int size() { return super.size(); };
```

is assumed to be present. Furthermore, we need to assume that instance variables which are used in lifters are declared public.[1] Also, the name self may not be used.

The main task of this translation is to compose the lifters, i.e. all lifters for one method have to be merged at once here. This can lead to more dense code, as all needed lifters are composed in one class, contrary to the inheritance translation.

An object creation

new $F_1(F_2 \dots (F_n) \dots)$

translates to

new $F_1 \_F_2 \_ \dots \_F_n$

For this, we first need the following base classes for each feature implementation $F_i$, $i = 1 \dots n$. For the type of self in the code below, we use the class $F_1\_F_2\_\dots\_F_n$. If no assumes statements are used, then just $I_i$ is sufficient and the class can be reused for other object creations. Alternatively, one can introduce an intermediate class with just the needed interfaces $I_i, I_i^1 \_ \dots \_ I_i^{l_i}$.

```
class Fᵢ implements Iᵢ {
    (F₁_F₂_..._Fₙ) self ;              // reference for delegation
    Fᵢ (F₁_F₂_..._Fₙ s) { self = s; } ; // constructor for this class
    Fᵢ.vardecls
    Iᵢ.t₁ θF₁.f₁;                      // function implementations
    ⋮
    Iᵢ.tₖᵢ θF₁.fₖᵢ;
}
```

---

[1] Note that public declarations are omitted throughout this presentation.

For delegation to work in the above, we need to apply a substitution $\theta$ which renames this to self:

$$\theta = [\text{this} \mapsto \text{self}]$$

With the above base implementations we construct the class $F_1\_F_2\_\ldots\_F_n$ via aggregation.

```
class F₁_F₂_...._Fₙ implements I₁, I₂, ..., Iₙ {
    F₁ b₁ = new F₁(this);                    // delegate objects
    ⋮
    Fₙ bₙ = new Fₙ(this);
                                             // now need to nest lifters
    I₂.t₁ δ₂F₁,₂.f₁;                         // lift feature 2 to 1
    ⋮
    I₂.t_{k₂} δ₂F₁,₂.f_{k₂};

    I₃.t₁ δ₃θ₂,₃F₁,₃.f₁;                     // lift feature 3 to 1
    ⋮
    I₃.t_{k₃} δ₃θ₂,₃F₁,₃.f_{k₃};
        ⋮
    Iₙ.t₁ δₙθₙ₋₁,ₙθₙ₋₂,ₙ...θ₂,ₙF₁,ₙ.f₁;     // lift feature n to 1
    ⋮
    Iₙ.t_{kₙ} δₙθₙ₋₁,ₙθₙ₋₂,ₙ...θ₂,ₙF₁,ₙ.f_{kₙ};
}
```

For simplicity, we only indicate the applications of nested lifters via unfolding operators $\theta_i$, where $\theta_{i,j}$ unfolds the lifter from $j$ to $i$, sketched as

$$\theta_{i,j} = [\text{super}.f_1 \mapsto F_{i,j}.f_1, \ldots, \text{super}.f_{k_i} \mapsto F_{i,j}.f_{k_j}],$$

and also passes the actual parameters. Unlike in the examples below, unfolding is in general more involved for functions, as we cannot have local blocks with return statements. Hence we also assume for simplicity that methods return void.[2]

Furthermore, we have to delegate calls to super to the delegate objects. For this purpose, $\delta_i$ shall rename the instance variables and method calls of methods in $I_i$ to super correctly to the corresponding $b_i$. For instance, super.pop() is translated to sf.pop(), where sf is the name of the instance variable in the following example. We show the translation for the combination of the three introductory features. First, new base classes are introduced (with suffix _ag):

---

[2] This is no restriction, as in Java objects of primitive type can be "wrapped" into an object in order to be passed as variable parameters.

```
class SF_ag implements Stack {
  Stack self;
  String s = new String();
  SF_ag(Stack s) {self = s;};
  void empty() { s = "";}
  void push( char a) {s = String.valueOf(a).concat(s);};
                  // self replaces this for proper delegation!!
  void push2( char a) { self.push(a); self.push(a);};
  void pop() {s = s.substring(1); };
  char top() { return (s.charAt(0)); };
}
class CF_ag implements Counter {
  Counter self;
  CF_ag (Counter s) {self = s;};
  int i = 0;
  void reset() {i = 0; };
  void inc() {i = i+1; };
  void dec() {i = i-1; };
  int size() {return i; };
}
class LF_ag implements Lock {
  Lock self;
  LF_ag (Lock s) {self = s;};
  boolean l = true;
  void lock() {l = false;};
  void unlock() {l = true;};
  boolean is_unlocked() {return l;};
}
```

A class for a composed object is shown below.

```
class LF_CF_SF implements Lock, Counter, Stack {
          // delegate objects
  SF_ag sf = new SF_ag(this);
  CF_ag cf = new CF_ag(this);
  LF_ag lf = new LF_ag(this);
          // delegate to lock
  void lock() {lf.lock();};
  void unlock() {lf.unlock();};
  boolean is_unlocked() {return lf.is_unlocked();};
        // delegate to lock
  void reset() {if (this.is_unlocked()) {cf.reset();}};
  void inc() {if (this.is_unlocked()) {cf.inc();}};
  void dec() {if (this.is_unlocked()) {cf.dec();}};
  int  size() {return cf.size();};
        // delegate to stack
  void empty()
```

```
        {if (this.is_unlocked()) {this.reset(); sf.empty();}};
  void push( char a)
        {if (this.is_unlocked()) {this.inc(); sf.push(a);}};
  void push2( char a) {sf.push2(a);};
  void pop() {if (this.is_unlocked()) {this.dec(); sf.pop();}};
  char top() {return sf.top();};
}
```

Compared to the first translation, we need fewer classes here, as the base classes can be reused. On the other hand, aggregation introduces another level of indirection, which may affect efficiency.

## 4 Parametric Features

In order to write reusable code, it is often desirable to parameterize a class by a type. In this section, we introduce parametric features, which are very similar to parametric classes. Due to the flexible composition concepts for features, we also need expressive type concepts for composition. For Java, parametric classes have just recently been proposed and implemented in the language Pizza [11], which will be the target language for our translations. Apart from other nice extensions, which are also used in some examples here, Pizza introduces a rather powerful extension for type safe parameterization. The notation for type parameters is similar to C++ templates [19]. A typical example is a stack feature parameterized by a type A as follows:

```
interface Stack<A> {
   void empty();
   void push( A a);
   void push2( A a);
   void pop();
   A top();
}
feature SF<A> implements Stack<A> {
   List<A> s = List.Nil;          // Use Pizza's List data type
   void empty() { s = List.Nil;};
   void push(A a) {s = List.Cons(a,s);};
   void push2(A a) { this.push(a) ; this.push(a);};
   void pop() {s = s.tail();};
   A top() { return s.head();};
}
```

Stacks over type char with a counter are then created via

```
    new CF (SF<char>);
```

Note that it is sometimes useful to make assumptions on the parameter for providing operations, e.g.

```
interface Matrix<A implements Number> {
  void multiply_matrix( ...);
  ...
}
```

Such an assumption is different from assumptions via **assumes**, as it refers to a parameter and not to the inner feature combination. The difference is that this kind of parameterization is not subject to liftings.

For translating parameterization into Java we refer to [11]. We here only aim at translating into Pizza. As we mostly use basic concepts, it is not necessary to go into the details of the Pizza type system.

## 4.1 Type Dependencies

For parameterized features new and interesting specification problems occur when combining features. Not only can features depend on each other, but the parameter types can also depend on each other. This gets even more complicated if more than two features are involved, as shown below. For instance, we may want to combine Stack<A> with a feature which only allows elements within a certain range. Its implementation maintains two variables of type A used for filtering. This feature Bound is parameterized by a numeric type:

```
interface Bound<A> { boolean check_bounds(A el); }
```

```
feature BF<A implements Number> implements Bound<A> {
  A min, max;
  BF(A mi, A ma) { min = mi; max = ma;};
  boolean check_bounds(A el) {...};
}
```

Clearly, we can only combine the two features when both are supplied with the same type. This can be expressed by liftings:

```
feature BF<A> lifts Stack<A> { ... }
```

Another example for such a dependency will be shown in Section 5. Note that in feature implementations, assumes conditions can also express type dependencies in the same way.

## 4.2 Multi-Feature Interactions and Type Interactions

In the following, we discuss multi-feature interactions and type interactions using the undo example. This will lead to a new aspect of lifting features, i.e. that lifting may change the type parameter.

The implementation of the undo feature is simple: save the local state of the object each time a function of the other features is applied (e.g. push, pop). Undo depends essentially on all "inner" features, since it has to know the internal state of the composed object. As we work in a typed environment, the type of the state to be saved has to be known. This multi-feature interaction is solved by an extra feature, called `Store`, which allows to read and write the local state of a composed object. (The motivation for store is similar to the Memento pattern in [5].)

We introduce the following interface for `Store`:

```
interface Store<A> {
    void put_s( A a);
    A get_s();
}
```

Note that the parameter type depends on the types of all instance variables of the used features. Consider for instance adding this feature to a stack with counter. Then for both features the local variables have to be accessed.

With the `Store` feature, we reduce the multi-feature interaction to a type interaction problem. This means that the parameter type of a feature has to change when a feature is lifted. The following solution makes these type dependencies explicit. We use the Pizza class `Pair<A, B>`, providing for polymorphic pairs, for type composition. In the following lifter, we state that the inner feature combination supports feature `Store<A>` for some type `A`. For this, we need a new syntactic construct, namely **assumes inner**. As feature stack ST adds an instance variable of type `List<B>`, we can support the store feature with parameter `Pair<List<B>,A>`.

```
feature ST<B> lifts Store<Pair<List<B>,A>>
              assumes inner Store<A> {
   Pair<List<B>,A> get_s()
        { return Pair.Pair( s,            // local state
                     super.get_s()); }    // inner state
   void get_s(Pair<List<B>,A> s) { ... }
}
```

The **assumes inner** however has some constraints. The lifted feature may not have instance variables or calls to self where the changed type parameter type is used. (This can be allowed if the type change is a specialization, which this is not the case in this example.)

This inner condition is implicit in other lifters and is only needed if the type parameters change. The lifting

```
feature F lifts F1<A> { ... }
```

can be seen as an abbreviation for

```
feature F lifts F1<A>
          assumes inner F1<A> { ... }
```

We show below how this change of parameters affects the two translations schemes of Section 3. Continuing with the example, we express that the counter CF adds an integer and LF a boolean variable with the following lifters:

```
feature CF lifts Store<Pair<A, int>>
          assumes inner Store<A> {
  ...
}
feature LF lifts Store<Pair<A, Boolean>>
          assumes inner Store<A> {
  ...
}
```

With the above lifters, we can assure that the store feature works correctly and with the correct type for any feature combination. All we need to add is a base implementation for store. As the base implementation cannot store anything useful, we introduce a Pizza type/class Void, which has just one element, void_el.

```
class Void { case void_el; }
```

```
feature ST implements Store<Void> {    //  base implementation
  void put_s(Void a ) {};
  Void get_s() {return Void.void_el; };
}
```

With the store feature, we can now write the generic undo feature, which can be plugged into any other feature combination. It is important that the store feature fixes the type of the state of the composed object. The undo feature can then have an instance variable of this type. Recall that this is not possible for store, as the type parameter of store changes under liftings.

The undo feature consists of two parts: storing the state before every change and retrieving it upon an undo call. The latter is the core functionality of undo, whereas the former will be fixed for each function with affects the state via liftings. First consider the undo feature and its implementation, which uses a variable backup to store the old state. Since there may not be an old state, we use the algebraic (Pizza) type Option<A>, which contains the elements None or Some(a) for all elements a of type A.

```
interface Undo<A> {
   void undo();
}
class Option<A> {
    case None;
    case Some(A value);
}
feature UF<A> implements Undo<A> assumes Store<A> {
  Option<A>  backup = None;
  void undo() {
        switch ((Option) backup) {
            case Some(A a):
```

```
                    put_s( a );
} } }
```

An alternative version of undo may store several or all old states. Due to our flexible setup, we can just exchange such variations.

For each of the other features, we have to lift all functions which update the internal state. As for lock, this lifting is canonical, e.g. for push:

```
void push(A a) {
   backup = Option.Some( get_s());
   super.push(a); };
```

Note that there is an interesting interaction between lock and undo: shall undo reverse the locking or shall lock disable undo as well? We chose the latter for simplicity and hence add lock after undo. Lifting undo to lock is canonical and not shown here. As an example, we can create an integer stack with undo and lock as follows:

```
new LF (UF<Pair<int,Void>> (SF<int> (ST) ))
```

### 4.3   Translation into Pizza

We show in the following how to translate the above extensions into Pizza. This will reveal another difference between aggregation and inheritance: for inheritance, we cannot cope with the change of parameters. Otherwise, the translation to Pizza is quite simple.

For aggregation, additional inner statements just translate into types of the instance variables of class generated for a combination. This is shown in the following code for a class generated for a composed object with both stack and store features. We first introduce a class SF_ag<A> for parametric stacks. As we do not allow calls to self for features whose type parameter changes during lifting, we do not use the usual delegation mechanism in the above class. Hence we use just ST. The class SF_ST<A> exports the interface Store<Pair<List<A>,Void>>, but uses a delegate object with interface Store<Void>.

```
class SF_ag<A> implements Stack<A> {
   Stack<A> self ;
   SF_ag(Stack<A> s) {self = s;};
   List<A> s = List.Nil;
   void empty() ...
}
class SF_ST<A> implements Stack<A>,Store<Pair<List<A>,Void>>{
   SF_ag<A>    sf = new SF_ag(this);
   Store<Void> st = new ST();
   Pair<List<A>,Void> get_s()
                 {return Pair.Pair(sf.s, st.get_s()) ; };
   ...
}
```

A further detail to observe is that all type variables have to be considered for the translation. This means that for the new class introduced, all type variables which appear as parameters in the desired set of features have to appear as parameters. For instance, for the combination F<A>(G<B>), we need a class F_G<A,B>.

For inheritance, an inner statement is an assumption on the extended class. If the parameter changes, this amounts to specialization for parameterized classes, which is problematic in typed imperative languages, as discussed in [11]. In Pizza, the problem in this example is that subtyping does extend through constructors such as List. For instance, we cannot translate the above feature combination to the following (illegal) code:

```
            // illegal ! Type conflict!
class ST_SF<B,A> extends ST<A>
      implements Stack<B>,Store<Pair<List<B>,A>> {
      Pair<List<B>,A> get_s() {
          Pair.Pair( s,                 // local state
                     super.get_s()); // inner state
      }
      ...
}
```

If the parameters do not change, the translation is straightforward.


# 5   Examples

In the following, we sketch a few more typical applications for feature-based programming. Some examples are freely taken from standard literature on design patterns [5]. We argue that for many of these typical programming schemata, feature-based implementations provide high flexibility and the desired reusability. This is particularly important if several features or design patterns are combined.


## 5.1   Adding a Cache

Consider implementing some functional entity, e.g. sets, where caching of the results of operations is a viable option. In the lines of [5], this can be viewed as a Proxy pattern. Clearly, a cache is an independent feature, and there exist many variations of caching. For instance, considering the data structures used and the replacement strategy. And it furthermore may depend on appropriate hash functions, which could also be provided via features.

When writing a reusable set of caching modules, the various cache implementations just implement the data structures and the access functions. Interaction resolution in turn modifies the access operations for the object to be cached and determines the type dependencies.

Consider writing this with classical object oriented languages: for each needed combination of a cached object, a cache, and a hashing function, a new (sub-)class has to be implemented.

A sketch of such an example is shown below. It shows how to add a cache to the parametric features Set<A> and Dictionary<A, B>. The feature implementation CacheI<A,B> (whose interface Cache is not shown here) caches mappings from A to B.

```
interface Set<A> {
   void put( A a);
   boolean contains(A a);
}
interface Dictionary<A, B> {
  Option<B> get(A key);
  void put(A key, B value);
}
feature CacheI<A,B> implements Cache<A,B> {
   ...
   void put_s( A a, B b) {...} ;
   boolean find_s(A a) {...};
   B get_s() {...};
}
feature CacheI<A,B> lifts Dictionary<A, B> {
               // adapt access functions to cache
  Option<B> get(A key)
    { if find(key)  return Option.Some(get_s());
           else  return super.get();  }
  ...
}
               // second parameter is just boolean here
feature CacheI<A,boolean> lifts Set<A> {
   ...
}
```

Note that the lifters express the type dependencies. For instance the set is viewed as a mapping from A to boolean.

## 5.2   Adaptor Patterns

The adaptor design pattern [5] glues two incompatible modules together. This design fits nicely in our setting, as adaptors should be reusable. Typically, there is some core adaption functionality, e.g. some data conversion, which we model as a feature. When adding this to another feature, we can just lift the incompatible functions with help of the core functionality.

An example is converting big endian encoding of data to little endian. For instance, if we output data on a (low-level) interface which needs big endian,

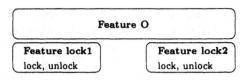

**Fig. 4.** Alternative Feature Composition

but we work with little endian, such a conversion feature can just be added. The adaptor feature provides the core functionality, here the data conversion, and interaction resolution adapts the operations of the object.

The following features and lifters sketch the solution of pluggable adaptors with features. The adaptor feature `Big_to_little_endian` adds a conversion function, which is used in the lifter to provide the put method with big endian data input.

```
feature Big_to_little_endian {
            // convert to little endian
  int big_to_little(int a) {...};
}
interface low_level_IO {  // assumes little_endian
  void put(int a);
}
feature Big_to_little_endian lifts low_level_IO {
  void put(int a) {super.put( big_to_little(a)); };
}
```

## 6 A Note on Feature Composition

When introducing our model of features, there is one important design decision for composing features: we assume that features are composed in a particular order. Only from the outside interface it is possible to view an object as composed of a set of features.

There are several reasons for this ordering. First, it is in the spirit of inheritance and it seems to be the simplest structure capturing the essential object-oriented ideas like inheritance.

Secondly, there are problems when viewing features as unordered citizens. We show in the following that, although intuitive, the idea of treating features without order is difficult wrt. liftings or inheritance. The problem seems to be similar to known problems with multiple inheritance.

Consider an example of an object integrating two unordered features, both implementing a lock. Such a configuration with lock1 and lock2, to which a feature O is added, is shown in Figure 4. The interaction is that closing lock1 should also close lock2 and vice versa. Hence we need liftings from the two features to feature O. The simple lifting model is to lift the functions of each feature to O, e.g. by applying all lifters corresponding to the other present features. The lifter of lock1 shall call `lock2.lock()`; and similarly the lifter for lock2 calls `lock1.lock()`; The problem is which version of lock should be called, the lifted or the original of the feature? If original is called, then all other liftings are ignored, e.g. if other features are involved. Or if the lifted version is called, then the procedure diverges.

In cases where features are fully independent it is not needed to order them. But still, there is no harm with an ordering in this case, and possibly a simple syntactic extension may alleviate the problem.

## 6.1 Related Work

We briefly compare the feature model to other approaches. Apart from the detailed comparison, we argue that the feature model provides maximal flexibility (with static typing) and is as simple as possible.

- Mixins [2] have been proposed as a basic concept for modeling other inheritance concepts. The main difference is that we consider interactions and separate a feature from interaction handling. If mixins are used also as lifters, then the composition of the features and their quadratic number of lifters has to be done manually in the appropriate order. Instead, we can just select features here.
- Method combination with before, after and around messages in CLOS [8] follows a similar idea as interactions. As with mixins, this does not consider interactions between two classes/features and gives no architecture for composition of abstract subclasses. Such after or before messages can be viewed as a particular class of interactions.
- Composition filters have been proposed in [1] to compose objects in layers, similar to the feature order in our approach. Messages are handled from outside in by each layer. The main difference is that we consider interactions on an individual basis and separate a feature from interaction handling.
- Several other approaches allow to change class membership dynamically or propose other compositions mechanisms [9, 20, 4, 16, 10]. Note that one of the main ingredients for feature-oriented programming, lifting to a context, can also be found in [16]. All of these do not consider a composition architecture as done here, and address other problems, such as name conflicts. Clearly, the idea of features can also be applied to dynamic composition, but this remains for future work.

## 7 Extensions

We discuss in the following a few extensions and issues which have not been addressed so far. As we have focused on feature composition, several interesting aspects have not been addressed.

- An aspect not yet considered is hiding. For instance, when adding the counter to a stack, we may not want to inherit the inc and dec functions, as they may turn the object into an inconsistent state. Such hidings can easily be provided by adding an appropriate interface and by disabling the others.
- Generic liftings via higher-order functions are possible in Pizza. In the stacks example it is easy to see that lifting to lock is schematic. It is natural to express this by higher-order functions. Consider for instance the following function for lifting lock, where ()->void is the Pizza notation for a function type.

```
void lift_to_lock( ()->void f)
        { if (this.is_unlocked() ) { f() ;};}
```

It can be used e.g. with

```
   void reset() { lift_to_lock( super.reset ) ;  };
//   replaces
//   void reset() {if (this.is_unlocked()) {super.reset();}};
```

This can be made to a default lifter, which is applied if no explicit lifters are provided.
- Another extension is to consider exception handling as a feature which can be added as needed. This is explored with (monadic) functional programming in [13, 14] and with first examples in Java in [15].

# 8 Conclusions

Feature-oriented programming is an extension of the object-oriented programming paradigm. Whereas object-oriented programming supports incremental development by subclassing, feature-oriented programming enables compositional programming, and overwriting as in inheritance is accomplished by resolving feature interactions.

The recent interest in feature interactions, mostly stemming from multimedia applications [21, 3], shows that there is a large demand for expressive composition concepts where objects with individual services can be created. It also shows that our viewpoint of inheritance as interaction is a very natural concept.

Compared to classical object-oriented programming, feature-oriented programming provides much higher modularity and flexibility. Reusability is simplified, since for each feature, the functional core and the interactions are separated. This difference encourages to write independent, reusable features and to make the dependencies to other features clear. In contrast, inheritance with overwriting mixes both, which often leads to highly entangled (sub-)classes.

Compared to other extensions of inheritance, the feature model contributes the following ideas:

- The core functionality is separated from the interaction resolution.
- It allows to create objects (or classes) freely by composing features.

– For the composition, we provide a composition architecture, which generalizes inheritance.

**Acknowledgments.** The author is indebted to the ECOOP reviewers for their helpful efforts to improve the paper. Also, M. Broy, B. Rumpe, and C. Klein contributed comments on earlier versions of this paper. M. Odersky made this paper possible by providing the Pizza compiler just in time.

# References

1. Lodewijk Bergmans and Mehmet Akşit. Composing synchronization and real-time constraints. *Journal of Parallel and Distributed Computing*, 36(1):32–52, 10 July 1996.
2. Gilad Bracha and William Cook. Mixin-based inheritance. *ACM SIGPLAN Notices*, 25(10):303–311, October 1990. *OOPSLA ECOOP '90 Proceedings*, N. Meyrowitz (editor).
3. K. E. Cheng and T. Ohta, editors. *Feature Interactions in Telecommunications III*. IOS Press, Tokyo, Japan, Oct 1995.
4. H. J. Fröhlich. Prototype of a run-time adaptable object-oriented system. In *PSI '96 (Perspectives of System Informatics)*, Akademgorodok, 1996. Springer-LNCS.
5. E. Gamma, R. Helm, R. Johnson, and J. Vlissides. *Design Patterns: Micro-Architectures for Reusable Object-Oriented Design*. Addison Wesley, Reading, MA, 1994.
6. James Gosling, Bill Joy, and Guy Steele. *The Java Language Specification*. Addison-Wesley, September 1996.
7. R. E. Johnson and J. M. Zweig. Delegation in C++. *J. of Object-Oriented Programming*, 4(3), November 1991.
8. Jo A. Lawless and M. Molly. *Understanding CLOS: the Common LISP object system*. Digital Press, Nashua, NH, 1991.
9. Ole Lehrmann Madsen, Birger Moller-Pedersen, and Kristen Nygaard. *Object-Oriented Programming in the BETA Programming Language*. Addison-Wesley, Reading, 1993.
10. Mira Mezini. Dynamic object modification without name collisions. In *this volume*, 1997.
11. Martin Odersky and Philip Wadler. Pizza into Java: Translating theory into practice. In *Proc. 24th ACM Symposium on Principles of Programming Languages*, January 1997.
12. W. F. Opdyke and R. J. Johnson. Refactoring: An Aid in Designing Application Frameworks. In *Proceedings of the Symposium on Object-Oriented Programming emphasizing Practical Applications*. ACM-SIGPLAN, September 1990.
13. Christian Prehofer. From inheritance to feature interaction. In Max Mühlhäuser et al., editor, *Special Issues in Object-Oriented Programming. ECOOP 1996 Workshop on Composability Issues in Object-Orientation*, Heidelberg, 1997. dpunkt-Verlag.
14. Christian Prehofer. From inheritance to feature interaction or composing monads. Technical report, TU München, 1997. to appear.
15. Christian Prehofer. An object-oriented approach to feature interaction. In *Fourth IEEE Workshop on Feature Interactions in Telecommunications networks and distributed systems*, 1997. to appear.

16. Linda M. Seiter, Jens Palsberg, and Karl J. Lieberherr. Evolution of object behavior using context relations. In David Garlan, editor, *Symposium on Foundations of Software Engineering*, San Francisco, 1996. ACM Press.

17. Lynn A. Stein. Delegation is inheritance. *ACM SIGPLAN Notices*, 22(12):138–146, December 1987.

18. Patrick Steyaert, Wim Codenie, Theo D'Hondt, Koen De Hondt, Carine Lucas, and Marc Van Limberghen. Nested Mixin-Methods in Agora. In O. Nierstrasz, editor, *Proceedings of the ECOOP '93 European Conference on Object-oriented Programming*, LNCS 707, Kaiserslautern, Germany, July 1993. Springer-Verlag.

19. B. Stroustrup. *The C++ Programming Language*. Addison-Wesley, Reading, 1991. 2nd edition.

20. David Ungar and Randall B. Smith. Self: The power of simplicity. *Lisp and symbolic computation*, 3(3), 1991.

21. P. Zave. Feature interactions and formal specifications in telecommunications. *IEEE Computer*, XXVI(8), August 1993.

# Genericity in Java with Virtual Types

Kresten Krab Thorup

DEVISE – Center for Experimental Computer Science
Department of Computer Science, University of Aarhus
Ny Munkegade Bldg. 540, DK-8000 Århus C, Denmark
Email: krab@daimi.aau.dk

**Abstract** This paper suggests virtual types for Java, a language mechanism which subsumes parameterized classes, while also integrating more naturally with Java's object model. The same basic mechanism is also known as virtual patterns in BETA and as generics in ADA95. We discuss various issues in the Java type system, issues with inheritance and genericity in general, and give a specific suggestion as to how virtual types should be integrated into Java. Finally we describe how to make an efficient implementation of virtual types based only upon the existing Java virtual machine.

## 1  Introduction

Java is a new programming language which is interesting for many reasons. First of all, it is not the result of a language-research project in the traditional academic sense. Java is the result of engineering work, assembling many useful features developed for other programming languages, most visibly language features of SIMULA [6], Objective C [24] and C++ [8]. In fact, it has been an expressed goal in the design of of Java to stick with programming language mechanisms that have already been proven through serious use.

Another interesting aspect of Java is that it reintroduces "safe programming," throwing away much of its heritage from C++: pointer arithmetic is gone and language-level protection mechanisms (such as private and protected) are enforced in the execution environment, unlike in C++ where such mechanisms can be worked around. Safeness, in this sense that programs should not be able to "crash," is another corner stone of the design of Java.

As an emerging standard programming language, Java is still open to enhancements. As such, there are several extensions and enhancements [7, 12, 22, 25] being proposed and developed, and this paper addresses one area where enhancement is needed namely the need for genericity. There is a wealth of ways genericity could be implemented in Java, e.g. by using parameterized types as it is known from C++ and EIFFEL [21], or by using functional polymorphism, as in ML.

The rest of this paper will progress as follows: Section 2 briefly introduces the notion of virtual types. Section 3 reviews the Java type system, and Section 4 discuss virtual types in context of issues with genericity and inheritance in general. Section 5 provides a detailed description of our design, and Section 6 outlines how to implement virtual types and describes some of the performance characteristics. Section 7 discusses related issues and work. Section 8 concludes.

# 2 Virtual Types

Our work is based on the ideas of *virtual patterns* in the BETA programming language [14, 18, 19]. A decade later, a similar mechanism is also found as *generics* in ADA95 [29], and as *creators* in [28]. As such, what we are about to present has already been in use for more than a decade in various programming languages.

However, in context of Java the mechanism does present several interesting challenges, particularly in the implementation because we have to generate Java programs that would be accepted by the type-inference integrity check performed by the execution environment.

## 2.1 An Informal Introduction

With our language extension, class and interface definitions can be augmented with virtual type declarations, each introducing a new type name as an alias for some existing type. The details are described later, but the general idea is that "typedef *Name* as *Type*" introduces an alias for type *Type* named *Name*, much like in C and C++. In the following example, class Vector declares a virtual type named ElemType.

```
class Vector {
  typedef ElemType as Object;
  void addElement (ElemType e) ...
  ElemType elementAt (int index) ...
  ...
}
```

For instances of this Vector class it would make no difference if the virtual type declaration was removed, and Object substituted for ElemType.

In context of a subclass however, a virtual type may be *extended* to be an alias for some subtype of the type it was an alias for in the superclass. The effect of extending a virtual type is that all inherited entities that are qualified by the virtual type in context of the superclass, will adopt the local alias of the virtual type when used in context of the more specific class. Now consider a subclass of Vector which extends the virtual type ElemType, to be qualified by Point rather than Object.

```
class PointVector extends Vector {
  typedef ElemType as Point;
}
```

For all the methods and fields inherited from Vector to PointVector, the alias type ElemType will be referring to Point rather than Object. So PointVector defines a vector of elements, which is statically typed to hold instances of class Point or subtypes thereof. Thus, where one today is limited to use code of the form:

```
Vector v = new Vector();
v.addElement (new Point(2,2));
...
Point p = (Point) v.elementAt(0);
```

Using the new class PointVector above, we could have written the following, without the explicit cast in the last line:

```
PointVector v = new PointVector();
v.addElement (new Point(2,2));
...
Point p = v.elementAt(0);
```

To facilitate recursive class types, a special virtual type called This is automatically available in all classes. This special virtual type always refers to the type of the enclosing class. Thus, in any given context, the dynamic type of the special variable this will always be the special type This. To illustrate this behaviour, consider a linked list element class:

```
class Link {
  This next;
  This prev;
  void insertBetween (This p, This n) {
    p.next = this; n.prev = this;
    prev = p; next = n;
  }
  ...
}
```

To use this Link class, it is subclassed and some interesting behaviour is added. In context of the subclass, the special type This is bound to StringLink.

```
final class StringLink extends Link {
  String value;
  ...
}
```

After which instances of StringLink can only be linked to other instances of StringLink, because calling insertBetween for an instance of StringLink automatically asserts that both arguments are also instances of that same class.

# 3 Java's Type System

Since we are suggesting changes to Java's type system, we will briefly review and critique of the existing type system. This is a rather dense description, so we have included references to material where further examples can be found.

## 3.1 A "Riddle" of Type Systems

The type system of any object-oriented programming language will always reflect some tradeoff between the following three desirable properties: *covariance typing*, *full static typing* and *subtype substitutability*. It is not possible to have all three, since supporting any two of these mechanisms in full, will mutually exclude the third. A more complete discussion of this conjecture can be found in [16, 17], but we will briefly illustrate it here with an example:

Consider an `insert` method in a `GeneralList` class and in a `PersonList` class. One would want to be able to have the argument of `insert` be qualified with `Person` in the latter, and `Object` in the former. If a type system allows this, it is said to allow covariance typed methods, or simply covariance. This is a desirable property of a type system, because in general, a more specific class would naturally require more specific types of arguments. We would also like subtype substitutability, i.e. assuming `PersonList` is a subclass of `GeneralList`, a reference to a `PersonList` object can be stored in a variable qualified by `GeneralList`. Seeking to allow both of the above as well as static typing introduces a problem because the `insert` method invoked for a variable qualified by `GeneralList` only requires an `Object`, while in reality, a `Person` is needed if it is referring to the more specific `PersonList`.

This riddle of type systems apparently was not described until 1990 [32], but understanding it's implications lets us understand different type systems much better.

## 3.2 Java's Tradeoff

While Java is indeed a typed programming language, we do not consider it fully statically typed since the execution of Java programs may still uncover type errors in the following two situations:

- When making explicit "down casts" also known in the literature as reverse assignments [11, §15.15]. This is allowed by the compiler if it cannot be statically determined that the cast will always go wrong. Such casts must be checked at runtime.

- When storing elements in an array of references [11, §10.10]. This may cause an exception to happen, because Java arrays are *covariant* typed, i.e. *array of Point* is a subtype[1] of *array of Object* iff *Point* is a subtype of *Object*.

Programs which would otherwise cause runtime errors beyond these two are rejected either by the compiler or by the execution environment itself, which performs a type-inference integrity test on loaded code before it is executed. Regardless of these safeguards, it is clear that Java is not statically type safe – and it is even described in the Java specification. In fact most popular object-oriented programming languages have runtime type checks in one way or another, including C++, SIMULA, EIFFEL and BETA.

---

[1]Throughout this paper, we will assume that any type is by definition a subtype of itself. We will use the term proper subtype to express subtypes that exclude the type itself.

Exactly like C++, Java implements *overloading* and *no-variance* with respect to methods. This means that when a virtual method is overridden in a subclass, the overriding method must have exactly the same types of arguments and exactly the same return type. If the types of arguments are different, it is considered to be a completely different method which is said to be *overloading* the original method.

Some readers might find it interesting that Java also has the flavour of contravariance. Part of a method declaration in Java can be a `throws` clause, which designates the exceptions that the method may cause. An overriding method is allowed to declare the same set of exceptions as the method being overridden, or a subset thereof.

Java allows declaration of `final` methods and classes, designating such methods that cannot be overridden, and such classes which cannot be subtyped. This feature can be used to reduce the (performance) implications of subtype substitutability, and as a protection mechanism. In essence, `final` bindings can narrow the general *open world assumption*. This mechanism is much like Dylan's sealed classes [3] and also has similarities to final bindings in BETA [19].

## 3.3 Critique

In our opinion, Javas type system reflects a rather ad-hoc mix of the three desirable properties (covariance typing, full static typing and subtype substitutability), of which only subtype substitutability is available in a coherent fashion. Covariance is only available for arrays – methods are no-variance typed, while the language as a whole is actually not statically type safe. Since the language is not fully statically typed anyway, we will argue that covariance typing for methods may as well be introduced; while still preserving a high degree of static type safeness.

The absence of covariance typing in particular leads to a programming style in which many things are typed simply as `Object`, or some other abstract superclass, and values are then explicitly *casted down* when needed. The same programming style is generally used in C++, which has a type system with many similarities with Java's type system.

While there will always be a need to rediscover the full type of an object when storing such in some kind of collection, it is our opinion that there are many situations where Java's type system forces programmers to use excessive amounts of casts. Indeed it is ironic from a programmer point of view to have to write casts that will never cause type errors. Consider for instance the case when the programmer knows that a certain collection of objects only contain instances of a certain class, all the casts necessary to access objects in the collection would be superfluous.

### 3.3.1 Virtual Types and Java's Type System

With virtual types most of these superfluous casts that would normally be necessary do not have to be written explicitly by the programmer. Based on virtual type declarations, our compiler inserts casts automatically "behind the scenes."

These casts are actually needed in the code to allow the Java execution environment to perform it's type-inference based integrity check. The compiled Java code is then annotated with enough information to let the execution environment eliminate these superfluous casts again, thereby making the code run faster. If the Java execution environment is not aware of virtual type annotations, the program will simply run a little slower than if it is.

While virtual types will not guarantee programs to be type safe, it does allow more programs to be statically type safe. Cf. the discussion above, since Java is already not statically type safe and never will be, we will allow ourself to introduce covariance; effectively allowing an overriding method to specify more specific types for argument and return types.

Virtual types can also explain the covariant behaviour of Java arrays. Arrays can be thought of as a class with a virtual type describing the constraint on the elements; consider:

```
class Array {
  typedef T as Object;
  T insert (int index, T elem) { ... }
  T get (int index) { ... }
}
```

For any particular parameterization of the array type, say String[], the Array class is specialized:

```
class StringArray {
  typedef T as String;
}
```

Which has the behaviour that any assignment into the array (using insert) is checked and can cause a type exception to happen.

# 4 Genericity and Inheritance

At present, the official Java language presents no way to express generic classes, i.e. classes which are polymorphic in one or more type variables, even though several proposals for such exists [22, 25]. Here we discuss some of the mechanisms that has already been deployed to obtain genericity in object oriented programming languages. A more encompassing review and critique of genericity in various programming languages can be found in [27, 139ff].

## 4.1 Parameterized Classes

In his often quoted paper [20] Bertrand Meyer presents parameterized classes as a programming language mechanism in Eiffel which combines the benefits of polymorphism, as in ML, and those of inheritance. Several other programming languages, including C++ [8] and Sather [26] implement similar features. As we see it, there are several conceptual problems in parameterized classes.

To illustrate these problems, assume for a moment that Java does have parameterized classes, allowing declarations of the form:

```
class Map<Key,Elem> {
  void insertAt (Key k, Elem e) ...
  Elem elementAt(Key k) ...
  int count ();
}
```

Which defines a generic class Map with two *type parameters*, key and element. This generic class can then be used to create any kind of map, like a map from Strings to Points as illustrated here:

```
Map<String,Point> map1 = new Map<String,Point>();
```

The variable map1 now refers to an instance of class Map<String,Object>, which is in turn an instance of the generic class Map. Because of this *instance of* relationship between classes and generic classes, there cannot be a straightforward subclass relationship between parameterized classes and regular classes, which seem desirable.

We consider it a conceptual problem that parameterized classes have to be *instantiated* in some sense to become "real classes," thus introducing another layer of abstraction in the model, somewhat like meta classes in CLOS and Smalltalk [10, 13].

Secondly, it is unclear what the relationships between parameterized class instantiations should be in these object models, especially if there is more than one type parameter. E.g. should List<Point> be a subtype of List<Object>, assuming Point is a subclass of Object? Getting back to our example, consider some other instances of the generic class Map:

```
Map<String,Object>
Map<Color,String>
Map<Point,Color>
```

And it is clear that only the first, i.e. class Map<String,Object> *may* have a sub-typing relationship to class Map<String,Point>.

Because of these conceptual problems, some programming languages either define explicitly *no* subtype relationship between such generic class instantiations as is the case in C++ or Pizza [25], or they define some kind of structural conformance semantics which is, in our opinion, only useful for one type parameter as is the case in both Eiffel and Sather, as well as the alternative proposal for parameterized types for Java by Myers, et. al. [22].

Like inheritance, conformance is yet another kind of mechanism which introduce types, and this will simply confuse the programmer. We find it compelling to think of inheritance itself as *the* mechanism for genericity. In some abstract sense, when a class is subclassed, it becomes less generic, while at the same time the original class acts as a "pattern" for the subclass. We use this similarity between inheritance and generic classes, implementing both through inheritance.

With our proposal the types that exist in a program are exactly those that are declared as classes, and the subtype relationship between these types is given explicitly in the inheritance hierarchy. Instead of creating another instantiation of a conceptual "template class" the programmer will simply write another class. While this may at times cause the code to be slightly more verbose, it is conceptually much clearer than parameterized classes.

## 4.2 Recursive Class Types

Another class of problems related to genericity and inheritance arise when a class need to refer to itself. Consider for instance, an `equals` method in a class hierarchy of Points and ColorPoints:

```
class Point {
  int x, y;
  ...
  boolean equals (Point other) {
    return (x == other.x) && (y == other.y);
  }
}
```

Nqw, what should `equals` look like in a subclass, say ColorPoint? One solution might be to write two methods, one for Points and one for ColorPoints.

```
class ColorPoint extends Point {
  Color c;
  ...
  boolean equals (ColorPoint other) {
    return super.equals (other) && c.equals (other.c);
  }
  boolean equals (Point other) {
    throw new Error ("TypeError");
  }
}
```

... and while this is indeed a solution to this problem, it would be nice if this kind of "type error" could be checked by the compiler. With virtual types self-recursive types are trivially supported by declaring the argument of `equals` to be of the special This virtual type available to all classes, as it was already outlined in Section 2. Understanding recursive class types has been a subject of research in computer science for several years, further discussions can be found in [4, 5, 27]. Several programming languages include specific support for recursive class types, such as Sather [26] which has a special type named SELF, and Eiffel's like Current mechanism [21].

### 4.2.1 Recursive Classes in Design Patterns

Mutually recursive classes, which often occur in design patterns can easily be programmed. Consider in this example due to Erik Ernst, a simple implementation of the Observer pattern [9] in the following example, which also shows how virtual types can be used in interfaces (example due to Erik Ernst):

```
interface Observer {
  typedef SType as Subject;
  typedef EventType as Object;
  void notify (SType subj, EventType e);
}

class Subject {
  typedef OType as Observer;
  typedef EventType as Object;
  OType observers[];
  notifyObservers (EventType e) {
    for (int i = 0; i < observers.length; i++)
      observers[i].notify(this, e);
  }
}
```

The usage of virtual types ensures that these classes work together, even in specializations of the presented classes. To use this design pattern in a particular context, the two classes would be subclassed "together," extending the various virtual types accordingly. A set of Subject/Observer classes for dealing with window events might look like this:

```
interface WindowObserver extends Observer {
  typedef SType as WindowSubject;
  typedef EventType as WindowEvent;
}

class WindowSubject extends Subject {
  typedef OType as WindowObserver;
  typedef EventType as WindowEvent;
  ...
}
```

Following which any class can choose to implement the WindowObserver interface and in assurance that it only receives events that are at least WindowEvents, which are originating from a WindowSubject or a subclass thereof.

The BOPL language described in [27] explicitly supports mutually recursive class types through "automatic" generation of groups of classes that are statically safe, similar to how we manually generated classes for the example above.

# 5 Design

## 5.1 Terminology Considerations

Before we dive into the details of virtual types, we will discuss our choice of terminology a little. As described in the introduction, the spirit of Java is to only use mechanisms that are well known, and can be understood by all programmers. There is no point in introducing a mechanism which is too hard to understand.

Since Java's terminology and syntax is heavily inspired by C++, we have chosen to explicitly take this point of view in this presentation, and bring forth the `typedef` keyword. In C and C++, `typedef` introduces a simple type alias. Thus, coming from a C background, a programmer already knows the basic meaning of the keyword.

One might consider using `virtual typedef` then, to designate that the typedef can be extended in a fashion much like virtual methods. However, since *all* methods are by default virtual in Java, that distinction is not natural – why should typedef's have to be declared explicitly virtual when methods do not? In BETA a virtual type *definition* is syntactically distinguished from a virtual type *extension*. We chose not to make this distinction since Java doesn't syntactically distinguish methods that override other methods, from methods that do not override.

As a general name for the feature, we chose the name *virtual type* because we find it clearly descriptive: the name associates with typing, i.e. a virtual type really is a type; and because it associates with virtuality, i.e. a virtual type can be redefined in context of a subclass. We anticipate however, that our choice of syntax may lead to this feature being known as virtual typedefs, but that wouldn't be too bad.

## 5.2 Virtual Types Specifics

Now we introduce the full syntax for virtual type declarations, and the following sections will informally introduce the semantics of various aspects of virtual types. The first thing we describe is where a virtual type is allowed to appear. A *VirtualType* as defined in the following can be used anywhere a *Reference-Type* [11, §4.3] can be used:

> *ReferenceType:*+
>   *VirtualType*
>
> *VirtualType:*
>   *TypeName*
>   `This`

Intuitively, this means that a virtual type can be used anywhere where a class or interface type could be used, e.g. to qualify instance variables, parameters, return values, etc.

## 5.3 Virtual Type Declarations

A virtual type declaration can have a *qualification* described by one or more classes or interfaces, a *name*, and optionally an explicit *binding*. A virtual type declaration has the following form:

> *VirtualTypeDeclaration:*
>   *Modifiers_{opt}* `typedef` *Name*
>     `as` *Qualification Binding_{opt}* ;

*Qualification:*
    *ClassOrInterfaceType*
    *Qualification , InterfaceType*

*Binding:*
    = *ClassType*

*Modifiers: one or more of*
    `final abstract`
    `public protected private`

Informally, the *Qualification* describes what you can assume about variables of type *Name*. The *Binding* is the class used when creating instances of the virtual type *Name*. The details of these is the subject of the following sections.

## 5.4 Virtual Type Qualifications

Any reference entity (variable, parameter, etc.) which is typed with the virtual type *Name* is allowed to refer to objects that are subtypes of all the types listed in the *Qualification* for the named type. The following defines the subtype relation $\subseteq$ between a type $S$ and a list of types $[T_1, T_2, \ldots, T_n]$, defined in terms of a subtype relation between singular types:

$$S \subseteq [T_1, T_2, \ldots, T_n]$$
$$\Updownarrow$$
$$\forall t \in \{T_1, T_2, \ldots, T_n\} : S \subseteq t$$

Intuitively, this means that in order to be a subtype of a list of types, the type in question must be a subtype of each type in the list.

Further notice that the qualification does not need to list any classes, it is allowed to list only interfaces. In Java the special `Object` class is a super type of all other reference types including interfaces, so `Object` is implicitly inserted as the class in the qualification, if only interfaces are listed. For the same reason, a virtual type qualified only with `Object` is effectively an unconstrained virtual type.

As an example of a qualification listing multiple types consider the following declaration of a variable that can hold a reference to an object which is an instance of a class implementing both the `Encoding` and the `Decoding` interface.

```
typedef Archivable as Encoding, Decoding;
Archivable a;
```

Next consider this class `ArchivablePoint`, which implements the two interfaces `Encoding` and `Decoding`:

```
class ArchivablePoint implements Encoding, Decoding {
  ...
}
```

Since `ArchivablePoint` is a subtype of both `Encoding` and `Decoding`, a reference of type `ArchivablePoint` is allowed to be assigned to a reference of type `Archivable`:

```
a = new ArchivablePoint ();
```

As we shall see later however, this assignment has to be dynamically checked in the case where `Archivable` may be extended in a subclass.

A similar notion of "structural qualification" exists in Objective C [24], where any *variable* can be qualified by a class, and zero or more interfaces.[2] For instance, in Objective C, the following declares a variable `var` qualified by class `View`, which implements both the `Encoding` and `Decoding` interfaces.

```
View <Encoding,Decoding> *var;
```

Such qualifications are very useful because they allow arbitrary combinations of interfaces for a particular situation, without having to introduce a new class.

## 5.5 Extending Virtual Types

When a virtual type has been declared in context of a class or interface, it can be *extended* in subclasses (or sub-interfaces) thereof. Intuitively, extension of types is similar to the notion that a virtual method can be overridden in subclasses.

When a virtual type is extended, the qualification of the extended type must express a subtype of the qualification of the type being extended. Since qualifications can be lists of types, we need to define the subtype relationship between two lists of types:

$$[S_1, S_2, \ldots, S_m] \subseteq [T_1, T_2, \ldots, T_n]$$

$$\Updownarrow$$

$$\forall t \in \{T_1, T_2, \ldots, T_n\} : (\exists s \in \{S_1, S_2, \ldots, S_m\} : s \subseteq t)$$

In natural language this simply means that for each element $t$ in the list describing the super type, there exists an element $s$ in the list describing the subtype, such that $t$ is a super type of $s$.

If the virtual type being extended is not declared `abstract` then it is allowed to be instantiated, as it will be discussed further in section 5.7. If this is the case then the constructors of the qualification class are exposed, so it must also be asserted that these are available in the more specific type. Since constructors are not inherited in Java, it is a further requirement that the same constructors are available for the qualification class in the extending type as in the type being extended.

The following is an example of using multiple types in the qualification of a virtual inspired by David Shang's cow example [30].

---

[2] Java's notion of interfaces originates from Objective C, where they are called formal protocols, as opposed to Smalltalk's informal notion of protocols. The mechanism was fostered by Steve Naroff at NeXT in 1991, and first released in NeXTSTEP 3.0 [23].

```
class Animal {
  typedef Edible as Food, Drink;
  eat (Edible e) { ... }
}

class Cow extends Animal {
  typedef Edible as VegetarianFood, Water;
  eat (Edible e) { ... }
}
```

These rules for extension of virtual types express subtype substitutability, i.e. the general notion that a subclass is more specific than it's superclass, while at the same time being "upwards compatible." A consequence of this rule is the introduction of *covariant* method typing, since we allow method arguments to be qualified by a virtual type.

If a virtual type is declared final, then it cannot be extended in classes or interfaces which inherit the given virtual type. It is trivially true that any member of a final class is automatically final as well, so a virtual type may also implicitly be final by appearing in a final class.

## 5.6 Virtual Type Casting

Virtual types can also be used in a dynamic cast expression. When either explicitly or implicitly introducing a cast to a virtual type of the form:

$var = (Name)\ expr\ ;$

then *expr* must be either null, or a reference to an object satisfying the qualification of *Name* as declared in the *dynamic* class of this.

Should the qualification for a virtual type be broken, then the runtime system will throw a java.lang.VirtualTypeCastException runtime exception. This is similar to the exceptions that may happen when storing elements in an array, or when casting values of reference type as described in Section 3.2.

A dynamic cast like the one above is sometimes inserted implicitly when passing an argument to a function where the parameter is declared to be of a virtual type. Specifically, it is not needed if the value being passed as an argument is already qualified by the virtual type, or if the virtual type is declared final in the given context.

## 5.7 Virtual Type Bindings and Instantiation

The effect of instantiating a virtual type is to create an instance of its binding. An instance of a virtual type is created using the following syntax:

$var = obj.\text{new}\ Name()\ ;$

where *obj* is a reference to an object declaring the virtual type designated *Name*. The "*obj*." prefix can be omitted if *Name* is accessible directly in the enclosing context (via this), as for other member accesses.

The optional *Binding* form in the declaration syntax allows an explicit specification of the class to be the binding of the virtual type. If no explicit binding is declared, and the *Qualification* lists exactly one element which is a *ClassType*, then the binding defaults to that class, i.e. "typedef *Name* as *C*" is shorthand for "typedef *Name* as *C* = *C*" for any class *C*.

Since constructors are not inherited in Java, it is not trivially true that the binding class has all the constructors available for the qualification class. Thus it is a further requirement that the binding must have *at least* the same constructors as the class in the qualification; a constraint that can easily be checked at compile time.

If a virtual type is explicitly declared abstract then it cannot be instantiated, similar to abstract classes. Alternatively, if a virtual type is *not* declared abstract, then it is always allowed to be instantiated. From this basic notion of abstractness we then derive rules for the cases where virtual type needs to have an explicit binding.

Virtual types declared in interfaces are never allowed to have bindings. This is similar to the notion that methods in an interface cannot have a body. When a class inherits an interface which declares a virtual type and that virtual type is non-abstract (i.e. is allowed to be instantiated), then the class must "implement" the virtual type by explicitly declaring the virtual type with a binding.

The constructors available for instantiating a virtual type are limited to those that are available for the class type appearing in the qualification, or if no class type is in the qualification list only the default constructor is available. This means that for all intent and purposes, the binding of a virtual type is not visible, only the qualification is.

As for any object with virtual type, the class appearing in the *Binding* form has to be a subtype of the virtual type, so the binding class also has to satisfy the qualification.

### 5.7.1   Instantiation of the special type This

Because the This virtual type is uniformly available for all classes, it's use for instance creation is restricted to only use the default constructor. This means that the virtual type This effectively adopts the same access protection level as the default constructor. The restriction that only the default constructor is available via This is not a problem in practice, because it is easy to decouple the initialization from allocation, writing a virtual init method which can take whatever arguments.

## 5.8   An Example

Below we bring a larger example using virtual types, defining a class Ring and related classes. This example was introduced in [20], and has been used in the literature to illustrate mechanisms for genericity [18, 19, 27]. This example also illustrates how the This virtual type can be used to statically type self referential classes.

```
abstract class Ring                    class VectorRing extends Ring
{                                      {
  public Ring() { zero(); }              typedef ElementType as Ring;
  void plus (This other);                ElementType e[];
  void zero ();                          VectorRing (int size) {
  void unity ();                           e = new ElementType[size];
}                                          for (int i = 0; i < size; i++)
                                             e[i] = new ElementType();
class ComplexRing extends Ring         }
{                                        void plus (This other) {
  double i, r;                             for (int i = 0; I < e.length; i++)
  void plus (This other) {                   e[i].plus (other.e[i]);
    i += other.i; r += other.r;          }
  }                                      void zero () {
  void zero () {                           for (int i = 0; I < e.length; i++)
    i = 0.0; r = 0.0;                        e[i].zero();
  }                                      }
  void unity () {                      }
    i = 0.0; r = 1.0;
  }                                    class ComplexVector extends VectorRing
}                                      {
                                         typedef ElementType as ComplexRing;
                                         ComplexVector (int size) {
                                           super(size);
                                         }
                                       }
```

# 6  Implementation

As for implementation, there are three major implications: dynamically checking that an object qualifies for a given virtual type; selecting where to insert such checks; and creating instances of virtual types. In the following we will outline how these are implemented. A full specification is beyond the scope of this paper.

Of primary concern in our design is to make virtual types integrate closely with the Java programming language as it is. In the implementation we have therefore explicitly chosen to restrict ourselves such as to:

- Perform translation into pure Java or translation directly to the Java byte code format.

- Make the translation in such a way that existing classes will not have to be recompiled to be used from a class with virtual types.

- Let the resulting generated classes be usable via a compiler that does not understand virtual types.

Since Java byte code format is tightly coupled with the language itself, there is technically very little difference between generating Java code and generating byte code. In this presentation the translation is presented as a source code mapping.

## 6.1 Substitution of Virtual Types with Real Types

For the compiler, the very first *ClassOrInterfaceType* appearing in the qualification of a virtual type definition is special. This type is substituted for every usage of the virtual type as the qualification of some other entity, such as an argument or a variable. This most general specific type of the virtual is also used for all applications of extension of this virtual type. Consider the following example:

```
class Vector {
  typedef T as Object;
  insert (T elem) { ... }
}
class PointVector extends Vector {
  typedef T as Point;
  insert (T elem) { ... }
}
```

The Object is substituted for the all the occurrences of T in the code, and when a method is overridden, an explicit cast is inserted yielding:

```
class Vector {
  insert (Object elem) { ... }
}
class PointVector extends Vector {
  typedef T as Point;
  insert (Object elem$0) {
    Point elem = (Point)elem$0; ...
  }
}
```

This imposes a non-trivial impact on the performance of the system, and since the compiler can guarantee that this cast will never fail, it can augment the generated byte code with extra information so the virtual machine may eliminate the redundant cast.

## 6.2 Dynamic Cast to Virtual Types

A dynamic cast to a virtual type is implemented by a virtual method call. For each *VirtualTypeDeclaration*, the compiler will generate a virtual method named "cast$*Name*", taking as argument and returning an object qualified by the first element in the qualification for that virtual type. This method will check that the object conforms to the given qualification by attempting to cast the incoming object to all the required types. For instance, for the virtual type declaration:

```
class Vector {
  typedef T as Observer;
  ...
  { ...; T var = (T)expr; ... }
}
```

The compiler will generate the following, "`return (Observer)o`" being the heart of the cast operation.

```
class Vector {
  Object cast$T (Object o) {
  try { return (Observer)o; }
  catch (ClassCastException e) {
   throw new
     VirtualTypeCastException (...);
  }
  ...
  { ...; Object var = cast$T(expr); ... }
}
```

If the cast fails the Java runtime will generate a `ClassCastException`, which in turn is translated to a `VirtualTypeCastException` by the code in the `catch` clause.

A virtual type declared in an interface will generate an abstract declaration for the according cast operation, thus imposing a requirement on implementors of that interface to actually implement the cast operation.

### 6.2.1 Compiling casts to This

The compiler automatically adds a virtual type named `This` to all classes, similar to how the `Ring` example used the class. For this, code of the form:

```
T var = (This)obj;
```

is translated to:

```
T var;
if (this.getClass().isInstance(obj))
  var = (T)obj;
else
  throw new VirtualTypeCastException (...)
```

Using this special implementation has the advantage that existing classes will not need to be recompiled in order to adopt the special `This` virtual type, and subclasses of the class containing the compiled code will automatically have the correct behaviour even if they are compiled with a compiler not supporting virtual types.

## 6.3 Insertion of Virtual Casts

Whenever a call is made to a method with arguments of virtual type or when a value is assigned to a variable of virtual type, the assigned value may have to be checked dynamically. However, for a large number of such situations, the check can be eliminated since it can be determined statically that the type is already right.

Because these casts are not necessary everywhere, the check is performed at the call site, rather than inside all methods taking virtual type arguments.

Consider the following example of making a call to `insert` of the `Vector` class, where we need to insert a dynamic check:

```
class Vector {
  typedef T as Object;
  void insert (T elem) { ... }
}
...
Vector l; ... l.insert (expr);
```

For which we generate the equivalent of:

```
Vector l; ... l.insert (l.cast$T(expr));
```

Because the variable `l` may be referring to a subclass of `Vector`, which has a more stringent qualification than visible directly by inspecting class `Vector`.

Of particular interest is all the situations where these checks are not needed. This is the case whenever the assigned value can be determined to be the same actual virtual type as required, as opposed to the declared virtual type as seen from the usage site. This is the case in the following two situations:

- When calling a method via `this`, with an argument already typed as the same virtual type $T$. In this situation both the formal parameter and the given value will have the type `this.T`.

- When the virtual type as seen from the usage site is `final`, either because it was declared so explicitly or because the class it appears in is declared `final`.

To illustrate the first case above, assume we extend the `Vector` class above with a method `insertIfAbsent`:

```
class Vector {
  typedef T as Object;
  void    insert (T elem) { ... }
  boolean includes (T elem) { ... }
  void    insertIfAbsent (T elem) {
    if (!this.includes (elem))
      this.insert (elem);
  }
}
```

In the translation for `insertIfAbsent`, the type of `elem` does not have to be checked for the two calls to `includes` and `insert`, because it has already been verified before entering `insertIfAbsent`.

The second case above is trivial to see, because it simply describes the situation where a virtual type is made non-virtual by declaring it `final`. For performance reasons it is often a good idea to make such classes `final`, which are not designed to be specialized, because this will also reduce the overhead of any regular method invocations to the cost of a regular function call.

### 6.4 Instance Creation of Virtual Types

As described earlier, if a virtual type is not explicitly declared `abstract` it must have a binding, i.e. be capable of being allocated. To facilitate this, any such virtual type will generate a set of methods named "new$*Name*", one for each constructor of the class listed in the virtual type qualification. If no class is listed in the qualification, only the default constructor is generated. Here is an example like above, except here we give T a binding to allow it to be instantiated.

```
class Vector {
  typedef T as Observer = WindowObserver;
  ...
  { ...; T var = new T(); ... }
}
```

The compiler will generate the following.

```
class Vector {
  Object new$T () {
    return new WindowObserver ();
  }
  ...
  { ...; Object var = new$T(); ... }
}
```

If the type T is extended in a subclass, then the method generated for the extension will override the method declared here.

#### 6.4.1 Compiling allocation of This

Similar to the case for casts above, allocation of the virtual type `This` is compiled especially. For this, code of the form:

```
T var = new This ();
```

is translated to:

```
T var = this.getClass().newInstance();
```

Using this special implementation has the advantage that existing classes will not need to be recompiled in order to adopt the special `This` virtual type.

## 6.5 Performance Impact

One place where virtual types introduce a non-trivial overhead is when calling a method with virtual typed arguments. Consider for instance the `insert` method in the `PointVector`, which has been used throughout this article. Here is an example using that method:

```
{ PointVector pv; Point pnt; ...
  pv.insert (pnt); ... }
```

Because of subtype substitutability, pv may refer to an instance of a subclass of PointVector, which may again *extend* the virtual type of the declared argument. In this case, our implementation inserts an extra call, asking pv to assert that the argument does indeed match the constraint it imposes on T. This generates the equivalent of the following:

```
{ PointVector pv; Point pnt; ...
  pv.insert (pv.cast$T(pnt)); ... }
```

Effectively making a virtual method call become two virtual method calls. While this is indeed a problem, we have made our implementation in such a way that a compiler using customization may inline one of the virtual calls effectively reducing this overhead to a dynamic cast. With customization, calls to `this` can all be inlined, so we introduce a new method in `Vector` which performs the cast-checks, and calls to `insert`. Calls to `insert` are then replaced with this call when needed. Because virtual `cast$T` method is then overloaded in `PointVector`, the check will do the right thing. The following code snippets illustrate how the check is rewritten. The two calls appearing in `check$insert` can both be inlined in a customizing compiler.

```
class Vector {
  Object cast$T(Object o){ return o;}
  void check$insert(Object o) {
    this.insert(this.cast$T (o));
  }
  void insert(Object o) { ... }
}

class PointVector extends Vector {
  Object cast$T(Object o) {
      try { return (Point)o; } ...
  }
}
```

It is not necessary to make this check when the type of argument can be determined to be sound, such as when calling the insert method with an argument already qualified by T, or when the type of T is final.

Much work has already been done to implement such compilers supporting customization as part of the SELF project [2, 31]. One such sophisticated Java virtual machine is described in [1]. Another similar Java virtual machine has been developed by Animorphic Systems which was recently acquired by JavaSoft.

If Java were to support *type exact variables*, i.e. variables that can only hold references to instances of a particular class but not its subclasses, then this qualification check could be eliminated because the exact qualification of a virtual type in objects referred to would be known. Sather is one of the languages that support type exact variables. In lieu of this, Java's final classes can be used to simulate type exact variables, since variables qualified by a class declared final can only refer to instances of that class. If PointVector was defined as the following, calling methods on this would be no more expensive than it is with todays collection libraries.

```
final class PointVector
    extends Vector
{
   typedef T as Point;
}
```

Similarly, this extra overhead can be eliminated by declaring the extended virtual type declaration final, like in the following:

```
class PointVector extends Vector {
   final typedef T as Point;
}
```

That way, it would still not cost extra to call the methods of PointVector with virtual type arguments, *and* the class PointVector can be subclassed.

## 6.6 The Cost of a Cast

Since the overhead we impose effectively is a matter of some extra casts, we have been trying to estimate the cost of dynamic casts in general. In an effort to estimate the cost of a regular dynamic cast in Java, we tried to run the same test program Myers et. al. used in [22] to determine that:

> "For a simple collection class, avoiding the runtime casts from Object reduced the run times by up to 17%..."—*Myers, Bank, and Liskov*

Their performance figures also compare the cost of "cast from Object" to "hard coded types", and they state that using hard coded types, i.e. not having to cast, is as much as 21% faster. We were not able to reproduce their results. For the following program, which resembles that in the paper of Myers et. al., we observed only on the order of 1-5% slowdown, with variations for various hardware and virtual machines. We tried running it using Sun's JDK on various SPARC platforms; as well as running it on a 486DX100 using the Microsoft JIT-based environment.

```
Vector v = new Vector ();
v.addElement (new Point (0, 0));
```

```
for (int j = 0; j < 100000; j++) {
  Object t = v.elementAt (0);
  t.equals (t);
}
for (int j = 0; j < 100000; j++) {
  Point t = (Point)v.elementAt (0);
  t.equals (t);
}
```

Since developing these results we have obtained a copy of the actual code used by Myers et. al. in their paper, which we have included below. While they state that their example is based on a "simple collection class" it is rather based on an "accessor method" for a single member variable in a tight loop, thus emphasizing the impact of a the cast. Given this, we still believe that our measurements presents a more realistic picture.

```
class CellElement {
  private Element t;
  public CellElement(Element t) {
    this.t = t;
  }
  public Element get() { return t; }
}

CellElement c = new CellElement();
c.add(new Element());
for (i = 0; i < 1000000; i++) {
  Element t = c.get();
  t.do_method();
}
```

In addition to replicating the test case used by Myers et. al we tried to run a performance test of the code generated for the Ring example above, comparing it to a "hand written" version which had no explicit casts. With that test case we saw a performance degradation on the order of one to two percent, depending on which configuration it was tested in. We believe that the performance of an average program is no worse than the Ring code in the example above.

While we have only performed very limited performance testing, we believe our results are much more realistic than those of Myers et. al. In order to obtain better figures for the run time performance impact of virtual types, one would have to write a large program twice, both with and without the feature, a job which has been beyond the scope of this project so far. Based on admittedly very limited tests, we see a strong indication that the performance overhead is in the order of one to two percent or less for any realistic application.

# 7 Discussion

While the previous sections presents a specific suggestion for how to include virtual types in Java which is complete in itself, we will here discuss some possible alternatives to our design ad identify some of the open issues. Finally, we will discuss related and future work.

## 7.1 Variations

Several reviewers have pointed out that it would be more in Java's spirit not to have the compiler insert the dynamic cast for method arguments of virtual type. Inserting these casts automatically is how BETA does it. Rather, they would like to require the programmer to insert explicit casts, so the invariant can be maintained, that run time errors can only happen in the two situations listed in Section 3.2, i.e., only at explicit casts and array-store operations.

This would indeed be very useful, but it would require significant changes to the current Java grammar. For instance, the syntactic category *VirtualType* would have to not only include "*TypeName*," but also "*AmbiguousName . Type-Name*" [11, §6.5], so that a virtual type can be accessed using dot notion for casts, such as in:

```
void m (PointVector pv) {
  Point p = new Point(2, 2);
  pv.insert ((pv.ElemType)p);
}
```

Which would then be generating the following code:

```
void m (PointVector pv) {
  Point p = new Point(2, 2);
  pv.insert ( pv.cast$ElemType(p) );
}
```

Secondly, the compiler would have to be able to decide that the value of pv in the example above does not change between the two applications of that variable. If the value of pv would change between the cast and the call to insert, then the cast is no good, since it may have been replaced by some other subclass of PointVector. This assertion is trivially true for constant, i.e., final declared, fields, variables and parameters [11, §8.3.1.2], or the special variable this which is always constant. One possible restriction could thus be to only allow remote virtual qualifications (and casts) via final variables or fields.

In our design of virtual types we have decided not to include remote casts because of these complications, and thus virtual types are only accessible implicitly via this. On the other hand, the dynamic check is only used when actually needed, as outlined in the implementation section it can be eliminated when calling a method on this, when invoking a method on a final class, or if the virtual type in question is declared final.

A major complication in the design is the fact that constructors are not inherited. One idea we have been playing around with was to introduce a kind of constructor which is automatically replicated in all subclasses unless explicitly redefined.

Another issue which we will not cover in detail in this paper is how to eliminate the "superfluous casts" that are inserted as part of the code transformations implementing virtual types. Intuitively, to make this possible the verifier will need to know about virtual types. To enable this, the compiler must add extra annotations to the .class file replicating the declaration of virtual types, and all their applications in method signatures and instance variables. By examining these in the same way the compiler did, the verifier can see "why" the compiler chose to insert certain casts, and thus it can also remove them again if they can be determined to be safe.

One of the weaknesses of our present design is that primitive types, such as int and long, cannot be used for qualification, and thus parameterization by simple types is not possible. While this is indeed a problem, it is based on an inherent notion in Java, that such simple types are *not* objects. Collections of simple objects can be made using the wrapper classes java.lang.Integer, java.lang.Long, etc.

Another weaknes is the fact that our support for recursive class types via This is limited to self-recursive types. It is harder to to support mutually recursive classes that support being subclassed, such as is often the case for design patterns. To do this the programmer has to emulate the equivalent of This for the recursive types and extend these appropriately in subclasses. The BOPL programming language [27] solves this problem in a clean and consistent, albeit very expensive, fashion.

## 7.2  Related Work

In their paper [22], Myers et. al. suggest a mechanism for implementing constrained genericity through parameterized classes in Java, where constraints are based on *where* clauses as in CLU [15]. Another recent paper by Odersky et. al. is [25] which describes the design of Pizza, implementing of F-bounded parametric polymorphism for Java in a fashion very similar to Myers et. al.

While both of these are very well documented indeed, they still have the conceptual problems with parameterized classes discussed earlier. In addition, since in [22] *where* clauses are based on conformance rather than declared relationships between types, a class may accidentally conform to (match) the where clause without the programmers intent. This introduces another class of "semantic type error" illustrated with this example due to Boris Magnusson: Consider a clause of a graphics related method requiring a draw method to be present at objects it accepts as arguments. Now imagine handing an instance of GunMan to this method.

One of the strengths of both their designs is that they allow parameterization by simple types such as int and float. However, their implementation it limited to 32-bit entities (thus excluding long and double), and it is tied to the fact that they provide their own implementation of the Java VM. In their paper they briefly describe how parameterization can be implemented using only the virtual machine, but forget to mention that it would also disallow parameterization with primitive types.

If at all possible, one should strive not to require changes to the Java Virtual Machine when designing changes to Java. There is already several dozen implementations of the Java Virtual Machine, so adding new virtual machine instructions is currently impractical, if not impossible. Myers et. al. argue that casts are too expensive to allow implementation of covariance typing without changes to the virtual machine. We believe this is wrong. Their position is supported with performance measurementns we believe to be carrying very little value, as already described in the section on performance above.

## 7.3 Future Work

We are currently investigating how the scheme presented herein could be generalized, so as to be usable for other languages with compilers targeted at the Java Virtual Machine. Since virtual types subsumes e.g. EIFFEL-style parameterized classes, and because it is very similar to generics in ADA it is concievable to that we can make one mechanism that can support such languages.

Another interesting feature would be to introduce *type exact variables*, i.e. variables that do not allow subtype substitutability. By using such variables, typechecking of covariance can often be eliminated so more programs can be statically typechecked. Sather and BETA are examples of languages which already implement type exact variables.

## 8 Conclusion

We have presented *virtual types*, a programming language mechanism known from BETA, as a means to provide the functionality of parameterized classes in the Java programming language. Virtual types can also be used to effectively express recursive class-types, structures which often occur in design patterns.

The real advantage of virtual types over "traditional" parameterized types is that virtual types provide a simple conceptual model for providing generic classes which very intuitive because the subtype relationship between all class-types in a given program are given directly by the inheritance hierachy. Other programming languages typically provide a mixture of typing features to obtain the same level of functionality, which may be confusing to the programmer.

Virtual types allow covariance methods, which is very useful and intuitive, in a style that can be statically type checked in many situations. When calling covariant final methods, the arguments can always be statically checked.

We have outlined our implementation of the virtual types mechanism. This is descibed as a transformation into the core Java programming language itself. As such, our translation does not require any particular runtime support, so the compiled programs can run in any Java execution environment.

Our implementation does impose some overhead. For passing arguments to methods which has formals declared of virtual type, the overhead is an extra virtual method call. In most situations, a execution environment with sophisticated inlining can eliminate this overhead. For other cases, the overhead is determined to be neglectable.

After having worked out all the details in this paper, it is clear that the relative complexity of Java itself makes it hard introduce changes to Java, which are consistent with Java and at the same time easy to explain. While Java at first glance seems like a neat little language, The Java Language Specification [11] is more than 800 pages, and it is an unsurmountable task to know it all.

## Acknowledgements

The author would like to present a special thank to BILL JOY and JOHN ROSE for their insightful comments and explanations of the finer points of Java. The author has also greatly benefitted from discussions, comments and encuragement from the following people: OLE LEHRMANN MADSEN, MADS TORGERSEN, GORDIE FREEDMAN, the anonymous reviewers, and last but not least my co-students who helped proof read the paper.

## References

[1] AGESEN, O. Design and implementation of Pep, a Java just-in-time translator. To appear.

[2] AGESEN, O., AND HÖLZLE, U. Type feedback vs. concrete type inference: A comparison of optimization techniques for object-oriented languages. In *Proceedings of OOPSLA'95* (1995), ACM Press, pp. 91–107.

[3] APPLE COMPUTER, EASTERN RESEARCH AND TECHNOLOGY. *Dylan: An object-oriented dynamic language*, 1st ed. Cambridge, MA, April 1992.

[4] CANNING, P., COOK, W., HILL, W., AND OLTHOFF, W. F-bounded qualification for object-oriented programming. In *ACM Conference on Functional Programming and Computer Architecture* (1989), ACM Press.

[5] CANNING, P., COOK, W., HILL, W., AND OLTHOFF, W. Interfaces for strongly-typed object-oriented programming. In *Proceedings of OOPSLA'89* (1989), SIGPLAN, ACM Press.

[6] DAHL, O. J., AND NYGAARD, K. Simula, an algol-based simulation language. *Communications of the ACM 9*, 9 (1966), 671–678.

[7] ELECTRONIC COMMUNITIES. The E Whitepaper. from http://www.communities.com/e, 1996.

[8] ELLIS, M. A., AND STROUSTRUP, B. *The Annotated C++ Reference Manual.* Addison-Wesley, 1990.

[9] GAMMA, E., HELM, R., JOHNSON, R., AND VLISSIDES, J. *Design Patterns: Abstraction and Reuse of Object-Oriented Designs.* Addison-Wesley, 1994.

[10] GOLDBERG, A., AND ROBSON, D. *Smalltalk-80 – The Language.* Addison-Wesley, 1989.

[11] GOSLING, J., JOY, B., AND STEELE, G. *The Java Language Specification.* Addison-Wesley, 1996.

[12] JAVASOFT. Inner Classes in Java 1.1. from http://www.javasoft.com, 1996.

[13] KICZALES, G., DE RIVIÈRES, J., AND BOBROW, D. G. *The Art of the Meta Object Protocol.* MIT Press, 1991.

[14] KRISTENSEN, B. B., MADSEN, O. L., MØLLER-PEDERSEN, B., AND NYGAARD, K. Abstraction mechanisms in the BETA programming language. In *Proceedings of POPL'83* (Austin, TX, 1983).

[15] LISKOV, B., SNYDER, A., ATKINSON, R., AND SCHAFFERT, C. Abstraction Mechanisms in CLU. *Communications of the ACM 20*, 8 (August 1977).

[16] MADSEN, O. L. Open issues in object-oriented programming–a scandinavian perspective. *Software–Practice and Experience 25*, S4 (December 1995).

[17] MADSEN, O. L., MAGNUSSON, B., AND MØLLER-PEDERSEN, B. Strong typing of object-oriented languages revisited. In *Proceedings of OOPSLA'90* (Ottawa, Canada, 1990), SIGPLAN, ACM Press.

[18] MADSEN, O. L., AND MØLLER-PEDERSEN, B. Virtual classes: A powerful mechanism in object-oriented programming. In *Proceedings of OOPSLA'89* (1989), SIGPLAN, ACM Press.

[19] MADSEN, O. L., MØLLER-PEDERSEN, B., AND NYGAARD, K. *Object-Oriented Programming in the BETA Programming Language.* Addison-Wesley, 1993.

[20] MEYER, B. Genericity versus Inheritance. In *Proceedings of OOPSLA'86* (1986).

[21] MEYER, B. *Object-Oriented Software Construction.* Prentice Hall International Series in Computer Science. Prentice Hall, Englewood Cliffs, NJ, 1988.

[22] MYERS, A., BANK, J., AND LISKOV, B. Parameterized types for Java. In *Proceedings of POPL'97* (1997).

[23] NAROFF, S. Personal communication. 1993–1996.

[24] NEXT COMPUTER, INC. *Object Oriented Programming and the Objective C Language.* Redwood City, CA, April 1993.

[25] ODERSKY, M., AND WADLER, P. Pizza into Java: Translating theory into practice. In *Proceedings of POPL'97* (Paris, 1997), ACM Press.

[26] OMOHUNDRO, S. The Sather Programming Language. *Dr. Dobb's Journal 18*, 11 (October 1993).

[27] PALSBERG, J., AND SCHWARTSBACH, M. I. *Object-Oriented Type Systems*. Addison-Wesley, 1993.

[28] SCHWARTSBACH, M. I. Object-oriented type systems: Principles and applications. from http://www.daimi.aau.dk/~mis, 1996.

[29] SEIDEWITZ, E. Genericity Versus Inheritance Reconsidered: Self-Reference Using Generices. In *Proceedings of OOPSLA '94* (1994).

[30] SHANG, D. Are cows animals? *Object Currents 1*, 1 (January 1996). http://www.sigs.com/objectcurrents/.

[31] UNGAR, D., SMITH, R. B., CHAMBERS, C., AND HÖLZLE, U. Object, message and performance: How they coexist in SELF. *IEEE Computer 25*, 10 (October 1992).

[32] ZDONIK, S., AND MAIER, D. *Readings in Object Oriented Databases*. Morgan Kaufmann, 1990, ch. 1: Fundamentals of Object-Oriented Databases, pp. 1–32.

# Tool Support for Object-Oriented Patterns

*Gert Florijn, Marco Meijers, Pieter van Winsen*

Utrecht University, Dept. of Computer Science
P.o. box 80.089, 3508 TB Utrecht, the Netherlands
E-mail: florijn@cs.ruu.nl

## Abstract

A software (design) pattern describes a general solution for a recurring design problem. The solution is mostly described in terms of an abstract design structure expressed in design elements such as classes, methods and relationships (inheritance, associations).

This paper describes a prototype tool that supports working with design patterns when developing or maintaining object-oriented programs. The tool provides three integrated views on a program: the code (classes, methods, etc.), a design view (abstraction of the code plus additional information not in the code) and occurrences of design patterns in the program.

The tool assists developers using patterns in three ways:

- Generating program elements (e.g. classes, hierarchies) for a new instance of a pattern, taken from an extensible collection of "template" patterns
- Integrating pattern occurrences with the rest of the program by binding program elements to a role in a pattern (e.g. indicating that an existing class plays a particular role in a pattern instance)
- Checking whether occurrences of patterns still meet the invariants governing the patterns and repairing the program in case of problems

Through the use of an existing refactoring package, the tool supports the use of patterns both in forward engineering and in backwards engineering, i.e. documenting occurrences of patterns in existing programs and modifying the program to better reflect the pattern's structure.

The tool is implemented in Smalltalk and has been applied to identify pattern occurrences in several non-trivial (Smalltalk) applications and to reorganize these subsequently.

## 1. Introduction

Over the past few years, design patterns have become a hot topic in the object-oriented community. A (design) pattern describes a general solution for a recurring design problem. The solution is described in a standard format (the pattern format) that consists of a generic design structure for the solution (expressed in some terminology of design elements) together with a textual description of the pattern, indicating, for example, when to use the solution or how to apply it in certain situations.

Though most patterns are not OO specific (i.e. they could be used in non-OO programs), the design structures are commonly expressed in object-oriented terminology, i.e. in terms of classes, interfaces, methods, attributes and relationships (inheritance, associations). This means that applying patterns in the development of object-oriented systems is - in principle - fairly straightforward, since the terminology can be mapped directly on language constructs.

Patterns offer several (potential) benefits when developing (OO) software. First, there is the issue of reuse. By applying a solution that has been developed and used before, we can avoid design work that would normally take place, especially the work invested in checking out solutions that do not suffice for the problem at hand. Using patterns also means that discussions are more focused on important decisions, such as "should we allow run-time variation of this behaviour?" or "where must the creation of these objects be localized". In a similar way, patterns make communication among developers more effective. By using pattern names we can avoid detailed discussions about why certain classes are organized and programmed in a certain way. Also, understanding a program written by others becomes easier when we know whether and where certain patterns are used.

**Problems when using patterns**

Using patterns when developing an OO program is not a trivial process. First, one has to identify the need for a certain pattern by recognizing a problem and choosing a particular solution. Once that is done, the pattern has to be integrated with the design/program that is already available. In general, this means that the design elements from the pattern description have to be mapped to and integrated with the design elements in the program. More specifically, a developer must decide which classes in a program will play the roles defined by the classes in the pattern description, which methods in the program classes will play the role of the methods defined in the pattern's classes, etc. Of course, this can also lead to situations where the design elements in a program play multiple roles, i.e. correspond to design elements in several patterns. For example, a class playing the role of "abstract factory" in the Abstract Factory pattern[1], could also play the role of the singleton class in the Singleton pattern.

Putting pattern occurrences in a design affects the overall organization of a program, i.e. which classes there are, how they are associated and how class-hierarchies are organized. However, the inverse is also true; the existing program structure influences how we apply a pattern. For example, many patterns define inheritance hierarchies. If we want to combine two of these patterns at the same place in our program (e.g. combine a composite with an observer), we may have to decide which of these two hierarchies is taken as leading and find a different solution for the integration of the other pattern.

---

[1] All pattern examples discussed in this paper are taken from [Gamma95]. The reader is assumed to be somewhat familiar with the patterns described there.

So, when applying a pattern, a developer must be aware of the overall organization of the program, and occasionally be prepared to reorganize it based on new insights. When this occurs, the developer must make sure that the semantics of the program are left untouched and that the pattern occurrences introduced earlier are still intact.

Finally, using a pattern somewhere in a program can impose constraints on the further development of the elements involved. If we, for example, have applied a Proxy pattern somewhere, we must ensure that the proxy class implements all operations defined in its super-class and delegates them - whenever necessary - to the object it represents. If, at a later point in time, operations are added to the superclass (possibly by another developer) the proxy class may have to be adapted also. However, if no precautions are taken (eg. through documentation), it is easy to forget this, and in some cases it may be hard to find the errors that are then introduced.

**Tool support**

The goal of our research is to explore how tools can make the use of patterns in OO software development easier. Our focus is not on the selection of suitable patterns for particular problems but on using patterns in the creation, reorganization and evolution of a design/program. Basically, we want to introduce patterns as first-class citizens in an integrated OO development environment.

Over the past year or so we have developed a first prototype of such an environment. It provides assistance for:

- generating program elements (e.g. classes, hierarchies) for a new instance of a pattern that is taken from an extensible collection of "template" patterns
- integrating pattern occurrences with the existing program by binding program elements to a role in a pattern (e.g. indicating that and existing class plays a particular role in a pattern instance)
- checking whether (modified) occurrences of patterns still meet the invariants governing the patterns and repairing the program in case of problems.

Through the incorporation of an existing refactoring package, the environment supports program reorganization operations and can also be used for "reverse engineering", i.e. documenting occurrences of patterns in existing programs and modifying the program to better reflect the pattern's structure. The environment is implemented in Smalltalk and has been applied to identify pattern occurrences in several non-trivial (Smalltalk) applications and to reorganize these subsequently.

**About this paper**

In the remainder of this paper we discuss the tool we have developed. Chapter 2 discusses some the key issues and requirements for pattern tool support. Chapter 3 gives an overall overview of our system, while chapter 4 discusses program and pattern representation. Chapter 5 illustrates some of the tools that are currently available. Finally, in chapter 6, we discuss some preliminary experiences and topics for current/future research.

## 2. Issues and requirements for pattern tool support

As mentioned above, the primary goal of our research is to develop a tool to support (OO) program development with patterns. The underlying idea is that design patterns could be regarded as a kind of coarse-grained building blocks for OO design. A tool that provides the ability to define, instantiate, interconnect, and rearrange these building blocks could well help in rapidly producing consistent, high-quality designs. This section discusses some of the fundamental issues and requirements that such a tool must address.

### The development model

A key decision to make is which role patterns play in the development environment. We have identified two models that could be used. In the first approach, the developer only works on the level of patterns, i.e. a system is developed by gluing instances of patterns together into a design. For this design, the tool could generate skeleton code (similar to the model in [Budinsky96]) in some programming language. While this approach is very interesting, it depends on the availability of a large catalogue of patterns which covers all possible design problems that can occur. At this moment, however, such a catalogue does not exist. Another drawback of this model is that it makes it more difficult to do reverse engineering of OO applications, i.e. to take an existing program, identify or put patterns in it, and reorganize.

In the approach we have chosen for our tool, a developer works on a program on different levels of abstraction (i.e. patterns, design, code) within the same environment. The environment provides three integrated and mutually consistent views on the underlying program. Each view supports operations particular to its level of abstraction. For example, on the pattern level the developer can instantiate patterns from a repository, on the design level she can split classes into a hierarchy, while on the code level she can add the code to methods. This approach does not rely on the availability of a comprehensive catalogue. Also, we can take an existing program into the environment and reorganize it subsequently.

Of course, this approach implies that a broad collection of tools has to be available, ranging from normal programming tools like code editors via design tools to pattern level tools.

### Representing patterns

The solution part of a pattern gives a (generic) design structure expressed in a vocabulary of design elements. In order to manipulate patterns, a system should be able to represent these elements and treat patterns as some organized composition of such elements.

The key question that must be addressed is: what are the elements needed to express design structures? Obviously, this includes basic OO constructs such as (abstract) classes, inheritance association/aggregation relations and (class) method and attribute declarations with particular access control. However, in existing pattern catalogues [Gamma95, Buschmann96] the pattern description codes more information.

Frequently, special graphical notations are used to highlight certain (dynamic) properties and relations like the fact that a particular class (or method) creates instances of another class. Also, a pattern can impose certain behavior on methods, e.g. the fact that a "notify" method in a subject must invoke the "update" method on all its associated observer objects in an Observer pattern.

In general, one can envisage that a pattern is expressed in a design vocabulary that is richer than that offered by programming languages or design notations. As an illustration, consider a hypothetical relation "co-located" placed between two classes, that indicates that objects of these two classes should reside on the same site in a distributed system. We can also imagine annotations for persistence or concurrency control. The conclusion therefore must be that a design environment should be open with respect to the design elements that can be expressed. Likewise, it should be possible to represent patterns as configurations of arbitrary design elements, not just of classes, relations and methods as is the case in the approach of Kim and Benner [Kim96].

## Dealing with programming language variations

To implement a pattern in a particular programming language, we have to find a suitable mapping from the design elements in the pattern to programming language constructs. In some cases the mapping is straightforward, and the design structure can be mapped directly to a (skeleton) program. In other cases, however, patterns can be implemented in completely different ways depending on the available language constructs. A good example is an Adapter, which can be implemented efficiently with multiple inheritance. If that construct is not available, we must use other mechanisms like interfaces (in Java) or delegation.

One of our long-term goals is to make the environment independent of a particular programming language, e.g. by using language-specific strategies and idioms to map configurations of design elements to language constructs. For the short term we assume a direct mapping between design elements and language constructs. This means that patterns must to be defined in terms of the design elements that can be mapped directly to the programming language used. Currently, we use the Smalltalk object model as a reference point, which means that constructs like multiple inheritance are not used. We will return to this issue later on.

## Instantiating and binding patterns

The pattern view of in the environment should allow the instantiation of predefined patterns from a repository and the binding of the design elements in the pattern to elements in the program. This binding is similar to the conformance declaration that specify how classes (partially) satisfy the rules of role specification in contracts [Helm90]. There are three different ways of instantiating and binding patterns:

- Top-down: given a pattern description, generate the necessary design elements in the program and bind them to the pattern. This is typically expressed by: "Give me an instance of the Observer pattern", after which the developer is given an initial set of classes (with methods, relations, etc.) that follow the canonical structure of the Observer pattern.

- Bottom-up: given a number of elements in the program, bind them to a new instance of a pattern. This addresses situations such as: "These classes (and their methods) together reflect the Proxy pattern; let's turn it into a Proxy pattern." The difference with the top-down approach is that no new design elements are created in the program, instead existing elements are used.

- Mixed: this approach differs from bottom-up in that the program elements that only partly meet a pattern structure may be combined with newly generated elements that are generated. An example of this is: "This structure closely resembles the Composite pattern; turn it into a Composite instance." In this case, the structure will be completed with new design elements that were missing.

### Program transformations and conformance checking

Since we do not assume that programs can be developed just by instantiating and composing design patterns, the environment must provide operations to edit the program on both the design level and program level. Thus, it must offer operations to add new classes, create new hierarchies, define associations, move method definitions; in short: to add, modify, move or delete arbitrary design elements.

Obviously, these operations can also affect the elements in the program that play a role in a pattern instance. For example, we could move the notify method of a subject class in an instance of the Observer pattern to a sub-class. Basically, such reorganizations are no problem. Patterns are not laws; they suggest a general solution that has to applied and specialized to the problem at hand. This also means that the design structure defined in a pattern is not the "one and only" configuration of elements that meet the pattern. Variations are possible, and sometimes even necessary, e.g. when the programming language used does not offer multiple inheritance.

On the other hand, some transformations and operations can cause situations where a program no longer meets the structural or semantic intentions of patterns that were put into it. For example, if we completely remove the notification of observers from the subject class, the program no longer meets the underlying contract of the Observer pattern. This also occurs if the developer adds a method to the common superclass of a Proxy pattern instance, and forgets to extend the proxy class with a new method that delegates to the real object. So, as pointed out by Kim and Brenner [Kim96]: "a design pattern must be used correctly" and a design tool should help the developer in doing just this, without enforcing him to a single solution.

To deal with such situations, the environment should be able to check whether the configuration of design elements in a program meet the requirements of the pattern(s) in which they play a role. In a sense this corresponds to conformance checking as defined for contracts [Helm90] and to the "pattern instantiation validation algorithm" in [Kim96]. If the program does not conform, the environment should offer the developer different strategies to deal with the situation, ranging from ignoring the problem to (semi-) automatic repair. Also, it may take quite some editing operations to take the program from one "consistent" state to another, so a transaction model and undo facility would be useful.

Clearly, such program transformation operations, together with the ability to check pattern conformance, are crucial for reverse engineering an existing application.

### Pattern specific operations

Besides editing operations on the program/design level, one could also imagine operations on the pattern level. One example could be the replacement of an entire pattern instance by an instance of another pattern that solves the same problem but in a different way. A slightly simpler situation occurs when a particular pattern can be extended in a certain dimension, but doing these extensions involves a lot of lower-level editing operations, such as adding a factory to an instance of the Abstract Factory pattern or adding a concrete builder to a Builder pattern instance. It would be convenient if each of these sub-elements of these patterns could be manipulated as a single entity and if the creation and removal of such sub-elements could be eased. In short, it should be possible to associate a set of pattern specific operations to perform tasks that are particular to that pattern.

### Miscellaneous issues

The points addressed above are among the core issues that must be dealt with. However, there are many other, issues that must be considered. For example it should be easy to add new patterns to the environment. Ideally, a developer should be able to take a particular configuration of design elements and translate it - without too many difficulties - into a new pattern for reuse in other situations. Furthermore, it should be possible to save, export and reload programs while retaining the information that was added in the environment. This involves the notion of documentation, so that in exported program code or design drawings we can, for example, identify which elements play a role for particular pattern instance.

## 3. Tool architecture

In the previous section we have identified the key issues and requirements that a pattern-based design environment must address. In this section we discuss the overall architecture of the environment we have constructed and that addresses most of the issues raised in the previous. Subsequent sections go into details about the various parts.

Figure 1 illustrates the key components of the environment. The basis of the environment is the *fragment model* and the corresponding *fragment database*. A fragment represents a design element of a particular type (i.e. class, method, pattern, association, etc.). Fragments have roles that can contain references to other fragments. The program being manipulated is thus stored as a graph of interrelated fragments of different types. Fragments (of a particular type) can also have behavior associated with them, such a checking consistency constraints or implementing pattern-specific operations.

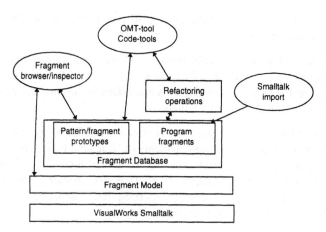

Figure 1: Key components in the environment

The pattern repository is a suite of prototypical fragment configurations that can be cloned into the program. Through editing operations on the fragment database, roles of pattern fragments can be bound to already existing fragments (of a particular type).

The fragment database can be inspected and manipulated directly with a couple of browsers. The *fragment browser* displays the available fragment graph and supports connecting fragments and invoking pattern/fragment specific operations and consistency checking. The *fragment inspector* shows details about one particular fragment and its type.

Besides these basic tools we have added higher-level tools. They support working on the three views on the program in the database. The central role is played by the *OMT-tool* which provides a (OMT) design level view of the program.

From the OMT tool the developer can perform edit operations (refactoring operations) on the program. She can also launch code-level tools, such as class browsers, which again work on fragments. In addition, the OMT tool provides more high-level support for instantiating and binding patterns into the program, and for viewing which parts of the design play a role in a particular pattern occurrence.

The development environment can be used to organize work through the creation of projects and diagrams. Projects are a means to have multiple programs loaded in the design environment. Within a project, the user can create diagrams, which are a subset of the design elements in the project. Basically a diagram is a sub-view of a program. They are mostly used for documenting and reorganizing existing programs. Finally, the tool supports import and export of Smalltalk programs into the fragment database.

## 4. The fragment model

Fragments play a pivotal role in our environment [Meijers96]. All design elements in the program - from pattern occurrences via classes and relations among them to methods and possibly even their code - are represented as (graphs of) fragments of particular types. Patterns (and pattern occurrences) are fragments (of a particular type) and the repository of available patterns is just a collection of prototype fragment structures which can be cloned.

We have decided not to adopt a multi-level model for handling patterns as is done in other pattern-tools such as [Kim96]. They make a distinction between the user design level that contains the classes, their elements and relationships, and the pattern level to which user-level design elements are bound.

The main reasons for choosing a single level system were flexibility and simplicity. In our model it is easy to add new design elements (or fragment types, see below) at run-time and to use these in pattern definitions. So, we are not limited to a fixed number of design elements defined on the "pattern level" (see also chapter 2). In addition, in a single level system it is easier to "promote" existing design structures to a pattern, just by copying them to the template repository.

**Fragment structure**

A fragment represents a design element of a particular type (determined by a delegation parent holding shared data and behavior) that holds particular information (e.g. the name of class in case of a "class" fragment) and behavior (in code slots) and that has roles that contain references that point to other fragments (e.g. the methods of the class).

The working of the fragment model works is best illustrated by an example. Figure 2 shows an instance of the Observer pattern together with a corresponding fragment structure[2]. Note that because the system is based on prototypes and cloning, the given pattern structure could stand for a pattern instance as well as for a prototype.

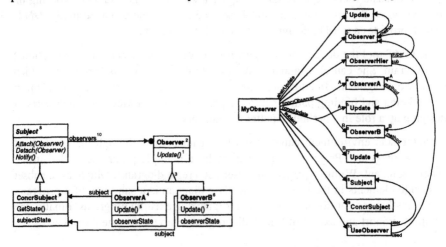

Figure 2: Observer instance and corresponding fragment structure

---

[2] Note that this fragment structure is not complete. Only the numbered items from the class structure have been depicted.

Fragments are connected by *roles* that are indicated by labeled arrows. A role is a typed container owned by a particular fragment. The fragments that are referenced by a role all provide a similar function to the role owner. A fragment that fulfills a role for another fragment is said to be an *actor* of that role. Note that a fragment may be actor and role owner at the same time. In our example, ObserverA fulfills the role "sub" for ObserverHier as well as the role "concreteObserver" for MyObserver, and in addition it is owner of a "method" role.

Roles are typed in order to constrain the actors of the role. For example, the Method role of a Class fragment can only be fulfilled by fragments of type Method. Additional constraints may be imposed on roles by defining the minimum and maximum cardinality to limit the number of actors linked to the role. In our example, at any time only one abstract observer class is allowed. This is expressed by setting both the minimum and maximum cardinality of MyObserver's abstractObserver role to one. The different actors of a role are distinguished by their actor IDs that uniquely identify them within the role. The A's and B's from the sample fragment structure denote the actor IDs.

Each pattern has one *root fragment*. In our example, MyObserver is the root fragment. Its main function is to hold all fragments that are relevant to the pattern instance. All the relevant fragments play a particular role for the pattern instance, otherwise it would contradict the fact that they are relevant to the pattern. To reflect this idea, all these fragments are linked to the root fragment by roles.

Root fragments are just like any other fragment. Therefore, they can also fulfill roles for other fragments. Root fragments serve as a sort of placeholders for pattern instances. The Observer fragment that is called MyObserver for example stands for an instance of the Observer pattern. All Observer fragments will descend from a single fragment called ObserverBehavior from which they inherit common behavior that is specific for the Observer pattern.

It is important to note that even relationships can be represented by fragments. For example, to model the inheritance relationship between classes we can use a separate Hierarchy fragment with two roles for the superclass and subclasses respectively (as is done in figure 2). An alternative way to model this is providing a subclass role to fragments of type Class, so the subclasses are directly connected to the superclasses. It is in fact this latter approach that we have used in the current modeling of patterns.

The example shown here contains only a single pattern instance. In practice such instances could overlap in arbitrary ways, e.g. when an Observer instance is combined with a Singleton pattern applied to one of its classes. That class would simply fulfill roles for the root fragments of both an Observer and a Singleton instance. In addition, both root fragments would fulfill the design role of the global root fragment. So our current model allows overlapping pattern instances almost trivially.

## Implementation model

Technically speaking, fragments are objects similar to those found in the Self programming language. Fragments have an identity, a number of slots and a pointer to a parent object to which messages that cannot be handled in the fragment itself are delegated. Fragments can share data or behavior by referring to the same delegation parent but can also override behavior locally whenever this is necessary.

Fragment slots can hold primitive values (Smalltalk objects), code or references to other fragments[3]. The code slots are Smalltalk block-closures that are evaluated with a context of the receiving fragment, the handling fragment and the parent pointer. The data slots in a fragment are used to record information about the fragment, such as the name of a class or a method, the (uninterpreted) code of a method or the type of an attribute.

Whenever we talk about a fragment "of a particular type" we actually refer to a fragment object with particular behavior defined in a particular delegation parent. Thus, a fragment is a "method fragment" if it delegates (directly or indirectly) to the fragment (called MethodBehavior) that holds the common data and behavior for methods. In a similar way, there is a "type" fragment for each pattern defined in the system, such as Observer. It holds the "intent" and the pattern specific operations for all observer patterns in the program (see figure 3).

## System structure

The complete fragment database is organized similarly as a pattern, as can be seen from figure 3. Note that this picture is not complete, but is only used to illustrate the overall structure of the system.

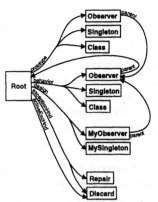

Figure 3: Fragment system structure

Like any other pattern, the system structure has a single root fragment to collect all fragments that are relevant to the system. We will subsequently refer to the root

---

[3] Roles are implemented as a particular kind of fragment object.

fragment of the system as the *global root*. All the relevant patterns are linked to the root fragment by roles.

The *prototype* role refers to the root fragments of all prototypes (of patterns and other fragments). The *behavior* role collects all fragments that define shared behavior for fragments of a particular type. For example, it holds the ObserverBehavior fragment contains all information and behavior that is shared by all Observer instances. All design elements in the program are registered in the *design* role. So for example, creating an instance of the Observer pattern and applying the Singleton pattern to the AbstractSubject class of it will result in the binding of both pattern instances to the design role. The remaining two system roles deal with exception handling. All handlers that are present in the system are registered by the *exceptionHnd* role. The exception handler that is currently active, which is at most one, is designated by the *activeExcHnd* role. More on validation and exception handling follows below.

The global root fragment performs yet another function besides collecting the relevant fragments. We have already mentioned that each fragment has a delegation parent. So a fragment's parent also has a parent, and so on. This delegation chain eventually ends with the system's root fragment as can be seen from figure 3. In other words, the global root fragment acts as the indirect ancestor of all fragments. The global root therefore provides default behavior with respect to cloning and other operations on fragments.

**Operations and transactions**

Operations on the fragment database are implemented by behavior slots in the fragments. Default behavior is provided to clone fragments and to bind/unbind fragments to/from roles. Pattern specific operations are defined in the shared behavior fragments for these patterns.

For Abstract Factory patterns, for example, there are four pattern-specific operations, i.e. adding and removing factories and products. An operation like addProduct involves creating and linking multiple fragments (a hierarchy with an abstract base class and a number of concrete product classes, creation methods in the various factories). These operations are programmed in code slots and use method calls to clone instances of existing fragments and bind them to the right roles.

To let these composite operations be treated as one unit the tool provides a nested transaction model. Validation checking is postponed until a (sub-) transaction is completed. Transactions are also used to let the user set check points to which the system can roll back if necessary. The user can issue commands to begin a transaction, end a transaction, and undo a transaction.

**Constraints and validation**

Using the basic operations defined above the structure of the "user design", i.e. the program being developed, will gradually evolve. As mentioned in section 2, this can also mean that the initial fragment structure of design patterns (as given by the prototype) is modified. This can lead to situations where the program does no longer conform to the patterns put into it.

To handle this problem we have to deal with two issues. First, how do we specify what a valid pattern occurrence is? Gamma et al. [Gamma95] use a rather informal notation to describe these constraints. They are often suggested by naming conventions or textual annotations to the class diagrams. In order to let a tool automatically check the constraints, a more explicit mechanism must be invented to describe them. Second, we must decide how to handle constraints, or more precisely, constraint violations. Do we attempt making sure that only correct configurations can be constructed with the given representation or do we check the validity of a configuration after it has been created? We have adopted the second approach, because for certain constraints it is difficult to build them implicitly into the representation.

Our initial attempt to was to hard-code the checks into a code slot called "validate" attached to the shared behavior fragment of each pattern. Each pattern instance has a number of roles, and the validation procedure checks whether these roles are correctly fulfilled by fragments of the right type and whether these fragments are well interconnected (e.g. whether instance access method for a Singleton pattern instance is bound toa class method fragment that plays a class method role in the singleton class).

Note that we use a per-pattern type validation procedure instead of one general algorithm as used in [Kim96]. This is caused by the fact that we do not have a two-level system, but also because patterns can involve arbitrary design elements, and because we wanted to handle sharing constraints as mentioned above.

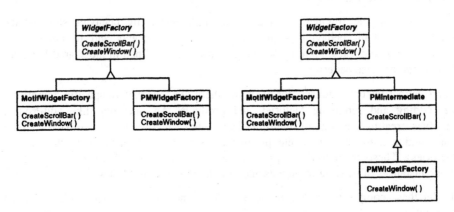

Figure 4: Example design variation

The structure checking based on role-types becomes problematic, however, when indirections are introduced, e.g. through inheritance or delegation. Consider the Abstract Factory pattern again. One of the constraints is that each concrete factory class must provide an implementation for the abstract factory class. This does not imply however that each concrete factory class must also be a *direct* subclass of the abstract factory class. The only restriction is that it must be a descendant, but it need not necessarily be a direct descendant (see figure 4). A similar situation appears when a particular class is supposed to provide a particular method. It is not necessary to require the method to be implemented by the class because it is valid to inherit the method from a superclass.

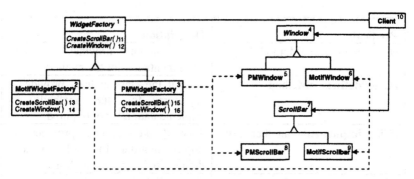

Figure 5: Abstract Factory pattern instance

A partial solution is to add such indirections to the constraint-checking, similarly to the use of the generalized path mentioned in [Kim96]. However, since our pattern structure can involve arbitrary design elements it was not easy to decide on a general approach as to whether (and which) kinds of indirections were allowed. As a consequence, the validation checking had to be modified constantly, augmenting the other drawback of procedural constraint coding: the code became difficult to write and maintain.

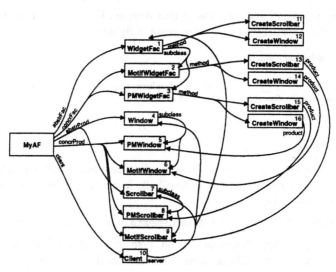

Figure 6: Fragment structure of the abstract factory instance in figure 5

In order to alleviate these problems we decided to use a declarative approach combined with a slightly different modeling of relations. As an illustration consider the abstract factory pattern instance shown in figure 5 with the fragment structure depicted in figure 6.

Constraints for patterns are now expressed as compositions of predicates defined on certain fragment types. The predicates are much like query operations; the most important ones are listed in table 1. For defining constraints, these predicates can be combined by boolean operators like and, or, not, plus the quantors forall, and exists.

| Predicate | Description |
|-----------|-------------|
| aClass **provides:** aMethod | True if the class provides a concrete implementation for the method. |
| aClass **defines:** aMethod | True if the class at least provides a signature for the method; an implementation is not required. |
| aClass **implements:** anotherClass | True if the receiver provides an implementation for all methods defined in the argument class. |
| AMethod **creates:** aClass | True if the receiver method instantiates the argument class. |
| aMethod **uses:** anotherMethod | True if the receiver directly or indirectly calls the argument method |
| aClass **contains:** anotherClass | True if the argument class is a component of the receiver class |

Table 1: Some fragment predicates

Now follows a possible specification of four Abstract Factory invariants based on the modeling of the Abstract Factory pattern given in figure 6:

$$\underset{f \in concrFac}{\forall} \quad f \text{ \textbf{implements:} } abstrFac$$

$$\underset{f \in concrFac}{\forall} \quad \underset{p \in abstrProd}{\forall} \quad \underset{c \in ConcrProd}{\exists} \quad \underset{m \in (f \; provides)}{\exists} \quad c \text{ \textbf{implements:} } p \wedge m \text{ \textbf{creates:} } c \wedge abstrFac \text{ \textbf{defines:} } m$$

$$\underset{p \in abstrProd}{\forall} \quad client \text{ \textbf{uses:} } p$$

$client$ **uses:** $abstrFac$

Note that for the sake of legibility, the constraints have been written in a formula-like format. In practice, they are written in Smalltalk, in a code-slot of a fragment; the first constraint then becomes:

```
_self concrFac  forall: [:f | f implements: _self abstrFac theActor]
```

Validation of a pattern fragment should take place if editing operations have (potentially) modified it. Validation must be performed on the instance to which the editing operation was applied and, in the case of role operations, it is the role owner that must be validated.

It might be necessary to propagate the validation signal further because relations might be fulfilled indirectly. The fragment that is in between in that case could well belong to an entirely different pattern instance. The only way to propagate the validation signal correctly seems to validate all the fragments to which the affected fragment is connected. This will finally end with the validation of the global Root fragment.

## Exception handling

What happens when constraints are violated? When something wrong is encountered during the validation process, an exception is raised. An example of such an exception is:

**typeErrorOnActor:** aFragment **ofRole:** aRole

Exceptions are sent to the active exception handler. As can be seen from the system structure of figure 3 there are a number of exception handlers one of which is active at a particular moment. The system can easily be extended with additional exception handlers, because they are simply represented by fragments linked to the `exceptionHnd' role of the global root.

Each exception handler uses a different strategy for handling constraint violations. The handlers we have considered and tested are:

- Ignore: This handler permits everything, it will not bother the user with messages or other actions; it simply ignores any violation. Of course, the behavior of the system after ignoring a violation is at your own risk.

- Discard: This option prohibits faulty actions. On exception, an error message is displayed and the action that causes the exception is rolled back.

- Warn: A warning message is displayed and the user is asked for confirmation. It provides the opportunity to cancel the action or to ignore the warning.

- Repair: Tries to repair the defect. This appeared to be very useful in practice. More on this option follows.

- Choice: Gives the opportunity to choose interactively among different strategies. When an exception is raised, the user is informed about it and can choose to cancel (and hence roll back) the action, to ignore it, or to repair it. This option is useful if the user prefers full control over the actions that are taken on each individual exception.

The repairer is like an intelligent assistant. On a "MissingLink" exception (i.e. when a role is not adequately bound to other fragments), for example, it will simply add the link that is missing and add a new instance of the right fragment type. If an exception occurs the user will not even experience it as something wrong, instead it looks like the system is completing his actions. Note that this technique can make the definition of pattern specific operations like adding a product to an Abstract Factory pattern a lot simpler.

There are certainly cases in which there is no automatic fix for the problem. In that case, an error message is still presented to the user. Furthermore, the user can be asked to make a decision if there is more than one way to repair a defect. Furthermore, it is often the case that a defect can be repaired in both a constructive and a destructive manner. On a MissingLink exception for example a bind operation can be applied to add the missing link. Alternatively, the fragment that requires the link could be removed in its entirety. The first approach is constructive, while the latter is clearly destructive. Both approaches could be useful in different situations. But when an exception occurs, what repair mode should be used? Constructive or destructive? In our opinion, it would be reasonable to link up with the type of action that caused the exception. If the nature of the action was constructive (e.g. the bind operation) then it is most desirable that the action is completed in a constructive way, so constructive repair must be used. On the other hand, if the user issues a destructive operation (e.g. destroy or unlink) then it would be highly annoying if the just removed link appears again because of the repair actions. So destructive repair is obviously preferred in that case.

## 5. Tools

This section discusses some of the tools that are available in the environment. Detailed descriptions can be found in [Meijers96] and [Winsen96].

**Fragment browser**

The fragment browser is depicted in figure 7[4]. The browser displays the fragments in a straightforward way. Fragments are depicted as boxes with labels in boldface. Because roles basically are fragments, namely container fragments, they are depicted by boxes as well. However, roles are labeled in italics whereas the other fragments are labeled in boldface. Roles are connected to the role owner by arcs and the same holds for the way actors are linked to roles.

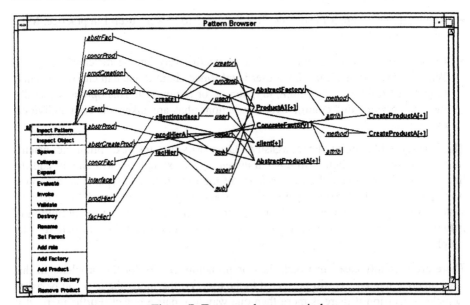

Figure 7: Fragment browser window

---

[4] This view was realized with the ObjectGraph package developed by Christopher Penney, Intelligent Systems Laboratory, Michigan State University.

The figure shows a browser window focused on an instance of the Abstract Factory pattern. Note that in this case the root fragment has almost entirely been covered by the popup menu.

The level of detail that is displayed in the browser can be controlled by collapsing and expanding nodes. In addition, one can spawn a separate browser on a subdesign rooted at a particular fragment in a separate window. Finally, the user can mark the nodes of a subdesign with a particular color.

What is displayed in figure 7 is the so called component view that shows how fragments are linked to other fragments by roles. There is yet another view mode however, namely the parent view, that reveals the delegation chain among fragments.

The fragment structure can be manipulated in the browser fully through menus. Standard menus provide a number of general operations, for example to change the view mode, to close the browser, and to control transactions. In addition, there is a context-sensitive menu that depends on the type of the fragment to which the cursor is pointing. Since menus are "inherited" through the delegation chain, the global root fragment provides a basic menu that is overridden or extended by descendants. Via this menu the user can perform actions such as inspect a pattern, expand, collapse or spawn a new browser on a subdesign, destroy and rename fragments, add roles, or invoke validation on a fragment. The context sensitive menu also allows the user to bind/unbind a fragment from a role.

The context-sensitive menus allow the invocation of pattern-specific operations. In the case of an abstract factory pattern this involves operations like adding a product or adding a factory. Also, one can add a new fragment to a particular role by selecting from a list of available fragment prototypes that meet the type expected by the role. In case of the *design* role of the root fragment, one can thus also add a pattern instance by selecting the appropriate name from the list. The complete fragment structure of the prototype is then cloned and added (with a supplied actor-id) to the design-role.

Adding pattern fragment copies together with rebinding allows top-down, bottom-up and mixed-mode pattern instantiation. As an example, consider applying the Singleton pattern to an existing class. First, we create a Singleton instance as described above. Then the class to which the Singleton pattern is to be applied, must be bound to the `theClass' role of the singleton's root fragment. This is done by issuing a Bind operation and selecting the same actor ID of the actor that was automatically provided, the latter will then automatically be replaced by the custom class. After that, invoking the validation operation on the singleton instance with the active exception handler set to "Repair" will takes care of moving the class method and class variable of the Singleton instance to the class designated as a singleton.

**Fragment inspector**

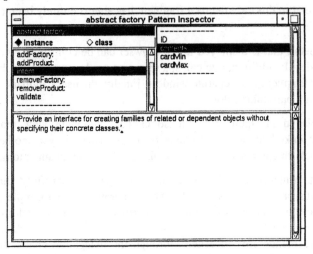

Figure 8: Fragment inspector window

Whereas the browser provides a global view on the fragment structure, the fragment inspector focuses on one particular fragment and reveals its details. Figure 8 shows a sample inspector window on the root fragment of an arbitrary Abstract Factory instance.

Like the standard Smalltalk browser[5] the pattern inspector can be set in one of two modes. In class mode the right subpane will list all properties of the fragment such as parent and type. On selection of a particular property, the corresponding value appears in the lower subpane. When put in instance mode, the right subpane lists the properties of a single slot that is selected from the left subpane. The corresponding value is again displayed in the lower subpane. In the sample figure the contents of the primitive slot named "intent"" is being displayed. In addition to being displayed, the value of any property can also be edited in the lower subpane.

Note that this means that code-slots can also be added and modified with the fragment inspector. Together with the binding operations in the fragment browser, this also offers the means to add new fragment types and thus new design patterns. The process is roughly as follows: First, we create a new fragment of an arbitrary type, give it a new name, add it to the behavior role of the root fragment and define particular behavior/data slots for it. Typically, for design pattern fragments, we would define a "validate" slot coded using the constraint-model defined earlier. Then we create a prototype fragment structure (by instantiating and linking the right fragments or by copying an existing structure) and let its root fragment delegate to the behavior fragment defined earlier (an operation provided in the browser). After that is done, the new pattern is available for use, and new instances can be added to the design.

---

[5] The fragment inspector is actually implemented by a subclass of the system browser.

## The OMT Tool

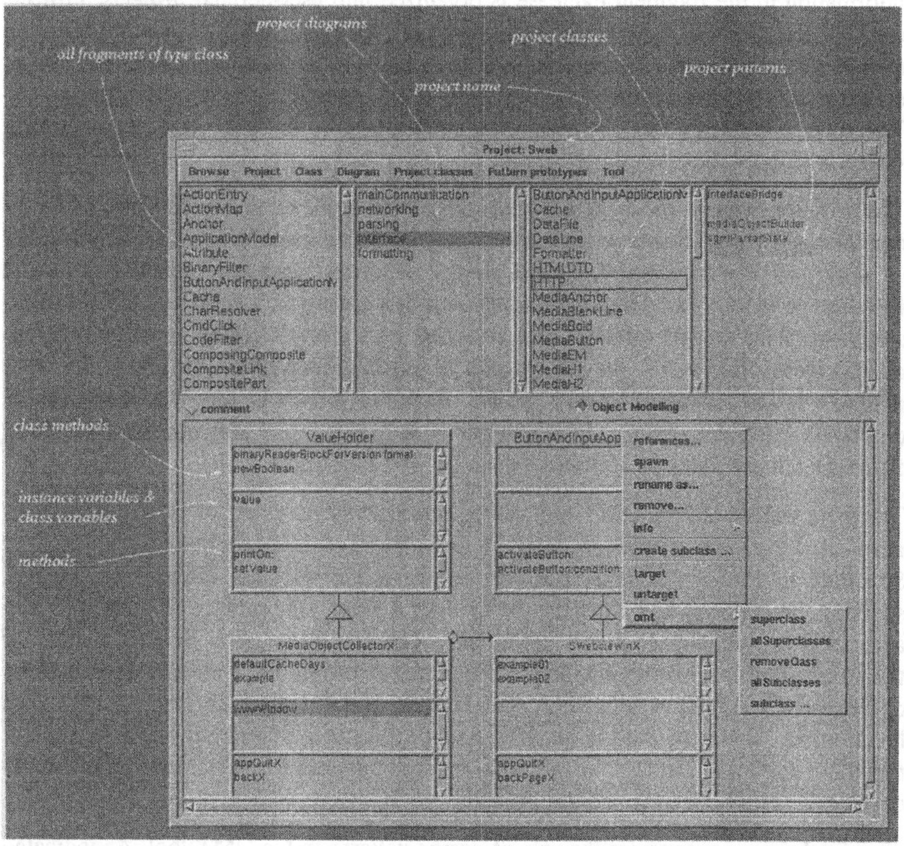

Figure 9: OMT-Tool main window

The fragment browser and inspector provide support for direct interaction with the fragment model and the fragment database. In principle, all the necessary functionality for manipulating the design and dealing with patterns is available through these tools. The OMT-tool is a first step towards a higher-level, and easier to use development environment working on the fragment database. The OMT-tool was primarily developed to support the identification of patterns in existing software and to reorganize these programs. However, new programs can also be developed with it.

The OMT tool is an extended version of the Smalltalk Refactoring Browser[6] developed at the University of Illinois, which on its turn is based on the work on design refactoring operations by William Opdyke [Opdyke92]. Obviously, the Refactory Browser has been "ported" to work on the fragment database, not the Smalltalk Image.

---

[6] See http://st-www.cs.uiuc.edu/users/droberts/Refactory.html

Figure 9 shows the main window of the OMT-tool. One of its key features is that the information in the fragment database is organized into user-defined *projects*. Projects can be focused on creating a new program but also on manipulating existing (Smalltalk) software that is imported into the fragment-database. Importing means that existing classes are transformed to class fragments, methods to method fragments, etc. The code, comments, etc. of the existing software is, in the latter case, automatically stored in slots of the created fragments.

The browser displays the available class-fragments in the fragment database. The user can then add these classes to the current project. More specifically, she creates views or *diagrams* that consist of certain design elements from the information in the fragment database. The diagram typically involves a view on a couple of classes, i.e. a selection of the (class) methods and attributes of a class, together with the relations among these classes, i.e. the inheritance or association/aggregation relations. Other relations/design elements stored in the fragment database can currently not be displayed. Each diagram can be displayed as an OMT object diagram (as depicted in figure 9), but one can also annotate a diagram with comments.

The main window of the OMT-tool serves as a starting point for launching other tools most of which are similar to (and in fact fragment-using derivations of) regular Smalltalk tools. For example, one can invoke a normal class browser on a class, showing the methods and attributes defined for a class. Obviously, one can there also add, remove and change these definitions. The OMT-tool also defines a suite of transformations to restructure and extends the program on a design level. These operations are called *refactorings*, and provide services like inserting a class in a hierarchy or moving method or attribute definitions across a hierarchy [Opdyke92]. Put together, these tools/operations provide enough support to edit the program under development on both code and design-level.

As a final point we consider the role of design patterns in the OMT-tool. As indicated in figure 9, a separate list of pattern occurrences in the current project is displayed in the main window. All these pattern occurrences are marked with a particular color. The other tools[7] annotate the program elements they display with markers in these colors if the program elements plays a role in a pattern. In this way, the developer can easily see which program elements were introduced as a consequence of applying a particular pattern. To find out which role a particular element plays, the user can pop-up an OMT-view of the pattern prototype in a separate window. After selecting the program element considered, the corresponding element in the pattern -view is highlighted.

Obviously the OMT-tool also supports instantiating patterns, using the fragment level implementation. Bottom-up definition is supported by adding a fragment structure for the pattern, and then using the OMT views of the pattern and the design to rebind the roles. In doing so, the user can check at any time whether all roles are already bound or not.

---

[7] Currently, this is only supported in the OMT view of the main OMT-tool window

# 6. Conclusions

This paper has described a prototype OO design environment that supports working with design patterns. The tool has been implemented in Visualworks Smalltalk. The implementation incorporates all the functionality described in the previous section. The system currently holds around 12 of the patterns defined in [Gamma95] and includes invariant-definitions for some of these. We are adding more pattern definitions as work continues and the need for them arises (e.g. in reorganizing an existing application).

Though we are still in the early stages, the experiences gained so far are quite good. The representation that was chosen (i.e. the fragment model) makes it easy to represent arbitrary program structures and design elements, including those that go beyond the regular OO constructs. It also means that we could handle patterns that incorporate less conventional design elements, such as fault-tolerance indications or timing constraints.

Until now we haven't encountered patterns that could not be represented in the system. However, most benefits occur when the structure of the pattern is the most prominent part, as is the case with patterns like Observer or Abstract Factory. In principle, this could also hold for patterns in which the behavior of methods is a key point (e.g. delegation). However this requires that the "code" of methods is represented as fragments. Experiments with this have not yet been done.

For patterns that focus more on methodical advice, such as Bridge, Mediator or - to some extent - Composite, support is inherently less advanced. For example, in a Composite pattern instance, a key issue is whether methods defined for item types are to be pushed-up to the level of the abstract base class for all item types. Such a decision cannot be made automatically. Only if the designer adds the method on the abstract base class, the system can - by validating and repairing constraints - add the necessary method fragments to all derived classes.

The prototype approach to represent and instantiate patterns works quite well in practice. Allowing design variations based on an initially consistent structure together with validation and (semi-) automatic repair seems a natural metaphor when designing/developing object-oriented programs. Obviously, capturing the "essence" of a pattern in an invariant requires is not always straightforward, and can be subject to discussion. Here too, the choice for a flexible system has its benefits. It is easy to represent multiple versions of the same pattern that differ only in the invariants. One could even adapt the invariants for a particular pattern occurrence.

Some of the metaphors used in the OMT-tool are appealing. Especially the ability to view which design elements are part of a particular pattern proved to be very useful when redocumenting the existing system.

The tool upto now has been mainly used in backwards engineering, i.e. to find patterns and reorganize a WWW-browser written in Smalltalk. This program with supporting software (after reorganization) involves around 150 classes stored in the fragment database. During reorganization several more or less obvious pattern occurrences were detected and documented (and subsequently made more explicit through refactorings) such as State, Builder, Memento and Bridge. See [Winsen96] for more details on this work.

This experience has made us somewhat skeptical about the possibility to automatically detect predefined patterns in existing software. Pattern occurrences were often "degenerated" in that many conceptual roles did not exist as distinct program elements, but were cluttered onto a few, more complex ones. For example, the idea of abstract coupling found in many design patterns was not encountered often, especially not if only one concrete sub-class existed. In such cases, the roles were collapsed into single concrete class. In some cases, the use of (Smalltalk) language-specific techniques obscured the existence of a pattern. A good example of this was a State pattern occurrence in which the state dependent behaviour was not defined in separate classes (one for each state) but in the original class itself, by using method names for the state sensitive operations that were prepended with the name of the state. So, instead of delegating the operation "display" to a state-object by an expression like "self currentState open" the code for the methods looked like this:

```
self perform: (currentStateString, "open")
```

Automatically recognizing a real State pattern from such a case appears difficult.

A different question is whether *new* patterns could be detected in a large body of software, e.g. by looking for similarities in fragment structures of a large body of software. We have not investigated this issue yet, though it seems technically viable. Whether such an experiment would provide interesting results remains to be seen. A priori, a serious problem is that original intentions of the designer are not fully represented in program code. It would seem that the interesting design patterns thus also cannot be seen. Recovering these intentions is the human part of any re-engineering effort.

**Open issues**

The current environment, addresses most, but not all of our design requirements. Currently we are working on some extensions/new issues:

- The support for visualization of design elements in the OMT-tool should be extended. Especially non-conventional design elements (creation relation, etc.) should be represented. As a special case of this, we will consider a visualization of a program purely in terms of pattern instances.

- It is necessary to derive more design information from programs loaded into the system (e.g. associations, creation relations, etc.). Currently, we only show the information that can directly be derived from Smalltalk code without any analysis. Applying the environment for statically typed languages like C++ or Java will make gathering of this kind of information easier.

- More aspects of the program should be represented as fragments. In particular we are considering the "fragmentation" of method code, so that we can distinguish fragments like message-sends or instance creation. This opens the possibility to do behavioral conformance checking in pattern validation, i.e. the checking of causal obligations as defined in [Helm90]. Also, we can then annotate parts of the code with indications that it plays a role in a particular pattern

- A related, but as yet unresolved, issue is to see how we could make the use of the environment less language dependent or even language independent. The general idea is to map a design with patterns automatically to constructs in a particular programming language. More in general, we would like to see how one pattern description could be mapped to multiple object models. The approach we are currently considering is to create a description of a language in relevant programming constructs (inheritance model, access control mechanisms, static vs. dynamic typing information, etc.) and to explore what a mapping function could look like. Specifying parameters that generate implementations as is done in [Budinsky96] will be considered.

- We are also studying "high-level" design refactorings that are based on certain design patterns. Basically, these operations transform the existing design by introducing and integrating a particular design pattern. To illustrate the idea: the designer identifies a particular class and indicates that he wants to have a proxy for it. The system then should instantiate the proxy pattern (with the hierarchy involved), derive the interface methods for the base class and generate the basic delegation code in the proxy.

# References

[Gamma95] E. Gamma et.al., Design Patterns - Elements of Reusable Object-Oriented Software, Addison Wesley, 1995

[Buschmann96] F. Buschmann, et. al. Pattern-Oriented Software Architecture - A System of Patterns, Wiley and Sons Ltd., 1996.

[Helm90] Richard Helm, Ian M. Holland and Dipayan Gangopadhyay, ``Contracts: Specifying Behavioral Compositions in Object-Oriented Systems,'' pp.169-180 in Proceedings of the 1990 OOPSLA/ECOOP Conference, ed. Norman Meyrowitz (October 1990).

[Kim96] Jung. J. Kim and Kevin M. Benner, "An Experience Using Design Patterns: Lessons Learned and Tool Support", Theory and Practice of Object Systems, Vol. 2, No. 1, 1996, pp. 61-74.

[Budinsky96] F.J. Budinsky et.al., "Automatic code generation from design patterns", IBM Systems Journal, Vol 35, No. 2, 1996.

[Meijers96] Marco Meijers, Tool Support for Object-Oriented Design Patterns, Master's Thesis, Utrecht University, CS Dept, INF-SCR-96-28, August 1996.

[Winsen96] Pieter van Winsen, (Re)engineering with Object-Oriented Design Patterns, Master's Thesis, Utrecht University, CS Dept, INF-SCR-96-43, November1996.

[Opdyke92] William F. Opdyke, Refactoring object-oriented frameworks, University of Illinois, Urbana Champaign, 1992.

# A Model for Structuring User Documentation of Object-Oriented Frameworks Using Patterns and Hypertext

Matthias Meusel, Krzysztof Czarnecki, and Wolfgang Köpf
Daimler-Benz AG
Research and Technology
Ulm, Germany
E-mail: m.meusel@str.daimler-benz.com
{czarnecki, koepf}@dbag.ulm.DaimlerBenz.com

**Abstract.** Adequate documentation of an object-oriented framework is the prerequisite to its success as a reusable component. The overall design of a framework and its intended method of reuse are not obvious from the source code and thus have to be addressed in the documentation. Most importantly, the documentation of a framework has to be structured in such a way that it guarantees the adequate support of three major audiences: users selecting a framework, users learning to develop typical applications based on the selected framework, and users intending to modify its architecture.

This paper presents a model for structuring the documentation of an object-oriented framework. The model integrates existing approaches such as patterns, hypertext, program-understanding tools, and formal approaches into a single structure that is geared towards supporting the three audiences. The model will be illustrated using HotDraw, a Smalltalk framework for drawing editors, as an example. We also give a preliminary evaluation of the model.

## 1 Introduction

Object-oriented frameworks are reusable designs that leverage simple code reuse. One of the advantages of frameworks is the high degree of adaptability that is achievable through specialization. Unfortunately, experience has shown that both the development of a framework and its specialization are difficult. Specialization of a framework is difficult since it usually requires the modification of the framework (e.g. through subclassing), and this kind of reuse presupposes detailed knowledge of its design. We refer to this as the *framework understanding problem*. On the other hand, frameworks represent a state-of-the-art technology which can be used to develop components for easy bottom-up integration (e.g. [Tra95]). Such components are more self-contained than framework classes and avoid framework usability problems—yet often at the cost of lower adaptability.

The overall design of a framework and its intended method of reuse are not obvious from the source code. For this reason, adequate framework documentation is a necessary prerequisite to successful framework reuse. The biggest challenge, however, to documenting a framework is that it must support users with varying backgrounds and different levels of experience in using the framework. We observed this problem with the documentation of in-house frameworks developed at Daimler-Benz. The need for adequate documentation is even more urgent if the frameworks are intended to be reused as standard components throughout the corporation. In this context, a framework has to be viewed as a product.

This paper presents a model for documenting object-oriented frameworks that was developed to address the needs of adequate documentation of standard frameworks within the corporation. The model integrates existing approaches such as patterns [Joh92], hypertext, program understanding tools, and formal approaches into a single structure which is geared towards supporting different types of users. We also give a preliminary evaluation based on a case study that used this model to document Hot-Draw [Bra95], a moderately-sized Smalltalk framework.

This paper is organized as follows: Section 2 defines the requirements for user documentation of object-oriented frameworks. Section 3 introduces "the pyramid principle", a text structuring approach which our model is based on. The documentation model is presented in Section 4. Section 5 lists the related work, and Section 6 reports on some preliminary evaluation of the model and indicates directions for future research.

## 2 Requirements for User Documentation of Object-Oriented Frameworks

The general problem of *program understanding* is defined as the process of developing a mental model of a software system's intended architecture, meaning, and behavior [Mül96]. Methods to support program understanding include *documentation* as well as *program understanding* and *reverse engineering tools* such as static and dynamic analyzers, browsing and visualization tools that extract knowledge directly from the actual system.

*User documentation* is the type of documentation that is packaged with the final product. Some information for user documentation is extracted from the *development documentation* which is maintained throughout the project. But as a rule, user documentation has a different focus than development documentation. Development documentation records all the information pertinent to the developed product and its development process. User documentation, on the other hand, should contain only the information that enables the user to make the best use of the final product. Therefore, user documentation requires special effort to assure its value to the end-user.

According to [SAN88] (see also [AS90]), documentation adequacy is constituted by its *accuracy, completeness, usability*, and *expandability*. In the context of structuring user documentation, we are chiefly interested in usability. This can be further divided into *logical traceability* and *understandability*:

- **Logical traceability** is defined as the ability to follow the logical train of thought in the documentation through all of the pertinent parts, regardless of whether the parts are contiguous or not [SAN88]. A user must be able to find everything he needs, making adequate *search facilities* and *references* an absolute necessity.

- **Understandability** (also known as *Comprehensibility* or *Logical Readability*) is defined as the ease with which the documentation can be comprehended [SAN88]. User documentation is written for people. For this reason, the available knowledge of the process by which people construct mental models of the world has to be taken into account when structuring documentation. This knowledge includes issues such as the way people organize objects and the typical capability of short-term memory. In terms of text structuring, factors influencing understandability include *modularity, conciseness*, and *redundancy appropriateness* (i.e. when to repeat an item of information and when to use a reference). Appropriate writing style, term consistency, and physical readability (i.e. format, print, etc.) are also important but are not considered in this paper.

The adequacy of documentation has to be evaluated in the context of its user and his goals. In particular, user documentation has to be structured so that it is useful to users with different levels of experience in using the software. Johnson differentiates among three types of audiences which the documentation of a framework needs to address [Joh94]:

1. **users deciding which framework to use:** These users should be able to quickly asses the scope of the framework and to tell if the framework is adequate for the application to be built. No information on how to use the framework is needed. Quick and accurate evaluation can prevent unnecessary costs.

2. **users wanting to build a typical application:** This audience needs to learn how to use the framework in order to develop a standard application. This involves customizing the appropriate "hot spots" [Pre95] by configuring concrete classes, filling in contracts by implementing abstract methods, etc. The amount of reading that is required for the user to be able to build simple applications has to be minimized.

3. **users wanting to go beyond the typical use:** These users intend to add new components and features, modify the architecture, etc. They need the detailed descriptions of the framework design and the algorithms. This type of documentation has to explicitly include the design assumptions underlying the framework architecture. This type of user needs to be able to find very specific information quickly.

## 3 Pyramid Principle

As already stated, the way people build mental models of the world needs to be taken into account when structuring documentation. In fact, this requirement applies to any document whose purpose is to communicate something useful to the reader. An ex-

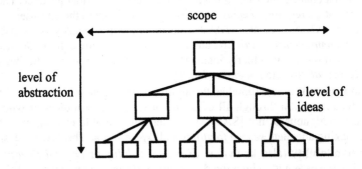

**Fig. 1.** Pyramid structure of a document

ample of a document-structuring approach that follows this requirement is the *pyramid principle* [Min91]. This approach has been developed primarily for structuring business documents. It is based on the concept that any grouping of ideas is easier to comprehend if this grouping is pre-sorted into a logical, top-down structure. This structure reassembles a pyramid with a main idea at the top and the remaining ideas arranged into levels (see Figure 1). Each idea in the pyramid raises questions that are then answered at the lower level. The relationships between statements across two levels are called vertical relationships, whereas the relationships within one level are horizontal relationships. The latter can be further divided into deductive or inductive relationships.

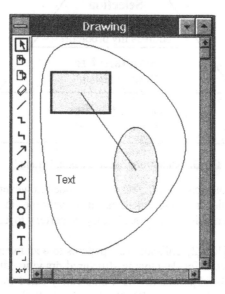

**Fig. 2.** Sample HotDraw application

The pyramid shape corresponds to the bottom-up abstraction process, i.e., to the process of clustering ideas to come up with more general ideas, which is typical for any development and discovery process. However, the presentation of ideas should always proceed in a top-down fashion since it focuses the reader's attention. Presenting an idea will create questions in his mind that have to be answered at the lower level. This process should be similar to carrying on a conversation.

The shape of the pyramid is determined by "The Magical Number Seven Plus or Minus Two". This famous number, introduced by Miller, indicates the typical number of things that a person can store in his or her short-term memory [Mil67]. If more than seven ideas at one level support an idea at the higher level, then it will most probably become necessary to insert a new level grouping the supporting ideas into logical classes between the other two levels.

The concept of abstraction represents the way people think and lies at the heart of hierarchical software [Par72]. Documentation needs to be structured in the same modular and hierarchical way.

## 4 Model of User Documentation for Object-Oriented Frameworks

Our model of framework documentation is based on the pyramid principle. In fact, every documentation has this structure whereby the structuring units are usually

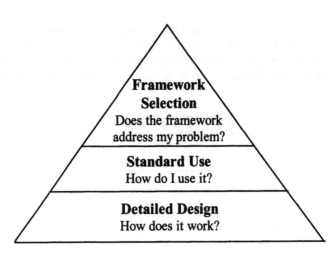

**Fig. 3.** Framework Documentation Pyramid

books, chapters, sections, paragraphs, etc. In our model, however, the ideas within the documentation pyramid are represented, as far as possible, in the form of patterns [GHJV95]. The pyramid is implemented using hypertext to capture the references between patterns.

In his seminal paper [Joh92], Johnson used patterns to document HotDraw. HotDraw is a Smalltalk framework for developing structured drawing editors, such as the one shown in Figure 2 [Bra95]. HotDraw is a moderately sized framework. The implementation of HotDraw described in [Bra95] has about 90 classes. We decided to use HotDraw as a case study for our documentation model, as it is an extremely useful framework, and it is not difficult to find users who would like to use HotDraw. Our hope was to receive feedback on the documentation from a variety of users.

In our model, the documentation pyramid has three main levels that correspond to the three different audiences defined in Section 2. At the top of the pyramid, there is the *Framework Selection Level* that addresses the scope of the framework using a *catalog pattern* (see Figure 3). The transition from top level to the *Standard Usage Level* is initiated by the question: *How do I use the framework?* The Standard Usage Level uses a system of *application patterns* to answer this question. Finally, the question *How does the framework work?* is addressed at the *Detailed Design Level*.

We will now discuss the three documentation levels using the HotDraw documentation as an example.

## 4.1 Framework Selection: Catalog Pattern

The *catalog pattern* is a concise, structured description indicating the framework's name, type, its application domain, main features, scope (illustrated by citing examples of typical applications), the main ideas behind its design, and related frameworks. The catalog pattern, as any pattern, has a problem-solution format and can be used as an entry in a component repository. In fact, its structure reassembles the structure of so-called design records [Tra95] that are used to describe components in a repository. Figure 4 shows the structure of the catalog pattern for the HotDraw example. Our hypertext implementation uses HTML frames to present the structure of a pattern and the selected section at the same time (as in Figure 8). A more elaborate format for catalog patterns can be found in [SW96].

| Framework name | HotDraw |
|---|---|
| Type | application framework, white-box with some black-box elements <br> *<other possible entries are* support framework *or* framework toolkit*>* |
| Keywords | object-oriented semantic-based graphic editor, diagrams, drawings, Smalltalk, white-box framework |
| Problem description | *<short description of the application domain>* |
| Solution | *<main features and design concepts of the framework>* |
| Examples | net editors, diagram editors, drawing editors, two-dimensional object visualization *<list of typical applications>* |
| Documentation | *<short description of the parts of documentation, possible and suggested entry points for reading>* |
| Other frameworks | SmallDraw, UniDraw for C++ |

**Fig. 4.** Catalog pattern for HotDraw

When documenting a framework toolkit, i.e., a set of related frameworks, it is necessary to create at least two levels of catalog patterns. For example, the ACE toolkit [Sch96] is a framework toolkit consisting of a number of support frameworks for distributed systems. The Framework Selection Level for ACE would consist of one main ACE catalog pattern and a number of other catalog patterns, each describing one of the ACE frameworks. As a general rule, depending on the complexity of the software which is documented, any of the three main pyramid levels can contain multiple sublevels.

## 4.2 Standard Usage: Application Patterns

Patterns have been proposed as a documentation technique which minimizes the amount of reading in order to solve a problem [Joh92]. The pattern approach to documentation corresponds to a cookbook and cookbooks have been successfully used to document e.g. MacApp [App] or VisualWorks [PPD]. We refer to patterns for documenting frameworks as *application patterns* as opposed to e.g. design patterns [GHJV95], since they describe how a framework is used to develop a typical application and not how the framework was developed. Application patterns are basically cookbook recipes with a certain standard format, and co-relationships. A system of application patterns describes the *standard application design space* of a framework. This design space can be thought of as determined by the framework's "hot spots" [Pre95].

There are many different pattern formats that usually depend on their area of application (e.g. design, architecture, system analysis, programming, planning and management, etc.; some example formats can be found in [CS95]). The format we used for the HotDraw application patterns is shown in Figure 5.

| Application Pattern 1: Creating a Semantic Graphic Editor | |
|---|---|
| **Context** | HotDraw is a framework for structured, two-dimensional drawing editors. The elements of the drawing can have constraints between them, they can react to user commands, and they can be animated. The editors can be the complete application, or they can be embedded into a larger application. |
| **Problem** | How can a drawing editor be created using HotDraw? |
| **Solution Flowchart** | **Explanations** |

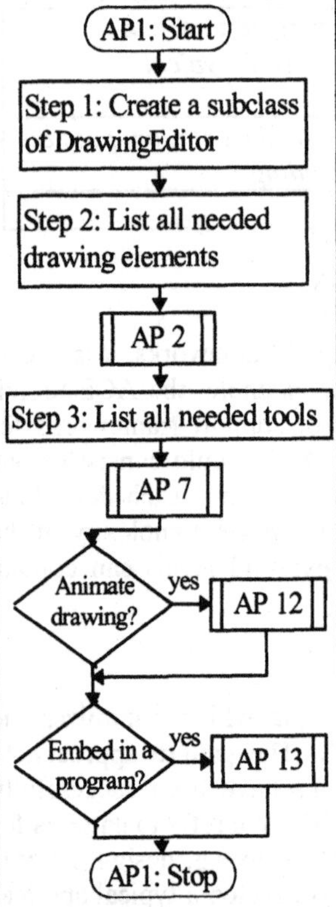

**Step 1:**
HotDraw provides DrawingEditor as a standard superclass for all drawing editors. You will need to create a subclass of DrawingEditor to represent your editor, e.g.:

```
DrawingEditor subclass: #MyDrawingEditor
        instanceVariableNames: ''
        classVariableNames: ''
        poolDictionaries: ''
        category: 'MyCategory'
```

**Step 2:**
Each drawing consists of a number of drawing elements, such as lines, circles, and rectangles. You will need to create a list of drawing elements that are needed for your problem. Use <u>Application Pattern 2</u> to define the needed drawing elements.

**Step 3:**
Tools are used to create and manipulate drawing elements. They are located on the tool palette. You will need to create a list of tools that are needed for your problem. Use <u>Application Pattern 7</u> to define the needed tools.

**Decision 1:**
If you need to animate your drawing, refer to <u>Application Pattern 12</u>.

**Decision 2:**
If you need to embed your drawing in other program, refer to <u>Application Pattern 13</u>.

| **Examples** (references to concrete implementation steps) | <u>PERTChart</u> <u>DrawingInspector</u> |
|---|---|
| **Design Information** | <u>HotDraw Architecture</u> |

**Fig. 5.** Example of an application pattern

Each application pattern has a flowchart presenting the steps for solving the problem. Conditional decisions can be annotated with forces, i.e. factors that the framework user has to consider when deciding which branch to follow. Some steps in the flowchart are local to the application pattern, e.g. Step 1 in Application Pattern 1 (Figure 5). The explanations of the local steps may include diverse diagrams, e.g. class or interaction diagrams. Other steps represent "calls" to other application patterns, e.g. AP2. The boxes representing such steps can be hyperlinked to the corresponding application patterns. The complete "calling structure" for the HotDraw application patterns is shown in Figure 6. The pattern names were left largely unchanged compared to the original names in [Joh92]. Six patterns, however, had to be added and the bodies of the original patterns had to be updated to adequately represent the new HotDraw design as described in [Bra95].

Application Pattern 1 (AP1) is the initial pattern (see Figure 5 and Figure 6). The

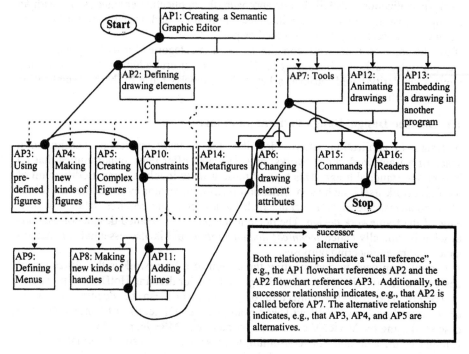

**Fig. 6.** System of application patterns for HotDraw and tutorial trail for PERTChart

original set of patterns in [Joh92] also had an initial pattern; however, we split it into the catalog pattern and the new initial pattern AP1, so that AP1 contains only the top level steps for creating a drawing editor.

Each application pattern references a concrete implementation step which is part of a tutorial covering the implementation of a complete application. A sample application for HotDraw is PERTChart. PERTChart is a simple editor for nets representing real time events and timing relationships between them (see [Bra95]). The PERTChart editor can be developed by applying twelve HotDraw patterns. The implementation steps for the PERTChart example are shown as a trail traversing the application patterns in Figure 6. A framework documentation may require more then one tutorial, so that each application pattern references at least one concrete implementation step.

Ideally, the examples can be run out of the tutorial. A configuration management system, such as Envy [OTIa], can also be used to store each implementation step as a new version of the sample application. This way, one can browse through the source code of the application whose degree of completion corresponds to the currently viewed implementation step. We used a simple HTML server running in the Smalltalk environment in order to to invoke class browsers and other Smalltalk applications by clicking on a hyperlink in a HTML browser.

Tools for visualization of the examples, such as in [LN95], could be used at this level. In fact, so called *exemplars* have been proposed as a top-down approach to framework specialization [GM95]. In this approach, the application engineer starts with an exemplar that is similar to the intended application and visually customizes the framework by selecting classes for the hotspots.

If the documented framework contains large class categories for its hotspots, a class retrieval tool, such as ClassExpert [CHEK96], is a useful addition. ClassExpert deploys a similarity-based retrieval schema that supports reuse by both specialization and modification.

## 4.3 Detailed Design: Design Patterns and More

A system of application patterns describes the standard application configuration space of a framework. Frameworks, however, also offer reuse opportunities that go beyond the standard usage. This type of reuse usually involves some modification of the framework itself, such as modification of its architecture by including new kinds of components, altering some standard behavior, etc., and requires detailed knowledge of the framework design. The documentation of the detailed design corresponds to what is typically called *technical documentation* and is also essential for maintenance and re-engineering purposes.

A possible approach to documenting the design of a framework is the utilization of design patterns [GHJV95]. A set of design patterns for deriving HotDraw is presented in [BJ94]. The overall architecture of a framework can be documented using *architectural patterns* [BMR+96]. For example, the architecture of HotDraw is best described using the Model-View-Controller pattern [BMR+96, p. 125].

It might be difficult and time-consuming to present all the design information in the form of patterns. Therefore, some of the information could be presented simply as a set of related design documents that describe some selected topics (similar to the online help of Visual C++).

The design documentation has links to a class reference guide that describes the interfaces of framework classes. If class interfaces are properly commented, a complete class reference guide can be automatically generated from the source code. This approach is based on the idea of *literate programming* (see [Knu92]). In fact, commercial tools which generate HTML from Smalltalk code, for example, are available (e.g. Envy/QA [OTIb]), and some environments (e.g. Smalltalk/X [STX] ) generate such interface descriptions dynamically, thereby keeping the documentation synchronized with the environment.

As Johnson suggested, formal approaches are most appropriate at the detailed design documentation level. Examples of formal approaches for documenting frameworks include *contracts* [HHG90], *structural relationships* [PPSS95], and *ObjChart*

[GM95]. Such approaches could support the automatic verification that certain architectural assumptions are not violated by the client code. Another useful approach to combat this problem is *reuse contracts* [SLMD96].

Since the framework documentation can achieve only a limited degree of detail, program understanding and reverse engineering tools which extract design knowledge directly from the source code are extremely useful at this documentation level. Such tools include class and instance browsers, cross reference tools, debuggers, interaction diagrammers (e.g. [KM96]), method invocation coverage tools, path coverage tools, slicing tools (e.g. [TCFR96]), etc. These tools can also be hyperlinked with the documentation.

## 4.4 Overall Structure

The overall structure of the framework documentation is shown in Figure 7. The Framework Selection level contains a catalog pattern. The Standard Use Level consists of an application pattern system and tutorials (there are two tutorials in Figure 7). The Detailed Design Level contains a set of design patterns and design articles. The documentation should be supplemented with a glossary of domain concepts. Examples of domain concepts for HotDraw are *drawing elements* and *constraints*.

The list of contents on the initial page of the documentation should include the entry points indicated in Figure 7. These entry points are appropriate for a systematic topdown strategy to program understanding. To support other strategies, such as opportunistic strategy or iterative hypotheses refinement [TPS96], a search engine has to be provided. A search engine could also dynamically synthesize documentation pages that match certain user profiles in response to a query.

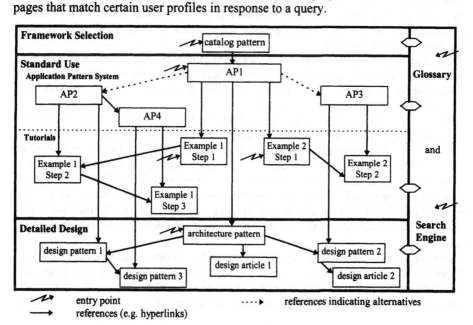

**Fig. 7.** Overall structure

In the foreseeable future there will be the need for a hard copy, therefore an appropriate facility for flattening of the hypertext for hard copy is required. The pyramid structure of the documentation guarantees its printability as a sequential document. Hyperlinks can be replaced by text references.

It is important to note that the completeness of the information in the lower parts of the pyramid can quickly lead to a "scope explosion". In order to adequately support the typical end-user, it is essential to adhere to the systematic, pyramid structure at the Framework Selection Level, Standard Usage Level, and in the upper part of the Detailed Design Level. This goal is achievable since the scope of the pyramid at these levels is still manageable. In large pyramids, the details in the lower parts of the Detailed Design Level are usually best accessed through a search engine.

# 5 Related Work

Johnson used patterns to document the standard use of HotDraw [Joh92], and Beck and Johnson used design patterns to document the design of HotDraw [BJ94]. Our work builds on both approaches and integrates them into a single model using hypertext. Our model distinguishes clearly between three documentation levels and defines the vocabulary for the documentation elements.

In [SW96], Silva and Werner propose patterns and hypermedia for packaging reusable components. The patterns described in their paper correspond to the catalog patterns in our model and are implemented using ToolBook, a hypermedia toolkit.

The types of documents that are usually packaged with object-oriented libraries or frameworks (such as VisualWorks) include the user's guide, cookbook, tutorials, technical documentation, and class reference guide. Our model contains all of these document types except for the user's guide, the contents of which are distributed over the three documentation levels.

The framework documentation techniques presented in [CI93] include documenting the class hierarchy, protocols, control flow, synchronization, entity relationships, and configuration constraints of the framework. These techniques can be classified into the Detailed Design Level of our model.

Probably the most ambitious approach to documenting frameworks are active cookbooks [PPSS95]. In the active cookbook approach, implementing steps are carried out automatically. This approach is complementary to our model. In fact, as indicated in the following section, active guidance and some bookkeeping functionality in the framework documentation system are desirable. However, the application of expert system technology to the documentation problem certainly needs more research. Our prototypical HTML implementation of the documentation model for HotDraw demonstrates the practicality of the model that is ready for pilot trials in industrial projects.

There has been a considerable amount of research on class retrieval techniques (see [CHEK96]). Such approaches clearly do not solve the framework understanding problem; yet, as indicated in Section 4.2, they are a useful addition to the documentation of a framework that contains very large class categories.

## 6 Discussion and Future Work

A complete evaluation of our documentation structuring model requires an elaborate empirical evaluation in an industrial environment that would enable a statistically valid conclusion to be drawn. Such an evaluation was beyond the scope of our project. Nevertheless, we have distributed our HotDraw documentation (in German) over the World Wide Web (see Figure 8).[1] A variety of users have viewed and used this documentation. Their subjective evaluation was basically positive even though there were some reports of problems.

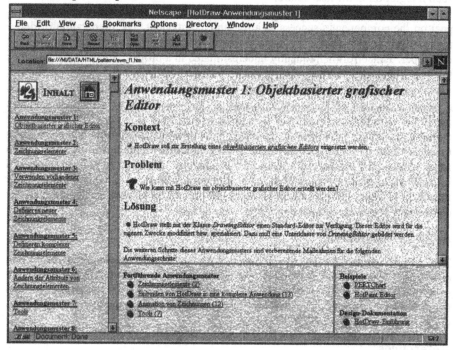

**Fig. 8.** Application Pattern 1 viewed in a HTML browser

Most of the users complained about the cognitive burden that results from keeping track of the path which was traversed through the system of application patterns while applying them. For example, after completing the step corresponding to the application pattern AP2 (in Figure 6), the user has to go back to the "calling" application pattern AP1 and resume at Step 3 (in Figure 5), which he has to remember. In order to solve this problem, a facility must be provided for keeping track of the executed steps. One possible scenario would be to let the user mark a step by clicking on an associated checkbox. The active cookbooks approach [PPSS95], however, seems to be a better solution.

---

[1] The HotDraw documentation is available in German at http://nero.prakinf.tu-ilmenau.de:80/
~czarn/doku.html.

We also learned that it is important for hypertext documents to be largely self-contained in order to minimize the need for jumping back and forth in the "hyperspace", although the required degree of self-containment depends on the user's background. Research on *adaptive hypertext* (e.g. [Bru96]) might provide an adequate solution to this redundancy appropriateness problem in the long term.

An area that we did not cover is the problem of integrating our model into the industrial software development cycle. As one of the authors is currently involved in an industrial project to document a framework, we hope to derive the requirements for such integration in the near future.

Documentation affects the overall quality of a component and has a substantial impact on the component's success as a reusable component. The preparation of documents requires enormous effort which is often viewed as a burden, especially by the developer. This effort is frequently underestimated in a project. Some information for the user documentation (especially for the technical part) can be extracted from development documentation, although user documentation has a different focus than the development documentation. For this reason, our position is that user documentation has to be written by a documentation expert. At the heart of component-based development lies the principle that developing the components costs more than assembling them, so that the extra cost for documenting reusable components pays off in the reuse part of the software life cycle. Unfortunately, in many cases, we observed a lack of willingness to invest this extra amount of effort in documenting in-house frameworks. This situation manifests some cultural problems that are symptomatic of component-based development in large corporations.

## Acknowledgments

The authors would like to express their thanks to Ralph Johnson, John Brant, and others for making HotDraw publicly available over the Internet and thus providing an extremely useful tool as well as a case study for the research community. We also thank Frances Paulisch and Ulrich Eisenecker for providing us with valuable comments on an earlier version of this paper.

## References

[App]       Apple Computer. *MacApp Programmer's Guide*. 1986

[AS90]      J.D. Arthur and K.T. Stevens. Document Quality Indicators: A Framework for Assessing Document Adequacy. Technical Report, No. TR90-60, Virginia Polytechnic Institute and State University, Blacksburg, VA, USA, 1990

[BJ94]      K. Beck and R. E. Johnson. Patterns Generate Architectures. In *Proceedings of the ECOOP'94*, Springer Verlag, Berlin, 1994, pages 139-149

[BMR+96]  F. Buschmann, R. Meunier, H. Rohnert, P. Sommerlad, and M. Stal. *Pattern-Oriented Software Architecture: A System of Patterns*. John Wiley & Sons, 1996

[Bra95]     J.M. Brant. HotDraw. Master's Thesis, University of Illinois at Urbana-Champaign, 1995. HotDraw is available at http://st-www.cs.uiuc.edu/users/brant/HotDraw/HotDraw.html

[Bru96]     P. Brusilovsky. Adaptive hypermedia, an attempt to analyze and gener-
            alize. In *Multimedia, Hypermedia, and Virtual Reality*, P. Brusilovsky, P.
            Kommers, and N. Streitz, Eds., vol. 1077, Springer-Verlag, Berlin, 1996,
            pages 288-304

[CHEK96]    K. Czarnecki, R. Hanselmann, U. W. Eisenecker, and W. Köpf.
            ClassExpert: A Knowledge-Based Assistant to Support Reuse by Spe-
            cialization and Modification in Smalltalk. In *Proceedings of the 4$^{th}$ In-
            ternational Conference on Software Reuse*, M. Sitamaran, ed., IEEE
            Comp. Soc. Press, 1996, pages 188-193

[CI93]      R.H. Campbell and N. Islam. A Technique for Documenting the Frame-
            work of an Object-Oriented System. In *Computing Systems*, vol. 6, no. 4,
            Fall 1993, pages 363-389

[CS95]      J. Coplien and D. Schmidt, eds. *Pattern Languages of Program Design.*
            Addison-Wesley, 1995

[GHJV95]    E. Gamma, R. Helm, R. Johnson, and J. Vlissides. *Design Patterns: Ele-
            ments of Reusable Object-Oriented Software.* Addison-Wesley, 1995

[GM95]      D. Gangopadhyay and S. Mitra. *Understanding Frameworks by Explo-
            ration of Exemplars.* In *Proceedings of the International Workshop on
            Computer-Aided Software Engineering (CASE'95),* 1995

[HHG90]     R. Helm, I.M. Holland, and D. Gangopadhyay. Contracts: specifying
            behavioral compositions in object-oriented systems. In *Proceedings of
            the OOPSLA/ECOOP'90,* SIGPLAN Notices, vol. 25, no. 10, 1990,
            pages 169-180

[Joh92]     R. E. Johnson. Documenting Frameworks using Patterns. In *Proceedings
            of the OOPSLA'92,* ACM SIGPLAN Notices, vol. 27, no. 10, October
            1992, pages 63-76

[Joh94]     R. E. Johnson. Documenting Frameworks. In Frameworks Digest, vol. 1,
            no. 13, Oct. 26, 1994, available at ftp://st.cs.uiuc.edu/pub/FWList/v1n13

[KM96]      K. Koskimies and H. Mössenböck. Scene: Using Scenario Diagrams and
            Active Text for Illustrating Object-Oriented Programs. In *Proceedings of
            the 18$^{th}$ Int. Conf. on Software Engineering*, IEEE Comp. Soc. Press,
            1996, pages 366-375

[Knu92]     D.E. Knuth. Literate Programming. Center for the Study of Language
            and Information, Stanford University, 1992

[LN95]      D.B. Lange and Y. Nakamura. Interactive Visualization of Design Pat-
            terns Can Help in Framework Understanding. In *Proceedings of the
            OOPSLA'95,* ACM SIGPLAN Notices vol. 30, no. 10, October 1995,
            pages 342-356

[Mil67]     G.A. Miller. The Magical Number Seven Plus or Minus Two. In *The
            Psychology of Communication: Seven Essays*, G.A. Miller, New York:
            Basic Books, 1967

[Min91]     B. Minto. *The Pyramid Principle. Part One: Logic in Writing.* Pitman
            Publishing., London, 1991. First published by Minto International Inc. in
            1987

[Mül96]     H. A. Müller, Understanding Software Systems Using Reverse Engi-
            neering Technologies: Research and Practice. Tutorial Notes, 18$^{th}$ Int.
            Conf. on Software Engineering, 1996, page 2-12

[OTIa]      Object Technology International Inc., *ENVY/Developer R3.01.* User Manual, 1995

[OTIb]      Object Technology International Inc., ENVY/QA, see at: http://www.oti.com/briefs/qa/qabrief.htm.

[Par72]     D.L. Parnas. On the Criteria To Be Used in Decomposing Systems into Modules. In *Communications of the ACM*, vol. 15, no. 12, December 1972, pages 1053-1058

[PPD]       Parplace-Digitalk, Inc. *VisualWorks Cookbook.* 1995

[PPSS95]    W. Pree, G. Promberger, A. Schappert, and P. Sommerlad. Active Guidance of Framework Development. In *Software—Concepts and Tools*, no. 16, 1995, pages 136-145

[Pre95]     W. Pree. *Design Patterns for Object-Oriented Software Development.* Addison-Wesley, 1995

[SAN88]     K.T. Stevens, J.D. Arthur, and R. E. Nance. A Taxonomy for the Evaluation of Computer Documentation. Technical Report, No. TR88-38, Virginia Polytechnic Institute and State University, Blacksburg, VA, USA, 1988

[Sch96]     D.C. Schmidt. The ADAPTIVE Communication Environment: An Object-Oriented Network Programming Toolkit for Developing Communication Software. Available at http://www.cs.wustl.edu/~schmidt/ACE.html

[SLMD96]    P. Steyaert, C Lucas, K Mens, and T. D'Hondt. Reuse Contracts: Managing the Evolution of Reusable Assets. In *Proceedings of the OOPSLA'96*, ACM SIGPLAN Notices, vol. 31, no. 10, October 1996, pages 268-285

[STX]       eXept Software AG, Smalltalk/X, see at: http://www.informatik.uni-stuttgart.de/stx/stx.html

[SW96]      M.F. da Silva and C.M.L. Werner. Packaging Reusable Components Using Patterns and Hypermedia. In *Proceedings of the 4th International Conference on Software Reuse*, M. Sitamaran, ed., IEEE Comp. Soc. Press, 1996, pages 146-155

[TCFR96]    F. Tip, J.-D. Choi, J. Field, G. Ramalingam. Slicing Class Hierarchies. In *Proceedings of the OOPSLA'96*, ACM SIGPLAN Notices, vol. 31, no. 10, October 1996, pages 179-197

[TPS96]     S.R. Tillay, S. Paul, and S. B. Smith. Towards a Framework for Program Understanding. In *Proceedings of the 4th Workshop on Program Comprehension*, A. Cimitile and H.A. Müller, eds., IEEE Comp. Soc. Press, 1996, pages 19-28

[Tra95]     W. Tracz. DSSA (Domain-Specific Software Architecture) Pedagogical Example. In *ACM SIGSOFT Software Engineering Notes*, vol. 20, no. 4, July 1995

# Using Patterns for Design and Documentation

Georg Odenthal and Klaus Quibeldey-Cirkel

Department of Electrical Engineering and Computer Science
University of Siegen, D-57068 Siegen, Germany
{odenthal I quibeldey}@ti.et-inf.uni-siegen.de

**Abstract:** The dovetailing of design and documentation is characteristic for many mature engineering disciplines. In electrical engineering, for example, a circuit diagram is a means and technique for both designing and documenting. Software engineering falls short in this respect, especially when it comes to *architectural* issues. Design patterns can help here. Using both *form* and *content* of design patterns promotes the principle of *documenting by designing*. Our experience report presents some examples of this principle taken from an evaluation project at SAP, Germany.

**Keywords:** object-oriented design patterns, pattern form, software documentation

**Overview:** In Section 1, we clarify what we mean by the principle of documenting by designing. In Section 2, we outline the aim of the evaluation project. We then generalize the steps of *instantiating* a pattern to solve a particular design problem and of *identifying* a pattern candidate in a given design to gain some flexibility. To demonstrate these pattern-related *activities*, we discuss two examples in more detail. Section 3 enlarges on documentation using patterns. We discuss the central role of hypertext and give two forms (templates): one for the documentation of pattern instances, and an extension for documenting frameworks. In Section 4, we summarize our experiences in using patterns for design and documentation contrasting them to experiences from literature. We conclude our report with some remarks on further research activities.

---

## 1 Introduction

Design patterns are generally welcome for their pragmatism:

- capture and reuse of design expertise and experience [1, 9, 10, 12, 13, 15],
- design and documentation of frameworks [3, 14, 16, 17, 22, 24],
- economy and clarity of expression [4, 27].

In this experience report, we stress the *dual* nature of the pattern approach: it is both *generative* and *descriptive*.[1] Kent Beck and Ralph Johnson give a reliable definition [3]:

> *Alexander's patterns are both a description of a recurring pattern of architectural elements and a rule for how and when to create that pattern. [...] We call patterns like Alexander's that describe when a pattern should be applied 'generative patterns'.*

---

[1] See the mailing discussion on "Generative vs. Descriptive Patterns" and "Designs Documented as Patterns?", the latter initiated by Robert S. Hanmer:
http://iamwww.unibe.ch/~fcglib/WWW/OnlineDoku/archive/DesignPatterns/1171.html

In ontological terms, the attribute *generative* refers to a pattern's *content*, that is the recurring thing itself (classes constituting a micro-architecture). In epistemological terms, *descriptive* refers to a pattern's *form*, that is the way we capture and articulate this thing (by formats like problem-context-forces-solution). It is the dual function of design patterns, the interplay between form and content, that we experienced worthwhile in the context of documenting software.

## 1.1 The Guiding Principle of "Documenting by Designing"

In mature engineering disciplines, the design of an artefact is dovetailed into its documentation, and vice versa. Architects and electrical engineers, for example, get a great deal of their product documents *in passing*, that is as a by-product of the design process. The main reason for this is that circuit diagrams or blueprints describe *material* artefacts, i.e. hardware such as buildings and circuits. Their structures can be easily made explicit as geometric models or schematic diagrams. The mode of designing the product is the mode of documenting it. On the other hand, software engineers have to struggle with *immaterial* constructs, i.e. data structures and algorithms. The *essence* of software complexity, as Frederick Brooks has coined it [6], lies in the mixture of data structures, algorithms, and function calls.

Although today's software engineers have far more expressive constructs at their disposal, such as inheritance and polymorphism, they still lack architectural constructs with clear semantics. *Categories* [5], *Subjects* [11], or *Clusters* [20] aim at grouping semantically linked classes. However, these terms are used notationally. They are of little value as architectural vehicles for they function only as *ad hoc* containers: What is put into them is at the will of the designer. It is this lack of architectural constructs that makes class libraries, and especially frameworks, so hard to design and difficult to comprehend and maintain (see Fig. 1).

Obviously, it was the deficit of conceptual structures beyond the boundary of individual classes that has initiated the search for an "Architecture Handbook" of software engineering; first articulated at OOPSLA '91. And it was the framework context, where design patterns were first identified for documentation purposes (see Erich Gamma's thesis [14]). The GoF ("Gang of Four") authors of the best-selling standard pattern text [15] have gained their expertise in the development and documentation of well-known frameworks (ET++, UniDraw, and InterViews). Design patterns are both a means and technique to design and document *micro-architectures* that can be easily identified and reused. By establishing a further level of abstraction, patterns can reduce the *accidental* complexity (again, in Brooks' terms) of system description. This has been regarded as a further indirection, and therefore as a disadvantage. With documentation, however, the advantages overwhelm. Documents are living products that should be allowed to evolve *together* with the iterative and incremental design cycle. Using patterns in both ways – generative and descriptive – promotes this principle of documenting by designing.

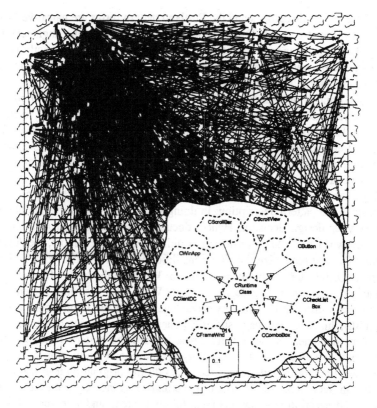

**Fig. 1.** In need of architectural information and guidance[2]

## 1.2 The Interplay between Form and Content

If we relate the pattern form to software documentation, we should be ready to give some pragmatic answers to "What constitutes *good* software documentation?" To sum up the literature [5, 20] and one's experiences [23], characteristic of good software documentation is a sound *mix* of formal and informal means of description: graphic versus textual notations; natural versus formal languages. As an empirical fact, most designers are reluctant to rigid formalisms of description. On the other hand, however, documenting a design in natural language has psychological constraints of its own – the "white paper" barrier, for example. Additionally, many designers associate bureaucratic activities with documenting. Moreover, for documentation in a natural language there is only little systematic CASE support; mostly restricted to fragmented and distributed annotations of individual design components. In contrast to traditional means of documentation (use cases, CRC cards, class diagrams), the pattern *form* as a natural prose style is systematic, disciplined, cohesive, and more comprehensible. Re-

---

[2] What is shown here resulted from reverse engineering the MFC framework into a Booch diagram. Zooming into this mass of classes does not reveal any architectural structure that could be easily recognized, or directly used for documentation.

garding prose style, Alexander's and the Portland pattern forms are narrative, while the GoF form is more structured. The latter seems to better reflect the engineer's writing mentality. Besides, documents structured in the GoF form can be directly supported by hypertext techniques and retrieval systems. In contrast to paper documents, a fine-grained and consistent information system is feasible.

Form and content of a pattern stimulate design and documentation *in concert*. Its content motivates documenting by its very nature: it helps the designer to reflect on his decision. Either by way of confirmation or by contrast, he will document his current design. Let us elaborate on this point: The GoF pattern form comprises more than a dozen sections such as Applicability, Consequences, and Implementation. In the process of instantiating a pattern of this form in your design, you will refer to the original pattern description. Documenting the resulting class structure, you will, *again*, refer to the pattern description. In doing so, you self-critically validate, justify, or dismiss your design decision. Hence, documenting your design *rationale* in the pattern form will make you reconsider its validity. Take, for example, the Applicability section: Do you recognize the situations described there? Does your design fit to the context? Or take the Consequences section: What are the trade-offs and results of instantiating the pattern in your design context? What aspects of your system structure does the pattern instance let you vary independently? Or the Implementation section: What pitfalls, hints, or language-specific issues should a maintenance programmer reading your document be aware of? Thus, besides the pattern form, the pattern's content, too, will help you produce the design documents. Finally, your growing experience in using a certain pattern will feed back to the original pattern itself (we will discuss this in Section 3.1 on the role of hypertext). It is the *dual* nature of a pattern – generative and descriptive – that lets form follow content, and vice versa. Documenting with the pattern form helps justify one's design rationale to oneself and to others, and might reveal design alternatives otherwise not taken into account.

### 1.3 Pattern Activities

How are design patterns related to the software development process? According to our approach of documenting by designing, we can differentiate and localize the following main activities of applying design patterns to the development cycle (Fig. 2):

- **Pattern Instantiation**. This is *standard* pattern practice: choosing a design pattern to *generate* parts of a design (a process driven by analysis efforts).

- **Pattern Candidate Identification**. This is *non-standard* pattern practice: locating a given class structure to insert a design pattern instance for *flexibility* reasons (a process initiated by design walkthroughs, code inspections, or changed requirements preparing the ground for a framework development).

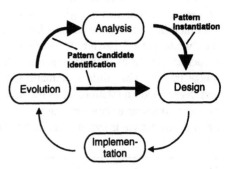

**Fig. 2.** Pattern-related activities

A third pattern activity, not argued in this report, is loosely related to design but closely related to documentation: Mature designs can be made more reusable and self-explaining by documenting the patterns used. The popular InterViews framework [19] for example, would be a worthwhile candidate for this activity of *reverse* documenting. It was designed with design patterns in mind[3], their use and the resulting pattern instances, however, have never been annotated in the documents (as far as we know). In the following section, we will discuss the first two activities in the context of non-trivial design examples.

## 2  Pattern-Oriented Design

In standard pattern texts, the authors unanimously point out that patterns alone do not constitute a design *method*. Patterns are (mental) *building blocks* that support the designer in certain phases of the software development cycle. They can, however, put some of the decision processes in a concrete form, which would otherwise remain vague and without guidance. In the following, we will demonstrate this guidance by examples. We emphasize the less typical pattern practice, i.e. pattern candidate identification. Additionally, we argue that reducing a pattern's original flexibility can be opportune in a particular design context.

### 2.1  The Evaluation Project

The aim of the project was to develop an object-oriented interface to interoperate between the SAP-R/3 Business Object Repository (BOR) and the Open Scripting Architecture (OSA) from Apple/IBM. OSA is comparable to Microsoft OLE Automation. The Business Object Repository is the managing unit for Business Objects, which are mainly used by the SAP Business Workflow. Business Objects allow an object-oriented access to and modification of R/3 data. With the Business Object Repository, a client can make up object types from data fields and ABAP functions (corresponding to the attributes and operations of a class). It was agreed from the beginning of the project to apply patterns of the GoF form for both design and documentation. Fig. 3 illustrates the components designed in the project. Two of them, i.e. "Storing Business Object Types" and "Process Control", will be taken as examples in Sections 2.3 and 2.4.

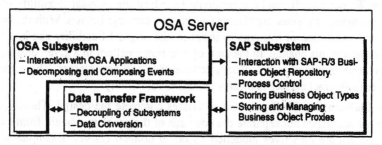

**Fig. 3.** Components of the OSA server

---

[3] This framework is often mentioned in the Known Uses section of the GoF form [15].

## 2.2  Steps for Instantiating and Identifying Patterns

In the previous section, we have differentiated between two main pattern activities: (1) designing with patterns and (2) making a design more flexible through patterns. The first one is standard practice, generally called "instantiating a pattern". The second one is *non*-standard practice that we call "identifying a pattern candidate" in a given class structure. Both activities can be divided into four major steps. While the first two steps refer to *decision-making problems*, the latter two refer to *structural changes*. Nota bene: The steps are not meant to represent a design method – our intent is to make the cognitive and technical processes of using patterns explicit.

**Step 1: Searching and Choosing.** The designer looks for a suitable design pattern in a pattern catalogue, or tries to identify a candidate for a pattern in a given design. Instantiating a pattern takes place in the initial phase of a design, while identifying a candidate follows first experiences with a prototype or working system. For example, some features of a design component have proved to be insufficient and shall be made more flexible by incorporating a pattern into the class structure. Both activities presuppose a thorough knowledge of patterns. The more patterns a designer knows, the more he will cover his design by instances of patterns; or in the case of a given design, the more likely he will find a pattern that matches a problem identified in the class structure. Generally, there will be several alternatives, so that the process of choosing or identifying implies a decision-making problem. The *Forces* section of a design pattern may function here as a first guidance.

**Step 2: Planning and Allocating.** The process of instantiating a pattern poses the following questions: What are the pattern's classes called in the problem domain? What additional responsibilities must be assigned to the pattern's classes? Generally, the assignment will be *complete* since there is no fixed design to be taken into account. In the case of identifying a pattern candidate, the questions are: Which roles do the given classes, operations, and attributes play in the pattern? Do they all play a role? In this case, the assignment will often be *incomplete* since some classes, operations, or attributes do not fit. This may lead to the question: Does the pattern really match at all? The problems encountered should not be solved in this step, just properly documented. The documentation of this planning stage will guide the next steps of structural changes.

**Step 3: Fitting.** Instantiating a design pattern might involve changes to its original structure. Sometimes, it can be appropriate to reduce the original flexibility of a pattern by changing or dismissing classes (we give an example below). With the help of a proper documentation of this pattern instance, the original flexibility can be restored, should requirements change. In the case of inserting a pattern in a given design, it will often be necessary to change a class' interface or to add new classes. These are likely the pattern's abstract classes that carry the desired flexibility.

**Step 4: Elaborating.** Finally, technical classes complete the design. They won't add any further semantics but separate the concerns of the problem domain from technical issues and coding directives modelled so far in domain classes. Examples are container classes like lists or sets from a class library. Additionally, an extension to a class' interface might be necessary, e.g. to add dynamic type checking. It is up to the designer to state the completion criteria.

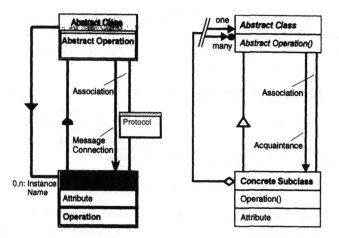

**Fig. 4.** Coad's notation used in *objectiF*® vs. OMT used in the GoF book

Some remarks on the graphic notations: We have used a mix of Coad's notation of class diagrams [11] and the OMT-based notation as used in the GoF book [15]. Handling different notations has two reasons:[4] First, the OMT notation of steps 1 and 2 is used to keep the original association of the GoF pattern alive. This facilitates communication among designers: both pattern and field experts are able to judge the design effort. Our extended OMT notation of step 2 also reflects the *interfacing* quality of the diagram. The concepts of both domains are annotated to the classes, separated by a colon (*pattern* concept : *field* concept). If an assignment is unclear or impossible, a question mark is annotated. Elements not used at all are crossed out. The diagrams of these steps can be freehand or drawn with the help of some semantic graphic editor. The second reason for using different notations is to make the transition from planning (steps 1 and 2) to developing (steps 3 and 4) explicitly clear. In the latter steps, a development tool with a notation of its own is involved (in our examples, this is Coad's notation as used in *objectiF*® V 1.1 from microTOOL, Berlin, see Fig. 4).

Annotating a pattern's instance is still an issue of debate. We have chosen the "Pattern:Role" labelling of Gamma assigning the pattern's name and its role names to the corresponding classes. A Venn diagram, however, is more suitable when the interplay between several instances of different patterns is to be illustrated (for a first impression, see Fig. 11). We argue against the current UML proposal (V.0.9) to annotate a design pattern as a Jacobson's Use Case, as this would lead to overloading both the term and the graphic design representation.

## 2.3 Example of Instantiating a Pattern: "Storing Business Object Types"

*Context*: The object type (class) of a SAP Business Object is defined and maintained in the Business Object Repository. The interface of such a class comprises a list of attributes and operations. An operation, on the other hand, comprises a list of parame-

---

[4] Admittedly, the pragmatic reason is sort of *willy-nilly*: At the time of the project, there were three different notations, i.e. of Booch, Coad, and Rumbaugh, spread over the CASE tools we had at our disposal.

ters. The *problem* is to develop a unit maintaining and storing the classes' interfaces. *Solution*: Regarding the hierarchical structure of the data, the *Composite* GoF pattern is a likely choice. An intuitive instantiation of the pattern is shown in Fig. 5; for the original GoF structure see Fig. 6, step 1.

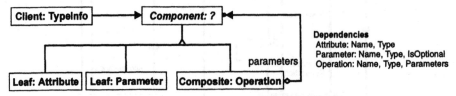

**Fig. 5.** A first try with the *Composite* pattern

*Forces*: Considering the dependencies of the context, we modified our first try (see step 2 of Fig. 6): a separation between attributes and parameters is not necessary. Being convinced that the *Composite* pattern will work, we transferred it into the design (step 3). Further adapting the structure of the pattern, we realized that we could do without a *Leaf* class at all. Hence, we changed the *Component* class from abstract to concrete. By that, we somehow reduced the original flexibility of the *Composite* pattern for reasons of simplicity. However, if requirements will change and we wish to restore the pattern to its full potential, we can simply achieve this by inserting *Leaf*

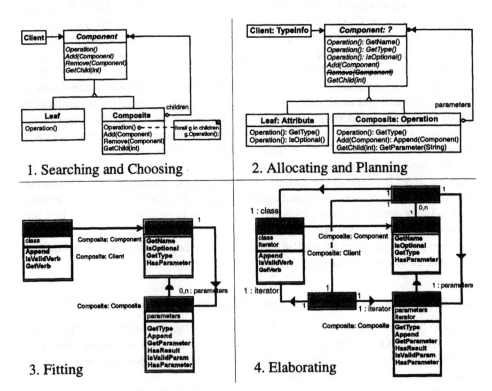

**Fig. 6.** Steps of instantiating the *Composite* pattern

classes. This presupposes, of course, that the pattern instance is clearly annotated and documented. Finally, the resulting design has to be elaborated upon to make it work. Thus, the technical task of storing parameters is delegated to class templates, i.e. *List* and *Iterator*, taken from a standard library (step 4).

## 2.4 Example of Identifying a Pattern Candidate: "Process Control"

Decoupling was an important goal in the development of the OSA server. The sub-systems to be designed for interacting with SAP R/3 and OSA were to be strictly separated from one another. The aim was to guarantee easy substitution of the interoperability interface. Decoupling was to be achieved for the flow of both data and control. In this example, we will concentrate on the control flow, i.e. the reaction to an OSA event. Fig. 7 (upper section) depicts the design fraction representing the general problem: How is the control flow maintained between the receiver of an event (OSA-Dispatch) and the class representing the BOR component of the SAP system? For an orientation, we bring the motives behind the requirements to the fore:

- Early feedback from rapid prototyping: decoupling of subsystems; process control between OSADispatch and BOR.
- A postponed requirement from analysis: The SAP subsystem represented by the BOR class is considered not to be changed. OSADispatch should be easily substitutable by another interoperability interface, e.g. OLE.
- An extension to prior requirements from analysis: one-to-many relationship between OSADispatch and BOR so that several SAP systems can be addressed simultaneously by a single OSA event.

In short, these requirements aim at improving the quality of the design by inserting additional *flexibility*. With this aim in mind, there are initially several design patterns at our disposal:

- *Facade* encapsulates a subsystem and defines a generalized interface to make the subsystem easier to handle.
- *Adapter* converts the interface of a class into something a client expects.
- *Chain of Responsibility* chains several receiving objects to one sending object. A request is passed along the chain of receivers until an object handles it.
- *Observer* defines a one-to-many dependency between a "Subject" and one or more "Observers" ensuring that all Observers are notified when the Subject changes state.

Choosing a pattern is the most important step as (a) all subsequent changes to the given design and (b) the quality of result will depend on it. To make a choice, the designer has to rely on his knowledge of design patterns and his understanding of the requirements of the problem. A deep understanding of a pattern's potential, its *essence*, can only be gained through practising the pattern several times. The lower section of Fig. 7 represents the essence of the *Observer* pattern:

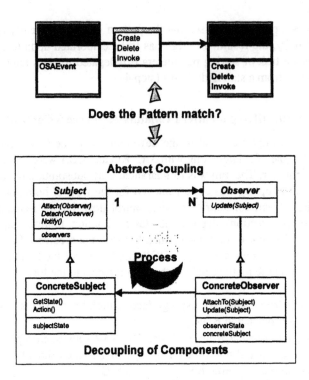

**Fig. 7.** Step 1: In search of the right match

- Dividing the components' interactions into two parts: an unchangeable abstract coupling (upper part) and the specific request from a ConcreteObserver to a ConcreteSubject (lower part).
- One-to-many relationship between a subject and its observers
- Intuitively, the proceeding is clockwise:
  AttachTo() → Action() → Notify() → Update() → GetState().

Some remarks on our decision-making: *Facade* and *Adapter* are not suitable in our context as they are primarily structural patterns. The behavioural aspect, i.e. the control flow between OSADispatch and BOR, is paramount. *Chain of Responsibility* does not fit either: The essence of this pattern lies in the ability of objects to pass a request along their class hierarchy. Incorporating a subsystem's classes into an inheritance relationship that is semantically not justifiable – just to insert a pattern in the design – makes little sense. Finally, the *Observer* pattern seems most suitable. Its transfer into the design will be discussed below.

We first examine the existing design (upper section of Fig. 7): After receiving an event, the OSADispatch class passes the request to BOR's interface. Thus, BOR plays the role of a server, while OSADispatch is the client. This approach turns out to be disadvantageous as the responsibility lies with OSADispatch concerning control of communication and the selection among several SAP systems. Additionally, a client component is the easier to replace the leaner it is. By changing the roles of client and server, the design becomes more flexible and is closer to the framework idea: "don't call us, we'll call you". Thus, the flow of communication within the OSA-Server will be reversed (see Fig. 10). OSADispatch now functions as a server. Having received an event, it only forwards a message of notification (Notify()) saying that something has changed. All SAP subsystems attached to Subject get an update message and can individually decide which one is meant. Afterwards, additional information will be requested from OSADispatch (GetCommand()).

In step 2 (see Fig. 8), it is obvious that the whole interface of the BOR class, i.e. Create(), Delete(), and Invoke(), could not be allocated to the pattern's functionality. As a consequence, we changed BOR's interface as shown in Fig. 9. Now, BOR's previous functions cannot be called any longer by a client. They have become protected member functions and are called via Update(). Thus, being notified, BOR itself will take control of this function. Finally, in step 4 we have inserted technical classes, such as List<Observer> and Iterator<Observer>.

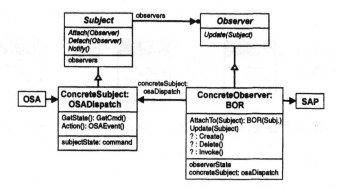

**Fig. 8.** Step 2: Allocating and Planning

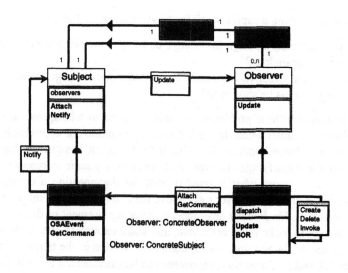

**Fig. 9.** Steps 3 and 4: Fitting and Elaborating

Taking this approach, the responsibility of process control is with the SAP subsystem that has been considered fixed. Hence, as a by-product, the one-to-many relationship has come along by inserting the *Observer* pattern.

To fulfil the requirement of making OSADispatch easily replaceable, the instantiation of the *Observer* pattern would have to be realized as a framework. For this, an abstract message dispatcher (AbstractDispatch) would be inserted to define a protocol of communication between BOR and AbstractDispatch. Before that, communication was handled by the operation GetCommand(). With communication getting more complex, GetCommand() would gain a symbolic meaning. A concrete dispatcher like OSADispatch would be derived from Subject and AbstractDispatch. For a translation of the communication protocol, the *Adapter* pattern could be applied. The steps described here clearly indicate that the original approach has been made more flexible and that a shift of responsibility has taken place: a smooth transition to framework development is mapped out (Fig. 10).

**Fig. 10.** Change of roles: Seamless transition to framework design

# 3 Pattern-Oriented Documentation

With software becoming a capital stock for many companies, two problems aggravate:

- How can a company's design knowledge and experience be preserved in the face of fluctuation (braindrain)?
- And how can we effectively integrate a newcomer into a design team, i.e. how can the learning process be shortened?

It is well known that these problems are closely related to widespread negligence of proper software documentation. In the following, we outline our approach to using design patterns for documentation. The aim is to document designs for better understanding and for identifying, evolving, and applying *reusable* components. From a designer's point of view, what is most needed for documenting a complex object-oriented design is an abstract layer right above the class level (see Figures 11 and 12). The components at this *Pattern level* meet a major requirement of design reuse: they are large enough to make reuse economic, and small enough to stay in the realm of a designer's concerns. In addition, with a slight modification of the templates introduced in Sections 3.2 and 3.3, *domain components* can be documented as well. In this case, the annotation of patterns and domain components often will overlap.

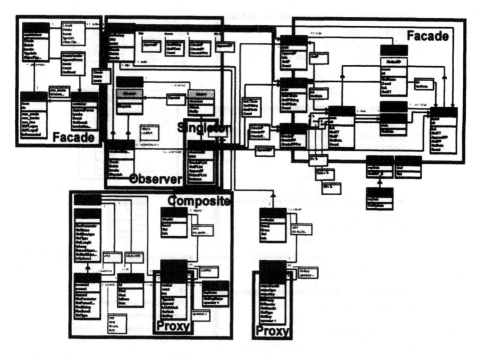

**Fig. 11.** Reducing descriptive complexity by covering the design with pattern instances[5]

Our pattern-oriented approach to documentation concentrates on the *reflective* use of (on-line) pattern texts, be they proprietary or standard. It does not aim at finding and describing new design patterns. Pattern-oriented documenting logically continues pattern-oriented designing: Covering a design partly by pattern instances (see Fig. 11, which shows the project's overall class structure), these instances *simultaneously* lay the foundation for documenting the design. They structure the system under development at a higher level of abstraction. Hence, the design is structured independently of the problem domain, establishing a *meta*-level documentation: For those designers who are not familiar with the problem domain, but familiar with design patterns, there is a *neutral* access to understanding the system. Pattern-oriented documentation supplies a *link* between the general description of design patterns and their instances in the problem domain: This link documents why, in which context, and how a design pattern has been instantiated – that is the *rationale* of a design decision. The most suitable technique for a pattern-oriented approach of documenting is *hypertext*. We will discuss the tool aspect below.

---

[5] Compare with Fig. 1: Imposing a Pattern level there could break the complexity barrier of understanding. Unfortunately, as far as we know, patterns were not used for the design of the MFC framework.

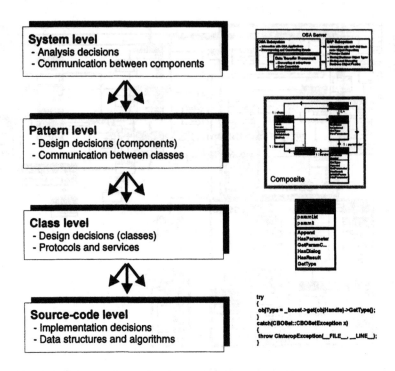

**Fig. 12.** Levels of system description: A hierarchical hypertext

### 3.1 The Role of Hypertext

Recapitulating the interplay of a pattern's form and content, what is needed for an efficient and comfortable medium to quickly switch from one aspect to another is hypertext.[6] Fig. 12 illustrates the description levels we differentiated in our project. Both aspects of system description, design and documentation, are accessible by hypertext techniques. With the help of hypertext, the items of interest can be made *sensitive* for design navigation, searching, filtering, and modification.

Consider this: The description of standard design patterns is available as hypertext. You are in the process of instantiating a design pattern. The hypertext documentation system will support you directly: It will generate a documentation frame to function as a *cardinal point* for the emerging texts, graphics, even source code. While you are instantiating design patterns or identifying pattern candidates – being involved in the steps of searching and choosing, allocating and planning, fitting, and elaborating (see Section 2.2) – the documentation *evolves*. Moreover, the content of a design pattern may evolve, too. Take, for example, structural changes that you have found appropriate and worthwhile in your current project. You probably will document these changes in the Consequences, Applicability, or Implementation sections of the original pat-

---

[6] Authors of standard pattern texts have emphasized this point before [9, 15, 22], but mainly with regard to an on-line version of a pattern catalogue.

tern's description. In fact, a *new* pattern might evolve. A pattern-driven design will eventually lead the designer to *unknown* patterns of his problem domain, particularly when his repertoire of patterns proves to be insufficient. If the items of design and documentation are captured as a hypertext, some kind of *yo-yo* access is supported: You can dive into the highest system description, inspect some component's pattern description by penetrating its class structure as deeply as to code fragments, and come up to the system level again taking a changed perspective of the design under development, and so forth.

For lack of space and because a linearized hypertext does not disclose its potential, we would like to direct the reader's interest to the on-line *WinHelp* version of the project's hypertext documentation.[7]

## 3.2 Template for Documenting Pattern Instances

In the following, we concentrate on the document's structure at the Pattern level (see Fig. 12). For our project, we found the following hypertext template appropriate for documenting pattern instances. What is most important, is the *consequent* use of the same template at a certain level of description. This will enhance the reader's familiarity with the documentation as a whole.

**Overview.** Give a reference to a class diagram or produce some other kind of visualization for a first orientation in the design context.

**Intent.** State the reason why you have instantiated just this design pattern.

**Motivation.** Describe the design context in more detail. Give a survey on the design component. It is very useful to illustrate the design actions that have led to the actual instantiation of the pattern (as shown in the examples of Sections 2.3 and 2.4). If possible, state the references to documents from the analysis phase, e.g. the relationship to analysis patterns of the problem domain [13].

**Roles.** Label the classes of the pattern instance with "Pattern:Role". This will quickly inform the reader on the role-specific assignments. Briefly outline each role and how it contributes to the pattern's essence.

**Collaborations.** Describe the interaction between the client and the pattern instance.

**Consequences.** Argue the pros and cons, e.g. design issues like extendibility, contrasting them with other design alternatives.

**Implementation.** Point out special features of your implementation and make references to the corresponding sections of the source code.

## 3.3 Extended Template for Documenting Frameworks

The second main pattern activity that we exemplified in Section 2.4 supplies a further argument for a pattern-oriented approach to documentation: The need to document those parts of a design that have been made *more flexible* by inserting a pattern. This

---

[7] http://www.ti.et-inf.uni-siegen.de/Entwurfsmuster/

is especially the case when flexibility is intended for *framework* development. We took this argument into account by the following extension to the previous template:

**Hot Spots vs. Frozen Spots.** For the documentation of a framework, a detailed description of the parts not to be changed and the parts to be extended by the user is essential [22, 24]. State clearly what degree of flexibility is offered and what the conceptual constraints are.

**Recipe.** Sketch the use and adaptation of the framework in a cookbook style with an example [16, 18]. If possible, give a ready-to-use example to test the framework by running it. To enhance one's practical understanding, a pre-configured debugger session could help. If your framework is designed for a certain run-time environment (e.g. an OLE component), consider an interactive on-line support (assistant or wizard) for adaptation and use of your framework. This would be the optimum help for the user.

**Integration.** State briefly (e.g. by making references to the corresponding locations in design and implementation) which assumptions the would-be environment of the framework has to fulfil.

**Known Uses.** List all successful uses (and typical misuses, too!), so that a prospect can quickly assess the potential of the framework for his requirements.

**Structural Extensions.** Mention the aspects that you consider limiting the framework's current design and implementation. If you have any solutions or hints for follow-up extensions, write them down. Localizing all relevant hot spots of a framework requires several design cycles in (ideally) slightly different environments. This section can document the history of these efforts.

Finally, some remarks on omissions: We have omitted here those links of the hypertext template that refer to the library management of pattern texts. For lack of space, we also left out the links to the information by whom and when the design pattern was instantiated in the process model (aspects of version control and process management). Similar templates for structuring documents can also be used at the *Class level* (see Fig. 12) to document attributes and operations. We did this, too, in our project [21].

# 4 Experiences Gained

Comparing our experiences with those from literature [4, 7, 8, 25, 26, 27], we can name the following two categories: Category A for experiences gained in applying design patterns *generatively* (where ours are similar to those from literature) and category B for experiences gained in applying a pattern's *form and content* for "documenting by designing". Let us contrast A with B: Identifying a candidate class structure to be merged with a design pattern for some flexibility reasons is harder than "just" instantiating a design pattern. As Booch observed: "Identifying involves both discovery and invention" [5]. In the case of "pattern instantiation", there is no fixed design context the designer has to take into account. Especially, when it comes to allocating class roles, the case of "candidate identification" leaves a couple of design decisions open to the designer. For example: Which of the classes' roles of the given design can be matched by the abstract design pattern? Which new roles are there to be taken over from the pattern? Finally, there are also *synergetic* experiences gained from both categories, A *and* B, confirming the principle of documenting by designing.

## Category A: Using Patterns for Design

- Cohesive and comprehensive documentation of *design decisions* (trade-offs, forces, context, etc.).
- Higher degree of reusability (making explicit the flexibility locations in a design (*hot spots* according to Pree [22]), facilitating maintenance).
- Potential pitfalls: patterns must have been *internalized* before they can be applied effectively. A basic knowledge of design patterns is sufficient to understand existing designs that refer to these patterns. However, when software is to be designed in the pattern fashion, design patterns must have been utterly understood and practised several times before.

## Category B: Using Patterns for Documentation

- A design covered with pattern instances is accessible for understanding from both sides: (a) from an in-depth knowledge of the problem domain and (b) simply with design patterns in mind. The pattern documentation functions as the "missing link" between the meta-level of pattern annotations and the problem domain.
- Systematic support of natural language documentation enhances the stimulus for documenting in general.
- Alleviation of descriptive complexity: documenting a complex design with patterns draws one's attention to the *architectural* structures of interest and, hence, facilitates one's understanding of the design.
- The design *rationale* (i.e. compensation of forces and fitting to the problem's context) is made explicit.
- The guiding interplay of a pattern's form and content animates documentation and reduces the time spent for it.
- Hypertext is the ideal medium to take full advantage of the *dual* nature of design patterns: it facilitates navigation through design documents and is a guiding instrument during the design process.

## Categories A and B: Using Patterns for Design & Documentation

- Synergetic effect: Designers documenting their designs with the pattern form will be more inclined to apply patterns, and vice versa.
- Smooth transition to framework development: in contrast to prior experiences from literature, this is a transition from a *given* design to a framework; other reports stated a transition from scratch [3], or documented the framework's rationale with patterns afterwards [16].

- Improvement of software documentation: Instead of *reverse* documenting a design, a design is documented while it evolves, that is, when design knowledge is at its highest.
- Potential pitfall: if a design pattern has been changed *structurally* to make it fit to a particular design context, all changes should be properly documented. Otherwise, the pattern instance will be difficult to recognize and its potential flexibility may not be seen any longer.

## 5 Concluding Remarks

*Componentware*, especially frameworks, will have a tremendous impact on software engineering in the years to come. On the one hand, the development of complex applications will be accelerated by visually configuring standard components. On the other hand, however, documenting the demanding design of such components will become a crucial factor to realize their *ilities*: applicability, reusability, extendibility, maintainability. We have tried, in this report, to show the correlation between design and documentation. The pattern-related design activities sketched in Section 2.2 also produce parts of the design documentation. Such a documentation will show the path that was followed from the initial design problem to its final solution: the design traps and pitfalls, the trade-offs, and the final rationale of a design are documented *in passing*, and, hence, can be easily traced back by another designer.

The spreading knowledge and acceptance of patterns will change our current *culture* of designing and documenting: There is a need to explicitly document the designer's patterns of thinking and doing. Eventually, this need will establish a new level of abstraction, what we call the "Pattern level" (see Fig. 12). It helps to put design reuse on a firm footing and will function as a *meta model* for documentation systems to come.

The project's results sketched in this experience report have encouraged us to keep on using patterns for design and documentation. Currently, we are *reverse* documenting a mature manufacturing framework [24] in the hypertext fashion of Sections 3.2 and 3.3. Besides, we consequently follow our principle of "documenting by designing" in a framework project for scheduling at universities [2].

**Acknowledgements:** We would like to thank the anonymous reviewers for their helpful suggestions and comments.

## References

[1]  Alexander, C., et al. *A Pattern Language: Towns, Buildings, and Construction*. Oxford University Press, New York, 1977.

[2]  Baumgart, M., Kunz, H.P., Meyer, S., and Quibeldey-Cirkel, K. Priority-driven Constraints Used for Scheduling at Universities. In *Proc. of the 3rd Int. Conf. on the Practical Application of Constraint Technology*, London, UK, 1997 (accepted for publication).

[3]  Beck, K., and Johnson, R.E. Patterns Generate Architectures. In *Proc. of ECOOP '94*, Bologna, Italy, 1994, 139-149.

[4] Beck, K., Coplien, J.O., Crocker, R., Dominick, L., Meszaros, G., Paulisch, F., and Vlissides, J. Industrial Experience with Design Patterns. In *Proc. of 18th Int. Conf. on Software Engineering (ICSE '18)*, Berlin, Germany, 1996, 103-114.

[5] Booch, G. *Object-Oriented Analysis and Design with Applications*. Benjamin/Cummings, Redwood City, CA, 1994. 2nd Edition.

[6] Brooks, F.P. No Silver Bullet: Essence and Accidents of Software Engineering. *Computer 20*, 4 (1987), 10-19.

[7] Brown, K. Using Patterns in Order Management Systems: A Design Patterns Experience Report. *Object Magazine*, Jan. 1996.

[8] Budinsky, F.J., Finnie, M.A., Vlissides, J.M., and Yu, P.S. Automatic Code Generation from Design Patterns. *IBM Systems Journal 35*, 2, 1996.

[9] Buschmann, F., Meunier, R., Rohnert, H., Sommerlad, P., and Stal, M. *Pattern-Oriented Software Architecture: A System of Patterns*. Wiley, New York, 1996.

[10] Coad, P. Object-Oriented Patterns. *CACM 35*, 9 (Sep. 1992), 152-159.

[11] Coad, P., and Yourdon, E. *Object-Oriented Analysis*. Englewood Cliffs, Yourdon Press, Prentice Hall, 1991.

[12] Coplien, J.O. *Advanced C++ Programming Styles and Idioms*. Addison-Wesley, Reading, MA, 1992.

[13] Fowler, M. *Analysis Patterns: Reusable Object Models*. Addison-Wesley, Reading, MA, 1996.

[14] Gamma, E. *Object-Oriented Software Development based on ET++: Design Patterns, Class Library, Tools* (in German). Ph.D. thesis, University of Zurich, 1991.

[15] Gamma, E., Helm, R., Johnson, R. E. and Vlissides, J. *Design Patterns: Elements of Reusable Object-Oriented Software*. Addison-Wesley, Reading, MA, 1995.

[16] Johnson, R.E. Documenting Frameworks Using Patterns. In *Proc. of OOPSLA '92*, Vancouver, BC, Canada, 1992, 63-76.

[17] Keller, R.K., and Lajoie, R. Design and Reuse in Object-Oriented Frameworks: Patterns, Contracts, and Motifs in Concert. In *Proc. of 62nd Congress of the Association Canadienne Française pour l'Avancement des Sciences*, Montreal, QC, Canada, 1994.

[18] Krasner, G.E., and Pope, S.T. A Cookbook for Using the Model-View-Controller User Interface Paradigm in Smalltalk-80. *JOOP 1*, 3 (Aug./Sep. 1988), 26-49.

[19] Linton, M.A., and Calder, P.R. The Design and Implementation of InterViews. In *Proc. and Additional Papers, C++ Workshop*, Santa Fe, NM, 1987. USENIX Association, El Cerrito, CA, 1987, 256-268.

[20] Meyer, B. *Object-Oriented Software Construction*. Series in Computer Science. Prentice Hall, Englewood Cliffs, NJ, 1988.

[21] Odenthal, G. *Design and Implementation of an Interface between the SAP-R/3 Business Object Repository and the Open Scripting Architecture (OSA)* (in German). University of Siegen, Master thesis, 1996.

[22] Pree, W. *Design Patterns for Object-Oriented Software Development*. Addison-Wesley, Reading, MA, 1994.

[23] Quibeldey-Cirkel, K. *The Object Paradigm in Computer Science* (in German). Teubner, Stuttgart, Germany, 1994.

[24] Schmid, H.A. Creating the Architecture of a Manufacturing Framework by Design Patterns. In *Proc. of OOPSLA '95*, Austin, USA, 1995.

[25] Schmidt, D.C. Experience Using Design Patterns to Develop Reusable Object-Oriented Communication Software. *CACM 38*, 10 (Oct. 1995), 65-74.

[26] Schmidt, D.C., and Stephenson, P. Experience Using Design Patterns to Evolve Communication Software Across Diverse OS Platforms. In *Proc. of ECOOP '95*, Aarhus, Denmark, 1995.

[27] Special issue on Software Patterns. *CACM 39*, 10 (Oct. 1996), 36-82.

# Going Beyond Objects with Design Patterns

Erich Gamma

Object Technology International
Zurich, Switzerland

**Abstract.** A design pattern systematically names, explains, and evaluates an important and recurring design. This idea for capturing design experience has progressed rapidly from cult to mainstream status. Design patterns become a catalyst for design reuse and enable to understand a design at a higher level than individual objects. This talk reports experience on how design patterns can address challenges of software development.

# Author Index

# Springer
# and the
# environment

At Springer we firmly believe that an international science publisher has a special obligation to the environment, and our corporate policies consistently reflect this conviction.

We also expect our business partners – paper mills, printers, packaging manufacturers, etc. – to commit themselves to using materials and production processes that do not harm the environment. The paper in this book is made from low- or no-chlorine pulp and is acid free, in conformance with international standards for paper permanency.

Springer

# Lecture Notes in Computer Science

For information about Vols. 1–1169

please contact your bookseller or Springer-Verlag

Vol. 1208: S. Ben-David (Ed.), Computational Learning Theory. Proceedings, 1997. VIII, 331 pages. 1997. (Subseries LNAI).

Vol. 1209: L. Cavedon, A. Rao, W. Wobcke (Eds.), Intelligent Agent Systems. Proceedings, 1996. IX, 188 pages. 1997. (Subseries LNAI).

Vol. 1210: P. de Groote, J.R. Hindley (Eds.), Typed Lambda Calculi and Applications. Proceedings, 1997. VIII, 405 pages. 1997.

Vol. 1211: E. Keravnou, C. Garbay, R. Baud, J. Wyatt (Eds.), Artificial Intelligence in Medicine. Proceedings, 1997. XIII, 526 pages. 1997. (Subseries LNAI).

Vol. 1212: J. P. Bowen, M.G. Hinchey, D. Till (Eds.), ZUM '97: The Z Formal Specification Notation. Proceedings, 1997. X, 435 pages. 1997.

Vol. 1213: P. J. Angeline, R. G. Reynolds, J. R. McDonnell, R. Eberhart (Eds.), Evolutionary Programming VI. Proceedings, 1997. X, 457 pages. 1997.

Vol. 1214: M. Bidoit, M. Dauchet (Eds.), TAPSOFT '97: Theory and Practice of Software Development. Proceedings, 1997. XV, 884 pages. 1997.

Vol. 1215: J. M. L. M. Palma, J. Dongarra (Eds.), Vector and Parallel Processing – VECPAR'96. Proceedings, 1996. XI, 471 pages. 1997.

Vol. 1216: J. Dix, L. Moniz Pereira, T.C. Przymusinski (Eds.), Non-Monotonic Extensions of Logic Programming. Proceedings, 1996. XI, 224 pages. 1997. (Subseries LNAI).

Vol. 1217: E. Brinksma (Ed.), Tools and Algorithms for the Construction and Analysis of Systems. Proceedings, 1997. X, 433 pages. 1997.

Vol. 1218: G. Păun, A. Salomaa (Eds.), New Trends in Formal Languages. IX, 465 pages. 1997.

Vol. 1219: K. Rothermel, R. Popescu-Zeletin (Eds.), Mobile Agents. Proceedings, 1997. VIII, 223 pages. 1997.

Vol. 1220: P. Brezany, Input/Output Intensive Massively Parallel Computing. XIV, 288 pages. 1997.

Vol. 1221: G. Weiß (Ed.), Distributed Artificial Intelligence Meets Machine Learning. Proceedings, 1996. X, 294 pages. 1997. (Subseries LNAI).

Vol. 1222: J. Vitek, C. Tschudin (Eds.), Mobile Object Systems. Proceedings, 1996. X, 319 pages. 1997.

Vol. 1223: M. Pelillo, E.R. Hancock (Eds.), Energy Minimization Methods in Computer Vision and Pattern Recognition. Proceedings, 1997. XII, 549 pages. 1997.

Vol. 1224: M. van Someren, G. Widmer (Eds.), Machine Learning: ECML-97. Proceedings, 1997. XI, 361 pages. 1997. (Subseries LNAI).

Vol. 1225: B. Hertzberger, P. Sloot (Eds.), High-Performance Computing and Networking. Proceedings, 1997. XXI, 1066 pages. 1997.

Vol. 1226: B. Reusch (Ed.), Computational Intelligence. Proceedings, 1997. XIII, 609 pages. 1997.

Vol. 1227: D. Galmiche (Ed.), Automated Reasoning with Analytic Tableaux and Related Methods. Proceedings, 1997. XI, 373 pages. 1997. (Subseries LNAI).

Vol. 1228: S.-H. Nienhuys-Cheng, R. de Wolf, Foundations of Inductive Logic Programming. XVII, 404 pages. 1997. (Subseries LNAI).

Vol. 1230: J. Duncan, G. Gindi (Eds.), Information Processing in Medical Imaging. Proceedings, 1997. XVI, 557 pages. 1997.

Vol. 1231: M. Bertran, T. Rus (Eds.), Transformation-Based Reactive Systems Development. Proceedings, 1997. XI, 431 pages. 1997.

Vol. 1232: H. Comon (Ed.), Rewriting Techniques and Applications. Proceedings, 1997. XI, 339 pages. 1997.

Vol. 1233: W. Fumy (Ed.), Advances in Cryptology — EUROCRYPT '97. Proceedings, 1997. XI, 509 pages. 1997.

Vol 1234: S. Adian, A. Nerode (Eds.), Logical Foundations of Computer Science. Proceedings, 1997. IX, 431 pages. 1997.

Vol. 1235: R. Conradi (Ed.), Software Configuration Management. Proceedings, 1997. VIII, 234 pages. 1997.

Vol. 1238: A. Mullery, M. Besson, M. Campolargo, R. Gobbi, R. Reed (Eds.), Intelligence in Services and Networks: Technology for Cooperative Competition. Proceedings, 1997. XII, 480 pages. 1997.

Vol. 1240: J. Mira, R. Moreno-Díaz, J. Cabestany (Eds.), Biological and Artificial Computation: From Neuroscience to Technology. Proceedings, 1997. XXI, 1401 pages. 1997.

Vol. 1241: M. Akşit, S. Matsuoka (Eds.), ECOOP'97 – Object-Oriented Programming. Proceedings, 1997. XI, 531 pages. 1997.

Vol. 1242: S. Fdida, M. Morganti (Eds.), Multimedia Applications, Services and Techniques – ECMAST '97. Proceedings, 1997. XIV, 772 pages. 1997.

Vol. 1243: A. Mazurkiewicz, J. Winkowski (Eds.), CONCUR'97: Concurrency Theory. Proceedings, 1997. VIII, 421 pages. 1997.

Vol. 1244: D. M. Gabbay, R. Kruse, A. Nonnengart, H.J. Ohlbach (Eds.), Qualitative and Quantitative Practical Reasoning. Proceedings, 1997. X, 621 pages. 1997. (Subseries LNAI).

Vol. 1245: M. Calzarossa, R. Marie, B. Plateau, G. Rubino (Eds.), Computer Performance Evaluation. Proceedings, 1997. VIII, 231 pages. 1997.

Vol. 1246: S. Tucker Taft, R. A. Duff (Eds.), Ada 95 Reference Manual. XXII, 526 pages. 1997.

Vol. 1247: J. Barnes (Ed.), Ada 95 Rationale. XVI, 458 pages. 1997.

Vol. 1248: P. Azéma, G. Balbo (Eds.), Application and Theory of Petri Nets 1997. Proceedings, 1997. VIII, 467 pages. 1997.

Vol. 1249: W. McCune (Ed.), Automated Deduction – Cade-14. Proceedings, 1997. XIV, 462 pages. 1997.

Vol. 1250: A. Olivé, J.A. Pastor (Eds.), Advanced Information Systems Engineering. Proceedings, 1997. XI, 451 pages. 1997.

Vol. 1251: K. Hardy, J. Briggs (Eds.), Reliable Software Technologies – Ada-Europe '97. Proceedings, 1997. VIII, 293 pages. 1997.

Vol. 1253: G. Bilardi, A. Ferreira, R. Lüling, J. Rolim (Eds.), Solving Irregularly Structured Problems in Parallel. Proceedings, 1997. X, 287 pages. 1997.